The Course of Gay and Lesbian Lives

Worlds of Desire: The Chicago Series on Sexuality,
Gender, and Culture
Edited by Gilbert Herdt

ALSO IN THE SERIES:

The Course of Gay and Lesbian Lives

Social and Psychoanalytic Perspectives

Bertram J. Cohler and
Robert M. Galatzer-Levy

THE UNIVERSITY OF CHICAGO PRESS
CHICAGO AND LONDON

Bertram J. Cohler is the William Rainey Harper Professor of Social Science at the University of Chicago.
Robert M. Galatzer-Levy is a lecturer in the Department of Psychiatry at the University of Chicago.
The authors are also on the faculty of the Institute for Psychoanalysis.

The University of Chicago Press, Chicago 60637
The University of Chicago Press, Ltd., London
© 2000 by The University of Chicago
All rights reserved. Published 2000
Printed in the United States of America
10 09 08 07 06 05 04 03 02 01 00   5 4 3 2 1

ISBN (cloth): 0-226-11303-5

Library of Congress Cataloging-in-Publication Data

Cohler, Bertram J.
    The course of gay and lesbian lives : social and psychoanalytic perspectives /
    Bertram J. Cohler and Robert M. Galatzer-Levy.
        p.   cm.
    Includes bibliographical references and index.
    ISBN 0-226-11303-5 (alk. paper)
    1. Homosexuality—Psychological aspects.   2. Homosexuality—Social
aspects.   3. Psychoanalysis and homosexuality.   4. Sexual orientation.   5. Gender
identity.   I. Galatzer-Levy, Robert M.   II. Title.
RC451.4.G39 C64   2000
306.76'6—dc21
                                                                          99-087700

⊗ The paper used in this publication meets the minimum requirements of the American National Standard for Information Sciences—Permanence of Paper for Printed Library Materials, ANSI Z39.48-1992.

For Bill Hensley,
with thanks for patience and understanding
—B. J. C.

and

In memory of
Mike Sussholtz (1943–1989)
Died in New York City
Also on his way to freedom
—R. M. G.-L.

Contents

Preface

Human sexuality is amazingly malleable and can organize itself in many sorts of ways. How that desire is understood and hence experienced is what counts. Only in some societies and eras do desires coalesce into a social role, or identity, that gets labeled homosexual, or gay, or lesbian, and that corresponds to how individuals organize their emotional, intimate, and erotic lives. And for reasons that still can only remain speculative, the modern West appears to be one such place and time. (D'Emilio [1983] 1998, 254)

A group of friends and family recently gathered to celebrate the commitment to each other of a gay couple. Both of these men were involved in important work in the community, using their professional education to improve the lives of the least advantaged, and now they sought to celebrate their partnership. They exchanged vows they had written themselves, exchanged rings, and then celebrated their union with a tender and passionate embrace which reflected their love. Those present broke out in applause, then toasted the couple. Among the guests were several other gay couples, whose own enduring commitment implicitly affirmed the vows these caring, talented young men exchanged.

This celebration of mutuality took place the same week that a leader of the United States Senate compared all gay people to "kleptomaniacs" and a national newsweekly featured a cover story on "ex-gays" who, while acknowledging continuing homosexual desire as expressed in fantasy, claim conversion to heterosexual behavior on the basis of fundamentalist religious-political conversion (as we show in the present book, there is little evidence that such conversion of sexual orientation is possible). Clearly, we live in a time of paradox. Ever larger numbers of men and women are celebrating their gay sexual identity and commitment with their partners, and more organizations, public and private, are providing partner benefits, yet this validation of lesbian and gay relationships is largely ignored by those who would deny the civil rights of people whose sexual orientation differs from their own.

This book is all about this paradox and the men and women who experience a gay sexual identity. In the afterword for the 1998 edition of his book *Sexual Politics, Sexual Communities,* John D'Emilio well portrays this paradox. In contemporary Western society some men and women organize their lives and their sexual identity in terms of desire for others of the same gender. However, one cannot presume that identity has been organized in the same way in other times and places. Our colleague Gilbert Herdt (1997) portrays what he terms sexual lifeways, the alternative sexualities scripted in a culture. In this book we add to the lifeway presently described as being gay or lesbian the concept of life course, a developmental course which may be described within the society of the modern West. At the same time, following the social theorist Karl Mannheim ([1928] 1952), we consider how social change may lead gay men and women of different generations or cohorts to understand the trajectory of this life course in somewhat different ways. How people interpret the meaning of these possible lifeways may change both over historical time and across the course of an individual life (Elder 1996). The meaning of being gay, lesbian, bisexual, or straight varies across cultures but also, within any one culture, across generations and social circumstances.

Thus, it is difficult to generalize about the expression and presumed origin of same-gender sexual orientation across cultures and times. Further, while time and place provide the template within which meanings are constructed, the subjective experience of being gay or lesbian, and the understanding of this aspect of self, cannot be predetermined. Indeed, as George Chauncey (1994) shows in *Gay New York*, the very terms used to portray variation in sexual lifeways vary over time within a given society. The concern with origins, including the presumed biology of homosexuality, has political overtones for both the right and the left and is itself a reflection of beliefs resulting from living in a particular time and place. We have attempted to consider both historical time, reflected in social change, and the particular experiences of a lifetime as elements in the construction of sexual orientation. Indeed, we believe that it is among the tasks of clinical psychoanalysis to understand the meanings of presently constructed sexual orientation in the life story told by a particular analysand at a particular time and in a particular place.

Work focusing on the concept of "lived experience" (Schutz and Luckman 1973, 1983; Berger and Luckmann 1967) has highlighted the significance of understanding founded in social life. The social philosopher Michel Foucault (1975, [1976] 1990, [1994a] 1990, [1984] 1990) showed how ideas in the modern West were founded on a particular relation of power and knowledge implicit in all aspects of social life. From this perspective, the very concept of sexuality and of sexual pleasure is informed by shared conceptions which arise from dominant forces within society. Judith Butler (1997) extends Foucault's focus on the social origin of ideas to the very concept of subjectivity itself. It is not only in these shared conceptions of self founded in a diffuse discipline of presumed knowledge but also in the way we understand our own lives that this power is manifest. Butler maintains that the concept of power goes well beyond those of socialization or internalization and is founded on a self-discipline that mirrors the relation between power and knowledge within the larger society.

These issues of intentionality, will, and the regulation of desire are central to discussions of the origins of same-gender sexual desire (T. Stein 1996). Those seeking an answer to what "causes" homosexuality will find this book disquieting. We suggest that concern with the question of causality, so often posed by gay men and women and their families, by mental health professionals, and by the larger society, is a reflection of scientism, which attempts to reduce meaning and morale to issues of cause and to replace the authority of religious belief with the authority of scientific belief (Bauman 1992; Toulmin 1990; Weber [1904–5] 1955). Discussions of same-gender sexual orientation inevitably lead to questions of the origin of desire. Clients seeking psychotherapy (particularly gay men) inevitably ask "how I got that way" (Drescher 1998; A. Sullivan 1998) and explain their same-gender sexual desire in terms of either upbringing (Isay 1989) or genetic determinants (Hamer and Copeland 1994, 1998).

As Andrew Sullivan (1998) has observed in a particularly cogent essay, biological factors such as genetic predisposition may be necessary but not sufficient to lead to sexual orientation as gay or lesbian. Work of Simon and Gagnon (1984, 1988) and of Plummer (1995) highlights how we learn scripts or narratives of the origin of sexual desire. This issue confounded Freud in his own effort to understand the origins of sexual orientation. Freud wisely recognized that an infinite number of factors might contribute to same-gender sexual orientation and ultimately decided to focus on issues of meaning and intent for the analysand rather than on theories of causation. Drescher too sagely cautions the analyst to explore with the analysand the many meanings involved in this question; at least one such meaning is to be found in resolving the question "Why do I feel differently from everybody else?" (1998, 81). As with other questions of origin in psychoanalysis, the focus of the psychoanalytic work shifts from a culturally constructed concern with "origin" to helping analysands understand the meanings for them of being lesbian or gay and the place of such meanings in a presently recounted life story (Drescher 1998; Schafer 1980, 1981).

Our conclusions may seem unduly partisan to those who believe that insufficient attention has been paid to the possible adverse impact on personality and adjustment of "nonnormative" sexual orientation (Schafer 1995). On the other hand, many people express surprise that the relation of homosexuality and mental health remains an issue within the mental health professions. Indeed, careful review of the available evidence supports our view that there is little support for any assumption that nonnormative sexuality is tied to maladjustment or psychopathology, except as influenced by stigma on the part of the larger community (I. Meyer 1993, 1995; Nungesser 1983).

The intense political pressure of the present time—reflected in the "ex-gay" movement, the reemergence of discussion about nonnormative sexuality, and continuing legal challenges to nondiscrimination ordinances around the country by the religious right—suggests the need for a detailed review of same-gender sexual orientation and mental health across the course of life. Following the lead of Herek (1991, 1996), who has so ably commented on the impact of antigay prejudice for the mental health professions, it is important at this time to refute the presumption, often implicit within psychoanalysis and psychodynamic psychiatry, of an inevitable association between nonnormative sexuality and psychopathology.

This book is founded on two particular intellectual disciplines, life-course social science and psychoanalysis, extending the integrative position described by Galatzer-Levy and Cohler (1993). From the perspective of life-course social science, well articulated in the systematic study reported by psychologists Paul Baltes and Warner Schaie (1968; also Schaie 1995), by sociologist Glen Elder ([1974] 1998, 1995, 1996, 1997), and by both Dannefer and Uhlenberg (1999) and Settersten and his colleagues (Settersten 1999; Settersten and Hägestad 1996; Settersten and Mayer 1997), psychological development must be understood not only in terms of particular life circumstances but also within a social and historical context (Plath 1980).

For example, the meaning of being gay is quite different for today's adolescents (Herdt and Boxer 1996) than it was for young people coming to adolescence in the postwar era (A. Kantrowitz [1977] 1996; T. Miller 1997; Reid [1973] 1993; P. Robinson 1999). While such significant events as the Stonewall Inn riots in New York in June 1969, which marked the emergence of the contemporary gay and lesbian civil rights movement (Clendinen and Nagourney 1999; D'Emilio [1983] 1998; Duberman 1993; I. Young 1995), affected all gay men and women, their impact was quite different for those who were young adults and those who were in midlife at the time. From the life-course perspective, it is difficult to make any claims about the significance of psychological changes associated with any particular point in the course of life independent of "cohort effects."

The concept of generation or cohort brings together study of individual psychological development, social structure, and social and historical change (Clausen 1993; Dannefer and Uhlenberg 1999; Elder and Caspi 1990; Settersten 1999). Psychoanalysis adds further to the understanding of lifetimes within this social context (Galatzer-Levy and Cohler 1993). Understood as a method of study, clinical psychoanalytic perspectives provide a means for systematically understanding the manner in which persons make sense of lived experience within the context of social change, as they struggle to maintain a coherent account of a presently remembered past, an experienced present, and an anticipated future. Some readers will ask why psychoanalysis is included as an intellectual perspective in the study of gay and lesbian lives, while other readers, psychoanalytically sophisticated, may lament that this book is not sufficiently psychoanalytic. These later readers might claim that psychoanalysis is concerned with issues of subjectivity beyond consideration of the time and context in which persons lead their lives.

Foucault ([1966] 1970) has described psychoanalysis as the premier human science precisely because of its focus on the manner in which persons make and maintain meanings of lived experience, but psychoanalytic perspectives have been much misunderstood within both the mental health professions and the larger society. Freud's own scientist worldview was a product of his early exposure to the mechanistic philosophy of science prevalent in the last third of the nineteenth century and has little relation to the issues of wish and meaning that he explored in his pioneering study of mental life (Galatzer-Levy and Cohler 1990; Gay 1988). Concepts of fixation, regression, and deficit stand outside of the clinical context and, as Freud himself acknowledges in his biographical study of Leonardo da Vinci ([1910c] 1957), should be understood as metaphorical. These terms were borrowed by Freud from his reading of neurology, particularly the work of the British neurologist Hughlings Jackson (Stengel 1963; Sulloway 1979). Contemporary critiques of psychoanalysis often fail to recognize that it is a method of study founded on a unique collaboration between analyst and analysand engaged in the study of the analysand's particular life story.

As a method of study, clinical psychoanalysis is distinctive in its concern with not only the content of a life story but also both proximal and distal circumstances related to telling and listening. Central to this narrative activity is the ambiance of the setting in which the story is told and the meaning each participant, analyst and analysand, makes of the encounter (Schafer 1981, 1992). Contemporary psychoanalysis emphasizes the "two-person" psychology (Gill 1994) implicit in Freud's own work (Lipton 1977). The analyst contributes to the ambiance of the therapeutic or working alliance (Greenson 1965; Zetzel 1958) within which the analysand recounts a life story. It is as a result of his or her own personal analysis that it is possible for the analyst to maintain awareness of the personal significance of the analysand's account, including those aspects which lead to feelings of anxious discomfort (Devereux 1967; Kohut [1959] 1978).

In circumstances outside the analytic setting, the gay or lesbian analysand has most likely learned that other people will be made uncomfortable by aspects of this life story and so may presume that the analyst will similarly be unable to maintain an empathic attitude in listening to his or her account of becoming gay. But as a result of the analyst's personal psychoanalytic experience, entailing an encounter with her or his own wishes and fears, it is possible for the analyst to reflect on the very experience of listening to a life story, to engage in vicarious introspection or empathy (Kohut [1959] 1978) and maintain a listening attitude, recognizing that any sense of anxiety and dysphoria is in response to tasting the storyteller's own lived experience (Fliess 1944, 1953). At other times, an analysand's life story may interact with pressing, unresolved issues in the analyst's own life; this may interfere with the analyst's maintaining an empathic attitude and create what is experienced by the teller of the life story as an empathic break or disruption of the ambiance of the situation. Optimally, the analyst's personal analytic experience and continuing self-inquiry makes it possible for the analyst to become aware of and resolve this intrusion (Gardner 1983; Racker 1968).

As contrasted with the metaphorical basis of other aspects of his theory, Freud discovered the concept of ambivalence directly through his reflexive response to his father's death. The concept of a nuclear conflict (enshrined after 1910 as the so-called Oedipus complex) was a guiding principle for a first generation of analysts following the First World War. Later psychoanalytic theories continued to emphasize how early development shapes later experience. This book is not concerned with the validation of one or another psychoanalytic theory of development as a guide to explaining the emergence of same-gender sexual desire, either as pre-oedipal deficit or as evidence of unresolved oedipal psychopathology. Indeed, as both the sociologist and psychoanalyst Nancy Chodorow (1992) and the psychoanalyst Jack Drescher (1998) suggest, all expressions of sexual desire share equal valence as modes of experience. Furthermore, speculations about origins and developmental course draw us away from a focus on the meaning of sexuality for any analysand, gay or straight.

Efforts to align a behavioral outcome in an analysand's story with a particular "cause" reflects the analyst's own anxiety, dealt with through recourse to a preferred mode of explanation. A part of what is troubling about reparative or conversion therapy, sometimes claimed to be a psychoanalytic perspective, is that the analyst presumes at the outset both to know the cause of same-gender sexual orientation and to know the desired outcome. In analysis we do not presume any ideal outcome beyond that which the analysand comes to value after a period of intensive self-reflection.

It is possible that a gay, lesbian, or bisexual analysand might opt for a different sexual lifeway following a period of intensive self-reflection in psychoanalysis. But because antigay prejudice is so strong in contemporary society, and is inevitably shared by analysand and analyst alike, whether gay or straight (Herek 1996; Malyon 1982), one must ask in such cases whether antigay prejudice, instead of becoming a focus of analytic study, may have silently guided assumptions regarding the ideal analytic outcome. Even among gay analysts, if this prejudice is not the subject of continuing self-inquiry, the analyst's own self-criticism (J. Butler 1997; Kris 1990) may lead the analyst to encourage the analysand to adopt a normative sexual orientation. However, conformity with such norms most often does not fit with the analysand's own world of desire and merely enhances the analysand's sense of a false self (Winnicott 1960a). Our view is that the goals of clinical psychoanalysis include enhanced self-understanding, personal integrity, and vitality. Compliance and the process of fostering a false self, so prevalent in the present "ex-gay" movement, sap such personal vitality and deny the reality of desire.

Acknowledgments

This book began as a report commissioned by the Executive Council of the American Psychoanalytic Association. The association, confronted by the reality of a quarter century in which homosexuality had continued to be regarded by psychoanalysis as a prodromal index of psychopathology, long after other mental health professions had changed their views on this issue, was pressed to address the scientific status of same-gender sexual orientation understood as a way of life rather than as an expression of personal psychopathology.

In response to such vexing scientific and ethical issues, a subcommittee of the Committee on Scientific Issues was charged with preparing a report to be submitted to the Executive Council. Judith Schachter, then president of the association, both initiated the idea of a report and supported the substance of the report as it emerged in earlier drafts. The report eventually submitted to the Executive Council of the American Psychoanalytic Association provided the foundation for several recommendations for action by the association. The report was in part a response to the early efforts of Richard Isay and, more recently, those of Ralph Roughton, whose imagination and courage led the association to a new recognition of the importance of dealing with same-gender sexual orientation as an intellectual and therapeutic concern. As first chair of the association's Committee on Homosexual Issues, Roughton brought dignity and scholarly thoughtfulness to the debate, which made it possible, in the wake of the association's overwhelming vote to exclude sexual orientation per se as a factor in determining suitability for psychoanalytic education, for member institutes to plan in a systematic manner the recruitment of gay and lesbian candidates.

We would like to acknowledge the tremendous assistance provided by Jeanne Galatzer-Levy in carefully reading and clarifying issues posed by this discussion. As a science writer her work is a model of clarity. This book would not have been possible without the assistance of Jack Celia and the staff of the Seminary Coop Bookstore at the University of Chicago, arguably the best bookstore in the nation, with superb collections in psychology, sociology, and gay and lesbian studies. A number of colleagues read all or part of the manuscript and made important suggestions for revision: Henry Bach-rach, Alice Brand Bartlett, Jack Drescher, Stuart Hauser, Gil Herdt, Tony Kris, George Klumpner, Paul Lynch, Linda Mayes, Paul Mosher, Henry Nunberg, Robert Perlman, Ralph Roughton, Alan Skolnikoff, Joe Schocter, Susan Vaughan, and Robert Waldinger. We would like to thank the Executive Council of the American Psychoanalytic Association for their continuing support for the goals of this project.

Both students and fellow volunteer therapists at Horizons Community Services Center, which provides psychodynamically focused psychotherapy for the gay, lesbian, and bisexual community in Chicago, provided important insights regarding many of the issues raised in the book. Bruce Aaron and Norman Bonk, previous directors of Horizons Psychotherapy Service, and Mark Contarno, the present director, have been colleagues in the discussion of clinical cases, providing important insights reflected in the present book. Horizons' lesbian and gay clients and men and women participating in community focus groups contributed in countless ways to the human dimensions of this work. We would particularly like to acknowledge the contributions of the late Andrew Boxer, who was a wonderful colleague. Serving as the founding executive director of the Evelyn Hooker Center for Gay and Lesbian Mental Health, Andy set a standard for clinical and scholarly endeavors which continues to inspire us all. Student colleagues in the Committee on Human Development at the University of Chicago, particularly Jeff Beller, Samantha Bergman, David deBoer, Andrew Hostetler, and Andrew Suth, read and commented critically on both clinical and developmental issues considered in the book. Finally, we are indebted to Doug Mitchell, our editor at the University of Chicago Press, whose vision and enthusiasm for this project was important in seeing it through to completion, and Joel Score, whose careful and helpful copyediting made this a more readable book.

Part One

Homosexuality and Psychological Inquiry

One

Gay and Lesbian Lives and Psychoanalytic Inquiry

In 1973, following a complex scientific and political debate, the membership of the American Psychiatric Association voted by a significant majority to remove the category of homosexuality from the Diagnostic and Statistical Manual (DSM-II). Their action reflected the reality of a changing view of homosexuality within the larger culture. Across the twentieth century, there had been much controversy regarding men and women who enjoyed intimate relations with others of the same gender. Such relationships formerly had no name, but coining of the label "homosexuality" in the late nineteenth century, it became possible to study the phenomenon systematically. Earlier discussion of the moral status of homosexuality was then transformed into discussion of homosexuality as a medical problem. Since realization of intimate relations between persons of the same gender was not within the execrable outcomes of sexual identity socialization, it was assumed that such ties must reflect deviance and psychopathology (Katz 1995).

In the period following the Second World War, these assumptions were challenged for the first time by such homophile groups as the Mattachine Society (Loughery 1998). However, since significant stigma was attached to acknowledgment of homosexuality, much of the early opposition to the view of homosexuality as psychopathology was quiet and anonymous. Even in the early 1970s, a psychiatrist speaking at a meeting of the American Psychiatric Association about the effects of stigma resulting from being homosexual believed it necessary to disguise his appearance (Bayer 1987; Kutchins and Kirk 1997). However, following patron resistance to a police morals raid on a gay New York bar, the Stonewall Inn, in June 1969, and the emergence of "gay liberation" in the months following the ensuing riot, the quiet opposition of the prior decade became vocal (Duberman 1993), and within three years the American Psychiatric Association reversed its stance on homosexuality as evidence of psychological illness.

Following declassification of homosexuality as necessary evidence of psychiatric distress, it became possible to talk openly about sexual orientation and to study systematically many of the assumptions which fostered antigay attitudes and stigmatization of gay men and women. Journals focusing on issues of sexual orientation, psychological development, and social under-standing of same-gender sexuality provided a first publication source for many of these studies. Subject to peer review, this research increased in qual-ity over the succeeding decade; at the same time the number of available books grew.

A new era of study and debate arose in the early 1980s, in response to evidence, reported in the media and in medical journals, that a virus was responsible for transmission of the progressive, ultimately fatal syndrome now known as AIDS and the realization that sexual practices designed to prevent contact with bodily fluids of one's partner would be important in preventing further spread of the disease. At the same time, evidence that gay men in particular might have multiple sexual partners, and thus inadvertently spread the virus, again raised the question of whether homosexuality might reflect psychopathology.

Subsequent studies of psychological development, however, have raised doubts regarding the supposed association of gay sexual identity with wide-scale promiscuity (Herek 1991; Weston 1997). The majority of gay men and women report relationships similar in many respects to those of heterosexual counterparts (Blumstein and Schwartz 1983). Their relationships are beset by tensions similar to those reported among men and women in straight relationships. Moreover, little evidence of differences in psychological ad-justment or psychopathology has been reported in a large number of studies contrasting the mental health of gay and straight adults on a number of indi-ces of adjustment (Herek 1991). Where impairment in adjustment was re-ported, findings showed that the differences could be attributed in large part to exposure to antigay prejudice and stigma which had become a part of the conception of self reported by gay men and women.

What emerged from several cross-sectional studies of gay adolescents and adults was that, in communities in which there was less antigay prejudice, the course of development among lesbians and gay men did not differ in significant respects from that of straight counterparts. The studies showed the emergence of a subculture, such as might be found among any stigmatized minority group, and there was a difference in gay adolescents' time and man-ner of entry into expectable adult roles, but such difference was not shown to be equivalent to deviance or psychopathology. Particularly in large cities where formal and informal sources of social support and legal protections against discrimination on the basis of sexual orientation fostered a safe envi-ronment, gay men and women were able to publicly acknowledge their sex-ual orientation and to feel affirmed in their personal and collective identity.

Like other adolescents and adults, lesbians and gay men reported problems in adjustment as a consequence of both expected life changes, such as retirement, and unexpected adversity, such as the untimely death of a parent, partner, or friend. The AIDS epidemic—exacting a high toll in terms of mortality of partners and friends as well as persons' own discovery of their HIV-seropositive status—has created significant issues for mental health intervention, which are still not fully understood (Blechner 1997; Shelby 1995). Additional issues for mental health study arise from the effects of aging on members of a generation or birth cohort affected by both past stigma because of sexual orientation and by a present lack of services for gay and lesbian elders (Herdt, Beeler, and Rawls 1997).

This book provides an overview of what is presently known of the foundations for becoming gay or lesbian, together with the course of development, from childhood into later life, among persons acknowledging a gay or bisexual identity within appropriate contexts. The book reviews extant findings regarding sexual orientation and psychological adjustment and concludes with a discussion of issues posed for the psychoanalytic process which are related to the analysand's identity as gay or bisexual. While issues related to acknowledging a lesbian or gay sexual identity persist over time, the focus of this book is on the life course of those women and men who are able to recognize their same-gender sexual orientation and who have managed in at least some contexts to integrate their sexual identity with other aspects of adult life. Issues of first, recognition and, later, disclosure of same-gender sexual identity within accepting circles of relatives, friends, and colleagues may remain salient across the course of life.

This book is not specifically concerned with the lives of women and, particularly, men who experience some same-gender sexual desire as "breakdown products" accompanying particular stressful life changes (Elson 1986; Isay 1989; Goldberg 1995). Rather, it focuses on men and women who have deliberately chosen a gay or lesbian sexual identity and the manner in which they rewrite their life stories as a consequence of the developmental pathways associated with that choice. At the same time, it is important to emphasize that this choice is itself only possible as a result of social changes over the past three decades which have made it possible for gay, lesbian, and bisexual adults to find comfortable and safe opportunities at work and in the community.

This book also does not address in detail the issues associated with AIDS. Without doubt, this pandemic has created misery and suffering beyond imagination for many men and women within the gay community (Paul, Hays, and Coates 1995). Even as this book is written, it is not clear how long the current aggressive regime of medication, itself a demanding and painful process, will remain effective in permitting HIV-positive men and women to lead something like normal lives. Within the larger community, moreover,

AIDS has often become a metaphor for the gay experience (Herek 1999; Herek and Capitanio 1999). This metaphor has been a means for the expression of antigay prejudice, even, at times, within the gay community.

As AIDS continues to spread within both gay and straight communities throughout the world, its significance for person and society alike will require detailed discussion beyond the scope of the present book. The meanings of HIV for self and lived experience are explored in reports by Cohen and Abramowitz (1990), Odets (1995), and Shelby (1997, 1998). Issues of partner loss, grief, and living beyond loss have been explored by Hildebrand (1992), Shelby (1995), and Stein et al. (1997). Several recent collections (Blechner 1997b; Cadwell, Burnham, and Forstein 1994) explore psychodynamic perspectives on psychotherapy with gay men who are HIV-positive or suffering episodes of AIDS. Clinical reports by Fishman (1994), Hildebrand (1992), Petrucelli (1997), and Shapiro (1997) have discussed the particular impact upon the therapist of work with men and women with HIV or AIDS.

This book offers another perspective on gay and lesbian lives. It argues less that gay men and women are "virtually normal" (A. Sullivan 1995) than that there are a number of developmental pathways or lifeways (Herdt 1997; Hostetler and Herdt 1998) which offer gay men and women sources of satisfaction at school and work and in relations with friends and lovers. This book considers these alternative lifeways in terms both of larger community norms and of the unique stressors that arise as a result of being a member of a sexual minority. Indeed, as we suggest in this book, antigay prejudice and the withholding of support for enduring same-gender sexual commitment (or marriage) (Carleton 1999; Rivera 1991) compromise any effort to understand the lives of gay men and women within the terms of the larger society.

Psychoanalysis and Sexual Orientation

In part due to a long history of regarding homosexuality as evidence of impairment in psychological development, psychoanalysis has found it difficult to respond to the social changes that have, since the mid-1960s, led to enhanced visibility of gay and lesbian lives. Guided by his philosophy of science rather than clinical study, Freud ([1905–24] 1953) regarded homosexuality as evidence of psychological immaturity, as a different resolution than would be expected of the nuclear conflict accompanying the shift from early to middle childhood. But he did not believe that such difference necessarily amounted to psychopathology. Others within the first generation of psychoanalysis sometimes misread or misunderstood Freud's work and assumed that the concept of "immaturity," relevant to all aspects of either homosexual or heterosexual arousal not leading in a Darwinian sense to continuation of the species, must indicate pathology (Rado 1949). Having been taught that homosexuality reflected personal psychopathology and social deviance, their students found it difficult to reconsider the issue; psychoanalysis as a discipline has traditionally regarded the wisdom imparted in clinical teaching as unquestioned truth (Socarides and Volkan 1990).

While same-gender sexual orientation may be nonnormative in a statistical sense (Schafer 1995), it is not now presumed to be evidence of deviance, psychopathology, or personal immaturity. The perspective of the present discussion is that same-gender sexual orientation represents an alternative developmental course no more different from heterosexuality than being left-handed is different from being right-handed. While the personal meanings of both heterosexuality and homosexuality are relevant to psychoanalytic inquiry and intervention, neither modality is to be privileged as the ideal developmental course. Psychoanalytic study of same-gender sexual orientation must rely on the same methods and goals as those generally characteristic of psychoanalytic study of wish or intention (Chodorow 1994).

Intensive study of the meanings and realization of same-gender sexual orientation provides additional understanding of both the manner in which sexuality is organized across the course of life and the complex interplay of life circumstances and sociohistorical context as factors relevant in sexuality and personal development (Boxer and Cohler 1989). The present study addresses such questions as why a man or woman might adopt a lesbian or gay lifestyle in middle or later life, and what the impact might be of a gay analysand's lifelong experience of stigma upon the emerging transference in psychoanalytic work.

A younger generation of psychoanalysts has questioned the assumption of a necessary relation between so-called psychological immaturity and psychopathology (Domenici and Lesser 1995). Further, clarification of the place of Freud's philosophy of science, as a result of changes in both clinical theory and understanding of psychoanalysis as a human science, has led to questioning of the very assumption that homosexuality is evidence of "immaturity." Together with findings from developmental study of the lives of gay and lesbian adolescents and adults, this has encouraged psychoanalysis itself to reconsider long-held views regarding the inevitable relation between sexual orientation, psychological development, and psychopathology, as well as regarding the most appropriate stance for intervention when working with gay and lesbian adolescents and adults.

Psychoanalysis does not prejudge any particular intention or action but is concerned with the manner in which the analysand understands choices made over the course of life. Sexual orientation is in no way privileged as beyond understanding in terms of its meaning for the analysand's lived experience. However, given the heterosexism present in contemporary society, often implicitly shared by analysand and analyst alike, questions regarding changes in sexual orientation must be subjected to particular scrutiny in terms of transference and countertransference issues. Precisely because of these issues, and because clinical psychoanalytic intervention is focused on questions of meaning, directed efforts at changing sexual orientation, in advance of collaborative study of the issue by analyst and analysand, are not consistent with the ethos of psychoanalysis.

Some analysts, however, have continued to insist that change in a gay analysand's sexual orientation must be a part of any satisfactory resolution of the analysis. This position has been buttressed by anecdotal claims of "success" in pursuing such conversions. Nonetheless, it is impossible to predict at the outset of any analysis what the conclusion will be. As analyst and analysand join in examining the life experiences of the analysand and the meanings with which these experiences are presently endowed, they arrive together at new understandings of the analysand's life story. Their conclusions, presumably, facilitate the analysand's enhanced understanding of self through greater realization of wishes or intentions that, while not necessarily in awareness, guide fantasy and action.

It is possible that enhanced understanding of lived experience might lead an analysand who had previously adopted a gay or bisexual identity to seek an identity as a straight man or woman, just as a man or woman who was ostensibly straight at the outset of analysis might later adopt an identity as gay or bisexual. The problem is that self-criticism consequent to growing up in a heterosexist society may lead the analysand to comply with the wishes of an analyst who, likewise influenced by the antigay prejudice prevalent in society, believes that conformity with heterosexist norms is requisite for a good life; the analysand may then adopt a solution which compromises his or her "true self" (Winnicott [1960a] 1965). As a result, the analysand may later experience a personal crisis and even more confusion in personal and sexual identity, leading to greater feelings of depression and anxiety or even to suicidal ideation.

The National Association of Social Work has long maintained that *any* directed effort to change sexual orientation is unethical. Recognizing the possible adverse outcome of conversion therapy, the American Psychological Association, in 1997, and the American Psychiatric Association, in 1998, both adopted the position that, while not unethical, such efforts are generally not effective (as Freud originally observed) and are to be strongly discouraged. Based on the available evidence, there can be little justification for an analyst's pursuing the directed goal of changing the analysand's sexual orientation. Although it is possible that the analysand would conclude following analysis that heterosexuality might be preferable as a means of satisfying desire and realizing partnership and intimacy, this outcome should not be a goal explicitly held by the analyst at the outset of analysis. The analyst must be particularly careful to appreciate the analysand's feelings of self-hatred based on the experience of growing up in a heterosexist society and must be careful not to join with those self-hating aspects of the analysand's person by introducing directed change as a goal of the analytic process.

This book speaks to issues associated with same-gender sexual orientation: the course of development from early childhood through later life of gay women and men, the psychological adjustment of these men and women, and the implications of these findings for psychoanalytic intervention. It summarizes what is known regarding both psychological development and mental health outcomes related to sexual orientation among lesbians and gay men. Although we have sought to provide a balanced understanding of the issues involved in study and treatment, review of extant findings has led to several conclusions which inform the book. In the first place, while genetic influences *might* play some role in determining sexual orientation, evidence reported to date does not permit such a conclusion. Neither do extant studies of biological factors such as hormonal changes in prenatal life among men later identifying as gay support the hypothesis that such factors have an important role in explaining same-gender sexual orientation.

Findings from developmental studies suggest that sexual orientation is much more fluid across the course of life than has often been recognized. Many lesbians and gay men first become aware of desire for same-gender intimacy only in their adult years. These men and women are then able to find partners and establish long-term, satisfying relationships—and those who were previously married and are parents of young children, to maintain parenting alliances with their former spouses—as well as divorced heterosexual counterparts (R. Cohen and Weissman 1984). Moreover, there is little evidence of adverse mental health outcomes among children raised by gay or lesbian couples (Patterson 1992, 1995b). Additional issues for mental health study include the interplay of aging, membership in a generation that experienced stigma because of sexual orientation, and lack of services for gay and lesbian elders. Here again, available evidence from cross-sectional developmental studies suggests that, apart from issues of stigma, gay men and women's adjustment to middle and later life is not significantly different from that of straight men and women of their generation or birth cohort. While men and women seeking same-gender partnership face some unique issues in the timing of transitions into expectable adult roles, such differences must not be considered as indicating psychopathology.

In sum, there is very little evidence that same-gender sexual orientation is intrinsically related to impairment in mental health; however, extrinsic factors, particularly antigay prejudice within the family or community, may adversely affect personal adjustment (I. Meyer 1995). As this book is written, for example, the lesbian and gay community is struggling with the murder of a gay college student in Wyoming, chilling evidence of the continuing virulence of antigay prejudice.

Except to the extent that prejudice has interfered with their course of development, gay and lesbian adolescents and young adults are more like their heterosexual counterparts than different from them. Few differences appear when adult gay and straight counterpart groups are compared on measures of personality, adjustment, or evidence of symptoms characteristic of psychopathology as evaluated through structured assessment. However, methodological problems compromise the conclusions which can be drawn from many of these studies.

Analysis of gay women and men presents particular challenges to the psychoanalytic theory of technique and highlights the complex role of the analyst's own personality as a factor related to the process of personality change. Psychoanalytic intervention with gay men and lesbians challenges preconceptions about factors presumed requisite for psychological well-being, and elicits a countertransference response less often encountered in the analysis of ostensibly straight men and women. Analysis of men and women who have experienced HIV seroconversion or who have been diagnosed with AIDS entails responses by analyst and analysand alike to issues of illness, loss, and the experience of grief. The analysis of lesbians and gay men thus has much to offer to clinical psychoanalytic theory and technique regarding determinants and expression of desire over time.

The Scope of This Discussion

This book provides both an overview of present understandings of the origin and course of desire, focusing particularly on same-gender sexual orientation, and a consideration of the implications of these understandings for clinical psychoanalytic intervention. From the outset, psychoanalysis has struggled with the issue of same-gender sexual orientation. Freud stated clearly both that homosexuality did not necessarily reflect psychopathology and that heterosexuality was not privileged as a mode of sexual expression. Indeed, writing from the perspective of Darwin, whose work he much admired, Freud identified not just homosexuality but such aspects of heterosexuality as kissing and foreplay as representations of psychosexual immaturity, a view that is clearly evident in successive revisions of his *Three Essays on the Theory of Sexuality* ([1905–24] 1953).

Freud's views were much influenced by the sexology of his time, particularly the views of Havelock Ellis (Katz 1995; Sulloway 1979). However, the concept of psychosexual immaturity is experience-distant and not relevant either to understanding lived experience as a whole or to explanations of the meanings of sexuality within the psychoanalytic process (Kohut [1959] 1978). In our own time, the focus of study and intervention has been less on questions of maturity and immaturity than on the significance of same-gender sexual orientation for the presently told life history, including that constructed within the psychoanalytic relationship itself. Clinical psychoanalytic intervention is also concerned with the significance of particular modes of self-expression as a means for enhancing personal vitality, integrity, and self-awareness.

Same-gender sexual orientation has raised significant issues for psychoanalysis from the time of Freud's first writings. Categorizing variations in the expression of desire, Freud differentiated between men and women who sought another of the same gender as the object of desire (inversion) and those who substituted some symbolic object for intimacy with another person (perversion). Freud's own effort to understand same-gender sexual desire in scientific terms, following the earlier work of Ellis, fostered emergence of a category of experience known as homosexuality in the first decades of the twentieth century. Prior to this time there had been no specific label attached to sexual experiences between persons of the same gender. This attempt to understand same-gender sexual desire in scientific terms followed both from Freud's effort to explain all aspects of present experience in terms of the coactive presence of the personal past and from the effort to rephrase the emerging moral critique regarding same-gender desire as a medical problem (Chauncey 1994; Katz 1995).

Following Freud's pioneering study, and particularly in the years following the Second World War, another perspective developed which emphasized study of same-gender sexual orientation as medical-psychiatric illness and led to the view that homosexuality represented either oedipal or pre-oedipal fixation founded on problematic relationships between parents and offspring (Bieber et al. 1962; Ovesey 1969; Rado 1949). A third approach to the discussion of same-gender sexual orientation, founded at least partially on the first systematic study of the lives and present adjustment of men and women indicating preference for a partner of the same gender (Blumstein and Schwartz 1983, 1989), as well as on changes in understanding of sexuality within the larger culture, has emerged over the past two decades. This reconsideration of the psychoanalytic understanding of the place of sexual orientation in the course of life reflects more enduring social and cultural changes in the period beginning in the mid-1960s. This shift was reflected within mental health professions other than psychoanalysis by the decision more than two decades ago to remove same-gender sexual orientation as an expression of psychopathology within the official psychiatric nomenclature.

The present book reviews this century-long struggle to understand same-gender desire within psychoanalysis. This discussion assumes at the outset that the task of psychoanalysis is to understand all forms and expressions of desire, regardless of the gender of the person who is the object of such desire, and that heterosexuality itself is an outcome which must be understood (Chodorow 1992). Homosexuality is here understood as explicit awareness of sexual desire regarding others of the same gender. While it is possible that such awareness may not be associated with action, within contemporary culture it is most likely that men or women who define themselves as gay or lesbian will also have had at least transitory sexual experiences with others of the same gender.

Over the past three decades, historical study (Foucault [1976] 1990; Chauncey 1994; Weeks 1991; D'Emilio 1998), together with systematic study within the human sciences (Bell and Weinberg 1981; Blumstein and Schwartz 1983; Gonsiorek 1991; Herdt and Boxer 1996), has both influenced and been influenced by larger cultural changes. Formerly a taboo topic, likely to engender anxiety and often leading gay men and women to seek psychiatric intervention, same-gender sexual orientation is now generally understood as but another developmental pathway (Herdt 1997; Hostetler and Herdt 1998), one mode of lived experience, which must be understood in terms of the meanings which persons make of desire and its realization (A. Sullivan 1995).

This discussion posits that issues of sexual orientation cannot be understood apart from issues of historical and social change (Elder 1997; Mannheim [1928] 1993), particularly the remarkable changes that have occurred over the past four decades. The focus is on the changes which have taken place in our understanding of sexual orientation among gay men and women, including both those seeking psychoanalytic or psychotherapeutic intervention and those not expressing need for such assistance. The discussion is necessarily limited to issues of sexual orientation among men and women coming to identify as gay or lesbian and seeking others of the same gender for social and sexual intimacy. Issues of gender identity disorder or gender dysphoria, such as are reflected in the desire to change sex and among transgendered or transsexual men and women, are not included in the present discussion.

The position of this book is both that sexual orientation and psychopathology are independent dimensions except as moderated by the impact of stigma (Herek 1991, 1995) and that being gay or lesbian reflects merely another developmental pathway through the life course. There are a number of ways in which gay men and women come to adulthood, and a number of ways in which they negotiate their adult years; these lifeways (Schutz and Luckmann 1973, [1983] 1989) lead to meanings of lived experience which can be systematically explored within the psychoanalytic situation. Finally, it must be emphasized that just as life-course study may benefit from psychoanalytic case studies of the manner in which persons refashion meanings within the context of social and historical change, as Hartmann ([1939] 1958) stressed, psychoanalysis must take into consideration parameters such as the context within which meanings are made.

The Controversy in Psychoanalysis Regarding Sexual Orientation

The present volume presumes that experience of same-gender sexual orientation is, for whatever reason, an important and "owned" aspect of present lived experience. The discussion focuses on issues in personal development and psychoanalytic intervention among gay men and women who, in the popular idiom, are "out" (of the closet) and feel little need to disguise their sexual orientation, except possibly in response to the realistic demands of the workplace. Often acknowledged by self and others as gay since childhood or adolescence, these adults report little need to disavow their sexual orientation and generally seek psychoanalysis for issues only tangentially related to sexual orientation. These men and women—who understand themselves as gay, lesbian, or bisexual and select as intimate partners persons of the same gender, but do not see themselves as otherwise different from their heterosexual counterparts—pose a challenge to psychoanalysis and the other mental health professions that formerly regarded selection of a same-gender partner as evidence of psychopathology, deviance, a deficit in personality development, or personal immaturity.[1]

This discussion of sexual orientation and psychoanalysis also presumes both that the analysand is aware of same-gender sexual wishes and that neither analysand or analyst feels much need to disguise or disavow these wishes except in response to community-based prejudice. Issues regarding the de-

---

1. Community surveys have shown that as many as 60 percent of gay men and 80 percent of lesbians report, at any one time, being in a committed relationship (Hostetler and Cohler 1997). Further, in the most detailed comparison to date of relationships among straight and gay couples, Blumstein and Schwartz (1983) reported few differences founded on sexual orientation. At the same time, the intellectual perspective underlying this discussion assumes that the meanings of sexuality are fluid across the course of particular lives and over periods of historical time. Accounts of both analysands and analysts are framed by inevitable participation within the larger culture; the analytic process focuses on the manner in which particular accounts of lived experience have led to a particular set of meanings, understanding which is the focus of collaboration between analyst and analysand.

velopment of awareness of same-gender desire across the course of life, including personal, family, and community acknowledgment, are considered. It is assumed that as a consequence of changes within the mental health community over the past two decades, there is less need than previously to disguise sexual orientation within the scientific and professional community.

Few areas of study in psychiatry and psychoanalysis have fostered the stereotyping and misunderstanding which has surrounded the discussion of homosexuality. As is now well known, the 1973 vote by the trustees of the American Psychiatric Association to declassify homosexuality as a form of psychopathology was accompanied by heated debate and bitter acrimony (Bayer 1987; Bayer and Spitzer 1982). The issue was only settled after the question was submitted to the entire membership of the association. This is the only time that the entire membership has been polled regarding a classification for the Diagnostic and Statistical Manual (only a decade later, in the fourth edition of the manual, was the category of "ego-dystonic" homosexuality eliminated). And dissent has persisted; a number of psychiatrists continue to assert that homosexuality reflects enduring psychopathology.

The American Psychoanalytic Association voted, within the past few years, to eliminate sexual orientation as a factor in selecting candidates for psychoanalytic education. Freud was explicit in stating that sexual orientation was not relevant to selection for psychoanalytic education; Lewes reports that in 1930 Freud, responding to a letter from Ernst Jones and Otto Rank informing him that the British society had rejected the application of an "overt homosexual," had stated:

> We cannot exclude such persons without other sufficient reasons, as we cannot agree with their legal prosecution. We feel that a decision in such cases should depend upon a thorough examination of the other qualities of the candidate. (Lewes [1988] 1995, 33)

However, many in psychoanalysis demurred from Freud's views, assuming that selection of a sexual partner of the same gender represented psychopathology. Some analysts continue to insist that such a choice inevitably reflects failure to resolve important issues in preadult development, most notably the nuclear conflict itself. Others insist that homosexuality inevitably reflects pre-oedipal personality deficits, which may, for some analysands, be resolved through psychoanalytic intervention. This view within psychoanalysis, that same-gender sexual orientation necessarily reflects psychopathology or immaturity, may become the foundation of the belief that a goal of psychoanalytic intervention is to change sexual orientation. The present discussion challenges this limited understanding of same-gender sexual orientation, citing both of findings from systematic human science study and an emerging clinical psychoanalytic literature focusing on issues of technique and relationship in work with gay and bisexual men and women.

The theory of psychoanalytic technique has changed dramatically in the past three decades, largely in response to broader social and historical changes. The psychological development of women, for example, has been the subject of intense scrutiny. The dynamics of change within psychoanalysis have also been reconsidered, with renewed attention given to the analytic relationship itself (Gill 1994; Hoffman 1998). Scrutiny has also been given to the question of sexual orientation as it relates to psychological development and adjustment (Schafer 1995). The removal of homosexuality from the Diagnostic and Statistical Manual of the American Psychiatric Association is but one example of this change. The decision by the American Psychoanalytic Association to remove sexual orientation as a consideration of suitability for psychoanalytic education is another.

The present book maintains that while the meaning of sexual orientation is always significant as a part of the psychoanalytic process, sexual orientation is independent of psychopathology. From a clinical perspective, the focus of the psychoanalytic process is to explore the meanings a particular mode of sexual expression carries for the analysand and to foster enhanced vitality and personal integration as a result of this exploration. Possible modes of sexual expression include choosing a person of the opposite gender with whom to realize intimacy, choosing a person of the same gender, or choosing a partner of the same gender at some points in one's course of life and a person of the opposite gender at other points. The question for psychoanalytic study concerns the meanings presently expressed regarding all forms of personal attraction.

As Stoller (1985), Lewes ([1988] 1995), and Chodorow (1994) all have noted, psychoanalysis focuses on the stories which account for all modes of intimacy and sexual expression. Chodorow observes not only that psychoanalysis does not have a theory of the development of "normal" heterosexuality but also that when such theories have been proposed, primarily from the genetic point of view (Rapaport and Gill 1959), they have been silent regarding differences in outcome with respect to choice of sexual partner as a reflection of the compromise formation emerging from the resolution of the nuclear neurosis of early childhood. From the perspective of psychoanalysis as a psychology of mental conflict, variation in sexual expression cannot be differentiated in terms of such outcomes as mental health or personal maturity. Since, as both Stoller (1985) and Person (1988a) have observed, love and desire are experienced across varieties of sexuality, the focus within psychoanalysis must properly be on the manner in which desire is experienced and on the meanings of desire for the analysand. Psychoanalysis attaches particular significance to the experience of all states of desire and their potential for enhancing personal satisfaction and integration; there is no place within psychoanalysis for privileging particular modalities for the expression of desire.

The first part of this book focuses on critical discussion of the biological and developmental literature, reviewing findings from evolutionary biology, behavioral genetics, developmental neuroendocrinology, and neuroanatomy, followed by discussion of the course of development of men and women who at some point become aware of sexual wishes directed toward others of the same gender. The second part focuses on issues of mental health and psychoanalytic intervention, viewed in the context of the biological and developmental literature. It considers not only the complex relation between psychoanalytic intervention and directed efforts to foster change in the analysand's sexual orientation but, more generally, problems for the analytic situation founded on the sexual orientation of analysand and analyst.

As the sense of stigma founded on sexual orientation has diminished in contemporary society, making it possible for younger cohorts of gay men and women to realize personal goals with less need than in the past to disguise important aspects of self and personal identity, it has become possible to appreciate the extent to which what formerly appeared as psychopathology was largely the consequence of enduring prejudice (Young-Bruehl 1996). Younger gay men and women have the opportunity to grow up gay or lesbian and to understand their lives as but one of a number of pathways into adulthood (Herdt 1997; Herdt and Boxer 1996). They do not necessarily express conflict regarding sexual orientation (Cohler 1996). However, the meanings these young adults make of their sexual orientation, like those made by their straight counterparts, are an appropriate focus of psychoanalytic study, but psychoanalysis must first reconsider its long-standing assumptions about the inevitable interplay of psychopathology and sexual orientation.

A second issue, consequent to the first, concerns the significance of the analysand's choice of sexual orientation for the emergence of transference and countertransference across the course of clinical psychoanalytic intervention. Discussion of this issue involves consideration of the role of analysis in maintaining or changing sexual orientation. One group of analysts continues to maintain with considerable passion that same-gender sexual orientation reflects profound psychopathology and that psychoanalytic intervention should be directed toward a change in sexual orientation. Without doubt, there are some analysands for whom a particular expression of sexuality does reflect profound personal struggle; sexualization of relationships, including repetition of this effort within the transference, may be the expression of a "breakdown product" (Elson 1987; Khan 1974, 1979; Kohut 1977). But this is as true in selection of opposite- as of same-gender sexual partners.

To date, there is little clear understanding of the significance of sexual orientation either for lived experience or for the enactment of the life story within the psychoanalytic situation. The findings reviewed in the present book should foster more informed future debate regarding these issues. However, it is critical that this discussion take place in the context of abiding respect for those holding contrary views. Persons who have suffered lifelong discrimination, due to religious preference, ethnicity, or sexual orientation, are understandably sensitive to allegedly scientific perspectives which are little more than a disguise for continued discrimination (Young-Bruehl 1996). It is essential that there be open discussion of the scientific issues involved in so-called reparative or conversion therapy, efforts directed at change of sexual orientation. It is important that this discussion be respectful of the particular problems of stigma confronted by gay men and women, and not serve as yet an additional source of stigma (Malyon 1982).

The larger issue for psychoanalysis, as this discussion continually emphasizes, concerns the meanings for analysands of any particular expression of sexuality as an aspect of lived experience. In part, the problem of assessing the role of psychoanalytic intervention in determining subsequent sexual orientation arises from the assumption within clinical psychoanalysis that the outcome of an intervention cannot be presumed either at the outset or in the course of the collaborative psychoanalytic process. Decisions regarding the place of sexual orientation as desire and action, while clearly informed by the meanings which analysand and analyst together fashion of such aspects of lived experience as sexual desire and its expression in the life-world, should instead be made following conclusion of the formal analytic work. However, as de Monteflores (1986) and Herek (1991, 1996) have shown, the very heterosexist bias which characterizes contemporary society, inevitably shared by analyst and analysand, may prejudice decisions about both meaning and choice of sexual orientation. From this perspective, the danger of efforts to change the analysand's sexual orientation, which Freud ([1935] 1951) acknowledged as impossible, is that such conversion would reflect an implicit, unanalyzed transference/complementary identification countertransference (Racker 1968), which itself requires analysis.

The focus here, as in psychoanalysis more generally, is the manner in which analysand and analyst share the meanings which the analysand makes of particular aspects of lived experience. The present discussion recognizes that there are some men and women for whom sudden awareness of same-gender desire, characteristically in middle adulthood, may reflect some form of distress. Whether evoked as an effort to resolve the nuclear conflict of early childhood, realized anew with the advent of midlife and a growing awareness of finitude (Munnichs 1966; Marshall 1975; Neugarten 1979), or as a response to continuing concerns regarding personal identity, exacerbated by characteristic midlife concerns, this expression of distress is most often characterized by ego-dystonic wishes and actions leading to shame and embarrassment (J. K. Meyer 1985, 1995; Isay 1989). Clearly, this distress becomes a subject for analytic inquiry. At the same time, community study of sexual orientation and aging shows that there are many middle-aged men and women whose first awareness of same-gender desire is not a particularly distressing experience; while they seek psychoanalysis, their reasons for seeking help are not focused specifically on awareness of same-gender desire.

Finally, this book considers the implications of this perspective for the psychoanalytic process and the two-person psychoanalytic relationship (Gill 1994), focusing particularly on issues of transference and countertransference, including the many factors within the analytic relationship itself that contribute to the analysand's present understanding of his or her sexual orientation at the conclusion of the formal analytic work. The book concludes that the clinical psychoanalytic process represents an important means for studying the meaning of sexual desire across the course of life, that at the outset of the analytic collaboration the meaning of particular modes in which desire is expressed should be a focus of analytic study, that the goal of psychoanalysis should be to foster an enhanced sense of personal vitality, coherence, and self-awareness, and that the analysand's preference for intimate ties with persons of either the same or the other gender should be informed by such enhanced self-awareness. Clearly this outcome is related to the larger issue of both transference and countertransference, including the nature of the analyst's own complementary and concordant identifications (Racker 1968).

The present discussion challenges more traditional views of same-gender sexual orientation as necessarily indicating immaturity, deficiency in personality development, psychopathology, or the failure of prior psychoanalytic intervention. The evidence this book is founded on suggests that the bias entailed in regarding heterosexuality as "normal" and, thus, not in need of understanding or explanation may direct both analysand and analyst from the important task of seeking to understand the meanings of all aspects of wish and action.

Two

Perspectives on the Study of Sexual Orientation

Psycho-analytic research is most decidedly opposed to any attempt at separating off homosexuals from the rest of mankind as a group of a special character. . . . [A]ll human beings are capable of making a homosexual object-choice and have in fact made one in their unconscious. Indeed, libidinal attachments to persons of the same sex play no less a part as factors in normal mental life, and a greater part as a motive for illness, than do similar attachments to the opposite sex. . . . From the point of view of psychoanalysis the exclusive sexual interest felt by men for women is also a problem that needs elucidating and is not a self-evident fact. (Freud [1905–24] 1953, 145–46)

Discussion of same-gender sexual orientation, generally referred to as "homosexuality," has a complex history in both psychoanalysis and the larger culture. Few topics arouse such passion and philosophic difference as avowed preference for sexual intimacy with others of the same gender. Psychiatry has attempted, in the past century, to shift the understanding of homosexuality within the larger culture from a presumption of moral failing to a diagnosis of psychological illness or immaturity (Chauncey 1994; Greenberg 1988; G. Sullivan 1990). In psychoanalysis, perhaps more than anywhere else, discussion of homosexuality reflects the interplay of changing social and historical circumstances. Indeed, as a consequence of such changes psychoanalysis has had both to reconsider its theory of technique and to develop a new perspective in which same-gender sexual orientation is seen as but another developmental pathway, nonnormative but neither deviant nor pathological (Schafer 1995).

The term "homosexuality," was first used by Prussian jurist Karl Maria Kertbeny in an 1869 letter to the ministry of justice urging abolition of provisions defining same-gender sexual contact as criminal conduct under the Prussian code (Katz 1990; Mondimore 1996). Kertbeny suggested that same-gender sexual orientation may be innate and so not subject to legal and moral censure; as we will see, his argument remains important to this day. Work by other German jurists and medical scientists similarly reflected the new spirit of scientific inquiry, replacing earlier moral condemnation with compassionate understanding of illness. The distinction between homosexuality and heterosexuality was later immortalized in Krafft-Ebing's (1889–90) detailed medical study of the varieties of sexuality, and the terms soon entered the public idiom.

In England the study of same-gender sexual orientation was less directly associated with legal issues (Mondimore 1996). Focus on the significance of men having sex with other men as a distinctive matter stems from work late in the nineteenth century, particularly that of John Addington Symonds (1840–93), a British historian of the Renaissance who wrote a memoir (1984) detailing his sexual experiences with other men. After encountering a paper by the British physician Havelock Ellis on Walt Whitman's *Leaves of Grass,* Symonds wrote Ellis about his own erotic sensitivities. Ellis, in turn, coined the term "inversion" to refer to Symonds's same-gender sexual interests, and the two entered into a plan to write a book on the subject. When Symonds died suddenly early in their collaboration, Ellis finished the book alone (Ellis and Symonds 1897). Symonds had introduced Ellis to others of his circle; their histories, published in a disguised form, are significant for being normal, in the sense of being about men leading ordinary lives and not seeking psychological intervention. Ellis clearly distinguishes same-gender desire from neuropathology (Sulloway 1979).

Freud, fluent in all the major European languages, read Ellis's work in English and used it, together with that of Krafft-Ebing and Moll, as the foundation for his own discussion of the development of the libido. He adopted Ellis's term "inversion" in the *Three Essays on the Theory of Sexuality* ([1905–24] 1953) and his psychobiographical essay on Leonardo ([1910c] 1957). Freud first met Ellis in 1898, just as the initial volumes of Ellis's seven-volume study of sexuality were being published. They seem to have agreed about much regarding sexuality (Sulloway 1979).

The work of Freud and his English and German colleagues has continued to have a significant impact on the discussion of same-gender sexual orientation. Their discussion of sexual inversion provided the basis for the later discussion of homosexuality as a mode of sexual experience distinct from heterosexuality. During most of the nineteenth century there was not even a term for same-gender sexual expression (Chauncey 1994). The "love that dared not speak its name" simply had none. The effort to understand homosexuality as an attribute of personality (H. Ellis 1897) was a response to the Victorian view of homosexuality as morally reprehensible. Viewing same-gender sexual desire as a medical rather than a moral condition was important to Freud's ([1905–24] 1953) interest in nonnormative sexual expression. Supporting Freud's emphasis on so called bisexuality (better understood as "pansexuality"), Kinsey and his colleagues in fact argued for a continuum of expression of same-gender sexual desire (Kinsey, Pomeroy, and Martin 1948).

As part of his general program of explaining adult function as a product of early development, Freud sought to understand homosexuality in terms of the dynamics of the child's early experience in the family. However, recognizing that same-gender sexual orientation may originate in the dynamics of the family is very different from viewing it as pathological or reflecting a deficit in development. Foucault (1976), Weeks (1991), and Chauncey (1994) all note, however, that the attention paid to same-gender sexual desire as a distinctive social and medical problem helped create the sense that there was something to be explained, that men's sexual interest in other men was not merely a matter of taste, like a preference for women of various ages, body builds, or coloring. Consistent with Gay's (1998) portrayal of concepts of acceptable sexuality in late-nineteenth-century society, Suppe (1997) suggests that the continuing discussion of "homosexuality" and the search for its "cause" is an extension into the present of the late-Victorian preoccupation with the idea of "normal love," heterosexual romantic love that requires no explanation.

Psychoanalysis and Homosexuality—An Uneasy History

The discussion of sexual orientation, mental health, and psychoanalytic intervention has generated intense controversy since Freud's initial collaboration with Fliess. Critical reading of Freud's work suggests that he regarded variation in gender of sexual partner to be of interest primarily as support for his "archaeological model" of psychic development rather than as evidence of psychopathology (Jacobsen and Steele 1979). Freud viewed all aspects of sexuality apart from mounting and penetration in the missionary position as reflections of the infantile past as coactive in determining present pleasure. His argument was from analogy to Schliemann's excavation of Troy, Haeckel's ([1868] 1968) observation in natural philosophy that phylogeny recapitulates ontogeny, and his own earlier detailed laboratory study of the eighth, or acoustical, nerve as it enters into the medulla (Sulloway 1979; Wolf and Nebel 1978). This philosophical position, the foundation for the genetic point of view in psychoanalysis (Rapaport and Gill 1959), was never grounded in the clinical theory.

In the most detailed and best documented account to date of the influence of nineteenth-century natural philosophy on Freud's construction of his metapsychology, Sulloway observed:

> Freud's implicit endorsement of this [Haeckel's Fundamental Biogenetic] law constitutes perhaps the least appreciated source of *a priori* biological influence

in all of psychoanalytic theory. For if the developing child recapitulates the history of the race, it must likewise recapitulate the *sexual* history of the race. In other words, the prepubertal human being must have the innate potential to experience all of the archaic forms of sexual pleasure that once characterized the mature life stages of our remote ancestors. Not only did this biogenetic logic underlie Freud's earliest (mid-1880s) insights into the "extended" and "polymorphously perverse" nature of infantile sexual activity, but it also gave him, in later years, his most irrefutable justification for these views. (Sulloway 1979, 259–260 citing Freud [1916–17, 354])

Freud elaborated on this assertion when he maintained in other writings that each major substage in the child's "pregenital" phase of sexual development has preserved a specific legacy of this phylogenetic influence.

Abraham's collaboration with Freud extended this perspective (Abraham [1916] 1927, [1921] 1927, [1924a] 1927, [1924b] 1927), and revisions of the *Three Essays* reflect this collaboration. However, as Sulloway has shown, Freud inspired Abraham's efforts in the direction of an epigenetic psychology founded on his own continuing interest in archaeology and, by analogy, developmental neurobiology. Sulloway faults psychoanalysis as a method of psychological intervention because it is founded on a natural science philosophy with no empirical support. However, except as analogy, Freud's "archaeology of the mind" (Jacobsen and Steele 1979) had little impact upon his clinical theory, which focused on the study of meanings, wishes, and desires as reported by analysands (G. Klein 1976). From this epigenetic perspective, sexual inversion was a "normal" part of heterosexual intimacy on the same level as foreplay.

While Freud explicitly excluded sexual orientation as a factor relevant to selection for psychoanalytic education, many analysts persisted in assuming that selection of a sexual partner of the same gender represented psychopathology which might be modified through psychoanalytic intervention. Over the past two decades, though, there has been a shift in the views of the larger society regarding sexual orientation (Lewes [1988] 1995), stemming from the social and intellectual revolution of the period from the mid-1960s to the mid-1970s. Psychoanalysis is never immune from larger social and historical changes (Schafer 1995); indeed, each generation shapes knowledge as a consequence of such changes (Mannheim [1923] 1952), and changes within individual lives can only be understood in terms of these cohort-related changes.

Our discussion focuses on variation in sexualities as alternative pathways to intimacy and sexual pleasure. Freud ([1916–17] 1963) believed all modes of object choice must be explained, but Chodorow (1992) notes that subsequent study privileged heterosexuality as not needing explanation and instead focused on explanation of homosexuality as a departure from this norm. As a result, psychoanalysis lacks a coherent theory of the development of "normal" heterosexuality; moreover, to the extent that such theories exist, notably in a genetic context, they fail to relate differences in partner's gender to a compromise formation emerging from the resolution of the nuclear neurosis of early childhood.

Psychoanalysis, as a psychology of mental conflict, cannot differentiate particular variations in sexual expression as mentally healthy or personally mature. Since, as Stoller (1985) and Person (1988a) observe, love and desire are experienced in all varieties of sexuality, psychoanalysis must focus on how desire is experienced and its meanings for the analysand, with the goal of enhancing his or her experience of personal satisfaction and integration. There is no place in psychoanalysis to privilege a particular mode of expressing desire. From a clinical psychoanalytic perspective, each mode of sexual expression carries meanings for the analysand based on a lifetime of experience. Psychoanalysis focuses on wish and intent in the stories which account for all modes of intimacy and sexual expression (Chodorow 1992), without any value judgment favoring particular stories of personal relationships.

There can be little question that the broad social and historical changes of the past three decades have had significant impact upon both psychoanalytic understanding of the human condition and modes of intervention. This perspective is nowhere better represented than in the response within psychoanalysis to the larger culture's reduced perception of homosexuality as a moral failing or psychological derangement. Organized psychoanalysis itself has experienced tension, particularly in the past decade, in the process of coming to terms with larger social change with respect to such concepts as "normality" of sexual orientation.

Toward a Psychoanalytic Understanding of Homosexuality

Few concepts in psychoanalysis and the human sciences have been as much discussed and as little understood as "homosexuality."[1] Emphasis on same-

---

1. The complexity of any discussion of sexual orientation is illustrated by the problem of the words to be used in discussing this issue. Life-course studies of men and women self-identifying as of same-gender sexual orientation have highlighted major generational or cohort differences in preferred terms. Older men and women may use the term "homosexual," while middle-aged men and women may either use the term "gay" or distinguish between "gay men" and "lesbians." Young adults generally prefer the term "queer," which has particular political implications: (Jagose 1996; Warner 1993). Many young adults reject the distinction between gay and straight in a manner that harks back to the traditional nineteenth-century view, which made no arbitrary distinctions between men and women who at least sometimes sought intimacy with others of the same gender. Indeed, many young adults portray themselves as queer, which they explain means that they are not stereotypically straight/heterosexual. "Queer" best summarizes this particular perspective. The present discussion uses the term "gay" in referring to those men and women who understand themselves as

gender sexual desire, separate from sexual expression generally, is distinctive to the past century. In an effort to foster consideration of such expression of desire apart from moral and legal codes, the term "homosexuality" was fashioned as a description for the realization of sexual satisfaction with persons of the same gender. More recently, it has also been applied to a lifestyle associated with this preference or orientation. The definition poses four problems: (1) realization and enactment of same-gender sexual desire may be continuous with, rather than separate from, sexual desire more generally, (2) same-gender sexual desire involves both particular and shared meanings, (3) desire refers to subjective states and fantasy as well as actions in the world, and (4) form and expression of sexual desire shows marked variation in meaning for people within their own lives and across generations. These four qualifications make it difficult to define the concept of homosexuality, yet a presumed unitary concept of homosexuality is the basis of much discourse in psychiatry and other fields of mental health study.

Definition of Same-Gender Sexual Orientation

As understood in psychoanalysis and the human sciences that focus on the study of wish or intent (G. Klein 1976), and consistent with the issues that instigated the present review of what is known about same-gender sexual orientation, the scope of the present discussion is limited to a definition of homosexuality in terms of *presently acknowledged awareness or recognition of sexual desire toward another person of the same gender, whether or not realized in action, at any point across the course of life, together with the adoption of identity thought to be associated with this desire.* Several aspects of this definition are important to note. First, it focuses less on intrinsic or essential characteristics of individuals than on the interplay of society and history and particular life circumstances. Some men and women are exclusively gay or straight across the course of life; others seek same-gender sexual partners at one time and partners of the other gender at another time. Our perspective does not view sexuality from an essentialist perspective. This view contrasts with more traditional views regarding sexual orientation within psychiatry and allied fields of mental health study and practice.

Second, "being homosexual" entails more than simply having same-gender sexual desire. Rather, it means adopting an identity that integrates wishes, actions, and relationships characterized as a particular sexual orientation. There are many men and women who at some point in their lives have had sexual experiences with a person of the same gender who do not see

---

having a same-gender sexual orientation. We further differentiate between gay men and lesbians where there is need for explicit distinction between the genders.

themselves as gay or lesbian. In an exhaustive review, Shively, Jones, and De Cecco (1984) report that while most studies define homosexuality in terms of physical sexual activity, although others also emphasize erotic attraction and realization of a close affectional relationship with another of the same gender as important aspects of a gay or lesbian identity.

Much of the focus of recent accounts is less on realization of an identity as gay, bisexual, or straight than on the nature and quality of relationships, including the meanings or experience of self and other inherent in these relationships. As De Cecco and Shively (1984) observe, focus on relationships rather than identity as such is congruent with psychoanalytic perspectives on meaning and wish or intent and also recognizes the necessary intersection of particular lives and social context over time (Cass 1984).

It is important to distinguish between the concepts of sexual orientation and gender identity (Friedman and Downey 1994). The present discussion is limited to sexual orientation, particularly its implications for psychoanalytic intervention among men and women who explicitly acknowledge themselves as of alternate sexual orientation. A person's sexual identity, as gay, straight, or bisexual, may be consonant with sexual orientation. However, sexual identity is independent of and must be differentiated from gender identity. Views of oneself as masculine or feminine are not necessarily related to sexual orientation.

Understanding of oneself as gay, bisexual, or straight enters into one's self-definition and may enter into performance of particular social roles. While many gay men and women elect not to discuss their sexual orientation within the larger world of work and family, others are more comfortable with their sexual orientation and readily acknowledge being gay in many contexts. Their partners may take part in family events or be discussed at work as a heterosexual spouse might be. The experience of being gay, the relationship with one's partner, and the psychological issues raised by a gay identity in relation to work and family may all be subjected to the process of self-scrutiny that comprises psychoanalytic interventions, but such aspects of social life are of obvious relevance for clinical psychoanalytic intervention regardless of sexual orientation. Issues of particular concern for gay men and women entering analysis often include questions of whether, where, and when to disclose and discuss their sexual orientation.

Third, following Kinsey, the focus of this definition is on subjective experience, particularly recognized fantasy. Kinsey, Pomeroy, and Martin (1948) recognized the importance of erotic fantasy in their use of a seven-point scale (0–6), with zero referring to persons with absolutely no sense of erotic arousal regarding others of the same gender and six to those who, in the present popular idiom, "can't even think straight." Persons who regard themselves as predominately homosexual, or gay, are generally considered to be classified within groups four through six, characterized by sexual fantasies pertaining nearly exclusively to others of the same gender.

This scale was later extended by Klein, Sepekoff, and Wolff (1985) to include seven separate elements of sexual orientation: sexual fantasies, sexual behavior, emotional preference, sexual attraction, social preference, self-identification, and heterosexual-homosexual lifestyle preference. Further, recognizing that sexual orientation is fluid across the course of life, each of these seven elements was rated on a seven-point scale for lifetime to date and for the immediately preceding year. De Cecco and Shively (1984) suggest that we need to shift away from definitions based on the mechanics of sexual acts and focus on personal attitudes and expectations. Shively and De Cecco (1977) highlight the significance of distinguishing between gender identity, or basic conviction of being male or female, and sexual-role identity, or definition of oneself in terms of sexual preferences.

However, it is important to emphasize that these are not categories inherent in persons, that the content and expression of sexual fantasies show considerable variation within particular lives, and that social and historical factors are intrinsically involved in the definition of sexual orientation. For example, among the present generation of late adolescents and young adults, it is common for men and women to report with relative comfort sexual fantasies regarding both same- and other-gender individuals and to act upon these fantasies in sexual relations with both genders. A larger group of persons, often termed "bisexual," portray their sexuality in this manner than in prior generations.

It is important in this context to emphasize that, for the present cohort of those seeking expression of desire with others of the same gender, the terms "homosexual" or "gay" refer only to those aspects of persons which are related to expression of sexual desire and a search for intimacy. Related to this understanding of the expression of same-gender desire as but one aspect of personhood, and in contrast with much prior usage, particularly within psychoanalysis (Moore and Fine 1990), "homosexuality" and related terms all refer to *explicitly experienced* wishes and the many ways in which these wishes are enacted, including search for same-gender sexual partners and identification with the community of others sharing similar desires.

Finally, this definition of homosexuality includes, but is not limited to, expression of sexual desire, understood in the present context as a part of both lifestyle and characteristic intimate relationships. As is the case with heterosexuality, sexuality is expressed within the context of enduring ties to a partner; physical contact is but one aspect of affectional ties. Much of the discussion of homosexuality is biased in the direction of emphasizing not just desire, but desire expressed in desperate, promiscuous encounters; however, like their straight counterparts, gay men and women most often seek partnership within an enduring relationship.

The present discussion focuses primarily on issues of development and clinical intervention among those men and women who at some level understand their sexual orientation. Moore and Fine (1990) distinguish between latent and manifest, or unconscious and conscious, homosexuality. This distinction presumes that—related to unresolved aspects of the nuclear neurosis, and in response to fear of castration and the adoption of a "negative" attitude—there may be an unrecognized wish/fear dilemma represented as a latent wish which represents a defense against subsequent issues of rivalry or competition and is expressed through enhanced enactment or fear of passivity.

We assume in this volume that persons are aware of the content of their sexual fantasies. This awareness may be more or less troubling or egodystonic, and may be intrusive at times when such fantasies are not welcome or are related to particular other persons. Particularly in the years immediately following medicalization of the discussion of sexual preference, referring to homosexuality as a mode of sexual expression apart from "normal" heterosexuality led to a view of same-gender desire as deviant and dangerous. This view, in turn, was reflected in delusions such as Freud (1911) reports in the Schreber case. Today, when the expression of same-gender desire is less often stigmatized, particularly in urban settings, it is less often disavowed, appearing instead as an enactment within clinical psychoanalytic inquiry among men and women who have acknowledged their same-gender desire at the outset of their analyses. At the same time, for analysts who maintain the importance of the manifestation and resolution of the nuclear neurosis, including evidence of the "negative oedipal constellation," interpretation of this negative oedipal element and its impact upon present life may be an important aspect of the resolution of issues related to competition and professional achievement as well as self-esteem and personal inhibition.

Furthermore, within the transference, at least part of the reenactment of the nuclear wish or oedipal neurosis may well include efforts at enacting the "negative" solution of offering oneself sexually to the analyst in an effort to forestall anticipated retaliation. Interpretation of this enactment leads to enhanced understanding of characteristic modes of relating to others and of the reasons or causes for a particular mode of relating in the life-world. However, shared understanding and interpretation of this enactment (Chused 1991; McLaughlin 1991), while clearly relevant to the expression of same-gender sexual fantasies, must be differentiated from desire for others of the same gender as experienced in fantasy and in the life-world.

Among men and women who acknowledge themselves as gay or lesbian, the expression of sexual wishes toward others of the same or opposite gender may be a source of distress, but the content of these wishes is generally not kept out of awareness. In the past, at least to some extent, prevailing attitudes in both Europe and America made it difficult even to talk about these wishes, which had to be inferred from the content of associations within clinical psychoanalysis. Among those who seek psychoanalytic intervention within personally painful lives, homosexual wishes or enactments may be themselves a source of distress or a means of portraying other sources of distress. As Isay (1989) shows, awareness of desire for others of the same gender may first appear, associated with other life changes, at any point across the course of adult lives and may raise issues which are relevant to psychoanalytic understanding. What is troubling, however, is the awareness of these wishes and associated fantasies, which may be disavowed but which remain potentially in awareness, symbolically expressed in a manner which may be decoded by analyst and analysand within the transference.

The Significance of a "Master Narrative" for Being Gay

It is import to note some qualifications at the outset of this discussion: the concept of "being gay" (Isay 1996a) refers to states of desire. As already noted, the relation between fantasy and action is complex and is governed by present understandings of self and by important relationships within family and community. The process of "coming out," or disclosure of this desire, often associated with an effort to connect desire and action, reflects first acknowledgment to oneself of desires for same-gender partnership, which is commonly followed by an effort to realize this desire. Since sexual orientation is not a visible aspect of identity in the manner of gender or color, gay men and women often seek out safe or accepting places in the community, such as clubs and bars, where they might meet other gay men and women. Later, they may begin selectively disclosing their gay identity, coming out to friends and family. Often, these men and women report feeling more integrated and affirmed when they no longer feel the need to hide an important aspect of their lives from those they care about. This process of acknowledging to themselves and others an important aspect of who and what they are raises important issues which may be addressed in psychotherapeutic work.

What is most significant in the study of homosexuality and the life course is the diversity of these men and women whose only common link is a preference for sexual intimacy with others of the same gender. This diversity is reflected in the time of awareness of same-gender sexual orientation, in the role of being gay, lesbian, or bisexual in present adjustment and ties with others, in preference in partnership, and even in the significance of same-gender sexual orientation for present lived experience. One woman may be a highly effective associate in a law firm, concerned with her prospects for becoming a partner and paying little attention to her own sexuality. Another woman, a physician involved in the problems of women contracting AIDS and their children born with the disease, may have a partner with whom she shares an interest in community activism and be visible in social and political activities.

Over time, stereotypes have emerged regarding the "dyke" or "femme" lesbian and the effeminate gay man. Central to these stereotypes is the presumption that same-gender sexual orientation can be understood as a reversal of sex roles. From this perspective, gay men are really feminine like women and lesbians masculine like men. To a large extent, these stereotypes are shared in the gay community itself, where internalized homophobia plays a significant role as a consequence of a larger social preoccupation with issues of sexuality. Closely related to these stereotypes is the concept of a "master narrative" regarding the origins and development of same-gender sexual orientation. This dominant or master narrative (Plummer 1995) has been given support by both gay and straight investigators in the biological and social sciences who have attempted to confirm a series of stereotypes through scholarly study (Savin-Williams and Cohen 1996).

For example, a common master narrative for "being gay" holds that gay men were born gay and as boys were already gender-atypical in their interests. Particularly in earlier generations, growing up with the pressure of a heterosexist society, these men were forced to conform to the ideal in which boys play sports and shun artistic and quiet activities. If, as adults, they tend to enjoy football, baseball, and other stereotypically masculine activities, such interests are viewed as defensively constructed. This master narrative derives support from studies suggesting a biological foundation for same-gender sexual orientation, either in genetic transmission or untoward maternal stress during pregnancy which interferes with hormonal factors responsible for masculinization. Feelings of alienation and personal distress ensue during the school years, followed by the discovery, in early adulthood, of the gay world; the struggle to come out to family and friends; the search for partnership, which often entails additional distress over affairs early terminated; and, finally discovery of a life partner. The master narrative for lesbians has been less clearly described than that for gay men. Unexplained factors presumably lead to "tomboy" interests in early childhood, followed by masculine identifications in adulthood.

Clinical psychoanalytic/psychotherapeutic and community study alike suggests that there are few generalizations which may be made on the basis of presently reported sexual orientation. Just as there are many pathways into expression of same-gender desire, there are many variants of being gay, lesbian, or bisexual, and these too are affected by social and historical forces. For example, the significance of being a gay adolescent boy is very different for those attending socially and ethnically diverse urban high schools in the 1990s than it was for those attending homogeneous suburban high schools in the 1960s. Ability to integrate sexuality with other aspects of life may be easier for a young man who is an actor, artist, or musician than for his counterpart who is a banker or teacher. The significance of being gay, and also the story told about coming out, is very different for the gay man who "discovered" aspects of same-gender sexual desire while in college and a counterpart who first discovers the nature of such desire at midlife.

Above all, it is important to emphasize that gay men and women are no less diverse than straight men and women. While some gay men may be effeminate, other gay men are masculine, with political and social interests, leisure interests, and vocations no different from straight counterparts. Sexual identity and gender identity are independent dimensions; efforts to portray straight men as masculine and gay men as effeminate, or lesbian women as either masculine or hyperfeminine, do not capture the diversity and complexity of the interplay between sexual orientation and other aspects of the lives of people of all sorts. There is much more to life than sexual orientation. As an analysand recently observed in connection with a discussion at lunch with straight coworkers: "I'm not a gay man. I am a man who is gay, but there is much more to me than that. Why is it so hard for people to see beyond what I want to do in my bedroom?"

It is critical that, when attempting to understand factors related to the origin and course of the expression of desire, the variety of life paths of lesbians, gay men, and bisexual men and women also be acknowledged (Williams 1999). Study of master narratives is important because they provide the framework for the presently told life story. Men struggling to come to terms with their sexuality often read case reports and discussions of this master narrative in magazines and books, and may even hear from friends or family stories framed in the terms of the master narrative, which then provides them a means for rewriting their own life stories. Without doubt, there are many men whose memory of lived experience closely conforms to this master narrative. However, it is critical that we be able to account for the variety of life paths or biographies characterizing men and women who have little in common beyond realization of desire centered on another of the same gender.

Psychoanalysis, Homosexuality, and Society

From the outset, understanding the interplay of the intrapsychic and the social has posed problems for psychoanalysis. How the curative dynamic of the psychoanalytic process is portrayed reflects larger social and historical changes; for example, between the Marienbad meetings of the International Psychoanalytic Association of 1937 and the Edinburgh meetings of 1961, the focus of the portrayal of therapeutic change shifted from modification of the superego to the mother–child bond (Gitelson 1962). This reflected the impact of the Second World War and a decade of postwar research on the impact of early childhood on the resolution of oedipal conflicts (Friedman 1988).

Some psychoanalytic theorists (Reich [1933] 1949) viewed psychoanalysis as a means to foster radical Marxist reform. Recognition that increased self-awareness promotes empathy and appreciation for the plight of others has been viewed as a signal contribution of psychoanalysis to social change from the time of Freud's proposal that all school teachers in Vienna be analyzed to free them from unconscious conflicts that interfered with understanding children. More recent work—from Kovel's (1989) discussion of the dynamics of capitalist society to Odets's (1995) moving discussion of psychoanalytic therapy with HIV-negative gay men—all provides ample testimony to the usefulness of psychoanalysis in understanding the significance of social life.

The significance of social change for the meanings persons make of lived experience, which is so essential for the scholarly and scientific project of psychoanalysis, is commonly overlooked (Stewart and Healy 1989). Psychoanalysis is in a unique position to provide understanding of how people make sense of social and historical change, through its intensive study of meaning making in the psychoanalytic situation and the expression of this meaning-making activity in the transference.

Social and historical change also affects the external reality that analysands confront. For example, changes in the sequence and timing of transitions into adulthood across the postwar period increasingly delayed young people's entrance into the world of work. The emergence of a period termed "youth" (Erikson 1959, 1968; Keniston [1960] 1965) posed particular issues for the psychoanalysis of young adults, in that such early life experiences have an impact on how adults understand themselves at midlife. These events define a cohort for a generation of people.

The significance of social changes in the period roughly from 1965 to 1975 has not been fully appreciated by psychoanalysts and the human sciences. Over little more than a decade, major changes occurred in intellectual and social discourse, reflecting both a generational shift and such historical events including the war in Vietnam, the civil rights struggles, and the assassinations of John and Robert Kennedy and Martin Luther King Jr. These changes profoundly impacted the expression of desire and intimate relations (Tipton 1982; Gitlin 1987; Echols, 1989; Duberman 1993). The extent to which the new conservative movement of the 1990s, with its emphasis on traditional sexual values including strong disapproval of homosexuality, will affect people's values and actions remains unclear.

Accompanying the social changes of the 1960s, a new form of the study of social life emerged in America and Europe. This study questioned long-held assumptions about age, ethnicity, gender, and sexual orientation. At the same time, the dramatic and rapid nature of social change, observed largely among younger adults, led to a reconsideration of the interplay of generation and social change. Some psychoanalysts and other students of personality development shifted their focus from continuity or stability to change and factors associated with greater or lesser predictability of personal development. What was most interesting in the study of lives was no longer the extent to which people stayed the same over time but the extent to which they changed (Neugarten 1969). This shift had a profound impact on psychoanalysis as a developmental psychology (Emde 1981, 1983; Cohler and Freeman 1993; Cohler and deBoer 1996). From this perspective, what is significant about lives is less the extent to which early childhood factors directly shape adult expression of wish and desire than the means people use to maintain a sense of personal continuity or coherence over time; sexual orientation, then, is but one of several factors salient to understanding lives over time.

Generation and Social Change

Social change has reshaped how society in general and psychoanalysis in particular approaches sexual orientation and identity and relations involving gender. Conceptions of the roles of men and women in society have changed. Formerly urgent distinctions in the treatment of the sexes have become socially, and at times legally, prohibited. It is no longer considered appropriate to insist that baby boys be dressed in blue and baby girls in pink.

From the earliest elementary grades, boys and girls share common physical education activities and participate equally in activities such as Little League. The high school years are less marked by the rigid dating patterns of past generations; social groups include young men and women together, and young people have assigned new meanings to sexuality, which is seen as pleasurable and an ordinary part of many midadolescents' lives. While only a few decades ago guards separated male and female college students, enforcing rules designed to ensure the women's celibacy, men and women in college housing now often live on the same floors and share bathrooms. College-age men and women also commonly share apartments, sexuality being just one of many issues to be negotiated among roommates.

Life Course and Personal Narrative

This rapid social change has also been reflected in a significant change in the study of lives, from a life-span or life-cycle to a life-course perspective. The life-cycle approach to developmental study focuses largely on age/stage-ordered processes, presumed to be intrinsic, and sequential negotiation of age-related tasks. The life-course perspective assumes an open system shaped by social and historical processes, as well as expectable and eruptive life changes within individual lives (Elder 1995, 1996, 1997; Elder and Caspi 1988; Neugarten 1979, Neugarten and Hagestad 1976; Hagestad and Neugarten 1985; Mannheim [1928] 1993; Pearlin and Lieberman 1979; Stewart and Healy 1989). The life-course perspective makes few assumptions about the tasks or issues to be resolved or negotiated over time. Rather, it views people as inevitably confronting challenges or concerns relevant in their own lives as a consequence of their present social life (Dannefer 1984).

Earlier studies often assumed that the life history had an existence outside the social and historical context within which the narrative was constructed (Rosenwald 1993). Like physical development, it followed a normative course which might be disturbed by outside influences but which was fundamentally independent. Following Marx ([1845] 1978), the work of the Russian psychologist Vygotsky ([1924–34] 1987), the Russian literary theorist Bakhtin (1981, 1986), and others (Wertsch 1991; Kozulin 1990; A. Wilson and Weinstein 1992, 1996) emphasizes the intrinsic interplay between person and society in the construction of the person's story. Social and historical change fundamentally shape and reshape the life story of the individual and the shared life stories of each cohort. Founded on this dialogic perspective, recent study of the life story has emphasized the extent to which any account is necessarily coconstructed by teller and listener and, subsequently, in the interaction between reader and text (Ricoeur 1971; M. Freeman 1985). The change in the construction of life stories related to experience of sexual orientation is dramatically illustrated in collections of the life stories of gay men across the last half century (Hall Carpenter Archives 1989; Porter and Weeks 1991).

Generation, Cohort, and Life Course

The concept of generation is central to the life-course perspective (Cain 1964; Ryder 1965; Settersten 1998). Following Mannheim ([1928] 1993), Troll (1970), Bengtson, Furlong, and Laufer (1974), and Laufer and Bengtson (1974) have all defined generation with reference to three age-linked characteristics: position within a cluster of four or five groups alive contemporaneously; period or point in the course of life, such as youth or middle age; and cohort, or persons of a given birth year who have experienced similar social and historical events. The age distribution in a given society at any one time creates groups of individuals with particular understandings of self and others, determined in part by shared interpretations of historical events. These collective interpretations, in conjunction with expectable and eruptive life changes, largely shape the course of individual development over time (Cohler and Boxer 1984; Pearlin 1980; Pearlin et al. 1981).

It is particularly important in the study of lives to focus on the distinction between period and cohort in life-course study, and to recognize the significance of social and historical change as factors largely governing the sequence of transitions into and out of major social roles across the course of adult life (Hogan 1981; Hogan and Astone 1986; Dannefer 1984; Marini 1984; George 1993, 1996). Generation understood as cohort refers to a unit of developmental analysis founded on birth year (Schaie 1984, 1995; Elder [1974] 1998, 1996; Elder and Caspi 1990; Settersten 1999; Tuttle 1993). For example, as Easterlin (1987) has shown, people growing up in a large birth cohort, such as the postwar "baby boom" cohort, face greater competition throughout life for resources ranging from preschool programs to medical and social services for the elderly.

The capacity to understand the impact of social change is aided by recognition of the significance of cohort in defining how people understand their selves and experience in social life. Schaie's (1984, 1995) summary of his work on the Seattle Longitudinal Study highlighted cohort differences in psychometric test performance. Elder and his colleagues have shown the role of cohort in understanding how generational influences can directly impact understandings of lives over time. Reanalyzing archival data from the longitudinal studies at Berkeley's Institute of Human Development, Elder ([1974] 1998) showed the differential impact of the Great Depression on the adjustment of groups of preschool and adolescent boys and girls. As Elder and Caspi (1990) observe, age understood as an index of birth year serves to locate persons in history and suggests the range of events likely to have had an impact upon their lives.

This impact may derive from discrete events or from the "pileup" of events in a particular sequence (Elder and Caspi 1990). A prime example of such a pileup would be the combination of events that confronted those individuals born after the Second World War, who arrived at midadolescence during the turbulent years of the 1960s. The adolescent experiences of this '60s generation were vastly different from those of adults who were adolescents either ten years earlier, during the prosperous, repressive, and peaceful Eisenhower years, or two decades later, during an era of conservative backlash and ultraindividualism. Life circumstances and the sociohistorical context of adolescence appear to have particular influence on lived experience of the second half of life (Livson and Peskin 1980; Schuman and Scott 1989; Clausen 1993). There is a difference in the way preschoolers, teenagers, and middle-aged adults experience war or natural disasters (Tuttle 1993).

There may be little value in describing modal personality patterns or developmental tasks for a given age or point in life except as they relate to cohort-specific sociohistorical changes and events. It remains important to be aware of the difficulty of determining the boundaries of a cohort (Rosow 1978) or of significant intracohort effects (Elder 1996). Life circumstances affect members of the same birth cohort differently. For example, military conscription has different impacts on individuals depending on socioeconomic and marital or parental status (Elder 1986, 1987; Elder and Hareven 1993; Elder, Shanahan, and Clipp 1994; Sampson and Laub 1996). The life-history or narrative method provides means to disentangle period and cohort through a focus on the meanings of larger-scale social changes in lived experience.

Social Time, Expectable Transitions, and the Organization of Personal Experience

The concept of cohort organizes persons into groups of consociates (Plath 1980). "Social time" organizes individual lives into patterns of sequential role positions. In conjunction with cohort-specific effects, the subjective experience of social time shapes how individuals understand the sequence and timing of life events. Following Durkheim's ([1912] 1995) discussion of time and the ritual life of the community, study of how people understand the course of life suggests that persons maintain an internal timetable for expectable role transitions (Sorokin and Merton 1937; J. Roth 1963; Hazan 1980; Neugarten, Moore, and Lowe [1965] 1996; Neugarten and Hagestad 1976; Hagestad 1990; Hagestad and Neugarten 1985). Neugarten, Moore, and Lowe, for example, demonstrated agreement on the definition of age among concurrently living generations. Though older adults are somewhat more tolerant than younger adults of variation in the timing of certain role transitions, there is broad agreement on what constitutes childhood, adolescence, adulthood, and later life.

Persons continually compare their own development, including realization of particular, expected social roles, to a socially shared timetable. They determine whether they are "on-time," "early," or "late." Even very young children are familiar with the sequence of expectable life transitions, from school entrance through graduation, first job, parenthood, retirement, widowhood, and death (Farnham-Diggory 1966). This sequence provides a context for understanding personal experience. Even unpredictable life changes—adverse or positive—occur in the context of this expectable sequence. More eruptive life events, such as widowhood in the fourth versus the eighth decade of a woman's life, pose particular problems because there are few consociates to provide support and assistance (Plath 1980; Kahn and Antonucci 1981) and because there has been little opportunity to rehearse this life change through observation of others in a similar position (Neugarten 1979).

Seltzer (1976) and Cohler and Boxer (1984) suggest that positive morale or life satisfaction is largely determined by the sense of being on-time for expectable role transitions. The sense that life changes are consistent with those experienced by other members of a cohort or generation enhances the sense of personal congruence and well-being. Although individuals may eventually overcome difficulties associated with early off-time transitions, the initial adjustment is often extremely challenging (Furstenberg, Brooks-Gunn, and Morgan 1987). On the other hand, being late off-time may have certain advantages. Men who make a late off-time transition to parenthood are more settled in their careers and more comfortable with themselves than men who make this transition on-time (Nydegger 1980, 1981; Daniels and Weingarten 1982).

Hagestad (1996) discusses a fourth possibility, being "outside" or "out" of time. Based on her own experience of prolonged illness and her sense of being excluded from professional and social events, Hagestad described the feeling of living outside the continuity of time. While her friends and colleagues may have been acting out of consideration for her welfare, not wishing to burden her during her illness, the result was a strange sense of depersonalization. Hagestad's observation, however, also concerns individuals who may be "out of time" in two senses: people with a terminal illness of uncertain duration face the difficulty of planning for a future with an unknown terminus. These people are out of time not only in the sense of confronting the finitude of life earlier than was characteristic of recent cohorts, but also in the sense that it is difficult to reckon time when its future duration is unpredictable.

There may be differences in the timing of role transitions, both within cohorts—according to race, class, education, and a variety of other demographic characteristics—and across cohorts. For the generation of young adults born in the late 1960s and early 1970s—the so-called Generation X—the underemployment characteristic of the late 1980s and early 1990s seemed to shift the beginning of careers to the late twenties. This led to postponement of such other expectable role transitions as marriage and parenthood (Hogan 1981; Hogan and Astone 1986; Marini 1984; George 1993, 1996). Comparing their attainments to those of preceding generations, Generation Xers experience lower morale and express frustration at being late off-time for these role transitions. However, when they compare themselves to other members of their own generation, things seem less bleak. The impact of cohort or generation and social timing are best appreciated through the study of how these building blocks of lived experience, necessarily embedded in history, are reflected in meanings integrated into a life story which itself inevitably changes across the course of life.

Cohort, Sexual Orientation, and Gay Identity

Concepts of cohort, timing, and social change are important in considering issues of sexual orientation among both men and women (Cohler and Boxer 1984; Cass 1984; Parks 1999). Within the oldest living generation of men and women, sexual orientation is generally conceived in essentialist terms, as biologically determined and binary (homosexual or heterosexual). Men and women within this cohort identified themselves as "homosexual," although some men have adopted the term "gay," used by younger cohorts, and some women use the term "lesbian." Older lesbian women often view their sexual orientation as much in social terms as in terms of sexuality. These men and women may have seen service in the Second World War and were middle-aged at the time of the social change of the years 1965–1975.

History, Cohort, and Gay Identity

For many older homosexual men, sexual orientation as such is not a prominent issue (Cohler, Hostetler, and Boxer 1998). Like their heterosexual counterparts, these men have partners of many years, hold jobs in which sexual orientation plays little role, and engage in social activities with other couples. Stigma has played little role in their lives since they have kept their sexual orientation separate from their work life and take part in few community activities in which their sexual orientation would pose a challenge to others. They find appropriate religious congregations, often of other older gay and lesbian couples. Men and women within this older cohort expected

little from society in terms of understanding or accommodation of their sexual orientation and are not distressed by such social indifference.

Men and women in the cohort of presently middle-aged adults see themselves as characterized by same-gender sexual orientation. They have had a
different life-course trajectory from those in the oldest cohort. This generation came of age in the midst of the social changes of the years 1965–1975.
Generally forced by social pressures to take a stance either for or against the
war in Vietnam, confronted with issues of the draft, and witness to the social
unrest of the late 1960s, this generation became visible as a social activist
generation (Tipton 1982). This generation was presented with choices previously less widely accessible, including nonalcoholic recreational drugs and
a greatly relaxed attitude toward sexuality and sexual orientation. From the
civil rights marches to the antiwar protests and rock concerts, this generation
was confronted by at times overwhelming choices and opportunities.

Within this cohort, concepts of race and gender, as well as sexual orientation, became the subject of redefinition. This was the generation which
founded the gay rights movement and moved activism from the nearly secret
Mattachine Society to Gay Pride. Symbolic of this shift was the response to
a June 1969 police raid on Stonewall, a tough homosexual drag dance bar in
New York's Soho neighborhood. Police raids on homosexual bars had been
common in New York and many other cities. This time, however, consistent
with the climate of social activism, patrons fought against arrest and chased
the police out of the bar (Duberman 1993; D'Emilio 1998). The resulting
standoff between the police and the socially marginal patrons became, over
the next decade, symbolic of the gay community's resistance to harassment,
the explicit acknowledgment of same-gender sexual orientation, and the
right to elect a lifestyle.

As this generation grew to middle age, gay men and women enjoyed dramatic advances in civil rights and acceptance from the larger community of
same-gender sexual orientation. A colleague tells of a meeting of the American Psychiatric Association in the late 1960s at which he had to hide his face
while presenting a paper on the adjustment of homosexual men. In 1973,
the concept of homosexuality was removed as a diagnostic category from the
Diagnostic and Statistical Manual (Bayer 1987; Bayer and Spitzer 1982). In
subsequent years gay and lesbian psychiatrists formed an interest group in
the American Psychiatric Association and soon assumed visible national
leadership positions.

In the wider society, annual gay rights parades in major American cities
have brought out as many as half a million participants and spectators. Being
"out at work" became a rallying point for young professionals, as law firms,
businesses, and even public school systems began to actively recruit talented

gay men and lesbians, and concepts changed regarding what it meant to be gay or lesbian. Increasingly, American corporations offer partner benefits to employees in same-gender relationships similar to those provided for employees in heterosexual marriages. Members of an emerging community of gay men and lesbians now have little concern about being public about their sexual orientation; pictures identifying gay and lesbian participants in community activities are common within a visible gay press, and gay and lesbian couples publicly celebrate their union as domestic partners.

The cohort of presently middle-aged gay men and women helped foster changes that, together with the civil rights movement and the women's movement, caused same-gender sexual orientation to become a visible element of public life in a period of less than two decades. The struggle to achieve these civil rights was not without its costs. Many more middle-aged than older gay men and lesbians report problems with stigma and social stereotyping at work or in their families (Cohler, Hostetler, and Boxer 1998). These men and women have had to confront and combat beliefs that, for example, gay men were inevitably effeminate and lesbians inevitably masculine, or that gay men and women were preoccupied with sexuality to the exclusion of all other aspects of life. The currently middle-aged generation experienced and fought prejudice in ways that were inconceivable to the older cohort of gay men, who led their lives quietly, out of the glare of public proclamation.

The generation of presently middle-aged men was the first to encounter the specter of HIV/AIDS. Like their straight counterparts, many gay men enjoyed multiple sexual experiences. The new, visible gay bars were no different in organization from those frequented by young heterosexual men and women looking for companionship and, perhaps, a sexual encounter. It was in this context that the HIV virus circulated silently in the gay community for a decade until it came to the attention of public health officials in the early 1980s. With tragic irony, just when this generation of gay men was enjoying its attainments in the area of civil rights, a dreadful disease raged silently and unchecked, affecting more than a million victims before it was even identified. Most gay men have had to face the question of being tested for HIV seroconversion. Issues of anxiety about HIV and sexuality have become intertwined. Nearly every gay man and woman of this generation, and many straight people as well, have known friends or fellow workers who have died of AIDS. Indeed, issues of grief and mourning have become major mental health concerns in the gay community. HIV/AIDS has also become a rallying point for those who are uncomfortable with the rapid pace of social change and who view the epidemic as proper retribution for the supposed promiscuity of the gay community.

The generation of gay men and lesbians who are presently young adults grew to adulthood in a society in which sexual orientation was more honestly discussed than previously. Many high schools and colleges, particularly in urban communities, have created gay pride youth groups. While some young adults use the occasion of college entrance as the time to adopt a same-gender sexual orientation, many others come to college having publicly acknowledged their sexuality since junior high school. This generation of young adults sees sexual orientation as a less central part of a life that includes seriousness of purpose regarding educational and career goals. Sexual orientation is seen as not necessarily limiting their hopes and aspirations.

The present generation of young adults, particularly those living in urban and suburban communities, have an ease about sexuality uncharacteristic of zlprevious generations. Many of them define themselves as "bisexual, queer, or spectrum." The role of bisexuality in the present discussion is complex and is reviewed at several points in terms of its implications for the study of personal development and therapeutic intervention. Suffice it to say now that the current cohort of young adults does not feel constrained, as earlier generations did, to limit sexual experimentation to one gender. This was never an absolute constraint in postwar American society (Kinsey, Pomeroy, and Martin 1948; Kinsey et al. 1953). However, no previous generation has felt as easy as the present one in expressing desire toward both same- and other-gender partners. Identifying oneself as bisexual reflects the view that the gender of one's partner is less significant than emotional commitment and satisfaction with the relationship.

Questions must be raised regarding the role of aging and social change among presently younger and middle-aged adult cohorts (Levine, Nardi, and Gagnon 1997; Odets 1995; Schwartzberg 1996; Sontag 1989). The now middle-aged cohort will arrive at later life with a history of setting trends which will lead to new conceptions of gay aging. These same men and women will have experienced multiple losses stemming from the AIDS epidemic. The present generation of both gay and straight young adults has grown up in the shadow of the AIDS epidemic. Many communities begin health education in elementary or junior high school. Study of the HIV virus, its predictable mutations, and the need for personal protection against "getting" the virus is commonplace in schoolroom discussions. These young adults have grown up with an appreciation for the importance of personal responsibility in matters sexual, but also with increased appreciation for the variety of pathways to personal satisfaction. They have grown up more concerned than prior generations with issues of decency, with an awareness of variation in ethnicity and sexual orientation and of the political and social equality of men and women at home and work. In many cases, their mothers and fathers have both worked since their offsprings' earliest childhood. They expect that gender and work will be only loosely tied. Issues of gay and lesbian parenthood pose little problem for this generation. Finally, with in-grained awareness of the importance of taking responsibility for their sexual-ity and aware of the means of transmission of the HIV virus, gay men in this young adult generation should escape much of the grief at midlife that characterized the lives of the present cohort of middle-aged gay men.

Cohort, Identity, and Sexual Orientation

Up to this point we have discussed sexual orientation in terms of selection of partners of the same or opposite gender. However, we must address how adults define their sexuality and the relationship of sexuality to other aspects of their lives, including family, work, and community. We will use the term "sexual orientation" to refer to the gender of the partner in sexual wishes and actions, for homosexuality has often been discussed in terms of sexual or gender identity or of sex role. It is important to clarify these terms.

The term "identity" was introduced into the psychoanalytic literature by Erikson ([1951] 1963, 1958, 1959). Erikson studied young adults showing signs of what appeared to be the breakdown of personality into psychosis, which he believed to be evidence of profound and fundamental questioning of meanings and belief. He introduced the term ego identity as

> something in the individual's core with an essential aspect of a group's inner coherence . . . the young individual must learn be most himself where he means most to others—those others who have come to mean most to him. The term identity expresses such a mutual relation in that it connotes both a persistent sameness within oneself (selfsameness) and a persistent sharing of some kind of essential character with others. (1959, 109)

Erikson notes elsewhere that "personal identity . . . includes a subjective sense of continuous existence and a coherent memory . . . a sense of same-ness and continuity as an individual ([1951] 1963, 61). In sum, the concept of ego identity reflects the experience of personal coherence with the shared goals of a larger group. Erikson believed that this issue was highlighted in adolescence, which necessarily must be a moratorium, or time at which questions of meaning and belief are suspended until endowed with new un-derstanding as a result of personal questioning. While some late adolescents and young adults seem stuck in a diffuse or negative identity, unable to re-solve the questioning and uncertainty characteristic of this point in the course of life, others are too ready to avoid questioning.

From the outset, Erikson's concept was faulted as slippery and founded on superficial and manifest, rather than latent or unconscious, personality processes (Abend 1974, 1995). However, it is useful to review Erikson's concept of identity in light of the renewed focus on the psychoanalytic process as the rewriting of the life story in a manner likely to lead to an enhanced sense of personal vitality and coherence (Schafer 1980, 1981). Reviewing Erikson's concept in terms of more recent psychoanalytic study, Abend suggests that the term "identity" should be limited to the

> loosely organized set of conscious and preconscious self-representations that serve to define the individual in a variety of social contexts. Included in its composition we would expect to find ideas regarding specific professional, social and sexual roles and preferences, aspects of the person's political and religious ideology and other unique values, and his more important personal interests and avocations. (1974, 620)

Identity is an issue most salient in adolescence and young adulthood, where it is associated with issues of futurity (A. L. Greene 1986, 1990). It may become relevant again at later times when people are compelled to review their life history. One's sense of identity is reflected in a story told to oneself and to others, integrating the elements of lived experience into a reasonably coherent, sensible narrative, that is both "tellable" and "followable" (Ricoeur 1977). Ponse (1978) calls the effort to construct a coherent life story "identity work" and observes that people try to organize aspects of their life into a coherent life story that legitimizes their place within the family and community.

The concept of a gay or straight sexual identity is part of this larger concept of identity (S. Epstein 1987). Cass (1984) suggests that gay identity reflects the current integration of the person's interpretation of his or her desire and relationships with others, as experienced in the past, present, and anticipated future. Successful realization of a positive gay identity includes the remaking of experiences of a lifetime to date into a story that is personally coherent and socially adaptive. A gay identity optimally includes a conception of oneself as a sexual person with acknowledged desires and as a positive participant in a relational world of people with similar interests and concerns (Cass 1984).

Gay identity is constructed over time in the context of a shared understanding of what constitutes being gay or lesbian. The currently popular term, "coming out," reflects this integration of desire and relationality. Consistent with Abend's (1995) psychoanalytic perspective on identity, De Cecco (1982) and Epstein (1987) suggest that, at its core, identity is constituted relationally through involvement with and incorporation of significant others and integration into the larger community. Sexuality and awareness of the importance of same-gender desire is more than a biological essence. Desire itself, a sensation of attraction and arousal, is culturally constructed—the expression of desire reflects the interplay of biological and cultural factors as a wish. This wish requires the presence of others, at least in fantasy, for its realization. It is possible to realize a gay identity apart from action. However, it is in the connection of wish and involvement with others as partners and as members of a larger community that gay identity is expressed and affirmed.

A positive gay identity (integrated with other personally and socially relevant elements of the presently told life story) represents a significant part of "who I am." A gay identity and the particular elements of the life story used to support the construction of this identity are themselves socially constructed on the basis of shared social understandings both of sexuality and life history. For example, many current coming-out stories of younger and middle-aged adults, including stories told in psychoanalytic or psychodynamic psychotherapeutic situations, emphasize themes of knowing from early childhood that one was different or enjoyed non–gender-stereotyped activities (Savin-Williams 1997). This understanding of the foundations of being gay becomes a significant element in the life stories of many gay people.

Realization from earliest childhood of a sense of self as vital and effective (Kohut 1977; Kohut and Wolf 1978) provides a matrix for a positive gay identity across adolescence and adulthood in the context of an affirmative family and community. Consider an example:

> The oldest son of university-educated, psychologically minded liberal parents living in a diverse urban community, he became aware of his attraction to other boys during junior high school. His private school had several gay and lesbian faculty and an active gay-lesbian-straight student alliance. Summoning the courage to talk with one of his teachers whom he knew to be gay, this student felt sufficiently affirmed to approach his parents, who were understanding and supportive of his emerging gay identity.
>
> In high school he dated another gay student, with whom he spent much time. His parents and the parents of his partner, also accepting and affirmative of this relationship, became friends and the two families spent much time together, including a memorable celebration of their high school graduation. The two were active in promoting school and community resources for gay and lesbian teens and won recognition for their efforts.
>
> Attending college a continent apart, these two gay high school activists decided it was best not to continue such an intense relationship. Now a third-year undergraduate, comfortable with being gay and feeling little need to disguise his identity, this young man has done well academically, was active in revitalizing the gay and lesbian student alliance, and serves as coordinator of the college hot line. He is involved in a relationship with a beginning graduate student in his field of interest in the biological sciences and plans on a career in medical research.

This vignette describes a charming, intellectually able young man who took advantage of optimal circumstances to find an identity as a gay student leader. Consolidation of this identity was promoted by an environment that in-

cluded accepting, supportive parents, a progressive school unusually understanding of the psychological needs of students, and an elite university also
committed to respect for and affirmation of diversity. With this support, the
student has been able to acknowledge his same-gender desire, integrate this
desire in the context of family, and become an effective participant in his
school and community. A contrasting situation has been described by a patient:

> A talented young man, an accomplished classical violinist, attended a state uni-
> versity near the community where he grew up. He had been aware since high
> school of an interest in other young men and had a number of brief relation-
> ships in college. His father, a politically active minister in a mainline, conserva-
> tive Protestant sect, and his nervous mother were aware of his personal struggles
> but sought to deny what they knew.
>
> In his traditional high school boys were expected to achieve in sports and
> business. Serious discussion of sexuality was absent and even taboo. This young
> man experienced his high school as an extremely homophobic environment.
> His parents urged him to succeed in athletics and discouraged his interests in
> music. They also urged him to go out with young women from families they
> knew. After he disclosed his sexuality to his best friend, the other boy, troubled
> by this announcement which conflicted so with community values, had little
> to do with him during his senior year.
>
> Moving after college to an urban area, where his musical talents were already
> being recognized, he met another gay musician. After a year in which he lived
> almost full-time in his friend's apartment, the two decided formally to live to-
> gether as a gay couple. Enjoying intimacy with his partner, who was orphaned
> early in life, and feeling uncomfortably duplicitous about not acknowledging
> the life that he was leading, he disclosed his sexuality to his parents. He had
> planned to bring his partner home for Thanksgiving to meet his family and
> enjoy his mother's wonderful cooking. However, his disclosure precipitated
> marked family conflict, which has continued over time. Psychotherapy has fo-
> cused on his sense of disappointment and loss, and also on his contribution to
> his family's difficulties, which include lengthy telephone conversations marked
> by rancor and dramatic confrontations in which his mother has fainted and his
> father has accused him of destroying the family.

This gifted, attractive young man has been struggling with his identity as gay
in the context of a family and community that was not affirmative across the
adolescent years and a college environment that while not actively hostile
was indifferent to the students' psychological needs. He struggles to realize
a positive gay identity. Though he reports a satisfying and caring relationship
with his partner and little concern about his sexuality, he cannot integrate
his sexuality with his relationship to his family and the world from which
he came.

As Abend (1995) has observed, the terms sex role, sexual identity, and
sexual identification are often used in confusing ways. Sometimes under-

stood in boys as the "heir of the Oedipal complex" (Freud [1910a] 1957, [1910d] 1957), or in men and women as an ego attribute referring to learned ways of managing conflict founded in characteristics of family and environment (Freud [1923] 1961; Cohler and Grunebaum 1981), identifications include the means learned for managing tension and conflict as well as means for managing relations with others. Identifications include values and skills learned in the family and community, which often guide a sense of lifelong well-being.

Realization of positive identity, often expressed as feelings of comfort with who and what one is, is a developmental achievement separate from sex-role identifications or a sense of masculinity and femininity. Sex-role identity and sexual orientation are separate concepts. A part of the confusion in this area stems from the issues of transgendered or transsexual life. There are men and women who believe from early childhood that they are of the other gender and were born into the wrong body (Garfinkel [1967] 1984). These men and women often seek surgery in order to realize conformity between their sex-role identification and their body.

> A young man came for a psychological assessment as a part of a lengthy process which could lead to transsexual surgery. He reported that he had always felt himself to be female, played with dolls as a child, sought the company of girls, and enjoyed being a cheerleader in high school because he could associate with the most feminine girls in his traditional small-town high school. After college he had started to work in the theater as a dresser, arranging the clothes for the actors. In his spare time, he enjoyed dressing in drag and was involved in a group of men whose social life was defined in terms of cross-dressing. Most recently, he had begun a course of estrogen therapy designed to grow his breasts and provide him a more feminine appearance. His sexual life had been satisfactory; he had found women who were attracted to him. In intercourse, he was finally able to ejaculate when he could fantasize that he was the woman receiving the penis. He had no interest in other men and had never had a homosexual encounter. His sole desire was to have surgery in order to have the vagina for which he had longed since early childhood.

This man was ultimately approved for surgery and had enjoyed life as a woman for more than five years when last interviewed. While still somewhat masculine in appearance (large hands and angular features), she is able to enjoy sexual relations as a woman and can experience some sexual pleasure. She has found several men who are attracted to her and has had a brief lesbian affair with a woman who had been lesbian since early adolescence.

This man (now woman) expressed female sexual gender identity and saw herself as feminine since earliest childhood. The many biopsychosocial factors leading to identifying oneself as of the other gender are complex and have not been well studied. Suffice it to note in the present discussion that what this man had sought while still a man was identification with the woman who received the penis, not the penis itself. Within a group of twelve men evaluated for transsexual surgery, only one had even a transient homo-sexual relationship. This is in marked contrast with gay men who find erotic arousal within the experience of being with other men, whose fantasies are of intense physical pleasure from sexual intimacy with other men, and who identify with male rather than with female sexuality. These are men seeking other men rather than men wishing they were women and seeking men who will satisfy them as women. Gay men fantasize about sex between two men. Transsexual individuals have heterosexual fantasies of sex between a man and a woman or lesbian fantasies of sex between two women.

One social stereotype holds that gay men are "feminine" or "effeminate." This stereotype is founded in part on the experiences of persons seeking psychotherapy and in part on the fantasies of heterosexual men who have difficulty understanding gay and lesbian sexual orientation. As we will discuss at greater length later, there is absolutely no necessary relationship between masculinity or femininity and sexual orientation. Many gay men are very masculine in appearance and identity, while many straight men may be said to be effeminate. Many lesbian women are stereotypically feminine, while others are more masculine in appearance and interests.

Many gay men, particularly those seeking psychotherapy, report so-called gender-atypical activities since childhood. Again, this issue must be discussed in greater detail when considering what is known about the development of gay men and lesbians as contrasted with straight counterparts. The young violinist seeking psychotherapy for issues related to coming out to his family found that his musical talents were defined by the small town in which he grew up as gender-atypical, although in a more urban milieu such interests would not be so narrowly construed. While he was able to win recognition from his family and community for his athletic accomplishments, he experi-enced these achievements as not really a part of who and what he was and he derived little satisfaction from the recognition. As he observed, reflecting on his high school years,

> I looked so damn normal and heterosexual, but clearly my family knew some-
> thing they weren't talking about because there was a whole lot of pressure for
> me to keep doing these athletic things. It was like, if I could be so successful as
> an athlete I couldn't possibly be gay like those effeminate men my parents used
> to imagine when criticizing what was taking place in television and the movies.

Gay men and women may be most likely to seek psychotherapy when their experience of their own identity conflicts with expectations of family and community. Feeling themselves in some way different from straight counterparts, they may report gender-atypical interests which in other contexts would not have been seen as gender-related. There is no support from systematic study for assumptions linking sexual orientation to sexual identity or gender orientation.

Conclusion

Within the present cohort of young adults, under optimal circumstances where family and community accept variation in the developmental pathway to adulthood, realization and emergence of same-gender sexual orientation becomes an integral part of the life story. Under these circumstances, being gay or lesbian has a significance similar to other social attributes, such as political affiliation or ethnicity. As this cohort of young adults who have realized a positive gay identity moves through the life course without the distortions in development imposed by heterosexism and stigma (Herek 1991, 1995, 1996; I. Meyer 1995; Seidman, Meeks, and Traschen 1999), issues of realizing partnership and of integrating sexuality with other spheres of adult life will pose fewer problems than they have for the present cohorts of middle-aged and older gay men and lesbians.

Many of these younger gay men and women living with caring partners in committed relationships will adopt children or arrange to have children, who in turn will grow to adulthood, no more or less likely than children within counterpart straight families to be gay or lesbian, but likely to be more open in their attitudes toward same-sex desire (Patterson 1992, 1995a; Patterson and Chan 1996). Other gay men and women may elect not to have children or to remain single. It is difficult to predict how this generation of young people fortunate enough not to experience distortion in their development will enter middle age and later life. What is clear from the present discussion is that same-gender sexual orientation need not disrupt realization of positive identity.

Part Two

The Question of Origins and the Course of

Psychosocial Development

Three

Biology, Sexuality, and the Foundation of Human Sexual Orientation

The biological importance of sex and many people's sense that desires are beyond psychology combine to suggest that sexual orientation must be biologically rooted. From his first discussion of same-gender desire, Freud ([1905–24] 1953) emphasized a "complementary series" of causes in experience and biology. Today many investigators endorse an open-systems perspective emphasizing the interaction of body and behavior (Kandel 1998), but much of the study of the causes of same-gender sexual orientation ignores this principle. This line of work, starting with Krafft-Ebing's (1889–90) work on sexual pathology and Albert Moll's (1897a, 1897b) discussion of "contrary" sexuality,[1] focuses on a reductionist search for innate biological factors that "cause" homosexual behavior.

The Biology of Homosexuality

Our culture favors essentialist-biological explanations of wishes and actions, explanations emphasizing how biological causes produce qualities that are part of a person's core nature. Freud's emphasis on the biological substrate of personality reflects this view (Sulloway 1979). From his early work on aphasia (Freud [1891] 1953) through the "Project for a Scientific Psychology" (Freud [1895] 1966; Pribram and Gill 1977) to the posthumous Outline of Psychoanalysis (Freud [1937] 1964), the reductionist scientific world view learned as a student in Brücke's physiology laboratory inspired Freud's search for a biological substrate for psychological phenomena (Sulloway 1979; Gay 1988), even as he asserted the interaction of biology and environment.

Many of today's psychoanalysts continue in this tradition. In every discipline, each new generation of scholars learns not only the content of the discipline but also an approach to knowledge (Mannheim [1923] 1952; (Toul-

---

1. Krafft-Ebing and Moll studied the sexual lives of psychiatric patients. Moll, like Freud, studied with Charcot and tried to treat "sexual pathologies" with hypnosis. Influenced by Darwin and Krafft-Ebbing, Moll stressed the neuropathology of the sexual organs themselves. He used the term "libido" to refer to sexual development. Freud's personal library included a heavily annotated copy of Moll's study of sexual libido (Sulloway 1979).

min 1990). The enormous material success of the rational physical sciences and the desire to avoid the irrationality that produced the recent horrors led scientists and physicians educated just after the Second World War to embrace rationalist assumptions of Descartes' "New Science." For investigators coming of age during this era, as for those at the end of the nineteenth century, uncertain and rapid social and political change made biological explanations for psychological phenomena particularly attractive. We do not believe that this point of view is invalid because of these origins but do think it important to clarify the context in which the work arose, especially since this perspective helps explain the enthusiasm with which findings that otherwise might have seemed unimpressive were received. We are also aware that the postmodern critique of knowledge applies equally well to ourselves, writing as we do from a point of view shape by the history of the late twentieth century.

The search for biological factors initiated by Karl Ulrichs ([1864–79] 1994), which continues to this day, is also driven by moral and legal concerns (Kenen 1997; Murphy 1997). Since no moral community can punish people for being as biology destines them, the construct of biological homosexuality as a discrete, essential entity should protect homosexual men and women from legal prosecution and other persecution (Chauncey 1994; Foucault [1976] 1990; Weeks 1985, 1991). The biological-essentialist view of gender orientation has been closely tied to the idea that laws and moral opprobrium against homosexuals cannot be defended if sexual orientation is not a matter of choice. In the United States the Christian right has taken a position that mirrors this idea, claiming that since, in its view, sexual orientation can be altered by therapy, negative attitudes and actions toward gay and lesbian people are justifiable. In addition to noting the moral implications of a biological view De Cecco and Parker (1995) suggest that finding biological origins for homosexuality would resolve the ambiguity of social constructionist views, with all their disconcerting implications about the role of sex and gender in society.

The search for a biological origin for same-gender sexual orientation finds encouragement in several groups of observations as noted by Byne and Parsons (1993):

1. Experimental animals whose prenatal hormone levels are altered often adopt mating positions which are presumed to be gender-atypical. Assuming that rodent and human behaviors are analogous, human sexual orientation might be accounted for by hormonal changes in the uterine environment.
2. Gender nonconformity often emerges in early childhood, suggesting that gender orientation may be inborn.

3. The resistance of sexual orientation to change through psychotherapy and behavior therapy could mean that sexual orientation is "hard wired."
4. The inadequacy of nonbiological explanations, particularly in contrast with the power of presumed biological explanations (A. Bell, Weinberg, and Hammersmith 1981), suggests, by default, that explanations of sexual orientation should be biological.

Byne (1997a, 1997b) notes that much of the biological study of same-gender sexual orientation assumes that homosexual men and women fall at an intermediate point between male and female, that they are, in some sense, intersex (see, for example, Gladue, Green, and Hellman 1984). Often it assumes that same-gender sexual orientation results from permanent immaturity, defective biology, or early socialization (Ellis, 1996b, 1997). Studies of so-called prehomosexual boys and girls, who are described as gender-atypical from early childhood, generally assume that biological factors directly or indirectly lead to this atypicalness (Paul 1993).

There are three major types of biological models of same-gender orientation (Byne and Stein 1997). Formative experience models assume biology shapes the organizing and interpretation of life experiences, including sexual desire. Direct effects models hold that factors like genetic predisposition or prenatal hormones produce brain circuits determinative of sexual orientation. And indirect models suggest that biological factors like temperament, not directly related to sexuality, indirectly shape sexual orientation. Direct effect models involving behavioral genetics, hormonal influences, and regional brain studies have gained particular prominence in the last decade.

Whatever their intrinsic merits, searches for a biological bases for homosexuality have been plagued by the difficulty of finding reliable and valid means to identify clear groups differentiated by sexual orientation. As Kinsey, Pomeroy, and Martin (1948) noted long ago, it is difficult to define the phenotype to be studied in such genetic research.

Homosexuality and Intersex

Nineteenth-century biological studies of homosexuality did not differentiate physical contact from affectional bonds nor did they consider differences between male and female homosexuality (Herrn 1995). It was assumed that the organization, mode of expression, and significance of same-gender sexual orientation was similar in men and women. This trend continues today in many biologically oriented discussions of sexual orientation, which treat female and male homosexuality as arising through symmetrical mechanisms.

Same-gender sexual orientation is often conceptualized as a person's having an attribute, sexual orientation, of the other gender. Thus homosexuality is viewed as an intermediate state between masculinity and femininity: gay men are presumed to be feminine and lesbians masculine (Oudshoorn 1995; Pillard 1991; McFadden and Pasanen 1998). Studies reporting that seemingly feminine boys who do not enjoy "rough-and-tumble play" are more likely than more gender-typical youngsters to mature into gay men (R. Green 1987) are taken to mean that femininity and male homosexuality are closely linked. In our culture, people have come to expect gender nonconformity in the childhood of homosexual individuals (Pillard 1991; Plummer 1995); life stories of homosexual adults often reflect this expectation, and historical events are commonly interpreted as being consistent with this view. For example, a gay musician in his late forties reported that in junior high school he preferred playing the clarinet in an orchestra and a jazz band to playing football or baseball. At the time of the interview he viewed this preference as "feminine." On reflection, it is unclear why making music should be regarded as a gendered activity, but, influenced by current theories of homosexuality, this self-report seems to support an intersex theory. (In fact, there is little data suggesting that in our society attitudes toward contact sports are associated with sexual orientation.)

Herdt and Boxer (1996) found that the interests of a social group of gay urban teenaged boys not referred for therapy did not focus on "feminine" pursuits but ranged from alternative music to professional basketball. Moreover, gender nonconformity is similar across groups of various sexual orientations; neither current or traditional gendered interests correlate significantly with actual sexual orientation. Social-historical factors further confound attempts to find such correlations, since what is considered to be a gender-typical behavior changes dramatically over time.

The commonest naive view of same-gender sexual desire is that gay men are like women and lesbians are like men. Indeed, much of the biological discussion still assumes that gay men have women's brains and lesbians have men's brains (Dörner 1976; De Cecco and Parker 1995). Another view, implicit in much of the work on the relation between the brain and sexual orientation, suggests that homosexuality, like such conditions as schizophrenia, results from a diseased brain (Harrison, Everall, and Catalan 1994). It is critical in reviewing discussions of biological hypotheses about desire directed toward persons of the same gender that we differentiate between gender identity disorders like that of the "sissy boy" (Green 1987) and same-gender sexual orientation. Currently, there is little evidence to suggest that these phenomena are related, and it certainly should not be assumed in biologically oriented studies. Animal models (discussed below) that demonstrate atypical mating resulting from abnormalities in the brain or its development cannot be equated with meanings and intentions in humans because we have no way of knowing what intentions, if any, are associated with the animal behavior. It is difficult to imagine that a male rat would frame something equivalent to the idea "I wish to be engaged in sexual activity with another male rat." Because meaning is at the center of human sexuality, extrapolation from animal to human sexual behavior, if attempted at all, requires great care.

The idea that same-gender attraction reflects an individual's having aspects of the opposite gender's normal brain function does not fit well with the phenomonology of homosexuality. Gay men do not view their desire as feminine, nor do lesbians view their desire as masculine (Jones and De Cecco 1982). Further, same-gender sexual orientation bears little relationship to the desire to be of the other gender ("gender dysphoria"). Homosexual fantasies do not involve images of one party's being transformed into a member of the opposite sex but concern the sexual engagement of two people of the same gender. Were the homosexual individual to be sexually like a person of the other gender we would expect fantasies of heterosexual activity.

The misunderstanding of homosexuality as adoption of the heterosexual orientation of the other gender has long led to a search for ways in which people with same-gender desires are like persons of the other gender. A recent example of this approach is found in the work of McFadden and Pasanen (1998). They studied a convenience sample of university students, men and women self-identified as gay or bisexual, with regard to otacoustic emissions (OAEs), weak sounds produced by elements in the inner ear. They compared groups differing in gender and sexual orientation. Previous work showed that in mixed-sex fraternal twins the pattern of the females' OAEs are more like those of boys than in singleton female births. As a result of the presence of the male twin, the female fetus in this situation is exposed to higher levels of androgen in utero than it otherwise would be. The authors hypothesized that lesbian sexual orientation might result from increased intrauterine androgen exposure and so predicted that patterns of OAEs among lesbians would be similar to those of straight men. Finding the predicted difference, they concluded that "prenatal exposure to higher-than-normal levels of androgens in homosexual and bisexual females produced a partial masculinization of both their peripheral auditory systems and some brain structures involved with sexual orientation (1998, 2712). The authors do not explore the impact of their sample on their data, reasons for the hypothesized increased intrauterine androgen levels, the relationship of androgen production to OAEs, or the brain structures that are supposed to be changed. Though consistent with the hypothesis that elevated intrauterine androgen may produce brain changes that contribute to same-gender sexual orientation in women, the authors' data do not rigorously support their hypothesis. Yet the study produced headlines in the national press.

An additional flaw in this study is the assumption, common to many biologically oriented investigations, that the direction of causation is from the biological to the psychological (Gladue 1988). Yet sexual wishes, fantasies, and behavior are likely to affect brain and endocrine processes. If the season of the year is able to alter the size of such neuroanatomical structures as the nuclei of the anterior hypothalamus (Swaab, Gooren, and Hofman 1992), meditation and stress to effect testosterone levels (MacLean et al. 1997), and stress to alter luteinizing hormone levels (Varnes et al. 1982), it is reasonable to expect that other aspects of experience, including one's sexuality, might impact brain structure, function, and hormonal production.

Sexual Orientation and Evolutionary Theory

Another group of common assumptions in the biological explorations of sexuality relates to evolution. Same-gender sexual orientation has been described as "unnatural" or "abnormal" because it appears opposed to reproduction and preservation of the species (Byne 1995). Based on his understanding of and commitment to Darwinian evolutionary theory Freud ([1905–24] 1953) adopted a similar position the *Three Essays on a Theory of Sexuality* (Sulloway 1979; Ritvo 1990). E. O. Wilson (1975) brings a similar perspective, based in a more sophisticated view of evolution, to the study of behavior, though with different conclusions. This view, that sexual function should be assessed by its impact on species reproductive fitness, is unique to the scientific Western intellectual (Dickemann 1995).

Following American cultural stereotypes, sociobiological discussions of homosexuality often assume that gay men have feminine characteristics that promote the reproductive fitness of near relatives (Ruse 1982; Weinrich 1976). The extent to which this view is culture-bound is suggested by societies ranging from classical Greece to the Sambia of the highlands of Papua New Guinea (Herdt 1981, 1997) that viewed sexual activities between men as the most characteristic of masculine activities.

The similarity of the evolutionary perspective to the perspectives of the eugenics movement in implicitly equating goodness with biological fitness poses significant ethical issues for the scientific search for the origins of same-gender sexual orientation. Defending the social evolutionary perspective against the charge that it makes homosexuality a kind of genetic psychopathology, Weinrich (1995) states that, in its current formulation, this view focuses on how individuals become adapted to their "niche" in the natural and social world. It predicts that in a community polymorphism will promote the survival of the gene pool. In particular, homosexual individuals aid in sustaining the gene pool from which they come. Though this view appears to counter negative attitudes toward gay people, it continues to rest on the questionable equation of moral right and evolutionary adaptation. Weinrich maintains that science must be ethically neutral and that sociobiology merely takes advantage of shared understandings of phenomena like homosexuality. We are struck, however, by how easily this view can slip into a biological explanation of presumed deviance and from there into a "scientific" rationale for rectifying that deviance.

Sociobiological Models and the Adaptive Value of Same-Gender Sexual Orientation

In a careful review of evolutionary biology perspectives on the "purpose" of homosexuality in populations, Ruse (1982) found four distinct models: balanced superior heterozygote fitness, kin selection, parental manipulation, and (male) homosexuality as a maladaptive side effect of intensive natural selection for superior heterosexual males.

The first model is founded on the work of the ecologist G. Evelyn Hutchinson (1959). He argued that a heterozygous individual might have an adaptive advantage over individuals who were homozygous for certain traits. The classical example relates to sickle-cell anemia. Individuals who are homozygous for the gene that produces the sickle-cell form of hemoglobin suffer from a devastating illness, but individuals who are heterozygous—that is, who carry one sickle-cell gene and one normal gene—are less susceptible to malaria than people both of whose genes code for normal hemoglobin. Since the probability of being homozygous for sickle-cell disease is very much smaller than the likelihood of being heterozygous, the presence of sickle-cell genes is an overall advantage to populations living in areas where malaria is present. Though no other clear instances of heterozygous advantage are known in humans, the capacity to make two forms of a protein that could result from a heterozygous state could be adaptive in some circumstances.

Homosexuality may be considered in this context. Imagine a homosexual and a heterosexual gene with the latter being dominant (i.e., a person with one each of these genes would be heterosexual) but with the heterozygous state conferring a reproductive advantage over the state of being homozygous for heterosexuality. In this situation the homosexual gene, in proper proportion, would confer an evolutionary advantage to the population in which it existed, even though people homozygous for the condition would not transmit the gene to the next generation. Thus, McKnight (1997), in a detailed review of the sociobiological evidence, maintains that if homosexuality continues to exist in the population then it must have an adaptive value. He argues that heterozygosity confers enhanced reproductive vigor and is therefore adaptive for the population even though those few persons who have two homosexual alleles have little chance of reproducing. McKnight attributes this increased vigor to qualities that he believes to be present in homosexual men: elevated sex drive compared to heterosexual men; enhanced potency; enhanced sexual aggressiveness; shorter refractory periods between orgasms; enhanced response to novelty, ensuring more numerous sexual partners; and larger penile size, which together with greater erectile potency leads both to enhanced effectiveness in transmitting sperm in the sexual act and to ejaculation of fresh sperm, which are likely to be more effective in conception. In addition to these specifically sexual qualities, McKnight (who states that he is a straight man) believes that homosexual men are particularly intelligent, cultured, charming, sexually attractive, responsive, and skilled at finding sexual partners. These capacities lead to the prominent role of gay men in the arts.

Despite the advantages his vision of homosexuality confers, McKnight maintains that men do not like being homosexual. Citing the study of Weinberg, Williams, and Pryor (1994), he claims that proportionally more homosexual than bisexual or heterosexual men seek to change their sexual orientation. Thus, in his view, there is little danger that all men will seek to become gay; the population can enjoy the benefits of the heterozygous state with regard to the homosexual gene without the reduction in fertility that would result if a large part of the male population became homosexual. McKnight presents little evidence other than fragmentary data from a study by Weinberg and Williams (1974) for his various claims about homosexual men, and one is left to speculate about the origins of his image of homosexual virility. Futuyma and Risch (1984) found no evidence that homosexuality is genetically transmitted in the manner McKnight proposes or that male relatives of homosexual man are particularly reproductively competent.

Were McKnight's views merely idiosyncratic we could easily put them aside, perhaps with some amusement at his belief in gay sexual supermen; there is little need to review the sampling problems, reliance on hearsay, and other issues of method that undermine McKnight's argument. His work is interesting, however, in that it illustrates, albeit in an extreme way, how extraordinarily low the standards for discourse about the biology of homosexuality are compared to those in allied disciplines. In particular, the tolerance for questionable empirical data and the willingness to build theories on loose and insufficiently considered analogies seems high in this area.

The second model, founded on concepts of kin selection (Hamilton 1964), posits that genes may continue to circulate in the population without conferring survival advantage. As with the first model, the prevalence of homosexuality is limited to levels that do not interfere with the group's overall reproductive capacities. At the same time, through acts like helping to support nieces and nephews and occupying high–status social roles, homo-sexual men and women raise the fitness of the families to which they be-long—like "sterile worker-bees in that they reproduce through relatives rather than directly" (Ruse 1982, 11; see Weinrich [1976] for a similar view). Though less effective in passing on their own genes, homosexuals contribute to the reproductive success of relatives with whom they share many genes their supposed superior intelligence, enhanced capacity for empathy (Salais and Fischer 1995), and ability to get ahead in society. The sociobiological model endorsed by Weinrich is largely silent on the question of homosex-ual women.

For the theory to work, the quantitative increase in reproductive fitness of relatives sharing the genetic endowment of homosexual individual would have to be such that the overall result would be increased survival of that individual's genes. However, it remains unclear what specific actions by homosexual men commonly help biological family members (Ruse 1982). Moreover, current findings on temperament, intelligence, and social role performance of gay men as contrasted with straight men do not support the model's assumptions. There is no evidence that gay men are either less physi-cally adept or more intelligent than their straight counterparts. Reported differences in their capacity for empathy are, most likely, a response to the stigma they have experienced.

The third model, parental manipulation, is founded on the assumption that parents seek to maximize the transmission of their genes to the next generation by fostering their offspring's reproductive effectiveness (Trivers 1974). From this point of view, effectiveness refers not to the number of children produced by each child but the total number of children produced by the siblings. If one additionally assumes that parents recognize the altruis-tic actions of the homosexual offspring as functionally beneficial to the family another sociobiological model of homosexuality emerges. Reproduction by one child might be "sacrificed" to increase the reproductive efficiency of the others.

Work such as that of Bieber et al. (1962) and Bell, Weinberg, and Ham-mersmith (1981) suggests that parents "make" a child homosexual to achieve this goal (Ruse 1982, 12). In this model parents, recognizing that some off-spring are less biologically fit, seek to protect these offspring from challeng-ing life experiences, and by overprotecting them direct them toward a homosexual outcome. From this perspective, it would be good if mothers became overprotective and fathers withdrew, at least to the extent of not encouraging typical masculine activities, from their ostensibly less robust sons, so these boys might become homosexual and not produce offspring (Ruse 1982). Evidence about parents making a child gay or lesbian is contradictory and is largely founded on clinical and anecdotal studies. This hypothesis assumes a degree of casual relationship between preadult socialization to masculinity and adult sexual orientation that is not supported by the literature on psychosocial development across the life course (Cohler and Freeman 1993).

The fourth evolutionary model, also focused largely on homosexual men, posits that the gay man is fundamentally less biologically effective (active and aggressive in seeking woman partners for reproduction) than heterosexual men (R. D. Alexander 1975). Since males must compete aggressively for female mates, aggressive, competitive, and successful men, able to conquer the most desirable women, are most likely to insure a robust species. Thus, it is better for the species that less aggressive men not reproduce. Those males who are likely to be less successful in attracting mates are diverted into homosexuality through masturbation and a resulting preoccupation with the bodies of men rather than of women. Neither of the assumptions on which this model rests, that future homosexual men are less effective than future heterosexuals and that masturbation leads to homosexuality, have found empirical support.

The Four Models in Review: Critique of Evolutionary Perspective

Evaluating these four models, Ruse (1982) finds little evidence for their common assumption that homosexual men differ genetically from heterosexual men in such a way as to be biologically unfit to reproduce (Futuyma and Risch 1984). Many individuals who see themselves as gay or lesbian have been married and had children. Furthermore, all four models largely ignore the question of female homosexuality. The assumption that men's attributes are more important that women's because women are essentially passive in the reproductive process seems unlikely as a reality (as opposed to a social pretense) and is not empirically supported. However, Ruse's major critique of these models is that the gene-environment interplay is more complex than sociobiological perspectives seem to recognize.

While recognizing the limitations of simple biological models, Ruse does believe in the importance of a biological perspective on the foundation of same-gender sexual orientation. His claim is founded on his review of studies concerning the heritability of homosexuality, including twin studies, findings that more younger than older sons are homosexual, and findings that more sons of older than of younger parents are homosexual (perhaps resulting from mutations that become more common with advancing age, as do some chromosomal abnormalities, such as that associated with Down's syndrome). Ruse himself provides primarily a deficit model of homosexual men, who from earliest childhood are bright and socially adept but athletically and sexually weaker and less competent than their heterosexual counterparts.

Sociobiological assumptions are particularly difficult to subject to systematic test since they make broad assumptions about the nature of populations, the purpose of life, and the functions of behavior, which are difficult to specify in terms of discrete lifestyles or ways of acting. All four evolutionary models largely reviewed by Ruse (1982) reflect stereotypes about homosexual men's biological fitness that are inconsistent with systematic findings (Dickemann 1995). By treating social stereotypes as if they were scientific data and embedding them in seemingly scientific discourse, these investigators reinforce existing prejudices.

Similarly, by treating homosexuality as a deficit which, at best, may serve as an aid to heterosexual fecundity, these investigators support a negative view of homosexuality. It is important to recognize that, when framed in this manner, Darwin's emphasis upon "survival of the fittest" can easily become a misplaced metaphor supporting stereotyped and biased views of same-gender sexual orientation. These arguments have the potential for profound social impact, and responsibility for this impact cannot be avoided by evoking the neutrality of science. At the very least, knowledge of their potential and historical impact should lead investigators operating within this model to particular scrupulousness about the adequacy of their data.

Behavioral Genetics and Sexual Orientation

Pioneers in the study of male homosexuality, Magnus Hirschfeld (1932) and Havelock Ellis (1936) noted a "family disposition" toward homoerotic interest (Mondimore 1996; E. Stein 1999). Using a classical means to differentiate genetic inheritance from other causes for traits to run in families, Franz Kallman (1952) built on these anecdotal clinical findings by systematically comparing sexual orientation among monozygotic (MZ) and dizygotic (DZ) twins.

Kallman was convinced that Mendelian inheritance could account for many aspects of behavior and that deviant conditions like schizophrenia and homosexuality likely resulted from individuals being homozygous for a single recessive gene. He reported nearly perfect concordance rates for homosexuality among MZ twins, and a correspondence rate of about 10 percent among DZ twins, which he took to support this hypothesis. Kallman's work has been criticized on many levels. The concept that one gene controls one behavior, especially a behavior as complex as same-gender sexual orientation, seems, on the face of it, unlikely (Lewontin, Rose, and Kamin 1984).

Methodological flaws in Kallman's work have led even investigators who believe that available evidence points to the heritability of sexual orientation to hold that Kallman overstated his case (G. Allen 1997). For example, Kallman failed to study randomly selected MZ and DZ twin pairs raised apart, which Farber (1981) insists is critical for behavioral genetics study.

McGuire (1995) and Allen (1997) provide detailed methodological critiques of the past two decades of studies of the heritability of homosexuality. They carefully consider anecdotal reports, particularly those of twins reared apart, which are essential for differentiating genetic from environmental factors (Haynes 1995). They find that much of the anecdotal literature on the sexual orientation of twins is ambiguous since subjects were not systematically interviewed regarding their sexuality.

Research on the heritability of sexual orientation has focused almost entirely on men. Since, even if there are heritable factors that result in same-gender orientation it would seem extremely unlikely that they were the same for men and women, we can only conclude that there is essentially no data on the inheritance of homosexuality in women.

Following Kallman's dramatic findings, more careful investigations led to reports of about 40 percent correspondence in gay sexual orientation among MZ twins in a carefully designed registry report (Heston and Shields 1968). Psychiatrist Richard Pillard and his colleagues have explored the sexual orientation of brothers of gay men. Pillard and Weinrich (1986) recruited volunteers through newspapers, including papers that targeted a gay male audience, and questioned them about their own and their brothers' sexual orientation using the Kinsey scale. The siblings were either interviewed or classified according to the respondent's report. Perhaps because of the way the sample was selected, the authors found perfect agreement between the two sources of information about brothers' homosexuality. Approximately a fifth of gay men had gay or bisexual brothers.

In another study Bailey and Pillard (1991) recruited gay men with twins or sibs through gay newspapers and interviewed them about their own and their sibling's sexual orientation, twin zygosity, Kinsey scale rating, and scales of childhood gender typicality. Nearly two-fifths of these interviews were conducted by telephone. These investigators found that half of MZ twins shared a gay sexual orientation, while 22 percent of brothers and 11 percent of adopted brothers also reported a homosexual orientation. They found little relationship between childhood gender conformity and sexual orientation. However, there was a nearly perfect match between gender nonconformity among respondents and among their MZ twins. While the DZ twin sexual-orientation correspondence of about a fifth is greater than reported elsewhere, the correspondence in sexual orientation among gay men and their nontwin adopted brothers was less than reported by Pillard and Weinrich (1986). Whitman, Diamond, and Martin (1993) report an even greater, two-thirds concordance rate for homosexuality among MZ twins, contrasted with a concordance rate of about one-third for DZ twins.

Bailey and Benishay (1993) and Bailey, Pillard, et al. (1993) tried to replicate findings from the study of gay men in lesbian twins and report concordance rates approximating those for gay men. About half of MZ twins, 16 percent of DZ twins, and 14 percent of nontwin biologic sisters reported a homosexual orientation. Gender nonconformity was unrelated to twins' sexual orientation. Other reports have found either a higher or lower correspondence; Whitman, Diamond, and Martin (1993) report that three out of four MZ lesbian twins were concordant for homosexuality. But King and McDonald (1992), using a small convenience sample of both gay and lesbian MZ and DZ twins, report a concordance rate of about 20 percent among MZ twins; this study did not report findings by gender of the respondent.[2]

Critique of Study of Heritability of Sexual Orientation

This review of findings appears to support the position that heritability plays a role in sexual orientation (Bailey and Dawood 1998). However, to date, studies of the heritability of homosexuality have been methodologically problematic; with the exception of Heston and Shield's report, all have used samples recruited through advertisements and, significantly, relied on respondents' reports of their siblings' sexual orientation. Further, while there is little reason to assume that heredity might play a similar role in male and female homosexuality, to date only one group has gathered a sufficiently large group of lesbians and their twins to make any reliable claim.

Reviewing findings to date, Pillard (1996, 1997) is certain they show markedly greater concordance for sexual orientation among MZ twins than among DZ twins and that this supports the argument for heritability. Findings reported by Hamer and Copeland (1994) lead them to estimate that a brother of a gay man has a 14 percent probability of being gay, as contrasted with a 2 percent probability among men without gay brothers, and even claim that heritability is more pronounced within the maternal than paternal lineage. However, Meyer-Bahlburg (1997a) has recalculated rates reported by Buhrich, Bailey, and Martin (1991), and finds that differences between concordance rates for MZ and DZ twins lack statistical significance.

The value of the comparative study of MZ and DZ twins rests on the

2. Hamer and Copeland (1998, 188) review findings of both Nicholas Martin and Michael Bailey suggesting that since MZ and DZ twins do not differ in rates of lesbian self-identification, shared (social) environment is more important than genetic factors in determining sexual orientation among women. However, these behavioral genetics investigators fail to recognize the significant role played by such social factors among men who self-identify as gay. This issue is discussed in greater detail in chapter 4.

assumption that MZ twins share an identical genotype leading to correspondence in traits in the absence of interfering environmental factors (Farber 1981; Haynes 1995). However, no behavioral trait subject to genetic study is completely independent of environmental influences, which determine the manner and mode of expression. Farber maintains that the twin method applies only when twin pairs are randomly selected and when members of each twin pair are randomly assigned to different rearing conditions. Farber (1981), Haynes (1995), McGuire (1995), and Allen (1997) all concur that few of the studies on human twins really meet these conditions; clearly these conditions have not been met in twin research on homosexuality.

The twins in these studies were raised together, making it difficult to separate environmental and genetic factors (Allen 1997; Lidz 1993; Pillard 1996). Features of the psychological situation of twins, and particularly MZ twins, could easily skew the findings of twin studies and lead to the observed concordance figures. For example, Lidz (1993) notes that twins often mirror each other and that MZ twins are commonly raised with the *expectation* that they will be strikingly similar in all regards. Whitman, Diamond, and Martin (1993) note that the fantasy of sex with a twin is not rare in gay men and women, so that twins reared together might engage in sexual activity and thereby influence each others' sexuality and orientation. King and McDonald (1992) found that 15 percent (7) of twin pairs they studied, all presumed to be heterosexual, acknowledged a sexual relationship, often continuing over years and sometimes continuing despite marriage. Of the twin pairs with such relationships six were MZ, one DZ. Whitman, Diamond, and Martin's (1993) study included three MZ twin pairs who were raised apart— two were concordant for sexual orientation, one was not (although both members of this pair had some atypical erotic interests).

While more than half of MZ twins in the research reported by Bailey and Pillard and their colleagues were concordant for same-gender sexual orientation, only 9 percent of nontwin brothers and 22 percent of the DZ twins were. The genetic hypothesis predicts equal rates of homosexuality among DZ twins and brothers generally (Byne and Parsons 1993). Ironically, adopted siblings were more likely than biological siblings to report same-gender sexual orientation; the percentage of adopted siblings of gay men reporting being homosexually oriented (11 percent) is more than double the proportion of men as a whole self-identified as homosexual (Byne 1994), which is about 5 percent (Michaels 1996). Byne and Parsons (1993) conclude that the higher rate of homosexuality among MZ than DZ twins may be accounted for by similarity of environment rather than genetic factors. This familial relationship suggests that nongenetic factors may account for a large part of the concordance.

Providing a careful assessment of the genetic studies of Pillard and Bailey and their colleagues, Byne and Parsons (1993), McGuire (1995), and Meyer-Bahlburg (1997) all conclude that the combination of problems of method—including the way subjects were located, reliance on indirect reports about the sexual orientation of some siblings, use of various means (face-to-face interview, telephone) to obtain direct reports, focus on behavior rather than fantasy, measurement of zygosity by self-report, use of an untested variant of the Kinsey scales, unusual ways of interpreting the scales, and the very small sample sizes—render conclusions from this work problematic. In addition the limitation of the studies to educated gay men leaves in question a range of factors likely to be influenced by gender and socioeconomic status. McGuire concludes that "the greater MZ vs. DZ correlations could be due to differential environmental effects, recruitment bias, substantially shared environments, additive genetic effects, or substantial non-additive genetic effects. The fact that biological brothers and adoptive brothers show the same incidence of homosexuality strongly suggests that it is entirely environmental in origin. . . . The evidence for a genetic component for homosexuality is hardly overwhelming" (1995, 139–40).

The observed concordance in MZ twins suggests that any existing genetic effect involves several genes rather than a single gene (Byne and Parsons 1993; Meyer-Bahlberg 1997). The high rate of discordance of the trait of same-gender sexual orientation among MZ twins in the studies of Pillard and his colleagues, Bailey and his colleagues, and King and McDonald suggests that much of the variance must be founded in environmental factors or, more likely, in a complex interplay of life experiences and polygenetic determinants. Present methods for the study of this interplay are inadequate. Like many studies of homosexual issues, investigations of heritability implicitly assume that the axis from same- to opposite-gender sexual interest is both significant and stable. Haynes (1995), McGuire (1995), and Allen (1997), however, question the use of Kinsey seven-point scale, which emphasizes a continuum of sexual behavior and fantasy between the dichotomous values of gay and straight. The Kinsey scales may not reflect the very different understanding men have of their sexual orientation a half century after the Kinsey Institute's pioneering work. For example, the concept of bisexuality, significant among the present generation of young adults, plays little role in the initial reports of Kinsey, Pomeroy, and Martin (1948).

The Search for the "Gay Gene"

Great media interest in the heritability of homosexuality followed the study of genetic linkages reported by Hamer et al. (1993) in *Science* and elaborated in LeVay and Hamer (1994) and Hamer and Copeland (1994). Genetic theory predicts that if a trait is inherited through a single gene then relatives who share the trait will share the gene more often than expected by chance, and that genes close together on a chromosome are almost always inherited together. Thus, even though the gene responsible for a trait may not itself be identified, it may be shown to exist by the transmission of another clearly inherited quality to which the trait is linked. Linkage studies are standard tools in the study of inheritance. Hamer and his colleagues studied forty families with two gay sons. Focusing on a gene located on the X chromosome which is transmitted from the mother but expressed only in men, the investigators located a marker in the region of Xq28 that was concordant for thirty three of the forty pairs of gay brothers; in a large group of presumably straight brothers the marker was randomly distributed. The chance of this association is less than one in ten thousand.

Further evidence for the association of this gene with male homosexuality came from studies of maternal relatives. Correcting for the fact that people generally know their maternal relatives better than their paternal relatives, gay men identified more maternal than paternal uncles and cousins as gay, a finding consistent with the location of a gene for male homosexuality on the X chromosome.[3] (If it is assumed that the same gene causes homosexuality in men and women then, since women have two X chromosomes, the incidence of homosexuality in women would be expected to be the square of the rate of men [W. J. Turner 1995].) Failure to use controls limits the conclusions in the research reported by Hamer and his colleagues. The presence of Xq28 markers among the nongay brothers in the families of the forty pairs of gay siblings was not studied (McGuire 1995; G. Allen 1997). Finally, as in all disciplines correlation is not causation (Byne 1994, 1996). Research in behavioral genetics has traditionally proceeded by contrasting offspring in each generation who do and do not show a particular trait. Hamer further biased his study by assuming in calculations an unusually low frequency of homosexuality, about 2 percent of the population, when, as Michaels (1996) notes, the more accurate frequency of exclusively homosexual men is about 5 percent. McGuire (1995) notes that Hamer's method of recruiting participants for his research suffers the same sampling problems noted for the family studies: the reliance on volunteers, including men attending an HIV–positive support group, and on pairs of brothers both agreeing to participate. Other methodological limitations are also similar to those affecting the family re-

3. It could be argued that this difference arises not because a "gay gene" is located on the X chromosome but because gay men have lower fertility than straight men. If the gene were located on an autosomal chromosome and inherited from the father's side, the father's side of the family would be smaller for that reason, and so would contain fewer gay men.

search discussed early: the Kinsey scale was administered in a less than systematic manner (some respondents were interviewed in person, others by phone, and some through mail-in questionnaires), the subjects reported a range of more or less homosexual behaviors yet were dichotomized as gay or straight, and the impact of ethnicity and life experience were not addressed.

Rice et al. (1999) report failure to replicate Hamer's work. This research group was unable to find a link between male homosexuality and Xq28, and maintains that gay brothers are no more likely than straight counterpart brothers to share the Xq28 genetic marker. Further, this group found little evidence supporting Hamer's claim of maternal transmission. Wickelgren (1999) reviews findings reported at the 1998 meetings of the American Psychiatric Association which also failed to replicate the findings of Hamer and concludes that there is very little evidence supporting the hypothesis that Xq28 is a genetic marker linked to homosexuality.

Hamer and Copeland (1994) and McKnight (1997) speculate, consistent with the sociobiological argument discussed above, that the gay gene's presence on the X chromosome increases the reproductive fitness of women who carry it. These researchers purport both that homosexual men are particularly potent and successful in finding male partners and that women carrying the gay gene will share these traits. Thus, for the population, the gene's benefits outweigh its reproductive costs, even though men carrying the gay gene are unlikely to father children.

Hamer and Copeland note that the "gay" gene has not been isolated and that "Xq28 plays some role in about 5 to 30% of gay men. The broad range of these estimates is proof that much more work remains to be done" (1994, 146). Among the work that remains incomplete is an empirical study of Xq28 linkage in brothers not concordant for homosexuality (as opposed to the theoretical analysis on which the high improbability of observed linkage was based). Marshall (1995) has reported in *Science* that Ebers and Rice at the University of Western Ontario were unable to replicate Hamer's findings and found no evidence for such a linkage. Reanalysis of Hamer's data fails to support the claim of differential heritability of male homosexuality from the maternal and paternal lines (McGuire 1995). Further, McKnight (1997) reports that Bone (1995) has challenged Hamer's sampling methods, and Marshall (1995) has stated that the NIH Office of Research Integrity was investigating Hamer's research.

Thus, while it seems likely that heritable characteristics play a role in fostering same-gender sexual orientation among men, such characteristics are far from being the major determinants. The biologist R. C. Lewontin and his colleagues (Lewontin, Rose, and Kamin 1984) criticize the general approach to behavior genetics on which Hamer and his colleagues base their work. They argue that the importance given to behavioral genetics findings is disproportionate to their scientific merit and attribute this disproportionate to the implicit political use being made of these findings. Lewontin and his colleagues share with Allen (1997) a concern that studies such as that of Hamer on the Xq28 allele fail to consider the complex interplay between behavioral genetics and social context because to do so would serve a political agenda less well. While in the paper published in *Science* Hamer and his colleagues claim only to have found an association between markers in the Xq28 region and a behavioral outcome (homosexuality), in more popular writings (Hamer and Copeland 1994, 1998; LeVay and Hamer 1994) they blur the distinction between association and causation in a way that more strongly suggests a genetic basis for homosexual behavior (Allen 1997).

Reviewing the behavioral genetic study of sexual orientation, Allen (1997, 1999) and Pattatucci (1998) criticize its predominantly mechanistic, materialist approach. Like McGuire (1995), they note that the presumption of genetic influences independent of the environment, implicit in much behavioral genetic research, does not accurately reflect current general ideas about the relationship between genetics and environment. Genes are less fixed blueprints of persons than elements in an open system involving a complex set of biological and environmental factors. The assumption of a necessary relationship between gene and phenotype fails to recognize the intrinsic feedback loops between DNA, genetic expression, and environment.

Schüklenk and Ristow (1996) also observe that efforts at showing a relationship between genetic factors and sexual orientation are extraordinarily politicized. Many gay men and lesbians and their families welcome evidence that sexual orientation is predetermined and that personal choice, preference, and environment play little role. The politics of the genetics of homosexuality parallels those surrounding the genetics of such psychopathologies as schizophrenia and affective disorders—an entirely biological explanation for these conditions spares all concerned the anxieties associated with questions of meaning, morality, or ambiguity. If homosexuality is a genetic condition there can be no argument, at least in our contemporary society, about the inappropriateness of discrimination against gay people. Thus, genetic and other biological investigations can be used as a dodge to avoid confronting confusion and hostility about same-sex orientation. For this reason Schüklenk and Ristow question the value of biological research until we move beyond a concept of same-gender sexual orientation as a deficit or a disease in need of cure. The infrequency of reports of replicated findings, combined with the intense publicity given findings in this area, suggests that these publications serve mainly to reinforce hoped-for but unproven assumptions rather than to clarify the issues they purportedly address (Byne 1996; Byne and Parsons 1993). From a psychoanalytic perspective, these attempts to provide a genetic basis for homosexuality, independent of life experiences, currently discourage the search for meanings inherent in sexual orientation and hinder analysts' efforts to help analysands realize an enhanced sense of personal integration and freedom through exploration of these meanings.

Hormones and Homosexuality

Generations of investigators have explored the relationship between same-sex orientation and hormonal function (Byne 1996; L. Ellis, 1996a, 1996b; L. Ellis and Ames 1987; Ehrhardt 1978; Meyer-Bahlburg et al. 1995; Meyer-Bahlburg 1997; Reinisch and Sanders 1984). Older studies, consistent with the view of homosexuality as an intersex phenomenon, explored deficiencies and excesses of sex hormones as causes of homosexuality. When this approach proved inadequate the question shifted to whether same-gender orientation might result from exposure to a variant hormonal milieu, such as might result from biosocial stress, during critical developmental periods (Kinsley, Lambert, and Jones 1997). The observation that in the absence of fetal androgens the external genitalia develop as female led to the speculation that masculinization of brain centers also required the presence of these hormones.

Sex Determination in Prenatal Life

A model of same-gender sexual orientation based on prenatal hormonal influences has many advantages. It could build on known biological determinants of gender (Imperato-McGinley, Peterson, et al. [1981] 1985; Gooren, Fliers, and Courtney 1990; R. C. Friedman and Downey 1993a, 1993b), employ appropriate analogies with animal behavior, and avoid both the either-or of essentialist biological perspectives and the relativism of social constructionist approaches (Gooren, Fliers, and Courtney 1990).

Much is known about the intrauterine development of sexual differences (L. Ellis 1996a, 1996b, 1997; Ellis and Ames 1987; Fausto-Sterling 1995). The processes involved in development of typical male characteristic are better understood than those leading to female characteristics. We will not review these processes here except to note that the development of masculine features depends on appropriate levels of testosterone being present at critical times in development. From the point of view of the study of homosexuality, a particularly important occurrence is the development of sex-hormone receptors outside the genital apparatus during the fourth through seventh months of gestation. Appropriate levels of testosterone appear to be necessary for these receptors to develop.

The possible impact of disturbed intrauterine testosterone levels, such as might result from unusual stress or other environmental factors, has been the object of ongoing study and speculation. Aberrations in the hormonal receptor sites that might be caused by such changes would not manifest themselves until the time when those receptors would ordinarily begin to function. For example, males who had partially failed to develop testosterone receptor sites might not show the changes in muscle mass and strength that ordinarily accompany puberty. Testosterone and its metabolite DHT are necessary for male sexual arousal, so abnormal hormonal receptors might also influence sexual arousal.

Intrauterine Androgens and Adult Sexual Orientation

The impact of the failure to produce testosterone on the development of masculinity has been studied in laboratory experiments, primarily using rats. Female rats ordinarily exhibit lordosis in preparation for mating, arching the back and thrusting the rear up, ready for the characteristic male behavior of mounting, thrusting, and insertion. Experiments have focused on the impact on mating position of intrauterine androgen insufficiency, created either by manipulating hormone levels or by inducing stress in the mother rat during pregnancy. The central finding is that such insufficiency leads male rats to behave in the female pattern.

Researchers relating these findings to human same-gender sexual orientation assume that the adoption of the opposite-sex mating behavior in rodents may be equated with homosexual orientation in humans. They further argue that stressed human mothers would be likely to experience endocrine effects similar to those seen in rats and that their male fetuses might have subnormal intrauterine exposure to androgens. The brains of these fetuses would be expected not to be masculinized in the way that brains of male fetuses exposed to normal androgen levels would and so to develop along a female line. This could result in gender-atypical interests or even a preference for gender-reversed activities (Dörner 1988; Dörner, Geiser, et al. 1980; Ward 1977).

This hypothesis is open to many questions. McKnight (1997) notes, for example, that while maternal stress may block fetal testosterone and lead to changes in copulation position in rats, there is little overall change in other sex-typical behaviors. Direct data about the impact of intrauterine androgen insufficiency in humans is limited; reduction in effective intrauterine androgens, which occurs in several pathological conditions, can lead to the birth of boys with femalelike genitalia, and these individuals do have some greater tendency to later homosexual ideation.

Generally, experimental manipulation of postnatal sex steroids has contributed little to understanding sexual orientation. However, investigators have found what appears to be a correlation between a normal difference in male and female endocrine response and same-gender orientation. In adult women estrogen administration stimulates the production of luteinizing hormone (LH), a positive estrogen feedback effect (EFE). In men, administration of estrogen leads to reduced LH, a negative estrogen feedback effect. In rodents stimulated with exogenous sex steroids a positive EFE is associated with lordosis, a negative EFE with mounting and thrusting. Exposure to increased androgen levels during a critical period of prenatal life leads to later failure to respond to exogenous sex steroids with a positive EFE. It seems reasonable to assume that positive and negative EFEs are associated with different brain states. The association is further suggested by studies of castrated macaque monkeys, who lacked both mounting behavior and negative EFEs characteristic of intact males.

These animal studies suggested that the study of EFEs might illuminate a biological basis for human sexual orientation. In a series of publications, which initially attracted much attention, Dörner (1980) and Dörner, Döcke, et al. (1987) found an EFE intermediate between those of women and those of self-identified straight men in a group of self-identified gay men. They inferred that homosexuality in men may result from an altered intrauterine endocrine environment that permanently changes the fetus's brain. The conceptual basis for the assumption that there is an irrevocable prenatal determination of positive or negative EFE is questionable. These investigators did not explore the possibility that sexual behavior changes EFE. Even intense exposure to abnormal intrauterine androgen environments do not necessarily alter adult sexual function in an expectable way. For example, exposure to large quantities of androgen prenatally does not necessarily alter women's menstrual cycle (Gooren, Fliers, and Courtney 1990).

Specific studies of EFE bring Dörner's hypothesis into question (Hendricks, Graber, and Rodriguez-Sierra 1989). First, variation in EFE may be induced postnatally (Gooren 1986a, 1986b, 1990). Second, transgendered men and women, who would be presumed to be more intermediate in the neuroendocrine status than gay men, show the same EFE as their biological counterparts prior to surgery. After hormonal treatment and surgery, male-to-female transgendered people show the characteristic male EFE (Gooren 1995). Thus it appears that the EFE depends on the individual's current endocrine status and is not immutably set during a critical period of intrauterine development as Dörner and his colleagues posit. Gooren (1995) further faults these studies because the investigators should have studied LH response to synthetic luteinizing hormone-release hormone (LHRH), which is the physiological releasing hormone of pituitary LH.

Dörner's studies are problematic in many other ways. The original studies have not been replicated, the original sample was small, and the within-group variance was large (McKnight 1997). Only a third of the group of gay men showed the predicted effect, and over half of the group could not be differentiated from the straight comparison group. Many heterosexual men exhibited the "homosexual" pattern of response. The research does not control for or adequately address other factors known to effect LH response including reduced testicular functions due to aging, drug use, or viral infections. When homosexual and nonhomosexual men are matched on these factors, there is little difference in EFE response (Gooren 1995).

An increased LH response to LHRH following exposure to estrogen is an essential element of the positive EFE associated with the stereotyped female position adopted by rodents in sexual intercourse. This increased LH response was not observed by Gooren and his colleagues (Gooren 1984, 1986a, 1986b; Gooren, Fliers, and Courtney 1990). None of the gay men in this study showed increased LH, while all lesbian women did show this effect, as would be predicted by the gonadal sex of the subject rather than by sexual orientation: LH secretion does not appear to be a reliable indicator of sexual differentiation in the brain.

Finally, one investigation suggests a correlation of higher intrauterine androgen levels with same-gender orientation. Forger and Breedlove (1987) report that a morphological index of early fetal testosterone exposure (survival of motoneurone in Onuf's nucleus) supports a view that gay men have more rather than less fetal androgen exposure than straight counterparts. In addition they argue that since gay men begin puberty at a somewhat earlier age and engage in more sexual activity with more partners than straight counterparts, gay men must not experience androgen deficiency during fetal life, since otherwise they would not show the intense sexual response associated with higher testosterone levels.

Prenatal Maternal Stress and Gender-Atypical Development

Dörner and his colleagues (Dörner, Schenk, et al. 1983) have maintained that baby boys born in wartime are more likely to become homosexual men; they attribute this phenomenon to the increased stress on their mothers during pregnancy, which results in a drop in fetal androgen levels. Available evidence does not support a correlation of pregnant women's stress during war and same-gender orientation in their grown sons (McKnight 1997; Schmidt and Clement 1995). Ellis et al. (1988) retrospectively interviewed mothers of self-identified gay, straight, and bisexual undergraduate men and women about stress during their pregnancies. They found little association between such stress and the students' sexual orientation. On one measure of stress (using a liberal probability value) they did tease out differences showing greater stress during the second trimester of the pregnancy of gay men and lesbians as contrasted with other groups. However, the long interval between pregnancies and interviews and the marginal significance levels of the data do not inspire confidence in this finding.

Bailey, Willerman, and Parks (1991) did not find higher pregnancy stress experience correlated with Kinsey rating in their retrospective interviews with mothers. They did find a statistically nonsignificant retrospective relation between maternal psychosocial stress during pregnancy (primarily household moves) and reports of later boyhood gender nonconformity among their sons. Even were the finding more robust, such a correlation might reflect the mothers' attempts to provide a reason for the gender nonconformity.

Despite the problems noted in Dörner's work, other researchers have built on conclusions implicit in these findings emphasizing the significance of boyhood gender nonconformity and lack of "rough-and-tumble play" for the emergence of homosexuality among gay men. R. C. Friedman (1988) and Friedman and Downey (1993a) suggest that the preference for gender-atypical play—including avoidance of aggression, sports, and rough-and-tumble play (RTP)—among boys who later become homosexual men is an indirect effect of a reduction in intrauterine androgens resulting from maternal stress during pregnancy. Friedman writes, "Research thus suggests that childhood behavioral dimorphism involving rough-and-tumble activities reflects of influence of prenatal androgenization" (1988, 17). The biopsychosocial viewpoint explicit in the work of Friedman and Downey suggests that diverse pathways lead to same-gender sexual orientation and that biological factors such as prenatal trauma in the mother might be partially responsible for the preference for same-gender sexual activity.

Friedman and Downey argue, by analogy to the impact of maternal stress in rats on male offspring's copulatory behavior, that the "experience of the pregnant mother during a critical time interval could trigger physiological reactions in the male fetus that irreversibility alter the sexual behavior of the offspring during adulthood" (1993a, 134). Friedman and Downey further maintain:

> It is credible to hypothesize in the light of powerful effects of androgen on the organization of the CNS substrate that controls rough-and-tumble play, that decreased RTP among pre-homosexual children might reflect focal androgen deficit, perhaps at the level of the amygdala, during a critical prenatal developmental phase. . . . A mechanism of this type would not be detectable through assessment of the hypothalamic-testicular axis during adulthood. (1993a, 139)

This hypothesis is consistent with the observation that homosexual men and women do not show abnormalities in peripheral sex hormone production.

In an otherwise detailed report of the effects of stress upon the development of the nervous system and such "downstream" effects as sexual arousal and behavior in rats, Kinsley, Lambert, and Jones (1997) are much less specific regarding the relevance of their findings for humans. Reviewing evidence regarding the later indirect effect of prenatal hormones and sexual orientation, Banks and Gartrell have concluded that "at this time the literature does not support a causal connection between hormones and homosexuality" (1995, 263). Pointing to the methodological difficulties, some of which are cited above, they find no empirical evidence for partial nor complete prenatal androgen insufficiency being associated with sexual orientation.

OFFSPRING OF DES MOTHERS AND CAH GIRLS. Another intrauterine state that has been studied as a possible influence on sexual orientation is the disruption of estrogen in prenatal life caused by administration of diethyl-stilbestrol (DES) (Meyer-Bahlburg et al. 1995). Before being banned in 1971 because of its harmful effects on the fetus, DES, a synthetic estrogen, was widely used to manage high-risk pregnancies. DES prevents inactivation of estradiol, with the consequence that androgen receptors are not fully inactivated. Consequently it may be hypothesized that daughters prenatally exposed to DES will have a more masculine orientation than otherwise similar girls and that boys of DES mothers will be more feminine.

Follow-through study of women exposed to DES in utero shows some trend among DES daughters in some of the groups prenatally exposed to DES to express more masculine interests and bisexual fantasies than women not so exposed. Some investigators have taken these ambiguous findings to show that "estrogens are, indeed, directly involved in the usual prenatal organizational processes of the central nervous system that are assumed to underlie the development of sexual orientation" (Meyer-Bahlburg et al. 1995, 19). However, Yalom, Green, and Fisk (1973) report that the gender behavior of six-year-old boys of DES mothers cannot be differentiated from the comparison group of boys of non-DES mothers. Only teacher-rated six-year-old boys of DES mothers might be less assertive and athletic, and sixteen-year-old boys appeared to be less masculine than counterpart boys of non-DES mothers on several measures. Hoult (1984) suggests that psychosocial rather than biological effects might be responsible for these findings since the DES mothers were all chronically ill and were particularly overprotective.

Another state in which the impact of prenatal sex hormones can be studied occurs when the adrenal gland fails to synthesize sufficient cortisol but instead secretes excessive amounts of androstenedione, an androgenic precursor hormone. This leads to the clinical syndrome of congenital adrenal hyperplasia (CAH) (Slipjer 1984). Girls with this syndrome may be born with masculinized genitalia. This problem may be treated with continuing cortisone replacement therapy and appropriate surgery, leading to physiologically normal adolescence. However, Friedman and Downey (1993a) report that the childhood play of these girls was more atypically masculine and sexually avoidant than the play of their unaffected sisters.

However, in their careful review of both DES and CAH studies, Friedman and Downey (1993a) report little association between these hormonal factors and sexual orientation. Little information is provided about the erotic fantasies of these women and only anecdotal reports suggest a somewhat greater proportion of homosexuality than among women in the general population (Gooren, Fliers, and Courtney 1990; Friedman and Downey 1993a). Boys with CAH appeared hypermasculine and were particularly attracted to sports and rough outdoor activities, but overall those effects did not extend to adult sexual orientation. Data concerning the slightly masculinized CAH girls does not allow differentiation between hypothesized prenatal androgen effects on the developing brain and gender-atypical behavior encouraged by parents confused about the child's gender at birth (Breedlove 1994). Reviewing findings from their own study together with other reports, Berenbaum and Snyder (1995) note little association between early androgen and childhood activity preference.

PSEUDOHERMAPHRODITE BOYS. Other evidence about the impact of hormonal factors on human sexual orientation is founded on study of "pseudohermaphroditism" or 5-alpha-reductase (5-A-RD) deficiency syndrome, a genetic disorder causing a deficiency in the hormone dihydrotestosterone during pregnancy. Boys with this disorder show gonadal ambiguity. However, at puberty, boys with 5-A-RD deficiency develop masculine secondary sex characteristics. Studies in the Dominican Republic, where the syndrome is particularly common, find that even if boys with this condition are raised as girls, after puberty they show typical heterosexual interests (Imperato-McGinley, Guerrero, et al. 1974; Imperato-McGinley, Peterson, et al. 1979), whereas Byne and Parsons (1993) have shown that in other cultures these boys, when raised as girls, maintain a feminine identity after puberty. One difference is that in the Dominican Republic these boys are maintained gonadally intact, while elsewhere surgery to "correct" genital abnormalities may result in castration of the boy and, hence, no typical male androgen surge at puberty. However, purely cultural factors are also important. It may be significant that Dominican culture emphasizes the superior social standing of men and thus may direct these children into the adoption of a characteristic masculine presentation of self.

Reviewing comparative data from Highland New Guinea people with the Dominican Republic studies, Herdt and Davidson (1988) note differences in the significance of this biological anomaly across culture. Of fourteen informants suffering from 5-A-RD deficiency, five were raised as girls until adolescence. The remaining nine, despite their female appearance, were recognized at birth as pseudohermaphrodites or a "third sex" by sharp-eyed midwives. These boys were raised as boys in anticipation of the pubertal transformation. However, they were not regarded as normal and were excluded from the rituals in which younger boys gain masculinity from older ones by fellation. As young men they may be accepted into the men's cult but have a difficulty marrying and becoming householders. Some are regarded as shamans, held in public esteem but privately ridiculed. Herdt and Davidson note that, in contrast with the report from the Dominican Republic, where gender switching after puberty was possible, in a culture where fear of women and concern with semen depletion is particularly salient, lifelong stigma remains even when gender switching occurs. Herdt and Davidson emphasize how culturally encoded concepts of gender are more salient than hormonal changes at puberty in determining how these persons will be regarded in society.

CRITIQUE OF THE ANIMAL MODEL PERSPECTIVE. Byne and his colleagues (Byne 1995, 1996, 1997b; Byne and Lasco 1997) and Fausto-Sterling (1995, 1997a) have reviewed the science that first led to the use of animal models in the study of human sexual orientation. Phoenix et al. (1959) had published a paper reporting the effects of injection throughout pregnancy of testosterone propionate (TP), an androgen facilitator, in guinea pigs. Offspring were born with genitalia altered in size and form. After rearing and weaning, which were not controlled in this study, gonads were removed from all animals. The animals were then injected with estradiol benzoate (EB) and either progesterone or testosterone, and patterns of mating behavior were observed (rear-end mounting was viewed as characteristically male and lordosis as characteristically female). Injections of EB and progesterone brought the female animals into heat, at which time lordosis is most readily observed. Prenatal injection of androgen suppressed the capacity of female animals for lordosis. Phoenix and coworkers explicitly saw their experiment as forming a foundation for a theory of sexual behavior differentiation, as well as showing the impact of prenatal hormones on adult sexuality.

Birke (1982) noted several problems in using animal models, particularly laboratory rats, as models of human sexuality. These include biological variation between strains of rats, problems with generalizing from rat studies to humans, and the equation of copulatory position with sexual orientation.

Fausto-Sterling (1995) notes that the steroids used in these studies diminish sexual interest and reduce the size of the vagina, induce neuromuscular changes, and increase the animals' size, all of which also make mounting more difficult. Increased testosterone affected the female's odor, which slowed the male's ejaculation. Further, rat pups raised by altered mothers were licked less, which may have interfered with the neurological base of their sexual responses (Moore, Dou, and Juraska 1992). A host of other factors including the impact of rearing and handling also alter sexual responses in these animals.

The idea that intrauterine androgens are needed during a critical period of brain development is brought into question by investigations such as those showing that implanting testosterone pellets postnatally in the preoptic area of the hypothalamus increased mounting behavior (Christensen and Gorski 1978).

Problems of Method and Subject Selection in the Study of Hormones and Sex Role

In a lucid critique of the literature on prenatal hormones and determination of human sexual orientation, Byne (1995, 1997b) and Byne and Lasco (1997) note that there is no evidence that the brain regions that regulate copulation in rodents have an equivalent in humans. Animal studies explore situations in which biologically altered rodents attempt copulation in a fashion typical of the opposite gender. This corresponds but slightly to the complex thoughts, feelings, and behaviors typical of same-sex orientation in humans. Animal studies do not even investigate the rat's sexual preferences (if such a concept applies to rats) by providing a choice of partners. The animals' behavior is observed only during opportunities for heterosexual mating.

Findings from many studies of hormones and homosexuality have been compromised by poorly matched subject groups, insufficient control of factors influencing hormone levels, questionable means of assigning ratings of sexual orientation, and variable laboratory techniques (Meyer-Bahlburg 1984, 1997a; Purifoy and Koopmans 1980; Banks and Gartrell 1995). For example, failure to control for such health issues as HIV status among men or for the complex interplay of lifestyle and hormone production in women seriously compromise findings from such hormone studies. Dörner's (1976) findings were complicated because some of the homosexual male subjects were being treated for venereal disease and testicular disease could affect hormone levels. Gladue's (1988) report included at least some men who were HIV-positive, which would affect testosterone response to increased LH (Banks and Gartrell 1995; Meyer-Bahlburg 1997b).

Even more problematic, while rodents may show positive EFE, rhesus monkeys do not show a marked effect of prenatal androgen levels on LH regulation (Meyer–Bahlburg 1997b). Baum et al. (1985) report that positive estrogen feedback among nonhuman primates is not determined prenatally and can be manipulated by estrogen administered postnatally. Meyer–Bahlburg also notes that findings from studies of prenatal hormone levels and postnatal sexual or reproductive life have been contradictory. Interspecies differences are so great that findings from such studies can only be generalized to other species with the greatest caution. To cause same-gender orientation without other neuroendocrine effects, intrauterine androgen deficiency would have to operate with pinpoint precision. Yet as Meyer–Bahlburg (1997b) notes, homosexual men and women show normal sex hormone levels and do not report somatic symptoms of intersexuality (Banks and Gartrell 1995).

Even rodent studies are far less clear than they first appear. Dörner's (1976) findings were based on rats studied after gonadectomy and testosterone administration in adulthood. Intact experimental rats showed little change in reproductive position in response to intrauterine androgen deficiency.

Responding to critiques of their research, Dörner, Popper, et al. (1991) suggest that adding the idea of genetic vulnerability to the prenatal stress hypothesis strengthens their argument for intrauterine effects leading to same-gender orientation. They found that levels of a cortisol precursor, 21-deoxycortisol or 21-DOF, were elevated after adrenocorticotropin (ACTH) stimulation among homosexual men, women, and their mothers in contrasted to a heterosexual comparison group. They suggest homosexual men may have a genetic predisposition to androgen-dependent homosexuality. However, women with classic CAH, which is attributed to high levels of 21-DOF, do not show increased homosexuality. In general, human neuroendocrine responses are not fixed but vary over time depending on many factors including diet and exercise.

On reviewing available evidence, several investigators (Gooren, Fliers, and Courtney 1990; Byne 1996; Byne and Lasco 1997; Byne and Parsons 1993; Meyer–Bahlburg 1984, 1997b; Ricketts 1984) reach similar negative conclusions about the relevance of research on prenatal development of rats to human same-gender sexual orientation: "None of the available studies permit us to fully exclude a confounding of the prenatal hormone factor with putative social factors" (Meyer–Bahlburg 1984, 390). Even were the correlations more clear, correlation is not causation. As Birke (1982) and Ricketts (1984) note, even demonstrating that groups differing in sexual orientation also differ on some other characteristic would not prove causality.

The entire program of research concerning animal hormonal models for human homosexuality is questionable. It ignores the relative independence of human sexuality from reproductive function and the systems of meaning that so profoundly affect human sexual life. The assumption that sexual positions have the same meaning in rodents and humans seems doubtful and the idea that same-gender orientation entails adoption of the other gender's normal copulatory position (whatever that may be) is, at its center, obviously wrong.

The assumption implicit in these investigation, that same-sex orientation is an aspect of an intersex state, has impaired efforts to understand homosexuality from a biological perspective. For example, much biological research presumes that one may differentiate between gay men who prefer the role of anal penetrators ("tops") and those preferring anal reception ("bottoms"). While it might be argued that "bottoms" were adopting a typically female position in copulation, which in itself would demand a high degree of confusion about genital anatomy, the behavior of "tops" could not be explained as an adoption of a female copulatory position. In any case it is more common for gay men to enjoy both activities than to have a rigid preference in this regard. Nor is the social stereotype that gay people are particularly likely to show physical or psychological characteristics of the other gender borne out. When biologically oriented investigators focus on intersex models of homosexuality they miss the opportunity to explore the more interesting question of the biological contribution to sexual interests.

Positions for sexual acts are so rich in meaning that, with the possible exception of anatomical feasibility, it is difficult to be convinced that biological factors play a very strong, much less a dominant, role in people's choice of sexual position. Cultural definition arguably plays a greater role in the choice. For example, Carrier (1989) reports that Mexican culture defines the "bottom" partner in a male couple as homosexual but the "top" as simply a man with sexual desire. Similar observations have been reported by Murray (1995a, 1995b, 1995c).

Anthropologist Clifford Geertz's (1973, [1974] 1983) advocated a focus on the informant's point of view, but there has been little inquiry into gay men's views of the significance of "top" or "bottom" positions and their relation to ideas of masculinity and femininity. Contemporary gay men in the United States appear not to equate sexual position with gender (Byne and Lasco 1997). As one community informant observed:

> Giving it to my partner, and feeling my partner inside of me . . . they are both a real turn on. It [anal intercourse] feels good, and sometimes I feel like doing one thing and sometimes the other. It depends upon what my partner and I both feel like at the time. When you're doing it, I just think about how good his body feels and how good it feels to be one with him, to have him inside me

or for me to be inside of him and to be close, holding each other, and enjoying
each other's body.

A patient described by Corbett (1997) states, "When Alex is in me, it's like
I feel filled up with him. Like his cock reaches all the way through to mine,
as though we are one." Such lived experiences are not adequately addressed
from stereotypes, often based on crude models of heterosexual interests,
about the meaning of sexual positions for participants. Too much of the
study of homosexuality has relied upon mechanistic measurement and stereotyped fantasies of what variation in position during sexual encounters
must mean, in the absence of exploration of the meaning of activities to
the participants.

It is striking how different reports of lived experience are from the presumptions of investigators who explore same-sex behavior as though it were
a variant of heterosexual behavior and as if the preoccupations, of the participants were the same as those of a hypothetical heterosexual man imagining
himself engaged in same-sex activities. Such presumptions appear to reflect
the heterosexist bias in contemporary society (Herek 1996).[4]

In sum, while the prenatal hormonal environment may influence mating
positions in some rodents, the significance of these findings for human sexuality is obscure. As the study of 5-AIRD deficient pseudohermaphrodites
shows, in humans even the strongest biological influences are reshaped by
culture. Available data do not support an important role for the hypothesis
that intrauterine hormonal influences contribute significantly to sexual orientation.

Brain Structure and Sexual Orientation

A fourth biological perspective in the study of the determination of sexual
orientation, sexual dimorphism in brain anatomy, has received considerable
media attention, largely as a result of a report in *Science* (1991) and a popular
book, *The Sexual Brain* (1993), by the neuroanatomist Simon LeVay. LeVay
described autopsy findings in men with the same-gender sexual orientation
in which he found features of the third interstitial nucleus of the anterior
hypothalamus (INAH3) not found at autopsy among heterosexual counterparts. LeVay's work followed reports by of Allen, Hines, et al. (1989) and
Allen and Gorski (1992) that INAH3 was larger in women than among men

---

4. The situation is strikingly similar to early developments in the psychoanalytic theory of feminine psychology. Freud plausibly observed that a little boy seeing a girl's genitals might regard her as
a castrated boy. However, this statement about a boy's fantasy was generalized to an idea that female
sexuality was a negative complement of male sexuality and that women needed to accept this inherently unsatisfactory situation.

and a tentative report by Swaab and Hofman (1984) that the suprachiasmatic nucleus appeared larger at autopsy in a group of male AIDS patients, presumably homosexual, than in counterpart heterosexual men.

Investigations like those of Swaab and Fliers (1985) suggested that the hypothalamus, long thought to be important to sexuality, is sexually dimorphic. It is therefore reasonable to ask whether differences would be found among men of differing sexual orientations. Further, Alexander and Sufka (1993) report EEG activation patterns on tasks of spatial and facial-emotion recognition and verbal and emotive word-pair judgment that in very small groups of self-identified gay men students were similar to those of straight women but different from those of straight men. These findings were extended to even more sensitive neuromagnetic measures by Reite et al. (1995).

McKnight (1997) concludes that available data support the idea that gay and straight men differ in brain anatomy but rejects the possibility that sexual orientation might affect EEG and MEG findings. However, while each study describes an anatomical difference, no two studies pinpoint the same difference and some studies of hypothalamic differences contradict others (Breedlove 1994). Further, brains studied at autopsy are often compromised by disease and brain harvesting methods, which might affect the size of a particular brain area. The number of brains studied is uniformly small, and factors such as age which are known to affect brain anatomy have not been taken into account.

Sexual Dimorphism, Sexual Orientation, and Neuroanatomy

Study of brain sexual dimorphism leads us back to the problem of intrauterine androgen exposure because there is some evidence that the size of INAH3 in rats depends on prenatal androgens during a critical period, that this area is critical for rat sexual functioning, and that reported differences in the size of the INAH3 nucleus in the human anterior hypothalamus are consistent with the prenatal stress–androgen effect hypothesis. LeVay reasons that gay men are like women in preferring men as sexual partners, so this nucleus, larger in women than in men, should be larger among gay than straight men.

The foundation for research on sexual dimorphism in the anterior hypothalamus is the study by Bleier, Byne and, Siggelkow (1982) showing that particular areas of the preoptic area of the hypothalamus of the rat brain contain more cells in one gender than in the other. It was assumed that this gender dependence indicated that these areas play some role in sex and reproduction, possibly in copulatory position. Summarizing subsequent research, Harrison, Everall, and Catalan (1994) note that three research groups have extended this initial finding: Gorski and colleagues report on the anterior commissure and several nuclei of the anterior hypothalamus (L. Allen and Gorski 1992; Allen, Hines, et al. 1983; Allen, Richey, et al. 1991; Gorski et al. 1978), Swaab and colleagues report sexual dimorphism in INAH1 of the anterior hypothalamus (Swaab and Fliers 1985; Swaab and Hofman 1984; Swaab, Gooren, and Hofman 1992; Swaab et al., 1997), and LeVay reports on the anterior hypothalamic nucleus INAH3 (1991, 1993). With the exception of findings about the INAH3, found sexually dimorphic by Allen, Hines, et al. (1989) and replicated by LeVay (1991), findings reported by one research group have not been replicated by other groups. Where replication is reported, methodological problems seriously qualify the significance of the findings. Research in this area has many of the problems we have discussed regarding genetic and endocrine research, only the difficulties with the neuroanatomical research seem more severe. Most significantly as Harrison, Everall, and Catalan (1994) note, there is little evidence that the hypothalamus plays any role in human sexual orientation.

These issues are of particular relevance to LeVay's (1991, 1993) research because he argues so strongly for a link between sexual dimorphism and homosexuality and claims to have found reliable differences in the size of INAH3 between gay and straight men. In a review not unsympathetic to LeVay's underlying logic, Friedman and Downey (1993a) summarize well the evidence for and against LeVay's hypothesis. One problem is that there is an enormous cross-species difference in the size and location of brain structures controlling sexuality and reproduction. Even solid findings from rats can only be generalized to humans with great caution. A second problem is that to date, there have been no replications of LeVay's finding; Byne (1994) reports that Manfred Gahr at the Max Planck Institute has tried unsuccessfully to replicate LeVay's findings. Moreover, the other interstitial nuclei in the anterior hypothalamus vary in size, in part in relation to seasonal factors, suggesting that these structures are not so immutable as LeVay's research appears to assume. More than three dozen studies have failed to confirm LeVay's (1991) claim that the corpus callosum is larger in male homosexuals than in heterosexual men. This is particularly troublesome since LeVay's sample was faulty from the outset—sixteen of the nineteen subjects in the study had died of AIDS or AIDS-related complications, and AIDS is known to cause changes in brain neuronal density (Everall, Luthert, and Lantos 1991). Factors such as concurrent illness, the impact of a wide range of medications, and even seasonal variation all might influence the size of the nuclei studied (Everall, Luthert, and Lantos 1991). Thus it is hard to see how the investigator could be confident that what he was observing correlated with the subject's sexual orientation.

During the past century, numerous researchers have tried to find anatomic factors differentiating the male and female brain. To date, only one reliable difference has been found—regardless of sexual orientation, men have slightly larger brains than women (Byne 1994, 1997a; Byne and Parsons 1993). Byne (1996) reports that a cell group straddling the medial preoptic and anterior of the hypothalamus is larger in the female than in the male rat and that damage to this preoptic region decreases male mounting behavior in a number of species, while its electrical stimulation increases mounting behavior. The meaning of these findings for human sexuality, if any, is unclear (Gooren, Fliers, and Courtney 1990). Byne (1996) reports that these studies implicate an area other than that often presumed to influence mounting behavior. Damage to this area has unpredictable effects on male monkeys. Some shun females and others seek more contact with females. Allen and Gorski's (1992) report that the anterior commissure of gay men was significantly larger than that either of heterosexual men or of women has not been replicated.

Critique of Research on Sexual Orientation and Neuroanatomy

It is not clear what role the anterior commissure might play in sexual orientation other than fostering sensory integration of the right and left brain. The finding reported by Allen, Hines, et al. (1989) and Allen and Gorski (1992), the foundation for LeVay's work, has itself not been replicated. While findings from Gorski's research group and Swaab and Fliers (1985) and Swaab and Hofman (1984) all report on some sexually dimorphic nucleus in the anterior hypothalamus, the location of this nucleus has not been agreed upon and, in any event, it has not been shown that a gender-correlated size difference has any relevance to human sexual orientation.

The extensive methodological problems in using cadaver materials from AIDS-infected people are noted above. But even if these problems were resolved and the observations replicated, the relationship of the anatomical differences to sexual orientation would remain unclear. Further, parallel postmortem comparative study of lesbian neuroanatomy has not been reported.

Harrison, Everall, and Catalan (1994) caution that there is little scientific basis for any explanation of sexual orientation as a "hardwired" phenomenon and that there has been little careful study of the reciprocal influence of brain and behavior, which would be necessary to understanding the causal dimension of any neuroanatomical—sexual orientation correlations that might be discovered. Causal connection in the opposite direction, that is, behavior causing changes in neuroanatomy, must also be considered. As Kandel observes, "Development, stress, and social experience are all factors that can alter gene expression by modifying the binding of transcriptonal regulators to each other and to the regulatory region of genes" (1998, 464).

Conclusion

Biological perspectives on the determination on sexual orientation are much less informative and explicit than either popular or scholarly writings suggest. Fundamental issues, like the definition of same-sex orientation, are almost entirely ignored in biological studies (Breedlove 1994; Kenen 1997). Animal copulatory positions have little to do with human sexual orientation (Breedlove 1994; McKnight 1997). Much of the biological work claiming to show a relation between biology and human sexual orientation does not live up to prevailing standards of assessment in the biological and social sciences (Suppe 1994, 1997). This, along with the purposes to which it has been used, suggests a motivation for research different from that expected in scientific study. A morass of ethical and political concerns propels the search for a biological "cause" of same-gender desire among men and women (Doell 1995; E. Stein 1994; Hamill 1995; Haumann 1995; T. Murphy 1997).

This chapter has highlighted a number of problems in the methodology and underlying assumptions of research addressing the issue of same-gender sexual orientation from biological perspectives. Byne, Suppe (1997), and Stein (1999) have well summarized the state of current knowledge. As Byne has observed:

> We are a long way from understanding the factors that contribute to sexual orientation. Even if the size of certain brain structures does turn out to be correlated with sexual orientation, current understanding of the brain is inadequate to explain how such quantitative differences could produce qualitative differences in a psychological phenomenon as complex as sexual orientation. Similarly, confirmation of genetic linkage would make clear neither precisely what is inherited nor how the heritable factor influences sexual orientation. . . . As research into the biology of sexual orientation proceeds, we should ask why we as a society are so emotionally invested in its outcome. . . . Perhaps the answers to the most salient questions in this (biological) debate reside not in the biology of human brains, but within the culture those brains have created. (1997b, 78–79)

In an elegant and sophisticated review, E. Stein assessed methods and findings from the four research traditions most prominent in the biology of homosexuality. He concludes:

> Although the main studies in this [emerging research] program are well-placed, widely cited, and their conclusions are even more widely believed, I argued that there are serious methodological and interpretive problems facing each of them. Studies in the emerging scientific program embrace—explicitly or

implicitly—a problematic account of what a sexual orientation is; have problems finding an appropriate subject pool to study; accept unjustified assumptions about the base rate of homosexuality; and make a variety of implicit, widely varied, and unjustified assumptions about homosexuality. (1999, 226)

Stein notes that there may well be some biological factors, principally genetic, which contribute to the expression at some point across the course of life of same-gender sexual orientation, but that research to date has not provided evidence to support such a conclusion.

McKnight (1997) has carefully reviewed the problems of method in genetic, hormonal, and anatomic studies related to homosexuality. He concludes that, even though these studies involve serious methodological problems, the preponderance of the evidence suggests that some biological factors have a role in shaping the course of sexual orientation. We do not agree. No matter how numerous, unconvincing studies do not sum to convincing conclusions. It might even be argued that the failure to find convincing evidence for biological causes of same-gender orientation, despite intense and impassioned efforts to do so, weights against their existence. Our review of these studies suggests that problems of method and analysis so compromise them that little can be concluded about the biology of sexual orientation. The strongest findings are in the area of behavioral genetics, where it appears that for some gay men and women there may be increased genetic loading which, together with other factors, might account for same-gender sexual orientation in adulthood. As Breedlove (1994) notes, society, personal meaning, and brain function are likely to interact in so complex an area as human sexual orientation with causal connections going in all directions.

Studies of the biology of sexual orientation have assumed that sexual orientation is innate and independent of individual motivation. Some gay scientists and activists have rallied behind that assumption since it clearly entails that gay men and women cannot "help" their desire. Since no decent society could censure people for a characteristic beyond their control and a good society would protect them from discrimination, this assumption of biology could provide the basis for protection in law from discrimination. (The view that sexual orientation is immutably determined early in life carries similar moral consequences [Breedlove 1994].) Since, as we will show in chapter 8, same-gender orientation is not associated with impaired personal adjustment or effectiveness any such discrimination says more about the motivation of those expressing antigay prejudice. Yet, the attractiveness of a biological viewpoint as an argument for treating gay people decently does not validate the viewpoint. Using invalid scientific concepts for good ends not only confuses scientific understanding, it may also short-circuit or at least postpone addressing important moral issues. As Breedlove (1994) and T. Stein (1997) observe, from the social policy perspective it matters little how much sexual orientation is subject to volition. Respect for others who may differ in some respect from ourselves need not be justified by biology but should be an intrinsic element of our life together within a community of shared values.

Biological predispositions, ranging from genetic influences to prenatal development, may influence sexual orientation to a varying extent, although such influence remains undemonstrated. Some gay men and women feel different early in life and associate early gender atypicality with later same-gender orientation. However, studies by the Chicago research group on gay and lesbian lives across the second half of life (Cohler, Hostetler, and Boxer 1998, in press; Hostetler and Cohler 1997; Herdt, Beeler, and Rawls 1997) suggest that many men and women do not become aware of same-gender desire until middle or later life. There is little reason to presume that biological factors are more salient in those men and women aware earlier in life of their same-gender desires. It is possible that there may be biological "sleeper" effects, predispositions which affect fantasy or action only later in life, but findings to date do not appear to support the claims made by Breedlove (1994) or McKnight (1997), either that sexual orientation is necessarily determined early in life or that it is not a matter of individual choice.

Murphy (1997) and Stein (1999) pose a further ethical question: Presuming there were a demonstrated technology for prenatally determining or altering sexual orientation, would it be desirable to insure that no boy or girl would grow up to be gay or lesbian? What impact would that technology have on the lives of gay men and women? Stein suggests that rather than attempting to alter sexual orientation, we should work toward social change which will make it possible for gay men and women to lead lives free of stigma and prejudice. In such a setting sexual orientation would not interfere with morale.

Consistent with Gay's (1998) discussion of acceptable sexuality in late-nineteenth-century bourgeois society, Suppe (1997) suggests that the only reason for the continuing search for a cause of same-gender sexual orientation is a preoccupation in contemporary society with late-Victorian theories of "normal love." This nineteenth-century perspective assumes that heterosexuality is the ideal expression of romantic love. It simultaneously discourages the consideration of the origins of heterosexuality and focuses concern on issues of homosexuality (Gay 1998). In the end, as Freud observed, "Recognition of the organic factor in homosexuality does not relieve us of the obligation of studying psychical processes connected with its origin" ([1922] 1955, 230).

Four

Storied Accounts and Psychoanalytic Understandings of the Childhoods of Gay Men and Women

I always knew I was different. I hung around with the other kids, but somehow there must have been something different. When I was in second grade, my teacher warned my mother I was going to turn into a "fag." She got so scared that she put me into every athletic program in town. My real interests were in theater. I was a star athlete but didn't really like it. In college I was finally able to work in the theater, where I met a guy and began a relationship. It lasted until graduation, then I went to Chicago to work in theater and he went to the west coast to do screenwriting. I knew then that I had been gay my entire life.

—TWENTY-SEVEN-YEAR-OLD MAN IN ANALYSIS

My wife began working in D.C. She'd come home weekends, but the kids and I felt it was pretty hard to keep the family going. . . . We had been married for more than twenty years and had a pretty good relationship, but my wife had gone back to school, graduated successfully, and was pretty ambitious about her career. My wife and I decided to get a divorce. She stayed in Washington and I took the kids and stayed here. I guess I was pretty lonely, and one of my friends in the office invited me out with him and some friends. They took me to Sidetrack [a gay video bar]. It was a Monday night, they were doing show tunes and everyone was singing along. It was pretty much fun. I looked around at all these guys, ordinary guys just like me and thought, they're all gay but they're just like me. I got to talking with a friend of my friend from work; we went out to dinner a few days later and ended up at his place. I didn't know before this that I was gay, but it was wonderful being with him and the sex was incredible. One thing led to another . . . now we've been living together for five years. My two kids [both in high school] live with us too. They're pretty cool about it.

—FORTY-FIVE-YEAR-OLD MAN SEEKING PSYCHOTHERAPY

These vignettes from the life stories of two gay men portray the paradox of understanding the emergence of sexual identity as a gay or bisexual man or woman. The comments of the first man represent what might be considered the "master narrative" of gay lives in our time (Plummer 1995, 82). This story emphasizes the gay man's feelings of always having been different from other men (although not effeminate). The parents too are aware that their son is different and make presumably well-intentioned efforts to steer him into the kind of activities expected of "normal" boys his age, but at the cost of some distortion of his "true self" (Winnicott 1960a). His eventual realization of gay sexual identity emerges at college. The focus is less on the personal struggle to accept same-gender sexual desire than on the feeling of coercion and denial on the part of other family members, as well as the first realization of this desire upon leaving home.

The report of the man at midlife poses a challenge to this master narrative, told within the gay and straight communities alike (Savin-Williams and Cohen 1996). Same-gender desire is presumed to be intrinsic and omnipresent from the time of a presumably different childhood through its first realization in relationships beginning in adolescence. Yet this man had not been aware of same-gender desire prior to his divorce, which was prompted by factors not associated with the sexuality of either husband or wife. Sometime subsequent to his divorce he began a relationship with a man and found that it met his needs for intimacy and sexuality. Therapeutic work has shown this man's rage in response to his wife's desertion, which he believes to have played some part in his interest in developing a relationship with a man. Coming from a close-knit middle-class family in which his mother had stayed home with the three children while his father worked in a neighboring suburb, this man had assumed he would have a "typical" marital career in which he and his wife would grow old together, enjoying their adult offspring and their grandchildren.

The present discussion understands "homosexuality" as the experience of (sexual) desire directed at others of the same gender, which may be expressed through creation of intimate ties of some duration. Following Kinsey, Pomeroy, and Martin's (1948) pioneering effort to define homosexuality, and consistent with psychoanalytic perspectives, this discussion emphasizes wish and accompanying fantasy; the realization of fantasy, in such actions as the search for an intimate partner, participation in political and social activities in the gay community, and definition of one's lifestyle as "gay," is clearly governed by life circumstances. While social and historical forces are intrinsic to the enactment of desire, encounter with the life stories of more than forty gay men and women during the second half of life suggests that these forces interact with the totality of life experiences not only in the enactment but also in the formation of same-gender desire (Cohler, Hostetler, and Boxer 1998, in press; Hostetler and Cohler 1997).

Far too often, discussion of same-gender sexual orientation has been restricted to the study of adolescence and young adulthood. This focus may reflect the prior prevalence of younger men and women in bars and other gay public spaces. Less is known about the course of lesbian, gay, and bisexual lives through the second half of life. It is assumed that at some point, perhaps in their mid-thirties, gay men and women find long-term partnership; as among their straight counterparts, the locus of social activity may move from public space to home. Present cohorts of gay women and men are likely to be more visible in social and political activities as they reach middle and later life than were former cohorts of gay men, because they have been involved in the community throughout their young adulthood. However, it is important to consider gay and lesbian lives across the course of life as a whole. While Kimmel (1978) and Plummer (1981, 1996) have urged more detailed study of sexual orientation and the course of middle and later adulthood, it is only within the past decade that systematic study has taken place (A. D'Augelli and Patterson 1995; Savin-Williams and Cohen 1996). This trend may reflect both the graying of the population and an increased sophistication in understanding the impact of history and social change across the course of life (Baltes, Cornelius, and Nesselroade 1979; Elder 1995; George 1993, 1996).

History and Life History: Telling the Gay Story

Review in chapter 2 of contemporary perspectives regarding sexual orientation and sexual identity was based on a perspective in the social sciences founded on Marx's ([1845] 1978) emphasis on the role of historical factors in determining the consciousness of a particular time, and on Mannheim's (1928) discussion of the sociology of knowledge. Viewed from this perspective, the social and historical forces present in society at any one time provide the template or foundation for the particular meanings which men and women alive then impart to their own subjectivity or lived experience (Schutz and Luckmann 1973, [1983] 1989).

The rapid social change of recent decades has been reflected in a significant change of focus in the study of lives, from a life-span or life-cycle to a life-course perspective. The life-cycle approach to developmental study focuses largely on presumed intrinsic, stage-ordered processes culminating in sequential negotiation of additional age-related tasks. By contrast, the life-course perspective assumes an open system shaped by social and historical process, as well as by both expectable and eruptive life changes within individual lives (Neugarten 1979; Hagestad and Neugarten 1985; Pearlin and Lieberman 1979; Stewart and Healy 1989). This perspective makes few assumptions regarding necessary tasks or issues to be resolved or negotiated over time. From this later perspective, persons inevitably confront challenges or concerns relevant to their own lives as a consequence of present social life (Dannefer 1984).

The implications of the life-course perspective for the study of particular lives has been reviewed by Dannefer (1984), Elder and Caspi (1990), Rosenwald (1993), and Alwin (1995). In brief, the four or five generations of men and women alive at the same time all experience the same major social and historical changes. However, the impact of these changes upon understanding of lived experience for each of these generations depends upon their members' age at the time the changes occur (Plath 1980; Elder [1974] 1998, 1995, 1997). Findings from the study of collective memory and the course of life by Schuman and his colleagues (Schuman, Belli, and Bischoping 1997; Schuman and Scott 1989) suggest that adolescence and young adulthood represent the period most significant in determining which larger-scale social and historical events will be recollected during the adult years as particularly salient for the life story told then (Fitzgerald 1996).

This finding, that youth is a particularly important time for the construction of the personal past used in the future, is consistent both with studies of the use of time across the course of life by Cottle and Klineberg (1974), Greene and her colleagues (A. L. Greene 1986, 1990; Greene and Wheatley 1992), and Clausen (1993), and with the study of life stories (Cohler 1982). This study suggests ways the experience of time changes during adolescence; if the transition from early to middle childhood may be characterized as a time when the past is forgotten, and middle childhood as a time of living in the present, then youth is a time when the future is first experienced as real and connected with a presently remembered past and experienced present. It is during youth that there arises anticipation and an interest in planning a future which connects family traditions with the larger society.

This perspective on the impact of a shifting context in understanding the course of lives over time has important implications for psychoanalysis, generally, including the psychoanalytic study of the meanings of variation in the expression of sexual desire. Social and historical forces provide the context for telling and reading stories, both those the analysand brings to psychoanalysis at the outset and that which is coconstructed by analysand and analyst across the course of their collaboration (Schafer 1992). Analyst and analysand, listener and teller, share a context which makes possible the concept of vicarious introspection or empathy, as portrayed by Kohut ([1959] 1978); however, each participant brings to the psychoanalytic encounter, as to any telling and listening, understandings shaped by both period and cohort.

To the extent that constructions of life course and lived experience are differ across cohorts, it may be difficult for the listener to empathize with the text provided by the analysand or other teller. As Mannheim ([1928] 1952) observed, a point supported by Toulmin's (1990) discussion of the sociology of knowledge, formal education fosters a generationally founded understanding of a discipline. In the case of psychoanalytic education, this entails particular ways of understanding sexuality, normality, and adjustment. Reconsidering long-held tenets regarding psychoanalytic theory and practice, whether in response to larger-scale historical and social change or to reformulations of clinical theory, may be painful. (We know very little about how the dynamics of personal change in attitudes and values accompanying larger-scale historical and social change affect life story and understanding of self, others, and the course of development. This is an area in which the psychoanalytic method, focusing on empathic observation of transference enactment, could make a significant contribution to social theory.)

From this perspective, present understanding of the dynamics of the psychoanalytic process reflects the interplay of generationally defined understandings of self and others. The analysand's expression of wish and intent is founded in a presently told life story, a narrative weaving together social context and particular life circumstances. The analyst's empathic response to this account, including a particular interpretive stance, is also based on present, contextually defined understandings of lived experience (Toulmin 1990). The very shape of the transference is codetermined by the life histories of analysand and analyst, as told in a particular time and place.

It is as a consequence of that larger historical context that study of wish and meaning becomes so particularly complex. Nowhere is this more evident than in the study of sexual orientation. There is considerable variation not only in the manner in which being straight, gay, or bisexual is understood within the larger society, but also in the understandings successive cohorts have of their own sexuality, over historical time and over the course of particular lives (Boxer and Cohler 1989; Chauncey 1994; Chodorow 1992; Katz 1990, 1995).

In a particularly moving account of his discovery of his own same-gender sexual wishes, the writer Arnie Kantrowitz ([1977] 1996) narrates the personal pain and desperation which he felt about growing up gay during the 1950s. Kantrowitz reports feeling so stigmatized and ashamed that at one point he attempted suicide. Half a century later, urban young people are able to relax in the context of supportive youth groups for lesbian and gay youths. Out to their family and friends, often active in gay youth groups in their suburban high schools, these teenagers live within a society far more tolerant and understanding of the varieties of sexuality than in former times. While stigma within the larger community is still a factor (Martin and Hetrick 1988), the lives of young people living in privileged and affluent communities, headed toward elite liberal arts colleges providing active support for lesbian and gay students, are far different than those of previous generations of gay youth. It is nearly impossible to compare the experience of growing up gay at the present time with the experiences of former cohorts. Porter and Weeks (1991) have made a similar point in their collection of personal accounts portraying changes in the experience of being gay in England over nearly a century.

However, even within historically adjacent cohorts, social and historical change can lead to quite different experiences of self and others. For example, community resistance to the police raid on New York's Stonewall Inn, a rough gay bar, in June 1969 (Clendinen and Nagourney 1999; Duberman 1993; D'Emilio [1983] 1998), had an electrifying effect, particularly on the young adult generation of lesbians and gay men also caught up in the broader social upheaval of the 1960s. As in many cities, the police had routinely raided New York's gay bars; the decision by a number of patrons to resist being arrested merely because they were dancing with others of the same gender led to far-reaching changes hardly envisioned by the down-and-out drag queens and leather men congregating in the bar that day.

Resistance to the Stonewall raid became an icon for the gay community and led in New York and elsewhere to the emergence of a "gay liberation movement." In the succeeding decade, young men and women experiencing same-gender desire came to see an alternative to the harassment of former times (Patterson 1995c; Plummer 1981). Their newfound courage was inspired by the larger civil rights movement, resistance to the war in Vietnam, and other cataclysmic changes taking place in American society in the years 1965–1975. This social activism, which in turn affected arts and letters, the social sciences, and psychiatry (including psychoanalysis), continues to have an impact in contemporary society. For good or for ill, virtually all of us have had to reconsider our lives, our values, and our personal goals in the social and intellectual turmoil of the past three decades.

For the cohort of youth coming of age in the 1970s aware of same-gender desire, gay liberation made it possible to find others facing similar struggles. There were places to go and opportunities to read and talk about the gay experience. In larger cities, where diversity of lifestyles supported a variety of communities, the emergence of a culture open and accepting of gay and lesbian lifestyles had an impact on everyone who was gay or lesbian. Once a community was established, successive cohorts coming out found a place of ready acceptance. One Chicago bar owner, in a neighborhood that now has about one-third lesbian and gay residents, opened a gay bar in 1979 which had large plate-glass windows. Reflecting already changing attitudes within the larger urban community, this gesture also fostered further social and personal change by affirming that there was no need to be secretive. This anchor tenant became part of the basis for an urban neighborhood experienced by lesbians and gay men as a safe space.

History, Lived Experience, and the Construction of the "Good" Life Story

Narratives of lived experience, whether oral or written, are founded on a presently understood history of one's life. Within our own culture, a life history is supposed to include an account of both origins and outcomes. As suggested in the preceding chapter on biology and homosexuality and again in the present discussion of childhood and family circumstances, the emergence of a lesbian, gay, or bisexual lifeway is presumed to have an origin, understood in terms of both personal predisposition and experiences during childhood. The content of this dominant narrative of "how I became gay" shifts over historical time and with social change but remains consistent with our understanding of what constitutes a "good" or followable story (Ricoeur 1977).

A life story is evaluated by both teller and listener in terms of presently shared understandings of what constitutes a good story. Indeed, one of the ways in which the clinical psychoanalytic situation can be understood is in terms of a story brought to the analysis by the analysand and subject to revision by way of the collaboration of analyst and analysand (Ricoeur 1977; Schafer 1980, 1981, 1992). Optimally, analyst and analysand share a view regarding criteria for a good story, which fosters the goal of helping the analysand realize an enhanced sense of personal integrity.

As with all historical accounts, the life story may be understood as a narrative (H. White 1987) which includes a sequence of events reflecting particular intentions portrayed through a presently remembered past, experienced present, and expected or assumed future, organized according to socially constructed understandings of time and space (Ricoeur 1977; MacIntyre 1984; Carr 1986). Following Bruner (1990), Kenneth Burke ([1945] 1969, [1950] 1969) has suggested that a narrative (1) inherently refers to a sequence of events in which people are featured as actors; (2) must be evaluated in terms of an internal plot or story line rather than an extralinguistic reality; (3) provides points of connection between the exceptional and the ordinary, which renders ordinary that which is exceptional; and (4) shows a literary quality or, in the case of the life story, portrays some dramatic quality or "tension" referring to a problem which needs to be resolved. Events constituting a narrative, like historical events more generally, are of little significance or meaning apart from their placement within the story (Mink 1965; H. White 1980, 1981, 1987). The task of both the author and reader or listener is to construct an emerging plot or story line based on the sequence of recounted events.[1]

1. The critic E. D. Hirsch (1976) has pleaded for recognition of "authorial intent." Presumably, the author arranges events in a particular sequence in a particular manner based on some intention. Hirsch is concerned that this intent fails to emerge when the task of constructing meaning is placed on the reader (Mink 1981; Schafer 1980, 1981). Similarly, listeners of a life story, as in the clinical psychoanalytic encounter, strive to understand the principles leading the analysand to place events together within a particular fabric or "story." However, as Ricoeur (1971) and M. Freeman (1985, 1993) have observed, there is a continuing and open dialogue between text and reader, with the very significance or meaning of an account shifting over time as elements are added or as shifts in theory,

MAKING A "GOOD" STORY. The life story, as read or as heard, is evaluated in
the same terms as other stories in our culture (Ricoeur 1977). Starting from
somewhat different theoretical positions, Geertz (1973, [1974]) 1983, Bertaux (1981a), Bertaux and Kohli (1984), Mandler (1984), Polkinghorne
(1983, 1988) and Bruner (1990) all have maintained that a central concern
of the human sciences or social studies (Cohler 1988) is to study the life story
just as other stories are studied, focusing both on the ordered sequence of
events which is narrated and on the context, frame, or plot which the author
employs in providing coherence or narrative integrity (Labov and Waletzky
1967). Appreciation of shared symbolic understandings, historical events,
modes of production, and dominant idea systems are also significant in evaluating the life story as a text. Ricoeur has noted in this context that

> narrative intelligibility implies something more than the subjective account-
> ability of one's own life-story. It comes to terms with the general condition of
> acceptability that we apply when we read any story, be it historical or fic-
> tional. . . . A story has to be "followable" and, in this sense, "self-explanatory."
> (1977, 869)

Ricoeur's discussion highlights issues of narrative intelligibility leading to
an increased experience of personal integrity or coherence. One's sense of
identity is reflected in a story told to oneself and to others which integrates
the several elements of lived experience into a narrative which is reasonably
coherent, which "makes sense" and is both "tellable" and "followable" (Ricoeur 1977). Freud ([1937] 1964) too emphasized the necessity of an enhanced sense of conviction as the means for evaluating all narratives, including that constructed within clinical psychoanalysis itself.

Ponse (1978) has portrayed the construction of a coherent life story as
"identity work," observing that persons seek to organize aspects of their life
into a coherent life story which legitimizes their place within family and
community. Thus, attainment of a positive gay sexual identity, as integrated
with other personally and socially relevant elements of the presently told life
story, represents a significant part of "who I am." Still, it is important to
recognize that realization of a gay identity, and the use of particular elements
of the life story to support construction of this identity, is itself socially constructed on the basis of shared understandings of what constitutes sexuality
and one's life history. At present, for example, the "coming-out" stories of
many younger and middle-aged adults, including those stories recounted

---

external to the text, give rise to new means for making sense of the story line. Appeals to authoritorial
intent are understandable given the anxiety generated by lack of certainty and a fixed point of departure for interpretation (Devereux 1967). It is important that we recognize this anxiety in order that
we may be free to focus on the task of interpretation in a manner akin to Freud's ([1912c] 1958)
concept of "evenly suspended attention."

within a psychotherapeutic context, emphasize themes of knowing from early childhood that one was different or enjoyed non–gender-stereotyped activities.

This shared theme for representing the foundations of being gay becomes an element significant in the life stories of lesbians and, in particular, gay men. The experience of fragmentation, or loss of personal integrity, may be understood as the failure to maintain an acceptable or followable personal historical narrative or life story (Ricoeur 1977; G. Klein 1976; Kohut 1977). Schafer (1980, 1981) has maintained that analyst and analysand actively collaborate in constructing a new life story which is more convincing, coherent, and integrated, than that told by the analysand at the beginning of analysis.[2]

The "reality" of events comprising the life story is necessarily less of a concern than the construction of a plot, based on a particular ordering of those events as presently recounted. In successive historical cohorts and at successive stages within an individual life, marked variations will be found both in the principles used to render the life story presently coherent, or interpretable by teller and listener, and in the ordering of events itself. As in any historical account, facts are unimportant apart from the narrative based on the events they purport to describe. Whether a story is recounted by the person to whom its events are said to have happened or by another, in the form of a biography it is subject to the same expectations of intelligibility (Schafer 1980, 1981; Lejeune 1989). Autobiographical stories are in no way privileged over other historical accounts; they must be evaluated by the same criteria as other narratives (Mandler 1984; Mandler and Johnson 1977; C. Peterson and McCabe 1983; Slavney and McHugh 1984; N. Stein and Policastro 1984)[3] and to be held to the same standards of coherence and internal consistency (Ricoeur 1971; Cohler 1982, 1988; M. Freeman 1985, 1993). The fundamental focus must be on the attribution of meanings to a presently experienced past and present and anticipated future, resulting in a life story that preserves a sense of continuity portrayed as the self (Kohut 1971).

Bruner (1986, 1987, 1990) comments that a good story or narrative presents the reader or listener with a tension or problem which appeals to psy-

2. Kohut ([1959] 1978) has noted the significance of empathy, or vicarious introspection, as the single most important element in the psychoanalytic "cure." The experience of telling the life story to another who struggles to understand this account has positive therapeutic value although it is not sufficient to bring about resolution of personal distress apart from interpretation of emergent transference enactments.

3. Peterson and McCabe (1983) provide a systematic comparison between three modes of evaluating narratives, showing that young children are able to tell narratives which may be judged according the criteria outlined by Bruner (1990) but finding that coding systems yield somewhat different findings. The "good" narrative requires systematic study from more than one perspective.

chological curiosity regarding both self and others. This perspective on the personal narrative or life history as story, which provides an important means for linking humanistic and social science study, is reflected in much contemporary inquiry in developmental psychology as well as in history and literature. There has been little systematic study specifically of the presently recounted personal account retold to oneself and others over a lifetime or told within the complex personal-change situation of clinical psychoanalysis; however, findings regarding what constitutes an acceptable story within our culture generally may be of some assistance in understanding the criteria used in evaluating the adequacy of the presently told life story.

Polanyi (1989) notes that we must be provided with sufficient detail to understand the nature of the changes which have taken place and the relationships between events in the story. Formal aspects of the story, including how the story is told, are implicitly evaluated in terms of their contribution to making the story coherent and culturally acceptable. Stein and Policastro (1984) have reviewed more than twenty definitions of the concept of story in our culture; much of variation between definitions concerns the role of intention and novelty, or unexpected complicating events, as defining characteristics. Similarly, adequate resolution of problems posed by unanticipated adversity may be seen as a defining element of the life story.

Distress seems to be a major organizing factor in the life story within our own culture: Miller and Sperry (1988) report that recounting of adversity and difficulty is among the earliest uses children make of the past in their own life stories. Peterson and McCabe (1983) report that narratives of young children judged as "good" most often (75 percent) referred to sad and unpleasant events rather than to happy ones, although no such difference was found among narratives judged as "bad." It is common for those seeking intervention for psychological distress to "blame" their past and to seek explanations for present difficulties founded upon earlier adversity. At least a part of the interpretive activity of psychoanalysis and psychoanalytic psychotherapy consists of making sense of this experienced affliction so that it need not continue to dominate the present, as well as integrating adversity into a life story fostering better adjustment in the present. This reliance upon past adversity as the basis of the narrative account is also reflected in much psychological theorizing regarding critical periods early in life which are presumed to shape later outcomes (Lorenz [1937] 1965; Erikson [1951] 1963).

Construction of a life story or narrative focusing more or less explicitly upon past affliction, together with a present effort to make sense of this affliction (and we know even less about differences in awareness of efforts to overcome affliction), is characteristic of life-history accounts within our culture.[4] Guidelines for the construction of narratives differ across cultures; one of the few universal human characteristics of these narratives appears to be the maintenance of a sense of self as coherent within the meanings provided by a particular culture. Failure to maintain a sense of personal integrity and continuity leads to feelings of depletion, culminating in the experience of fragmentation and disorganization. Stories regarding response to affliction provide a means for integrating the presently remembered past, experienced present, and anticipated future into an account which makes sense of lived time, providing the foundation for the study of both continuity and change across the course of life, as well as a foundation for therapeutic intervention (Jaspers 1963). The life story based on a "narrative of affliction" may, however, provide increased coherence at a particular time at the cost of satisfactory adjustment to subsequent life experiences (Maas and Kuypers 1974), which may challenge present maintenance of meaning and personal integrity and require reevaluation of one's history (R. Butler 1963; Lieberman and Tobin 1983; Tobin 1991). For example, Henry Adams ([1907] 1961) portrays his own life in terms of two periods of unanticipated adversity which required reconsideration of the story of his life as previously understood, resulting in feelings of increased integrity and narrative certainty.

It is clear from Adams's account that the personal adversity he experienced represented a challenge to the narrative continuity of a previously followable life story, presenting both a need and an opportunity for its revision. Affliction provided the opportunity for telling a more compelling, or better, life story than previously, but this revision was also required in order to maintain a sense of personal integrity. In the case of the coming-out stories discussed by Plummer (1995), in which lesbians and gay men struggle to make narrative sense of their own sexual wishes, antigay prejudice and stigma create a social climate in which one's sexual orientation may be experienced as a kind of affliction, which in turn becomes the foundation for a good or followable story. The story is then elaborated in terms of shared presumptions within our society regarding the foundation of same-sex desire either in innate predisposition or, as reviewed in the present chapter, in the child's experience with family and community.

4. E. Kris's (1956) initial study of the life story suggested that narrative life accounts could be differentiated from some external, observable reality. Consistent with more recent study of history and life history (Cohler 1988), the significance of historical or life events outside of experience may be questioned. The existence of a verifiable life event may be less important than the meaning attributed to that event and its changing significance across the course of life (Schutz and Luckmann 1973, [1983] 1989). The important issue posed for study of the life story concerns factors leading to shifts in the meanings attributed both to particular events and to the stream of events as part of a more or less coherently organized narrative of the course of life.

The narrative approach to the study of affliction and the management of meaning provides an important means for understanding subjectivity. Focus on the life history as story connects concepts and methods from the social sciences and human studies with those of the humanities. Interpretive approaches pioneered in anthropology (Geertz 1973, [1974] 1983; Crapanzano 1980), history (H. White 1972–73, 1980, 1981, 1987) and psychoanalysis (Freud [1937] 1964; Schafer 1980, 1981), together with concepts used in criticism (Crane 1953; Booth [1961] 1983; Ricoeur 1971, 1977), further assist us in understanding the role of narrative in managing meanings reflected in the life story.

MAKING A GOOD GAY LIFE STORY. The dominant narrative in life stories recounting the assumption of a gay or lesbian identity emphasizes the sense that, from early childhood on, the teller felt different from other boys or girls. After a period of hesitancy and perhaps some personal distress, having learned from others to label this experience as "homosexual" (Plummer 1975), he or she makes an effort at public acknowledgment or disclosure of this sexual identity, a process referred to as "coming out" to family, friends, and coworkers. This master narrative of coming out is associated with cohort effects: gay men and women who grew up before Stonewall have tended not to follow this master narrative (Hall Carpenter Archives 1989; Porter and Weeks 1991), while those coming of age following the Stonewall resistance have generally organized their life story in terms of this sequence of stigma, selective disclosure, and realization of a true self (K. Cohen and Savin-Williams 1996; Savin-Williams 1996; Savin-Williams 1990, 1997; Fricke 1981; Fricke and Fricke 1991; A. Kantrowitz [1977] 1996; Shyer and Shyer 1996).

Plummer (1995) suggests that coming-out stories follow in the modernist tradition; as in stories more generally, there is a journey or progression through stages, suffering to be endured, a contest to prevail over misfortune and stigma, the search for transcendence or mastery over evil, and finally the establishment of a new identity which leads to an enhanced sense of a cohesive self (in the terms used by Kohut [1977] and extended to the study of coming out by Gonsiorek and Rudolph [1991]). Nonetheless, the terms used in constructing and telling this story are those of a particular time, with its own prevailing metaphors and material culture. The issue of coming out will be discussed in greater detail later in this section; the focus here is how, in our own time, the coming-out story has become a master or dominant narrative, a cultural script or story which men and women rely on as the foundation for understanding personal experience.

TELLING AND LISTENING: THE DIALOGIC PERSPECTIVE. The present discussion focuses on the socially located discourse (Bakhtin 1981, 1986) of first telling and listening, then writing and reading, as this doubly dialogic process relates to the task of making sense of the life story. It is informed by discussions within ethnography that focus on the relationship between informant and ethnographer, by recent developments in criticism that focus on the relation of reader to text, and by recent psychoanalytic perspectives on the use of the past in the collaboration between analyst and analysand.

Over the course of the past two decades, in fields ranging from developmental psychology to literary study, there has been increased appreciation of the "jointness," or dialogic perspective, inherent in the study of lives. Particularly as founded in the work of Russian psychologist Lev Vygotsky ([1924–34] 1987) and Russian literary theorist Bakhtin (1981, 1986) and in interpretations of their work by Wertsch (1985, 1991), Kozulin (1990), and Wilson and Weinstein (1992, 1996), study in much of the past decade has emphasized the extent to which any account is necessarily coconstructed by the participants.[5] This concept of both social life and text as founded within a social context, implicit in Mishler's (1986b) discussion of the interview, suggests that there can be no life story apart from the particular collaboration between teller and listener or text and reader, apart, that is, from the dialog of story production and reception. There are two further consequences of this dialogic position: a process takes place between reader and text parallel to that between the original teller and listener, and the life experiences, wishes, and intents of each participant enter into this social construction as an intrinsic element (Gergen 1994).

Understanding the life stories of gay men and women, as with any account of lived experience, inevitably takes place within the context of telling and listening, even if the listener is oneself, as in a diary or in oral history accounts (P. Thompson [1978] 1988; Tonkin 1992). Accounts of lived experience, central to both the ethnographic and the psychoanalytic situation, focus on telling and listening to stories about the past, but the nature of the account which is provided is dependent upon both historical context and present circumstances. In relating the story of disclosing one's sexual identity as "gay," the difficulty of reconciling this identity with oneself when confronted

5. Within psychoanalysis, there has been increased emphasis upon the concept of intersubjectivity (Atwood and Stolorow 1984; Stolorow, Atwood, and Brandchaft 1994), initially founded in Husserl (1960) and Schutz and Luckmann (1973, [1983] 1989). While this concept emphasizes the extent to which psychological processes are founded within a relationship, it focuses primarily upon personal psychological processes, in particular experience of self and others as founded in the child's earliest experience of the mother. The more inclusive concept of dialogic process stresses not only the social foundation of thought but also the extent to which continuing social life modifies all thought as a function of life with others.

by the heterosexism of the larger society (Herek 1995, 1996; D. Moss 1997b), and the process of deciding how and to whom to reveal one's identity, all contribute to the context of the telling. The relationship of teller and listener must be considered together with the social and historical context of the particular act of telling and listening.

Clearly, the account of a young adult analysand telling of her sexual identity as a lesbian or bisexual woman is understood in quite different terms than it would have been prior to gay liberation and the emergence of an understanding of same-gender sexual orientation as a lifeway (Schutz 1970; Schutz and Luckmann 1973, [1983] 1989). Plummer has observed that

> for narratives to flourish there must be a community to hear; that for communities to hear, there must be stories which weave together their history, their identity, their politics. The one-community-feeds-upon-and-into-the-other story. There is an ongoing dynamic or dialectic of communities, politics, identities and stores which have their roots in the nineteenth century but which reach a critical "take-off" stage by the middle of the twentieth. . . . The development of a gay personhood and a gay culture proceed incrementally, in tandem and feeding upon each other. (1995, 87)

Nowhere is the concept of a dialogic process better portrayed than in this discussion of the manner in which the gay story is told, listened to, and told anew in an ever changing manner as a consequence of larger social and historical change. Such changes, for example the AIDS epidemic and the social turmoil associated with the emergence of same-gender marriage, have, over the past two decades, fostered revision of the account of what it means to be a gay man or woman, both as told and as heard by others (Odets 1995; Schwartzberg 1996; Sturken 1997).

Teller and listener each have a goal in hearing this account, whether ethnographic or therapeutic. As Devereux (1967) has noted, anxiety on the part of the listener may disrupt the telling of the life story, just as anxiety on the part of the reader may disrupt the process of reading the life story as context becomes text (Ricoeur 1971). Kohut ([1959] 1978) has noted that such anxiety makes it difficult to maintain that attitude characterized as "vicarious introspection" or empathy, which is critical to the success of the psychoanalytic or psychotherapeutic interview. Racker (1968) has distinguished between "complementary" identification within the psychoanalytic situation, which represents a reciprocal enactment out of awareness in response to the process of listening, and "concordant" identification, which represents vicarious introspection and "tasting" of the analysand's communications (Fliess 1944, 1953).

To the extent that the listener can sustain empathy or vicarious introspection while listening to an account (Kohut 1959), it is possible to facilitate the telling of the life story within this dialogic situation. The problem is that telling the gay or lesbian sexual story (Plummer 1995) almost always evokes anxiety for both teller and listener, who inevitably share heterosexism because of the stigma attached to the concept of a gay identity within the larger society (De Monteflores 1986; Herek 1995, 1996; Malyon 1982; Moss 1997a, 1997b; Young-Bruehl 1996). As a consequence, this anxiety emerging both in listener and teller may disrupt the telling and is experienced by the teller (analysand) as the listener's disapproval or lack of interest in the story (Kohut 1959; Racker 1968). At the very least, whether for purposes of study or psychotherapeutic intervention, it is important to remain aware of the possible effects of this anxiety on teller and listener as they strive to understand the listener's telling of the life story (Devereux 1967; A. Wilson and Weinstein 1996). Moreover, as Foucault (1975) has cautioned, there is the additional requirement that the listener be aware of the extent to which such power dynamics might shape the further course of the telling (Foucault 1975; Plummer 1995).

SOCIAL CHANGE AND THE "GOOD" GAY LIFE STORY. Earlier studies assumed that the life history had an existence outside of the social and historical context within which the narrative was constructed (Rosenwald 1993). Following Marx ([1845] 1978), as well as Vygotsky, Bakhtin, and their commentators, this tradition has emphasized the interplay between person and society in the construction of the story which is told. Clearly social and historical change may lead over time to quite different rendering of life stories, both within particular lives studied over long periods of time and within succeeding cohorts, whose stories may be very much influenced by prior accounts.

Generation, Being Gay, and the Life Story

Life stories reflect the interplay of lived experience with the particular social and historical context of period and cohort (Bertaux and Kohli 1984; Orbuch 1997). Indeed, as Dannefer (1984), Elder (1995, 1996, 1997; Parks, 1999) and others have emphasized, it is difficult to isolate the personal narrative from this larger context. The particular story of lived experience makes use of signs and symbols associated with role identities, or conceptions of how a person likes to think of himself being and acting (McCall and Simmons 1978, 65). Simon and Gagnon (1984, 1988) have referred to these role-based life stories as "scripts," which they view as metaphors for conceptualizing the production of behavior within social life. The life story as told, then, is an intrapsychic script, a presently narrated account of meanings attributed to oneself and one's place in the world. This intrapsychic script is necessarily dependent on context for the building blocks which are used to make sense of particular lived experience.

Intensive study of autobiographical memory has shown the extent to which present lived experience shapes the story which is presently told about the past (Conway 1990; B. Ross 1991; Rubin 1996; Singer and Salovey 1993). Recent reports show that children as young as two may be induced to tell a story about the past which is experimentally induced (Fivush, Haden, and Reese 1996). The study of recall of things past in adulthood also shows the extent to which the past might be remembered in ways which are shaped by cohort and history (Schuman and Scott 1989).

Spanier (1976) has reported that faulty recall is common in retrospective reports of sexual history, whether due to motivated forgetting, the wearing away of details, or the interplay between memory and present proximal and distal life circumstances within an open system. Of particular relevance for the present context, changes over the course of life in the understanding of sexual orientation or sexual identity may themselves shape the story which is told of the personal past. Further, as Mishler (1986b) has shown, the relationship between interviewer and respondent, even in studies using highly structured interviews, may also color the details which are provided in the life story.

Ross (1980) has noted the implications for studies of homosexuality of the reality of an open system comprising memory, history, and society. Ross studied changing conceptions of sex role within randomly selected groups of Swedish and Australian gay men. As expected, the Swedish men reported much less pressure to conform to stereotypical sex roles than did the Australian men, who reported greater pressure toward gender-appropriate behavior, with heterosexuality regarded as the norm. This differential socialization pressure shaped the nature of the men's recollections of the extent to which they deviated from gender-appropriate activities in childhood, with gay Swedish men showing much less concern with regard to sex-role conformity either in childhood or in adulthood. In sum, socialization pressures lead to particular patterns for recalling in adulthood various childhood experiences, including patterns of play, discovery of lesbian or gay identity, and the subsequent course of sexuality within lived experience.

Because persons living at a particular place and time share certain experiences, some of their life stories may be sufficiently congruent as to be viewed as manifestations of a master narrative. The current master narrative among gay men and women, which involves overcoming stigma and realizing a sense of "true self," meets the criteria for a good story (Davies 1992). At the same time coming-out narratives, particularly among older cohorts and adolescents living in less tolerant and supportive communities, may end in tragedy, even in attempted or realized suicides (Gibson 1989; Schneider,

Farberow, and Kruks 1989; Savin-Williams and Cohen 1996). As these narratives are fashioned within a particular cohort and context, they implicitly include conceptions of self and other, the course of life, and the management of adversity. Stories of how one became gay or, for that matter, straight (Chodorow 1992) all make use of a master narrative (Savin-Williams 1996c).

Gonsiorek and Rudolph (1991) trace the term "coming out" to Sengers's (1969) discussion in the psychiatric literature. Coming out is generally portrayed as a stepwise process, in the manner popularized by Erikson's ([1951] 1963) modification of Abraham's (1921, 1924a, 1924b) epigenetic model. Plummer (1995) suggests that the master narrative of the coming-out story is a linear progression starting in childhood, which is seen as an unhappy time marked by feelings of being different from other children. With the onset of adolescence, there is the experience of desire increasingly discordant with mainstream heterosexist society and the subsequent emergence of problems, often those associated with guilt and secrecy. These problems are overcome, most often through becoming a part of a social network of gay or bisexual teens or young adults, which leads to affirmation of a gay identity. The construction and telling of this story itself may provide an enhanced sense of personal integrity. Identification of various steps or stages in the process of coming out has been reviewed by Plummer (1981), Minton and McDonald (1984), and Gonsiorek and Rudolph (1991).

Once again, it is clear that accounts of the development of gay and lesbian sexual identity must be understood in the context of the social and historical factors. The resistance to police raids at the Stonewall Inn has become part of an oral tradition (Tonkin 1992) or "collective memory" (Connerton 1989; Gillis 1994; Sturken 1997; Halbwachs [1952] 1992). Indeed, as Plummer (1995) has observed, the historical event, as retold over the intervening three decades, has become a part of a new master narrative of protest, struggle, and realization of both personal and public identity as a gay man or woman.

Social Change and Pathways into a Gay or Lesbian Identity

The change in the construction of life stories related to experience of sexual orientation is dramatically illustrated in the collections of the life stories of gay men across more than half a century assembled by the Hall Carpenter Archives (1989) and Porter and Weeks (1991). Recent study of the life story, founded on a dialogic perspective, has emphasized the extent to which any account is necessarily coconstructed by teller and listener and, subsequently, by reader and text (Ricoeur 1971; Freeman 1985).

What is most striking in the study of homosexuality and the life course is the diversity reflected among men and women whose only common link is a preference for sexual intimacy with others of the same gender. Nevertheless, over time stereotypes have emerged regarding the "dyke" or "femme" lesbian and the effeminate gay man. Central to these stereotypes is the presumption that same-gender sexual orientation can be understood as a reversal of sex roles. From this perspective, gay men are really feminine and lesbians masculine. These stereotypes are shared, to a large extent, within the gay community itself and, notably, are reflected in the coming-of-age master narrative previously discussed. This dominant narrative (Plummer 1995) has been given additional support from both gay and straight investigators in the biological and social sciences who have attempted to confirm through scholarly study a series of stereotypes (Savin-Williams and Cohen 1996).

This master narrative, for example, holds that gay men were born gay and, as boys, were already gender-atypical in their interests. Isay (1986a) reports that each of the forty gay men he had seen in psychoanalysis or psychoanalytically oriented psychotherapy to that time had reported "knowing" from early childhood that he was different from his peers: more sensitive to the feelings of others, interested in nature and artistic and creative pursuits, disterested in competitive athletics. These men reportedly began to develop a gay identity, including explicit awareness of same-gender sexual fantasies, while still children. Their sexual identity became consolidated at adolescence in manifest homosexual activity. This increasing realization of same-gender sexual desire and activity was accompanied by recognition of intolerance for this emerging sexual identity among their peers and an increasing sense of shame and self-criticism. This enduring sense of shame was at least partially resolved when these men eventually found a community of others with a similar sexual identity.

This prevailing master narrative derives support from studies suggesting a biological foundation for male same-gender sexual orientation founded either in genetic transmission or in maternal stress during pregnancy which interferes with hormonal factors responsible for masculinization. (The master narrative for lesbians has been less clearly described than that for gay men. Unexplained factors presumably lead to "tomboy" interests in early childhood, followed by masculine identifications in adulthood.) But clinical and community study alike suggests that there are few generalizations which may be made on the basis of presently reported sexual orientation. Just as there are many pathways into expression of same-gender desire, there are many variants of being gay, lesbian, or bisexual, each of which is characteristic of some gay men and women. It is important to emphasize this diversity, which is as great among gay men and women as among straight men and women. Sexual identity and gender identity are independent characteristics. As Jones and De Cecco (1982) have noted, efforts to portray straight men as masculine and gay men as effeminate, or to portray lesbians as either masculine or hyperfeminine, ignore the complexity of the interplay between sexual orientation and other aspects of particular lives. Without doubt, there are many men whose memory of lived experience closely conforms to the master narrative. However, it is critical that we be able to account for the variety of life paths followed by men and women who may have little in common beyond realization of desire centered on another of the same gender.

As discussed previously, personal narratives of the course of development are subject to the same evaluative criteria as other stories. Listeners or readers regard a good story as one involving struggle, particularly one in which some adversity is overcome; and indeed, the dominant narrative in life stories of gay men and women involves overcoming the experience of stigma—without doubt, a powerful force in the lives of gay men and women in earlier cohorts (Herek 1995, 1996; I. Meyer 1995; D. Moss 1997; Young-Bruehl 1996). What is significant in understanding the life story is *how* persons have experienced this stigma, and how it may have distorted their development. While at least some young people, growing up in fortunate circumstances within liberal and tolerant communities, are able to escape this sense of stigma, issues of stigma are still characteristically the primary form of adversity to be overcome (Neff 1997). Other expressions of adversity which may anchor the life stories of gay men and women include an early history of physical and sexual abuse, problems in establishing and maintaining intimate partnerships, and, within present cohorts of gay men and women, the impact of the AIDS epidemic (Odets 1995; Schwartzberg 1996; Sontag 1989).

Understood as a story, the development of sexual orientation, like any other story in our culture, is presumed to have a beginning, a middle, and an end or outcome. Discussion of development begins with a review of Freud's signal contributions to the study of the development of same-gender sexual orientation, founded largely on his philosophy of science and retrospective study within the context of the clinical psychoanalytic process, then reviews contributions to date regarding the prospective developmental course of gay and bisexual men and women. It is important to recall Freud's own caution when considering the systematic literature on the development of gay and bisexual identity:

> So long as we trace the development from its final outcome backwards, the chain of events appears continuous, and we feel we have gained an insight which is completely satisfactory or even exhaustive. But if we proceed the reverse way, if we start from the premises inferred from the analysis and try to follow these up to the final result, then we no longer get the impression of an inevitable sequence of events which could not have been otherwise determined. We notice at once that there might have been another result, and that

we might have been just as well able to understand and explain the latter. The synthesis is thus not so satisfactory as the analysis; in other words, from a knowledge of the premises we could not have foretold the nature of the results. . . . The chain of causation can always be recognized with certainty if we follow the line of analysis, whereas to predict it along the line of synthesis is impossible. (Freud [1920] 1955, 167–68)

Psychoanalytic Accounts of the Development of Homosexuality

A number of recent accounts have attempted to explicate the many explanations Freud provided for same-gender sexual desire (Isay 1989; Lewes [1988] 1995). Perhaps the most detailed and faithful review is that provided by Lewes. It should be noted that virtually all such discussions focus on selection of a same-gender sexual partner among men. The significance of same-gender partnership among women and its possible origins in psychological development have been largely overlooked by psychoanalysis. It would appear that our culture finds intimacy among men a greater source of distress than intimacy among women.

Further, while Freud ([1935] 1951) himself observed that homosexuality was neither a virtue nor a vice, most psychoanalytic writers since Freud have cast same-gender sexual orientation as not only a different line of psychological development but also, necessarily, a disordered line (Lewes [1988] 1995).

Lewes finds at least four distinct "explanations" for selection of same-gender sexual orientation among men in Freud's writings: (1) outcome of castration anxiety resulting from realization that his mother lacks a penis, leading to distaste and loathing for women; (2) overvaluation of the mother and the care received from her, leading to a search for a love object he can love as he was once loved by his mother; (3) continuation of the "negative" or "inverted" nuclear conflict, leading a man to offer himself to another man in a passive manner in order to avoid possible castration as a consequence of so-called oedipal wishes; and (4) converting a possible rival of whom one feels jealous into a loved object as a reaction formation.

Common to these four explanations is the suggestion that a man selects a same-gender sexual partner not as an expression of a particular desire, but rather as a means of protection from the horror of mutilation. Further, just as in Freud's characterization of moral development among girls, if the primary identification is with the mother, then the boy's ability to attain an ethical sense, reflected in superego development, is not possible. However, psychoanalytic study of same-gender sexual orientation suggests that neither of these conditions characterizes the present generation of gay men. Their attraction to other men is positive rather than negative, and there is little evidence that they are less able to maintain a strong moral position than their straight counterparts. However, while Freud's efforts to understand the choice of a same-gender sexual partner is phrased primarily in terms of developmental arrest, his concern with explicating the dynamics of sexual orientation is significant. That mode of inquiry, which is distinctive of psychoanalysis, may be employed in a continuing effort to understand the dynamics of the selection of any partner, whether of the same or opposite gender, as well as the very significance of intimacy for the analysand's experience of self and other.

Lewes has also noted that in attempting to tie the origins of same-gender sexual orientation principally to disturbances in the boy's relationship with his mother, Freud ([1905–24] 1953) subordinated his own concern with the meanings of instinctual life, and the impact of society and history upon the expression of desire, to a Darwinian concern with biology and reproduction. Many subsequent psychoanalytic discussions of homosexuality, as well as contemporary studies in sociobiology, have likewise turned to a natural science perspective and away from the human science perspective more generally characteristic of Freud's effort to understand desire (R. C. Friedman 1988, 1977; Friedman and Downey 1994). This initial framing of the discussion in terms of biology, which was in reality a reification of the Darwinian perspective, interfered with the discussion of same-gender sexual desire as an important factor in the particular life history (Sulloway 1979; Ritvo 1990).

Much of the psychoanalytic discussion regarding same-gender sexual orientation over the past half century has focused on the implications of sexual orientation for the psychoanalytic situation and will be discussed elsewhere in this work. Suffice it to say that while Freud regarded the inversions as evidence of the immaturity of libidinal development, this purported immaturity was of interest primarily because it supported his concept of epigenesis, quite apart from issues of adjustment. The concept of immaturity was implicit in Freud's philosophy of science but had little relevance to lived experience. In fact, as already noted, Freud ([1921b] 1977, [1935] 1951) made it quite clear that he believed sexual orientation was immutable but that it did not in itself constitute psychopathology. Much of the subsequent debate within psychoanalysis regarding homosexuality has been framed within a more recent discourse which has reified Freud's concept of immaturity as developmental arrest in a way far different from what Freud intended in his discussion of development (Socarides 1978, 1988).

Is Childhood Destiny? Preadult Socialization and Sexual Orientation

Systematic study of the development of boys and girls experiencing same-gender sexual orientation at some point across the course of life finds little guidance from Freud's many accounts of the origin of homosexuality. In part, the problem stems from the ambiguous definition of the term as used by Freud: at times he refers to wish, at other times to action. For example, in his case study of a purportedly homosexual young woman (Freud [1920] 1955), he dealt with the young woman's preoccupation with an older woman. However, viewed from present perspectives, there is little evidence of sexual desire; rather, the younger woman's infatuation with an older career woman may be understood as the expression of a youthful search for ideal-ization (Kohut 1977, 1979; Magid 1993). At the time it was still difficult for women to realize career aspirations, and the older women embodied quali-ties which the younger woman desired. Understood in these terms, the in-fatuation takes on quite a different quality.

As in so much of Freud's writing about women, issues of female homosex-uality were seen as simply symmetric to those of men. There was little discus-sion then, as now, regarding the development of a lesbian identity. To date, much of the literature on the development of gender orientation has focused on issues of sexual expression rather than on the lived experience of adoles-cents and young adults struggling to make sense of their sexuality, and it is still the case that more of this literature has concerned the development of boys who later become gay than girls who become lesbian or either boys and girls who choose the bisexual option. Finally, it is worth noting that, while a "tomboy" phase is regarded as normal for girls, a boy's being a "sissy" is presumed to be predictive of a later gay sexual orientation. This presump-tion of assumed continuity between effeminacy in childhood, presumably biologically determined, and adoption of a gay male sexual orientation in adulthood reflects the most pronounced concern in the developmental liter-ature to date (R. C. Friedman 1988; Bem 1996, 1997).

FAMILY STRUCTURE AND SEXUAL ORIENTATION. Much of the study of lesbi-ans and, principally, gay men has focused on the role of family dynamics in the construction of sexual orientation. The presumption of an association between offspring outcome and the characteristics of the family has been widespread throughout the bourgeois West from the Enlightenment to the present (Foucault [1961] 1988; Freud [1909a] 1955, [1909b] 1959, [1909c] 1955, [1910a] 1957, [1910d] 1957; Rousseau [1762] 1979). This position, focusing on parents' forward socialization practices in relation to particular personality constellations in offspring, was actively pursued in the intellectual ferment following the Second World War, as psychiatry sought to become a systematic science through the study, first, of family and psychopathology and, later, of the presumed biological substrate for aberrant behavior.

In early studies of family factors presumed to lead to psychopathology (Mishler and Waxler [1965] 1968), Lidz and his colleagues at Yale (Lidz 1973;

Lidz et al. 1965) had studied a group of young adult schizophrenics and their parents. Focusing on parental marriages which were either skewed, with one parent protecting the other parent who suffered from some psychopathology, or schismatic, in which parents continually fought, Lidz suggested that the emergence of schizophrenic psychopathology in offspring was a response to these skewed and schismatic marriages.

When Wynne and his colleagues at the National Institute of Mental Health and the University of Rochester (Wynne 1981; Wynne, Singer, et al. 1977) showed that offspring psychopathology reflected a learned "nonrationality" evident in amorphous and fragmented communication in the forward socialization of offspring, Lidz and his colleagues included this perspective in their family study. Relying upon codes based on Rorschach protocols obtained from parents of young adult schizophrenics, Wynne, Singer, and their colleagues were able to differentiate between psychologically well and troubled offspring on the basis of parental transactional styles, reflected in the manner in which parents communicated what they saw on the Rorschach blots. They developed the concept of the schizogenic parent who was presumed to induct offspring into disordered patterns of communication, fostering episodes of disturbance as the young adult tried to communicate in ways other than sensible (M. J. Goldstein 1983, 1987; Goldstein, Hand, and Hahlweg 1986; Leff and Vaughn 1985).

Even as these models based of forward socialization were advanced to "explain" the onset of schizophrenia, the first systematic studies, such as that of Mishler and Waxler (1968), were showing few differences in observed interaction between families including a schizophrenic member and comparison families with psychologically well offspring. Further, Waxler (1974) showed that the performance of parents of a psychologically well young adult on an experimental cognitive task deteriorated when they had to perform with a schizophrenic young adult. The performance of the parents of young adult schizophrenic did not suffer when they worked with a psychologically well young adult.

Findings from Waxler's study suggested that the purportedly nonrational communication observed among the parents of young adult schizophrenics may have been a consequence of reverse socialization, in which parents learned to communicate in apparently irrational ways in order to maintain communication with their troubled offspring. Similarly, offspring may induct parents into new roles or into reconsideration of their adult role portfolio across the course of adult life (Hagestad 1974). Studies such as those of Mishler and Waxler were followed by the advent of a consumer movement in which parents began to decry the continuing effort of mental health professionals to blame them for the illness of their offspring.

In the intellectual milieu of the postwar epoch, however, studies focused largely on forward socialization and presumed that family structure and processes were responsible for a variety of adult characteristics ranging from psychological adjustment to definition of sexual orientation. For example, assuming that homosexuality reflected psychopathology and that gender roles were learned in the context of preadult socialization within the family, and influenced by early reports from family study of a purported link between family dynamics and the onset of serious psychopathology among offspring, the psychoanalyst Irving Bieber, his psychotherapist wife, and a group of colleagues known as "the Committee" (Bieber et al. 1962; Bieber and Bieber 1979) undertook a major, systematic study of family relations among gay men in psychoanalysis and their parents. They used the pioneering approach of ratings by the analyst founded on his or her understanding of the analysand. The committee collected constructed information on a group of 100 self-acknowledged gay men in analysis as well as 106 self-reported heterosexual analysands over the preceding postwar period. These analysands were highly articulate, gifted, and artistic; most had grown up outside of New York and moved to the city as adults.

Based on the analysts' ratings, the Biebers and their colleagues concluded that homosexuality within offspring was the outcome of a unique family constellation which they portrayed in a "triangular system" hypothesis. Mothers of the homosexual analysands were portrayed by their analysts as seductive, controlling, and dominating to a greater extent than was reported by analysts evaluating mothers of the heterosexual analysands. The impact of this seductive, controlling mode was to inhibit emergence of heterosexual desire among their sons. These same mothers were also presumed to have interfered in the emergence of the "normal" rough-and-tumble play of boys:

> The data from our study strongly suggest that closeness and over-intimacy combined with hostility, minimizing attitudes, and apparent rejection have the effect of inhibiting generally orientated heterosexuality among these men. (Bieber et al. 1962, 82)

Fathers of the homosexual analysands were portrayed as hostile and detached from a relationship with their sons. In each and every instance, analysts reported defective relationships between their homosexual analysands and the analysands' fathers, to a significantly greater extent than among the heterosexual analysands and their fathers. Fathers of homosexual analysands were reported to have spent little time with their sons, to have failed to show them affection or encourage emergence of typical masculine interests, and to have stimulated feelings in their sons of both fear and resentment of their power. Summarizing the findings of these analysts on the father-son relationship, Bieber and his colleagues concluded:

> A detached pattern of father-son relatedness obviously promotes a defective relationship. . . . [The child] may develop a cognitive awareness of a lack of paternal affection, warmth and interest, or he may be unable to formulate the lack and may experience a vague hunger or yearning for something he cannot identify . . . the child may attempt a way out by seeking other reparative relationships to fulfill his yearning—often with other males. Thus, the pathologic seeking of need fulfillment from men has a clear point of origin in fathers who were detached. (1962, 114)

According to Bieber and his colleagues, the father's withdrawal and failure to protect the son against the mother's intrusiveness both magnifies the purportedly destructive maternal behavior and deprives the child of a masculine role model. Schismatic marriages, in which parents are often in open conflict with little respect for each other, create a situation in which the prospectively homosexual boy ends up protecting his dominating mother from his father's often futile efforts to control the family, ultimately leading to the father's hostile detachment. They conclude that "the chances appear to be high that any son exposed to this parental combination will become homosexual or develop severe homosexual problems" (1962, 172). Bieber and Bieber (1979) report a replication of their initial work founded on psychiatric interviews anecdotally reported with "well over 1000 male homosexuals," most of whom were presumably in psychotherapy (Bieber and Bieber 1979, 409). The Biebers conclude:

> We have never interviewed a male homosexual whose father openly loved and respected him. . . . A boy whose father is warmly related and constructive will not become a homosexual. (1979, 411)

CHALLENGING ASSUMPTIONS ABOUT FAMILY AND CHILDHOOD GENDER SO-CIALIZATION. According to the Biebers' portrayal, adult homosexuality emerges as a result of growing up in a schismatic family or with an overprotective and dominating mother who blocks her son's access to usual boyhood developmental experiences. The father fails to counteract this malignant maternal control or to serve as a positive masculine role model, instead expressing a dangerous hostility. According to this perspective, the boy destined to become homosexual develops fears and phobias in response to his father's omnipresent but distant hostility. Siblings become resentful of the increasing focus on the boy, particularly of his apparently exclusive tie to the mother. Coates (1985) suggests that since mothers tend to be overprotective of frail and sissy boys, domineering protection may be evoked in part by the child's own state (Lerner and Busch-Rossnagel 1981).

The prospective homosexual boy worries about his own masculinity and fears paternal retaliation, which leads to excessive fear of injury (presumably a displacement of the perceived threat of castration by the oedipal father, perhaps the consequence of the close mother-son coalition) together with a fixation on ideas of a big and powerful penis. The choice of girls as play partners is a consequence of these inhibitions and fears and of a sense of frailty, clumsiness, and vulnerability, as well as a desire to be a girl, which is presumably expressed later in the boy's deviant sexual orientation.

This significant research effort by the Biebers and their colleagues stimulated much additional research on family dynamics and sexual orientation. West (1959), following Freud's ([1909a] 1955, [1909b] 1959, [1910a] 1957, [1910d] 1957) initial formulation of the nuclear conflict, viewed male homosexuality as the consequence of inhibition of the desire for women following from failure to resolve the nuclear conflict. Nash and Hayes (1965) maintained this pattern was most salient for those men preferring the "passive" position in homosexual intercourse (as previously noted, the assumption that men have an exclusive or nearly exclusive preference for one or the other role in the homosexual encounter is erroneous).

However, much of the focus in replication studies has been on the presumably critical role of the father-son relationship for the development of the boy into later homosexuality (Bancroft 1975; Bane, 1965). This has been supported in quite different ways in the reports of several other groups of clinical investigators reporting on findings from the study of men seeking psychotherapy or in prison or psychiatric hospitals (Apperson and McAdoo 1968; Friedman and Stern 1980; Freund and Blanchard 1983; Snortum 1969; Isay 1986a, 1986b, 1989, 1996a, 1996b). Evans (1969) relied upon a group of 185 self-identified homosexual men in the Los Angeles area reached through contacts in the psychiatric community and a matched comparison group of purportedly heterosexual men who had volunteered for a cardiac study. Based on self-report measures, Evans reports that gay men were more likely to describe themselves as having been frail and clumsy during childhood, as being less athletic, and as having fathers who they feared would harm them and who avoided them. These men also reported retrospectively having had mothers who were seductive and who preferred them to their fathers as companions. Homosexual men who considered themselves more masculine also reported having had more favorable home environments.

Freund and Blanchard (1983) report that, while the quality of the recollected father-son relationship of childhood has little to do with such particular characteristics as masculinity, disturbance of the childhood tie of son to father does lead to feminine gender identity. However, in an effort to replicate with a nonclinical group the findings of Bieber and associates (1962) regarding the significance of the father-son tie in early childhood for adult sexual orientation, Friedman and Stern (1980) wrote that based on respondent self-reports all seventeen of the gay men studied had had poor relations with their fathers and had lacked a masculine role model, as contrasted with twelve of seventeen men self-identifying as heterosexual (a finding highly statistically significant according to our calculation using the Fisher's exact test).

The gay men interviewed by Friedman and Stern had reported childhoods in which they felt rejected by their peer group as "sissies." Nine of the seventeen men reported their fathers to be hostile and detached, while other fathers were portrayed as indifferent or caring but absent following divorce. All seventeen retrospectively reported awareness of same-gender sexual wishes since middle childhood, and nearly all said their mothers had worked to foster a masculine identification in their son. This contrasts with the claim of the Biebers and their colleagues that mothers of homosexual men interfered in masculine development through their domineering actions. Overall, Friedman and Stern maintain that their subjects' recall of same-gender sexual fantasies during childhood is indicative of other than a usual developmental course and point to the possibility that the apparently absent or negative relationship with the father is the source of later same-gender desire.

These seventeen men were known to the authors or their colleagues and represent biased group of respondents. The report of the Biebers and their colleagues (1962) had become well known and influential throughout the psychiatric community and among gay men as well. Indeed, the domineering mother, distant or hostile father, and childhood marked by distress as a consequence of lack of athletic prowess and typical boyishness had become part of the master narrative of becoming gay. Friedman and Stern's (1980) report is thus testimony to the power of a master narrative to shape respondents' recollection of presumed childhood experiences. Without doubt, there are gay men whose childhood experiences within the family have been as portrayed by the Biebers and their associates (Bieber et al. 1962; Bieber and Bieber 1979) and also by Friedman and Stern (1980). However, except within a shared story of earlier life experiences, it is difficult to conclude that same-gender sexual orientation in men is an inevitable consequence of a domineering mother and a distant or hostile father.

It is worth noting that most of these studies focusing on family dynamics, preadult socialization, and the construction of homosexuality appeared in the 1960s; the focus shifted following the intellectual and social changes of the early 1970s. It is only since then that psychiatry and other mental health professions have recognized differences in sexual orientation as something other than psychopathology.

Within the context of the 1960s understanding of choice of same-gender intimacy, the logic of the study undertaken by the Biebers and their colleagues makes sense. From the outset, however, its significance was compromised by reliance on reports of persons in analysis; even assuming the reported pattern of domineering mother and aloof father accurately characterizes the families of the gay analysands studied, the generalizability of these findings must be called into question. Bell, Weinberg, and Hammersmith (1981), interviewing comparison groups of gay and straight men who were not seeking psychotherapeutic intervention found little support for the triangular family hypothesis of the Biebers and their colleagues. Their statistical study showed that aspects of family constellation as portrayed by the Biebers and their colleagues bear little relationship to adult sexual orientation. As Weinberg, Bell, and Hammersmith observe, "Our causal analysis convinces us that the tendency for homosexual males to perceive their fathers in a relatively negative fashion has little eventual influence on their sexual orientation" (1981, 61–62). As the authors note, while there is some tendency for conflict with fathers to be associated with gender nonconformity in childhood, there is little evidence of an association between any aspect of men's experience with either parent and adult sexual orientation. Their community study provides little support for the views of the Biebers and their colleagues regarding the significance of family factors as determinants of adult sexual orientation.

Zuger (1980) has suggested that the triangular system identified by Bieber's group has not been supported by prospective study and may reflect the needs of their gay analysands to provide such accounts. Further, this paradigm of parental relations is so global as to be equally applicable to the life stories of straight young adults. The report by the Biebers and their colleagues received so much attention from the popular press and the gay community that it entered into the dominant or master narrative (Plummer 1995) as the set of factors presumed to lead to gay adult sexual orientation.

The study reported by the Biebers and their colleagues presents other problems of interpretation beyond the fact that it is founded on the study of men in analysis, which limits the validity of any generalizations that might be drawn about the course of development. The fact that the conclusions reported are founded on analysts' interpretation of the lived experience of their analysands—not to be confused with concordant identifications (Racker 1968) or vicarious introspection (Kohut [1959] 1978)—is indicative of at least part of the problem. The analysts participating in the research ("the

Committee"), influenced by Rado's (1949) views regarding the adaptational significance of sexual behavior, were hardly unbiased observers and viewed same-gender sexual orientation as evidence of psychopathology. Further, the pattern of domineering mother and distant-hostile father, considered by the Bieber group to be modal for the emergence of homosexuality in adulthood, is found in slightly more than a quarter of the analysts' reports. The replication of the initial study (Bieber and Bieber 1979), though it makes use of direct reports, still relies on gay men in psychotherapy and may be biased by the authors' wish to replicate their earlier findings.

Friedman (1976a) has reported on the case of a man whose relationship with his parents fit the triangular system model put forward by the Biebers and their colleagues (1962) as prompting the later emergence of homosexuality. While this man reported a brief period of cross-dressing as a child, however, he showed little evidence of homosexual wishes across the course of psychiatric intervention. Responding to this case presentation, Bieber (1976b) qualified his earlier claim regarding the triangular system hypothesis, observing only that this was the most frequent pattern observed within the group of analysands whose histories were rated. He did question whether the period of cross-dressing indicated the potential for a homosexual adjustment which Friedman had disregarded. In response, Friedman raised important questions regarding the bias present in the selection of cases for the 1962 report and suggested that the report was significantly biased by the manner in which analysts selected cases for presentation (1976b, 381).

CONTRASTING CLINICAL AND NORMATIVE PERSPECTIVES ON SEXUAL ORIENTATION. Of particular relevance for the present discussion, Friedman, reviewing Hooker's (1956, 1957, 1969) findings on the similarity of adjustment of homosexual and heterosexual men living in the community, as shown on semistructured tests, suggests that homosexual men seeking analysis may not be comparable in their adjustment with men in the community not seeking intervention. Anticipating Isay's (1989) concerns, Friedman (1976a) questions whether psychodynamic formulations really assist in understanding the emergence of a same-gender sexual orientation, particularly when founded only on the study of persons who experience personal distress and seek psychiatric intervention.

Siegelman (1974) reviewed much of this literature, seeking to replicate and extend findings from the work reported by the Biebers and their colleagues, and observed, consistent with Hooker's findings, that virtually all prior research on relations between homosexual men and their parents had relied upon groups of men in prison or in psychiatric treatment. Clearly, this treatment experience would be expected to have some impact, which has not been assessed. Hooker (1969) noted, for example, the similarity of family psychopathology in the report by the Biebers and their colleagues (1962) with the characterization of the schizogenic family portrayed by Lidz and his colleagues (1965). Greenblatt (1966) reported in a similar vein, that the pattern of disturbed family relations associated with the triangular systems hypothesis was not reported among either homosexual or heterosexual men whose profiles on the Minnesota Multiphasic Personality Inventory (MMPI) were within the normal T-score range. However, both homosexual and heterosexual men with deviant MMPI profiles retrospectively reported patterns of disturbed relations with parents during childhood. Further, Schofeld (1965) reports greater incidence of reports of troubled relationships with their parents among gay men seeking psychological services than among gay men who had not sought such services.

Studying respondents who had not sought psychotherapy, Siegelman divided a group of more than three hundred self-identified gay men in New York into two groups, psychologically distressed and not troubled, on the basis of a score on a "neuroticism" scale. While the troubled men's reports of early childhood parental relationships replicated the triangular system described by the Biebers and their colleagues, this was not the case within the group of gay men not reporting psychological distress. The New York study was subsequently replicated with a group of British respondents (Siegelman 1972b). Less neurotic men were not found to differ from their heterosexual counterparts in terms of their recollections of parent-child closeness during childhood; there was no support for the triangular system hypothesis that disturbed relations were tied to later homosexuality.

Perhaps what is most interesting about these early studies of preadult socialization is the complex interplay between society and science. Across the past two decades, as homosexuality has increasingly come to be viewed as merely another developmental pathway or sexual lifeway, independent of psychopathology, the focus of study has shifted away from presumably pathogenic factors in the early experiences of children who in adulthood adopt a same-gender sexual orientation. Further, our understanding of the role of the family in development has shifted emphasis from forward socialization, from parent to children, to reciprocal socialization, in which each generation seeks to influence the other and offspring may induct their parents into new understandings of roles and relationships within the family.

Within more recent cohorts of gay men and women and their parents, there are many young people who report positive and close relationships with parents who are able both to accept the sexual orientation of their offspring and to be supportive of this developmental course. The thousands of families that have joined Parents and Friends of Lesbians and Gays (PFLAG) attest to this quite different response to the struggles of gay and lesbian young adults (Herdt and Boxer 1996; Beeler 1997).

Isay (1986a, 1986b, 1989, 1996a, 1996b) implicitly views a disturbance in the tie between father and son as responsible for at least some expressions of same-gender desire in adulthood, although he is explicit in stating that such same-gender desire is independent of psychopathology. While in apparent agreement with the Biebers and their colleagues (1962), R. C. Friedman (1988), and Friedman and Stern (1980) regarding the significance of the absence of the father, his explanation relies less on forward socialization processes than on the consequences of reverse socialization. His explanation follows on the accepted account within psychoanalysis of the significance of the boy's experience of the nuclear conflict, related both to the wish for intimacy with his mother and to fear of retaliation in the form of emasculation should this wish be realized. This fear of castration is presumed to lead both to the effort during middle childhood to learn the skills necessary to finding such intimacy and to the active search for intimacy outside the family following adolescence.

Writing from within a very traditional drive psychology, Isay suggests that this paradigm is reversed in the instance of some, perhaps all, boys who later become homosexual. His study of forty gay men in analysis with him supports the view of Green (1987), Friedman (1988), and others who argue that the childhood of the prospectively homosexual boy is characterized by adoption of a feminine position in relation to his father in the "oedipal" years marking the transition from early to middle childhood. While agreeing with the Biebers and their colleagues (1962), Freund and Blanchard (1983), and Friedman and Stern (1980) that the boy and his father have a strained relationship and even supporting Green's (1987) views that the boy may not enjoy such typical interests as competitive athletics, Isay (1986a, 1986b, 1989, 1996a, 1996b) maintains that the strained relationship is a consequence of the boy's reversed resolution of the nuclear conflict. Rather than regarding the mother as a love object and the father as a rival, the prospectively homosexual boy regards the father as a love object and his mother as a rival for his father's attention and affection. The father—who may himself harbor uncomfortable wishes which are evoked anew by the attentions of his son or who may be responding in terms of culturally engendered homophobia—reacts adversely to the little boy's bid for affection and attempts to distance himself, becoming avoidant and hostile. Later, in adulthood, the boy may seek to realize the close father-son tie missing in earlier life in a relationship with another man. The experience of his father's rejection may also become a source of internalized homophobia stemming from the belief that if he were "normal" his father would not have withdrawn.

Isay's findings, like those of other psychoanalytic observers, follow from work with men unhappy with their lives, shameful regarding their sexual orientation, and seeking an enhanced sense of personal integrity as gay men. But, following the perspective of Hooker (1969), Siegelman (1974, 1981), and Herdt and Boxer (1996), it is difficult to generalize from clinical to non-clinical groups; it is important to begin study among gay men in present cohorts of young adults in order to determine the significance of psychoanalytic perspectives for the course of development. Important in Isay's (1989) portrayal is not only the reformulation of the basis for the father's withdrawal and absence, but the reformulation of the course of early childhood development among at least some boys who later adopt a same-gender sexual orientation.

Isay suggests that for some boys, the effort to resolve the oedipal configuration results in what Freud ([1914–18] 1955) termed the "negative oedipus constellation" in his discussion of the Wolf-Man case. There has been little study of this phase in the resolution of the nuclear conflict of early childhood. Presumably the boy, fearing castration, offers himself to his father as a sexual object with the goal of forestalling his father's retaliation. Lewes ([1988] 1995, 41–42) suggests that Freud saw at least three possible determinants of this so-called negative constellation: the effect of (biologically based) constitution, a nonnormative developmental pathway perhaps the consequence of accidental factors co-occurring, or a neurotic compromise. Lewes notes that it was only following Bergler's (1949, 1956) formulation of homosexuality as psychopathology that this third aspect of Freud's initial speculations came to be emphasized. The concept of the negative oedipal constellation need not be regarded as regression from the effort to resolve the nuclear conflict but may be considered another developmental pathway through this conflict, which marks the transition from early to middle childhood; subsequent choice of a same-gender partner is then not necessarily "perverse" or pathological (Gillespie 1964; Isay 1989, 1996a, 1996b; Lewes [1988] 1995).

This effort at resolving the nuclear conflict soon succumbs to a solution in which the little boy gives up any effort at intimacy with his mother and develops an identification with his father's skills, which facilitates emergence into school and community and development of attributes which will permit him to find a woman like his father married. However, there appear to be at least some boys who take their father as the source of affection and regard their mother as the rival. These boys develop an intense longing for their father which cannot be explained through invocation of the concept of the negative oedipus constellation.

For example, one young man entering analysis in response to problems in realizing professional goals vividly recalled a time when, as a preschool child taken on vacation with his parents, he had been required to shower with his father prior to going swimming. This man remembers looking with longing at his father's penis and wishing that his father would have intercourse with him. This wish was less a defensive response to fear of castration than a positive longing for intimacy with his father, parallel in many ways to the wishes for intimacy with their mothers recollected by other men in analysis. The relationship between father and son was in other respects not remarkable except for the periodic longing which the analysand had experienced for his father, who appears not to have recognized this desire. Father and son had continued a respectful and mutually supportive relationship, although they were not particularly close. Beginning in late adolescence, this analysand developed a long-term partnership with a man about fifteen years his elder. He especially enjoyed experiencing his partner's penis inside him, in the manner in which he had formerly sought his father's penis, and reported feelings of particular closeness and intimacy when the couple went away for a holiday, tracing this particular satisfaction to an association with his awakening to sexual wishes toward his father while on holiday.

Goldsmith (1995) and Lewes (1998) concur with Isay's focus on the father-son relationship as the nexus for at least one dynamic leading to adult same-gender desire among men. However, Lewes suggests what he terms a plicate, or "folded," Oedipus complex (1998, 347) in which the father is experienced by the preschool aged boy as both the source of desire and the prohibitor of desire. This dual experience of the father is founded in the little boy's wishes (presumably founded on some temperamental characteristics) and may have little to do with his father's personality. As a consequence, the little boy is unable to fully resolve the nuclear neurosis or oedipal conflict which, among straight counterpart boys, is marked by diminution of sexual urges until adolescence and eventual identification with the father's skills and talents in order to marry a woman like his mother. Lewes maintains that the outcome of the plicate oedipal configuration is that many prospectively gay men recall their early school years as a time of continual sexual excitement rather than the expected diminished sexuality.

Lewes agrees with Isay that the outcome of this folded oedipal configuration is that the father becomes uncomfortable with the boy's seductive overtures and turns away from him. Further, Lewes agrees that the little boy's experience of his father's rejection provides the foundation for the sense of shame that so often characterizes the lives of gay men. Both Goldsmith and Lewes note that accounts such as that of Socarides ([1978] 1989, 1988), which suggest that gay men turn away from women because of unresolved issues of individuation with their mothers (Mahler, Pine, and Bergman 1975), do not account for the reality that many gay men enjoy congenial relations with women.

Schwartz (1999) maintains, however, that Lewes's elaboration of a plicate oedipal experience among at least some prospectively gay men further reifies normative sexual development, with its stereotypical outcome of the hetero-sexual man. Schwartz maintains that the very concept of the oedipal phase of development is founded in Freud's endorsement of Darwin's concept of evolution, in that the function of the oedipal phase is to ensure that men will desire women and reproduce the species (Ritvo 1990; Sulloway 1979). From this perspective, heterosexuality is presumed the ideal maturational outcome of psychological development and same-gender desire is relegated to the realm of psychopathology. Given this perspective, Schwartz maintains, it is inevitable that gay men harbor an enduring sense of shame about their same-gender desires. The alternative is that the sense of shame so often experi-enced by gay men is a consequence of their realization that their desire for contact with other men is socially taboo because of what such contact means in terms of masculine ideals. For Schwartz, the issue of personal discomfort with being gay is less the outcome of the oedipal phase of development than of our culture's views of same-gender desire among men as a sign of feminin-ity and of associated gender anxiety within the community. If gay men are other than feminine, it must be that they experience conflict regarding ex-pression of their feminine self. As a result, gay men who enjoy same-gender desire but are not necessarily feminine must be riddled with conflicts.

Masculinity and the Concept of the "Sissy Boy"

While there has been extensive study of sexual orientation in adolescence and young adulthood, there has been much less study of sexual orientation and child development. This neglect is due in large part to the problems of studying the topic of gender orientation among young children, which is largely taboo in contemporary society. Study to date has generally been guided by the assumption that the gay adult male presents in childhood as effeminate (Bradley and Zucker 1997; Coates 1985; R. Green 1987; R. C. Friedman 1988; Zucker 1990). More recently, this presumed difference be-tween the boyhood of gay men and their straight counterparts has been char-acterized as "gender atypicality."

This characterization of boys who later become gay men as effeminate is based both on the study of gender dimorphic determinism (founded on the "fetal androgen incomplete masculinization" hypothesis reviewed in chapter 2) and on theories of childhood socialization which suggest that, regardless of cause, some boys present as feminine even in infancy and are socialized into a feminine gender identity (M. Bailey and Zucker 1995). The biological hypothesis assumes that, perhaps as a consequence of maternal stress sometime in the second trimester of pregnancy, there is a disruption in the process of masculinization controlled by androgens. The socialization hypothesis, not necessarily in conflict with the biological hypothesis, assumes that gender identity is equivalent to sexual identity or sexual orientation. This understanding is founded on work by the biologist John Money and his colleagues (Money and Ehrhardt 1972), which focused on sex assignment and particularly on parental response to hermaphroditism in childhood.

As noted in the critique of the literature on biology and sexual orientation, Byne (1995, 1996) and Fausto-Sterling (1995, 1997a) have provided detailed critiques of the androgen demasculinization hypothesis; they note that the development of endocrine regulation of gender is not parallel in rodents and humans and also that the processes leading to sex determination during fetal development are more complex and interactive than has been reflected in the literature to date. Much of the problem of those following in the tradition of Money and his colleagues is the confabulation of core gender, or sense of oneself as a man or woman, and sexual identity, or acknowledged desire for intimacy with a person of the same or other gender. For example, Coates (1985) assumes that confusion regarding core gender identity (Stoller 1968; P. Tyson 1982) is the precursor of adult same-gender sexual orientation; lesbians and gay men, that is, seek same-gender sexual partners because they are uncertain whether they are men or women. While her findings may be relevant to the emergence in adulthood of transsexual and transvestite interests, she fails to differentiate between homosexuality, or same-gender sexual orientation, and gender identity disorders in which, for example, men who identify with the woman's role in personal and sexual intimacy seek not partnership with other men but to become women.

There is reason to question the concept of the effeminate boy necessarily growing into a gay man. In the first place, if same-gender sexual orientation is a behavior or phenotype, there may be many routes that lead to it, founded on the complex interaction of biological, psychological, and social factors. One route may indeed be characterized by effeminacy in boyhood, but other boys may adopt a same-gender sexual orientation based on quite different developmental antecedents. The present master narrative of "growing up gay" reflects a reading of the biological literature in support of innate determinants in large part because of the presumed political implications: if homosexuality is innate, then change in sexual orientation is not possible and society should accommodate the particular needs of gay men and, presumably, gay women.

COHORT, SOCIAL CHANGE, AND TYPICAL BOYHOOD INTERESTS. The master narrative of "growing up gay" has shifted somewhat over the past few years, the term "effeminate" being replaced by "gender-atypical." The gender-atypical boy is presumed to shun sports in childhood, preferring theater, music, and the visual arts, or to be sophisticated beyond his years in such academic pursuits as literature, history, or even politics (Hanson and Hartmann 1996). Criticisms of this argument may be founded both on sampling issues and on the issue of retrospective study so well noted by Freud ([1920] 1955). Without doubt, gay men volunteering for research through universities and community organizations represent a group of highly educated men with atypical interests, which may or may not stem from childhood. And while it is not clear that theater and the arts reflects a specifically gay sensibility, it may be that men and women participating in the arts are unusally experimental in all aspects of their lifestyle, including sexuality. In any case, social and historical changes have led present cohorts of young adults generally to be more experimental in determining their lifestyle than was characteristic of the cohort of older social and biological scientists who have studied this issue. The question they have posed concerns the number of boys preferring their studies and the arts to sports who become gay, or more generally, what discernible variations in adult sexual orientation among men correspond to boyhood interests that are more or less gender-atypical. It must be noted, however, that the very concept of gender typicality changes over time. Participation in athletics may now be more characteristic of the lives of both boys and girls than in past times, while participation in scouting, 4-H, and other activities may have declined.

The first study to raise the question of effeminacy among boys who grew up to be gay was reported by Green (1987). Influenced by the work of Money, and preferring socialization to biological explanations for the emergence of homosexuality among the feminine boys he has studied, Green has devoted much of his career to the study of these boys and their adult outcomes. His stated reason for focusing on feminine boys rather than tomboys is that there is greater stigma attached to effeminacy among boys than to some "boyishness" among little girls. Saghir and Robins (1973) had reported on an earlier cohort of gay men recalling a childhood preference for playing with girls and a desire to be feminine. Drawing on their findings and following nearly two decades of his own study, Green (1987) maintains that boys who later seek same-gender sexual partners begin life as effeminate and prefer play more characteristic of little girls.

In an effort to avoid problems of retrospective recall, which had been evident in the report by Saghir and Robins, Green recruited a group of so-called feminine boys (cross-gendered) as nominated by physicians and mental health professionals in the greater Los Angeles area. These boys were presumed to show sexual identity conflict. A matched comparison group of boys was recruited through newspaper advertisements. The cross-gendered sexual identity of the feminine boys was evaluated through playroom observations and parent interview. These boys were followed in an informal longitudinal study through early adulthood, when their sexual orientation was presumed to be fixed. Though he was writing at a time when same-gender sexual orientation among boys was presumed to be the outcome of the familial constellation of controlling mother and aloof father, together with marital conflict (Bieber et al. 1962), Green was hesitant to endorse this formulation.

FEMININITY, PASSIVITY, AND THE "GIRLYBOY." Coates (1992), reviewing Green's (1987) report, noted that Green assumes that psychopathology among feminine boys is the consequence of parental withdrawal and discomfort with their sons' effeminate manner: Green describes both parents as remote and avoidant of their feminine sons. The work of Bieber and his colleagues (1962) has been so often cited that it has entered into the master narrative of several successive cohorts of gay men, who tell life stories not only emphasizing feminine pursuits in childhood (more recently termed gender-atypical) but also characterizing their mothers as domineering and their fathers as passive and distant. At the same time, it is important to note that neither systematic study (Bell, Weinberg, and Hammersmith 1981) nor a detailed study of life histories of gay youth growing up in the southern United States in the postwar period through the 1970s (Sears 1991) provides much support for the Bieber hypothesis.

Studying a group of boys involved in psychiatric treatment, Green (1987) reports that parents, particularly mothers, rated their feminine sons as more beautiful but also as more sickly during infancy and early childhood than parents of nonfeminine sons in the comparison group. The feminine boys were reported to have watched and even emulated the application of cosmetics. At the same time, both fathers and mothers of feminine boys spent relatively less time with them than parents of boys in the comparison group. Fathers appeared to be particularly remote. Both parents of the feminine boys reported wishing for a girl (1987, 71–72). Fathers who themselves had reported a less masculine boyhood were more supportive of their sons' cross-gender attributes.

Following the feminine and nonfeminine boys through early adulthood, with a loss of about a third of each group, Green finds that, while statistical correlations between childhood feminine role behaviors and adult homosexual fantasy do not reach an acceptable level of significance (the magnitude of correlations is greater when combining the feminine and nonfeminine groups because of the greater variability of the measures), anecdotal study suggests that highly feminine boys showed increased homosexual fantasies and wishes to become a woman. Indeed, nearly two-thirds of the volume is devoted to such anecdotal reports. On the basis of these detailed reports, Green posits a model which includes the androgen demasculinization and social learning perspectives, arguing that family, school, and peer group all support emergence of a gay identity among boys who early in childhood show a preference for more typically feminine pursuits.

Green is properly suspicious of perspectives which focus overly on stereo-typed family dynamics while believing that parents may subtly, often un-knowingly, support cross-gender actions among those more beautiful, feminine-appearing boys. While not supporting Stoller's (1968) observations that mothers tend to be more attentive to feminine boys, Green reports that fathers tended to shun more feminine boys who, in turn, reported greater feelings of alienation from their fathers; still, it is their femininity and not the lack of parental attention which best predicts a homosexual outcome.

Green has identified a particular group of boys who are particularly beau-tiful as infants, although rather frail and sickly, who show preference early in life for "girlish" pursuits, whose parents, who would have preferred to have had girls tend to be avoidant because of their dashed hopes for daughters and the atypical interests of their sons. Green speculates that the initial wish for a girl may have had something to do with the socialization of these boys into a feminine sex role. Coates (1985) reports additional study of feminine boys, primarily those seeking to become transsexual (taking the role of a woman) as adults; she has shown these boys to be particularly troubled. Their parents are ambivalent regarding their offspring's girlish interests and respond to im-plied community pressures by seeking to reverse such expressions of cross-gender identity.

More than half of these boys had suffered lengthy separations from their parents early in life due to hospitalizations, and their mothers felt so depleted and overwhelmed during the first years of their children's lives that they showed signs of clinical depression. Coates also suggests that mothers of boys with a conflicted sense of being male were also overprotective and devalued men, in an effort to overcome their feelings of hostility toward the boys. Fathers, for their part, were both remote and violent (Coates 1985, 117). Coates concludes that extreme boyhood femininity is part of a larger constel-lation of significant psychopathology manifest not only in the child but also within the larger family context. However, the family psychopathology por-trayed by Coates (1985) and Green (1987) is experienced by the child as ma-ternal withdrawal and disappointment rather than the domineering mother portrayed by Bieber and his colleagues (1962).

Green's study implicitly follows an earlier line of developmental research which attempted to link aspects of childhood sex-role interests and identifications to adult gender roles and sexual orientation (Bieber et al. 1962; Chang and Block 1960; Gebhard et al. 1965; Holeman and Winokur 1965). Developmental hypotheses elaborated in Green's (1987) study are concerned with whether and how gender identity precedes the emergence and development of sexual orientation, albeit in a clinically constituted sample. However, as E. Stein (1999) has observed, Green's study has little relevance for understanding the basis of same-gender sexual orientation among men without markedly atypical childhood interests. Further, these boys may have been subjected to unusual stereotyping by family and community, which would increase the possibility that they would opt for a gay sexual orientation. The predominant paradigm of this study is child-centered, with major emphasis on longitudinal changes in gender-atypical "sissy males" (a term employed by Green to describe a constellation of atypical behaviors, i.e., a syndrome), examining parent and child variables which predict adult homosexuality.

A major problem of method apparent in this study is the quite different sources of data employed for childhood and adult measurements. While there are statistically significant correlations between some child and adult variables, overall they account for little explained variance. The sample selection procedures themselves precluded examination of gay men who did not manifest effeminate behavior in early childhood (for a critical review of these issues, see De Cecco 1987 and E. Stein 1999).[6] Because of the selection criteria, this study of men may represent one type of homosexuality while excluding many others. Green's work is not, in contrast to the focus of our discussion, primarily concerned with gay or lesbian identity development and the life course of youth subsequent to adolescence. The focus on origins and causes in this line of research meant that Green was unable to provide more detailed description and understanding of the life course subsequent to childhood.

The problem for present consideration of the developmental pathways of boys who become gay men is that many investigators working in this area of study, most notably Green but also Coates (1985) and Bailey and Zucker (1995), conflate sex role, gender role, and sexual orientation in their discussion of boyhood effeminacy and its consequences for adult psychosocial development (Paul 1993). As R. C. Friedman noted in a panel presentation (Bernstein 1993), and as noted by both Stoller (1968) and Tyson (1982), we

---

6. Green's study illustrates our earlier point regarding the difficulties of changing theoretical perspectives within the history of a longitudinal study. The original purpose for this work, as he has indicated (R. Green 1987), was to understand the development of transsexualism.

must distinguish core gender identity, awareness of oneself as man or woman, from both gender role, or overt behavior with others, and orientation in selection of sexual partners. Green (1987) is not always clear which of these perspectives he is adopting. Particularly in discussing adult outcomes, he fails to distinguish between core gender identity and sexual orientation, that is, between boys who seek other boys or men as sexual partners and those who see their core gender identity as women, wish to become women, and adopt a transsexual expression of their sexuality. A boy's emulation of his mother's application of cosmetics and wish to dress as a woman is an expression of conflict regarding core gender identity and is not equivalent to being homosexual. While there are gay men who present as effeminate (known in gay circles as "queens," they enact a lifestyle known as "camp"), their coquettishness is but one pathway into a gay identity. Green's conflation of characteristics and portrayal of gay men as effeminate is unfortunately common in the study of homosexuality among men; Bailey and his colleagues (M. Bailey and Zucker 1995) and Bem (1996) similarly presume that all gay men have a fictive feminine sex-role identity manifested by gender-atypical interests, and a presumptive feminine gender identity which leads them to seek other men as sexual partners.

Other studies of the boyhood of gay men have followed in the tradition of Green's longitudinal report (M. Bailey and Zucker 1995; Bakwin 1968; Lebovitz 1972; Zuger 1966, 1974, 1978, 1984; Zuger and Taylor 1969). Only one such study (Zuger 1984) has followed gay men from boyhood. However, the value of this report is compromised both by the process of selection (all fifty-five cases were drawn from the psychiatric practice of the adults) and by the indirect manner in which adult outcome was determined (reports of physicians or family members regarding adult psychosexual status). Most mothers were aware of their son's "aberrant" feminine interests in early childhood; boys with problems in core gender identity (wishing to be like girls) all were reported to have become homosexual (1984, 92).

Inspection of the clinical criteria for selection of twenty of these cases, involving effeminate boys ranging in age from four to sixteen years at first evaluation (Zuger 1966, 1100–1101), shows that several different criteria were employed. Six or seven boys showed a disturbance of core gender identity at first evaluation and expressed the wish to become a woman when grown; these boys may have been showing the precursor of what in adulthood is a transsexual disorder, different from same-gender sexual orientation. The remaining boys expressed concerns characteristic of the retrospective reports of gay men in the cohort that grew up in the 60s regarding their childhood. These boys reported feelings of attraction to other boys and being subject to stigma at school. The fact that a boy wants to be a hairdresser when adult or enjoys baking does not, in itself, qualify as effeminate. Zuger and Taylor (1969) maintain that boys who are truly effeminate show a more stable pattern of feminine interests than counterpart boys, whose feminine interests are fleeting. There is some suggestion that boys with more enduring feminine interests may have had some physical problems in early childhood (Zuger 1974).

As in Green's (1987) study, the term "homosexual" was applied in the work of Zuger and of Lebovitz (1972) equally to boys seeking to be transsexual and to boys attracted to other boys as sexual partners. Only Bakwin (1968) sought to differentiate boys likely to become transsexual from boys likely to become homosexual. Bakwin observes that "although many homosexuals show general behavioral traits characteristic of the opposite sex, the term homosexual does not necessarily imply effeminacy. . . . Many male homosexuals pride themselves on their masculinity, and, similarly, many female homosexuals prize their femininity" (1968, 627). Bakwin also cautions that "those homosexuals in whom the deviation is limited to erotic behavior being otherwise normal are not detectable in childhood" (1968, 627).

Little effort was made in studies such as those of Bailey and Zucker (1995), Lebovitz (1972), or Zuger (1978, 1984) to differentiate as urged by Bakwin between boys with gender-identity disorders and so called "girlyboys" (Corbett 1997, 1998, [1997] 1999). In part, this reflects the effect of a particular historical time upon what is considered to be effeminate. Playing with dolls and an interest in cooking among boys may once have been considered signs of effeminacy, but even the most casual observation of boys and girls playing together in a contemporary nursery school would show that these are interests common to both genders. (Indeed, as Bettelheim argued in *Symbolic Wounds* [1954], boys are often envious of the creative capacity of girls and seek to emulate them in their play.) It is difficult to make sense of the findings of these studies because so many interests were grouped together as purportedly feminine or, in terms of the master narrative previously discussed, as fostering early awareness of being different from other boys: creative or scholarly interests, desire to cross-dress, playing with dolls, or overt expression of the wish to be a girl—apparently only boys with an interest in sports are "typically" masculine! The fact that the boys studied were seen in psychiatric practice suggests that other factors may have been involved in both childhood and adult outcome. At the very least, it would be difficult to claim that creative, scientific, or aesthetic interests among boys are associated with adult sexual orientation.

In their review of research in the area of boyhood effeminacy and adult adjustment, Bailey and Zucker (1995) also confuse gender identity and sexual identity. Indeed, they assume not simply that feminine boys will be homosexual but specifically that they will be anal receptive (a "bottom" in the language of the gay community). If the bottom is a man with a gender-identity disorder stemming from early childhood, how are we to characterize his partner? This stereotype, which is so problematic in studies of the biology of homosexuality, continues in the literature in the absence of systematic study of the actual gender identity of these men as adults and in spite of the reality that most gay men do not identify themselves as exclusively either a top or a bottom.

Further, while appropriately critical of studies relying upon retrospective reports, which are subject to the distorting effects of history and memory, Bailey and Zucker's (1995) meta-analysis of such studies claims to show highly significant effect sizes for the association between boyhood effemi-nacy and homosexual adult outcomes. Their meta-analysis, however, not only inherits from its component studies the problem of retrospective reports but amplifies it by combining reports compiled over a period of more than half a century, each reflecting the particular stereotypes regarding the origins of sexual orientation prevalent at a different point in time. Meta-analytic studies are only as valid as the component studies they include. Problems of method of study inevitably compromise the real-world significance of a statistically reliable finding.

Bailey and Zucker (1995) selected forty-one studies reporting on gender identity prior to age twelve and including contrasting groups of women and men with homosexual and heterosexual outcomes, standardized for lack of variance within the heterosexual groups. The effect size for men far ex-ceeded that for women, suggesting that homosexual men are particularly likely to report cross-gender interests in childhood and reflecting both a par-ticular focus in the literature on femininity in boys as a source of enduring stigma. However, the significance of the meta-analysis is compromised by great variability in what is deemed to constitute homosexuality in adulthood (confusion of same-gender sexual orientation with gender identity disorder) and to constitute cross-gender interests in childhood (confusion of pursuits such as doll play among boys with such interests as involvement in the cre-ative arts).

Other retrospective reports of the boyhoods of gay men show little more than that there is a master narrative which frames the life stories of many gay men. Bailey and Zucker (1995) claim that the lack of association in their meta-analytic study between effect size and year of publication of the com-ponent studies shows that there is not a cohort effect. However, linear anal-ysis does not permit determination of nonlinear effects, particularly the sig-nificance of having grown up before and after an epochal event like the 1969 Stonewall riots.

Whitam (1977) reports on findings from a 1974 study of homosexual and heterosexual men in a cohort growing up in the 1940s and 1950s, in which homosexual men reported greater interests than heterosexual men in girlish activities. Within this cohort, the stronger one's homosexual inclinations were reported to be, the greater was the childhood focus on sissy activities. Whitam does recognize a group of homosexual men whose childhood was not distinct from that of their heterosexual counterparts except for an early awareness of sexual attraction to other boys. Whitam believes the camp life-style to be an intrinsic aspect of homosexuality, reflecting a continuity into adulthood of feminine interests and pursuits.

Based on a paper-and-pencil inventory of earlier and later childhood interests, completed by men and women volunteers, ages sixteen to seventy-four from Los Angeles–area homosexual groups, and matched groups of heterosexual volunteers, Grellert, Newcomb, and Bentler (1982) report that homosexual men reported typically feminine childhood interests (playing house and dolls was not differentiated from jacks or school interests at a young age) as contrasted with the interest in sports reported by most heterosexual men. Homosexual women were also portrayed as having cross-gendered childhood interests more like those of the heterosexual boys. Considering the heterogeneity of the groups, particularly the broad age range, which combines several generations or cohorts, it is difficult to interpret these findings.

Corbett (1996, 1998, 1999) has questioned the assumptions underlying the presumption that the sissy boy is necessarily feminine. In the first place, just as argued by Schwartz (1999) the presumption treats the feminine as a disvalued category: to be like a woman is to be weak, to suffer a disorder. In the second place, it ignores the variety of developmental pathways leading to a gay or lesbian sexual orientation in adulthood; the sissy boy portrayed by Green (1987) or "girlyboy" portrayed by Corbett reflect one such pathway and must be differentiated from boys experiencing gender dysphoria or gender-identity disorder (S. Coates 1992). As Corbett has observed:

> Homosexual boyhood as a conceptual category does not exist. The existence of homosexual boys has until now either been silence or stigmatized. Bullies identify sissies. Psychiatrists identify sissy-boy syndromes. There has been virtually no effort to speak of the boyhood experience of homosexuals other than to characterize their youth as a disordered and/or nonconforming realm from which it is hoped they will break free. The fate of these boys is contemplated with the kind of hushed charity that obscures antipathy. (1999, 108)

Corbett maintains that the "girlyboy" who does not pursue traditional gender interests such as competitive sports and rough-and-tumble play, poses a dilemma for a society which insists upon categorizing gender roles as either feminine or masculine. He suggests that the paradox and mystery of homo-sexuality is that it questions this binary categorization of gender roles.

Corbett cautions a rush to judgment regarding the meaning of nontradi-tional gender interests: "I wish simply to propose that early cross-gendered experience is interimplicated with later developing homosexuality in com-plex ways that remain unaccounted for within current developmental theo-ries" ([1997] 1999, 111–12). For example, as his clinical vignettes suggest, the mere fact that a little boy plays with dolls says little about gender and sexuality; indeed, the doll play of his child patients is most often the enact-ment of conflicts within the child's life which he is unable to master. Corbett cautions against definitions of gender-identity disorder such as those ad-vanced by Friedman (1997), Coates and Wolfe (1995), and Bailey and Zucker (1990), which assume that gender is fixed. Girlyboys do not define themselves as girls, although they may enjoy some activities once regarded as stereotypically feminine. However, they also do not define themselves as boys in the manner most often portrayed by the larger society. Indeed, they maintain strong identifications with attributes and interests of both mothers and fathers and, in this way, challenge accepted psychological theories re-garding the development of gender identification.

As Stoller (1968) and Tyson (1982) have both emphasized, consistent with Corbett's caution regarding gender interests and sexual orientation, it is im-portant to distinguish between gender identity and sex role. The mere fact that a boy enjoys needlepoint or shies away from physical fights does not necessarily mean that he is uncertain or confused about his gender. Clearly, the fact that some boys refuse to fight, do not like sports, and avoid rough-and-tumble play makes many parents, teachers, and therapists anxious (per-haps lest the boys be seen as having feminine traits, which in contemporary bourgeois society are disvalued). Corbett suggests that Friedman's (1997) en-dorsement of "rough-and-tumble" play as evidence of expected boyhood development put misplaced emphasis on the value of aggression as a proto-typic masculine attribute. This critique is founded on Friedman's explicitly biological explanation for such play (R. C. Friedman 1997, 490). Friedman accuses Corbett of lacking familiarity with this biological literature, while Corbett (1997) challenges Friedman's essentialist model of psychobiological development. (The problems with this biological perspective are reviewed in chapter 3). As Corbett observes:

> [Friedman] has focused on the adaptational role of juvenile aggressivity in mas-culine development, and has shown a marked interest in the hypothesized rela-tionship between aggressivity and the postnatal behavioral effect of prenatal androgens. (1997, 498)

Corbett's remarks highlight the problems with prenatal biological explanations for development, in which masculine aggressivity is presumed to be essential for reproduction of the species. Recent writing on the struggles of boys growing up in contemporary America have highlighted the high cost to their well-being of being required to sustain this stereotypic image of masculinity (Kindlon and Thompson 1999). The gender-nonconforming boy, however, is not necessarily in distress, except as a consequence of the experience of stigma. As Corbett notes: "We are in need of a developmental theory that can account for pattern while simultaneously duly noting the role of variance, and even chaos, in psychic structure and health" (1996, 435).

Indeed, Corbett maintains that the "girlyboy," as one variation of expectable childhood development, does not regard himself as a girl but rather seeks the passive experience of total merger with another. Across the adult years, at least some girlyboys seek others of the same gender as partners, sharing in sexual intimacy. The satisfaction of being the receptive partner in anal intercourse should not be regarded as evidence of an identification with femininity such as is reported by gender-dysphoric or transsexual men seeking to be women (it must be emphasized again that most gay men do not identify exclusively with one or the other position in anal intercourse). Passivity as a concept must be differentiated from femininity. Two lovers, either gay or straight, may enjoy the sense of merger which is a part of sexual intimacy, feeling one with another, without feeling that that merger is necessarily associated with issues of gender.

Older gay men learned a master narrative in which they were purported to have been effeminate as children; the post-Stonewall generation may tell stories of lived experience which similarly evince less interest in such stereotypic masculine interests as competitive sports than in aesthetic or creative interests, but without seeing these interests as necessarily feminine. Indeed, with the emergence of coeducational physical activity in schools and the elimination of all required athletic participation in many communities, it is likely that the emerging generation of gay and straight men alike will define masculine and feminine in ways different from earlier cohorts (Maccoby 1998). Once again, the significance of a life-course social science perspective is essential if we are to make sense of the lived experience of successive generations moving through history and social change. This perspective is particularly well manifested in Sears's (1991, 1997) discussion of the experience of growing up gay in the southern United States during the past half century.

EXOTIC BECOMES EROTIC. Many of these problems of confusion of core gender identity are also present in the work of Bem (1996, 1997), which again traces a route from boyhood effeminacy to same-gender sexual orientation in adulthood. Bem seeks an integration of the perspective that the homosexual man is first an effeminate child and that his effeminacy is founded in temperament. This predisposition to effeminacy is assumed to be expressed in gender-atypical childhood interests and avoidance of stereotypically masculine rough-and-tumble play and competitive athletics. As a result, the boy is taunted by peers for being a sissy and develops a fear of gender-conforming boys, who are then regarded as exotic and hence the source of erotic interest. This interest is then translated into attraction or same-gender sexual orientation. Bem cites the San Francisco study of Bell, Weinberg, and Hammersmith (1981) based on retrospective reports by gay men that as boys they had preferred hopscotch and playing jacks to competitive sports to a greater extent than heterosexual men, and had enjoyed playing with girls. Bem maintains that these boys then become erotically or romantically attracted to those who were dissimilar or unfamiliar to them in childhood (1996, 325). Physiological arousal provides cues for feeling emotion, and anxiety-producing scenes have been shown in experimental study to evoke particularly strong sexual responsiveness. Since other boys had evoked anxiety among these boys who did not respond in gender-stereotyped ways, men become the source of a particularly strong erotic attraction. Over time, the anxiety disappears and is replaced entirely by the attraction. The same paradigm holds for girls and is presumed to explain same-gender sexual orientation among women. Finally, bisexual men and women represent those persons who may be erotically attracted to the same gender but romantically attracted to the opposite gender, perhaps due to negative conditioning or social learning (1996, 331).

Bem's argument rests heavily on the concept of the sissy boy. He attempts to resolve the paradox reflected in studies such as that of McKnight (1997), which claim that gay men are hypermasculine in their sexual life, with the demasculinization hypothesis, which assumes an effeminate boy socialized across the childhood years into either the role of the woman or a role intermediate between men and women. Again, core gender-identity becomes confused with sexual orientation; the boy who shuns competitive sports in favor of studies and creative expression need not be presumed to show a gender-identity disorder. There are clearly many men who are heterosexual but gender-atypical in their interests and other men who are masculine but who seek same-gender partnership (Zuger 1980). Same-gender sexual orientation is independent of core gender identity.

Cohort issues are also implicated in Bem's complex chain of reasoning. Bem claims that boys who are not gender-stereotyped enjoy girls' activities and play. Among present cohorts of elementary school–aged boys, it is not necessary to shun other boys in order to enjoy activities other than competitive sports. Further, nonteam athletic activities such as running track have become increasingly popular among both adolescent boys and girls. Indeed, contrary to Bem's own argument that the exotic becomes erotic, many gay men report as boys finding other boys with common interests, with whom they shared sexual experiences. With the significant social changes of the past two decades, many of these older gender stereotypes have disappeared. Boys and girls share gym classes from earliest elementary school. Boys are expected to learn such skills as sewing and cooking, while girls are explicitly socialized to become accomplished in science and mathematics. E. Stein (1999) has carefully and sympathetically reviewed Bem's paradigm for the emergence of same-gender sexual orientation. He concludes, however, that the theory has serious problems which have yet to be resolved. Most significantly, if the exotic becomes erotic, then boys who show gender-atypical interests in childhood should be attracted both to gender-typical boys *and* gender-atypical (masculine) girls. The reality is that we live in a society which is polarized along such dimensions as ethnicity, social status, and gender, and several decades of research shows that most people are erotically attracted to others like themselves in terms of these parameters. Bem's theory encounters even more problems in explaining same-gender sexual desire among women. As in study of the biology of homosexuality, most developmental study has focused on the origins of same-gender desire among men and has largely neglected comparable study of women (E. Stein 1999).

While Bem may have accurately characterized one subgroup within cohort of now middle-aged gay men, it is less clear that his "exotic becomes erotic" formulation may be generalized beyond this subgroup. Bem both conflates gender identity and sexual identity and relies upon concepts of effeminacy among little boys which presume questionable biological determinants. As the biologist Fausto-Sterling ([1985] 1992) has emphasized, the only difference in the central nervous system of men and women is brain size, and that difference seems related to mens' larger physical stature and has few functional implications. Earlier assumptions that girls were inherently less adequate in the realm of spatial abilities relevant to acquisition of scientific skills has been shown to be a consequence of differential socialization practices, which have also changed in the past two decades (Wittig and Petersen 1979). Likewise, the presumption that boys who focus on verbal or aesthetic interests must be like girls (S. Coates 1985) has been shown to be without basis. There is also a problem of selection bias reflected in many reports on sexual orientation. While there is little evidence that gay men are smarter or better educated than straight counterparts, gay men with intellectual or artistic interests are easier for researchers to locate because of their connection to higher education.

Psychosocial Development among Lesbians

There has been much less study of the childhood of women who ultimately define their sexual identity as lesbian than of gay men (Kirkpatrick and Morgan 1980; Downey and Friedman 1996b; Golden 1997). Indeed, Downey and Friedman observe that the "literature on female homosexuality is extremely sparse" (1996b, 3). It should be noted that such discussion as has been reported (Socarides 1962, [1978] 1989) has viewed female homosexuality in the same pathological terms as male homosexuality, although Wolfson (1987) and Glassgold and Iasenza (1995) begin to redress this bias. Missing in the discussion of womens' lives is the genre of extensive autobiographical reports about their childhood. Collections such as those of Jay and Young (1977), and Penelope and Wolfe (1989, 1993) characteristically contain brief vignettes, a few of which address the experience of childhood among women who later become lesbian.

While this neglect of autobiographical writing may be yet one more instance of what the British writer Virginia Woolf (1929) portrayed as a the penalty for not having a "room of one's own," even the recent literature on the development of femininity in society during and following adolescence has neglected discussion of women who seek other women as sexual partners. And much of what discussion there is of sexual orientation in the psychoanalytic literature on women's development (Benjamin 1995a, 1998; Burch 1993; Magee and Miller 1996a, 1997; O'Connor and Ryan 1993; A. Schwartz 1998) reflects an elaboration of postmodern feminist literary theory following either Lacan or, more recently "queer theory." Allusions to concepts such as "phallocentricity" and "patriarchy" lead to an experience-distant discussion of the lives of women, which has little relevance to understanding the lived experience either of girls growing up lesbian or women who turn from heterosexual to lesbian adjustment as adults.

There are a number of reasons for this disparity in the detailed study of the lives of lesbians and gay men. Foremost is Freud's own penchant for basing the study of men's development on findings from his own self-analysis (Freud 1897–1904). Downey and Friedman (1996b) suggest that Freud's discussion conflated homosexuality and the process of psychological development among boys. Concerned with variations in the emergence and resolution of the nuclear conflict, Freud ([1905–24] 1953) stressed the negative oedipal constellation as the source of homosexuality among boys. Much subsequent psychoanalytic exploration of same-gender sexual orientation has followed in the tradition of Freud's initial formulations in the *Three Essays on a Theory of Sexuality* (Ferenczi [1911] 1950; R. C. Friedman 1988; Isay 1989; Lewes [1988] 1995; Nunberg 1938; Socarides 1960). Indeed, Freud himself followed in the tradition pioneered by Ellis and Krafft-Ebing, each of whom had focused largely on homosexuality among men. Freud reported in detail only one case of a homosexual woman (Freud [1920] 1955). However, as previously noted, it is less likely that the younger woman experienced sexual desire for the older woman than that she idealized her as a competent professional woman at a time when women in Viennese society were expected to remain within the domestic sphere (Magid 1993).

This initial concern with same-gender sexual orientation among men was undoubtedly bolstered by the apparently greater antipathy evoked by men having sexual contact with other men than by same-gender sexual contact among women. Suppe (1994, 1997) has suggested that this concern is founded, at least in part, on the preoccupation, following Darwin, with the reproduction of the species, in which the man is presumed to be the active partner. Nungesser (1983) hints at a darker concern: There is an aspect to same-gender sexual desire among men that is far more personally frightening and threatening to other men than expression of same-gender sexual desire among women; this may have fostered both greater prejudice against gay men than against lesbians and greater awareness of the personal and social impact of being gay, which in turn has fostered more study. Following Foucault (1975), it might also be observed that men control production of knowledge in society and are able to direct attention toward areas of study which are of greatest concern to themselves.

Finally, and related to all of these concerns, virtually all of the study of the biology and development of homosexuality has focused on the presumed biological determinants of homosexuality among men. Indeed, following a report by Hu et al. (1995) on the failure to replicate a finding of Xq28 linkage markers among lesbians and their siblings, Hamer and Copeland (1998) asserted that homosexuality is genetically determined among men but culturally determined among women! A report by Pattatucci and Hamer (1995) indicating that more than two-thirds of "heterosexual" women college students volunteering for a study of their own sexuality reported sexual attraction to another woman, while very few "heterosexual" men reported same-gender sexual attraction, further suggested to Hamer and his colleagues that same-gender sexual attraction was expectable among women but not among men.

Other studies of heredity and same-gender sexual orientation have reported findings which contradict the conclusions of Hamer's group. Bailey,

Pillard, et al. (1993) report that the concordance rates for homosexuality among lesbians and their monozygotic (MZ) twins was little different from that earlier reported for homosexual men and their MZ twins. This finding suggested to Bailey and his colleagues that heritability of homosexuality was similar among men and women. While nearly half of the MZ lesbian twins were reported to be lesbian, only 16 percent of dizygotic (DZ) twins, and 14 percent of nontwin sisters were reported to be lesbian (the higher than expected concordance of homosexuality among DZ twins and nontwin sisters could also be used in support of an argument for homosexuality founded on experience rather than heredity).

Based on this study, Downey and Friedman (1996b, 18) assert that homosexuality is moderately heritable in women, implying that there are few gender-based differences in the heritability of homosexuality. Problems with Bailey's study have already been reviewed, in chapter 3; the nature of the sample and the method of study both raise questions regarding the significance of this genetic research. As Vance (1989), Suppe (1994, 1997), and T. Stein (1996) have noted, the fundamental problem is in seeking in biological study an explanation for the origins of homosexuality, presuming as an essential category a phenomena whose understanding has changed over time and across cultures.

A major focus for study of the development of homosexuality among men is the presumed effect of the interruption of androgenization upon forward gender socialization among young boys. As already noted, much of this study misguidedly conflates gender identity and sexual identity, ignores changing understandings of what constitutes appropriate activities for boys and girls, and presumes, based on earlier psychoanalytic speculation, that the masculine is active, the feminine passive, and that position in sexual intimacy can also be unambiguously categorized as active or passive. Since experimentally interrupting androgenization of rats destined to become male leads these males to assume a position in mating similar to that of the female rat, the researchers conclude that men who enjoy receptive anal intercourse with other men must show similar incomplete androgenization during fetal development. The misguided conclusion from this biological analogy is that men seeking sexual contact with other men, particularly the "bottom" in anal intercourse, must be similar biologically to normal women since both seek men as sexual partners.

The parallel argument, founded on study of hormonal factors presumed to impact the development of women, is that women who seek other women as sexual partners must be like men since both lesbians and heterosexual men seek women as sexual partners. Again, while virtually all of the early experimental study of hormonal factors and prenatal development focused on factors thought responsible for ambiguous gender identity and sexual identity among young men, a recent study by McFadden and Pasanen (1998) reported on differences among gay and straight women and straight men in click-evoked otoacoustic emissions and used the androgenization argument to explain differences in female sexual orientation.

McFadden and Pasanen (1998) reason that the similarity in lesbians' and straight men's responses, in contrast to those of straight women, could be explained by the presumption that the lesbian women had received too much androgen during prenatal life and had been turned into men. This "explanation" appealed without foundation in evidence to the same biological literature on sexual orientation and hormones whose problems were reviewed in chapter 3. The psychoacoustic significance of this report is beyond the scope of the present discussion. The point here is that the same argument was made in fishing for biological makers of differences in sexual lifeways among women as was made earlier for men. Downey and Friedman (1996b) adopt a similar position, arguing by generalization from the experimental literature on animal populations that incomplete androgenization leads to feminine gender identity among boys (R. C. Friedman and Downey [1993a, 1993b] follow in the tradition of R. Green [1987] in conflating gender identity and sexual identity), while masculine gender identity and homoerotic sexual identity among women must be the result of too much prenatal androgen.

This biological argument, founded on the presumed impact of prenatal hormonal factors on the course of development across the course of life, assumes that sexual orientation is a fixed and essential attribute. However, as Suppe (1994, 1997) and T. Stein (1996) have observed, and as study of both gay and lesbian adult lives reviewed in the present work shows, there may be marked variation in the expression of sexual desire across the course of life. Further, Kirkpatrick and Morgan (1980) have stressed the importance of viewing the dynamics of same-gender sexual orientation as different for men than for women. Golden (1997) has suggested that fluidity of sexual orientation may be even more characteristic of the lives of women than the lives of men, particularly as adolescent women move into the adult years. Golden observes, "My sense is that gay men do not experience their sexuality in the fluid manner that some lesbian and heterosexual women do. . . . I suspect that very few gay men could be characterized as elective homosexuals" (1997, 161).

This observation must be understood in context of women's perspective on their own development as primarily relational rather than autonomous (Baruch and Brooks-Gunn 1984; Brooks-Gunn and Petersen 1983; Chodorow 1978; Gilligan 1982; Gilligan, Lyons, and Hanmer 1990; L. Brown and Gilligan 1992). Support for its validity has been provided by Kitzinger and Wilkinson (1995), following Kitzinger's (1987, 1995) constructionist research regarding same-gender sexual orientation. Kitzinger and Wilkinson studied eighty women previously self-identified as heterosexual (more than two-thirds had been married) but now self-identified as lesbian. They report that these self-identified women are less likely to ask "Am I [a lesbian]?" than "Do I want to be a lesbian?" (1995, 102). The problem with this argument is that it continues the confusion of gender, sexual identity, and developmental study of gay and lesbian lives. Kitzinger and Wilkinson ironically end up supporting Hamer and Copeland's (1998) claim of an essentialist explanation for same-gender sexual orientation among men and a constructionist explanation among women. What is most interesting in the position of both Golden (1997) and Kitzinger and Wilkinson (1995) is that as focus shifts from study of childhood to adulthood, discussion of women's sexual lifeways becomes increasingly founded in the study of lived experience rather than feminist literary theory.

Downey and Friedman (1996b) similarly comment that there appear to be a greater number of alternative sexual lifeways open to women than to men across the course of life. Their argument rests in part on the interesting hypothesis that among men, sexual fantasies emerge prior to adolescence which provide a dominant narrative for the entire subsequent course of life. A boy aware of same-gender sexual fantasies in childhood uses these fantasies as the foundation for a life story rendered coherent by such preadolescent sexual fantasies. Downey and Friedman conclude (1996b, 26) that lived experience across the childhood years may be more important as the foundation of the succeeding life story among men than among women. This hypothesis suggests that it is easier for women than for men to move back and forth between same- and opposite-gender sexual attraction, supporting Kitzinger and Wilkinson's claim regarding the greater fluidity of sexual lifeways among women in contemporary society.

Downey and Friedman (1996b) suggest that a woman whose marriage fails in midlife is more likely than her work-preoccupied husband to seek emotional support from others of her same gender, which may turn into physical intimacy. However, study of the life-story accounts of middle-aged and older gay men and women (Cohler, Hostetler, and Boxer 1998; Cohler and Hostetler, in press; Hostetler and Cohler 1997) shows that fluidity of sexual orientation may be as characteristic of the lives of men as of women. For example, men's action following failed marriages at midlife may also lead to similar enhanced same-gender social ties, followed by discovery of the satisfaction of same-gender sexuality and development of long-term same-gender intimate partnership.

Conclusion

Discussions of the foundation of a particular sexual orientation are dependent on claims regarding gender-typical activities and childhood experiences, which inevitably reflect the social and historical context in which a particular generation grew up. Clearly, prior to the intellectual and social changes of the period 1965–1975, play and development among both boys and girls were more gender-stereotyped than they are at present. While it was once considered appropriate for gifts to be pink for newborn girls and blue for boys, such gender-coded gifts might now constitute a social gaffe. Not only are boys and girls socialized in a less gender-stereotyped manner than formerly but circumstances regarding gender orientation have changed markedly for recent cohorts (Fricke 1981; Herdt and Boxer 1996; Sears 1991, 1997). In an earlier historical time, it would have been unthinkable to come to the senior prom with a same-gender date, or to have one's same-gender partner attend a high school graduation. Clearly, gay and lesbian adolescents still face painful situations because of their gender orientation, particularly in more traditional communities, but at the same time, the pressure to conform to gender stereotypes may have diminished.

Of even greater significance from the life-course perspective on sexual orientation, men and women may have children at one point in the course of life and later turn to same-gender sexual orientation. Many gay and lesbian couples adopt children. Other gay and lesbian couples care for children from previous marriages of one or both partners. Patterson and her colleagues (Patterson 1992, 1995b, 1996; Patterson and Chan 1996) have shown that eventual same-gender sexual orientation is no greater among offspring raised by gay and lesbian couples than for the community as a whole, although these children appear to view sexuality in less stereotyped ways than counterparts raised by heterosexual couples. The most interesting aspect of findings such as Patterson's has to do with the process of preadult socialization rather than with the presumed moral consequences of the sexual orientation of offspring. From the perspective on which this discussion is founded, same-gender sexual orientation is but another developmental pathway.

Accounts to date have been relevant more as examples of the kind of "science stories" we tell in our culture than as a means for understanding the origins of sexual orientation (Paul 1993). As Hamil (1995), E. Stein (1999), and Young-Bruehl (1996) have noted, there may be political motivations for attempting to show or to disprove that sexual orientation has a biological foundation. In any case, it is important to realize that conceptions of both gender and the significance of selecting a person of a particular gender as an intimate partner vary across cultures and over time, on a personal and a historical scale. At least to some extent, focus on the presumed biological origin of sexual orientation occupies the same place within psychoanalysis as Freud's occasional appeal to a presumed biological origin of variation in character. The primary issue, however, is the meaning for the analysand of his present sexuality and the gender of his intimate partner, not the biological origins of this choice.

Ours is a culture in which essence is a fundamental question. This concern is implicit in questions of the determinants of sexual partnership as in many other aspects of culture and personal experience (E. Stein 1999). From a social constructionist perspective, the question of presumed biological substrates of sexual orientation is no different from such other questions as the choice of neurosis. At points at which Freud found himself beyond the evidence, he often invoked a presumed biological substratum, which played the same role in his argument as metapsychology or references to Goethe's *Faust*. Significantly, when questions arose regarding sexual orientation, Freud demurred from such speculation, focusing instead on the meaning of sexuality for the analysand.

Speculation regarding biological determinants of sexual orientation plays a role in a contemporary discussion which is more political than scholarly (Young-Bruehl 1996). It is often maintained that if a biological determinant of sexual orientation were found, such that persons varying from the social norm in selection of intimate partners were unable to choose another course, then discrimination against gays would be as patently indefensible as bias against the left-handed. As Mitchell (1996b) has noted, there are a number of problems with this essentialist perspective in the study of sexual orientation and clinical and developmental psychopathology.

First, psychoanalysis focuses on factors associated with choices of all kinds. The decision to seek a sexual partner of the same gender is a positive choice like any other. While gender of sexual partner is not privileged (Chodorow 1992), the meaning of this choice, indeed of every mode of sexual expression, is a proper focus for psychoanalytic inquiry, regardless of the gender of the sexual partner. The goal of such inquiry is to increase understanding and enhance the sense of vitality and engagement with one's sexuality. The goal is to enhance the capacity for intimacy and pleasure regardless of the gender of the sexual partner. While, inevitably, the psychological significance of the gender of the partner must be a topic of concern within the psychoanalytic process, the intent should never be to alter the analysand's sexual orientation.

Second, based on current knowledge in biology, there is little evidence to support the concept of a biological substrate as the foundation of the choice of intimate partner. Reviewing the literature on biology and purported determinants of sexual orientation, Friedman and Downey (1994) considered evidence from genetic, hormonal, and brain structure studies. While there appears to be a nonspecific genetic effect in the determination of the selection of sexual partnership, evidence regarding specific genetic determinants is fragmentary and inconsistent. Findings from hormonal studies are even less promising; as we have shown in chapter 3, there is little evidence in studies reported to date that sexual orientation is related in any direct manner either to hormonal factors or to brain anatomy (Byne 1996, 1997a, 1997b; Fausto-Sterling 1997a).

Friedman (1988) has suggested that prenatal androgen exposure might determine childhood attraction or aversion to stereotypically boyish play. However, since gender identity and sexual orientation are independent dimensions and there is little evidence that variation in attraction to rough-and-tumble play is associated with adult sexual orientation across historical cohorts, Friedman's effort to demonstrate a relationship between prenatal hormonal influences and adult sexual orientation appears problematic. Further, it is difficult to account for women's orientation toward same- or opposite-gender partnership on the basis of prenatal hormonal processes. Friedman's claim rests on the assertion founded in reports such as those of Maccoby (1990) and Pellegrini and Smith (1998) regarding so-called boyish activities, that gay men retrospectively report other than stereotypically boyish orientations in early childhood; this claim has not been substantiated by data other than anecdotal reports and retrospective claims (Bieber et al. 1962).

While some gay men report gender-atypical boyhood interests, others report a boyhood that did not deviate from the expected norm for boyish play. Again, for more recent cohorts of both gay and straight men and women, social changes such as the broadening of physical education, now coeducational, to include dancing, boating, golf, and other noncontact activities, have redefined normative masculinity and feminity. The argument—founded on a presumption that homosexuality is based in prenatal development—that gay men were necessarily effeminate, did not enjoy rough-and-tumble play, and were misunderstood by parents, peers, and teachers is at best a limited explanation for problems presented by gay men seeking psychoanalytic intervention. Many other gay men seeking psychotherapy or psychoanalysis, particularly presently young adults, report little distress founded on biased gender construction, apart from stigma and homophobia encountered now and while growing up. These gay men most often report difficulties in finding and maintaining same-gender intimate relationships or in finding satisfaction from their work.

It is critically important that gender identity be understood as independent of adult sexual orientation. Experience within the community of gay men not seeking psychotherapy provides consistent evidence that while some gay men report artistic or scholarly childhood interests, which would have been considered gender-atypical for an earlier cohort of children, other gay men report both typical boyhood interests, including rough-and-tumble sports, and devoted and appropriately involved parents. Social status and cohort are principal determinants of such interests. Working-class gay men seldom seek psychoanalysis; these men may not be different from their counterparts who prefer opposite-gender partnership. There is little evidence that "sissy" boys are more likely to grow up to prefer same-gender partnership than more characteristically masculine counterparts (R. Green 1987). Similarly, there is little evidence that lesbian women are more likely than counterparts seeking sexual intimacy with men to have been less than feminine as children. Indeed, studies of the current cohort of gay and lesbian adolescents, such as the account provided by Herdt and Boxer (1996) of a group of teens in a community center "drop-in" program, suggests that their interests differ little from those of so-called straight adolescents. Such pain as these adolescents experience associated with same-gender sexual orientation is a direct consequence of stigma and prejudice on the part of peers and teachers who may be threatened by their disclosure of their sexuality, or of the fear attendant on realizing in action what their desires tell them (Blum and Pfetzing 1997).

Further, across recent cohorts growing from childhood to adulthood, the very concept of what it means to be masculine or feminine may be changing and may continue to change in ways not yet understood (Boxer and Cohler 1989; Boxer, Cohler, et al. 1993). E. Stein (1999) has noted the many problems of retrospective accounts that seek to relate atypical childhood gender interests to adult sexual orientation. In understanding variation in sexual orientation it is important to move beyond stereotypes of all sorts, including one-dimensional characterizations of the role of socialization or family factors in the determination of adult sexual orientation. Gay men coming for psychoanalysis are likely to report conflict with other family members much like that reported by men with opposite-gender sexual orientation. Additional conflict may have been generated in previous cohorts as a consequence of parental response to their offspring's sexual orientation. However, as variation in sexual orientation becomes more acceptable within urban middle-class society, parents are more likely to be supportive than in the past. The advent of organizations such as Parents and Friends of Lesbians and Gays (PFLAG) reflects such cohort changes in understanding sexual orientation among offspring. Further, realization that sexual orientation is not fixed and may shift across the course of life adds to the complexity of understanding the role of family in selection of sexual orientation. As Isay (1989) has suggested, in at least some families, paternal distance from a gay son may be a response to the son's early sexual attraction to his father and the father's discomfort with such attraction.

A third biological factor believed possibly to be implicated in the origins of sexual orientation, neuroanatomy, has also been investigated, but absolutely no claims of an association between differences in brain structure and sexual orientation have been replicated across studies. The lack of replication of these studies, together with at best ambiguous findings regarding either genetic or hormonal factors associated with sexual orientation, casts doubt on such essentialist efforts. Indeed, the lack of findings hardly supports Friedman and Downey's tentative claim that "to some extent sexual orientation is determined by biological factors" (1994, 928). But regardless of the status of such essentialist research, the focus in psychoanalytic study of sexual orientation must be on the meaning for men and women of the selection of sexual partner regardless of gender (Mitchell 1996b).

Five

Adolescence and Youth:
Realizing Gay and Lesbian Sexual Identity

With Andrew Boxer and Floyd Irvin

It doesn't bother me that I am gay. I don't know why shrinks should get so upset about it. What bothers me is that people should have such a hard time believing it. This is a new time, and society has to learn to accept us as no different from anyone else. My roommate and friends understand that; my biggest problem was with my parents and my high school teachers, who never understood that teenagers can be gay but no different from anyone else. Everyone my age was very cool about it and I even took my boyfriend to the prom.

—FIRST–YEAR COLLEGE STUDENT

This gay college student represents a new cohort of adolescents and young adults who recognized during youth their same-gender sexual attraction within communities that acknowledged and supported this developmental pathway (Herdt 1997). After a period of struggle with his parents, who have since come to accept his sexuality, this young man completed high school and now plans to become a physician working on the forefront of the AIDS epidemic. He met his boyfriend at a high school science fair; the two were inseparable until this past summer when his boyfriend entered an elite college on the east coast. Following several months of intense discussion, they decided that since they were going to colleges so geographically distant it would be difficult to continue their close and exclusive relationship. However, they remain in touch by E-mail several times each week.

Gay and Lesbian Adolescence and Youth

It is important that society as a whole come to terms with this new generation of well-adjusted, competent young men and women, who differ from their peers in terms of sexual orientation but little else. It is also important to continue to study the course of gay and lesbian lives; clinical psychoanalytic study is critical as the premier method for understanding how these gay and bisexual men and women make sense of self and intention and maintain

Portions of this chapter appear in a different form in Boxer, Cohler, Herdt, and Irvin (1993).

an aspect of continuity over time. Such understanding has been facilitated both by studies such as those of Nemiroff and Colarusso, focusing on the psychodynamics of adult life (Colarusso and Nemiroff 1979, 1981; Nemiroff and Colarusso 1985a, 1985b, 1990), and by the accounts of analysts working with young gay men and women to understand their unique perspective (Isay 1996a, 1996b; P. Lynch 1999)

From Epigenetic to Developmental Perspectives on Adolescence and Sexuality

Abraham's (1921, 1924a, 1924b) use of the epigenetic model formulated in the several revisions of Freud's *Three Essays on the Theory of Sexuality* ([1905–24] 1953), founded at least in part on Abraham's own contributions to those essays, provided a paradigm over the succeeding half century for understanding normality and psychopathology, as well as intervention, from a psychoanalytic perspective. Indeed, Erikson's *Childhood and Society* ([1951] 1963) was an extension of the epigenetic model pioneered by Freud and Abraham from the period culminating in resolution of the nuclear conflict to the course of life as a whole. By replacing a concept of conflict with a focus on issues to be negotiated between a person and his or her caregivers and other intimate associates, Erikson sought to portray the totality of the life cycle within the model pioneered by Freud and Abraham (Vaillant and Milofsky 1980).

Erikson's portrayal of adult lives, like the epigenetic model of childhood development, is founded on a "life-cycle" perspective. Central to this perspective is the assumption of a series of issues arising out of maturational needs, to which caregivers respond in ways intended to facilitate adaptive resolutions (Hartmann [1939] 1958). Recognizing that, beginning in adolescence, social role largely replaces maturation as the foundation for forward socialization, Erikson portrayed four phases of youth and adulthood, defined like earlier life stages but determined by social rather than maturational factors: adolescence (identity versus identity diffusion/foreclosure), young adulthood (intimacy versus isolation), the "settled adult years" (Cohler and Boxer 1984) (generativity versus stagnation), and later adult life (wisdom versus despair). As in his precursors' discussions of the nuclear conflict, Erikson portrayed each of these epigenetic stages in terms of more or less adaptive resolutions.

Chapter 2 highlighted the difference between this first focus on life cycle and the emergent life-course perspective, which emphasizes not only change in psychological functioning over a lifetime but also the importance of understanding such changes in the context of both society and history. It is precisely this social definition of the course of life that distinguishes the two perspectives. Rather than stressing a sequence of tasks, the newer approach looks at transitions into and out of a series of linked social roles considered within present historical circumstances. The discussion here of gay and lesbian lives relies upon the life-course perspective described in detail in chapter 2 in seeking to understand the developmental pathways or sexual lifeways of gay and bisexual men and women from adolescence through oldest age. Psychoanalysis implicitly presumes a life-course perspective as the basis for understanding the meanings of adolescent and young adult lived experience as recounted in the life story at the outset of the psychoanalytic process.

Over the past few decades, much of the study of adolescence and sexual lifeways has focused on contrasting gay and lesbian adolescents with presently self-identified straight adolescents.[1] This study, in turn, reflects heightened awareness, both within society at large and among adolescents themselves, of the diversity of sexual orientation and lifestyle (Boxer, Levinson, and Petersen 1989; Csikszentmihalyi and Larson 1984). Initial study of the meanings of sexuality as constructed by both gay and straight adolescents has provided important findings on the impact of pubertal change on adjustment (Raymond 1994). These findings show that issues of body changes, and accompanying increased awareness of sexual wishes, pose problems for all adolescents. At the same time, adolescents are increasingly aware of the range of possible lifestyles and may be more accepting and understanding of different expressions of sexuality and intimacy than their parents' generation.

Most studies of gay and lesbian youth (and of gay and lesbian adults), however, portray slices of experience at one point in time, rather than their construction or development across time, largely relying upon retrospective methods. Asking adults about their adolescent past poses significant problems of method as a consequence of the continuing interplay of history and memory. Much of our understanding of the gay and lesbian life course has been constructed using cross-sectional and retrospective findings, inferring psychological processes across stages or age groups. For example, in the development of gay or lesbian identity, current "coming-out" schemas and ideal types are typically based on data gathered from respondents at one point in time and at varying points in this process.

Psychoanalytic study of sexual orientation must adopt the perspective pioneered in longitudinal (and, eventually, cross-sequential) study of the adult life course (Baltes and Schaie 1968; Schaie 1995). As noted in chapter 2, the developmental psychology of the gay and lesbian life course is largely a

---

1. In the present chapter, the terms "gay" and "lesbian" are used, respectively, to refer to homosexuality among boys and men and among girls and women. Some investigators (Murray 1984) use these terms interchangeably without sufficient recognition of the very different significance of homosexuality for men and women.

psychology of the presently remembered past and experienced present as recounted by men and women growing up at a particular time within a particular cohort. It is important to link studies of adulthood with those of adolescence through prospective research rather than inference. Therefore, the study of contemporary cohorts of gay and lesbian youth provides the opportunity to begin systematic investigation of individuals at a critical transition phase and to trace their development into adulthood and eventually old age. This mapping of gay and lesbian life-span trajectories will no longer rely on the reconstructed past.

The resulting picture of the course of gay and lesbian lives may be quite different from our current findings based on retrospective study. For example, previously reported gender differences in age at first homosexual experience (Troiden 1988) may be in part a result of the different cultural ideologies of men and women. Relationship and connection have been identified as more salient cultural categories for many women, whereas autonomy and differentiation have been more important for men (Chodorow 1978; Gilligan 1982); this may affect the ways in which adult men and women reconstruct the memories of their adolescent sexual experiences. Longitudinal study of gay and lesbian youth may yield a different picture, with a narrower range of gender differences.

Understood from a life-course perspective, the expanding visibility of gay and lesbian youth strongly suggests that the time has come to reassess certain key developmental concepts, including the process of coming out and the generalized concepts of "gay" and "lesbian" identity. Indeed, as Gonsiorck and Rudolph (1991) have noted, the term "coming out" is a recent coinage and stems from the work on self-acceptance by the Dutch psychiatrist Sengers (1969). In light of the first of the recent, developmentally informed investigations of homosexuality, however, these concepts now appear to have a static, ahistorical quality that will ultimately render them meaningless, unless such factors as historical time, social structure, and the individual's position in the life course are taken into account (Elder 1975, 1980). In a historical overview of adolescent studies, the sociologist Glen Elder has commented:

> Adolescence is intimately linked to matters historical: the evolution of social age categories, the emergence of youth related institutions, the impact of social change on lives. . . . In what sense can we presume to understand the psychosocial development of youth without systematic knowledge of their life course and collective experience in specific historical times? (Elder 1980, 3–4)

In studying historical changes in gay and lesbian life-course trajectories it is important to consider, for example, whether coming out in 1997 as a sixteen-year-old in Chicago is the same process as coming out in 1970 as a forty-year-old in San Francisco. Some researchers (Dank 1971; Kimmel 1978) have suggested that the 1969 Stonewall riots constitute a critical historical marker distinguishing the manner and significance of coming out for different cohorts of individuals. Moreover, to a large extent these processes have been studied independently of other life-span developmental issues. Too often we have presumed that creating a positive self-representation is the same for a middle-aged man or woman as for an adolescent or young adult (Cass 1979, 1983/1984, 1984; Plummer 1981; Herek 1985; T. Weinberg 1984).[2] A middle-aged man must reconcile the time already passed with his limited remaining time (Neugarten 1967). An adolescent, on the other hand, has yet to master the personal and social meanings of time but can look forward to his or her entire adult lifetime (A. L. Greene 1986, 1990).

Other research, reviewed by Herdt (1989), suggests significant differences in coming-out experiences between urban, suburban, and rural groups within the same historical period (see also F. R. Lynch 1987; Murray 1984; Troiden 1988). More frequently overlooked is the question of how the individual's identity has evolved in the years subsequent to the initial coming-out process.

As the student quoted at the beginning of this chapter observed, we have in large measure failed to recognize a significant shift in attitudes toward sexual orientation, and to differentiate between expectable struggles with sexuality in adolescence and the particular problems of stigma and stereotype faced by the gay and lesbian adolescent. Defining oneself as gay or straight may be less of a psychological issue than the social implications posed by this self-definition. For those adolescents self-identified as experiencing nearly exclusively homoerotic wishes adoption of a gay and lesbian lifestyle offers a positive resolution of the dual problem of increased psychological distress accompanying pubertal change and stigma accorded by society to homoerotic wishes. Study of gay and lesbian adolescents in a milieu accepting of their sexual orientation, suggests that their effort to make sense of pubertal changes and to come to terms with their sexual wishes does not differ from the personal struggles of their heterosexual counterparts.

Both historically and cross-culturally, formation of intense, intimate ties with others of the same gender, sometimes including satisfaction of sexual wishes, has been common in adolescence. Some young people ultimately rely exclusively or nearly exclusively upon a homosexual orientation as they continue into their adult years. Little is known of the determinants of exclu-

2. There are exceptions to this, such as Kimmel's (1978) studies of middle-aged and aging homosexual men, which examined certain developmental issues related to coming out, as well as the individual's position in the life cycle, in the context of cultural and historical influences (see also R. Berger 1982b; Kehoe 1986; M. K. Robinson 1979).

sive or nearly exclusive preference for intimacy with others of the same gender, of factors influencing the choice to continue such an orientation into adulthood, or of the mental health and well-being of gay and lesbian adolescents as contrasted with that of their heterosexual counterparts.

Social and Personal History and the Study of Adolescence and Youth

In few areas of study of the life course are the problems of the phenomenon to be studied and the time at which the study takes place so inextricably intertwined as in the study of gay youth. Prior to the late 1960s, discussion of a gay or lesbian lifestyle was largely taboo. While some pioneering reports, such as those of Evelyn Hooker (1965, 1967), provided important information on pathways into what is now regarded as the gay community, the few extant reports regarded same-gender sexual preference as evidence of impaired mental health. The very taboo nature of the subject provided both the foundation for reports of personal distress accompanying homosexual wish and action and the content of delusions among particularly suspicious psychiatric patients. It was unthinkable that adolescents might already have self-identified as nearly exclusively homosexual or that such self-definition might be made independent of mental illness.

The developmental study of adolescence, in general, is currently burgeoning. In part because of the increasing attention directed to its study by interdisciplinary researchers, adolescence is now the focus of varying kinds of new public attention, from both the humanities and popular journalism (Coons 1987; Spacks 1981). One example of this concern is represented by an issue of the *Journal of the American Medical Association* (26 June, 1987) devoted to research on adolescent health concerns. This accumulating body of research findings on adolescence has been useful in joining public health interventions with educational institutions and beginning to address national concerns such as teen pregnancy and parenting, substance abuse, school failure, and now, it is hoped, AIDS prevention. But none of this work has directly addressed the concerns of gay and lesbian youth. Without a "remapping" of adolescent development in the context of changing meanings of sexuality and sexual orientation for youth and society (Herdt 1989; Rust 1993), the experience and needs of a significant group of youth cannot be understood and addressed.

In spite of this neglect, a number of important findings relevant to the changing meaning of sexuality for contemporary adolescents have emerged as a result of longitudinal research. For example, evidence suggests that multiple, simultaneous transitions can be particularly stressful for adolescents (Simmons, Blyth et al. 1979; J. C. Coleman 1980). One large study found that the convergence of school transitions, pubertal development, and new social relationships resulted in particular difficulties for young adolescent girls (Petersen 1985; Petersen and Boxer 1982; Petersen, Tobin-Richards, and Boxer 1983). Longitudinal studies also suggest that while puberty may be an important "developmental organizer" for youth, the experience of puberty and its psychological outcomes are strongly influenced or mediated by the social and cultural contexts in which adolescents live (Clausen 1975; Petersen and Crockett 1985).

Longitudinal study of the adolescent epoch has shown that developmental trajectories through adolescence are quite variable. In one study of adolescent males (Offer 1969; Offer and Offer 1975), three developmental patterns were identified: continuous, surgent, and tumultuous. Such research has called into question earlier views regarding the turmoil presumed to accompany the adolescent decade and the inevitability of parent-youth conflict (Blos 1979; A. Freud [1936] 1946). This earlier perspective was founded on experience with young people seeking psychoanalytic intervention, particularly in the context of interwar European romanticization of youth. Within contemporary American and European society, many adolescents may experience time-limited perturbations in relations with fathers and mothers, but only a small percentage experience severe turmoil and conflict with their families (A. D'Augelli and Hershberger 1993; Steinberg 1981, 1985). Short-term longitudinal studies of adolescents' daily lives reveal that they may experience emotional highs and lows in different and perhaps more intense ways than adults (Csikszentmihalyi and Larson 1984; Larson, Csikszentmihalyi, and Graef 1980). The presumption of "raging hormones" resulting in a stormy and stressful adolescent phase appears to be a reality for only a small group of adolescents. Indeed, such research generally questions models of adolescent development which assume direct behavioral effects of hormonal changes without consideration of the maturational, psychosocial, and cultural processes that mediate these changes (McClintock and Herdt 1997; Petersen and Taylor 1980).

The realization that not all adolescents necessarily experience severe identity crises and accompanying turmoil has arisen on the basis of several developmental studies (Csikszentmihalyi and Larson 1984; Douvan and Adelson 1966; D. Kandel and Lesser 1972; Offer and Offer 1975). Yet the view that turmoil is inevitable persists among many of those working with adolescents, sometimes making it difficult for troubled teenagers to obtain care that addresses their particular concerns; because of this view major psychopathology may not always be differentiated by clinicians from concerns characteristic of the adolescent epoch. The needs of adolescents can only be addressed when service providers are informed by a broad understanding of development across the adolescent decade, including the complex interplay between maturational and personality processes, and the reciprocal impact of increasingly complex, socially defined expectations regarding major roles upon self-conceptions and individual well-being.

Despite these general advances, however, a developmental understanding of what is "normative" and expectable for gay and lesbian youth growing up in our society today, beyond the effects of antigay prejudice, is conspicuously missing (Raymond 1994). In understanding the problems of this group, we should consider both the nature of life changes and the means by which adolescents cope more or less effectively with such changes. Some evidence suggests that gay and lesbian teenagers are "at risk" for adjustment problems such as drug abuse, sexually transmitted diseases, physical abuse, prostitution, psychiatric disorders, and suicide (Gibson 1989, 1994; Hartstein 1996; Kourany 1987; Martin and Hetrick 1988; Roesler and Deisher 1972). For example, one recent, developmentally informed series of studies of self-identified gay male adolescents (Remafedi 1987a, 1987c, 1994a) indicates that they are at high risk for physical and psychosocial dysfunction as a result of experiencing strong negative attitudes (e.g., homophobia) from parents and peers. In addition, some of these youth reported verbal abuse, physical assaults, and discrimination.

Reviewing available findings regarding victimization of gay and lesbian youth, Di Placido (1998) and D'Augelli (1998) both expressed concern that as more young people begin to disclose their same-gender desire, and at ever younger ages, their very visibility may stir community reaction. The dilemma, as Di Placido (1998) observes, is that the belief that same-gender sexual identity must be concealed leads to continuing inhibition and psychological turmoil, while disclosing this identity may lead to discrimination, rejection by others, and even threats to personal safety. Consistent with Nungesser's (1983) observations, boys in junior high and high school disclosing their gay sexual identity may be particularly at risk for harassment and violence since gay sexual identity is perceived by the community, particularly by other males, as more threatening than lesbian sexual identity.

Questions of the relations between pubertal change and psychosocial outcomes dominated some of the earliest discussion of adolescence in G. Stanley Hall's (1904) pioneering work, which was informed, as was Freud's, by his reading of Darwin's evolutionary theory. Issues posed by Hall's study are still the subject of much research (Brooks-Gunn, Petersen, and Eichorn 1985; Boxer, Levinson, and Petersen 1989), particularly regarding the effects of pubertal timing on adolescent psychosocial development (there is marked interindividual variation both in the sequence of the appearance of such pubertal changes as secondary sex characteristics and in the time taken to com-

plete the process of pubertal change [Tanner 1971]). Pubertal changes generally take place gradually over a number of years and while, cumulatively,
these changes have an impact upon self-regard and the expression of wish
and intent, the impact is not nearly as dramatic as has been portrayed in classical psychodynamic formulations of adolescence (A. Freud [1936] 1946; Blos
1967, 1979). The relationship between pubertal changes and psychosocial
development is in fact more complex and less linear than initially assumed.
For example, most studies rate self-esteem as more negative among younger
than older adolescents (Simmons, Rosenberg, and Rosenberg 1973), with a
particularly marked drop in self-esteem among girls more likely to continue
into adulthood than a similar drop among boys (Petersen 1981). To date,
however, there has been little systematic study of pubertal and psychological
development comparing heterosexual and homosexual adolescents.

It is interesting to note that questions of pubertal status and psychological
change in adolescence were echoed as an early concern of Alfred Kinsey and
his associates. Kinsey viewed the onset of puberty and early adolescence as
important turning points, at least for male homosexuality. In his cross-
sectional sample, Kinsey found a high positive correlation between earlier
onset of puberty and occurrence of homosexuality during adolescence and
later life (Kinsey, Pomeroy, and Martin 1948, 317). This high correlation was
not found among female respondents. Kinsey linked this correlation to the
fact that the peak of sexual activity for males occurred between the ages of
sixteen and twenty; sexual behavior was thus viewed as reinforced by high
sexual drives.

Other associates of Kinsey have attempted to account for this correlation
by positing a kind of environmental-conditioning hypothesis (Gebhard
1965; Tripp 1975). This quasi theory states that boys who begin masturbating
early build a "crucial" associative connection between maleness and male
genitalia, and these in turn are linked to a set of associations which are sexually arousing. Tripp (1975) has hypothesized that these associations build into
an eroticism that is "ready" to extend itself to other male attributions and
later to a same-sex partner. Thus, heterosexual interests are preempted. The
retrospective, correlational data of Kinsey may, however, have been demonstrating a spurious correlation or, less likely, a result rather than a cause of
sexual orientation.

It should be noted that, while there has been little longitudinal study of
this issue, available findings do not suggest that pubertal timing is associated
with a higher incidence of homosexuality among youth. Rather, largely as a
consequence of social expectation, gay and lesbian teenagers become increasingly aware of being off-course in the object of their erotic desires,
rather than off-time in their pubertal development. All gay men and women

up to the present time have experienced this discontinuity. What is different today is that adolescents currently coming out now have the opportunity to integrate aspects of their sexuality with other components of their developing identities.

Sociohistorical events in recent decades have played an important role in altering the significance of homosexuality for personal adjustment in adolescence and adulthood. In the wake of the Stonewall riots and the emergence of the gay liberation movement, there developed a particular focus on the problems of gay youth together with efforts to provide community-based social support programs to assist adolescents struggling with their sexual identity. Comparison of memoirs such as that of Kantrowitz ([1977] 1996) with the account provided by Herdt and Boxer (1996) shows the remarkable change which has taken place as a consequence of the gay liberation movement, the emergence of a visible gay community, and the eventual extension of civil rights protections to gay and bisexual men and women. Indeed, the *New York Times* (21 June 1998) has reported on the emergence of a "post-gay" movement in which lesbian and gay activists have been pondering the future of gay activism as issues of antigay prejudice and stigma begin to recede and security in jobs and lifestyle increases.

Over the years since Stonewall symbolic urban communities have emerged which are characterized by homogeneity in lifestyle, residence, and services. Publications such as the *Advocate, Out,* and *Christopher Street* have helped legitimate identity as gay or lesbian and have provided timely and accurate information on subjects ranging from legal issues to AIDS. Indeed, the tragedy associated with AIDS has further strengthened ties within the gay community, as informal support services devised by caring community members have provided at least some of the care and assistance to parallel that which is customarily provided by family members (Schwartzberg 1996; Levine, Nardi, and Gagnon 1997).

The labels "gay" and "lesbian" as applied to adolescents appear to represent a unique emergence in history. It seems unlikely that groups of pre-Stonewall youth would have labeled themselves gay or lesbian, let alone had the opportunities for organized, collective socializing or socialization that some do today (Herdt 1989, 1997). What consequences this new phenomenon self-identification as gay or lesbian during adolescence will carry for later life-course development is as yet unknown. For that reason alone, developmental studies of gay and lesbian youth are a timely occurrence.

Legal and social protection won over the past several decades has enabled urban and suburban adolescents to seek understanding of their particular lifestyle through peer counseling and other informal support groups. Even public high schools in more sophisticated communities have provided staff and support services for gay and lesbian adolescents. However, little is known about the "career pathways" into a consolidated identity as gay or lesbian for these teenagers with long-term homoerotic orientations, or about the impact of different routes into a gay or lesbian identity in adolescence upon adult adjustment.

Being Lesbian or Gay in Adolescence

Increasing social recognition and legal protection of the gay and lesbian developmental course have fostered a more supportive milieu for urban adolescents predisposed to intimate relations with others of the same gender. Nonetheless, the issue of adolescent homosexuality remains little studied because of its taboo subject matter. Adolescent homosexuality is still presumed to reflect psychopathology and to be caused by sexual abuse, that is, by adults taking advantage of young people still uncertain of their own sexual orientation or constitutional vulnerability. This view is consistent with the belief, prevalent since the Enlightenment, that childhood is a time of particular psychological vulnerability and that children need a protected and measured environment if they are to grow into resilient adults. It is much more difficult for family and school to accept the possibility of a group of adolescents who early recognize their homosexual orientation and who seek a consistent lifestyle in the same manner as their heterosexual counterparts.

Youth and Sexual Orientation

Little systematic study has been reported regarding adolescents' understanding of variation in sexual orientation. While about 10 percent of adolescents self-define themselves as primarily or exclusively attracted to others of the same gender, the origins of this attraction are not clear. There does not appear to be any single, sovereign explanation for the origins of homosexuality in adolescence. Herdt (1991a, 1991b) has noted the variation in the expression of same-gender ties based on intimacy and desire which abound in our own and other cultures. Considering the "varieties" of homosexuality, and the variety of meanings constructed around same-gender sexual orientation, there seems to be little value in trying to find a common origin of homosexuality.

Continuing study by Warshaw (1990) does not support a hypothesis of childhood sexual abuse or neglect as a cause of adolescent homosexuality. Fewer than 10 percent of teens in this Chicago study (of more than two hundred gay and lesbian adolescents involved with a social service center support group) reported such earlier abuse.[3] Indeed, Warshaw reports that sexual abuse is more commonly associated with first sexual experiences among heterosexual women than among either gay men or lesbians. Regardless of stigma, stereotyping, and possible peer rejection, some adolescent boys and girls find the gay or lesbian sexual orientation to be personally compelling and satisfying. Recognizing this fact, it is necessary to study the impact of homosexuality upon personality development and adjustment into the adult years, and to find ways of providing gay and lesbian adolescents with the means to realize satisfying relationships with others.

While lacking the cross-sequential design essential in studying issues of adolescent sexuality and personal adjustment, findings reported by Boxer (1990) show that in a milieu lacking in stigma and stereotyping, gay boys and lesbian girls report little specific difficulty associated with selection of same-gender rather than other-gender partners for sexual satisfaction. More than half of the gay boys and lesbian girls in Boxer's study of homosexuality in adolescence reported marked satisfaction from their relationships. Fewer than one-fifth of these adolescents reported that coming out within the context of a homosexual encounter proved to be source of psychological distress. Reviewing findings regarding dating and romantic relationships among gay and lesbian adolescents, Savin-Williams (1995b) notes that most of these teenagers have a goal of living with a partner of the same gender for life; being in a same-gender relationship is a source of enhanced self-esteem and self-acceptance. D'Augelli (1991) has reported that more than half of a group of gay college students were living in partnered relationships, while Remafedi (1987a, 1987c) reports that a third of the students in his study of Minnesota youth were in partnered relationships and Savin-Williams (1990) reports that more than four-fifths of his sample of college youth were in partnered relationships.

In these studies of gay and lesbian adolescents, gay men were more likely than their lesbian counterparts to begin their romantic life with a same-gender partner. Boys who began relationships early in adolescence and have had several partners are more likely to publicly acknowledge that they are gay than other late adolescents choosing same-gender partners later in adolescence (Savin-Williams 1995b). Reports of initial attraction to others of the same gender varied from early childhood to adolescence itself. While a small number of gay boys reported being frightened by the realization that their

3. Issues of definition posed problems for the study of the sexual abuse hypothesis. The classic pattern is that of an adult, usually a family member, using a child for sexual gratification. This is quite different from intimacy between friends, one of whom is still in high school and one of whom is in college or working.

sexual fantasies were becoming focused on other men, this was not generally a problem for either boys or girls.

Life Story and Emergence of Alternative Sexual Lifeways

Over the course of the past two decades, the process leading to the disclosure to oneself and others of a gay or lesbian identity has been referred to as "coming out" (of the closet). The concept was fully explicated in the work of Dank (1971), referring to the fact of becoming homosexual, but as Herdt (1991a) has observed the concept is still not clear. Not only does "coming out" imply a process involving an individual rather than a cohort but also it perpetuates our Western concern with understanding the life course in terms of stages for transition into a homosexual identity (Troiden 1988, 1989). Introduction of stage and state models tends to impose artificial order on the life story and to reflect more on prevailing social expectations than on actual life experiences (McCall and Simmons 1978).

Stage models tend to reify and simplify transitions in lives, which are actually much more complex and occur over time. For example, in an otherwise sensitive portrayal of the assumption of a gay or lesbian identity, Troiden (1989) fails to consider the sequence by which gay and lesbian adolescents arrive at a self-definition as gay. However, as Boxer (1990) has shown, most homosexual adolescents go through a phase in their development in which they experiment with both heterosexuality and homosexuality before settling on a gay or lesbian sexual orientation. Boys appear more likely to experiment with first homosexual relationships rather than heterosexual relationships, before electing a homosexual identity, while girls identifying as lesbian are more likely to elect homosexuality following first heterosexual experimentation. Boxer's finding suggests that both gay and lesbian adolescents found heterosexuality to be less personally rewarding, meaningful, and intense than homosexuality. While, among lesbians, heterosexual intercourse was something that "just happened," gay boys actively sought out heterosexual experiences and then compared their response to gay and heterosexual experiences. It may be that the normative pressure toward heterosexuality in our society led these boys to check out heterosexuality in an effort to convince themselves of the inevitability of their homosexual adjustment.

Studying a group of gay and lesbian adolescents attending coming-out groups Herdt (1991a, 1991b) finds much relevance, for understanding the emergence in adolescence of a homosexual identity, in Van Gennep's ([1912] 1960) tripartite model of separation, liminality, and reaggregation. Van Gennep suggests that life-course transitions are marked by separation from the group, a period of time spent apart learning new conceptions of one's role, and, finally, reunion with the larger group, now with the new role conception learned and affirmed as a part of self. The concept of coming out, so often used in the literature on homosexuality (Plummer 1975; Troiden 1988, 1989), does not readily correspond to Van Gennep's portrayal of life-course transitions. Adolescents in the groups observed by Herdt (1997) and Herdt and Boxer (1996) had struggled for a long time before coming to the gay and lesbian services center sponsoring the group. Their willingness to enter the agency already marked a stage in the transition leading to separation from previously defined conceptions of self. Group members came to value the weekly meetings and the group for providing comfort and a time apart from the larger society. Obviously, all these issues of the transition into a homosexual lifestyle occur within a point in the course of life which is itself liminal. As Erikson (1959) has observed, adolescence in our culture is inherently a time marked by liminality and remaining apart from the larger society in order to arrive at a more clearly defined role identity.

Again, issues of acceptance both by self and others of the gay or lesbian lifestyle were a prominent feature of group discussions. Coming out involves first self-disclosure and then disclosure to friends and brothers and sisters and, ultimately, to parents. It is much less likely that either gay and lesbian youth or their adult counterparts would discuss these issues in the workplace. Comparative study of the experience of coming out among boys and girls shows that boys found it somewhat more difficult than girls to disclose their homosexuality. There was little of the organized and emergent acceptance of oneself as homosexual portrayed by Troiden's model, which progresses as follows: first, sensitization to subsequent self-definition as homosexual, then struggle between dissonant homosexual wishes and efforts to view oneself as heterosexual, followed by assuming the identity of gay or lesbian and finally committing to this sexual orientation and lifestyle as legitimate. Rather, issues attendant upon all three stages of Van Gennep's model were expressed together. The fact that separation, liminality, and reunion occurred within closer proximity than in the societies studied by Van Gennep, in which initiation ceremonies occurred over periods of many weeks or months, made it possible to continually contrast the transition taking place with participants' previous lives or the lives of straight counterparts.

Over the past several years, describing the process of coming out in adolescence has come to be regarded as less important than studying in detail how gay and lesbian adolescents negotiate issues regarding their own experience of an alternative sexual orientation. Reviewing studies reporting on sexual preferences in adolescence and young adulthood, D'Augelli (1996) reports that as many as 11 percent of girls and 9 percent of boys report awareness of same-gender sexual desire. However, a larger number of adolescents experiment with same-gender sexual expression before settling on a partner of the opposite gender. D'Augelli estimates that as many as 15 percent of both boys and girls in adolescence and young adulthood experience "nonheterosexual emotional and sexual attractions" (1996, 268).

As Savin-Williams (1995b) has observed, sexual orientation is not fixed with the onset of adolescence: there is considerable experimentation prior to establishment of a sexual identity as gay or straight in young adulthood. Further, within present cohorts of young people, an increasing number of adolescents and young adults prefer the term bisexual and acknowledge desire for both same and opposite genders. Indeed, bisexuality has emerged as a significant term for expressing both desire and lifestyle. Also, sexual identity may change across the course of life, even into oldest age. Citing figures from a Minnesota epidemiological study of sexuality in youth (Remafedi, Resnick, et al. 1992), Savin-Williams (1995b) notes that sexual activity is only one element in self-definition as gay or straight. Many adolescents arrive at this definition as a consequence of experienced desire rather than on the basis of realized sexual experience.

Two large-scale studies have been completed which focus on a cohort of adolescents coming out following Stonewall. Recruited in the mid- to late 1980s, the young people studied by Herdt and Boxer (1996) and by Savin-Williams (1990, 1997) represent urban and suburban youth. The 317 participants in the study reported by Savin-Williams were primarily college undergraduates in upstate New York who responded to questionnaires, while Herdt and Boxer and their associates (Gerstel, Feraios, and Herdt 1989; Herdt 1991a, 1991b; Boxer 1990; Boxer, Cook, and Herdt 1990; Herdt and Boxer 1996) reported on the lives of 202 adolescents, primarily high school students who participated in a drop-in program at the Horizons community service center in Chicago.

The latter group of young is noteworthy in that it includes a significant proportion of African-American (30 percent) and Hispanic (13 percent) participants. Indeed, Anglo-American study participants are a minority (40 percent) within the group. The report on the youth at Horizons is also unique in that it focuses on the daily lives of these gay and lesbian adolescents, together with the community in which they spend their time. Herdt and Boxer (1996) and Herdt (1997) view these issues within the context of contemporary cultural theory. Two additional large-scale community surveys have also been reported (Bradford, Ryan, and Rothblum 1994; A. D'Augelli and Hershberger 1993), together with studies of a much smaller group of gay adolescent boys (Remafedi 1987a, 1987b, 1987c, 1991; Remafedi, Farrow, and Deisher 1993) and of a group of lesbian adolescents, part of a larger panel of lesbian adolescents participating in a national survey study (Bradford, Ryan, and Rothblum 1994).

D'Augelli and Hershberger surveyed 194 gay and lesbian teenagers attending community survey centers nationwide; Remafedi and his associates surveyed a small group of twenty-nine gay adolescents living in the Minneapolis–Saint Paul metropolitan area and characteristic of this middle-class, Christian Minnesota community; Bradford, Ryan, and Rothblum summarize findings from a national survey conducted by the National Lesbian and Gay Health Foundation on adjustment problems and mental health needs of more than 200 lesbians, including 167 between the ages of seventeen and twenty-four. These survey findings complement and extend the more detailed studies of Savin-Williams in Ithaca and Herdt, Boxer, and their colleagues in Chicago.

Savin-Williams (1990) focused on issues of self-esteem in a psychological study, while Herdt and Boxer (1996) focused on the much larger issue of the gay youth culture within the larger community. The Horizons youth group studied by Herdt and Boxer is a self-selected group of adolescents, two-thirds of whom are in area high schools or the first year of college and who explicitly sought social support and the sense of community uniquely possible in a gay community social service agency. Significant in both studies is the atmosphere of normalcy which characterizes the participants. These are young people who are not "weird" or deviant. They do not seek psychiatric help and do not feel particularly unusual because they are gay or lesbian, although a significant number of participants in each study report incidents of insensitivity on the part of peers and teachers. Of course, study participants and their somewhat older community leaders have come of age and come out in the wake of the AIDS epidemic and are aware of the health problems posed by casual sexual contact. The participants in the Chicago study reported by Herdt and Boxer enjoyed participation in a larger gay community with an emerging geographic locus on Chicago's north-side Lincoln Park neighborhood, while the participants in the Ithaca study lived in or near a college community.

Much of the conversation in the Horizons youth groups concerns the social life of current participants, the response of parents and teachers to announcements that one is gay or lesbian, and occasionally issues of possible harassment within the larger community. Whether hanging out together at a neighborhood hamburger joint or pairing up for a Saturday night date, these teens are in many respects like their straight counterparts. They are, however, much more wary of the response of the larger society than would be characteristic of their straight counterparts. In other respects, members of the youth group are close to each other and able to talk about their feelings and desires in an articulate manner less characteristic of many of their straight counterparts. It is clear that the specter of AIDS and the problems of discrimination have together taken a toll on the innocence of this generation of gay and lesbian teenagers. At the same time, they clearly enjoy being together; the all-day (and often evening) meetings and socializing give group members strength to manage their day-to-day life in the community and at school for the remainder of the week.

The report from the Chicago study of Herdt and Boxer (1996) is ethnographic and follows in the tradition of Herdt's earlier cross-cultural study of a group he named the Sambia, who live in highland New Guinea (Herdt 1981, 1987, 1997). Because Sambia men believe that women rob and deplete men of their semen, it is necessary to arrive at adulthood with a lifetime stock, which is obtained by fellating older men and, in turn, sharing their semen with younger boys, who are themselves on the way to marriage and becoming householders. The erotic ritual of homosexuality is a part of a life course which leads into the expectable adult roles of work, marriage, and parenthood in Sambia society.

Following Margaret Mead's classic study of Samoan society ([1928] 1961), Herdt considers the homosexuality of these urban American youth in the light of the Western bourgeois presumption of youth as a time of tumult and rebellion on the way to normatively accepted adulthood. The youth in the Horizons project are not merely rebelling against prevailing norms; rather, they are pioneers in another developmental pathway through the adult life course as gay men and women. These youth report self- and public acknowledgment of their desire taking forms quite different from the coming-out models reviewed in the present discussion. Self-acknowledgment presents less of an issue than disclosing this self-acknowledged identity to others. These adolescent participants differentiate what is acknowledged to oneself from what is shared with parents, teachers, and peers.

These adolescents subtly engage in what Goffman (1959, 1963) has termed "impression management." They are skillful at discriminating in which contexts it is appropriate to acknowledge their sexual orientation. Consistent with observations of Savin-Williams (1990, 1995b), being in contexts where their sexual identity may be shared with others leads to enhanced self-esteem. Being able to disclose their sexual identity to peers was seen as a positive outcome; indeed, more than half of both gay and lesbian adolescents had made their first such acknowledgement to a friend of the same gender (the sexual orientation of that same-gender peer was less significant in the decision to disclose sexual identity).

Herdt and his colleagues (Herdt and Boxer 1996; Herdt 1997) understand this process of coming out in terms of life-course rituals as portrayed by Van Gennep and Turner and discussed in detail by Herdt (1989). Teenagers today are "betwixt and between" different social worlds (V. Turner 1967) as never before (Rust 1993) for lesbian and gay youth, this in-betweenness is represented by the ordinary heterosexual lifestyles of their parents, on the one hand, and the adult gay and lesbian community, on the other. To feel different and then direct oneself into new contexts opens up basic challenges, life crises, as suggested by Van Gennep ([1912] 1960, 21). From this cultural perspective, while adolescence more generally represents a time of liminality, when the rules are suspended with a transition from one state (childhood) to another (youth), gay and lesbian youth are particularly likely to emphasize this time "in between" in order to explore and consolidate their own sexual identity (Erikson 1958). At the same time, this cohort of gay and lesbian young adults is faced to a greater degree than their straight counterparts with coming to adulthood feeling alone and experiencing significant stigma and harassment from the larger society threatened by the struggles of these gay and lesbian adolescents and young adults. Herdt (1989, 1997) has suggested that, recognizing the stigma which persists in our society, the process of coming out is likely to be lifelong as gay and lesbian adults find means of realizing their own desires within an often hostile society.

Participants in the Horizons youth groups took great care and deliberated a long time before publicly acknowledging their sexual identities, but once they did so they reported an immediate sense of relief and improved sense of self-worth. Parents were generally informed after peers; most often, mothers were informed before fathers, in the belief that mothers would be more understanding. About a quarter of the boys and nearly half the girls reported some adverse reaction of the part of their parents, but fewer than a fifth reported any negative impact in their ability to study or their perception of their future as a result of either self- or public acknowledgement of their sexual identity.

What is particularly striking about the conversations which Herdt and Boxer (1996) report and about work more generally at the Horizons community service agency, where many members of the gay and lesbian community volunteer time and effort as professional counselors, staffers on the crisis hot line, or fund-raisers is that this pioneering generation is arriving at adulthood with a sense of purpose in which a commitment to a gay romantic and social lifestyle is but a part of a larger engagement in the world of work and community activity. The Horizons youth groups, their young-adult advisors, and the generation of now middle-aged adults who proceeded them as the first generation "out" after Stonewall is personally and professionally successful and concerned with issues of social welfare.

The group of study participants reported on by Savin-Williams (1990, 1997) differs from those in the Chicago study in being less activist within the community. Generally not living at home, these students have had a chance for a new beginning, remaking their lives within the context of a larger college community. While the Chicago study included a significant number of disadvantaged youth for whom involvement with Horizons led to the decision to continue with school and to avoid situations where personal safety and health might be compromised, the Ithaca study participants made their own community. The youthful participants in the Chicago study enjoyed the benefits of a generation explicitly and publicly acknowledging their gay and lesbian sexual identity through a yearly parade supported by the city and drawing large numbers of straight candidates for public office as parade participants.

The Ithaca study was centered around a bar which provided a haven for the local "queer" community (alternative sexualities) and a yearly picnic organized by study participants. Just as in the Chicago study, more than a fifth of study participants had significant heterosexual contact as well. Among gay men, positive self-esteem within this group was predicted by personal and academic success, perceived good looks, and close friends. Not surprising in a college community, academic success was highly correlated with feelings of enhanced self-worth. Among women, the capacity for expressing affection and understanding and being compassionate and romantic were qualities most closely related to positive self-worth; academic success, a romantic relationship, and continuing positive ties with parents were also important factors. While the teen women in the Chicago study were somewhat more explicit about the importance of sexual satisfaction in their lives, the somewhat older women in the Ithaca study were focused largely on issues of relationship, in the manner portrayed more generally for women in contemporary cohorts by Gilligan (1982).

Each of these two community studies provides important information regarding the process of coming out or the realization of a gay personal and sexual identity within a contemporary cohort of young adults. Herdt and Boxer (1996) use the term "developmental subjectivities" in portraying the processes important as persons adapt to socially defined roles and expectations, the meanings of which this process of adaptation engenders, and the mental health outcomes consequent upon their realization. In many respects this focus on developmental subjectivities continues a tradition of the adaptational point of view in psychoanalysis (Rapaport and Gill 1959) pioneered by Hartmann ([1939] 1958).

Gay men and women are confronted with the challenge of making their lives within the context of a nonnormative developmental pathway, together with the implications for morale and personal adjustment consequent upon particular solutions for this problem. At the same time, as a consequence of social and historical change, while issues of adaptation are posed, the content of this adaptation changes. Narrative reports (Fellows 1996; Hall Carpenter Archives 1989; Porter and Weeks 1991; Sears 1991, 1997) confirm the position of Herdt and Boxer regarding the importance of cultural and historical context in understanding both the challenge and response of persons with alternative sexualities. Indeed, the very concept of sexual identity presumes "culturally informed process of expressing desires in a social role and with socially shared cultural practices within a social context" (Herdt and Boxer 1996, 179).

The process of realizing a particular sexual identity, which includes both desire, or sexual orientation, and actual lifestyle, is governed both by time and place, including issues of generation or cohort, and by one's present place in the course of life. Negotiation of sexual identity is a lifelong issue which begins in childhood and extends through later life. Sexual identity is a fluid construct, not an attribute once constructed in childhood, then maintained forever. While some persons maintain a sexual identity as gay, expressing desire focused on others of the same gender through an appropriate (gay, lesbian, or bisexual) lifestyle, others may maintain a sexual identity as "straight" in early adulthood and as "gay" starting in midlife.

Coming out refers to the process leading to the first realization of a sexual identity alternative to that most generally accepted, which may take place at any age. Within contemporary society, this process characteristically is accentuated across the years of middle childhood to early adulthood. The most common pathway into an alternative sexual identity is realization during middle childhood of an attraction to others of the same gender and, subsequently, erotic experiences which confirm and strengthen this nascent sexual identity as gay, lesbian, or bisexual. As already noted, the problem with stage conceptions of the coming out process is that they reify a fluid process of a particular time and place as universal and do not account for the complex interplay between the lived experience of particular persons, their family, their friends and social context, and the particular time and place which define the meanings of erotic desire and personal development.

The young people in the Chicago study come to adolescence at a particular time, three decades after Stonewall, at a time when public recognition of homosexual identity has reached the point where the community of gay men and women has a known and protected geographic boundary, and at a time when the expression of erotic desire is conflated with a sense of danger and death due to the AIDS epidemic (Levine, Nardi, and Gagnon 1997; Odets 1995; Schwartzberg 1996; Sontag 1989). Indeed, the adolescents in

the Chicago study report an omnipresent sense of the dangers of sexual expression and of the need for careful personal protection where bodily fluids
might be exchanged. Herdt and Boxer (1996) focus less on stages than on
process within this cohort, recognizing that the process of awareness of an
alternative sexual identity within this cohort of young people is a reflection
of a meaning system within contemporary bourgeois society governing
experience of bodily states, expression of desire, and formation of ties with
others.

Most boys and girls within this cohort first became aware in middle childhood of same-gender desires, followed by more explicitly sexual fantasies
and, among most youth, overt same-gender sexual experience with a peer.
Boys have their first same-gender sexual experience younger than girls and
tend more often than girls to have first a sexual experience, later the emergence of a relationship. Significantly, both awareness of desire and even some
sexual experimentation occur before puberty, which is most often presumed
to be the point at which sexual wishes and realization of erotic desires first
arises. Significant in the Chicago study was a wide range of ages at which
there was first awareness of same-gender desire, ranging from the preschool
years through late adolescence.

The sexual fantasies of boys were more often erotic than those of girls.
Herdt and Boxer (1996) note that many of early recollected homoerotic experiences are shaped by a cultural construction, reified through the new
behavioral genetics and evolutionary psychology which attempt to explain
homosexuality as a trait adaptive for the population and presume that gay
men and women have stronger sex drives than their straight counterparts
(McKnight 1997). Youth recollecting a first sexual experience prior to adolescence recalled feeling particularly guilty about this experience because of
the shared view in our society, in spite of Freud's ([1905–24] 1953, [1909a]
1955) pioneering study, that children are not supposed to have sexual wishes
or to see sexual expression. Early pleasingly erotic childhood experiences are
followed by more clearly defined homoerotic relationships, characteristically
in early adolescence, with girls finding expression of this desire through dating and boys in more casual contact such as studying together for a test. The
overwhelming choice of a first partner was someone of about the same age.

More than half of the adolescents in the Chicago study had also had some
heteroerotic experiences while defining their own sexual identity. However,
most had by midadolescence settled on a sexual identity as a gay man or
woman. Their sexual identity was clear; less clear was how others in society
would respond to their explicit alternative sexuality. Most of these adolescents settle into a same-gender relationship with little personal conflict; the
primary determinant of their adult adjustment is the response to this alterna-

tive sexuality on the part of the larger society. For these fortunate youth living within an urban society which supports a diversity of lifestyles, as Weinberg and Williams (1974), Bell and Weinberg (1978), and Savin-Williams (1990) all have observed, there will be fewer such difficulties than are encountered by men and women in more traditional communities.

Traditionally within the psychodynamic perspectives, same-gender sexual preference has been understood either as a regressive response to the renewed conflict surrounding the nuclear (oedipal) wish with the appearance of sexual drives in adolescence (A. Freud [1936] 1946; Blos 1967) or as evidence of archaic personality elements interfering with heterosexual adjustment. Indeed, it is not just heterosexual adjustment which is troublesome among these young people. Many of these adolescents reflect impairment in the capacity for forming intimate relationships and need to feel a continued sense of excitement in order to forestall feelings of depression and personal depletion. The issue is less that of sexual orientation than that of problems in realizing closeness with others, which would leads to enhanced feeling of well-being.

The adolescents in the Chicago study, growing up in a cohort better able to express homoerotic desires than older cohorts who had to remain hidden, actively make their own history and their own lives. As Herdt and Boxer observe:

> The histories of Horizon youth suggest that they are actively choosing identities—ones which place a more positive stamp on their desires than ever before (and) suggest a new tradition of subjectification that gay and lesbian culture is providing. . . . The youth are seeing the possibilities of living with their desires . . . leading to greater creative fulfillment than they could have imagined at the beginning of the process. (1996, 201–2)

Within cohorts of urban youth at the present time, a new developmental pathway has been forged, largely by these youth who have made their own identity, in terms similar to those portrayed by the British historian E. P. Thompson (1963) in discussing the emergence of a working-class identity in the first half of the nineteenth century.

Pubertal Changes in Adolescence and Sexuality

While sexual play between boys or girls may be a feature of midchildhood realization of maturation, it also fosters enhanced desire and search for satisfaction. Further, while there has been some study of menarche and the negotiation of the girl's first menstrual period within the context of her relationship with her family (Petersen 1985), much less is known about spermarche or the adolescent boy's first ejaculation (Downs and Fuller 1991; Gaddis and

Brooks-Gunn 1985). While, among girls, there is some discussion of menarche among peers and within the family, a boy's first ejaculation is often a source of embarrassment and is not discussed among peers or within the family. The only two studies reported to date both show that boys report few feelings of distress or embarrassment following first spermarche. However, the report by Downs and Fuller (1991) reviews findings among men across the adult life course, disregarding possible cohort differences.

The report of Gaddis and Brooks-Gunn (1985) is based on cross-sectional accounts of boys in an elite and progressive high school. The authors note that there is seldom advance discussion of spermarche and that boys are most often surprised by its occurrence. They believe, however, that spermarche is less "traumatic" for boys than menarche for girls even though the experience is generally not shared with either parents or peers. Further, while attainment of menarche has important meanings for the adolescent girl and her family, with fantasies regarding complex bodily changes and the ability to have a baby accompanying this experience, the boy's first ejaculation is most often in connection with dreams or masturbation associated with wishes which may be a source of discomfort.

Although there has been little study of the issue, this may be a source of particular discomfort among boys whose first wet dream was associated with same-gender sexual wishes. Bell, Weinberg, and Hammersmith (1981) report from retrospective interviews with comparative "snowball" samples of gay and straight men and women in San Francisco in the 1970s few differences in age of first spermarche or first occurrence of a wet dream during sleep. More than a quarter of gay men (versus 3 percent of straight men) recalled a first sexual experience with a same-gender partner; more straight than gay men reported a first ejaculation in the context of a wet dream. These authors report from their statistical study little association between adult sexual orientation and circumstances surrounding a first ejaculation in childhood. Similarly, few differences in age of menarche or early sexual fantasies were reported among gay and straight women in this study; indeed, few differences were reported in sexuality among women in this group across the adolescent years.

Since the classic study of Mussen and Jones (1957), study of developmental process in adolescence has included pubertal timing in discussion of psychological development. Early maturing girls and late maturing boys are at particular disadvantage. Among early-maturing girls there are few consociates who are able to provide support; being early "off-time" is a problem here as elsewhere in the course of life. Late-maturing boys are at disadvantage in terms of physical prowess and self-image. Recognizing the problems involved in self-assessment of pubertal status, which may provide socially stereotyped estimates, Savin-Williams (1995a) recruited a group of gay or bisexual college students already completing pubertal change.

The group of men recruited by Savin-Williams (1995a) reported pubertal onset at just about at their twelfth birthday, with first orgasm occurring about eight months later, primarily as the result of masturbation. Pubertal change was associated with both awareness and enaction of same-gender sexual wishes. Early-maturing boys reported onset of pubertal change at about age eleven, while late maturing boys reported such changes only after about age fourteen. First same-gender sexual experience did not take place until about age fourteen, but the early-maturing boys reported a first same-gender sexual experience at about age thirteen, as contrasted with counterpart late-maturing boys for whom a first same-gender sexual experience did not occur until about age sixteen. However, after onset of pubertal change, few differences in terms of sexuality were reported between the early- and late-maturing boys.

Awareness and Realization of Sexual Orientation

Studies of adolescents by D'Augelli and Hershberger (1993) and Herdt and Boxer (1996) have focused on sexuality within the lived experience of teenagers. However, retrospective study of adult lives suggests multiple pathways into the awareness and realization of same-gender desire. There is some evidence that prospectively gay boys become sexually active at an earlier age than their straight counterparts. Bell, Weinberg, and Hammersmith (1981) report that a greater number of straight than gay men report a first sexual contact with another boy, although they also report less satisfaction from this first contact than was reported among straight counterparts. D'Augelli and Hershberger report first awareness of same-gender sexual desire among boys at about the age of ten. The group of boys in this study reported first same-gender sexual activity at about age fifteen, two years later than the group of boys in Herdt and Boxer's study of gay teens in a multicultural, sophisticated urban context.

While D'Augelli and Hershberger (1993) report few differences between the ages reported by gay men and by lesbians for their first awareness of same-gender desire or their first same-gender sexual experience, Herdt and Boxer (1996) report that gay boys are sexually active with others of their gender about two years earlier (about age thirteen) than lesbian teens (about age fifteen). Bell, Weinberg, and Hammersmith (1981) also note that gay women reports early sexual contact with both same- and opposite-gender partners at about the same age. Lesbian women were more likely than counterpart gay men to have experimented sexually with persons of each gender before expressing same-gender sexual preference. Boxer (1990) reports that gay and lesbian adolescents reported the same age (between eleven and twelve) as the time of first sexual awareness; however, boys reported fantasies which were more explicitly sexual than those of gay girls, which were more generally focused on closeness and sharing. Gay boys began their homosexual experience at an earlier age (thirteen) than gay girls, who began about two years later.

A small number of gay boys and lesbian girls reported homosexual fantasies but had not yet experimented with the expression of these sexual wishes within a relationship. First sexual experiences were overwhelmingly with a friend who was within three years of the age of the gay adolescent. A quarter of the boys and only about 10 percent of the girls in Herdt and Boxer's (1996) study reported being the instigator of the sexual experience, deliberately planning a liaison. For most of the boys and girls, the first homosexual experienced emerged naturally within the course of a deepening friendship. For example, one eighteen-year-old gay boy reports:

> It was beautiful. The sex wasn't planned. It was already a relationship. We'd just kissed and hugged before. I'm romantic. The relationship lasted two years. It was very romantic. I'd go to his house. We'd go out for dinner. (1996, 189)

Friendship was the most important element of the relationship for nearly half of the lesbian adolescent women but for only one-fifth of the gay adolescent men. Again, this is consistent with the culturally acknowledged role of men as more concerned with sexual satisfaction, and women as more concerned within a relationship with issues of intimacy and caring.

It is important to note that the significance of both cohort issues and same-gender sexual orientation may be different for gay boys and lesbian girls (Boxer 1990). Within the present generation of gay adolescent boys, as more generally within our culture, earlier stereotypes regarding appropriate masculine interests and lifestyles have become less effective. At the same time, it has become more permissible for women to engage in active athletic competition. The meanings of masculine and feminine in our own culture is presently being reconsidered, with increasing interest in such concepts as psychological androgyny (Spence and Helmreich 1978). At present, however, the very definition of gender in our society leads to differences in the expression of sexual wishes among men and women. A cultural construction of sexuality leads men to seek more frequent and intense sexual pleasure than women. Issues of gender-defined activity and passivity in sexual relations and the reality of sexual differences must also be considered.

There is some suggestion that same-gender sexual orientation may be a less encompassing and enduring self-definition in contemporary society, particularly among women, than has sometimes been assumed (Richardson 1981, 1992). Anecdotal reports of college women self-identified as lesbian suggest that, in time, these women may also marry and have children. The adult careers of these lesbian women are similar in some respects to those of the Sambia of the New Guinea highlands, who endorse a same-gender sexual orientation during youth while adults adopt a heterosexual orientation which fosters family formation. Gay men in our culture are less likely to marry and have children than their lesbian counterparts.

Social Life, Adjustment, and the Emergence of Gay Sexual Identity in Youth

The search for developmental continuities has implicitly characterized many investigations of adult homosexual men and women, which focus on delineating childhood correlates of adult sexual orientation. This is in striking contrast to the lived experience of many gay and lesbian adults, who require adaptive strategies for dealing with the many cultural discontinuities arising particularly from internalized societal expectations and early socialization experiences (Adams and Kimmel 1997; Bell and Weinberg 1978; Bell, Weinberg, and Hammersmith 1981; Cass 1979, 1984; Cerbone 1997; Humphreys and Miller 1980; Martin 1982; Minton and McDonald 1984; Troiden 1979; M. Weinberg and Williams 1974).

"Coming Out" as a Psychological Process

Questions of what leads to a realization of same-gender sexual orientation are particularly complex since, in the first place, such realization depends upon present understandings of this concept within the larger society (Irvine 1994). Where homosexuality is not recognized as a social category there is little effort made to define one's own sexual identity. For example, in ethnographic work in a bar frequented by African-American men seeking same-gender sexual contact it was difficult to get these men to portray themselves as gay in the terms used within the self-aware, prosperous community of Anglo men and women. It became clear that there was no term within this community for men seeking such same-gender intimacy.

Carrier (1989) and Murray (1995a, 1995b) have reported a similar phenomenon within Mexican culture, where there is no explicit generic term for men who prefer other men as sexual partners. The important distinction refers to position in sexual activity, with men electing the role of "bottom" defined as homosexual or feminine; there is little differentiation between men who prefer the top position and those who do not engage in same-gender sexual expression. Carrier's (1989) study suggests that many more

Mexican than American men have had same-gender sexual experiences and that issues of timing, availability, and cost of potential sexual partners may be the primary determinants in selecting a sexual partner. Finally, within our own culture, preference for the role of top or bottom is itself not fixed: men may play one role at one time and a different role at another time, with the same or a different partner. It is as a consequence of the effort to essentialize homosexuality that a stereotype has emerged regarding the purported sexual preferences of gay men and women. Within this culture, concepts of homosexuality and realization of sexual orientation as "gay" are most characteristic of urban men who have had some contact with cosmopolitan culture (Plummer 1995).

Within American and Western European culture, the social changes following the Stonewall riots and the advent of gay liberation both gave a name to same-gender sexual orientation and focused attention on the process leading to reflexive awareness of this sexual orientation. Since, it least initially, it was assumed that sexual orientation was biologically determined and became evident and fixed with the pubertal changes accompanying adolescence, much effort was devoted to study of the process of enhanced self-realization across the years of adolescence and young adulthood. Responding in part to the political pressure associated with an emerging social movement, a dominant or "master" narrative emerged (Plummer 1995, 82), in which the gay man or woman reported having felt different from peers since childhood, facing pressure from parent and school to conform to a heterosexist norm, rebelling against this norm, often in isolation, gradually recognizing a difference which could be put into words as being gay or lesbian (or more recently bisexual), and, after confronting oneself with this new identity, telling others, beginning with a close friend (among men often a woman friend), then brothers and sisters, mother, teachers, and, much later, father (D'Augelli and Herschberger 1993). D'Augelli and Herschberger also report that both gay and lesbian adolescents find their mothers to be more tolerant and understanding of their personal struggles than their fathers. Only about 10 percent of the gay and lesbian adolescents in their community study found their families to be supportive and understanding.

This process of acknowledgment of same-gender sexual desire, first to oneself and then to others, was given the term "coming out," the process of moving from an assigned heterosexual role learned early in childhood to a strong, positive, and accepting sense of oneself as gay (Plummer 1981, 101). It was first assumed to be intrinsic to adolescence, but ongoing study of gay and bisexual lives across the course of life has led to an increasing awareness that issues of coming out and self-acceptance may remain salient across the course of the adult years into later life. As with other stories of adversity and resilience, however, the story of coming out and of self-acceptance is not intrinsic to particular lives but is structured according to shared accounts of lived experience (Plummer 1995). It is important to locate stories of one's own lived experience within the terms of present social and historical context and within a particular culture characterized by a unique meaning system (Plummer 1981; Geertz 1973, [1974] 1983). Consistent with Plummer's (1975, 1981, 1995) perspective on the function of the master narrative for a community, learning the coming-out story from reading, from others in the community, or even from mental health professionals provides for the person searching after the meaning of enhanced same-gender desire some sense of coherence and integrity, while strengthening a sense of community among all of those sharing this narrative understanding. Particularly characteristic of present stories of becoming gay is the presumption of the dominance of heterosexist thought and thus of social stigma associated with homosexuality, which is reflected, in turn, by self-loathing among those who assume a homosexual identity. Enhanced identification with a gay community reduces the sense of personal isolation and stigma and provides enhanced social networking and support.

Within contemporary bourgeois Western culture, stories, like lives, are often portrayed in a linear manner, arranged like a novel from beginning to end (Ricoeur 1977). Lives thus portrayed are commonly divided into "phases" or "stages," analogous to the parts or chapters of a text. It is a reflection of our continuing fascination with lives that these phases or stages are presumed to provide an explanation, as if any such particular description could explain its subject. Nowhere is this more clear than in the portrayal of presumed awareness of sexual orientation. There have been four particularly clearly articulated portrayals of stages, those of Plummer (1981, 1995), extended by Troiden (1979, 1988, 1989, 1993), of Cass (1984, 1996), and of Minton and McDonald (1984), each of which, Bell, Weinberg, and Hammersmith (1981) note, regards adolescence as the point at which these stages of enhanced awareness of becoming gay are negotiated. Further, each of these stage theorists outlines a process leading optimally to a personally and publicly acknowledged existence as a person with a same-gender sexual orientation or an "identity" as a gay person (Erikson 1959).

Plummer (1981, 1995) delineates four stages on the way to a personally and publicly acknowledged gay identity: sensitization, signification, subculturalization, and stabilization. He also provides an example of the relevance of this stage conception in his discussion of present-day lesbian and gay youth in England (Plummer 1989). In the first stage people become aware of being a different kind of sexual person but not necessarily "gay." This may the most difficult stage since there is generally little social support associated with such awareness of difference. This recognition of a disruption in the usual or expected course of development within heterosexist bourgeois society, of being somehow apart from others, may lead to a discomforting sense of discontinuity in the life story or may be integrated into a life story always characterized by difference. The second stage, signification, is perhaps the most critical and may lead to greater discomfort, as persons become aware of the personal cost in a heterosexist society of adopting for oneself an identity of being sexually different.

The third phase, subculturalization, requires that a person come to terms with her or his sexuality, give a label to desire, and rewrite the life story in order to come to terms with and make sense of these sexual wishes. It is at this point that it becomes necessary to decide whether to tell others of this emergent identity as gay or bisexual, whom to tell, and in what order to tell them. Finally, in the fourth phase, persons presumably arrive at some greater sense of equanimity with their newfound identity as a gay or bisexual person within the terms of the dominant narrative characteristic of the time. This final phase, occurring within an affirming community, may be the least difficult step, contributing in significant ways to enhanced morale (Hammersmith and Weinberg 1973; Gonsiorek and Rudolph 1991).

Extending Plummer's delineation, but also recognizing Cass's (1984) contributions, Troiden (1979, 1988, 1989) has proposed a different four-stage model of coming out: sensitization, identity confusion, assumption of a gay identity for oneself, and commitment to homosexuality as a way of life. The first stage presumably occurs prior to adolescence and involves only feelings of marginality, feeling different from others of the same gender, and gender-atypical interests. However, it is only in retrospect that boys and girls become aware of this marginality, which becomes invested with new meanings; then the past is renegotiated during adolescence. This period is often marked by feelings both of confusion and turmoil and of erotic arousal in the presence of others of the same gender, awareness of stigma but a lack of knowledge of what it means to be lesbian or gay. Denial of same-gender sexual wishes, efforts to eradicate these wishes or to avoid situations where such feelings might be evoked, or even endorsement of a homophobic ideology all may be strategies employed in an effort to resolve this identity confusion. Other gay and lesbian young people redefine their awareness of dysphoric wishes as simply a temporary phase until, often after discovering that there are others with the same wishes, there is enhanced acceptance.

The third phase of this process as portrayed by Troiden is identity assumption in late adolescence or young adulthood. Defining oneself as gay or lesbian, and doing so in the company of others, is usually accompanied by increased contact with others in the lesbian/gay community, for example, through going to bars or learning that a friend is also gay or lesbian. Positive contact with other lesbian or gay friends reduces feelings of alienation and assists in management of feelings of guilt and stigma. A final stage, commitment to homosexuality as a way of life, is marked by more or less open same-gender relationships and acknowledgment of this newly adopted identity to those who may not themselves be lesbian or gay. Same-gender relationships are defined as a legitimate source of love, sexual satisfaction, and romantic attachment, and there is little regret regarding the decision to come out. There is an explicit effort to reduce stigmatizing perceptions among others, together with an enhanced effort to show that same-gender sexual orientation is but a part of who and what one is.

Minton and McDonald (1984) focus on three stages leading to a sexual identity, phrasing their program in terms of cognitive developmental theory, in which children are seen as moving from a more self-absorbed or egocentric modality to a more sociocentric modality in which their own needs are seen in the context of the larger community. They build on Plummer's portrayal of the process of coming out, as well as other portrayals in the literature (Minton and McDonald 1984, 95), and on the view proposed by Piaget, and extended by Kohlberg, of the shift from an egocentric to a differentiated understanding of one's own place in society and, optimally, to acceptance of who and what one is within the larger social world.

It is only with the advent of adolescence, and the capacity to understand the world from a more complex and differentiated perspective, that the young person is able to understand struggles earlier in childhood related to feeling different as a step along the way to becoming gay. The heightened awareness of homosexual identity, so important for Plummer's portrayal as a part of the resolution of the homosexual identity conflict, is reinterpreted by Minton and McDonald as evidence of a new awareness of society and one's place within it, leading to contemplation of general principles of social life and critical evaluation of one's place within society. Ultimately, homosexual identity is integrated with all aspects of self participating in the larger social world.

Perhaps the most detailed exposition of this stage perspective has been proposed by the psychologist Vivian Cass (1979, 1983/1984, 1990, 1996). Cass's work is informed by a perspective on the impact of stigma on lives. Cass poses a six-stage model, each stage associated with a number of possible pathways. The first stage is marked by identity commitment/confusion, in which there is a realization that one's own thoughts and actions are discordant with those of the larger society; this leads either to acceptance of a positive self-image or to a feeling that one's wishes and actions are not desirable, followed by a redefinition of these wishes and action in ways which change their meaning or that of the situation.

Regardless of the outcome of stage one, prospectively gay men and women recognize that they are part of an ostracized minority. The second stage, then, entails several possible pathways: one may choose to pursue this identity even recognizing the costs, proclaim the possibility of a bisexual or heterosexual adaptation, or, failing to resolve this dilemma, maintain a negative identity, possibly leading to suicide. The third stage, generality or tolerance, also posits a number of pathways by which one may attempt to reconcile personal needs with the demands of the larger society, with varying degrees of commitment to one's own particular identity. Stage four, identity evaluation or acceptance, reflects the process by which tolerance becomes acceptance and recognition of oneself as lesbian or gay with an enhanced self-valuation. Stage five, identity pride, results from increasing contact with others and adopting a them-versus-us perspective valuing homosexuality, perhaps at the cost of devaluing heterosexuality. Finally, in stage six, identity synthesis, feelings of anger and frustration are replaced by enhanced personal and public acceptance and recognition of the gay identity, together with the integration and self-esteem that makes it possible to also value those who are different from oneself.

In earlier work, Cass attempted to validate a four- to six-stage model using a questionnaire on sexual preference and the struggle to realize a personal and public recognition of oneself as a gay man or woman. Cass (1990) suggests that gay men and women negotiate a sexual identity in ways quite different from straight men and women due to the presence of stigma within the larger society. However, she also recognizes the inherent fluidity of sexual identity and, as a consequence, self-definition in terms of sexual orientation or preference.

Thoughts, feelings, and action are all involved in the construction of a homosexual identity, which can only be understood through appreciation of the manner in which these gay men and women make meanings out of lived experience. Cass maintains that meanings are closely tied to actions. She sees great possibility for change, even in the nature of wish or intention, as a quite deliberate activity and is among the few studying gay and lesbian lives to recognize that change in sexual orientation across the course of life is possible, although change from gay to straight is usually the consequence of a response to stigma. In this model, wish and desire are closely tied to the social circumstances in which men and women lead their lives. Attainment of a personal identity as gay or straight is closely tied to larger social circumstances which provide or deny affirmation of a gay or lesbian identity.

Affirmation by others is more important than behavioral expression and can arise even in the absence of the realization of wishes through action. In this sense, it is fantasy and self-image rather than overt expression of sexuality which is the determining factor in understanding sexual orientation and sexual identity across the course of life.

Gonsiorek and Rudolph (1991) have observed that these stage theories share certain common assumptions: a first stage is posited in which young people block recognition of their own wishes and seek to avoid acknowledgment of their sexual orientation. This is followed by a period of experimentation, leading to an increasing sense that such wishes are acceptable and normal, and eventually to acceptance of same-gender wishes and renewed positive self-regard. Depending upon prior adjustment and the extent to which social supports are available, the outcome of this process of coming out may be more or less favorable (Gonsiorek 1988). Socially defined expectations for men may accentuate the extent of the crisis experienced by adolescent boys coming out. Taboos on physical contact among men, together with the discouragement of intimacy, may lead men to feel greater discomfort than women in same-gender sexual intimacy. Consistent with this perspective, the emergence of a relationship between gay men is often characterized by sexual contact followed by romantic ties, while among women such romantic ties precede sexual expression (Gonsiorek and Rudolph 1991; Ponse 1978, 1980a; Sears 1991).

The problem with these stage models of coming out is that they are very much locked in time and place, largely reflecting the developmental experiences of a particular cohort of young people. These models are unable to account for changes taking place within the larger society which lead to changes in how sexual wishes are experienced across the course of life. As already noted, expressing same-gender sexual wishes was very different for an adolescent growing up in the south in the early 1970s and for an adolescent attending high school in New York or San Francisco in the 1990s. Reviewing findings on ages and stages of coming out, Savin-Williams (1990, 1995b) notes the diversity which characterizes contemporary youth cohorts. Findings regarding sexual awareness and experiences suggest that urban youth attain important psychological developmental milestones in recognizing same-gender sexual identity at an earlier age than young people in the rural south (Sears 1991).

Reviewing findings on gender differences in the experience of coming out, Savin-Williams (1990) notes that among adolescent and young adult women, being female takes precedence over being gay, while among men being gay is more important than being male. Political issues of feminism are also intertwined with the experience of being lesbian while political issues seem much less salient in the lives of younger gay men. Savin-Williams also reports that lesbian adolescents and young adults were more comfortable with their sexual identity than gay men counterparts. They also had more friendships with other women and were more likely to be and to remain in a love affair, more liberal and sports-minded, and more likely to have religious interests than their counterparts among gay men.

Among the first to study coming-out issues in a family context, Savin-Williams and Dubé (1998) have also questioned the value of stage models of parental adjustment to their offspring's disclosure of same-gender sexual orientation; first systematic study has suggested that there is great variation in parental response. Savin-Williams and Dubé report that many parents of adolescents were already aware that their interests were gender-atypical and had suspected the possibility of homosexuality. Findings reported by Robinson, Walters, and Skeen (1989) suggested that about a fifth of parents have some prior awareness of their offspring's alternative sexual lifeway. Parents often expressed shock and some sense of guilt or responsibility for their offspring's sexual orientation; this response appears to parallel feelings of greater shame among offspring in the process of coming out (Strommen [1989] 1993; Savin-Williams and Dubé 1998). Mothers appear more often to express guilt, while fathers more often use denial or express some feelings of rejection of their gay or lesbian offspring. Finally, DeVine (1984) has reported that young people disclose their sexual orientation slowly and carefully, first to the family member, usually a brother or sister, with whom they feel closest, then to mothers, and sometime later to fathers.

In contrast with portrayals in much of the popular literature of intense conflict among parents and their gay and lesbian adolescents following the offspring's disclosure of sexual orientation, Savin-Williams and Dubé (1998) report that few families in their study of college students had an extreme reaction, such as threatening to disown their offspring. This is consistent with findings reported by Herdt and Boxer (1996) based on their study of a drop-in adolescent group. Cramer and Roach (1988) report that when offspring disclosed their sexual orientation, relations between fathers and sons improved, with each reporting a greater sense of closeness. Murphy (1989) reported that while the majority of parents disapproved when learning of their daughters' lesbian sexual identity, when parents were able to be supportive, relations with their partners improved as well. While some parents continue to reject their gay offspring, with terrible emotional costs for both offspring and parents, most parents are concerned that they not become estranged from their offspring.

Consistent with the concept of reciprocal socialization (Hagestad 1974), some parents learn from their offspring what it is like to be gay and eventually join organizations such as PFLAG, where they receive support from other families struggling with this issue. Gay and lesbian offspring teach their parents new conceptions of the parental role, help their parents to feel comfortable with partners, and tell parents about what it is like to be part of the gay community. At the same time, and consistent with present stereotypes of gay lives, parents of gay sons often express particular concern about HIV/AIDS and health threats which their adolescent or young adult son might encounter.

Awareness of stigma, which Gonsiorek and Rudolph (1991), following Malyon (1982), regard as the primary determinant of the struggle associated with coming out, differs in its salience across cohorts and place. The advent of the AIDS crisis has provided a focus for much of this stigma expressed towards young people adopting a lesbian or gay sexual identity. Minority gay and lesbian youth face multiple stigma with regard to their ethnicity or race, their sexual orientation, and, in the case of lesbians, their gender (Espin 1993, 1997; Greene 1994; Savin-Williams and Rodriguez 1993; Savin-Williams 1994, 1996b). Studying a group of immigrant lesbian and straight women, Espin reports that the identity struggle related to becoming gay was accentuated by circumstances related to immigration and acculturation; sexism, racism, and heterosexism become confounded in the efforts of these lesbian women to realize a coherent life story.

Savin-Williams (1996b) reports similar confusion in realizing a coherent life story among lesbians within both East Asian and American culture. Savin-Williams's review of studies of gay and lesbian ethnic communities in the United States suggests that this discrimination founded on ethnic differences is even present within the gay community itself; minority gay and lesbian adolescents and adults maintain that their mainstream American counterparts don't understand their unique struggles, including the profound antigay prejudice characterizing immigrant families from traditional cultures such as those in East and South Asia and the Middle East. Caught between family expectations and their own search for acceptance as gay, young people whose origins are in these traditional communities may be particularly at risk for adverse mental health outcomes, including a profound sense of shame about their sexual orientation or suicidal preoccupation.

Models of coming out lesbian or gay implicitly assume that biological changes associated with puberty are a factor leading to increased awareness of same-gender desire (D'Augelli 1996). This perspective not only limits the importance of normative considerations of gender role–linked adolescent actions but also confines issues of coming out primarily to the adolescent decade rather than focusing on the process of attaining a gay or lesbian identity across the course of life. D'Augelli (1996) asserts that most adults who define

themselves as gay or lesbian do so by early adolescence. However, this observation merely reflects the fact that there have been few studies of sexual orientation across the course of life. Most study to date has focused on issues of
adolescent sexual orientation (Herdt and Boxer 1996; Savin-Williams 1990).

Not only do many gay men and women first become aware of same-
gender desire as adults, but also there is a greater fluidity in definition of
sexual identity than has been acknowledged in these models, which assume
an almost irrevocable transformation from uncertainly straight to gay. Many
men and women report same-gender desire in middle childhood or adolescence, then interest in a partner of the opposite gender, perhaps returning to
same-gender partnership in middle or later adulthood. Attributing this shift
simply to responses to heterosexism (Herek 1995, 1996) does not do justice
to the complexity of the search for intimacy and generativity across the
course of life.

Finally, coming-out models fail to account for variation in the manner in
which persons make sense of desire within their own life story. As a result of
turning the richness of lived experience into an abstraction, a model assuming stages, there is little opportunity for understanding the complexity of
personal experience. While gay and bisexual men and women are confronted with the task of making sense of desire that is not necessarily normative, this process need not be a source of conflict as presumed by the coming-
out model. Indeed, many adolescents and young adults in contemporary urban society do not report the struggle and search for reconciliation of desire
with expectation which is presumed by stage models.

PERSONAL DISTRESS AND SEXUAL IDENTITY IN ADOLESCENCE AND YOUNG
ADULTHOOD. In a self-conscious way, supported by their somewhat older
advisors, the urban adolescents participating in the ethnographic study of
Herdt and Boxer (1996) view being gay as "good" and are coming to adulthood with positive morale and an understanding of their sexuality as but one
aspect of their personhood. There is little evidence of the psychopathology
earlier presumed to characterize the process of arriving at a sexual identity as
gay, lesbian, or bisexual. Indeed, and of particular importance in this discussion of sexual identity and personal distress, it is important to realize that gay
and lesbian adolescents do not necessarily show greater psychopathology
than their heterosexual counterparts. Herdt and Boxer report that the participants in the Horizons youth groups did not differ from adolescents generally in their on measures of psychologic distress and resilience. Significantly,
those teenagers who had received affirmation and support for being gay or
lesbian reported less distress than those who felt more isolated.

There is also a complex interplay between mental health and sexual orientation in studies of gay and lesbian adolescents: in general, adolescents from

middle-class families, whether gay or straight, experienced relatively fewer stressful untoward life changes than lower-class counterparts or adolescents from families tracing their origins to such traditional cultures as East Asia (Savin-Williams 1996b). Adolescents publicly acknowledging their sexual orientation generally appear to be better able than those who remain more secretive to maintain a sense of positive self-worth, although public acknowledgment too early in adolescence appears associated with less positive mental health outcomes (Savin-Williams 1995b). Savin-Williams (1990) finds, based on his study of similar but somewhat older members of this cohort, that students from upper-middle-class professional families who were permitted to affirm their gay identity in the context of a supportive community reported higher self-esteem. This is in contrast to prior cohorts where, as a consequence of stigma, more explicitly visible persons in the community were forced to disguise their sexual identity.

The Chicago study (Herdt and Boxer 1996) and, to some extent, the Ithaca study as well (Savin-Williams 1990, 1997) reflect the emergence of a new developmental pathway for gay men and women marked by a self-conscious effort to make a new identity, not as secretive, isolated, guilt-ridden gay men and women but as self-affirming and vital members of a publicly acknowledged community in which sexual identity is but one aspect of its members' lives.

There is a pervasive stereotype within the larger community of wide-scale psychopathology among youth seeking an alternative developmental pathway that involves asserting an explicit sexual identity as gay, lesbian, or bisexual. This stereotyping and the resulting stigma poses more problems for young people than any struggle with awareness of same-gender desire. The young people in Herdt and Boxer's (1996) study well express the problems encountered with parents, themselves confused regarding their children's sexual orientation, and the heterosexism and even hostility expressed by teachers and school administrators (Martin 1998). One college student, seeking psychotherapy with one of the authors as a consequence of continuing conflict regarding his sexuality, reported:

> I finally decided last summer that it was time to tell Mom and Dad what was going on. . . . I had known for several years that I was gay, that I found some guys really attractive. . . . [David and I] had met at high school that year while working in the theater, and we were like one; our sex was incredibly wonderful. I was walking on air . . . but knew I had to tell my parents what was going on. So, while sitting around after dinner one evening . . . I told them I had something to tell them, that I was gay and that David and I were lovers.
>
> My mother, who teaches at my high school and knows David from class, burst into tears, shouted that I was not her son, that she could not bear having me at her school and have everyone know I was gay, and ran into the house. I could hear her sobbing. My father, who is a surgeon, at first said nothing, then

sighed deeply and said he would have to get used to my dying since I was bound to get AIDS. I left the house in disgust and rage. . . . It really affected my relationship with David and my sense of myself. Now I don't know what to do. It's not the gay thing, I really like that part. . . . Why can't people accept me for what I am?

This warm and caring young man, successful in his studies, a leader in several college organizations including the gay and lesbian student alliance, and deeply in love with his friend David, who attends another college in the same community, has suffered from the stigma expressed by parents and high school teachers. He sought counseling in an effort to deal with feelings of being hurt and rejected by his family, with whom he continues in a relationship marked by intense feelings on the part of each generation.

Without doubt, some adolescent confusion regarding sexual identity does reflect deficits in personality development, and may accompany other problems such as pervasive difficulties in making friends, conflict with family, and recurrent substance abuse. Lifestyle then becomes one more avenue in which rebellion may be expressed.[4] These more troubled adolescents must be differentiated from another group of young people who report being sexually attracted to others of the same gender from as early as they recall explicit sexual awareness. Some in this latter group recall same-gender sexual fantasies from their nursery years, while others first became aware of such wishes just prior to adolescence. However, regardless of the time of first awareness of same-gender sexual preference, by mid-adolescence these young people have chosen a lifestyle emphasizing same-gender sexual orientation, even though they may have had little or no actual sexual experience with either the same or the opposite gender.

These young people adopting a gay or lesbian lifestyle show little of the explicit impairment in their ability for realizing close relationships with others which has been assumed in much of the mental health literature. They have a number of friends with whom they can talk about fears, hopes, and dreams, and they relate well to adults, family, and peers. In the majority of families, where parents are able to accept the teenager's sexual orientation,

---

4. In recent years, there has been much discussion of the urban runaway. As a consequence of conflict with family and community, these young people leave home without permission or advice, often finding their way to socially disorganized areas of large cities. Stereotyped conceptions of the runaway lifestyle emphasizes heavy use of drugs and both heterosexual and homosexual prostitution. While some of these adolescent runaways show personality disorganization and psychopathology (J. C. Coleman 1980), others are simply fleeing from family patterns of neglect and abuse and return after a period of protest marked by physical absence. Boyer (1989) has shown that at least some young men engaging in homosexual prostitution are seeking affirmation of their gay identity using the only means which they presently know for contacting persons of similar lifestyle. With increased acceptance of the gay and lesbian adolescent and provision of appropriate support systems, the use of homosexual prostitution as a pathway into a gay identity should diminish.

and provide support for the development of age-appropriate intimacy with same-gender peers, good relations are maintained (Boxer 1990). Where problems have arisen, it is primarily the consequence of stigma rather than of deficits in the capacity for closeness or for soothing of tension states.

In the main, gay and lesbian adolescents do not fit stereotypes such as those advanced by Green (1987), who characterized many homosexual young men as effeminate. Again, cross-dressing and other transvestite behavior must be differentiated from the wishes and lifestyles of gay and lesbian adolescents. Much of the psychopathology attributed to the gay adolescent is a consequence of the stereotyping and homophobic preoccupations of their peers, teachers, and parents, who do not understand that gay and lesbian adolescents differ from same-age peers in little other than sexual orientation.

Harassment and Sexual Identity

A number of studies (Berrill 1990; D'Augelli and Herschberger 1993; N. Evans and D'Augelli 1996; Herek 1991; Hetrick and Martin 1987; Locke and Steiner 1999; Remafedi 1987c; Savin-Williams 1994) have noted the problems faced by gay and lesbian adolescents at school and in the community as a result of stigma and harassment. Remafedi (1987a) reports that more than half of his community group of gay teen men had suffered peer verbal abuse and more than a third had been physically threatened. D'Augelli's (1996) review of the development of gay and lesbian adolescents and young adults reports a number of studies showing rates of victimization in excess of half of those interviewed. Anecdotal reports from youth seen in drop-in programs (Martin and Hetrick 1988; James 1998) indicate similar problems of verbal and physical abuse on the part of classmates. Hershberger and D'Augelli (1995) review additional retrospective reports suggesting that verbal and physical harassment has been a long-standing problem for both gay teens and adults.

Gay and lesbian youth report problems with both peer and adult harassment. Peer verbal harassment is a source of particular distress for these adolescents, who share their classmates' concern for peer acceptance. Martin and Hetrick (1988) note that peer harassment was among the most frequent sources of distress among the several thousand teenagers visiting their urban help center. Similar reports of frequent verbal harassment by peers are reported in the more homogeneous small group of participants in Remafedi's (1987a) Minnesota study, and in Sears's (1991, 1997) report of growing up in the modernizing south in the postwar years through the 1970s. Even college youth report peer harassment (N. Evans and D'Augelli 1996; D'Augelli

1991; Hershberger and D'Augelli 1995); references to "fags" or jokes about homosexuals by teachers or peers can be interpreted by gay and lesbian adolescents as personally painful. Savin-Williams (1996b) recounts the problems for lesbian and gay adolescents of dating others of the same gender. Heterosexual dating has long been a marker of peer popularity. Lesbian and gay adolescents report concern about both being appropriate with peers and having to "fake" interest in the other gender for fear of harassment.

Anecdotal reports such as those of Fricke (1981) and Shyer and Shyer (1996), together with the life stories recounted by Sears (1991, 1997), provide detailed evidence of the personal cost of having to feign such interests and the attendant problems of not being able to perform in the sexually expectable manner when on a date. Several studies (D'Augelli 1996; Hershberger and D'Augelli 1995; Herdt and Boxer 1996; Savin-Williams 1996b) have reported that lesbian and gay youth go through a period of attempting heterosexual dating and even sexual intimacy before recognizing that this social and sexual conformity provides little sense of satisfaction or self-worth. Same-gender dating, however, presents the danger of additional harassment from peers. With few opportunities for same-gender dating, relations with other lesbian or gay adolescents tend to be secretive and guilt-ridden. These problems exacerbate the isolation and harassment many gay and lesbian adolescents report.

Hershberger and D'Augelli (1995) rely upon a structural modeling approach to show that support from family and feelings of acceptance and self-worth provide a buffer against the otherwise personally destructive impact of harassment. These findings are consistent with Meyer's (1995) study of the impact of experienced stigma more generally within the lives of gay men. Hershberger and D'Augelli also show that the experience of harassment and verbal abuse by peers is associated with suicidal attempts in youth.

Adult verbal harassment is also a source of distress for gay and lesbian adolescents and young adults. The problem of parents troubled at learning of their offspring's sexual orientation all too often leads to rejection and verbal accusations. This discussion has already reviewed information regarding heterosexism and the discomfort faced by gay and lesbian students. The combination of parental, teacher, and peer harassment poses a serious problem for the mental health of gay and lesbian adolescents totally independent of personal issues of sexual orientation. Reviewing findings from many studies, it becomes clear that most gay and lesbian adolescents and young adults are comfortable with their sexual orientation and have little interest in changing. They find meaning and satisfaction from relations with gay and lesbian peers and seek only the same acceptance as their straight counterparts. It is the stigma and hostility of the larger society, so often intolerant of ways of life different from those presumed to be typical, rather than experienced gender dysphoria which is the source of much of the personal distress that these young people report (Hetrick and Martin 1987; Martin 1982; Martin and Hetrick 1988; Savin-Williams 1994, 1995b, 1996c, 1997).

Society and the Problem of Self-Worth among Gay Adolescents

Hershberger and D'Augelli (1995) report that family support plays a critical role in reducing feelings of victimization and personal distress related to being gay in mid- to late adolescence. Family acceptance fosters enhanced feelings of self-worth, which is the critical determinant of positive adjustment for lesbian and gay adolescents. Unfortunately, self-help groups such as Parents and Friends of Lesbians and Gays (PFLAG) are generally not seen as a resource among those families who most need such support. A 1989 report of the United States Department of Health and Human Services makes clear the magnitude of this problem: nearly all students in American public high schools hear homophobic remarks as many as twenty-five times a day, 80 percent of gay and lesbian adolescents report experiencing social isolation, and more than 10 percent report physical attack from parents on learning that they are gay.

Even more sobering, more than four-fifths of teachers admit to very negative attitudes towards homosexuality and more than three-quarters of teachers polled would actively discourage any discussion of homosexuality in their classroom. Savin-Williams (1990, 1995a) notes that at least some of this negative sentiment is a reflection of the attitudes of the larger community: teachers fear parental retaliation should topics of alternative sexualities come up in their classrooms. The specter of HIV/AIDS has contributed to the experience of stigma among gay and lesbian youth and to even greater repression of discussion of sexual identity in school. One teenager reported that after learning he was gay, his homeroom and English teacher admonished him not to touch anything in the classroom lest he give AIDS to her or to other students!

The participants in Herdt and Boxer's study (1996) testified to the impact of such heterosexism on the part of teachers and peers on their own feelings of self-worth. While both girls and boys who had publicly acknowledged their sexual identity felt accepted by their own cliques, they believed that other students and, particularly, teachers were critical of them for being gay or lesbian. While it is commonly assumed that fellow students, struggling with their sexuality, would be particularly threatened by openly gay or lesbian classmates, Herdt and Boxer's findings suggest a cohort shift. Adolescents appear better able than their elders to accept diversity in lifestyle and ethnicity.

These problems of heterosexism and stigma do not end with the transition to postsecondary education. Evans and D'Augelli (1995) review findings from a previous study in which, among openly gay and lesbian college students, more than three-quarters had been subjected to harassment or homophobic remarks. Homophobia was particularly strong among undergraduate men, nearly half of whom thought gay students should not be admitted to college; more than four-fifths of straight students acknowledged making homophobic remarks (D'Augelli and Rose 1990). While these students, in their first year of study, were enrolled at a university which draws significant number of students from socially and culturally homogeneous semirural communities, many of the attitudes they conveyed are expressed to some extent in most colleges.

Media exposure and contact with diverse cultures within a larger urban public school is important in fostering enhanced tolerance for others within this recent cohort of young people. In the years since the detailed studies of Savin-Williams (1990) and Herdt and Boxer (1996), carried out in the late 1980s, gay and lesbian characters have become increasingly prominent on television and in motion pictures. When the popular television sitcom *Ellen* had its title character (and the actress herself) publicly announce her lesbian sexual identity, her struggles and successes became the talk of both high school and college classes. Variation in sexual identity is much less hidden than even a decade ago. Characters' gay and lesbian identities are increasingly being portrayed as merely a matter of lifestyle, in contrast with earlier portrayals which featured predominantly gay men infected with HIV, as in the film *Philadelphia*.

Considering the climate of stigma and heterosexism within community and school, surprising that being gay, lesbian, or bisexual in high school should pose particular problems. Herdt (1997), Remafedi (1994a), and Herdt (1997) all note the problems resulting from this discrimination. For example, failure to support same-gender dating among gay boys and girls may lead to a separation of sexuality and caring within relationships. In an effort to seek satisfaction for pressing sexual tensions, gay boys in particular may turn to anonymous sex because of the difficulty in finding appropriate partners in a setting where public acknowledgment of sexual orientation would be considered dangerous (Remafedi, Farrow, and Deisher 1993). Adolescents able to publicly acknowledge their alternative sexual orientation enjoy enhanced self-esteem (Savin-Williams 1995a); those forced to hide or to deny their own lived experience as self-acknowledged gay or lesbian pay a high cost in having to disavow a significant aspect of their identity (Sears 1991).

Being Gay or Lesbian and the Problem of Youth Suicide

Among adverse mental health outcomes associated with the stigma and stereotyping experienced by gay, lesbian, and bisexual adolescents, none is more tragic than suicide. For example, an activist gay teenager, Jacob Orozco, hanged himself just six days into the school year when the Salt Lake City school board continued to harass his gay-straight youth alliance (*Windy City Times,* 18 September 1997, 11). The death of this student highlights the consequences of stigma in contemporary society. Herdt and Boxer (1996) report that about 30 percent of the girls and 20 percent of the boys in their study of lesbian and gay adolescents reported making at least one suicide attempt prior to joining the Horizons youth groups. D'Augelli and Hershberger (1993) report that at least 60 percent of their group of gay and lesbian adolescents reported thoughts of suicide (comparative figures for straight adolescents were not provided for this study).

Savin-Williams (1994) emphasizes a problem endemic in contemporary bourgeois society, in which the experience of estrangement, stigma, and even verbal and physical harassment, including that from parents and other family members, leads lesbian and gay adolescents to suffer feelings of lowered self-worth leading to attempted suicide. Feelings of being overwhelmed, depressed, and anxious and experiencing low self-esteem were connected with the wish to take one's own life, as was lack of understanding on the part of parents and the feeling that the adolescent must hide his or her sexual orientation (fewer than a quarter of this group felt comfortable publicly acknowledging their sexual orientation). Evans and D'Augelli (1996) review findings showing that nearly two-thirds of lesbian adolescents have attempted suicide; the experience of stigma exacerbates the problems of growing up female faced by adolescent girls. Finally, as in Remafedi's (1991) report, feelings of lack of acceptance and understanding on the part of parents were the most frequent factor associated with suicidal ideation. Clearly, parental acceptance and understanding provides an important protective factor in reducing the risk for youth suicide.

Similar figures regarding suicide attempts among gay adolescents, ranging between a fifth and a third of all self-identified gay teenage boys, have been reported by Bell and Weinberg (1978). D'Augelli (1996), D'Augelli and Hershberger (1993), Gibson (1989), Kourany (1987), and Remafedi (1991), and Remafedi, Farrow, and Deisher (1993). Gibson (1989) report that gay and lesbian adolescents are up to three times more likely than their straight counterparts to attempt suicide, largely as a consequence of stigma experienced at home, at school, and in the community. D'Augelli (1996) and Remafedi, Farrow, and Deisher (1993) note further that problems between gay adolescents and their families appear to be major precipitants in nearly half of all reported suicide attempts among gay teens (Remafedi 1991). However, as Schaffer et al. (1995) caution, we should not presume that suicide attempts are a common characteristic of gay youth.

Suicide attempts among gay and lesbian youth, as among children and adolescents at risk more generally for suicide, may also reflect endemic problems within dysfunctional families in which issues of sexual identity as such are but one of many unsettled areas (Schneider, Farberow, and Kruks 1989). The difficulty of establishing a gay or lesbian sexual identity may also be compounded by problems associated with one's particular ethnic identity (Rotheram-Borus, Hunter, and Rosario 1994; Rotheram-Borus, Rosario, et al. 1995). Struggling with the issue of growing up in a minority ethnic group may further compound problems in maintaining a sense of who and what one is as an adolescent and across the course of life (Lewinsohn, Rohde, and Seeley 1994). These authors note that being gay or lesbian within ethnic minority communities has a particularly adverse impact upon mental health which is separate from problems otherwise associated with being a minority youth. These youth engage in risky sexual behavior, such as unprotected intercourse, and substance abuse at rates which appear to remain stable over time. The rates of problem behaviors among gay and lesbian youth are no greater than those reported in studies of other disadvantaged youth (Remafedi 1987a, 1987c, 1991; Roesler and Deisher 1972), but are further compounded by ethnic minority status (Epsin 1993, 1997; Savin-Williams 1996b).

Conclusion

It is important that future study of homosexuality in adolescence be approached with the concepts and methods of life-course social science. Concepts of social timing, careers and sequencing, and transition into a role identity as gay or lesbian must be studied over time and across cohorts. The dramatic impact of social and historical context on major life transitions of a particular cohort is particularly salient. Longitudinal life-span investigations (employing both predictive and interpretive methodologies) not only will have an impact on our understanding of vulnerability, resilience, and well-being for gay and lesbian youth and for adults, but also will have important implications for models, methods, and theories used in the study of lives within the social sciences (J. A. Lee 1987).

D'Augelli (1996) has noted that more lesbian, gay, and bisexual adolescents are now choosing to publicly acknowledge their sexual orientation and, given an atmosphere of increased acceptance of variation in sexual identity, choosing to do so at ever younger ages. This cohort of gay youth is particularly psychologically aware of the issues involved in being lesbian or gay, and has had the advantage of being able to confront these issues in their lives for a longer period of time than in prior cohorts. Greater discussion of the issue of sexual orientation, including more frequent portrayal of gay and lesbian characters in television sitcoms and in films appealing to a mass audience, have further pushed these issues into public awareness. As a result, it is very difficult for gay and lesbian youth in the present cohort to suppress or disavow their own desire.

From the vantage point of study of the life course, there are some critical questions which have emerged from our current knowledge regarding gay and lesbian youth. For example, what happens to adolescents after they have traversed the phases outlined by stage theorists of the coming-out process? How do gay and lesbian youth further negotiate their relationships with mothers and fathers during young adulthood, well after having come out to family members (Savin-Williams 1989, 1990, 1995a; Boxer 1990; Boxer, Cook, and Herdt 1990; Herdt and Boxer 1996)? How will the differing biographies and self-representations of "Jose" and "Pedro" in Mexico, elaborated by Carrier (1989), evolve as adults? How and in what form will the young lesbian discussed by Schneider (1989) create the life she desires as "normal and gay" (Schneider 1989)? More generally, what we do not yet know is how the experiences of gay and lesbian youth are evolving through the course of adolescence, how continuity and change are prefiguring their lives, how resilience and vulnerability are at work.

It is still not clear how the life experiences of present gay and lesbian youth may differ from those of gay and lesbian teenagers who have grown up in different settings and historical periods. For that matter, it is not clear how gay and lesbian adolescents differ from their heterosexual contemporaries. Is the normative adolescent "storm and stress" exacerbated among these youth? It is important to be sensitized to variations in development as a function of cultural and ecological factors (Barker 1968; Bronfenbrenner 1977), what used to be called the individual's "total life space" (K. Lewin [1946] 1964).

We are left, though, with the question of what happens to these youth over time: How will adulthood be affected by adolescent experiences within a particular cohort? More specifically, how will coming out in the current sociocultural and historical context shape expectations and hopes for the future (Irvine 1994)? How will intimacy, sexual expression, and friendships develop within a cohort of youth coming of age during the AIDS crisis and knowing no other historical context of life experience? How does a teenager's initial life adjustment to coming out relate to later outcomes, to patterns of achievement and cultural competence, to resilience and vulnerability during the time of young adulthood? How do those who fall victim to physical or emotional abuse because of their sexual orientation negotiate relationships later in adult life? Does the specific context of individual socialization into gay and lesbian communities relate to patterns of successful aging and life satisfaction during middle and later life? What kinds of effects do gay and lesbian-sensitive service providers have on the youth who make use of these, albeit limited, services?

Problems in talking to parents, together with verbal and often physical attack from peers at school and in the community, take their toll on feelings of self-worth among gay and lesbian adolescents. Bradford, Ryan, and Rothblum (1994) report that more than two-thirds of the lesbian adolescents in their survey study reported seeking counseling, while Remafedi (1987a, 1987c) reported that more than three-fourths of the adolescent and young adult gay men in his survey had sought counseling. Much of this need for service is directly related to problems of stigma and harassment within the community, together with lack of parental acceptance. At the same time, as Hershberger and D'Augelli (1995) have cautioned, many of the problems of depression and diminished sense of self-worth are no different from those among young people not defining themselves as gay or lesbian. Issues of stigma and harassment simply add to the already stressful life circumstances faced by young people in contemporary society.

The rise of AIDS both as an illness and as a historical context makes coming out in the 1980s unlike any other time in recent history. While we tend to associate the cultural ethos of AIDS only with individual illness outcomes, it is also part of a general cultural and historical context for both male and female adolescents. In a study of two hundred gay and lesbian youth in Chicago (Boxer, Cohler et al. 1993), one gay male adolescent, Marc, said in response to the question of how AIDS had affected his coming out:

> It has politicized me. It forced me or sobered me. I came out at a critical time. Six months earlier if I had come out, I might have gone through a slutty period. In my case it wasn't an option. People I met were into getting serious, not just dating. The tone of the community was alert and cautious. My sexual behavior didn't change. It's been consistent.

This young man's experience, inevitably, is both similar to and different from that of a gay man who grew up twenty years or even ten years earlier. In response to a question about his feelings regarding coming out he said:

> There was an awareness that things aren't always the way you are told they are. It's like being an expatriate in another country and you can view your own country from that distance. The isolation I experienced in being gay and feeling there was no one to go to resulted in my mustering up my own resources. Mustering up that fiber once was important.

Marc's perceptions on his own development highlight the importance of examining the impact of historical and cultural changes on the course of lives. This man discussed his relative ease in being open with others about being gay, after some initial reticence, while at the same time drawing on social support from "role colleagues" that he met at a gay and lesbian youth group, a setting quite different from what he would have encountered ten years earlier. He is also aware of the danger and constraints which AIDS has created. So while there is a component of danger to life associated with the expression of sexuality, there is also the opportunity for the expression and consolidation of his gay identity.

The cultural context of AIDS, obviously, has affected women as well, and may hold different meanings for them than for males. Jana, a lesbian youth in the Chicago project, put it this way:

> I'm concerned about it not only because males are getting it, but also because lesbians are getting it. . . . A friend of mine died of AIDS. We were really close. He was like seventeen. When he died I didn't know much about it. It really did scare me. Friends would say he was a fag, that's why he died of AIDS. It still scares me but not as much as it did before. I'm more educated so I feel a lot better about it. It's hard with lesbians—how do you have safe sex? I'm not sure what lesbians can do. I'm about as safe as I can get.

This cultural context becomes not only a fear of death and "plague" but also an adverse life event for peers, like Jana, who may experience various aspects of loss, grief, and bereavement.

It is important that both services provided for gay and lesbian adolescents and the study of these youths' adjustment across the adolescent decade include the family. Boxer (1990) and Boxer, Cook, and Herdt (1990) have provided important first findings regarding the manner in which gay and lesbian adolescents communicate their sexual orientation to their families. These findings point to a complex process of communication in the family marked by continuing efforts by each generation to influence the other. Adolescents socialized their parents into new conceptions of sexuality, while parents often communicated particular concern regarding their offspring's use of condoms as a part of their sexual behavior.

Mothers of both gay and lesbian adolescents maintained relationships with their offspring similar to their past relationships while, unexpectedly, the father-daughter tie was more often disrupted than that between fathers and sons. Where there was disruption in the mother's tie with offspring, Muller (1987) has reported that this disruption also occurs more often with daughters than with sons. In spite of the fact that the women's movement has provided a rhetoric of acceptance which ought to facilitate acceptance of a daughter's sexual orientation and lifestyle, it appears that both parents have particular difficulty with their daughter's adoption of a homosexual orientation. This may be related to disruption of parental hopes for a grandchild. This was an issue posing problems for parents of both sons and daughters and may be a more general issue in contemporary society, as marriage occurs at ever later ages and many adults decide to postpone or avoid parenthood. Again, only cross-sequential study, following groups of both homosexual and heterosexual adolescents in more than one cohort over time, will resolve this issue of the role of parental expectation in the course of intrafamily relationships.

There is little existing research on the development of gay and lesbian adolescents into adulthood. One exception is Lee's (1987) study following a group of middle-aged homosexual men for four years, examining aspects of their adult development and aging. Such study would help answer questions regarding the outcomes of youth who may be at risk for various biological, social, and psychological stressors. The relationship between life satisfaction and successful aging can also be examined by repeated study of cohorts of youth moving into adulthood. AIDS is now an especially critical factor to be considered. The use of longitudinal methods would provide an ideal way of delineating the psychosocial impact of AIDS on youth coming of age during the current epidemic (D. A. Feldman 1988; Millan and Ross 1987). The needs of groups of lesbians and gay males can only be determined through an assessment which examines changes in lifestyle, behavior, and development over time.

The concept of life course, which is socially structured, must be differentiated from such terms as life cycle or life span, which refer only to change over time, without consideration of the normative cultural element implicit in making sense of such change. It is clear that age as a chronological marker is of little significance for the study of the life course, except as represented by the socially shared biological and psychological meanings attached to particular ages and age changes across the course of life. Without such cultural and historical knowledge, age itself becomes an "empty" variable in the study of lives (Neugarten 1996). It is precisely this social definition of the course of life which transforms the study of the life span or life cycle into the study of the life course.

The present generation of gay and lesbian adolescents is confronting their sexuality and their relations with others in ways different from preceding generations. Absent at least some of the prior stigma, it is now possible to study such psychological stress and lowered morale as may be associated with selection of a particular sexual orientation and lifestyle apart from stigma and stereotyping. Life-course study, emphasizing cross-sequential research designs to evaluate the impact of generation, cohort, and place in the course of life, is essential in order to realize a revision of our current developmental understanding of gay and lesbian youth.

The first such studies of the contemporary cohort of gay and lesbian young people, informed by life-course perspectives but necessarily retrospective and anecdotal, suggest the need for revision in our understanding of mental health and adolescent homosexuality. There seems to be little explicit impact upon mental health resulting from selection of a homosexual orientation, which is different in its impact from the selection of a heterosexual orientation. To date there has been little systematic comparative study of heterosexual and homosexual adolescents; however, findings from the study of a group of gay and lesbian adolescents in Chicago (Herdt 1997; Herdt and Boxer 1996) show that the overwhelming majority (more than 80 percent) report little psychological distress accompanying the first actual homosexual experience. Where stigma and stereotyping are reduced, homosexuality itself does not appear related to increased personal distress. While clinicians encounter adolescents whose adjustment has been adversely affected by the possibility of a gay or lesbian sexual orientation and lifestyle, it is important not to generalize on the basis of this group of more troubled adolescents seeking mental health services.

Future studies will almost certainly lead to remapping gay and lesbian adult life-course trajectories (Herdt 1989, 1997). The developmental perspective can be a useful framework from which to examine the effects and interrelations of historical time and sociocultural context on individual development. This requires use of both quantitative and qualitative research strategies to better understand a previously hidden and neglected group of youth. Many past research findings, based on cross-sectional samples or retrospective methods, may be radically altered by studying lives over time.

Young adults today must negotiate a complicated series of decisions in the sequencing of events in the transition to adulthood (Greene and Boxer 1986). During late adolescence school, career, and family-related decisions appear to be interwoven, making late adolescence and young adulthood a time in which there is often a pileup of role changes. Gay and lesbian adolescents are faced with negotiating these decisions, as well as those related to the meaning, management, and expression of their nonnormative sexuality. The construction of personal expectations and anticipations for the future life course may be a unique developmental task for these youth (Raymond 1994). The first generation of gay and lesbian youth currently coming of age during the AIDS crisis are likely to become some of those with the longest lifetime histories of a gay or lesbian identity to date. It is now time, we believe, to embark with them as consociates, in developmental studies, as they grow up, enter adulthood, and grow old.

Issues raised in this discussion pose questions regarding methods presently used to study gay youth, including the validity of reliance on respondents' recollections of their childhood and adolescent experiences; inferences about developmental processes and outcomes made on the basis of cross-sectional samples; the time-specific, cohort-bound nature of many previous constructs and findings; and the persistent search for continuities between childhood gender behavior and adult sexual orientation. In consequence, the emerging body of theory is largely a developmental psychology of the remembered past. Strategies like those suggested here for longitudinal, prospective research on homosexual adolescents, shifting attention from child-based "casual" models to adolescent and adult-centered perspectives, may lead to important new understandings of the development of gay youth. Aimed at understanding life changes and the developmental processes and course of negotiating them, longitudinal methods will more accurately reflect the current experiences of gay and lesbian youth coming of age in a unique historical context. Findings from studies of the life course have direct implications for modification of current developmental theories, particularly those that inform gay- and lesbian-sensitive clinical services for all age groups.

The life-course perspective has highlighted the significant social changes, across the postwar period, which have affected our understanding of sexual orientation and its place across the course of life. At least within contemporary cohorts of gay and lesbian adolescents and young adults, it is clear that sexual orientation and identity itself need not pose problems for adjustment or mental health, and that being gay is but one aspect of the process of becoming adult and settling into the world (Cohler and Boxer 1984). For young people fortunate to grow up in communities that are supportive and understanding of variation in sexual orientation, there is little report of personal distress; rather, sexual identity is successfully integrated within the continuity of development across the years of high school, college, and beyond as these young people negotiate expectable tasks of adult life. The pioneers of this new cohort, young people like those whose lives are reported in Herdt and Boxer's (1996) unique study, pose a challenge to understanding sexual orientation within both life-course social science and psychoanalysis.

Six

Lesbian and Gay Lives across the Adult Years

With Andrew Hostetler

I was in my forties when I discovered I was gay. I really had never been aware of a guy's body in that way before. My wife was out of town a lot, I was lonesome and one of the other guys in the office invited me out with him and some friends to a gay bar. I met someone, went home with him, and we have been living together ever since.
—MIDDLE-AGED MAN NOW IN THE SIXTH YEAR OF A RELATIONSHIP

We have lived together as partners for more than forty years. We met quite by accident while working as young scientists for the government and it was love at first sight. Our life is pretty normal. I teach and he still works for the government, although both of us are about to retire. We bought some property near Santa Fe and plan to build there. Sometimes we invite friends to dinner, sometimes we just have a quiet evening at home. Most weekends we go to our cabin on the lake. Life has been pretty good to us. . . . we don't have much to do with the gay community. We just go about leading our own lives.
—OLDER GAY MAN DESCRIBING HIS PRESENT LIFE

I met my partner through one of my daughters who was then in the seventh grade together with my partner's daughter. Liz and I began talking, discovered we had a lot in common, and kinda just fell in love. I was a widow and she had recently been divorced. We and our kids have been living together for more than a decade.
—MIDDLE-AGED WOMAN DESCRIBING HOW SHE MET HER PARTNER

As these narratives attest, there is no inherent contradiction between a gay or lesbian sexual identity and the timely attainment of expectable adult transitions. These three individuals, part of a larger convenience sample, volunteered to participate in a study of gay and lesbian adult lives. Although each is at a somewhat different point in the course of life, they have all achieved a relatively normative adult role portfolio and they report high levels of morale. Their respective life histories reflect the variety of developmental pathways into an adult gay or lesbian identity and "sexual lifeway" (Herdt 1997; Hostetler and Herdt 1998): whereas one was aware of his sexual orientation while still in his teens, the other two were unaware of same-gender sexual attraction until chance meetings with individuals who would become their life partners. But despite this divergence in their early developmental trajectories, all three have carved out adult lives for themselves that are recogniz-able by all but the most homophobic of standards as healthy, balanced, and integrated. None report particular problems with acceptance and integration of their sexual orientation, and each reports high levels of life satisfaction and demonstrates an obvious capacity for a loving and caring relationship.

But while it is important to recognize that the adoption of a gay or lesbian identity can be perfectly compatible with the attainment of normative adults roles and developmental milestones, it is vital not to do so at the cost of denigrating less traditional-looking lesbian and gay adult developmental pathways. For just as there are divergent routes into a lesbian or gay identity, there are a variety of adult developmental trajectories, none of which should be assumed to be intrinsically more or less "healthy." This chapter considers these different developmental pathways, and the wide range of develop-mental issues faced by gay men and lesbians over the course of the adult years. Among the developmental issues addressed are intimacy and partnership, parenting, generativity and the midlife transition, and aging. The emphasis will be on the spectrum of normal developmental processes, including both continuities with and divergences from heteronormative development, which promote positive adjustment, morale, and general psychological well-being across the adult years of gay and lesbian life.

Understanding Gay Lives: Cohort, Social Time, and the Life Course Perspective

It is well known that ours is an aging society. With nearly 13 percent of Americans currently over age sixty-five and, a large, aging "baby boom" generation now in midlife, more than a fifth of our population will be over age sixty-five by the year 2025. Given the present median age of about thirty-three, we, along with much of the industrialized world, are becoming a middle-aged society (Myers 1990; U.S. Bureau of the Census 1993; Treas 1995). Shifts in the age pyramid interact with particular sociohistorical cir-cumstances, leading to changes in understandings of self and of one's place in the social order. Hence, it is difficult to generalize across cohorts and im-portant to study changes over time from a comparative perspective (Elder and Caspi 1990; Boxer and Cohler 1989).

Sexual identity is among those aspects of social life which appear most influenced by this complex interrelationship of culture, history, and demog-raphy. The organization of same-gender sexuality, in particular, reflects the dramatic social transformations of the past several decades. Thus, the study of gay development must begin with a recognition of the importance of historical events and cohort effects. The organization of same-sex desire around a homosexual identity, and later a lesbian or gay identity, became possible only during the course of the present century (Porter and Weeks 1991; Foucault [1976] 1990). The cohorts currently in middle and late adulthood came of age during an era in which there were no visible gay role models or other cultural resources to support their development. Indeed, older cohorts of gay men faced a kind of stigma and discrimination that is virtually unknown to the present generation of younger gay men and women (Vacha 1985).

In addition to emphasizing historical or cohort analyses, the life-course perspective recognizes the extent to which lives are shaped by both continuities and discontinuities, or expected and irruptive transitions. It is often assumed, for example, that sexual orientation and identity are stable across adulthood. However, there is increasing anecdotal and empirical evidence that, at least for certain individuals, sexual desires and identities can be fluid across the course of life. For example, several participants in the Chicago Study of Lesbian and Gay Adult Development and Aging (Cohler, Hostetler, and Boxer 1998; Herdt, Beeler, and Rawls 1997) claimed little awareness of same-sex desires until well into their adult years, before which time they felt very satisfied in their marital relationships and heterosexual lifeways. Similarly, Bozett's (1993) review of research findings indicated that a third of divorced gay men and more than three-fourths of divorced lesbians were unaware of their homosexuality at the time of their marriage. Thus, factors related to aging, cohort, and social context all enter into awareness and expression of same-sex desires, and issues of sexual orientation may be salient across the course of life.

But despite the reality of developmental discontinuity in lives over time, the life-course perspective also recognizes the existence of an expectable course of life, which resides in cultural narratives and the social institutions that support them. Knowing the expected duration of life, even young children construct a timetable regarding expectable life transitions (Farnham-Diggory 1966; Neugarten, Moore, and Lowe [1965] 1996; J. Roth 1963). Children and adults continually compare their own attainments with those expected in others of a particular age. Further, these transitions are linked in a particular sequence across the course of life. In contemporary bourgeois society, for instance, adult men and women are confronted with the linked tasks of work, marriage, and parenthood (Veroff and Feld 1970; Hogan and Astone 1986; Elder 1987, 1995, 1997). It is assumed that across the third and fourth decade of life, men and women have completed formal education, have found a vocation, married, and have had children. Cohler and Boxer

(1984) have portrayed this point in the adult life course as "settled adulthood." These shared understandings of the expectable course of life are often
referred to as "social time."

The concept of social time highlights shared patterns of sequential role
positions, developmental norms, and the meanings attached to them. In conjunction with historically specific factors, social time—which is also subject
to cohort shifts—contributes to the organization of personal experience. On
a symbolic level, the subjective experience of social time helps to determine
how persons understand life events, largely through processes of social comparison. On a structural level, the organization of social time provides the
basis for a seemingly ordered life course (and hence the semblance of predictable, intrinsic stages) and largely shapes individuals' interactions and patterns
of engagement with the social order.

Following Durkheim's ([1912] 1995) analysis of time and the ritual life of
the community, sociological study of the life course has suggested that persons maintain an internal timetable regarding expectable role transitions and
associated life changes (Sorokin and Merton 1937; J. Roth 1963; Hazan
1980; Neugarten and Hagestad 1976; Hagestad and Neugarten 1985).
Neugarten and her colleagues (Neugarten, Moore, and Lowe [1965] 1996)
have demonstrated agreement concerning definitions of age and age-related
social norms among concurrently living generations. Although older adults
are somewhat more tolerant than younger adults of variation in the timing
of certain role transitions (at the same time that they more strongly endorse
the existence of such norms), there is broad agreement upon what constitutes
childhood, adolescence, adulthood, and later life.

Across the course of life, persons continually compare their own development, including realization of certain social roles, to a socially shared timetable of expectable events. From these comparisons they determine whether
they are "on-time" or either "early" or "late" "off-time." This expectable
sequence of life changes provides the context for understanding personal
experience. As an example of the application of both cohort and social time
to an understanding of gay lives, gay men and women—and particularly
older cohorts—are likely to have resolved issues of sexual identity well after
their heterosexual peers. For many, this leads to being "off-time" with respect to the heterosexual majority. Prior to the gay liberation movement, and
the emergence of a public gay life course, (heterosexually) unmarried gay
men and women may even have had the experience of being completely
outside of normative time (Hagestad 1996).

Reflective of this cohort change in attitudes about homosexuality and in
the possibilities for leading gay and lesbian lives, the past twenty-five years
have been marked by increasing study of gay and lesbian lifeways (Herdt

1997; Hostetler and Herdt 1998). To date, scholarship on the topic has been primarily concerned with tracing the developmental processes involved in the disclosure to self and others of one's sexual orientation (or coming out), typically in late adolescence or early adulthood (Saghir and Robins 1973; Harry and DeVall 1978). Somewhat less study has been devoted to the consolidation of identity among gay men and lesbians across the years of stable adulthood (Cohler and Boxer 1984) and into middle age, and to other developmental issues confronted in middle and late adulthood.

General research on the second half of life has raised a number of questions regarding the impact of social context on aging, and has drawn attention to cohort changes in the personal and social significance of aging as important factors related to health, lifestyle, and psychological well-being (Cohler and Boxer 1984; Carney and Cohler 1993; Cohler and Nakamura 1996). As one example of the application of a contextual approach to the study of gay lives, the value placed upon youth and physical appearance in gay male communities has generated debates about "accelerated aging" (J. A. Lee 1987, 1991a; Sherman 1992) among gay men. More recent research (Bennett and Thompson 1990) indicates that gay men attribute this ageism to other gay men but do not internalize it themselves.

Otherwise, research on gay lives has typically failed to incorporate the insights of life-course social science, while the latter has also remained largely uninformed by the former. The above example notwithstanding, the study of homosexuality and aging has largely been ignored in the more general trend toward greater interest in the social and historical construction of the second half of life. Indeed, there have been fewer than a dozen systematic studies of older gay men and lesbians (Kimmel 1978, 1993; Garnets and Kimmel 1993; Quam and Whitford 1992), and most of the existing data was collected prior to the emergence of the AIDS epidemic, which has had wide-scale impact upon almost every aspect of gay life. Further, this research largely ignores the interaction of sexuality, ethnicity, and aging, focusing largely on affluent white gay men living in relatively visible, urban homosexual neighborhoods. The increasing visibility of a large generation of gay and lesbian baby boomers, and the emergence of the first generation of openly gay and lesbian elders, provide additional reasons for applying a life-course framework to the study of lesbian and gay lives.

The study of normative aging could clearly also be productively informed by the study of homosexuality and aging. Among the important comparative questions raised by "gay gerontology" are the impact of ageism and the AIDS epidemic on the subjective experience of aging, and the significance of social ties for morale across the second half of life (R. M. Berger 1980, [1982] 1996, 1984). As these examples illustrate, the marriage of life-course social science, which draws attention to the changing social contexts that shape lives over time, and the study of gay and lesbian lives could only benefit both.

Different Pathways into Gay and Lesbian Adulthood

As we have already indicated, gay and lesbian developmental research to date has largely focused on processes of identity development, typically theorized through epigenetic stage models (Lee 1977; Cass 1979; Troiden 1979; Coleman 1982). Although these models have provided many useful insights, they have been unable to account for individual and cultural variations in the attainment of a same-sex erotic identity. Instead, they tend to reflect the contemporary dominant narrative of having always known one was gay and of the continuity of same-gender desire throughout adolescence and into young adulthood (Plummer 1995; Savin-Williams 1996c). However, as both experience and empirical research have told us, there are a number of pathways into an adult gay or lesbian identity. Adult generations within contemporary American society include at least three cohorts of gay men and women who report some continuity between adolescent and adult sexual orientation (Herdt and Boxer 1996), although each has had quite different experiences of being and becoming "gay." At the same time, each generation has also produced gay or lesbian adults who report a much more discontinuous path into adult sexual identities and relationships.

Even among those individuals who have experienced continuity in their lives, self-identified as gay men and women, there have nevertheless been marked cohort differences in development. Cohorts of men and women currently in mid- and later life experienced particular stigma as "protogay" children and adolescents, stigma which often followed them into their adult lives. Within these two cohorts, men and women tell life stories that often revolve around shame, secrecy, and the fear of disclosure (A. Kantrowitz [1977] 1996; Sears 1991). For many, the pressures of lifelong socialization and the internalization of cultural norms hindered the healthy integration of their sexual and romantic desires, compromising their sense of personal integrity. Among members of the post–gay liberation, AIDS-era cohort, the resolution of sexual identity concerns and the adoption of a public gay or lesbian life course have been much less problematic and have generally occurred at much earlier ages.

Within the context of contemporary bourgeois life, young adults are expected to experiment with a number of relationships before establishing a more sustained, intimate relationship that will ideally culminate in marriage. Then, in their late twenties or early thirties, couples typically have their first child and assume the complete adult "role portfolio." For older cohorts of men and women, the achievement of a gay or lesbian identity in late adolescence or early adulthood typically led to a sense of being off-time, or even outside of time, with respect to the realization of these life tasks. Among younger cohorts, however, the emergence of a parallel gay social timetable may make it increasingly possible for gay and lesbian adults to experience on time, if still somewhat nonnormative development. Indeed, contemporary young gay adults are remarkably similar to their heterosexual counterparts in lifestyle. Both gay and straight individuals begin adulthood by exploring their sexuality in a variety of relationships. Indeed, many men and women experiment with both same- and opposite-sex relationships before settling on a heterosexual, homosexual, or bisexual identity (Golden 1996; Savin-Williams 1996a).

Given the emergence of public, semilegitimate lesbian and gay sexual lifeways, it is tempting to hypothesize that developmental continuity in gay and lesbian experience will become even more common. Although this may well be the case, the continuing heteronormativity of social institutions, particularly those involved in the socialization of children and adolescents, and the reality of sexual fluidity in the lives of many individuals seem to ensure that the path into—or out of—gay or lesbian life will remain discontinuous for some men and women. Like their straight counterparts, individuals who eventually develop same-sex desires are enculturated into a heteronormative social order, in which there are intense pressures and considerable incentives for individuals to conform to socially shared developmental timetables (although there has been little systematic study of the impact of sexual orientation on understanding of these timetables). Thus, despite early awareness of same-sex desires, many men and women pursue opposite-sex relationships, marriage, and family life in early adulthood, prior to the realization of a more ego-syntonic gay or lesbian identity.

Another pathway into gay or lesbian identity is reflected among those men and women who do not develop or become aware of same-sex desires until well into adulthood (Kimmel 1979–80). Such individuals are likely to have married and become parents. Two of the individuals quoted at the beginning at the chapter followed this pattern. As a consequence of a life change, such as divorce or the death of a spouse, and subsequent experiences, these men and women meet and fall in love with someone of the same gender and adopt a gay or lesbian identity, though not necessarily in that order (Charbonneau and Lander 1991; Crosbie-Burnett and Helmbrecht 1993). Clearly, the social timetable and developmental experiences of someone following this pathway is quite different than that of someone who first self-identifies as gay or lesbian in adolescence. Previously married men or women who come out in middle adulthood may find the path into a gay or lesbian identity, and the future course of family life—which may include the gay parent, the new same-sex partner, the ex-spouse, and children—to be particularly complex. Charbonneau and Lander (1991), describing the lives of thirty working- and middle-class women, have portrayed this complexity in detail. They found that the decision to adopt a lesbian identity and lifeway, arrived at only after much self-exploration at a time of personal pain, was precipitated by events more broadly associated with the advent of midlife. Women who made the transition to a lesbian identity subsequently reported higher self-esteem and an enhanced capacity to care for others. This developmental pattern is particularly likely to lead to reconstituted families (Coontz 1992, 1997; Gillis 1996), with one or both partners having children for which each assumes some degree of social and legal responsibility.

As but one other example of the different developmental issues posed by early versus late adoption of a lesbian or gay identity, stigma and discrimination may have interfered with completion of education and the establishment of a career, particularly among older cohorts, for those not pursuing a heteronormative course in early adulthood. Within the typical white-collar workplace, pictures of spouses and family are a silent marker of normality, and the discussion of family plans for weekends or holidays is an encouraged form of office discourse. Gay men or women have, in the past, frequently been unable to discuss their partners in the workplace, and younger gays and lesbians continue to change pronouns and invent stories of opposite-sex dating in the context of certain work environments. Particularly for men, the failure to establish oneself as a "family man" can interfere with career development and advancement. In recent years some large corporations have begun to offer domestic partner benefits, and lesbian and gay employee organizations, such as Out at Work, have started to spring up. Nevertheless, relatively few cities or states have enacted legislation protecting gay and lesbian employees from discrimination, and many gay men and women still find it difficult to integrate their personal and professional lives.

The following discussion reviews gay and lesbian lives in terms of expected adult roles, including intimacy or partnership, the realization of generativity (including, but not limited to, parenthood), entrance into work and retirement, and the experience of mid- and later life. We adopt the perspective that gay and lesbian lives represent but one set of developmental pathways, both similar to and different than the developmental trajectories of heterosexuals including the ever-single, the married childless, the married with children, and single men and women with children (Veevers 1979).

Sexual Identity, Intimacy, and Partnership

The study of same-gender intimacy has received increasing attention in recent years. This growing scholarly interest reflects a significant social transformation over the last three decades, during which time same-sex partnership has gone from invisibility to quasi-legal status. Current debates about same-sex marriage dramatically illustrate the social and political sea change that has opened up many more possibilities for the expression of same-gender love. However, at the same time that gay and lesbian relationships have begun to receive the kind of recognition and support so necessary for their ongoing maintenance, less traditional forms of intimate expression—both those which are emergent and those with a long history in gay communities—have become more marginal. As a result of this process of normalization, the gay or lesbian individual who is unwilling or unable to realize long-term same-gender partnership increasingly risks being seen as a developmental failure. While we recognize that many individuals encounter difficulties in realizing long-term partnership, and that this is an important topic for future academic and clinical research, we prefer not to privilege one developmental path over other viable alternatives. Thus, although the present discussion places somewhat more emphasis on enduring partnership, we also wish to highlight the diversity of "intimacies" that may contribute to well-being in adult life. The following review both summarizes the work that has been done and suggests directions for future research.

Given the difficulty of constituting a representative sample of gay men and lesbians (Herdt, Beeler, and Rawls 1997; Berger 1990; Gonsoriek 1982a; I. Meyer and Colten 1999), there is no way to precisely determine the rate of participation in same-sex relationships. Survey data, most of which is badly out of date, suggest that anywhere from 40 to 60 percent of gay men and 45 to 80 percent of lesbians are involved in committed relationships at any given time (Herdt, Beeler, and Rawls 1997; Kurdek 1995b; Bell and Weinberg 1978; Harry 1984a; Kehoe 1989; Nardi 1999; Jay and Young 1977). Herdt, Beeler, and Rawls, for example, reported that 46 percent of the gay men and 78 percent of the lesbians in their convenience sample reported currently being in a stable and committed relationship.

Despite the imprecision of the figures, two findings are consistently replicated: first, lesbians are much more likely to be in partnered relationships, and at rates which more closely approximate the heterosexual population, and, second, somewhere in the vicinity of half of gay men describe themselves as single at any given time. This latter finding suggests a "glass is half full" approach on the part of those who have focused exclusively on gay couples, and indicates that relational status may itself be an important source of experiential and developmental difference, particularly among gay men.

As we have already indicated, extant research on same-sex intimacy focuses primarily on the long-term couple. This research has been complicated by the lack of a universally agreed-upon definition of "same-sex couple" (Berger 1990). Early studies ran the gamut from the equation of same-sex relationships with short-term "affairs" (Saghir and Robins 1973) to definitions based on very restrictive criteria, such as cohabitation (Bell and Weinberg 1978). Echoing Berger (1990), it is important to recognize that, given the diversity among same-sex couples, self-definition as a couple is the most appropriate means by which to classify partners as such. However, given the possibility that an individual could report participating in more than one coupled relationship at a time, it is important to distinguish between primary and nonprimary relationships. Defining "single" is also somewhat complicated, as an individual involved in one or more casual relationships may or may not self-identify as single (Nardi 1999). Thus, in the absence of self-identification, classification as single should require the lack of a primary, committed relationship, while acknowledging both that any classification inevitably eliminates important differences within categories and that some individuals may not fall into either category.

Definitional difficulties notwithstanding, there have been numerous important studies of same-sex relationships, many of which compare same- and cross-sex couples on a variety of descriptive variables. This research has focused on a wide range of relationship issues, including partner selection (Kurdek and Schmitt 1987a,1987b; Harry 1984a, 1984b; McWhirter and Mattison 1984; Bell and Weinberg 1978), power and conflict (Reilly and Lynch 1990; Berger 1990; Howard, Blumstein, and Schwartz 1986; Peplau and Cochran 1990; Falbo and Peplau 1980; Harry and DeVall 1978), division of household labor (Kurdek 1994; Reilly and Lynch 1990; McWhirter and Mattison 1984; Bell and Weinberg 1978), relationship satisfaction (Kurdek 1988, 1994; Kurdek and Schmitt 1986; Blumstein and Schwartz 1983), parenting (Patterson 1995b, 1995c; Harry 1983; Kirkpatrick, Smith, and Roy 1981; Nungesser 1980; Bozett 1980a, 1980b; B. Miller 1979a, 1979b), and sexuality (Foulkes 1994; Blumstein and Schwartz 1983, 1989, 1990; Deenen, Gijs and van Naerssen 1994; Blasband and Peplau 1985; Harry and DeVall 1978; James and Murphy 1998). In general, the only significant differences to emerge from the comparative studies are a relatively more egalitarian division of labor (Kurdek 1994; Reilly and Lynch 1990; Blumstein and Schwartz 1983), less genital sex, and a higher valuation of affection (Blumstein and Schwartz 1990; Burch 1993; Jay and Young 1977) among lesbian couples, and a relatively higher incidence of sexual nonmonogamy among long-term gay male couples (Kurdek 1994; Kurdek and Schmitt 1986; Blasband and Peplau 1985; Harry 1984a, 1984b; Harry and DeVall 1978; McWhirter and Mattison 1984).

There have been few systematic comparisons of single and partnered lesbians and gay men. Bell and Weinberg (1978), in one groundbreaking study comparing single and coupled gay men, found that coupled gay men had fewer "sexual problems" than their single counterparts; this was in turn related to lower levels of regret concerning their sexual orientation. Men who described themselves as "coupled" also reported fewer sexual partners, while men and women who described themselves as "involved in a homosexual affair" (a category which likely includes some who would classify themselves as single and some who would classify themselves as coupled if given a dichotomous choice) reported higher levels of sexual activity.

Several other researchers have demonstrated a connection between relational status and psychological well-being (Berger [1982a] 1996; Kurdek and Schmitt 1987b; O'Brien 1992; Wayment and Peplau 1995). For example, O'Brien found that gay men who were in primary relationships experience less depressive symptomatology and greater well-being, but that relational status did not predict changes in these outcomes over time. And in a recent comparison of heterosexual and homosexual women, Wayment and Peplau (1995) report that women in partnered relationships—regardless of sexual orientation—score higher on measures of well-being than single women. Although these findings are supported by research on married versus unmarried heterosexuals (Gove, Style, and Hughes 1990; Veroff, Douvan and Kulka 1981), the reasons for the reported differences between single and partnered individuals remain largely unexplained, and are perhaps not as transparent as they seem. For instance, the psychological impact of normative societal expectations regarding permanent partnership is rarely considered.

Taken together, this research suggests general differences in the ways that gay men and lesbians construct their relationships in comparison to heterosexual counterparts, as well as significant diversity among gay men and women, both within and across relational categories (Trujillo 1997). Unfortunately, these differences have only rarely been the primary focus of study. Hence, the major task of future research must be to address the range of variation in the meanings and forms of same-sex intimacy.

The Diverse Forms and Meanings of Same-Sex Intimate Expression

As with development more generally, the course of same-gender intimacies may follow several different routes. Same-gender partnerships may either precede or, more commonly, follow heterosexual partnership or marriage, or they may follow a previous history of same-sex relationships. Important differences also exist across same-sex relationships, differences which often reflect the history of previous relationships. For instance, couples may choose to live together or apart, with both options potentially characterized by enduring bonds of intimacy and loyalty. Indeed, committed gay and lesbian relationships and those within the straight community are more alike than different (Blumstein and Schwartz 1983, 1990; Kurdek 1998). Among those individuals not currently in a relationship, some may be between relationships, some may be searching for but not yet have found Mr. or Ms. "Right," and some may choose to be single for shorter or longer periods of time.

And even though there are broad differences between single and partnered gay men and women, the wide range of lifestyles encompassed by these terms suggest that relational status should not be treated as a simple dichotomous variable. Within the category of partnered individuals there will be wide variation with respect to duration of relationship (even among individuals of the same age), current developmental issues or concerns, living and economic arrangements, relative distribution of resources and power within the couple, degree of sexual and emotional exclusivity, extent to which traditional relationship models are adopted (including gay marriage or domestic partnership), presence or absence of children, and so on.

Differences between partners—in terms of race, class, age, income, sexual identity (i.e., homosexual, lesbian/gay, bisexual, queer), and a variety of other psychological variables—also constitute an important area of research. Individuals within a couple, in addition to being at various points in the life course, will be distinguished from each other in terms of relationship history, current and future desire for remaining single versus finding partnership, access to social support, responsibility for raising children, degree of importance attached to relational status, and other factors.

Although the diversity of single gay lifestyles has received little systematic attention, there is a growing body of research on diversity among same-sex couples, some of which is cited above. This research has raised fundamental questions concerning the different meanings lesbians and gay men assign to their relationships, in comparison to both heterosexuals and other gay men and lesbians. For example, both Blumstein and Schwartz (1990) and Peplau and her colleagues (Peplau 1991; Peplau and Cochran 1990) have questioned the value of using heterosexual relationships as a model for understanding same-sex relationships. Peplau suggests studying same-sex relationships on their own terms, and not in terms of deviance from heterosexual norms of marriage and family. As she observes:

> Research findings indicate that it is no longer useful or appropriate to describe homosexual relationships in the value-laden language of "abnormal relationships" or "deviance." There is growing recognition of the wide diversity of "families" today. . . . Lesbian and gay partnerships should be included among this diverse array of family types. (1991, 182)

As Peplau observes, it is important that lesbian and gay relationships should not be assumed to be simple reflections—poor or otherwise—of gender roles in heterosexual models (Marecek, Finn, and Cardell 1982).

Related to the issue of definition, Peplau and Cochran (1990) argue against the stipulation of cohabitation as a necessary feature of relationships, heterosexual or homosexual. They argue instead for a functional definition of relationships based on interdependence and mutual influence. According to this definition, close relationships are characterized by mutual recognition of the importance of the tie, which is of some duration and is marked by some degree of intensity, frequent contact and shared experience in diverse activities, and inclusion in a wider circle of mutual friends (and/or family). Although this is a significant attempt at redefinition, self-designation by couples may yet be the best means for defining relationships.

Gender differences have also emerged from research on same-sex relationships, with gay men demonstrating a more widespread preference for sexual nonmonogamy and a greater valuation, in general, of genital sexuality (Klinger 1996; Nardi 1999); lesbians, in contrast, place a higher premium on intimacy and nongenital forms of sexual and affectional expression. Blumstein and Schwartz (1983) report a preference among lesbian couples for holding and hugging and other nongenital contact, while Jay and Young (1977) report very low rates of genital sexual contact within lesbian relationships. Taken together, these and other findings suggest that lesbians define sexuality somewhat differently than gay men, and perhaps place it within the larger context of relationality. Indeed, Nichols (1990) reports that both lesbian and straight women value relationality more than men. This is consistent with gender-role socialization, which continues to teach women to be kin-keepers (Firth, Hubert, and Forge 1970; Chodorow 1978; Gilligan 1982) and to manage expressive tensions within the family, while teaching men to be autonomous and to assume the role of instrumental task leader of the family. This may explain, at least in part, why lesbians appear more likely than gay men to be in relationships (Kehoe 1988).

In striking contrast with their lesbian counterparts, gay men are reported to be particularly sexually active, even more so than heterosexual men. Blumenstein and Schwartz (1983, 1990), Foulkes (1994) and Nardi (1999) observe that, in comparison to lesbians and heterosexual men and women, gay men are more likely to begin a relationship with a sexual encounter, with intimacy and romance emerging later. Further, gay men are more likely than their straight male counterparts to have sexual encounters outside of their primary relationship. In one study (Blumstein and Schwartz 1990), nearly four-fifths of the gay men reported such sexual contacts in the preceding year. Gay men are likely to maintain close friendships with former lovers which may even include some sexual intimacy (Nardi 1997) and may view sexuality in ways different from straight counterparts.

Harry (1983), Harry and DeVall (1978), Fowles (1994), and Nardi (1999) observe that gay men define partnership differently than either lesbian women or heterosexuals. These authors argue that gay male relationships are better described by a model of "best friendship," which assumes sexual nonexclusivity, than by a model based on heterosexual marriage. Nevertheless, these gender distinctions have probably been somewhat overdrawn, and there is reason to believe that, at least among younger cohorts, gay men and lesbians are moving closer together in their conceptualizations of relationships. For example, Nichols (1990) notes the emergence of lesbian "sex radicals" in the late 1970s, women who worked closely with gay men in the gay liberation movement and who were influenced by their free sexual expression. Although AIDS may have forced sexual radicalism of all types underground during the 1980s consistent with the perspectives of cultural studies, the continuing popularity of lesbian-oriented erotic magazines like *On Our Backs* and the emergence of new erotic magazines, anthologies, and even lesbian produced lesbian sexual videos all suggests that lesbian sexual radicalism is alive and well. This is but one example of cohort differences within the lesbian and gay community.

Despite the apparent prevalence of nonmonogamy among gay men, not all gay male relationships are nonmonogamous, and this is another important source of diversity. Studies variously indicate that anywhere from one-third to 100 percent of long-term gay male relationships are nonexclusive (Kurdek and Schmitt 1986; Peplau 1982, 1991, 1993; Mendola 1980; Bell and Weinberg 1978; Harry and DeVall 1978; Saghir and Robins 1973). However, the mere fact that a gay relationship is nonmonogamous says little about the quality of the relationship or the level of care, commitment, and respect between partners (Bettinger 1997). Although there is some evidence of greater psychological adjustment among monogamous or "closed" couples (Bell and Weinberg 1978), most studies have turned up few systematic differences between open and closed couples (Peplau 1991; Kurdek and Schmidt 1986; Blasband and Peplau 1985). McWhirter and Mattison (1984) and Harry (1984) have even suggested that nonexclusive relationships enjoy greater longevity. Kurdek (1998) reports that, contrasted with those of straight couples, gay and lesbian relationships reflect both a greater sense of intimacy and less commitment to a long-term relationship.

Preliminary data from our pilot interviews with approximately forty gay men and women over the age of thirty-five also indicate that nonmonogamy does not necessarily affect the quality of a relationship, with several men in successful relationships of three and four decades' duration reporting occasional or frequent outside sexual contacts. Clearly, the study of same-sex relationships should neither privilege certain relationship models over others nor make assumptions about the nature and quality of relationships which follow a nontraditional model. Moreover, given Blasband and Peplau's (1985) finding that only 20 percent of male couples reported a pattern of sexual exclusivity followed by nonmonogamy, a priori assumptions about the course of gay male relationships should also be avoided.

Among many other significant differences in same-sex couples is the seemingly superficial issue of what term the members of the couple use to describe each other and their relationship. The terms "friend," "significant other," "lover," "boyfriend" or "girlfriend," and "partner" signal subtle but potentially profound differences in meaning (Nardi 1999), as well as historical shifts in preferred relationship models (discussed below). In a study of ninety-two male couples, reported by Berger (1990), 62 percent of respondents preferred "lover," 22.5 percent preferred "partner," and 15.7 percent voiced a preference for other terms, such as "boyfriend" or "friend." Future studies should explore the different meanings associated with the use of these terms and what, if anything, the use of a particular term predicts about a relationship.

These are but a few potential sources of diversity among same-sex couples, and much more research is needed to establish the range of differences in the meanings of and models used for lesbian and gay relationships (Kurdek 1998). Equally importantly, the research void with respect to gay singlehood must be addressed. Little is known, for instance, about the differences between voluntarily and involuntarily single lesbians and gay men and why the latter group has difficulty finding partnership. Finally, it is important to recognize that categories of "single" and "partnered" are not static; there is obviously movement back and forth as previously single individuals enter coupled relationships and as formerly partnered individuals become single through the dissolution of relationships or the loss of a partner. These and other changes highlight the need to apply a developmental perspective to the study of same-sex intimacy.

Same-Gender Intimacy, Well-Being, and the Life-Course Perspective

It is clearly inappropriate to study either couplehood or singlehood at only one point in time. Stearns and Sabini (1997), who have addressed the need to study same-sex couples over the course of life, report suggestive age- or cohort-related differences in sexual/affectional conflict, as well as in the relationship between community involvement and dyadic cohesion. Relationships obviously change over time, with couples facing new sets of developmental issues together, from the initiation of the relationship to either its dissolution or the death of a partner. Despite what popular models of adult development, from Erikson ([1951] 1963) on, might lead one to believe, development does not cease in the absence of enduring partnership. Further, the experience of being single is itself different at different points in the life course. With respect to the development of relationships, several authors have proposed stage models to account for the transitions and changes experienced by couples (R. Hill 1986; Hill and Mattessich 1979). But while developmental study of relationships is important, it may be wise not to situate these developmental processes within the context of invariant and universal stages.

The stage model of development was inspired by diverse sources, including the field of education and family development (Havighurst 1948; Duvall [1951] 1971); psychoanalysis, as perhaps best exemplified by Erik Erikson ([1951] 1963); and the cognitive epistemology of Piaget ([1975] 1985). Common to these perspectives is the assumption of a relatively invariant sequence of tasks or issues in development, each of perspectives is the assumption of a relatively invariant sequence of tasks or issues in development, each of which must be mastered before one progresses to the next stage. Failure to adequately resolve a particular developmental task or issue represents fixation or inadequate development.

Little systematic evidence has been provided in support of such intrinsic stage models, either with respect to the life course as a whole or in the context of discrete areas such as work (Levinson 1978, 1996) and relationships (Aldous 1996; R. Hill and Rodgers 1964; McWhirter and Mattison 1984, 1996). Indeed, findings from the study of lives over time (Neugarten 1969, 1979; Emde 1981, 1983; Clausen 1993) suggest little support for any intrinsic or stepwise ordering of life phase or stages beyond socially expectable transitions in and out of particular roles, such as work and retirement (Elder 1997; Hogan 1981). Much of what is assumed to be orderly psychological development may actually reflect the way in which a particular cohort negotiates a particular role transition at a particular time. Application of stage models to relationships poses the additional problem of imposing an individual developmental model on relationships and complex family systems (Vaillant 1993; Cohler and Altergott 1995).

Further, by starting from the assumption—with minimal empirical validation—of invariant stages or role transitions, the study of lives presumes precisely that which should be the object of study (Vaillant and Milofsky 1980). This assumption of invariance over time is contradicted by the reality of social and historical change, which shapes understandings and experience of relationships across different cohorts. The AIDS epidemic and the changing context of gay parenthood—from nonexistence to raising biological children from a previous heterosexual marriage to adoption, artificial insemination, and the use of surrogate mothers—are but two examples of the social transformations that have impacted the experience of gay and lesbian couplehood. There have been corresponding changes in the experience of being single.

The problematic nature of stage models is illustrated in efforts to define and specify stages in gay and lesbian relationships (McWhirter and Mattison 1984, 1996; Slater 1999). McWhirter and Mattison, in their model of gay male relationships, identify the following six stages: blending, nesting, maintaining, building, releasing, and renewing. The McWhirter and Mattison model has been reviewed in detail (Kurdek 1995a; Peplau, Veniegas, and Campbell 1996). Although the authors have undoubtedly identified important developmental concerns in the lives of certain couples, this and similar models tend to smooth over significant differences and variations, both within and between given cohorts. For instance, the McWhirter and Mattison model seems less relevant for present cohorts than for those men who entered "settled adulthood" in the 1970s (Cohler and Boxer 1984). From AIDS to increased societal integration to the shifting meanings of same-sex relationships, historical or cohort-related factors largely shape the course of development. Much to their credit, McWhirter and Mattison (1996) acknowledge both the existence of variety in gay male relationships and some of the changes precipitated by the AIDS crisis. Nevertheless, these factors do not get included in their theoretical model.

Stage models also encounter difficulty when they attempt to specify, with any degree of precision, the length or duration of posited stages—a defining characteristic of some models. Not only does the expected duration of any life "stage" change over historical time; there is also an incredible range of variation within a given cohort. Developmental processes are far too irregular to be pinned down according to a set timetable. The seemingly straightforward and well-established finding among couples of diminished sexual interest over time provides but one example of developmental complexity. Although, as Blumstein and Schwartz (1983) have shown, both straight and gay relationships follow a pattern of diminished sexual contact over time, this issue must be understood in terms of the age of each partner as well as cohort-related factors such as HIV/AIDS, which may influence both the experience of sexuality within the relationship and the decision to be monogamous or nonmonogamous.

Perhaps most importantly, models such as the one proposed by McWhirter and Mattison disregard the subjective meanings of relationships or relational status. In the first place, straight men and women construct particular meanings of singlehood or partnership which may differ from those of gay men and women. Even within the gay community, these meanings vary according to cohort; to date, there has been little study of the meanings which younger, middle-aged, and older gay men and women ascribe to relationships and singlehood, or even of potential differences in meaning within couples. Commenting on the value of relationship stage models such as the one proposed by McWhirter and Mattison, Deenen, Gijs, and van Naerssen conclude:

> Some practitioners use McWhirter and Mattison's stage model (1984) in aiding gay couples. Our findings, however, question some basic presuppositions of this model. . . . It is not strange that in therapy some success is achieved using McWhirter and Mattison's model. In asking for help, some men are confronted with a theoretical model, and start to describe their lives in accordance with the model themselves and experience their relationship in accordance with their stage model. . . . Men who adapt to a theoretical model they are confronted with are not necessarily being helped. (1994, 429–30).

These authors highlight the importance of understanding the lived experiences of participants in a particular time and place. Such findings suggest that stage models may be of little value in the effort to portray the course of life among either heterosexuals or gay men and lesbians.

Adults experiencing same-gender desire have been among those most affected by social and cultural changes over the last several decades. This century has seen the creation of an Western category of identity based on same-sex erotic preference, and the continual transformation of that category, from invert to homosexual to lesbian/gay to—at least in some quarters—queer. Given these generational shifts, which also reflect changes in social acceptance and cultural integration, there have been radical cohort differences in the experience of being "gay" (Cohler, Hostetler, and Boxer 1998; Herdt and Boxer 1996). These differences obviously extend to the experience of both gay singlehood and partnership.

Perhaps the most important change is the gradual emergence of long-term, same-sex partnership as a viable, and increasingly public, life-course option. Although there have probably always been same-sex couples, their existence has been widely acknowledged only over the course of the last thirty years, and same-sex couples have been accorded semilegitimate status only in the last ten years or so. In terms of generational or cohort change, this has entailed a transition from widespread, compulsory heterosexual marriage to the common expectation, among younger gay men and lesbians, of a socially legitimated same-sex partnership. The profound experiential and developmental implications of this generational shift can hardly be overestimated. There are likely to be sharp cohort differences in the incidence of heterosexual marriage among gay men and lesbians, in how same-sex partnerships are initiated and the difficulties encountered in doing so, in the relationship models employed, and in the degree of openness and acceptance by family, friends, and colleagues (Townsend 1997).

For example, the centrality of the bar scene as the primary context for the initiation of relationships (R. Berger 1982b, 1990) has most likely diminished over the last thirty years as other options for meeting potential same-sex partners have opened up, both within and outside of the gay cultural scene. As already indicated, there have also been significant transformations in the meanings ascribed to and the models used for same-sex relationships. Among lesbians, there have been subtle historical shifts in relationship ideals, from the Boston marriage to butch-femme role playing to feminist-inspired egalitarianism (Nichols 1990; Harry 1983). Among gay men, sexual nonmonogamy was abandoned by many in the wake of AIDS (Berger 1990; Peplau and Cochran 1990; McKusick et al. 1985), but there are reasons to believe that nonmonogamy is making a comeback among male couples (Blumstein and Schwartz 1990). Among other changes, Deenen, Gijs, and van Naerssen (1994) report that younger men value emotional closeness to a greater extent than older men, noting that this may be attributed to cohort-related changes in the understanding of gay relationships. They also report cohort variation in the association between relationship duration and relationship commitment, with younger men reporting similar levels of commitment and intimacy irrespective of relationship length.

Despite the above-mentioned lack of consensus regarding the proper vocabulary for describing same-sex relationships, there have been clear historical shifts, from the euphemistic "friend" to the more sexually explicit "lover" to the more mainstream and neutral "partner." Additionally, there have been dramatic changes in the level of social and familial integration of the same-sex couple. Younger same-gender couples are free to express affection and to define their relationships in ways not possible for an earlier cohort of gay men and lesbians. The participation by family members in a same-sex wedding or commitment ceremony and the creation of corporate-sponsored benefits for same-sex partners were utterly unimaginable to the invisible, pre-Stonewall gay or lesbian couple.

Finally, the specter of HIV and AIDS has altered the way in which gay men in particular define the expectable course of life, including the course of significant relationships. In the Deenen, Gijs, and van Naerssen study (1994), the cohort of older gay men reported a larger number of sexual partners, suggesting that life in the age of AIDS has altered how gay men deal with sexual relationships. Among the cohort of gay men presently in midlife, who have been hardest hit by the epidemic, AIDS has led both to a foreshortened sense of time remaining (Borden 1989, 1992; Hopcke 1992) and to the expectation that one's own death may be preceded by "widowerhood" and bereavement at the loss of one's partner (Peplau, Veniegas, and Campbell 1996). HIV and AIDS have, in fact, altered gay male relationships in almost every area, including the reduction in the sheer number of available mates, the difficulty of negotiating safer sex, the decision to be monogamous or nonmonogamous, the fear and possible accusations of infecting one's partner, and coping with the illness and likely death of one or both partners.

The experience of being gay and single has also undoubtedly been altered by the events of the last several decades. Delay among younger cohorts in age of first marriage has made singlehood more common and acceptable among middle-class men and women in their twenties and early thirties (Glick 1989; Aldous 1996). Moreover, divorce rates continue to ensure a sizable (if temporarily) single population among individuals in midlife. And increased longevity notwithstanding, it is common for one spouse to outlive the other, producing a population of older "singles." This means that the approximately 50 percent of adult gay men who are single at any given time are in good company. On the other hand, as fewer gay men and lesbians reject more traditional relationship models on ideological grounds, the meanings of gay singlehood and its legitimacy as a lifestyle option (to the extent that it *is* an option) shift accordingly. To the extent that partnership becomes an "expectable transition" in an emerging gay life course, remaining single becomes more developmentally problematic.

At the same time, within the context of gay cultural norms, long periods of singlehood (as opposed to same-sex partnership) have not been unusual. The discourse of early gay liberation urged gay men and women to reject heterosexual norms of marriage and family (Wittman [1972] 1992), thus providing justification even for those who were involuntarily single. Given the increasing assimilation of lesbians and gay men into mainstream culture, and in light of recent legislative and judicial victories in the area of gay partnership and family rights (e.g., custody and adoption rights), it is very likely that we are witnessing the emergence of a lesbian and gay life course more closely modeled on heterosexual norms. This transformation could lead to a larger ideological and experiential rift between those who espouse and those who eschew traditional relationships, and to a devaluation of gay singlehood.

The consequences of such a cultural shift on the morale and well-being of single gay men and lesbians could be, if not disastrous, then at least less than positive. Seltzer (1976) and Cohler and Boxer (1984) have suggested that the experience of life satisfaction is largely determined by the sense of being "on-time" for expectable role transitions. The sense that the timing of changes in one's life is consistent with that for other members of one's cohort or generation contributes to an enhanced sense of personal congruence and well-being. As already reported, several researchers have found that part-nered individuals tend to score higher on measures of well-being than their single counterparts. This data can be interpreted in at least two, non–mutually exclusive ways: it could be that partnership is inherently more satis-fying and fulfilling than singlehood, but it could also be that the higher mo-rale and general well-being of partnered individuals reflects societal and personal expectations regarding appropriate life-course options. The future study of relational status must not only tease out the profound impact on development of societal expectations regarding normative life-course transi-tions, it must also be careful not to be prescriptive of these normative pathways.

On a more structural level, an individual's position within the socially reg-ulated timetable of expected roles and transitions largely determines his or her interaction with the social environment and influences his or her choice of social and institutional affiliations. For instance, married couples are more likely to have other married couples as friends and to have institutional affil-iations which reflect their interest in issues of marriage and the family. There is some evidence to suggest a similar pattern among gay men and lesbians. While almost three-quarters of the male couples in Berger's (1990) survey of the Couples National Network reported that the majority of their friends were also partnered, Herdt, Beeler, and Rawls (1997) suggest that partner-ship status is one of a number of important predictors in the selection of friends, including level of involvement with the lesbian and gay community. These authors also demonstrate the perception of the social organization they studied as primarily addressing the concerns of younger lesbians, gay men, and bisexuals, including coming out and finding partnership.

Even though roughly half of 50 percent of gay men, and an even higher proportion of lesbians, are apparently in relationships, institutions that con-stitute the lesbian and gay community are oriented toward the needs of single lesbians and gay men, or are at least perceived as such. As lesbian and gay partnership and family rights take center stage, and as a normative lesbian and gay life course involving partnership emerges, this may in fact change. Nevertheless, it seems likely that partnership status will continue to influence the social and institutional affiliations of lesbians and gay men, and may serve either to bring single and partnered gay men and women together or to drive them further apart. This is another very important area for future research.

Recognizing these and other cohort differences in the experience of being single or partnered, the developmental study of same-sex intimate expression must be historically and culturally grounded. To this end, stage models of development may be of limited use in understanding lesbian and gay lives over time, and the cross-cohort applicability of these models needs to be established. And considering the difficulty of distinguishing between cohort and age- or developmentally related differences, cross-sectional studies must be complemented with longitudinal data (Boxer and Cohler 1989).

Sexual Identity and Parenthood: Gay and Lesbian Parents and Their Offspring

Among all the policy issues posed by the increasing societal acceptance of homosexuality, those connected with family formation and the socialization of youth are the most difficult. Indeed, there is perhaps no institution in contemporary society that is more subject to ideological manipulation and nostalgic revision than the family. Adults often look back on their own childhood as a time of security and comfort, disregarding the inevitable problems and tensions of family life. Collectively, Western societies regard childhood as a time of innocence. Along with schools, the family is charged with protecting children from societies' ills, of which homosexuality has been considered a primary example for the greater part of the twentieth century.

Historians such as Aries (1962) and Demos (1986) have demonstrated the historically specific nature of beliefs regarding childhood "innocence," which was first portrayed by Enlightenment philosophers such as Rousseau ([1762] 1979), and they have challenged commonly held assumptions regarding the stability and cohesion of the immediate family. More recently, the social historians Stephanie Coontz (1992) and John Gillis (1996) have documented the presence of nostalgic biases in ideological constructions of the family, which they argue are a response to the rapid social changes of the last three decades. In her most recent work, Coontz (1997)—adding to the earlier work of Bane (1976)—offers clear evidence of diversity in family forms across time and space in American society. Significantly, Coontz also suggests that, if parental emotional engagement and empathy are essential for the promotion of optimal development, then many lesbian and gay couples are particularly well-suited for parenthood.

Parenthood is the most central of adult roles, and one that has long been considered incompatible with an openly gay or lesbian identity. However, given deeply entrenched heteronormative pressures to marry, along with the fluidity of the sexual life course, significant numbers of self-identified gays, lesbians, and bisexuals have already experienced parenthood in the traditional biological sense. And in light of recent legislative battles over gay adoption and the emergence of a "lesbian baby boom"(Patterson 1995a) made possible by advances in reproductive technology, it is clear that many other gay men and lesbians are choosing to make children part of their "families of choice" (Weston 1997). Although gay and lesbian parenthood is the subject of growing empirical and theoretical interest, we still know relatively little about the experiences of gay parents and their children, particularly as they relate to what we know about normative family development.

When considering gay and lesbian parenthood, it is important to situate the topic within the context of the expectable adult role portfolio in contemporary Western society, and the relation of such normative expectations to the experiences of gays and lesbians. Extant research on the expectable course of parenthood across the stable adult years and into midlife is useful in understanding the phenomenon of gay and lesbian parenthood, with the proviso that gay parenting raises additional questions not addressed by prior normative study (Cohler and Grunebaum 1981; Cowan and Cowan 1992; Cowan et al. 1985; Grossman, Eichler, and Winickoff 1980). As but one example, although the motives of gays and lesbians choosing parenthood may be somewhat different than those of their heterosexual counterparts, there have been no studies of the motivation for gay parenthood comparable to the classic studies of Benedek (1958), Bibring and her colleagues (Bibring 1959; Bibring et al. 1961), and Wyatt (1967, 1971).

Repeating a by now familiar refrain, there are many pathways into and through gay and lesbian parenthood. By far the most common pattern at present is for birth children to reside with the gay parent, who holds either joint or full custody and who may or may not have a partner (Flaks et al. 1995). Another common pattern is for gay men or lesbians, single or partnered, to adopt children from foster care. Often, these children are somewhat older and considered "difficult to place," and they may have special caretaking needs (which can place additional strain and burden on a couple.) A third, increasingly common pattern is for one or both members of a lesbian couple to become pregnant through donor insemination, with sperm coming either from a friend or from a sperm bank (Chan, Raboy, and Patterson 1998; Flaks et al. 1995; McCandlish 1987; Patterson 1994, 1995b; Steckel

1987). In exploring these different pathways, the following discussion addresses the range of issues typically considered in the normative study of parenthood, as well as the specific challenges of gay and lesbian parenting.

The Transition to Parenthood

In contrast with work and marriage, individuals receive relatively little preparation for the reality of providing complete care for another person (Entwisle and Doering 1981). It is hard for prospective parents to imagine the time and effort required for child care, or the extent of its effects on work and leisure. Indeed, it is the adult role that most radically reorganizes adult personal commitments, and, unlike other roles, there is no exit from it as long as there is memory (Benedek 1973). In addition to presenting new challenges, becoming a parent often evokes anew unresolved problems stemming from one's own early life experiences (Behrens 1954; Benedek [1958] 1973). Wishes and unconscious recollections related to one's early care may be stimulated by caring for a new baby. Among heterosexual men and women, repressed childhood fantasies of displacing the same-sex parent may be rekindled in assuming the parental role. Hence, it is not surprising that becoming a parent can be a source of much distress.

Gutmann (1975, 1987) and Chodorow (1978) have both argued that becoming a parent produces a sense of crisis and imperative unlike any other adult role transition, although they disagree about the consequences. While some research has questioned the assumption that the transition to parenthood is an inevitable source of challenge (Rossi 1968, 1972, 1980b; Jacoby 1969; Neugarten 1973; Osofsky and Osofsky 1984), the term "crisis" seems to apply well to the transition and to be supported by empirical research (Cohler 1984; McLanahan and Adams 1987). Although findings vary according to the group studied and the questions asked, most studies show that the transition to parenthood is a source of at least moderate personal crisis for both mothers and fathers. The nature and degree of the crisis is determined, at least in part, by the timing of parenthood.

As with most developmental transitions, parenthood fits into a larger social timetable. Although both marriage and parenthood have been delayed among younger cohorts, by their late twenties and early thirties many individuals feel increasing social pressure to marry and start a family (Sweet 1977; Hogan 1987). For women, the "biological clock" continues to set an upper limit for the realization of motherhood. Within these broad social and biological limits, however, there is a great deal of individual variation in the timing of parenthood, and this timing—whether "on-time," "early off-time" or "late off-time"—has important implications for the experience of

parenting. Although there has been no research on the impact of social timing on the parental transition among gays and lesbians, such effects are undoubtedly mediated by the specific pathway followed, whether prior heterosexual marriage, donor insemination, or adoption. Social conceptions of
parental roles are not static over time, and given the anxiety surrounding the
performance of this role, parents are especially sensitive to changing norms
and standards. Believing children to be fragile, American parents tend to
be preoccupied with professional child-rearing advice and the most recent
research findings (Clarke-Stewart 1978). Gay and lesbian parents of young
children may be particularly likely to immerse themselves in child development theory in an effort to "compensate" for any stigma they may confer on
their offspring.

Irrespective of the timing of parenthood, parents almost inevitably experience role strain and overload for at least a year following the birth of their
first child (LeMasters 1957, 1970; Dyer 1963; Hobbs 1965, 1968; Russell
1974; Grossman, Eichler, and Winickoff 1980; McLanahan and Adams
1987). In surveys, more than one-third of women with young children report marked loss of morale (Campbell, Converse, and Rodgers 1976; Hobbs
and Cole 1976; Weissman 1978, Weissman, Myers, and Hardin 1978; Weissman, Myers, and Thompson 1981). At least to some extent, this crisis results
from the geographic isolation of the nuclear and modified-extended family
in American society (Parsons 1949). Among gay and lesbian parents, such
problems may be amplified by isolation from supportive kin networks, although extended "families of choice" (Weston 1997) may be an important
source of emotional and material support.

Late off-time parents, particularly fathers, generally can tend better to the
role demands of parenthood than their younger, on-time counterparts, having established more stable personal and work identities. However, older
fathers, and to a lesser extent older mothers, complain that they lack role
colleagues. Older fathers feel that they should be associating with grandfathers rather than with new fathers who may be half their age. (Indeed, some
men starting a second family are both grandfathers and new fathers.) For
women, pressure to have children within the biologically imposed time
frame often conflicts with career building. Many professional women become mothers at critical times in their career development and thus experience a particularly strong conflict. Due to the relatively greater amount of
preparation and planning involved (Moses and Hawkins 1982; Falk 1989),
openly gay men and women who opt to become parents may also be older
and more secure in their work and personal lives at the time of the parental
transition, and thus may have much in common with their late off-time heterosexual counterparts.

Academic interest in the impact of child care on parents has increased over the last three decades, a shift largely motivated by a reconsideration of women's roles. While men may have become somewhat more involved with their young children there has been little change in the expectations placed on women, who are still overwhelmingly the primary caretakers (Rebelsky and Hanks 1971). Hence, despite the many gains of the feminist movement, the transition to parenthood remains, in actuality, the transition to motherhood (Rossi 1972; Chodorow 1978; Cohler 1984). The challenges of this transition are intensified for the growing number of women who work outside the home even during the preschool years. Although there is some evidence of a more equitable division of household labor and child care among gay and lesbian couples (Kurdek 1994, 1995b; Patterson 1995a, 1996), the biological parent—in the case of nonadoption—often shoulders the primary burdens of child care (Patterson 1996). Single gay adoptive parents may also experience a particularly difficult transition.

Although the increased role strain associated with the transition to parenthood is largely confined to the parent-child tie, marital relationships are obviously not unaffected. In general, husbands and wives show little enduring change in the nature of their relationship following parenthood (Meyerowitz and Feldman 1966; Russell 1974). However, most studies do report a modest, temporary decline in reported marital satisfaction among both husbands and wives after the first child's birth (B. Miller and Sollie 1980; Belsky and Isabella 1985; Belsky, Spanier, and Rovine 1983; Cowan et al. 1985; Cox 1985; Ventura 1987). Large numbers of children also lower marital satisfaction (L. Feldman 1971; Belsky, Spanier, and Rovine, 1983; Worthington and Buston 1987), particularly for women (Belsky, Lang, and Rovine 1985). Companionate marriages, characterized by strong complementarity of interests and intimacy, are particularly adversely affected by the transition to parenthood (Shereshefsky and Yarrow 1973); both parents see the baby as interference in their close relationship.

As the preceding review indicates, despite a large body of research on the transition into "normative" parenthood, we still know relatively little about the impact of this transition on gay and lesbian parents. For instance, we lack a good comparative study of the motivation for parenthood among lesbians with children from a prior heterosexual marriage, gay and lesbian couples adopting, and lesbian couples choosing donor insemination for one or both members of the couple. Ricketts and Achtenberg (1990) have suggested, for instance, that the decision-making process leading to adoption may be very similar among gay, lesbian, and heterosexual couples, but much more research is needed. In general, we need good comparative research on the different pathways into parenthood, both normative and nonnormative, and on the impact of the pathway chosen on this important developmental transition (Kirkpatrick 1996).

Diversity in Family Formation among Gay Men and Lesbians

As in the case of same-gender partnership, gay and lesbian parenthood should not be understood merely by reference to normative models, although the normative study of parenthood provides a necessary point of departure and comparison. The study of gay and lesbian parenthood must begin with the recognition of two points. First, the rapid social transformations of the past three decades have led to dramatic changes in every aspect of gay and lesbian life, including family formation, which is no longer open only to those gay men and lesbians who choose to marry heterosexually. Successful political and legal challenges to the hegemonic view that parental homosexuality is detrimental to children's adjustment and well-being have led to awards of custody based on factors other than sexual orientation. Further, sexual orientation is becoming increasingly irrelevant to foster care placement and adoption in many states. Second, as Patterson (1995b, 1996) and Pies (1990) have emphasized and as we have been arguing, there are many routes into parenthood among gays and lesbians, and gay parenthood can begin at different points in the life course of both parents and children.

The most common route into parenthood among gay men and lesbians is represented by the reconstituted family, that is, the same-gender couple and children from one or both partners' previous heterosexual marriages. Given that custody has typically been awarded to mothers, this pattern is more common among lesbian than gay male couples. However, a history of homophobic discrimination by the courts has long denied both gay mothers and fathers custody rights that might otherwise have been granted. A second route is for a single gay man or lesbian or a same-sex couple to participate in foster care or to adopt a child. A third route, increasingly common among recent cohorts of lesbians, is for one partner to become pregnant through a sperm donation by an acquaintance (inseminated artificially or "naturally" via intercourse) or through the services of a sperm bank. A variation, which allows for two "biological" mothers, is for one partner to donate the egg and the other partner to carry the baby to term. To date, there has been little research comparing lesbian couples who choose this route either to lesbians selecting other alternatives or to heterosexual couples employing various forms of artificial insemination (Pies 1990).

In the case of custody arrangements following divorce, the subsequent parent-child relationship varies in duration, depending upon both the duration of the parents' relationship and the age of the child when the gay parent or same-sex couple assumes either joint or sole custody. Gottman (1990) reports that as many as a million and a half lesbians and a million gay men are actively involved in the parenting of dependent children even when they don't have custody. Further, more than six million children are residing with gay or lesbian parents in committed relationships. Kirkpatrick (1987, 1996) estimates that about a third of lesbians have previously been in heterosexual marriages, and half of these women have young children. Most often, these children continue to live with their mother following divorce. In addition to reconstituted "gay" families, Patterson (1994) claims that thousands of women and their partners elect parenthood at some point during the same-sex relationship, although little is known regarding the process leading up to this decision. There is some evidence suggesting that lesbian women who become mothers may be more motivated to do so than their straight counterparts, since they must frequently overcome substantial social and legal obstacles (Falk 1989; Moses and Hawkins 1982; Pies 1990).

Given the greater likelihood that mothers, regardless of sexual orientation, will retain custody following a divorce, and given the wider range of parenting options open to lesbians (i.e., donor insemination), it is not surprising that the literature on "gay" parenting focuses more on lesbians mothers than on gay fathers. There is a growing body of systematic research comparing lesbian and heterosexual mothers, though much of the research to date has concentrated on divorced lesbians and divorced heterosexual "controls." Most studies have found slight to moderate differences between lesbian and heterosexual parents but also significant similarities. As Lewin (1993) emphasizes, there is much blurring of cultured categories between so-called lesbian parents and their presumed heterosexual counterparts.

Reviewing comparative studies of divorced heterosexual and lesbian mothers, Kirkpatrick (1987) finds few differences in previous length of marriage. However, relations with the former husbands may actually be more harmonious when the former wife is a lesbian. In this case, the divorced couple appears to be better able to maintain the "parenting alliance" (R. Cohen and Weissman 1984). Further, Kirkpatrick (1987, 1996) reports that lesbian women typically seek divorce due to lack of intimacy with their husband, whereas heterosexual women more commonly cite violence and family disorganization as precipitating factors. She also notes higher self-esteem among divorced lesbian mothers. Other studies support the idea that lesbians mothers experience a better postdivorce adjustment and are more likely than their heterosexual counterparts to be partnered and less likely to be socially isolated (Kirkpatrick, Smith, and Roy 1981; Golombok, Spencer, and Rutter 1983).

In a study by Green et al. (1986), lesbian mothers scored higher on measures of self-confidence and dominance, and a review by Falk (1989) indicates that lesbian women generally have lower rates of psychiatric distress and enhanced levels of self-confidence and self-sufficiency as compared to straight counterpart women. However, the somewhat better adjustment of lesbians following divorce apparently depends on acceptance of their new sexual identity; Rand, Graham, and Rawlings (1982) report that only those lesbian mothers who were comfortable with their sexual orientation experienced higher morale and a heightened sense of well-being relative to heterosexual mothers. Patterson (1996), however, comes to a somewhat different conclusion. Reviewing extant findings, and specifically citing the work of Gonsiorek (1991) and Falk (1989), she finds few significant differences in adjustment across the two groups. Leading quiet lives, lesbian mothers from older cohorts may have been less concerned about the possibility of losing custody due to their sexual orientation and partnership status. Lesbian mothers within the present cohort are likely to be more socially activist, less conformist, and less likely than straight counterparts to stereotype others based on ethnicity, social position, or sexual orientation. Similar results have been documented for both gay men and the offspring of gay and lesbian parents. Findings reviewed by Patterson (1995b) suggest lesbian mothers and gay fathers may both be more child-centered than their same-sex heterosexual counterparts. Further, divorced lesbian mothers are more likely to be living with a partner than divorced heterosexual mothers. While partnership may lead to conflicts, the presence of a partner may also alleviate some of the burdens of child care and the feelings of loneliness so frequently reported by divorced women, particularly those in single-parent households.

Women as a group are at increased risk for depression, as has been well documented in the literature (Weissman and Klerman 1978; Weissman, Myers, and Hardin 1978), and this risk appears to be accentuated by the advent of parenthood (Campbell, Converse, and Rodgers 1976; Gove, Style, and Hughes 1990; Shereshefsky and Yarrow 1973). Considering these findings, it is noteworthy that Green et al. (1986) and Siegelman (1972b) have reported that lesbian mothers were less depressed and anxious than their heterosexual counterparts. In fact, lesbians appear to fare better overall than heterosexual counterparts in their role as parents, experiencing lower rates of depression and higher global self-esteem. Kirkpatrick (1987, 1996) has suggested that the presence of children may actually enhance lesbian relationships. Although the biological parent in lesbian families is typically the primary caregiver (Patterson 1996; Gartrell et al. 1999) there is some evidence that partners in lesbian relationships are better informed about and more involved in child care than heterosexual fathers (Flaks et al. 1995), who in some cases may add to the perceived burdens of the wife and mother (Siassi, Crocetti, and Spiro 1974; R. Burke, Weir, and Duwors 1980).

In general, lesbian couples are better able than heterosexual couples to equitably divide household labor (Kurdek 1994, 1995b; Patterson 1995c). This sharing of household and child-care responsibilities reduces the role strain of the biological mother, decreases the risk for depression and disengagement from parenting tasks, and hence contributes to the overall adjustment and well-being of the child (Patterson 1995b). However, Gartrell et al. (1999) also report on role strain within the couple's relationship as a result of the advent of parenthood, similar to that experienced by straight couples. It should also be noted that virtually all research to date on lesbian couples has focused on relatively affluent and advantaged Anglo-American populations, often residing in highly supportive communities such as the San Francisco Bay Area.

Despite these and other differences, lesbian and heterosexual mothers were found to be quite similar on other indices, including personality measures and attitudes toward child care (N. L. Thompson, Schwartz, et al. 1973; Kirkpatrick, Smith, and Roy 1981; Patterson 1995b). Patterson, Hurt, and Mason (1998) report that both lesbian mothers and their offspring maintain close ties with their own parents (particularly the biological mother) as well as with the larger community. Moreover, few differences have been observed regarding gender-role socialization or future goals for offspring between these two groups of mothers.

As we have already indicated, there has been much less systematic study of gay fathers. To date, there have been two primary routes into gay fatherhood: fathers may have shared or sole custody of children following divorce or they may adopt. In general, gay fathers have found it much more difficult to retain custody following divorce than have lesbian mothers (Falk 1989; Patterson 1996). Indeed, far fewer gay fathers than lesbian mothers share a household with their children (Bigner and Bozett 1990). Gay fathers are typically more concerned about the impact of their sexual orientation on the development of their children and are less likely than lesbian mothers to see possible benefits for offspring, such as increased tolerance for diversity (Harris and Turner 1985/86). In a comparison of divorced gay fathers and divorced and married heterosexual fathers, Bigner and Jacobsen (1989a) found few differences in motivation for becoming parents, although gay fathers noted that societal expectations and pressures to assume this quintessential adult role made realization of the parental role even more significant for them than for heterosexual counterparts who had not had to overcome social barriers in caring for their children. These authors report that gay fathers were more committed than straight paternal counterparts to providing ongoing care and more motivated to maintain close ties with children. However, given that the comparison group contained both married and divorced men, another possible interpretation is that divorce enhances such motivation irrespective of sexual orientation.

The adoption route has only recently become available to gay singles or couples wishing to bring children into their lives. Ricketts and Achtenberg (1990) trace the history of social policies and legal decisions concerning gay adoption back to a 1973 revelation that the Illinois Department of Children and Family Services was placing difficult-to-adopt children in foster homes with gay men. Over the next decade, a number of states adopted similar policies, culminating in the decision by the Massachusetts Department of Social Services to place two boys no longer able to live with their own parents in the foster care of a gay couple, a decision that drew national media attention.

Regardless of formal state policies, adoption still poses particular problems for gay and lesbian couples. As Ricketts and Achtenberg (1990) note, such couples are usually at the bottom of the list of suitable placements and are frequently awarded children for whom foster care or adoption has not previously been possible or who have been removed from their natal homes following a serious crisis. These children may be older and particularly troubled, in stark contrast to the infants typically adopted by heterosexual couples. The children adopted by gays and lesbians are more likely to have experienced an unsettled developmental course, including a history of multiple foster home placements. Such late-adopted children may demand particular time and effort and may encounter significant problems at school. Recently, even heterosexual couples have encountered difficulty in finding suitable adoptions. As a result of increasing societal acceptance of abortion, there are fewer children available for adoption than in the past, and straight couples have often been forced to arrange off-shore adoptions from South America, Asia, or Eastern Europe. This has further reduced the adoption options of gay men.

Among lesbian mothers, partnership plays an important part in the management of the role strains and conflicts associated with becoming a parent (Gartrell et al. 1999). Harris and Turner (1985/86) suggest that partnered gay fathers may likewise receive more support and encounter fewer problems in their paternal role than gay fathers who live alone. Further, when the decision to adopt is mutual on the part of gay male partners, there is increased commitment to the parental role (Bozett 1993), with both partners devoting more time and effort to child care than is typical of straight fathers. However, partners of gay fathers appear somewhat less involved in child care than the partners of lesbian mothers (Patterson 1996). In those cases in which the father's partner is supportive and shares in child-care responsibilities, the father feels more secure in his parental role and the couple's relationship also benefits.

Finally, as with lesbian mothers, those gay fathers who are most open about and comfortable with sexual orientation fare best in the parental role. Gay fathers who are "out" in the context of their family life enjoy better relationships with their partners, their children, and their extended family, including the relatives of their former wives. At the same time, disclosure of sexual orientation appears to be a much more difficult issue for gay fathers than for lesbian mothers. Bozett (1980a, 1980b, 1993) has suggested that the task of public acknowledgment may be particularly complex among gay men. Using the concept "integrative sanctioning," he argues that the gay father must effectively come out twice, first by acknowledging his homosexuality in private and perhaps public spheres, and then by acknowledging his fatherhood in the context of the gay community. The integration of these roles is perhaps most challenging for divorced gay fathers of young children, who may have to contend with custody issues. Gay fathers of young children may also find it more difficult to achieve positive integration within the gay community, which has traditionally not been geared toward parenting.

Adjustment of Offspring of Gay and Lesbian Parents

Clearly, the major concern raised by gay and lesbian parenthood is the potential impact upon the adjustment and general development of offspring. This issue has been the subject of intense debate, as custody battles involving gay parents come before the courts and as states increasingly turn to gays and lesbians as a resource for children deemed difficult to place. Foremost is the fear that children raised in gay and lesbian families will themselves become gay or lesbian. Although we address this question, it is our position that sexual orientation as a developmental outcome is independent of mental health or adjustment. From this perspective, the sexual orientation of children raised by gay or lesbian parents is of interest only insofar as it raises questions concerning the determinants of gender-role socialization (R. Sears, Rau, and Alpert 1965). To take an opposing view would be to contradict the main argument of this book, namely that gay and lesbian identities and lifeways represent but one set among many developmental pathways across the course of life. Furthermore, the fact that an adolescent boy or girl presently claims a straight or gay sexual orientation may be of little relevance for adult life.

To date, there has been little longitudinal study of the children raised by lesbian or gay parents. In general, the developmental study of the children of gay parents must take into account the changing social and historical con-texts that shape the lives of both parents and children. Clearly, the gradual transformation of societal attitudes regarding both divorce and homosexual-ity, and the growing visibility of gay and lesbian communities and same-sex relationships, have contributed to the shifting developmental experiences of the children of gay and lesbian parents. Developmental research must also address the wide range of factors that contribute to the unique experiences of gay and lesbian families: for example, whether the child was adopted, brought into the home from a previous marriage, or the product of artificial insemination; whether the gay parent is single or partnered; whether the gay nuclear family unit has supportive or conflictual relations with extended families, including relationships and custody arrangements with ex-spouses; and how disclosure of parental sexual orientation is managed, both within and outside of the home (Eisold 1998; Hetherington and Clingempeel 1988; Maccoby and Mnookin 1992; Buchanan Maccoby, and Dornbusch 1966). Eisold's report is one of the very few discussions to date on the meanings children make of having two parents of the same gender. All of these factors have important implications for the adjustment and well-being of parents and children, and require much greater attention.

Although few differences have thus far emerged in comparisons of the different pathways into becoming the child of a gay or lesbian parent, the subjective experiences associated with these different developmental routes remain to be studied. On the other hand, the partnership status of the gay or lesbian parent appears to be an important predictor of developmental out-come. Steckel (1987) has observed that, regardless of developmental path-way, the young children of lesbian mothers with partners showed more se-cure attachments than the children of heterosexual marriages. The timing of parental disclosure of a gay or lesbian sexual orientation also seems to have important implications for children's adjustment. For example, Kirpatrick (1996) has found that maternal disclosure of a lesbian identity was easier for children in middle childhood or in late adolescence, but more difficult across the years of early to middle adolescence. Consistent with this report, Hug-gins (1989) has shown that children who learn of their mother's lesbian sex-ual orientation during childhood have higher self-esteem than children who first learn during adolescence. Having a father who is supportive of his for-mer wife's new identity is also associated with higher self-esteem among children.

In general, the comparative study of children raised by gay and straight parents has uncovered few significant differences. In a small number of stud-ies comparing children born to heterosexual parents and children born to lesbian mothers through donor insemination, the two groups were almost indistinguishable in adjustment across the childhood years. Steckel (1987) found that children of lesbian mothers managed issues of separation and individuation with greater ease than children within heterosexual families, but the availability of the father appeared more central in determining overall adjustment than factors specific to the mother-child relationship. In her study of children in preschool and early school years, Patterson (1994, 1995b) reported that the children of lesbian and heterosexual mothers were quite similar. Although the children of lesbian mothers experienced somewhat greater difficulty in their daily lives because of their mothers' sexual orientation, they also expressed a greater sense of self-confidence than their counterparts in "straight" families. Further, presence or absence of the father was apparently unrelated to the children's gender identity.

As we have already indicated, the most contentious question in the study of gay and lesbian parenting concerns the sexual orientation of offspring. The fear that gay parents will produce gay children continues to inform both custody decisions and adoption policies. Short-term longitudinal research through adolescence indicates that the offspring of openly gay parents become straight or gay in about the same proportion as the general population (M. Allen and Burrell 1996; Patterson 1995b, 1996; J. Bailey, Bobrow, et al. 1995; Bozett 1993; Hotvedt and Mandel 1982; Kirkpatrick, Smith, and Roy 1981; B. Miller 1979a), although there is some evidence that these adolescents are more tolerant or accepting of others than their counterparts in divorced and intact heterosexual families. As Patterson and Chan (1996) have noted, one of the most significant findings of the study by Bailey, Bobrow, et al. (1995), a behavioral genetics study study anecdotally focusing on offspring sexual orientation, was the lack of association between the length and depth of a relationship with a gay father and the sexual orientation of offspring. This finding contradicts a socialization perspective, which would posit a connection between frequent and intense childhood exposure to gay lifestyles and the development of a gay sexual identity in adulthood.

While the children of gay fathers or lesbian mothers are no more likely to be gay than children raised in more traditional family settings, children of gay fathers seem to have greater difficulty accepting their fathers' sexual orientation than children of lesbian mothers (Bozett 1988, 1993). Not only are gay male lifestyles and relationships more stigmatized, but gay fathers find it more difficult to manage disclosure of their sexual orientation and to integrate their identities as fathers and as gay men (Bozett 1988, 1993; G. D. Green and Bozett 1991; B. Miller 1979a; Patterson 1992, 1995b; Patterson and Chan 1996). In general, being a gay father is somewhat more complicated than being a lesbian mother, at least in part because child care has historically been considered the work of women. In addition, gay male life is commonly held to be incompatible with childrearing, and pernicious stereotypes continue to construct gay men as potential pedophiles or at the very least poor role models for children. These stereotypes have contributed to the continuing reluctance of courts to award primary custody to gay fathers following divorce. As we have already mentioned, gay fathers serve as the primary caregiver for children significantly less often than lesbian mothers, which means they have fewer role consociates.

Given these additional challenges, it would not be surprising if the children of gay fathers follow a more complicated path to adjustment. While foster-parenthood and adoption have become increasingly viable options for gay men wishing to be fathers, virtually all systematic study to date has focused on the offspring of separated or divorced gay fathers (G. D. Green and Bozett 1991; Patterson and Chan 1996). This research has primarily addressed the nature of the father's childrearing practices and the impact of his sexual orientation on the development of offspring, particularly sons. Crosbie-Burnett and Helmbrecht (1993) have suggested that the morale of teenage offspring of gay fathers is related to the quality of the relationship with their former wife. For both the parental and offspring generations, higher levels of morale were also predicted by the integration of the gay father and his partner into family life. Additionally, Miller (1979a) has shown that the father's comfort with his sexual orientation is a major factor contributing to the well-being of offspring: those fathers who were less able to acknowledge their homosexuality and less able to integrate sexuality with other aspects of their life tended to be particularly authoritarian and to have more strained relations with their school-age and adolescent children.

Gay fathers may try to compensate for any hardship their sexual identity brings to their children. Divorced gay fathers seem to make a special effort to be available to their offspring (Bozett 1987, 1988; Gottman 1990). They characterize themselves as especially warm and nurturant, as well as more likely to set definite limits on the behavior of offspring, as compared to the self-reports of heterosexual fathers (Bigner and Jacobsen 1989a, 1989b). Similarly, Bozett (1993) reports that divorced gay fathers are somewhat more nurturant and child-centered than divorced heterosexual counterparts, and also more self-aware of their parenting style. Finally, Harris and Turner (1985/86) and Bozett (1987, 1988, 1993) found that gay fathers focus particular attention on normative gender-role socialization, encouraging masculine behavior in sons and gender-appropriate play.

While there is no inherent advantage to being either gay or straight, it is interesting to note from the perspective of socialization theory that both gay fathers and lesbian mothers are careful to maintain ties to the socially dominant heterosexual culture and to stress realization of so-called gender-relevant sex roles (Nungesser 1980). Harris and Turner (1985/86) suggest that gay fathers work hard to ensure that their children have straight role models. Similarly, Kirkpatrick, Smith, and Roy (1981) report that lesbian mothers are particularly concerned that their children have contact with both gay and straight adults, and that they are more likely than divorced heterosexual counterparts to encourage the maintenance of ties between offspring and their fathers.

Finally, research has not borne out the commonly expressed fears that the offspring of gay fathers and lesbian mothers would be subject to ridicule and ostracization by peers. Drawing on children's self-reports and those of adult observers, Patterson (1992) presents evidence that the children of lesbian mothers have expectable social ties. Adolescent offspring, particularly those with gay fathers, may experience some degree of shame and embarrassment regarding public exposure of their parents' sexual orientation; social or school events where both the gay parent and his or her partner are present may be particularly difficult. Patterson and Chan (1996) suggest that adolescent offspring are made particularly uncomfortable to the extent that gay fathers openly express their sexuality, for instance, by commenting on the physical appearance of other men in public. Bozett (1993) has employed the term "boundary control" to describe the efforts of offspring to control information about their parents' sexual orientation. Overall, the offspring of gay and lesbian parents do not appear disadvantaged as a consequence of their parents' sexual orientation. Based on a meta-analysis of twelve studies meeting acceptable criteria for statistical analysis, which included a total of 572 boys and girls, Allen and Burrell (1996, 30) found little difference between homosexual and heterosexual parents on any measure contained within the study; whether the data are measured from the perspective of the parent, teacher, or child, no difference exists between heterosexual and homosexual parents. Baumrind (1995) reaches the same conclusion in her review of the literature, although she acknowledges the selection bias and the small size of comparison groups in research to date. While lesbian mothers seem to enjoy a relatively higher degree of integration within the larger society than gay fathers, and while the children of gay fathers encounter relatively more problems within family and community, many of these problems are mediated by the degree of comfort fathers have with their sexual orientation. Although the offspring of gay and lesbian parents appear somewhat less conventional than peers raised within traditional heterosexual families, they do not experience a greater frequency of adjustment problems. And perhaps most significantly, given the tenor of current debates, the offspring of gay and lesbian parents do not become gay or lesbian in greater numbers than would be expected given base rates of homosexuality.

It is not clear how this latter finding should be regarded. Given that sexual orientation is not related to mental health and adjustment outcomes except as mediated by experiences of stigma and discrimination, offspring sexual orientation should not be used as criterion by which to evaluate the child-rearing practices of gay and lesbian parents. As Eve Sedgwick (1992) has pointed out, current psychological thought seems to support the contradictory and ultimately untenable position that adult homosexuality and mental health are perfectly compatible but that healthy preadult development and homosexuality are not. The statistics regarding offspring sexual orientation do suggest, however, that heterosexist pressures within society at large continue to be powerful, and that boys and girls quickly learn expected gender roles and socially normative behaviors. Indeed, contrary to the fears of many, gay families seem to "promote" heterosexuality just as much as traditional families.

Gay and Lesbian Lives in Middle Adulthood: Generativity and Adult Lives

The normative study of generativity has typically assumed expectable transitions across adult life, including entrance into work or career, marriage, and parenthood (Hogan 1981; Hogan and Astone 1986; Marini 1984), and the generative efforts of individuals are thought to be focused in these areas. Given that the lives of gay men and women may not follow a expectable, normative course, gay and lesbian development challenges dominant understandings concerning the form, place, and significance of generativity in adult life. While many lesbians and gay men choose to parent, through one of the routes outlined above, others have elected partnership but not parenthood, and still others construct "families of choice" comprised primarily of friends. Each pathway has different implications for the experience of generativity. Hence, the study of lesbian and gay adult lives should enrich the broader study of generativity and midlife development.

Extending Erikson's original discussion of the midlife task of generativity versus self-absorption, Kotre (1984) attempted to construct a coherent and inclusive account of generativity based on the life-history narratives of eight men and women. While care for the next generation remains central to Kotre's view of generativity, sexual reproduction and parenthood are less central. Kotre adds two forms of generativity in his typology—technical (teaching skills and larger cultural traditions) and cultural (tending, modifying, and conserving culture). He also recognizes that social and historical change can reshape the nature of generativity, and that the diversity of individual lives makes theoretical generalization difficult.

Expanding on the work of both Erickson and Kotre, McAdams and his colleagues (McAdams 1985, 1993, 1996; McAdams and de St. Aubin 1992; McAdams, de St. Aubin, and Logan 1993; McAdams, Hart, and Maruna 1998; McAdams, Ruetzel, and Foley 1986) have clarified, revised and reworked the concept of generativity. They found that middle-aged adults expressed the need to feel close to and supportive of others. However, these and other researchers also found that generativity was less tied to age or place in the life course than earlier accounts suggested. Past research had described generativity either as a psychological response to the realization of mortality at midlife (Jaques 1965, [1980] 1993; Munnichs 1966; V. Marshall 1975, 1986; Neugarten and Datan 1974a) or as a midlife social role involving care for children and grandchildren and mentorship at work (Levinson 1978, 1996). In their 1992 study, McAdams and de St. Aubin suggest that generative actions are situated within a life story shaped by both personal attributes and socially constructed expectations. They reject the view of generativity as necessarily linked to midlife, and they argue that this connection reflects the societal mandate that adults take responsibility for the next generation. When individuals in their thirties or forties do not act in concert with this expectation, they are viewed as off-time in terms of expectable life transitions (Hagestad and Neugarten 1985).

We follow McAdams (1985, 1993, 1996) in defining generativity as belief and action that express concern for the welfare of the next generation. This concern is demonstrated in personal commitments to make life better for future generations and can take the form of political and social activism, careers in teaching, mentoring, public health, or environmentalism and conservation, or volunteering in social or political organizations that assist others. Parenthood leads to generativity only to the extent that it includes ongoing concern for the welfare of offspring. Finally, if the expression of generativity is more pronounced in midlife, it is because individuals by this time have typically realized those social roles, both at work and at home, in which generative commitment is expected. Clearly, however, many young adults are also deeply concerned with the welfare of the next generation, and thus generativity is not the exclusive province of the middle-aged and older individual.

The study of generativity within gay and lesbian lives must recognize that gay personality development is frequently off-time, or even outside of time, with respect to heterosexual norms regarding expectable life changes. Alternative gay developmental norms may also be emerging (Hostetler and Cohler 1997). The meanings and expression of generativity are further influenced by experiences of stigma and discrimination and the dramatic changes in gay and lesbian life over the last three decades. Finally, given that sexual identity is fluid in the lives of many individuals, who may pursue het-

erosexual and homosexual developmental paths at different times, generalizations about sexual identity and generativity become hazardous.

As indicated in the previous section, many gay men and lesbians become
parents through adoption, foster parenting, donor insemination, or previous
heterosexual marriages. For these individuals, the experience of generativity
may be strikingly similar to that of heterosexual parents (Kretzner and Sved
1996; Blumstein and Schwartz 1983). For gay men and women who, for one
reason or another, do not realize parenthood, the expression of generative
commitment may be more complex. Many members of the currently
middle-aged cohort did not resolve issues of identity and sexuality until well
into their twenties or even thirties, and so were well off-time with respect
to their heterosexual counterparts. Additionally, many gay men and women
faced career challenges as a result of their sexual orientation and were often
forced to choose between deceit and discrimination. For these individuals,
traditional avenues for the expression of generativity—including parenthood
and mentorship—may have been blocked.

Opportunities for gay men and women to be generative are further restricted by limitations placed on intergenerational contact, attributable both
to ageism within the gay male community and to the fear and stigma that
surround the bogus association between homosexuality and pedophilia. Finally, the AIDS pandemic has also made the realization of generativity
difficult for many gay men. AIDS hit the middle-aged cohort of men the
hardest, shortening their expectable life and leading to a telescoping of developmental tasks, including the loss of loved ones and the realization of the
finitude of life (Kelly 1980; Borden 1989, 1992; Bennett and Thompson
1990). For many men living with and dying from AIDS, there is little time
or energy to devote to the welfare of the next generation.

Nevertheless, many gay men do reach out to future generations through
teaching, social work, activism, and other forms of mentoring (Isay 1996;
Cohler, Hostetler, and Boxer 1998). Cornett and Hudson (1987) suggest
that childless gay men and women frequently seek commitments equivalent
to parental care. And, at the same time AIDS has devastated so much of gay
life, it has also, ironically, provided new opportunities for gay men and
women to be both nurturant and generative, as expressed in caring for the
sick and dying and in the shared dedication to ending the epidemic through
activism and prevention efforts.

In his important study of a group of John F. Kennedy's Harvard classmates,
Vaillant (1977) provides a particularly poignant example of a gay man's efforts
to be generative. Vaillant struggled to understand the adult life course of the
gay writer Alan Poe, divergent as it was from expectable norms. Poe told
Vaillant that he had read all of the papers thus far generated by the study, and

he pointed out that Vaillant and his colleagues had classified homosexuality as mental illness, alongside alcoholism and psychosis (1977, 352). Indeed, Poe himself had grappled with alcoholism in his early adult years and had seen the underside of life in ways uncharacteristic of his classmates. At the same time, having been originally employed as a high school English teacher, he had more recently attained modest success as a poet and dedicated part of each day to writing. Following several decades of personal struggle, Poe had achieved a sense of integrity which contrasted markedly with many of his contemporaries. Upon reviewing their conversation, Vaillant mused that what mattered most was that Poe "was happy and that he cared" (Vaillant 1977, 366). Cornett and Hudson (1987) suggest that Vaillant initially failed to appreciate Poe's capacity for development and growth following a troubled young adulthood because he assumed a heteronormative developmental course.

Homophobic discrimination and stigma, the different structure and timing of the gay life course, and the far-reaching effects of the AIDS pandemic have all contributed to a gay midlife experience that diverges from the heterosexual norm. Many members of the present generation of middle-aged gay men have already experienced the kinds of loss through AIDS that would be expectable at much later ages in the straight community. Having confronted so much loss, some of these men may be better prepared for subsequent losses of friends and relatives and for the transformation in use of time and memory associated with the "personalization of death" (Neugarten 1979; Neugarten and Datan 1974a).

Personality Development in Midlife

The course of life may be viewed as a series of potentially discontinuous transformations, as reflected in changes in the sense of time and the use of memory. The period roughly between the ages of five and seven, the so-called "five-to-seven shift" (Sameroff and Haith 1996; B. White 1965), marks the first of these transformations. This first shift is characterized by forgetting the past and focusing on the present (or what has been called primal repression). The advent of adolescence marks the second of these transformations and is characterized by a shift toward anticipating the future in more realistic terms (A. L. Greene 1986, 1990). The third transformation occurs in midlife, when there is renewed attention to the past, an attenuated sense of time remaining (Jaques 1965, [1980] 1993; V. Marshall 1975), and a corresponding use of reminiscence for problem solving (Lieberman and Falk 1971).

Whereas adolescents remember the past and look forward to the future in ways consistent with their life goals, middle-aged adults begin to use memory as a guide to solving current problems (Lieberman and Falk 1971). Then, sometime in the fifth or sixth decade, time begins to feel foreshortened and death is personalized (Neugarten and Datan 1974a), reflecting an increased awareness of the finitude of life (Munnichs 1966). (The advent of parenthood may also lead to the reordering of memory [Benedek 1958, 1973].) This development has also been referred to as "interiority" (Neugarten 1973, 1979). This crisis of finitude and the development of interiority are motivated by a growing acquaintance with mortality through the deaths of parents, other family members, and, increasingly, consociates (Jaques 1965, [1980] 1993; Jung 1933; Kalish 1971, 1989; Pollock 1989), and by comparison of one's own trajectory with socially shared expectations about the duration of life.

This heightened awareness of one's own mortality leads to a transformation in both orientation to time, with a shift of attention from time already lived to time remaining, and use of memory, with increased focus on the past and reminiscence. At first, reminiscence is used actively, in coping with life changes associated with career and family (Lieberman and Falk 1971; Tobin 1991, Lieberman and Tobin 1983). Then, at some point during the late forties or early fifties, individuals start looking to the past instead of the future for inspiration and meaning. With awareness of life's finitude, both men and women become more self-focused and less patient with demands placed on their time and energy, which are increasingly experienced as in short supply (Back 1974; Lowenthal et al. 1975; Cohler and Lieberman 1980; Cohler and Grunebaum 1981; Erikson 1982; Erikson, Erikson, and Kivnick 1987; Neugarten 1979; Hazan 1980; Kernberg 1980; Rook 1984). Realizing one's remaining goals and reworking one's life story to maintain a sense of personal coherence become particularly salient in late midlife, requiring the diversion of time and energy from other pursuits.

Unfortunately, we know very little about the place of interiority in the midlife experience of gay men and women. Undoubtedly, this developmental crisis has been precipitated earlier in the lives of many gay men, both those with and those without HIV, by the AIDS epidemic (Borden 1992; Odets 1995). In general, developmental shifts in time and memory may be somewhat different for gay men and women given their frequently nonnormative life courses. Among heterosexually identified individuals (Livson and Peskin 1980; Peskin and Livson 1981), the relationship between past, present, and future is reordered first in adolescence and then again in midlife, at which time it may constitute a crisis. For lesbians and gay men, however, the initial adolescent struggle with sexuality, identity, and the future may be so intense, necessitating such a profound restructuring of self in relation to time and social order, that it promotes psychological resilience in the face of the distress so commonly associated with midlife. Although this particular hypothesis has not been tested, a similar theory has been proposed to account for the relationship between sexual orientation and development in later life.

Personality Development and Well-Being among
Gay Men and Lesbians at Midlife

Above and beyond the developmental concerns typically associated with midlife, gay men and women face additional challenges and additional opportunities for growth. Although research on gay midlife has been very limited, given the preoccupation with youth in both the gay community and society at large, there are a growing number of important studies on the topic. Taken together, these studies suggest that lesbian and gay experiences diverge from each other somewhat in middle adulthood.

It is reasonably well-established in the research literature that gender significantly impacts the midlife transition (Back 1974; Gutmann 1975, 1987; Sinott 1982). Men grow increasingly concerned with personal comfort and interpersonal relationships, seeking succor from others and moving away from reliance on active mastery in solving problems. Women become somewhat more oriented toward active mastery and "instrumental-executive" activities, and less involved in caring for others (Firth, Hubert, and Forge 1970; Cohler and Grunebaum 1981; Gilligan 1982; Gutmann 1987). They define themselves less in terms of their roles as wife and mother, and more in terms of involvements beyond the home and family.

Although there are also important differences between gay men and lesbians at midlife, they do not appear to parallel the differences between heterosexual men and women. To date, the gay male midlife experience has been discussed primarily in the context of AIDS and the alleged ageism of the gay community. Gagnon and Simon (1973) and Frencher and Henkin (1973) were the first researchers to suggest that the heavy emphasis on youth in the gay male community may lead to a sense of premature or accelerated aging (Signorile 1997). Other research (Kelly 1980; Friend 1980, 1987; Berger [1982a] 1996, 1982b; Gray and Dressel 1985; Quam and Whitford 1992; Saghir and Robins 1973) has posited that gay men view midlife as beginning earlier than does the general population. For example, Friend (1980) advertised for "older" gay male participants for his interview study. Nearly all those who responded were younger than age sixty-four, some as young as their early thirties. However, many of these callers may simply have needed someone to talk with about their sexuality; thus it cannot be concluded that they thought of themselves as elderly. Reviewing personal ads placed in a west coast alternative newspaper, Laner (1978) did not find a particular preference among gay advertisers for younger partners, but he did note that fewer gay than straight advertisers mentioned their own age. From this latter finding, he concludes that older gay men may have been more likely to omit their age so as not to dissuade potential partners.

Other research has directly refuted the accelerated-aging hypothesis. Minnigerode (1976) found that three-quarters of gay men over age forty and all those over fifty portrayed themselves as middle-aged (and not "older"), approximating the findings reported by Neugarten, Moore, and Lowe ([1965] 1996) for the general population. Bennett and Thompson (1990) presented evidence that gay men defined mid- and later life for themselves in much the same way as straight men, but believed that other gay men defined middle age as beginning in the late thirties and old age as beginning in the fifties. With the exception of men in their mid-twenties, most gay men thought they were younger than they were likely to be perceived by others, believing others to be more youth-focused than they themselves were. Perhaps most significantly, a large group of men completely rejected the idea of age categorization, which they considered a form of stereotyping inconsistent with their own manner of relating to others. Kertzner (1997, in press) and Kertzner and Sved (1996) report little evidence of a sense of accelerated aging or personal distress in their study of gay men at midlife. Rather, as Kimmel (1978) had earlier suggested, these men reported that coming to terms with their homosexuality is a greater problem than aging.

Although these studies do not point to premature subjective aging as characteristic of gay men at midlife, it must be noted that they were all conducted prior to the AIDS epidemic, which has undoubtedly colored the experience of aging (Borden 1989; Odets 1995). Hence, these studies require replication. Systematic research has addressed the extent to which death has become increasingly personalized for many gay men as a result of the AIDS-related loss of lovers and friends. Clinical research by Borden (1989, 1992) and Odets (1995), and an ongoing life-history project at the University of Chicago (Cohler, Hostetler, and Boxer 1998; Hostetler and Cohler 1997; Cohler and Hostetler, in press), all suggest that AIDS has altered time perspectives, resulting in the increased personalization of death among middle-aged and younger gay men.

But while AIDS has complicated the developmental picture for middle-aged gay men, the unique life course of gay men may also provide a buffer against some of the adversities typically associated with middle adulthood. Toward the end of this chapter, we review the literature on "crisis competence," which suggests that the crisis surrounding acknowledgment and disclosure of a gay sexual orientation may produce a buffer against adversities associated with aging (Frencher and Henkin 1973). Further, since expectable adult transformations such as the "empty nest" may either be experienced off-time or not at all, gay men may steer entirely clear of the events typically believed to precipitate a "midlife crisis." Finally, given that gay "families of choice" (Weston 1997) frequently include friends of different ages, gay men may have both consociates and older role models to facilitate the midlife transition.

Indeed, it is important to consider the role of friendship networks, which often take the place of kinship relations in the lives of gay men and lesbians (Frencher and Henkin 1973; Weston 1997). Despite stereotypical portrayals, lesbians and gay men are not typically isolated from social support and resources, and their chosen families must be included in future developmental study. Moreover, being alone should not be equated with loneliness (Lowenthal and Robinson 1976; J. A. Lee 1987). As Winnicott (1958), Storr (1988), and Buchholz (1997) have convincingly argued, the capacity to tolerate solitude is a hard-won psychological ability. This observation may be particular pertinent to the midlife development of lesbians.

In debates about accelerated or premature aging, as in much of the developmental literature, the lesbian perspective has been largely overlooked. Presumably, the lesbian community does not focus on youth as much as the gay male community (Adelman 1990), and thus discussions of premature aging would be less relevant to the study of lesbian mid- and later life. Indeed, extant research suggests that midlife may be a particularly creative time for lesbian-identified women, who seem to enjoy an enhanced sense of autonomy and agency that they may be more free to express than their heterosexual counterparts.

In the two of the most comprehensive treatments of lesbian midlife to date, Kimmel and Sang (1995) and Bradford and Ryan (1991) report that lesbian women at midlife are professionally successful, emotionally resilient, and self-aware. Although nearly half of the women in Bradford and Ryan's national survey, which focused on health and well-being, reported physical or sexual abuse in childhood or adolescence, most believed they had overcome this early trauma by midlife through counseling and introspection. Similar to research on heterosexual women (e.g., Datan, Antonovsky, and Maoz 1981), results from both studies indicate that expectable midlife changes such as menopause have little adverse effect.

In the broader culture, married women with children tend to move in and out of the work force depending on family responsibilities (Hogan and Astone 1986). But the lives of lesbian women, and particularly those without child-care responsibilities, more closely parallel those of men. Women with children often enter full-time employment at later ages than their husbands, and their careers typically peak about a decade later. Not surprisingly, these women are likely to experience the midlife transformation, including the increasing awareness of finitude, at later ages than men. This midlife transformation appears to occur earlier for lesbians.

Indeed, Kimmel and Sang believe that lesbians, who may have major work commitments across the course of life, generally experience midlife differently than heterosexual women. Never-married lesbians are often immersed in work and derive great satisfaction from it. The lesbians they interviewed were also more concerned than heterosexual counterparts with balancing career and relationships, striving to maintain boundaries between work and personal life so as to foster close ties with their partners.

Many of these women described midlife as the best time of their lives. They claimed to be more fulfilled and to like themselves more than at younger ages. They felt more self-directed, better able to balance commitments, better able to understand and enjoy themselves and others (Dorell 1991), and, in the case of lesbian mothers, more satisfied in their relations with their children. They also enjoyed sexual relations with partners more than in the past, which they attributed to an increased capacity for closeness and communication. And because they had more than one source of satisfaction and fulfillment, the departure of young adult offspring did not produce the dramatic sense of role loss that is common among straight counterparts, who may have been less involved in work outside the home.

Although more than three-quarters of the lesbians in both studies were in committed relationships, many preferred to live alone and were more likely to rely on friends than on family for support and assistance. It should be noted, however, that research to date has focused primarily on successful professional women, who may be more involved in the lesbian community and thus better able to marshal community resources. But overall, the results of these studies suggest that many lesbians experience a relatively smooth transition to midlife, which for never-married lesbians may be less discontinuous than for heterosexual women, and they experience this period as a time of particular growth.

Although this review of extant research would seem to suggest that lesbians generally do better in midlife than their gay male counterparts (Buloff and Osterman [1995], however, have questioned this view of lesbian women at midlife as psychologically content), research on gay men has tended to be deficit-focused, or at least geared toward disproving stereotypes. Future research on gay men at midlife must also focus on potentially positive aspects of this transition. And there has been very little research comparing lifelong gay-identified individuals to those who come out in midlife, or comparing middle-aged gay and lesbian parents to nonparents. Given that childcare tends to delay entrance into full-time work, lesbian mothers would be expected to experience midlife in a manner similar to heterosexual women. However, to the extent that their partners participate more than husbands in childcare, they may maintain more continuous employment and have midlife experiences more typical of heterosexual men.

Most notably, research to date has tended to overrepresent the experiences of successful, relatively affluent, white men and women, who tend to be more involved in the institutions that constitute the gay and lesbian community (Cruikshank 1990). The gay and lesbian community is a largely hidden population, and those who have been particularly difficult to identify or convince to participate in studies—including those who are older, married, "closeted," of lower income or education, or living in small towns—have frequently been overlooked (Harry 1990). Thus, generalization to the wider population of lesbians and gay men has been problematic (Kelly 1977; Kimmel and Sang 1995). Clearly, future research must utilize more sophisticated sampling techniques.

Gay Women and Men in Later Life

Too often in contemporary American society later life is seen as a time of infirmity, illness, and loss—pathologies of later life have received far more attention in the research literature than usual or expectable development (Rowe and Kahn 1987). Furthermore, older adults are not a monolithic population; there are important distinctions between the "young old" (65–74), "old old" (75–84) and "oldest old" (over age 85). The "young old" may be focused on retirement-related concerns, while those over seventy-five are more likely to be grappling with significant loss (Neugarten 1979). Although most people over age seventy-five have some form of chronic illness, these "old old" individuals maintain high levels of morale to the extent that they are able to independently perform activities of daily life. Moreover, subjective evaluations of health may be more important for morale than objective measures of pathology (Kaplan, Barell, and Lusky 1988; Mossey and Shapiro 1982). Indeed, as Shanas et al. (1968) had earlier shown, the ability to manage the tasks of daily living may be a much better predictor of morale in later life than objectively rated health status. As one older participant told one of us in our study of aging and ethnicity in an urban community: "My doctor probably told you about all my problems [she had breast cancer], but you oughta see my neighbors. Compared with them I'm healthy as a weed."

It is also typically assumed that older adults are lonely. But as already noted, being alone and feeling lonely should not be conflated. There is little evidence that older adults are more likely to be lonely than their younger counterparts (Lowenthal 1964). Although most older adults must eventually endure the loss of spouse or partner, family, and friends, they continue to find solace in reminiscence for as long as memory allows. Indeed, reminiscence becomes increasingly important in later life. In this section we consider gay development in later life, addressing both expectable transitions related to ego integrity, reminiscence, and the crisis of survivorship and the specific challenges and strengths of older gays and lesbians.

Ego Integrity, Reminiscence, and the Crisis of Survivorship

In addition to the millions of baby boomers who will soon swell the ranks of the "young old," there is an unprecedentedly large cohort of individuals in their eighties and nineties. In fact, persons over age eighty constitute the most rapidly growing sector of the population, yet we know less about this age group than any other (Nemiroff and Colarusso 1985a, 1985b). There is an urgent need for research on personality development and adjustment in this population, particularly as they relate to problems of survivorship, including survivor guilt and feelings of grief (R. Butler 1963; Myerhoff 1978, 1979, 1992; Kaminsky 1984; Erikson, Erikson, and Kivnick 1986; Woodward 1984).

In the previous section, we discussed three postulated developmental shifts in the understanding of time and the use of memory. There may be a fourth such transformation, a crisis of survivorship that begins sometime during the eighth decade, as persons begin to outlive their cohort and to replace time/space relations (Novey 1968) with memories. This settling of past accounts, or life review (R. Butler 1963; McMahon and Rhudick 1964; Kaufman 1986), may involve increased mythological activity in the service of reconciling previous conflicts and controversies in favor of desired outcomes.

Older individuals often rework their life narratives in a "legitimation of biography," justifying a lifetime of decisions and actions to themselves (V. Marshall 1986). By convincing themselves that time was well spent and choices were well made in the past, individuals can look forward to the final chapters in a biography of personal coherence and ego integrity (Erikson [1951] 1963; Keith 1982; V. Marshall 1986). Whereas those who believe that life has not been fully lived can be plunged into depression and despair, those without regret can usually successfully grieve their lives. Many of the oldest old live within a time frame principally structured around daily existence. Though the comparison is perhaps unflattering, this experience of time is similar to that of prisoners or those held hostage. When faced with immanent death and all its attendant anxieties, the only way of coping may be to live moment to moment.

Although there is some debate about the extent to which elderly persons spontaneously engage in reminiscence, without prompting from a younger family member or well-intended researcher (Wallace 1992), it is clear that many older individuals do find comfort in their memories. Restrictions on physical mobility, decreased concern with the future, and the inherent richness and value of past experience all contribute to the increased prominence of reminiscence in later life. Unfortunately, reminiscence is too often mistaken for withdrawal, depression, regression, or loneliness. To date, relatively little is known about the value of reminiscence activity, particularly as it relates to a continuing sense of morale and personal integration. Clearly, older adults suffering from Alzheimer's or other forms of dementia are unable to realize the potential benefits of reminiscence. Indeed, the agitation and anxiety experienced in the early stages of Alzheimer's disease are at least partially attributable to the loss of memories, both meaningful and mundane.

Regardless of how salient reminiscence activity may be to the daily lives of older persons, there is obviously much more to later life than storytelling, and there are certainly important differences among the several cohorts of senior citizens. In general, research on normal aging has demonstrated that older adults typically maintain lifestyles characteristic of the overall course of their lives. For instance, there is little evidence that older adults "disengage" from major adult roles (Cumming and Henry 1961). Although there may be expectable role losses and exits, such as retirement in the seventh decade and widowhood in the eighth, older adults remain very much engaged in daily life, if more selective in how they deploy their limited energies (Neugarten 1973, 1979; Hochschild 1975). In addition to expectable and irruptive transitions, a myriad of factors bear on the adjustment, morale, and general well-being of older individuals. We now turn to a consideration of some of the factors contributing to well-being in the lives of older gay men and lesbians.

Social and Psychological Perspectives on Older Gay and Lesbian Lives

Unfortunately, much of the literature on older gays and lesbians seems to assume that being gay and being old are both problems requiring solution (Aguilera 1994; Sharp 1997; P. Thompson 1992). There is little evidence, however, that either homosexuality or aging represents a social problem in itself (Adelman 1987, 1990; Boxer 1997; Cruikshank 1991; Kimmel 1979–80; Reid 1995). Older gay men and lesbians confront many of the same concerns as their heterosexual counterparts (Adelman 1990; Kehoe 1989; J. A. Lee 1987; Minnigerode and Adelman 1978; Ehrenberg 1996), although a history of stigma and discrimination have complicated the experience of aging, particularly for older cohorts of gay men and women.

As in other groups of individuals, it is important to consider the interplay of aging and cohort (Baltes, Cornelius, and Nesselroade 1979; Schaie 1984). Much of what is presently known about gay aging is based on the study of a particular cohort of relatively successful and affluent adults who came of age well before the emergence of gay liberation. Given the social transformations we have discussed throughout this chapter, this research obviously cannot be generalized to younger cohorts of gay and bisexual men and women, who will arrive at later life with a largely different set of expectations and experiences.

Among the cohort of lesbians and gay men currently in later life, issues related to stigma have been particularly significant. Friend (1987, 1990a) has presented evidence that older gay adults who felt a need to hide their sexual orientation may experience a particularly difficult adjustment to the problems of aging. He proposes two developmental pathways, or modes of adjustment, that reflect prior experiences with stigma and the internalization of societal attitudes about homosexuality: the first group of gay elders internalized heterosexist values and remained secretive about their sexual orientation across the course of life, and they show relatively poor adjustment and morale in later life; the second group defied societal norms, were relatively open regarding their sexual orientation, and are now more active, happier, and better adjusted in later life. Sharp's (1997) qualitative and quantitative study of lesbian elders in Australia supports these findings. However, it should be noted that neither Friend nor Sharp considers the relation between the point in life at which the better and less well adjusted men disclosed to themselves and others their alternative sexual identity; those who remained secretive for a longer time may also be less able to adjust to the distinctive psychosocial issues posed by realization of later adulthood.

Older gay adults who actively participate in the social and political activities of the gay and lesbian community also appear to enjoy higher levels of psychological well-being (Berger [1982a] 1996; J. A. Lee 1987; Quam and Whitford 1992; Frencher and Henkin 1973). In fact, the men in Berger's study reported higher levels of morale than have been found among elders in general (Havighurst, Neugarten, and Tobin 1961). On the other hand, Gray and Dressel (1985) have suggested that frequenting bars and similar venues may actually be detrimental to the well-being of older gay men. In a magazine survey of middle-aged and older gay men, they found that attendance at bars and other sexually oriented venues accentuates age differences, leading older gay men to feel insecure about their physical appearance. This is a particularly significant finding given that participation in bar life tends to be the primary form of community involvement among older gay men, while older lesbians are more likely to be involved in political activity (Berger [1982a] 1996; Quam and Whitford 1992).

In contrast to the earlier cohorts represented in much of this research, the present cohort of middle-aged gay men and women, who came of age in the aftermath of Stonewall and gay liberation, expect more from their lives and from the society around them. However, their more explicit confrontations with homophobia and heterosexism have also produced a backlash, possibly intensifying the experience of discrimination and harrassment for some men and women (Kimmel and Sang 1995). As previously mentioned, this cohort was also the hardest hit by the AIDS epidemic. Among the older generation of gay men, who participated less in gay sexual culture at the time of mass infection, relatively few contracted HIV. The middle-aged cohort, on the other hand, has seen its ranks depleted by the epidemic. Many survivors will face their later years without the support of the friends and lovers who populated their earlier years, potentially posing problems for caregiving (Boxer 1997). Although it's too early to tell, these survivors may include some who lived long enough to benefit from the new antiviral medications but whose friends and consociates were not so lucky (Linsk 1997).

The availability of social support in later life will also depend upon the particular developmental pathway followed by the older gay man or lesbian (Berger [1982a] 1996; Berger and Kelly 1996; Kehoe 1989). For example, Kehoe found that lesbian women who came out later in life maintained closer ties with their relatives than women who had acknowledged their sexual orientation earlier. Those older gay men and women with children will likely enjoy more social support than those who remained childless (Herdt, Beeler, and Rawls 1997), and those with long-term same-sex partners may have a similar advantage relative to their widowed and single counterparts (Harwood 1997; Manasse and Swallow 1995; Hostetler and Cohler 1997). Nevertheless, those without partners or offspring are not necessarily alone or lonely. Several researchers have argued that friendship ties supplement or replace partners and children as a source of companionship in later life for many gay individuals (Friend 1980; Kehoe 1989; Raphael and Robinson 1980). Indeed, older adults often find friends to be a more satisfying source of support than offspring (Cohler and Lieberman 1980; G. Lee 1979).

In general, gay and lesbian adults come to later life with varied convoys of social support (Kahn and Antonucci 1981). As gay and lesbian lives become more visible, gay consociates provide an increasingly significant source of validation and support in the second half of life (Plath 1980). McWhirter and Mattison (1984) and Vacha (1985) reported high levels of companionship and mutual support among older gay men, and Quam and Whitford (1992) found a diminished fear of aging among gay men and women who receive support from other gay people. But it is also important to remember that lifelong friends and new friends are not necessarily equivalent sources of social support (Matthews 1986), a fact with particular significance for those presently middle-aged gay men who will reach later life having lost much of their early support network to AIDS.

Preliminary results from the Chicago Study of Lesbian and Gay Adult Development and Aging (Cohler, Hostetler, and Boxer 1998; Hostetler and Cohler 1997; Herdt, Beeler, and Rawls 1997) both support and contradict the findings of previous research. This ongoing study consists of several related research projects, including a life-history project, two surveys of middle-aged and older gay and lesbian adults, and data from focus groups and ethnographic research. The study adopts a life-course perspective and is grounded in the assumption that each point in the course of life poses particular challenges, with no one point necessarily having greater impact than any other. An analysis of narrative themes in the approximately forty life histories we have thus far collected, mostly from men, suggests that the older gay men (sixty and over) in our convenience sample are adjusting exceptionally well to later life. A majority of these older men were in long-term, committed relationships and had lived most of their adult lives "below radar," quietly gay and not visibly involved in the institutional gay and lesbian community. Nevertheless, these men did not view their sexual orientation as a shameful secret, unlike some of the participants in past studies (Friend 1980, 1990b). Nor did our participants report experiencing a "dual stigma" associated with being both older and gay (Berger 1990, [1982] 1996; Kehoe 1986, 1989; Kimmel 1979–80; Minnigerode and Adelman 1978).

Many of the men interviewed worked in low-profile positions as librarians, government bureaucrats, and engineers, and although they weren't necessarily "out" at work, they experienced little tension regarding their sexual orientation. Others worked in gay-identified jobs, such as hairdressing and interior design, and had generally supportive coworkers. Now in retirement, most of these men are indifferent regarding disclosure of their sexual orientation; they neither go out of their way to tell others nor hide it. Those older men with partners lead conventional and quiet social lives, hosting dinner parties for gay and straight friends, going to the opera, theater, and concerts, and spending weekends and summers at vacation homes.

With a few notable exceptions, these men do not believe that sexual identity has played a central role in their lives, and they were largely unaware of or indifferent to the events surrounding early gay liberation. Although they were not as hostile towards the gay rights movement as the older men described in Lee's (1987) study, these men chose to lead their lives quietly and apart from the social turmoil of the time. At the same time, they acknowledge that social and political change have made life easier for gay people. Two exceptions to this general lack of political involvement are a hairdresser who was an active participant in early homophile organizations, and a veteran of the Korean War who, after a lifetime of accommodation, became an outspoken leader in the local chapter of a national gay veterans organization in the wake of President Bill Clinton's infamous "don't ask, don't tell" policy on gays in the military.

Although many of the older men in our study reported being in good health, they expressed a great deal of concern about the possibility of needing the services of a nursing home or other long-term care facility. While sharing the same concerns about such facilities as their heterosexual counterparts (Kelly 1977; Lieberman and Tobin 1983; Tobin and Lieberman 1976), they also fear discrimination or at least a lack of sensitivity regarding their sexual orientation, including the fear that they will be separated from their partner. Berger ([1982a] 1996) and Kehoe (1989) both note similar concerns among the gay and lesbian elders they studied. But although both men and women in these studies feared declining health, other studies suggest that gay people's concerns about health are similar to those reported by older adults in general (Quam and Whitford 1992; Tobin 1991).

Taken together, existing studies indicate that gays and lesbians experience levels of adjustment and morale in later life similar to those of heterosexuals (Minnigerode 1976). Lee (1987) concluded that the present generation of gay men do not differ from their straight counterparts in terms of life satisfaction. And while the older men in his study were often alone, they did not report greater loneliness than the elder population at large. Summarizing his own research, Kimmel commented: "Homosexuality *per se* did not appear to have a negative effect on the respondents' adjustment to aging or satisfaction with life" (1979–80, 245).

However, it bears repeating that extant research has concentrated primarily on convenience samples of white, middle-class, urban-dwelling men and women, as Harry (1990) and others have noted. The Chicago study is unfortunately no exception. The voices of nonwhite, working-class, and rural-dwelling gays and lesbians have rarely been heard. As but one exception, Kehoe (1989) found that many older lesbians living in rural areas and lacking transportation feel isolated and lonely. Future research will undoubtedly unearth other important differences in the experiences of less visible populations of gay men and women.

The failure to demonstrate significant sexual orientation–related differences in aging has not been for lack of trying. In fact, the two most popular theories of gay aging are grounded in an assumption of difference, although the valence of this difference is not the same. We conclude the current section with separate considerations of "accelerated aging," which we have already briefly discussed, and "crisis competence."

Accelerated Aging and Age Norms

As we previously observed, much of the discussion of gay men and aging has centered on the presumed ageism and youth focus of the gay community. While gay and straight men may have the same conception of age norms more generally for their community, the accelerated aging hypothesis, which has been reported in numerous studies, suggests that gay men consider themselves old before their time (Friend 1987, 1990a; Frencher and Henkin 1973; Berger [1982a] 1996, 1982b; Gray and Dressel 1985; Quam and Whitford 1992; Saghir and Robins 1973). These studies suggest that gay men perceive both mid- and later life as beginning earlier than do heterosexual men.

As already noted, Minnigerode (1976), in perhaps the most systematic study to date, found few differences in the way gay and straight men define expectable points in the course of life, such as middle and old age. The gay men in her sample set the transition to middle age at about forty-one years and the transition to old age at about sixty-four, closely paralleling the figures reported by Neugarten, Moore, and Lowe ([1965] 1996) and Neugarten and Moore (1968) for the general population. Bennett and Thompson (1990) more recently suggested that gay men do not themselves internalize the ageism attributed to the broader gay male community. However, considering that much of this research was conducted prior to the AIDS epidemic, which has led to the earlier personalization of death among gay men (Bennett and Thompson 1990; Borden 1989, 1992), it is important to determine whether there has been a broader shift in gay men's understanding of age norms. When the presently middle-aged generation reaches later life, having endured a history of multiple early losses to AIDS, they may well feel older than their chronological ages.

Other groups of gay men may also be more prone to experience a sense of accelerated aging, including single older gay men and men for whom the bar scene provides their primary source of contact with the gay and lesbian community. Gray and Dressel's (1985) secondary analysis of data from Jay and Young's (1977) convenience sample of more than four thousand middle-aged and older gay men and women revealed an association between participation in gay sexual culture and negative feelings about one's physical appearance. However, more than half of the older men said they felt good about their looks. This data may also reflect a cohort effect, in that it was collected in the early 1970s, when bars, bathhouses, and related venues were among the only places gay men could congregate, and when intergenerational relations were made particularly tense by disagreements over gay liberation (Grube 1991).

Several researchers have noted that research findings are very much the product of the way in which they're collected (Friend 1990a; Gray and Dressel 1985; Harry and DeVall 1978; Weeks 1983). While older men who frequent bars, and particularly those of higher status, may express a preference for youth, men in committed relationships did not appear to have such a preference (J. A. Lee 1987). This finding is even more significant given that many older gay men have found partners and seldom, if ever, frequent bars (Kelly 1977). Nevertheless, American men as a whole celebrate the virtues of youth and beauty, and gay men are certainly no exception (Weeks 1983).

If accelerated aging is a concern for only a relatively small group of gay men, it does not appear to be of much concern at all among lesbians. Several studies indicate that lesbians are much less preoccupied than gay men with the physical effects of aging (Gagnon and Simon 1973; A. Bell and Weinberg 1978; Minnigerode and Adelman 1978). Further, Kehoe (1989) claims that there is greater intergenerational contact in the lesbian community than in the gay male community. However, the recent focus within the lesbian community on breast cancer, which is believed to afflict lesbians disproportionately, suggests that concerns related to health and aging are significant in the lives of both older gay men and lesbians, but not necessarily any more significant than in the larger community of elders.

Crisis Competence and the Presumed Double Stigma of Homosexuality and Aging

Another popular theory of gay aging seems to put a more positive spin on the experience of difference. According to the "crisis competence" hypothesis, lifelong battles with homophobia and heterosexism, and the specific experience of managing the "coming out" crisis, lead older gays and lesbians to be particularly resilient in the face of problems associated with later life (R. Berger 1984; Berger and Kelly 1996; Friend 1987, 1990a; Kimmel 1993; J. A. Lee 1987; Vacha 1985; M. Weinberg and Williams 1974; Sharp 1997). Although there is some evidence for this hypothesis, findings have thus far been contradictory.

Sharp (1997), in a study of older lesbians, found empirical support for the presumption that the hardening effects of coping with antigay prejudice over the course of a lifetime enhance well-being in later life. Weinberg and Williams (1974) report, however, that while the older gay men in their opportunity sample were more content with their lives than the younger men, there were few differences on general measures of adjustment. They found no evidence that combating stigma and prejudice increases the capacity of older gay men to manage the biological aspects of aging, such as illness and infirmity. Further, Lee (1987) indicates that successful adjustment among older gay men may be associated with "steering clear" of crises rather than facing them head on.

The crisis competence hypothesis also fails to take cohort effects into account. When currently middle-aged and younger cohorts of gay men and women reach later life, issues related to sexual orientation may be much less significant than at present. It is also possible that, having dealt more directly with homophobia and heterosexism in the workplace and the broader public sphere, the currently middle-aged cohort will demonstrate more crisis competence in later life than the current generation of gay elders. This question will have to be settled by future research. In sum, although it is an attractive hypothesis, there is limited evidence that the experience of managing stigma related to sexual orientation carries over to the management of age-related stigma.

These contradictory findings aside, it is unfortunate that research on older gay and lesbian lives has typically adopted the widely held belief that aging is a process of progressive and inevitable loss and decline. Given this grounding assumption, the elderly person portrayed in much of the aging literature is someone who merely reacts to loss. That aging is a problem, rather than one of many points in the course of life involving change, is very much open to question (Adelman 1987, 1990; Boxer 1997; Kimmel 1979–80; Reid 1995). Indeed, older adults face fewer unexpected life changes than younger adults, having lived beyond the "risk" period for irruptive transitions such as being laid off from work or experiencing the early off-time death of a spouse or child (Paykel, Prusoff, and Uhlenhuth 1971; Pearlin 1980).

Epidemiologic research (Robins and Regier 1991) demonstrates that older adults have also passed the risk period for the major mental disorders and generally have much lower rates of psychiatric impairment than younger counterparts. Cognitive changes in very late life represent the most significant source of personal distress. Consistent with these findings, Weinberg and Williams (1974) and Berger (1980, [1982a] 1996) found a negative association between age and both depression and psychosomatic symptoms among older gay men.

Fortunately, demographic trends promise to alter current stereotypes and further dissipate the stigma surrounding aging. As the populations of industrialized societies continue to age, there is an ever larger group of older adults (Boxer 1997). These "baby boomers" are already beginning to influence the ways in which aging is addressed, both in popular culture and public policy, and these changes will likely continue apace as their generation grows older.

Summarizing the research on gay and lesbian aging, it is clear that stereotypes about older gay and lesbian adults do not hold true. Reid maintains that the available literature, suggesting stereotypes of lonely, alienated and despondent older lesbians and gay men are incorrect. Rather, what emerges is a "picture of older gay men and lesbians who are active, selectively engaging in activities and interests of their choosing. . . . Some older gay men and lesbians prefer to keep their sexual orientation private, while others are open and highly engaged in public organizations and activities. These data underscore the reality of unique and individual adaptations as a result of different developmental experience and personal needs" (1995, 227).

Discrimination and stigma notwithstanding, the lives of older gay men and women are not unlike those of their straight counterparts. They enjoy levels of adjustment and morale similar to those seen at younger ages, and experience many of the same satisfactions in their relationships with family and friends (Berger [1982a] 1996), and in their sexuality (Pope and Schultz 1990). As this first generation of openly gay and lesbian elders age into the ranks of the oldest old, facing the possibility of long-term care and dependency, we can only hope that these trends continue.

Conclusion

From the life-course perspective adopted in the present chapter, there is little value in portraying development as a series of inevitable stages or tasks to be sequentially negotiated, and little evidence for the degree of developmental continuity that has been assumed by stage models. Applying catastrophe theory to psychoanalysis, Galatzer-Levy (1995) has argued for a framework for understanding the course of life based on patterns that emerge over time within particular structures. Far from being a nihilistic dismissal of epigenetic perspectives, this complex system theory assumes that there is organization and meaning reflected in the course of development, but that the particular course of development cannot be presupposed. The systematic study of lives over time (Clausen 1993) has provided support for this emerging perspective.

This chapter has reviewed the course of lesbian and gay lives across the years of adulthood, highlighting the diverse developmental pathways among adults realizing same-gender desire at some point in the life course. Some adults pursue a biography based on continuity of same-gender sexual orientation throughout life, while others become aware of these desires only in midlife or even later. The lives of recent cohorts of same-gender–loving men and women have unfolded in the context of dramatic social change, including gay liberation and the aging of the population in general. There are potentially millions of gay men and women among the large cohort of currently middle-aged adults who will compete in later life for scarce resources (Easterlin 1987, 1996).

But like the cohorts both before and after them, these gay baby boomers will arrive at later life by several different paths: some after a midlife change of course, having left behind a more heteronormative life; others side by side with their same-sex life partners, with or without children and grandchildren to accompany them; still others single but in the company of close friends.

Gay and lesbian adults experience a wide range of intimate relationships. As we have argued elsewhere (Hostetler and Cohler 1997), long-term same-sex partnership appears to be an integral part of an emerging "homonormative" (Spease 1999) life course. Indeed, a majority of gay men and women enjoy long-term, stable partnerships. Findings reviewed by Hostetler and Cohler (1997) suggest that approximately half of gay men currently have a significant other, with whom they may or may not reside, while estimates for rates of lesbian participation in partnership range from approximately half (Kehoe 1989) to as high as 80 percent. Hence, there is little evidence that gay and lesbian adults are unable to form lasting, intimate ties with others and little evidence that same-sex relationships necessarily differ from heterosexual relationships in terms of duration, stability, or overall quality (Blumstein and Schwartz 1983, 1990; Hostetler and Cohler 1997). And even the significant number of gay adults who presently report being single appear to be embedded within rich networks of supportive friends or family (W. L. Williams 1998; Weston 1997).

The intimate life course of gay men and women may be characterized by heterosexual marriage preceding same-sex partnership, by lifelong or serial same-sex relationships, or by serial singlehood occasionally punctuated by romance (and perhaps more frequently by sexual dalliance). Research also demonstrates variation in the meanings gay men and women attach to their relationships. For instance, although lesbian relationships typically involve sexual expression, lesbians appear to define sexuality somewhat differently than either gay men or straight men and women. Moreover, evidence to date suggests that intimacy, more broadly defined, is the primary determinant of satisfaction in lesbian relationships. For gay men, on the other hand, sexuality is at least initially a very important component of relationships, but gay male partners frequently make a distinction between sexual and emotional monogamy. In general, there seem to be important differences in the ways in which gay men, lesbians, and heterosexuals define relationships. These differences tend to be obscured by a narrow focus on relationship status.

Gay men and women also participate in parenthood in a multitude of ways, including foster care, adoption, donor insemination, and joint or sole custody of children from previous heterosexual marriages. But at the same time that many gay men and women realize generativity through the traditional route of parenthood, many others make contributions to the community and the next generation in other ways, including teaching, mentoring, and activism. By viewing generativity strictly in terms of parenthood, we fail to capture the variety of ways in which individuals, gay or straight, may "outlive the self" (Kotre 1984).

Among those gay men and women who do choose parenthood, there is growing evidence to suggest that they are as suited to the task as their heterosexual counterparts. Indeed, the offspring of gay and lesbian parents are almost indistinguishable from those children raised in the minority of households, mythology notwithstanding, that consist of both biological mother and father. Systematic research indicates that the offspring of gay and lesbian parents are no more likely than children from more traditional families to experience adjustment problems, at home or at school. In fact, there may even be certain advantages to being raised within a gay or lesbian household. Not only are the offspring of gay parents likely to more tolerant and accepting of others, but there is some evidence to suggest that the more equal distribution of parenting tasks among lesbian couples creates a more satisfactory home environment for all family members. Both the courts and child welfare and placement agencies have begun to acknowledge the fitness of gay and lesbian parents, suggesting that gay parenthood will be more accessible to future generations.

Although the transition to midlife does not appear to be inevitably more difficult for gay men and women as compared to heterosexuals, it does appear to be experienced differently by gay men and lesbians, and by those with and without children. While some research suggests that the emphasis placed on youth in the gay male community leads to a sense of accelerated aging among gay men, other research indicates that gay men do not in fact internalize this presumed ageism. AIDS has undoubtedly altered the way gay men think about aging, including the experience of finitude and the personalization of death, but most research on the topic was conducted prior to the start of the epidemic. It is also important to note that research on gay male aging has tended to be deficit-focused (Berger 1982). More recent research on the lesbian midlife experience has taken a more positive approach, and findings point to midlife as a potentially creative and transformative times for lesbians. Relatively less attention has been devoted to differences between gay parents and nonparents, or between those who came out in early versus middle adulthood. The future comparative study of midlife development among gay and heterosexual men and women should address the variety of pathways followed and should focus on the positive as well as the negative aspects of this transition.

In contrast to "accelerated aging," the concept of "crisis competence" points to a potential benefit of aging as a gay or lesbian person, namely an added resilience resulting from a lifelong struggle with stigma and discrimination. Despite its gay-positive slant, this theory nevertheless assumes that aging is a problem to be solved; current evidence does not support the theory, but rather indicates that gay men and women manage the tasks of later life in about the same way as their straight counterparts, with approximately the same levels of morale. However, those gay men and women who were compelled to secrecy regarding their sexual orientation and who were less active in the gay and lesbian community appear to have the lowest levels of morale. Fortunately for these men and women, it is never too late to come out. Indeed, if there is one point in the life course when sexual orientation becomes a matter of indifference to the larger community, it is in later life (Kehoe 1989).

In the next chapter, we apply the findings of developmental study to an understanding of the clinical psychoanalytic process. Both analyst and analysand share certain expectations about the normative course of life, but they may have very different commitments to the these expectations based on their life circumstances. It is important that we understand the life experiences of those gay men and women who seek psychoanalytic intervention, as well as the fact that life experiences unfold in an ever-shifting social context. Being gay or lesbian has meanings for particular persons living at a particular time and in a particular place. Social context and particular life circumstances provide the matrix in which meanings are refashioned over time, including the meanings attached to the analytic process itself.

Part Three

Gender Orientation and Issues in
Psychoanalytic Intervention

Seven

Sexual Orientation and Personal Distress: Shame, Stigma, and Homophobia

There is a presumption within the mental health professions, particularly psychoanalysis, that sexual orientation is inevitably related to well-being, and that persons with same-gender sexual orientation may also be characterized as showing impaired morale and enhanced psychopathology. As this work has tried to show, there is little evidence that sexual orientation is necessarily related either to developmental deficit or developmental immaturity. Rather same-gender sexual orientation reflects some interplay of fantasy and action, which may result in the search for same-gender interpersonal and sexual intimacy.

Part of the problem in discussing sexual orientation and psychological well-being is the shifting effect of social and historical circumstances in relation to the expression of same-gender sexual desire. Prior to the emergence of gay pride over the decade following the Stonewall riots of June 1969, acknowledgment of gay or lesbian identity was regarded as immoral and, often, illegal as well. However, in the wake of the social and intellectual changes that took place in the United States in the decade from 1965 to 1975, it became possible to acknowledge same-gender desire with a sense of security and personal freedom not characteristic across much of the present century.

At least within the middle-class European-American community, the normalization of same-gender desire has made it possible for men and women to realize same-gender desire with less shame than formerly, and with some support from family, school, and workplace. At the same time, because this desire is nonnormative in a heterosexist world, some sense of shame has persisted (D'Augelli 1991, 1994; Herek 1991, 1995; P. Lynch 1998). Survey studies across the past two decades have shown increasing tolerance for gay and lesbian persons and increased support for granting full civil rights protections to sexual minorities (Herek 1991). Within communities able to provide support for young people seeking to realize a positive alignment between same-gender desire and partnership, this increasing tolerance has made it possible for gay and lesbian youth to grow to adulthood free of much of the sense of shame and stigma that affected earlier cohorts. These young people show enhanced self-esteem and morale as contrasted with counterparts in prior cohorts (Herdt and Boxer 1996).

Shame, Stigma, and the Dynamics of Prejudice

Between 1980 and 1990 the landscape of homosexuality was forever changed with the appearance of HIV/AIDS. By the late 1980s this illness, first identified among gay men, had taken on the character of a public health crisis, regarded by some as a "gay plague" (VerMeulen 1982). The threat of a community backlash to the epidemic (Bayer 1987, 199) appeared to challenge an emerging view of homosexuality as but one of many developmental pathways across the course of life. Kutchins and Kirk (1997) suggest that one impact of the AIDS epidemic, and the presumed promiscuity of gay men, was to raise once again the question of whether homosexuality might constitute a psychiatric disorder. Indeed, Bayer (1987), never happy with the elimination of the category of ego-dystonic homosexuality, suggested that the existence of an epidemic affecting gay men proved that homosexual was a nonnormative adaptation. Further, renewed interest in the presumed biological origins of homosexuality also raised the possibility that a biological "cause" for homosexuality might be found which would also justify reinclusion as a diagnostic category within the American Psychiatric Association's Diagnostic and Statistical Manual (DSM).

Across the decade of the 1980s it became clear that even without promiscuity, sexual contact with one or two partners across the preceding decade might be sufficient to spread an infection whose presence became manifest only years later. The first phase of the epidemic reflected a lack of awareness of the potentially mortal dangers resulting from sexual intimacies. Controversial court rulings against aspects of a homosexual lifestyle, together with efforts at recriminalizing same-gender sexual relations, were part of a backlash that seemed to reverse much of the progress made in the previous decade regarding public recognition of gay men and women. Antigay prejudice surfaced in several southern and western states, with local governments voting against proposals to protect the civil rights of gay women and men in the workplace. More recently, the decision by courts in Hawaii to permit same-gender marriage has led to renewed controversy regarding the civil rights of gay and bisexual men and women and, in the wake of the backlash to such social change, more systematic study of the dynamics of this antigay prejudice.

Social Stereotypes and Antigay or Sexual Prejudice

In the aftermath of the Second World War, in an effort to understand the source of the atrocities of the Nazi era, there was careful study of the dynamics of prejudice, together with study of the means which might be used to change strongly held negative views regarding particular minority groups (Adorno et al. 1950; Allport 1954; Bettelheim and Janowitz 1950). Reviewing extant findings in the 1950s, Allport observed that prejudice is generally manifested in relation to rejected or minority groups and may be expressed in either attitudes or behavior. Elaborating on his definition, Allport observes that prejudice may be best understood as "an aversive or hostile attitude toward a person who belongs to a group, simply because he belongs to that group" (1954, 8). This attitude has been studied in terms both of shared intergroup attitudes and of individual dynamics.

Prejudice against a particular group, founded on such social categories as religion, national origin, or sexual orientation, may be expressed toward members of the group or against the group as a whole. Social psychology has portrayed this process of forming hostile feelings toward a minority group as "labeling," or tagging a person belonging to a minority group as bad, sinful, requiring social control and isolation (Becker 1963; Plummer 1975). The result of this process of labeling is stereotyping, or the expression of beliefs assumed to characterize persons identified with the targeted groups. The journalist and observer of social life Walter Lippmann (1922) had earlier portrayed the problem of prejudice in terms of "pictures we carry around in our heads," images of the world of public affairs, which may not square with reality. These pictures are "founded on a feeling, favorable or unfavorable, toward a person or thing, prior to, or not based on, actual experience" (Allport 1954, 7).

Ross (1978), Ross, Paulsen, and Stålström (1988), and Gonsiorek (1982b) have extended Allport's model, focusing on the impact of stereotyping and prejudice on minority groups, including sexual minorities. As Ross (1978) has noted, what is important is that gay men and women gain a psychological understanding of this prejudice. Such stereotyping has all too often been fostered by those within psychoanalysis, such as Bieber and Socarides, who work within the tradition of Rado's (1949) adaptational model, which castigates same-gender sexual orientation, and who have maintained that gay and lesbian people must by definition be characterized as having a deficit in personality development. This emphasis on a presumed association between same-gender sexual orientation and psychopathology contributes to stereotyping of gay men and women. Ironically, these mental health professionals, presumably concerned with psychological well-being, thus contribute to a political and social climate fostering greater prejudice, which in turn takes a toll on the mental health of persons in their community.

Psychoanalytically informed study of person and society is familiar with the problem of prejudice on the level of individual motivation. The question is how to understand the formation of public opinion founded on shared stereotypes or an illusory belief that particular characteristics are common to all members of a (minority) group (Herek 1991). It is ironic that Freud ([1921a] 1955), writing at the same time as Lippmann and relying upon earlier formulations by such French sociologists as Tarde and LeBon, had portrayed how such beliefs are intensified through identification with the leader and the group: idealization of the leader, and the subsequent effort of particular group members to enhance self-esteem through identification with the leader, inspires both beliefs and actions. This perspective was subsequently elaborated by Kohut (1976, 1985) and Offer and Strozier (1985). The historian Christopher Browning (1992) has relied upon a similar perspective in understanding the anti-Semitism and consequent atrocities against the Jews committed by a group of Nazi police during the period of National Socialism.

In the period following the Second World War, Adorno et al. (1950), Bettelheim and Janowitz (1950), and Allport (1954) all attempted integration of psychoanalytic and social psychological study, in an effort to understand the stereotyping of such groups as Jews and African-Americans in the context of what had happened in Europe and what was taking place in America with the emergence of the civil rights struggle. Much of this literature has recently been carefully and critically reviewed by Young-Bruehl (1996), who notes that this postwar commentary presumed the psychological attribute of displacement. This displacement was presumed to be the result either of the redirecting of aggression against the most convenient social group, such as the Jews in Germany prior to the Second World War, or of a conflict between personal desire and moral standards and the consequent attribution of those desires and presumed moral failings to an "outgroup."

Young-Bruehl (1996) notes that the concept of displacement as used in much of this early discussion of the psychodynamic basis of prejudice fails to distinguish between the two mechanisms of displacement and projection of unacceptable affects, such as aggression and psychic conflict, onto others viewed as different. She also notes that much of this earlier psychodynamic work relied on presumptions about preadult socialization—that having had an authoritarian father would cause an adult to have difficulty integrating desire and social norms, for example. Finally, she suggests that authoritarian and antigay attitudes are most often characteristic of men who are rigid in their conception of appropriate gender roles and who are prejudiced against all who are not like themselves. Antigay prejudice is but one aspect of this constellation of attitudes reflecting more general prejudice.

This focus on preadult socialization within the family as the basis for prejudice followed from the same perspective implicit in the work of Bieber et al. (1962), reviewed in chapter 4 of the present work, on the role of the parents in the presumed origins of same-gender sexual orientation in men. This perspective posed problem of levels of analysis: it is difficult to relate individual difference phenomena within the family to shared stereotypes. Allport is aware of this problem in his discussion of the origins of prejudice, which relies upon a "lens" model, beginning with shared views and moving to the level of individual differences—including factors which lead particular persons to feel threatened by their impulses and then to displace those unacceptable impulses onto a minority group, leading to formation of a stereotype. Allport defines stereotype as "exaggerated belief associated with a category. The function of a stereotype is to justify (rationalize) our conduct in relation to that category" (1954, 187). A stereotype is not the same thing as a category; rather, it is the idea which accompanies a category. Stereotypes both justify rejection of a particular group and provide a set of beliefs perpetuating this rejection.

Herek (1984a) has reported that antigay attitudes may best be understood in terms of the continuum between condemnation and tolerance. Expression of prejudice against those expressing preference for same-gender intimacy has long been noted. However, increasing visibility and activism within the gay community in recent decades may have led to enhanced expression of prejudice against this sexual minority group. Herek (1984b, 1991), discussing a antigay harassment suit against the Equality Foundation of greater Cincinnati, reports on a decade of antigay prejudice in the United States as demonstrated by the Ohio group. Herek (1991) reports that more than two-thirds of respondents in a national survey condemn homosexuality as a sin or as morally wrong. This figure shows little change over time. Further, findings from a 1992 American National Election Survey show that more than half of the electorate maintains very negative possible attitudes toward lesbians and gay men. No other minority group ever studied has elicited such "cold" and negative attitudes as lesbians and gay men. It should be noted that, to date, most polling has not differentiated between attitudes toward gay men and lesbians. Nungesser (1983), Herek (1984b), and Kite (1984) all report in separate studies that men are likely to hold more intense antigay or heterosexist attitudes with regard to gay men than with regard to lesbians.

At the same time, as Herek (1991) has observed, the electorate believes that protection of basic civil rights should be extended to lesbians and gay men; over the past decade, the proportion of those surveyed who support such protections has risen from a third to nearly three-fourths. This suggests that the increasing visibility of gay men and women has led to a change in public perception. A number of municipalities and states have extended enforcement of antidiscrimination laws to gay men and women and at least one state (Hawaii) supports legal recognition of same-gender partnership.

Based on this finding regarding the impact of personal contact with gay men and women on attitudes regarding homosexuality, Herek (1996) has differentiated between experiential and expressive bases of antigay attitudes. Experientially founded antigay attitudes are based largely on lack of familiarity with gay men and women. For example, Bayer (1987) reports on Spitzer's change in attitudes regarding homosexuality following his meeting with a group of respected gay colleagues within the APA. This familiarity became an important factor in Spitzer's decision to work for the removal of homosexuality as a diagnostic category from the DSM. Herek suggests, consistent with Smith, Bruner, and White's (1956) discussion of the function of anticommunist attitudes for the lives of persons reporting such prejudice, that the second, or expressive, basis for antigay prejudice has three different origins: in value-expressive, social-expressive, and defensive functions (Herek 1985, 1991, 1996). These three expressive functions may overlap—it is possible that value- or social-expressive functions also serve a defensive function.

Regarding the value-expressive function, Herek observes that those adults most likely to express antigay prejudice, and consequent stereotyping, live in small towns or rural communities, are older, are less well educated, and are of a conservative, often fundamentalist, religious background. They are likely to espouse values consistent with a conventional lifestyle and to exhibit the constellation of family and personal traits characteristic of the authoritarian personality. Antigay attitudes are but another reflection of this valuation of a conventional lifestyle. Children growing up within such communities receive wide-scale support for adopting similar conservative views leading to the stereotyping of minority groups such as gay men and lesbians, consistent with Herek's (1984b) observation regarding socialization into traditional norms within conservative small towns. Herek also notes, however, that the conservative attitudes learned within the family and school across the years of early childhood are themselves subject to change across cohorts. Increasing exposure in the media to gay men and lesbians who contradict implicit stereotypes, involvement in postsecondary education outside the community, and historical change itself all may alter these antigay attitudes learned in childhood.

The social-expressive function of antigay attitudes is founded on the need to gain acceptance or approval from peers, which leads to enhanced sense of belonging to the group. Consistent with Freud's ([1921a] 1955) discussion of the importance for followers of the admiration of the leader, and its extension in more recent work on leaders and groups (Kohut 1976; Offer and Strozier 1985), members of a group may maintain antigay prejudice in order to gain the approval of their leader. Based on the reports of D'Augelli (1991, 1996), this social-expressive function may be observed in school and college settings where students believe they will win approval from others if they express antigay attitudes.

The defensive-expressive function of antigay attitudes reflects the position of psychodynamic perspectives such as those of Adorno et al. (1950), Bettelheim and Janowitz (1950), and Bird (1957) that such attitudes reflect intrapersonal conflict such as that regarding experience and enactment of same-gender desire. Unconscious conflicts regarding sexual identity might lead to disavowal (Basch 1983) and projection of these personally unacceptable wishes onto sexual minority groups, a process portrayed by Bird as "incor-projection." According to this perspective:

> Prejudice is used by the ego specifically to prevent loss of desired objects and is called upon precisely when such a loss threatens to occur on account of feelings of envy, guilt resulting from that envy, and fear of punishment from reality or from the superego because of that envy. (Bird 1957, 504)

Bird notes that incorporation and projection are united in a single mechanism which protects against what otherwise would be a feeling of guilt resulting from envy and leads to criticism of others as if they were oneself. Prejudice reflects "self-criticism gone wrong" (Bird 1957, 511), or, as Sandler and Sandler (1987) and Kris (1990) have emphasized, an effort to maintain present equilibrium, transforming shameful feelings which might otherwise lead to self-criticism through projective identifications.

For example, envy of the presumed greater sexual freedom of gay men may lead to expression of prejudice as a function of self-criticism, now projected on those persons thought able to realize what is both wished for and viewed by oneself as wrong, making gay men and women the perceived source of the badness. This projective identification reflects the criticism against oneself, which is protected against by its being experienced as true of another. This perspective on prejudice is consistent with findings that antigay attitudes are most often expressed regarding others of the same gender (Herek 1984a, 1996; Isay 1989; Kite 1984; Nungesser 1983; Young-Bruehl 1996); as previously noted, men are more likely to express strongly negative attitudes toward other men who are gay than toward lesbians. Those men expressing antigay attitudes, a social-psychological experiment has shown, show greater physiological arousal associated with anxiety when told that they are talking to a gay man than when told they are talking to a heterosexual man or when viewing slides of men engaging in homosexual activities (Cuneot and Fugita 1982; Shields and Harriman 1984).

The advent of AIDS has lent a particularly tragic twist to antigay prejudice (Herek 1999). Treichler (1988) observed that the epidemic led to pronouncements from vocal groups within the media, members of Congress, and even public health authorities that gay men were addicted to sex, unable to control their impulses. Some conservative groups even asserted that they deserved their fate for having committed "immoral" acts. Sontag (1989), in an extension of an argument earlier made on the social construction of the significance of cancer, described how conservative elements in the community had turned AIDS into a moral message through analogies to such other phenomena as the plague of black death in medieval Europe. As portrayed by some conservative religious groups, the spread of the AIDS virus through the body parallels the way in which homosexuals have infected society and contaminated the public good. Epstein (1992) notes that the advent of AIDS enhanced the view of homosexuality as both morally wrong and a medical and sexual abnormality. Persons with AIDS and implicitly all homosexuals, were seen as dangerous and in need of quarantine from the larger society. Lewes (1992) notes that some heterosexual men developed an obsessive fear of gay men and the infection which they were presumably spreading (along with the feared and wished-for homosexuality) to the whole population.

Sontag's assessment of AIDS as a metaphor employed by the fundamentalist conservative community to highlight a presumably perverse, immoral, and life-threatening activity was supported in a report (Herek and Glunt 1988) detailing the extent to which Americans endorsed a view of AIDS as a homosexual infection. As Herek and Glunt note: "AIDS became socially defined as a disease of marginalized groups, especially gay men. Consequently, the stigma attached to AIDS as an illness is layered upon preexisting stigma" (1988, 887). Moss (1997a) notes particularly the focus of those conflating homosexuality and AIDS on bodily penetrations and attractive yet feared erotic dangers, which become the source of self-criticism repudiated through projective identification. As recently as 5 December 1997, the *New York Times* reported findings from public opinion polls showing that Americans have a greater dread of AIDS than of any other disease and continue to believe that this illness may be "caught" from casual contact such as shaking hands, or even from being in the same room with a person with AIDS.

From this antigay perspective, expression of same-gender sexual orientation becomes tantamount to having HIV/AIDS, and therefore to be gay is to have a fatal disease. In chapter 5 we cited the example of the physician father of a gay young man who commented when his son disclosed his homosexuality, "I might as well grieve for you now since you're sure to die of AIDS if you're gay." Although this man had ready access to information about the origins and course of HIV infection, his response to his son reflected the unquestioned equation of homosexuality with HIV/AIDS that was widespread within conservative elements of the larger community. The gay man, as others to whom wishes viewed as personally repugnant may be attributed, thus comes to be seen as dangerous, a source of infection. In this respect, antigay prejudice is structurally similar to such other well studied prejudice, such as anti-Semitism.

Stigma, Sexual Identity, Shame, and Morale

Studies of the impact of prejudice and stereotyping have highlighted their effects on the lives of members of minority groups. From the early studies of Kenneth Clark and Robert Coles regarding the impact of racism on self-esteem among African-American children to more recent studies of antigay prejudice, it has been clear that experiencing prejudice has significant psychological costs (Clark 1965; Coles 1967; Parsons and Clark 1966). The experience of being a member of a discriminated minority group was most thoroughly explored in Goffman's (1963) account of stigma. Goffman views stigma as "a special kind of relationship between attribute and stereotype" (1963, 4). Implicit in the concept of stigma is both the issue of abomination and such responses as disguise, disavowal, and disclosure. Central to Goffman's symbolic interactionist position is the concept of identity or experience of self, which is initially defined through social interaction.

Goffman (1959, 1963) and McCall and Simmons (1978) view identity in terms somewhat different from those entailed by Erikson's (1968) use of this term. As used by Goffman, McCall and Simmons and others within the social science tradition of symbolic interactionism, (personal) identity reflects a presently recounted life history, the nature of which leads to continuing revisions based on subsequent understandings of the presently recounted past. Personal identity must be differentiated from social identity or the way in which a person manages acknowledgment to others of this life history. Distortions or sensed incongruity are associated with a disrupted life history or a "spoiled identity" (Goffman 1963, 19). Subsequent life experiences, including those experienced as incongruous with a sense of who and what one is further, exacerbate this sense of spoiled identity.

Discrepancy between actual and virtual, or socially evident, self occurs in the context of stereotyping and leads to a sense of spoiled identity as a member of a shamed category of persons. Efforts at anonymity and avoidance of disclosure serve only to reinforce this sense. Keeping track of who does and who does not know about one's membership in the category of shamed persons leads to ever greater distortions of the life history. Goffman observes that, over time, stigma and the effort to manage it become fixed as an aspect of personal identity. Efforts to pass for normal become so automatic that their continuing impact upon identity may no longer even be recognized but accepted as a fact of life.

Recognition of one's membership in a shamed category of persons is learned through comparison with the socially defined "normal" state. As Warren (1980) has observed, both gay and straight children learn from earliest childhood a negative image of being gay. Kantrowitz ([1977] 1996) has portrayed the personal cost of such experience of stigma on his own well-being. Comparison of oneself with this socially defined norm leads to awareness of a shameful difference; attempts at disguise and disavowal and the formation of subterfuge; an effort to pass, or to maintain a "cover" as normal, as a means of self protection; and, finally, heightened vigilance, designed to obtain social information on the success of this effort to pass for normal. It is possible to become aware of one's membership in a shamed category of persons at any point across the course of life. Goffman's observation regarding stigma and life course is particularly incisive:

> The stigmatized individual may single out and retrospectively elaborate experiences which serve for him to account for his coming to the beliefs and practices that he now has regarding his own kind and normals. A life event can thus have a double bearing on moral career, first as immediate objective grounds for an actual turning point, and later . . . as a means of accounting for a position currently taken. . . . One experience often selected for this later purpose is that through which the newly stigmatized individual learns that full-fledged members of the group are quite like ordinary human beings. (1963, 39)

Persons within a shamed category construct stories of coming to be within that category which provide a sense of purpose and meaning for lived experience, such as the coming-out stories of gay men and women (Plummer 1995; Savin-Williams 1997).

Goffman wryly observes that "it is assumed that [one] must necessarily pay a great psychological price, a very high level of anxiety, in living a life that can be collapsed at any moment" (1963, 87). Nowhere is this more clearly evident than among those gay men and women who feel a continuing need to pass as "normal," in the sense of expressing normatively expected desired. Understood in terms of gay men and women, this sense of stigma and shame, sometimes referred to as (internalized) homophobia (Malyon 1982; Nungesser 1983; Shidlo 1994; Young-Bruehl 1996; G. Weinberg 1972), may be responsible for much of the psychopathology assumed intrinsic among persons experiencing same-gender desire.

However, Sagrin and Kelly (1980) question this assumption regarding the relation between community-based antigay prejudice and adjustment among gay men and women. Reviewing findings from Bell and Weinberg's (1978) study, and noting that at least some of the men and women who participated had a dysfunctional adjustment, even within a community in which same-gender sexual orientation was accepted and appreciated, these authors claim that labeling theory may not entirely account for the adjustment difficulties sometimes reported among gay men and women. All that might be claimed, then, is that same-gender sexual orientation need not be antithetical to satisfactory psychological adjustment. However, Sagrin and Kelly (1980) fail to appreciate the lifelong impact upon gay men and women of the labeling and antigay prejudice they had experienced before moving to a more acceptant community, which may account for at least some of the distress reported in Bell and Weinberg's study.

It is assumed that the dread shown by some heterosexual adults (primarily men) towards gay men and lesbians is internalized over time and becomes an element of their own self-loathing. It is difficult to live in a heterosexist society, stigmatized and stereotyped over time (Gair 1995; Glassgold 1995). Based on recalculation from national survey studies, Shidlo (1994) estimates that more than a third of lesbians and more than a quarter of all gay men feel a constant and enduring sense of shame associated with their sexual orientation. These feelings of shame are associated with greater distrust of others, difficulties in work and interpersonal ties, and problems in the realm of sexuality itself (Malyon 1982; Morrison 1999).

There has been much discussion in the psychoanalytic literature regarding the dynamics of shame (Lanksy and Morrison 1997; Morrison 1989, 1999; Morrison and Stolorow 1997; Goldberg 1995, 1999). Kohut (1971, 1977) initially observed that shame arose from the tension between goals or ideals and realized accomplishments. Lansky has observed:

> Shame arises . . . from the vast array of psychopathological dispositions and human experiences that involve awareness of failure to meet standards and ideals; from exposure as inadequate or deficient; from fantasied or actual denied or inferior status; and from awareness of oneself as dirty, inadequate, needy, empty, dependent, rageful, disappointing, shy, socially fearful or inept, humiliation prone and the like. . . . This wide range of the clinical phenomenology of shame has in common the origin of shame and points of exposure to self or others as . . . relegated to the status of inferior or to be rejected and cast out completely. (1999, 351–52)

Shame is perhaps the most powerful feeling state associated with the experience of a conflicted and socially disvalued identity such as being gay or lesbian. This sense of shame arises from the lifelong experience of stigma and prejudice, often leading to low-level depression or sense of lessened life satisfaction. Among both gay men and women this sense of shame is bound to arise again in the context the therapeutic relationship. Unless recognized and made an explicit aspect of the therapeutic situation, it is bound to interfere in the analysand's efforts to realize enhanced morale and personal vitality. Even those gay and lesbian therapists who are most overtly supportive of the gay community may harbor a sense of shame regarding their sexual identity, expressed as a complementary identification (Malyon 1982).

First efforts at portraying the effects of stigma resulting from membership in the shamed category of those expressing same-gender sexual orientation highlighted the process of labeling, through which persons most often learn of their membership in this category (Plummer 1975), together with the manner in which this labeling leads to rewriting or telling the life story in a particular manner (Plummer 1995), including the need for passing, as portrayed by Goffman (1963). Extending Goffman's observation, Plummer (1975) notes that same-gender sexual orientation is both an intense personal problem and a social problem, since society defines aspects of lived experience as a source of shame, which then becomes an important aspect of one's own life story.

Young-Bruehl (1996) extended Malyon's (1982) initial concept of internalized homophobia, noting that the problem of membership in a shamed category of persons is made more complex by the socially invisible nature of this particular stigma. Unlike other many other minority groups, in which there is some outwardly visible sign of membership, gay men and women look "virtually normal," in the terms used by the journalist Andrew Sullivan (1995) in his argument about the politics of homosexuality. Ironically, gay men and women are not intrinsically a recognizable minority but have been made one as a result of stigma.

Intrinsic to the antigay prejudice which is a consequence of stigma is an enduring sense of shame which has significant impact on self-esteem. Feelings of victimization as a result of antigay prejudice, stereotyping, and stigma, may lead to enhanced feelings of personal distress quite apart from the experience of being gay, lesbian, or bisexual. Nungesser (1983) and Herek (1991, 1996) show additionally that, to the extent that gay men or lesbians lack social support for their sexual identity, personal distress may be magnified. Reporting on a questionnaire study of a convenience sample of gay men, Shidlo (1994) reports that gay men who were lower in self-esteem were also more self-deprecating, had fewer social supports, and experienced a greater sense of loneliness. Those with greater self-esteem were better able to cope with adverse life changes; even HIV-seropositive gay men reporting less self-loathing and deprecation were better able to cope with the significance of their life-threatening illness.

While antigay prejudice serves protective functions for those who express it, it has significant costs for those against whom it is directed (Breakwell 1986). These costs have been explored in greatest detail by the epidemiologist Ilan Meyer, the social psychologist Lon Nungesser (1983), and the psychoanalyst Paul Lynch, who have examined in particular the process by which attributes of antigay prejudice become a part of one's view of oneself. This is the opposite of the incorprojection portrayed by Bird (1957) and leads to the sense of stress felt by persons who become the subject of prejudice. While there is certainly antigay prejudice within the gay community, what is most striking about gay men in particular is their sense of shame and self-criticism, which reflects acceptance of the criticisms of those expressing antigay prejudice.

Studying a large group of gay men in New York, I. Meyer (1995) shows a statistically strong association between, one the one hand, reports of stigma and the experience of discrimination and personal violence due to sexual orientation and, on the other, self-reported personal distress. Nungesser (1983) reports similar findings from a social-psychological study. The gay men in his study with the lowest self-reported sense of shame regarding their homosexuality had also experienced the least criticism and antigay prejudice from others, while those who experienced their homosexuality as most ego-dystonic had experienced the greatest amount of antigay prejudice. The experience of stigma and prejudice is inevitably costly over time for those experiencing such discrimination.

Meyer (1995), who devoted particular effort to locating a group of nearly 750 gay men living in the New York metropolitan area, including men not identified with particular homophile community organizations, reported little relation among measures he developed of personal disgust at being gay (internalized homophobia), sense of rejection and discrimination as a consequence of being gay (stigma), and self-reported encounters with antigay prejudice. Consistent with Shidlo's (1994) report on the significance of social networks as a means of counteracting the impact of self-criticism, those men reporting greater feelings of personal disgust regarding their sexual orientation tended to be less open about being gay and less identified with the gay community. Self-reported encounters of antigay prejudice were common D'Augelli (1992).

Using paper-and-pencil self-reporting measures of personal demoralization, guilt, sexual problems, and suicidal ideation, Meyer (1995) reported statistically significant relationships between measures of antigay prejudice and self-reported measures of personal well-being; sense of personal disgust is most strongly related to a diminished sense of well-being. Contrasting the effects of antigay prejudice among groups of gay men reporting more or less personal experience of prejudice and violence, Meyer found that those who reported encountering greater prejudice expressed a twofold increase in personal distress, including increased suicidal ideation. Antigay prejudice and the resulting experience of stigma has a direct impact upon self-regard.

Nungesser (1983) has suggested that persons learn attitudes early in life and that, in Goffman's (1963) terms, persons likely to be subject to prejudice develop the coping mechanism of "passing" in order to avoid stigma. Corbett (1997, 1998, [1997] 1999) has portrayed the impact upon the morale of boys with nontraditional or protogay gender interests such as theater, the arts, or cooking. These boys often experience rejection, hazing, and ostracism from their peer group, an experience which becomes the foundation of self-loathing founded in sexual orientation. However, there may also be an earlier problem in development fostering this sense of self-criticism. Isay (1986a, 1989, 1996a) and Lewes (1998) both have noted the problems stemming from the attraction which some boys experience toward their fathers, and the accompany effort on the father's part to distance themselves, emotionally and perhaps physically, from the relationship. Presumably, the father senses the boy's desire and is unable to tolerate the boy's bid for erotic closeness. These boys who will later seek other men as sexual partners experience their father's rejection of their bid for closeness as something wrong or bad in themselves. They become highly self-critical and develop an increased sense of shame as a response.

This early experience is compounded by the rejection by other boys across the school years and, later, increased awareness of a larger social rejection of desires which they feel as intrinsic to their being (Lansky 1999; Morrison 1989). The resulting self-criticism and even self-loathing expressed by many gay men leads to such difficulties in adult adjustment as poor self-esteem, difficulties in forming continuing intimate relationships, lowered morale, depression and anxiety, increased substance use, and even disregard of safer-sex practices (Allen and Oleson 1999; Meyer and Dean 1998). Some, as observed by Garnets, Herek, and Levy (1990), turn to such less safe sexual practices as unprotected anal intercourse (barebacking) with the intent of punishing themselves for being gay and even for having same-gender sexual desire. Nungesser (1983) further suggests that prospectively gay women and men becoming aware of their own same-gender sexual desire soon learn the social consequences of expressing wishes that may be subject to criticism from others. Over time, continuing exposure to antigay prejudice and stigma takes a toll on self-esteem, as gay men and women, complying with antigay prejudice and the resulting sense of membership in a stigmatized group, come to see themselves as the embodiment of stigma. They come to believe that they must resemble the stereotype imposed by others, and create a shameful sense of self consistent with learned childhood prejudice. This belief, that their wishes truly are reprehensible, exemplifies to the experience of internalized homophobia (Malyon 1982). Findings from systematic studies reported by Nungesser (1983), Meyer (1993, 1995) and Meyer and Dean (1998) concur that gay women and men with larger social networks, perhaps countering antigay prejudice and affirm a positive view of same-gender desire also had better morale and self-regard. Indeed, while noting some degree of continuing self-criticism or internalized homophobia as a consequence of being gay, Meyer and Dean suggest that the intensity of this self-criticism within the lesbian and gay community may be less intense than has been claimed. Findings from other studies may have been distorted by relying upon groups of gay men and women seeking psychotherapy, who may be particularly likely to experience such distress. However, inevitably, antigay prejudice learned early within family and community takes its toll over time, leaving a residue of self-criticism and shame which is difficult to resolve (Allen and Oleson 1999; Lansky 1999).

The feeling that one must pass as straight or disguise and disown wishes that would otherwise be a source of enhanced vitality leads to sense of depletion and shame (Basch 1983; Breakwell 1986; Cohler and Galatzer-Levy 1996; Drescher 1997c; Kohut 1977; P. Lynch 1999; Meyer 1993). Consistent with Simmel's ([1908] 1950) concept of the stranger and Bauman's (1991) portrayal of the construction of ambivalence within society, gay men and women are likely to be viewed in an ambivalent manner by family and the larger society. Having the freedom of the outsider, gay men and women are regarded by bourgeois society as indeterminate in terms of normative sexual definitions, and even dangerous, because unfamiliar. This unfamiliarity challenges presumed lifeways, including those of normative sexuality. As a consequence, gay men and women experience uncertainty regarding their place in society. They must struggle to attain individual identity, which is "never securely and definitely possessed—as it is constantly challenged and must be ever anew negotiated" (Bauman 1991, 201). As Bauman observes:

> The stranger's unredeemable sin is, therefore, the incompatibility between his presence and other presences, fundamental to the world order; his simultaneous assault on several crucial oppositions instrumental in the incessant effort of ordering. It is this sin which throughout modern history rebounds in the constitution of the stranger as the bearer and embodiment of incongruity. . . . The stranger is, for this reason, the bane of incongruity. (1991, 60–61)

Bauman notes that stigma, emphasizing difference, becomes the most frequent manner for dealing with the incongruous stranger. Stigma emphasizes exclusion and the effort to keep the stranger "outside." However, because it is at odds with the precepts of modern liberal society, it is practiced on the sly. Following Bauman's discussion, society becomes impatient with indeterminate categories, such as nonnormative sexual orientation, and resolves the ambivalence reflected in such diversity through inclusion and assimilation. Within the family, over time, gay men and women become accepted once again, their status as indeterminate stranger resolved into being "one of us." This acceptance may also be accorded to the partners of gay offspring, who are welcomed in the same manner as the spouses of straight offspring.

While the metapsychology of this internalized criticism is not as well understood as that of the incorprojection of such criticism (Adorno et al. 1950; Bettelheim and Janowitz 1950; Bird 1957; D. Moss 1992, 1997a), the effect of this criticism in fostering an enduring sense of shame on gay men and women has been well documented. For example, Lynch (1998) has reported on the effects of early learned sense of shame in the analysis of two gay men. One of these analysands, Brian, was well known in the gay community for his tireless efforts on behalf of others. Indeed, his whole family was actively involved in gay issues; his father was president of his community's PFLAG group (Parents and Friends of Lesbians and Gays). The analysis revealed, however, that underlying an ostensibly positive affect and community involvement (of the sort that Shidlo [1994] reports as important in reducing feelings of self-criticism), this community activist maintained a sense of profound shame, expressed as continuing self-criticism (Lansky 1999). This focused both on feelings of responsibility when relationships with other gay men failed to lead to greater sense of intimacy, and on anonymous sexual encounters, which he saw as demonstrating what an awful person he was. Consistent with Morrison's (1989, 1999) and Lansky's (1999) discussion of the dynamics of shame and Kris's (1990) discussion of the analysis of feelings of self-criticism, Lynch was able to foster in his analysand enhanced awareness of the origins of his extraordinary self-criticism in a profound sense of shame and self-loathing first experienced during his childhood years. The analysand recalled his parents' urging him, throughout his adolescence, to date, as well as continuing feelings that what he most desired was forbidden and shameful. Remembering and working through these recollections led to reduced self-criticism and an enhanced sense of personal vitality (Freud [1914c] 1958).

Stigma, Self-Criticism, and Psychoanalytic Situation

Perhaps the single most significant common factor in the adjustment of gay and bisexual men and women is the lifelong experience of antigay prejudice and stigma resulting from pursuing a nonnormative developmental pathway. Some members of the current cohort of young adults have been fortunate enough to grow up in liberal communities and attend elite colleges, so that their personal experience of overt prejudice is small. These young people are like blacks and Jews who grew up in communities where overt prejudice was socially forbidden but who were nonetheless affected by the knowledge that aspects of their identities would be likely to provoke prejudice and even violence beyond the confines of their communities. But many middle-aged and older adults who grew up in less enlightened environments experienced firsthand incidents of hatred, torment, and assault because of their sexual orientation or, perhaps equally distressing, experienced hiding a major part of their personality for fear of such treatment.

Self-Regard and Antigay or Sexual Prejudice

Antigay prejudice and the experience of stigma maybe the most significant common factors affecting the mental health of gay men and women across the course of life. Lynch (1998) has shown how this prejudice and stigma may become part of the self-structure even of gay men who publicly affirm their sexual orientation. The psychological impact of prejudice shows itself in gay men and women in the form of self-hatred and "internalized homophobia" (Malyon 1982; Drescher 1996b, 1998b, in press a; Frommer 1994a). Therapeutic intervention with gay and bisexual men and women often confronts the problem that patients have identified with antigay prejudice to the extent that it has become internalized and is repeatedly enacted as self-debasement. Such identifications can lead to personally degrading actions, lack of reasonable care for personal health or safety, or substance abuse.

Individuals with deficits in personality development are likely to further magnify such self-criticism and its effects (J. Smith 1988). For example, in studying twenty gay men recovering from alcohol abuse, mostly through Alcoholics Anonymous, Kus (1988) traced the beginnings of several of his subjects' heavy drinking to efforts to deal with self-criticism for being gay. He found that the men he studied began drinking before going to gay bars and used alcohol "to make the pain go away" (1988, 32). Some reported feeling so guilty about sexual wishes that they drank before a sexual encounter to overcome their inhibitions. (It should be noted that while alcohol abuse and lack of self-acceptance of being gay were closely linked, sobriety preceded these men's self-acceptance as gay. Their process of recovery involved, first, determination to remain sober. They then found AA groups comprised largely of other gay men. In these groups they met men who did not fit their stereotypes and who had often themselves struggled with issues of self-criticism. These men provided social support for being gay and, thus, helped overcome the ongoing need for alcohol.)

Issues related to antigay prejudice are particularly significant in work with adolescents and the elderly. Smith (1988) suggests that characteristic adolescent struggles with a sense of self may intensify self-hatred and lead to distress about same-sex erotic desire. Martin and Hetrick (1988), reviewing their experience at a crisis intervention center serving several thousand young people, found that foremost among the problems facing gay youth are isolation resulting from lack of information about available community resources and support services, isolation imposed by the necessity of remaining silent, feeling inferior in high school or college where heterosexuality is the norm, and finding other gay and bisexual men and women with whom to share even nonerotic companionship. These gay youth fear that discovery of their sexual orientation will lead them to be expelled from their social group. Having to hide their sexuality, they become ever more hidden from others and from their own desire. Hiding and fear of discovery becomes a way of life. They feel emotional isolated—more than 95 percent of gay and lesbian young people complain that there is no one with whom they can share their concerns. Martin and Hetrick (1988) suggest this isolation contributes to depression and preoccupation with self-criticism. At the same time these young people must often deal with stigma at school and within the family.

Older adults face similar problems (G. McDougall 1993). Gay elders are like other older adults in being marginalized and losing significant social roles. In addition, the present cohort of gay and lesbian elders experienced more intense antigay prejudice than younger individuals. Many of these men were less well educated than are the younger men who participate in the urban gay community and in so many of the convenience studies presently reported (I. H. Meyer and Colten 1999). Our culture generally, and the gay subculture particularly, values youth. This may affect older gay men who show high degrees of self-criticism and even hatred (G. McDougall 1993). Older lesbian women feel less stigmatized by age, have denser social networks, and may also be more physically adept. Both gay and lesbian elders, however, complain about the lack of senior facilities acceptant of their particular needs (Kimmel 1978).

Traditionally, analysts have been reluctant to work with older people (Cohler 1998). As Wylie and Wylie (1987) observe, Freud's (1905b) doubt about analysis during the second half of life, which probably resulted from his fear of aging and his pessimism about personality change in middle age and after, has been accepted as a rationale for avoiding psychoanalytic work with older adults. Freud's assumptions were based partly on the demographics of the society in which he lived and partly on the absence of an adequate life-course psychology. However, there is little evidence that older adults, including gay and lesbian elders, do not make good analytic patients because of their age.

Issues of shame commonly emerge in the transference during psychoanalysis. In depth, much of the self-reproach and shame expressed by gay and lesbian analysands is no different from that expressed by all analysands.

The problem is that this sense of shame is buttressed by attitudes common in the larger society, for which reason it may resonate with the analyst's own values. Malyon (1982) described "internalized homophobia," which includes unconscious self-criticism and conscious negative attitudes toward homosexuality. He notes that this conscious and unconscious attitude of criticism influences both the sense of self and relations with others. Further, this criticism becomes a part of superego functioning, fostering a sense of guilt and punishment toward the self.

Frommer (1994a), reporting on analyses of gay men, maintains that the analyst must take an actively affirmative stance supporting the analysand's sexual lifeway in order to facilitate enhanced self-regard. Cornett (1993, 1995) makes the same recommendation for psychodynamic psychotherapy. In contrast, Renik (1994) cautions that this stance is insufficiently focused on the analysand's needs: fostering self-esteem as a gay man may reflect the therapist's rather than the analysand's agenda. Renik views these interventions as a form of corrective emotional experience founded on the analyst's authority and power.

Herek (1996) notes that the term "homophobia" is a misnomer. The antigay prejudice in our society is not a clinical phobia, which is an individual disturbance, but a shared prejudice. Herek prefers the term "heterosexism" to refer to the social bias for heterosexuality and "psychological heterosexism" for the individual realization of this shared bias. Heterosexism becomes a part of the self-regard of many gay people, often manifest as self-criticism that leads to self-disparagement and the adoption of the idea that being gay or lesbian represents an unacceptable, disappointing, or pathological outcome of development.

Prevailing social attitudes provide the context in which men and women explore their own sexual desire and its realization, and the psychoanalytic situation must take these contexts into account in exploring the meanings of sexuality. For many middle-aged and even younger gay men and women the internalization of the heterosexist attitudes of the communities in which they grew up fosters shame. For fortunate gay women and men who grew up in families able to admire and support their children's competence and who later accepted the child's lesbian, gay, or bisexual orientation, this sense of shame may be significantly muted but is still present. Lynch's (1998) discussion of the sense of shame reported by a gay analysand who was a community activist in a very accepting family lucidly demonstrates the sense of shame that results from antigay prejudice. Living within a community with a supportive social network (I. Meyer 1993, 1995) helps combat shame but does not eliminate the need to acknowledge and work through the personal significance of society's antigay prejudice during analysis.

Clinical Psychoanalytic Perspectives concerning
Sexual Orientation and Self-Regard

Clinical and social-psychological study point to the inevitability of shame
and self-criticism about sexual orientation in gay and bisexual women and
men in our society (Herek 1991, 1995, 1996; Lynch 1998; I. Meyer 1995).
While shame and self-criticism are a ubiquitous problem for analysands, they
are particularly intense problems for many lesbians and gay men (C. Thompson 1947; Downey and Friedman 1996b). The function of shame in analysis
is often complex. For example, manifest shame about sexual orientation may
express underlying shame about other matters or it may be used to rationalize
a reluctance to talk about sexual orientation and identity in the analysis.

SHAME. Shame in psychoanalysis is often understood as reflecting deficits
from early childhood in the sense of self-worth. Freud ([1914b] 1957) described these problems in terms of narcissism (libido directed toward the
self). Kohut (1971, 1977) shifted the discuss to variation in self-esteem, unrelated to libidinous interests. Among gay and lesbian persons, where core
aspects of self are disapproved of by the larger society, shame and humiliation
may reflect less a deficit in personality organization than the self-criticism
engendered by lifelong social criticism, often repeated by the psychoanalyst
(Lynch 1998).

> A young professional sought treatment because of a long-standing sense of pes-
> simism and low morale. This man was well regarded for his technical expertise
> and was employed by a "gay friendly" firm. He publicly acknowledged being
> gay at work, lived in a "gay" neighborhood, and actively participated in gay
> political efforts. Still, he found it difficult to talk about being gay in a therapeu-
> tic situation, which was clearly gay-affirmative. His comments about himself
> and the gay community were always derogatory, reflecting society's antigay
> prejudice.
>
> When he started to talk about being gay, he often fell silent. In contrast to
> his public stance, in therapy he was reluctant to admit that he was gay. During
> the weekend before one session, he met a man and returned to his apartment,
> where they talked intensely and were sexually intimate. The next morning dur-
> ing breakfast with this man he felt ashamed. The man seemed an eligible and
> appropriate partner for a long-term relationship (similarly educated, having
> similar social and political views, about the same age, and also a professional)
> and the couple had had mutually pleasurable "safer sex," but in treatment he
> found it difficult to speak of his experience. After a long silence, he admitted
> feeling terribly ashamed of going to a neighborhood gay bar intending to
> "cruise" and his success in meeting a man toward whom he felt strongly at-
> tracted and bringing him home.
>
> The patient was puzzled by his shame in the face of what seemed such a

positive experience. How should we understand this shame? Does it result from internalized heterosexism, unresolved early feelings of shame that have attached themselves to the current sexual situation, or some other source.

Consider another young man. He sought psychoanalytic psychotherapy to understand his "compulsive" sexual cruising of an area in which men waited in their cars to meet someone for a "blow job" and a "hot" bar where he often found men with whom he had casual sex. Rather than providing pleasure, these activities left him feeling ashamed and depleted in self-esteem. Exploration of these activities suggested that this young man needed to debase himself and put what he saw as justified self-criticism into action. Spankings, which sometimes accompanied sex, while pleasurable, felt like deserved punishment for being gay. Looking back on his loving and caring family, who fully accepted and affirmed his sexual lifeway, he believed they should have criticized him and not been accepting. Therapeutic work on his self-esteem led to a marked diminution in cruising and enhanced pleasure from sexual encounters, which were no longer accompanied by the extensive self-hatred. (Lynch [1998] describes a similar phenomenon in two gay men he analyzed.)

Freud ([1923] 1961, [1933] 1964) introduced the concept of the superego as the agency of both loving and critical attitudes toward the self (Schafer 1960), focusing on self-criticism in the struggle to resolve the nuclear conflict of the preschool years. Freud ([1924] 1961) observed that there are people who thrive on suffering, a phenomenon he explained using the concept of moral masochism. As Freud observed, "The true masochist always turns his cheek whenever he has a chance of receiving a blow" ([1924] 1961, 165). The resulting suffering satisfies an unconscious sense of guilt and is part of the self-punitive function of the superego.

Freud maintained that the wish for punishment (by the father) is sexualized (in men) as moral masochism and reflects a regressive desire for sexual relations with the father. Moral masochism may lead persons to commit "sinful" acts, which are then subject to superego reproach and punishment. From this perspective, the self-reproach or self-criticism of gay men and lesbians may use social prejudice to express unconscious guilt about wishes of the nuclear neurosis. In this view, gay men or women seek same-gender ties to satisfy unconscious guilt, then look to the analyst to further condemn these acts and assuage their unconscious guilt.

Bergler (1949, 1956, 1961) extended the concept of moral masochism. Following the pattern of the postwar trend, he focusing on the infant's tie to the mother rather than the nuclear conflict (Gitelson 1962; R. C. Friedman 1988) as the source of this unconscious guilt. Bergler's (1956) formulation of homosexuality posits that in men, continuing rage about the loss of the breast, together with a need for reparation for this rage, is satisfied by turning to men. Men offer an escape from the constellation of frustration-rage-reparation stimulated by intimacy with women, who remind the homosexual of his mother. At the same time, through fellatio, the homosexual man finds a substitute for the lost breast. Guilt over aggressive wishes toward the depriving mother leads the gay man to seek torture from his lover. "The homosexual, in short, is unconsciously a masochistic injustice collector who has shifted the power to mistreat from woman to man" (Bergler 1961, 66). This unconscious need for punishment is reflected in excessive self-reproach and the abuse which Bergler regards as inevitable in homosexual relationships, and is enacted in the transference as the analysand seeks criticism from the analyst. All this is intended to produce the pain-pleasure of punishment for imagined crimes associated with frustration and anger over the loss of the breast in infancy or with wishes from the nuclear conflict of the preschool era. When Bergler was writing, disclosure of same-gender sexual orientation could ruin personal or professional reputations, so engaging in dangerous, exciting homosexual acts could be interpreted as evidence of moral masochism. Consider, for example, the following situation:

> Despite warnings against doing so by gay friends, a professionally visible middle-aged man decided that his personal integrity demanded that he publicly disclose his gay sexual identity in a work situation where diversity was poorly tolerated. He was surprised at the negative responses and implied threats that his disclosure could limit his promising advancement. His actions could be interpreted from the viewpoint of moral masochism as unconsciously arranging for self-punishment, and exploration of that possibility would be important in his treatment.

Bergler interpreted moral masochism, which he viewed as the foundation of all neuroses, by showing the patient how he inflicted pain on himself. Problems with Bergler's formulations lie in the assumption that painful experience is always unconsciously arranged and that a single mechanism accounts for a wide range of psychological disturbance, including all neuroses and "perversions."

SHAME, SELF-CRITICISM, AND THE THERAPEUTIC ENCOUNTER. Unconscious self-criticism among gay men and women may foster negative therapeutic reactions, for instance, the worsening of symptoms in response to accurate interpretations because of unconscious guilt for receiving assistance (Downey and Friedman 1996b; Freud [1923] 1961). Thus recommendations like Malyon's (1982), to present an affirmative perspective on the gay experience, may paradoxically lead to greater desperation and problems in using the accepting psychoanalytic setting. An actively accepting attitude by the analyst may lead to an analytic stalemate: the analysand fails to learn from this stance because of unconscious guilt, and the analyst grows increasingly frustrated with the analysand's failure to respond to his enthusiasm.

Analysands from the present cohort of middle-aged gay men and women may be particularly ashamed of their sexual orientation and self-critical in ways less characteristic of younger gay people, who have experienced less intense stigma, or older gay people, who are more likely to view stigma as expectable and, without shame, consciously try to organize their lives to avoid it. A gay man who had not disclosed his sexual orientation at work described a situation in which a group of coworkers made crass jokes about gay men. He cringed inwardly while maintaining a smooth facade. He felt deeply ashamed of his sexual identity and critical of himself for being gay and for the difficulties it posed, as well as angry at himself for feeling that way.

Analysands of all kinds struggle to avoid shame, embarrassment, and humiliation in the psychoanalytic situation (Basch 1983; Kohut 1977, 1979, 1984). Morrison (1989, 1999) and Sandler and Sandler (1987, 1994, 1997a) contribute to the understanding of the dynamics of shame in the analytic situation with the concept of primary and second censorship. They begin with the topographic model, which describes the mind as involving conscious, preconscious, and unconscious areas. The first censorship (also called the repression barrier) keeps repressed material from entering the preconscious; the second (or present) censorship limits access of certain preconscious thoughts to awareness. Typically the oedipal conflict is barred from the preconscious by the first censorship, so that it is only manifest in disguised compromise formation. The second stands between material that is available to awareness but is not currently in awareness. It addresses primarily present experiences, albeit modeled on expectations based in past experiences, especially experiences with caretakers (Schafer 1982; Sandler and Sandler 1994, 1997b). At a particular moment matters generally available to consciousness become partly or completely unavailable because of the second censorship. We may refer to this aspect of the mind as the "present unconscious." The present conscious should be understood not as superficial but as the totality of the life history as presently experienced and narrated in the context of the psychoanalytic process.

One function of the second censorship is to maintain self-regard by permitting only those aspects of present life circumstances that are consonant with positive self-regard to enter into awareness. It maintains the integrity of the presently told life story by keeping out of awareness or disavowing thoughts, fantasies, and experiences that are inconsonant with this narrative (Basch 1983; Schafer 1992). As Sandler and Sandler (1987, 1994) note, analyst and analysand both implicitly recognize this second censorship and even its role in avoiding shame and humiliation. Kohut (1977, 1987) described a very similar clinical phenomenon as a "vertical split." Consistent with his overall approach, Kohut held that such splits in awareness are resolved as analysands establish a sense of a coherent self within the relationship to the analyst, which includes an affirmative ambiance toward the analysand. Kris (1990) maintains that fostering understanding of the origins and activity of split-off shame occurs best when the analyst maintains functional neutrality.

Self-criticism plays a primary role in the sense of shame, which is managed through the second censor. In the description above of the sessions with the young professional man reluctant to discuss his sexual orientation in analysis, it was this second censorship that made it impossible for him to relate the sexual encounter of the previous weekend to his analyst. For him, as for many gay people, despite his activist stance, a deep-seated shame founded on the experiences of being gay within a heterosexist society persists (Hostetler and Herdt 1998). Like Lynch's (1998) patient, benign experiences within the family and in the workplace were not sufficient to relieve this sense of shame. Only analytic work that provided the patient with an awareness of how he attempted to avoid shame, and the working through of experiences of a lifetime in which similar feelings had been evoked, brought relief.

Self psychologists have emphasized how each person recollects shameful life experiences and tries to keep them out of awareness, even at the cost of disavowing important aspects of the self. Wolf (1994) notes that a persistent lack of safety leads to a pervasive sense of shame, which interferes with a sense of vibrantly sexual self.

Discussing the therapeutic alliance (Greenson 1965; Stone 1961; Zetzel 1958) and the analyst's contribution to the analysand's increasing capacity to tolerate and integrate feelings of shame, Kohut maintains that the analyst must promote an analytic ambiance that makes possible the reintegration of blocked-off sectors of the personality. Often, though, issues related to the alliance remain implicit. Kohut (1977, 1984) recommends that the alliance and ambiance be an explicit focus of analytic investigation within the analysis. Such focus leads to greater comfort and a sense of acceptance and helps overcome the sense of shame maintained by the process variously called second censorship or vertical splitting.

An important implication of this perspective on shame in work with gay women and men is that rather than emphasizing reconstruction of the infantile past, as advocated by Bergler (1956), attention is directed to the "here and now" of the psychoanalytic relationship. Through the analysis of the here and now of the transference, the significance of the past becomes most real and personally significant. Certainly for men and women whose unresolved childhood psychological issues foster shame, which is exacerbated by social prejudice and resulting stigma, an appropriate therapeutic alliance is needed to make these censored or disavowed thoughts and feelings available to awareness. The process of second censorship is shaped by the past and present and can only be understood through an analysis of both (Sandler and Sandler 1987).

> A lesbian analysand recently graduated from a program in the theater arts began talking about job prospects. About halfway through the hour she paused and shifted her talk to a phone call of the day before with her mother in which they disagreed about her choice of a career in theater. She wondered aloud why she had not started the hour with this pressing problem, which she was sure related to her mother's continuing concern with her sexual lifeway and her partner. She said she had "forgotten" to tell about this earlier in the hour but was relieved to realize she still had some time to begin to talk about it now.
>
> Older perspectives on transference would suggest this "forgetting" resulted from the patient's unconsciously placing the analyst in the role of the critical mother of childhood. The perspective of the present unconscious would suggest her forgetting was caused by shame about her lesbian identity. Over the next several hours it emerged that the forgetting did originate in shame about her lesbian identity, which overwhelmed her as she auditioned for the role of a heterosexual woman. Her sense that her mother's concerned remark about her chances in the highly competitive world of the theater masked a reference to her sexual orientation was a displacement from her own long-standing shame and humiliation, which also led her to censor these incidents. The forgetting was best understood in terms of present rather than past unconscious.

Kris (1990) criticizes Kohut's (1977, 1984) focus on the ambiance of the analytic situation, including the analyst's provision of the person of the analyst as a source of idealization or mirroring. However, at least in the analysis of socially disenfranchised group such as gay men or lesbians, where there has been a lifetime of experienced antigay prejudice and sense of stigma, issues of ambiance are central to the analytic process. Experiences such as that of the man distressed but unable to respond to the powerful sense of stigmatization, shame, and self-doubt inspired by the apparently innocent banter of work colleagues suggest particular sensitivities and concerns about feeling safe and understood. The hope of finding an analyst who knows how painful such experiences can be leads many gay people to seek gay analysts.

Kris asks which factors in the psychoanalytic situation facilitate the analysand's understanding of shame and associated self-criticism, particularly important issues among men and women with nonnormative sexual orientation who have experienced shame and stigma for much of their lives. Kris emphasizes the significance of divergent conflicts, or resistance to awareness and resistance to resolution of psychological conflict, in a manner consistent with Gill's (1982) discussion of resistance to awareness and resolution of the transference.

Gill (1982, 1994) and Kris (1982, 1990) describe the pain of mourning and putting to rest the past, including that of the psychoanalytic situation itself. Gill views the analysand's reluctance to acknowledge the analyst's importance and the significance of losing this relationship as emanating from the first censorship and the analysand's efforts to satisfy the wishes of the nuclear conflict in the here and now of the psychoanalytic situation. From the perspective of the Sandlers (1987, 1994, 1997b), this reluctance may arise from the second censorship and the feelings of shame inherent in acknowledgment and resolution of these wishes. Kris (1990) views this resistance as a way to avoid painful affects and emphasizes their resolution through exploration of these affects.

None of these theories addresses the impact of a lifelong history of being misunderstood and stigmatized and of identifying with the dominant society's reproaches, such as is common among gay people. They would need to be extended to address this issue if they were to be used to understand the common difficulty of gay or lesbian analysands in exploring excessive self-criticism.

The gay person seeking analysis is confronted with the problem of how the issue of shame is likely to be managed by a potential analyst. Awareness of the history of analytic ideas about same-gender orientation will not give this person much comfort. Few writers about homosexuality retained Freud's ([1905–24] 1953) distinction between inversion and perversion. Instead, psychoanalytic authors described same-gender attraction as resulting from early developments in the personality, such as the rapprochement subphase of the separation-individuation process, gone awry (Socarides 1968, [1978] 1989, 1988) or avoidance of oedipal conflicts through regression to a "pre-oedipal" phase. Many analytic formulations begin with the assumption that same-gender orientation is a perversion (Lewes 1995; Socarides 1995; Gillespie 1956). On the other hand, some more recent analytic writing implies that homosexuality is psychologically meaningless (since founded in biology) except for the stigma it brings (R. C. Friedman 1988; Frommer 1994a). Is it any wonder that gay potential analysands anticipate that the shame and stigma they have experienced throughout life will continue in the analysis, when psychoanalytic theory treats their most important wishes and intents as either intrinsically pathological or meaningless.

Changes in the larger society have forced many analysts to reconsider the significance of same-gender orientation (Kwawer 1980; S. A. Mitchell 1981, 1996b; Schafer 1995; Shelby 1994a, 1997). These contributions have emerged largely from self and relational perspectives which have been particularly receptive to reconsideration of personal development across the course of life, the dynamics of the psychoanalytic situation, and the exploration of shame.

Conclusion

Social and cultural changes of the past three decades have significantly changed our understanding of important aspects of sexuality, including same-gender sexual orientation. Once regarded as psychopathology in need of remediation or cure, it is now widely recognized as another developmental course, nonnormative but also nonpathological. This changing understanding of the significance of the same-gender sexual lifeway poses unique challenges for psychoanalysis. In the first place, the genetic point of view emphasized the extent to which same-gender sexual orientation represented developmental immaturity. Over the postwar period, with the advent of developmental study and a focus on the importance of the child's tie to the mother, much of the variation in human development was reinterpreted in terms of dyadic development. Failure of the resolution of issues posed by dyadic development was presumed to lead to a deficit in development that became significant only later, as the child was confronted with the biosocial changes of adolescence and the psychosocial challenges of adulthood itself. Viewed from this perspective, and assuming heterosexuality to be the expectable outcome of the developmental process, homosexuality was presumed to reflect not just immaturity in development but, of greater significance for adult adjustment, a developmental deficit with a malignant outcome.

One of the most misunderstood issues within the mental health disciplines concerns the presumed connection between same-gender sexual orientation and a variety of forms of psychopathology, ranging from defined psychiatric syndromes such as depression or substance abuse to inability to form relationships with others except as they are seen as extensions of oneself. Antigay prejudice has been evident in the bourgeois West throughout the past century, since the first labeling of same-gender desire as "homosexuality." Once desire had a name it could be described as an entity, then viewed in moral terms, either as social deviance or as psychopathology. This is the point of Foucault's ([1976] 1990, [1984a] 1990) critique of the approach to the study of sexuality within the social and medical sciences.

With a label attached to fantasy focused on same-gender desire and its enaction in erotic relationships, it became possible for the psychiatric community to respond to this entity as illness and for the public to express hostility leading to stigma and isolation of those aware of such socially unacceptable desires. Antigay attitudes directed against gay men seem to be particularly prevalent among men (Nungesser 1983). A number of studies have suggested that men may be more threatened by the expression of same-gender sexuality, and much less able to tolerate it, than are women with regard to same-gender sexual orientation among either men or women.

This stigma, in turn, is learned early in life and becomes the basis for self-revulsion, particularly among boys beginning to recognize their own same-gender sexual wishes (Reid [1973] 1993; Savin-Williams 1997; J. Sears 1991) and men and women first becoming aware of same-gender sexual desire at any point in the course of life. First portrayed by Malyon (1982) as "internalized homophobia," this sense of stigma may be so pronounced and so ingrained within bourgeois Western society that it colors all discussions of the meaning of same-gender sexual orientation, even within the psychoanalytic situation itself.

As this chapter has illustrated, stigma and its consequence—in terms of internalized homophobia, heightened self-criticism, and self-abasement—takes a toll on the mental health of gay men and women. Part of the impact of stereotyping and stigma, as Carol Nadelson commented in remarks from the floor at the 1984 panel of the American Psychoanalytic Association on lesbian lives (Wolfson 1987), is that it has led to much inaccurate information regarding the association between sexual orientation and mental health and has contributed to the development of a personal sense of shame and the consequent need to disavow and disguise salient aspects of oneself.

While such issues of method as sample selection have confounded nearly all studies, most studies reveal few differences in mental health or adjustment when comparing groups of gay and straight men and women. While there is some indication that suicidal wishes may be more common among gay adolescents and lesbian women than among their respective straight counterparts, and that alcoholism and depression may also be more common among gay men and women than among straight adults, this issue is confounded by the all too easy solution of selecting convenience samples of gay men and women from bars within the gay community, who may not reflect the life course of gay men and women more generally.

The issue of a possible relationship between psychopathology and sexual orientation is further clouded by cohort issues; gay men and women within the present cohort of young adults are able to be more visible than those within prior cohorts and find it less difficult than was characteristic of prior cohorts to develop social support through formal and informal community networks. This chapter has suggested that the presence of social networks ameliorates at least some of the sense of stigma still too often encountered in the community (Herek 1984a, 1984b). Finally, as both Nungesser (1983) and Meyer (1993, 1995) have shown, experience of stigma accounts statistically for much of the variance in mental health outcomes reported when urban-living gay adults as contrasted with counterpart gay men and lesbians living in small towns and rural areas. Pressure to conform to an expectable heterosexual lifestyle is particularly strong within rural areas, while possibility of realizing social support from other gay men and women is reduced.

Earlier psychoanalytic views regarding homosexuality as a developmental deficit were consistent with antigay social prejudice and only confirmed that gay men and women should hate themselves (Gonsiorek 1982a; M. Ross, Paulsen, and Stålström 1988). Growing up in a society characterized in large measure by antigay prejudice, with support for such prejudice affirmed by strident voices within psychoanalysis itself, gay men and women understandably viewed psychoanalysis with suspicion. Not only were efforts to convert sexual orientation largely a failure but, more significantly, such attempts did not address the reasons gay men and women did seek psychoanalytic intervention: to resolve personal distress associated with issues such as realization of enhanced intimacy with partners, or for assistance in resolving grief attendant upon losses.

The emergence of psychodynamic therapy designed to support and affirm gay and lesbian sexual lifeways was countered by those who maintained a view of homosexuality as psychopathology. It was tragic that the only group within psychiatry favoring continued categorization of homosexuality as a mental illness within the DSM-II were a group of analysts unable to resolve the conflict between their own psychoanalytic education and the changing social milieu. Even more tragic within a discipline designed to foster enhanced well-being, psychoanalysts actually provided written testimony opposing extension of civil rights to gay and lesbian people. To date, much more effort has been devoted to condemnation of homosexuality as disease than to consideration of what psychological environment might be most supportive of the struggle of gay men and women to realize an enhanced sense of vitality and integrity in their search for interpersonal intimacy and enhanced satisfaction from work and from social relations.

It is only in the past few years that first efforts have been undertaken within psychoanalysis to provide a milieu in which analysands may with some sense of safety consider what their sexuality and all other aspects of their life means for them. While first efforts may have been more political than clinical, over the past few years there has been increased attention to the unique transference and countertransference configurations reported in the analysis of gay men and women, together with serious study of such issues as compatibility of analyst and analysand in terms of gender and sexual orientation, management of the erotic transference, and interpretation of idealizing and mirroring transference configurations among gay men and women working with gay and straight analysts. This chapter has outlined some of the major dimensions of this psychoanalytic work with gay men and women experiencing personal distress and seeking enhanced self-understanding and resolution of lifelong feelings of self-hatred in order to realize a life story fostering a enhanced sense of personal vitality and integrity.

Traditionally, psychoanalytic perspectives have clarified few of the issues regarding possible relations between sexual orientation and psychopathology. While Freud distinguished between inversion, characteristic of homosexual adults, most of whom maintain positive adaptations and are capable of warm, intimate relations with others, and perversions such as fetishes, which represent disturbances in such ties, he did regard any sexuality not directed at reproduction of the species as evidence of psychological immaturity. Subsequent psychoanalytic reports turned inversion, or difference, into pathology and failed to maintain the distinction, which Freud had initially made in the *Three Essays on the Theory of Sexuality* ([1905–24] 1953), between inversion and perversion. Fanciful and fearful outcomes were sometimes posed within psychoanalysis as the presumed consequence of adopting an identity as gay or lesbian.

In responding to the significant social changes of the past two decades, however, psychoanalysis has reconsidered these earlier formulations. Much of contemporary psychoanalysis recognizes that difference in sexual orientation need not imply psychopathology (Schafer 1995). The concern of clinical psychoanalysis should be with the exploration of meanings of sexuality, as with all aspects of experience, over a lifetime, within the psychoanalytic situation. The next chapter considers issues of clinical technique posed in psychoanalytic intervention among gay men and women within contemporary clinical psychoanalytic study.

Eight

Sexual Orientation and Evaluation of Personal Adjustment

Over the course of the past three decades there has been a dramatic shift within American society in attitudes regarding same-gender sexual orientation. While it is still the subject of significant social criticism, particularly from conservative religious groups, community attitudes have shifted in the direction of greater acceptance of sexual lifeways other than those normative for the community. The previous chapter suggested that aspects of the social surround, particularly extensive antigay prejudice, serve to distort self-regard and foster a sense of shame, which has a lasting impact upon adjustment. This stigmatization was supported by the mental health professions as well until the emergence of gay liberation in the aftermath of the Stonewall riots in June 1969. In the years immediately following Stonewall, psychiatry, psychology, and social work all reconsidered prevailing attitudes regarding homosexuality and personal adjustment.

This change was symbolized by the removal of homosexuality as a diagnostic category from the Diagnostic and Statistical Manual (Second Revision) of the American Psychiatric Association. The decision was supported by research reported over the preceding decade showing few differences in mental health outcome between gay men and women living in the community, and not seeking psychotherapy and their straight counterparts. This chapter reviews the debate regarding the significance of sexual orientation in personal adjustment, discussing first factors leading to the removal of homosexuality from psychiatric nomenclature, then systematic studies of the relation between same-gender sexual orientation and personal adjustment.

Sexual Orientation and Psychopathology: The Struggle over the DSM

Much of the historical change in attitudes regarding the necessary association of psychopathology and same-gender sexual orientation was reflected in the decision by the American Psychiatric Association to remove homosexuality as a diagnostic classification from the second revision of the Diagnostic and Statistical Manual (DSM-II) and in the subsequent conflict over including any reference to homosexuality as a form of personal distress in the third revision, initially drafted during the late 1970s. This later controversy led to inclusion of a category of ego-dystonic homosexuality in the initial publication of DSM-III, in 1981, and then to the quiet removal of any explicit diagnostic category in the 1987 DSM-IIIR (Bayer 1987; Bayer and Spitzer 1982).

The social and intellectual changes that took place over the decade from 1965 to 1975, including the Stonewall riots of June 1969 and the emergence of gay liberation, were at least partially responsible for prompting reconsideration of homosexuality as psychological illness. The history of the revision and ultimate removal of any mention of homosexuality as a form of psychiatric disorder reflects the complex interplay of social change, voluntary association politics, and personal charisma. The story of this struggle, over a period of nearly two decades, has been narrated by Bayer (1987) in a revision of a 1981 review, by Kutchins and Kirk (1997) in their discussion of psychiatric diagnosis as political process rather than science, and in greatest detail by Clendinen and Nagourney (1999) in the history of the American gay rights movements. These authors show quite clearly that the controversy over homosexuality and the DSM may have had less to do with the empirical study of psychiatric illness than with social change and the response of organized psychiatry to psychoanalysis.

On the one hand, the rise of empirical psychiatry over the postwar period brought increasing disenchantment with diagnostic formulations founded on what were purported to be untested assumptions drawn from psychoanalytic theories of development. This opposition to psychoanalysis was reflected in the effort to rebuff those within psychoanalysis who sought, on the basis of a stereotyped and somewhat dated conception of development and psychopathology, to retain homosexuality as a classification of psychiatric illness. Although previous editions of the DSM had been much influenced by drive conceptions of personality organization and psychiatric disturbance, the goal of those responsible for drafting DSM-III was to construct a diagnostic manual founded entirely on evidence from systematic, purportedly scientific psychiatric study of the major mental disorders. Thus, the deletion of homosexuality as a diagnostic category at least partially reflected the loss of prestige of psychoanalysis within psychiatry.

Psychiatric Diagnosis and Homosexuality

The origins of the struggle regarding the classification of same-gender sexual orientation as a form of psychiatric illness lay in the personal and social changes of the period from 1965 to 1975, when many aspects of postwar values were being questioned. Since 1935, the American Psychiatric Association (APA) had sought to systematize the classification of mental disorders and had included homosexuality as one of many forms of sexual deviation within the group of personality disorders. However, the 1968 revision of the Diagnostic and Statistical Manual for the first time included homosexuality as a separate diagnosis within the category of sexual deviations. In their careful review of the events leading up to the removal of homosexuality from the diagnostic nomenclature, Kutchins and Kirk (1997) view the events following the 1969 Stonewall riots and the emergence of the gay liberation movement as significant.

Ironically, however, the initial target of the protest was not organized psychiatry but a group of psychiatrist-psychoanalysts within the APA who maintained that homosexuality was a psychological illness characterized by failure of individuation and subsequent emergence of family psychopathology. This was at a time when the work of Margaret Mahler and her colleagues was particularly influential within psychoanalysis (Mahler, Pine, and Bergman 1975). Empowered by post-Stonewall social activism, gay activists disrupted the 1970 APA meetings in San Francisco, which has one of the country's most visible gay communities, and demanded that their voice be heard. While this disruption of a scientific meeting enraged many attending the convention, there was increasing realization, as a group of more liberal colleagues assumed leadership positions within the APA over the next few years, that the demands of the demonstrators had to be recognized. Kutchins and Kirk (1997) suggest that the APA as a professional organization has been particularly easily influenced by concern about the public perception of psychiatry as a medical specialty. Practice is directly affected by the views of the community in any medical specialty, and the APA has been as image-conscious as any medical professional group.

The demonstrations continued at the 1971 Washington meetings, where gay activists demanded, among other things, the complete removal of homosexuality as a diagnostic category from DSM-II. The following year, in Dallas, a panel which included senior psychiatrists discussing the controversy regarding homosexuality and mental health controversy; one panelist, Dr. H. Anonymous, appeared in cloak and hood to conceal his identity and reported that he was one of more than two hundred homosexual psychiatrists in an informal social group (Clendinen and Nagourney 1999). Continuing pressure on the APA leadership from feminist groups and even veterans returning from the Vietnam conflict led to recognition that the organization must be more responsive than formerly to community demands.

As a result, the APA scheduled a presentation at the 1973 Honolulu meetings intended to air all sides of the controversy; soon thereafter the exchange was published in the prestigious *American Journal of Psychiatry* (Stoller,

Marmor, et al. 1973). More than a thousand conference participants gathered to hear this symposium. While Robert Stoller and Judd Marmor were identified with both psychoanalysis and psychiatry, the concern they expressed at the symposium was principally with the issue of homosexuality viewed as a diagnosable form of psychiatric illness. They simply could not accept such a formulation. This symposium, together with its rapid publication and the increasing awareness that a significant number of their junior and senior colleagues were themselves gay or lesbian, represented a turning point in the attitudes of APA members regarding homosexuality and changed the tone of the debate on homosexuality as psychiatric illness.

Consistent with Freud's own rejection of the classification of homosexuality as a form of psychiatric illness, expressed in the *Three Essays on the Theory of Sexuality* ([1905–24] 1953), and anticipating Chodorow's (1992) epochal paper of some two decades later, Stoller's presentation at the 1973 symposium acknowledged the significance of understanding *all* forms of sexuality as a compromise formation. Marmor's contribution focused largely on issues of cultural reception of nonnormative sexuality. Anticipating more recent study, Marmor observed that "much of the dis-ease that [homosexuals] suffer from is not intrinsic to their homosexuality but is a consequence of the prejudice and discrimination that they encounter in our society" (Stoller, Marmor, et al. 1973, 1209). Marmor also cautioned that care should be taken to differentiate between persons presenting for psychiatric intervention and persons living in the community with little felt need for such intervention. Gay activist Ron Gold pleaded at the meeting for tolerance. He noted the impact of gay liberation in fostering enhanced morale and reported that his own sense of coherence had been fostered through joining together with others sharing common interests and concerns.

While the psychoanalysts Bieber and Socarides repeated the position with which they had by then come to be associated, that homosexuality was a form of psychiatric illness originating in childhood and should be so recognized in the DSM, the psychiatrist Richard Green delivered a scathing critique of psychoanalysis and psychoanalytic presumptions regarding development and psychopathology as related to homosexuality. Robert Spitzer, emerging as the spokesperson for a descriptive psychiatric nomenclature, questioned whether there was any validity at all in assuming homosexuality was a form of personal distress within psychiatric classification.

Kutchins and Kirk (1997) and Clendinen and Nagourney (1999) have suggested that it was Spitzer who was critical in changing the attitude of the APA central committees and Board of Trustees toward homosexuality as a psychiatric disorder. Spitzer had been educated in psychoanalysis; however, as an academic psychiatrist identifying with the systematic, empirical study of the origin and course of major mental disorders, he believed that the traditional reliance on psychoanalytic approaches to classification of psychopathology must be abandoned. Spitzer was instrumental in organizing the symposium at the 1973 meetings, which was initially organized as a response to demands by Ron Gold and other gay activists at the Dallas meetings.

Gold's passionate remarks at the 1972 meeting and Spitzer's heated discussion with him immediately after the panel had both shaken and positively impressed Spitzer. Bayer (1987) recounts that Spitzer told Gold that he had never actually met and talked with a gay psychiatrist, so Gold brought Spitzer along to a meeting of the then informal association of gay psychiatrists following the panel. Although many in the group were afraid that they would be "outed" as a result of Spitzer's appearance, when they recognized the positive impact that the symposium and the opportunity to exchange views with respected colleagues, often senior, had on Spitzer, the gay psychiatrists felt affirmed and appreciated. And Spitzer ultimately changed his views regarding any necessary association between same-gender sexual orientation and psychopathology. Spitzer now recognized that if obviously sound and competent colleagues could be gay, then homosexuality and psychopathology need not be related (Clendinen and Nagourney 1999). Indeed, Spitzer assumed a leadership role in recommending to the APA Board of Trustees that homosexuality as a diagnosis be removed from the DSM-II.

Although opposed by the New York regional group, composed largely of psychoanalysts who maintained a firm belief in the association of same-gender sexual orientation and psychopathology, the New England regional group, comprising articulate and well-published psychiatrists, provided a coherent report arguing against this presumed association. Spitzer attempted to forge a compromise between the opposing views of the New England and New York groups (which ultimately failed), suggesting that the revision of the DSM might include the diagnosis of sexual orientation disturbance, referring to those persons explicitly troubled by their expressed (homosexual) sexual orientation; a number of statutory groups within the APA reviewed several proposals drafted by Spitzer. Ultimately, the views of the New England group prevailed, and in December 1973 the APA Board of Trustees by a vote of 13–0, with 2 abstentions, adopted the position advocated by Spitzer that classification of homosexuality as psychiatric disorder should be removed from the DSM-II, to be replaced by the concept of sexual orientation disorder, adding a clause stating, "This diagnostic category is distinguished from homosexuality, which by itself does not necessarily constitute a psychiatric disorder" (Bayer 1987, 137). Further, the APA Board of Trustees adopted Spitzer's proposal for a strong statement advocating protection of the civil rights of homosexual adults.

The New York group, including Bieber and Socarides, had attempted with passion to defend their view of homosexuality as a "suboptimal" condition and was outraged by this turn of events. Invoking the APA by-laws, this group demanded that the decision of the Board of Trustees be put to a vote of the entire APA membership. Some of these New York psychiatrist-psychoanalysts believed they had reliable evidence that homosexuality was a form of psychopathology, and others adamantly objected to what they saw as the tendency of the American Psychiatric Association to abandon science in favor of current political fashion and opportunism. Obtaining the necessary names on a petition circulated at the association's fall meetings, Bieber and Socarides were able to force the APA to poll the entire membership on the Board of Trustees' vote to remove homosexuality as necessary evidence of psychopathology from the psychiatric nomenclature.

Bieber maintained that science could not take place using the mechanisms of a popular referendum. Indeed, even the referendum was riddled with politics. The leadership of APA, now consisting of liberal, well-published, primarily academic psychiatrists, drafted a statement defending the actions of the APA Board of Trustees. This informational statement was mailed to the entire APA membership with funds supplied by the National Gay Task Force, whose leader, Ron Gold, had earlier spoken at the 1973 symposium (Stoller, Marmor, et al. 1973). However, the role of this gay activist group in paying for the mailing was not disclosed in the mailing itself. When the New York group learned of this support, they went to the media, which then reported on the complex politics of the statement and the APA struggle regarding the declassification of homosexuality. However, the membership was angered that internal political issues had surfaced in the media; more than a thousand APA members voted 58 percent to 37 percent to support the actions of the APA Board of Trustees. It may be argued that what the membership was voting for was the strong civil rights statement accompanying the proposal to remove homosexuality as a diagnostic entity from the manual. At the same time, the APA had not yet acknowledged that same-gender sexual orientation was simply another developmental pathway and in itself a sign neither of immaturity of personality nor of developmental deficit.

Ego-Dystonic Homosexuality and the Revision of the DSM

The issue of homosexuality and psychopathology was presumably resolved when specific reference to homosexuality as a diagnostic entity was removed from the DSM-II. However, with continuing advances in biological psychiatry requiring a descriptive nosology in order to classify patients for clinical trials, there was continuing effort to revise DSM-II. Following his work on the declassification of homosexuality, Spitzer's administrative talents had become evident and he gradually assumed leadership of the effort to revise DSM-II in the direction of a descriptive nosology no longer founded on phenomenology, no longer influenced by the epigenetic perspective of psychoanalysis, which led to construction of hierarchial models of personality development and psychopathology. During the late 1970s the nomenclature project developed a series of working groups charged with the task of providing descriptive nosology for each of the mental disorders.

Clearly, the working group on sexual disorders would have to struggle once again with the issue of homosexuality and psychopathology. Not content with the category of sexual orientation disturbance approved for the DSM-II, Spitzer proposed a variety of terms to the drafting committee, which included several noted psychiatric clinical investigators of homosexuality, at least one of whom publicly acknowledged his homosexuality. The next version of the Diagnostic and Statistical Manual, DSM-III, published in 1981 (and partly supplanted in 1987 by DSM-IIIR), included within the category of psychosexual disorders the term "ego-dystonic homosexuality" (J. K. Meyer 1985). While Spitzer had recognized that heterosexual functioning was not an appropriate criterion for determining adjustment, he did believe that adequate sexual functioning was a criterion of positive mental health: interference in realizing sexual satisfaction in homoerotic activity was as significant in providing evidence of classifiable personal distress as interference in realizing heterosexual arousal (Spitzer 1981).

Spitzer advocated inclusion of ego-dystonic homosexuality in the nomenclature as a compromise between the two extremes of the increasingly activist gay community and a group of psychoanalysts, including Socarides, who continued to insist that homosexuality was evidence of "suboptimal" functioning. Correspondence between Spitzer and members of the drafting group (Bayer and Spitzer 1982) reveals the intensity of opinion of those in favor of and those opposed to this inclusion. This category of ego-dystonic homosexuality presumed that some men and women were impaired in their capacity for heterosexual arousal and experienced same-gender sexual arousal as a source of distress. These patients presumably had experienced limitations in their capacity for realizing personal fulfillment and believed that something was missing in their lives. However, former APA president Judd Marmor (1980), expressing his dissatisfaction with the category, argued that it permitted psychiatrists with antigay attitudes a diagnostic label for what is simply another developmental course. Echoing sentiments Freud expressed in a 1915 footnote appended to the *Three Essays on a Theory of Sexual-*

ity ([1905–1924] 1953, 145), Marmor indicated his concern that the term continued the tendency to separate homosexuality from other aspects of sexual behavior and thus furthered the stigmatization of gay men and women.

Response to this classification within DSM-III, although buried within the category of psychosexual disturbances, was a sense of frustration among both gay and lesbian APA members and those who supported reform of the APA perspective on same-gender sexual orientation (Krajeski 1996). Over the preceding decade, accompanying social change more generally, gay and lesbian psychiatrists had become more visible in APA, forming the Association of Gay and Lesbian Psychiatrists in 1978 and often assuming leadership positions within the complex APA organizational structure. Some members of the drafting committee, together with increasingly vocal gay activist APA members, maintained that there ought to be a parallel category for ego-dystonic heterosexuality (Bayer and Spitzer 1982), which led to the response that no one had ever deliberately tried to become gay. Anticipating Chodorow's later (1992) detailed exposition, Stoller noted that *all* forms of sexual expression inevitably reflected a compromise formation (Bayer and Spitzer 1982, 44–45). However, Spitzer (1981) wryly noted that few heterosexual men or women sought to become homosexual, and insisted that homosexuality was a nonnormative mode of sexual arousal.

Spitzer's casual observation, not supported by evidence, led members of the drafting committee to respond that not only did some formerly straight women and men seek same-gender sexual ties but, more generally, the experience of homosexuality as ego-dystonic was simply the response of gay men and women to lifelong experience of stigma and stereotyping. Writing to Spitzer, Marmor observed that such conflict as Spitzer had portrayed "stemmed primarily from the fact that as homosexuals they felt severely disparaged and excluded from the mainstream of society. Their distress about their homosexual 'impulses' were not *inherent in the impulses* . . . but in the *consequences* of expressing these impulses" (Bayer and Spitzer 1982, 43). Others suggested that distress was not the same as psychopathology, the presumed province of the DSM, and that psychopathology consequent upon stigma might be included under the category of adult adjustment reactions.

Defending his position regarding the importance of including ego-dystonic homosexuality within DSM-III, Spitzer (1981) acknowledged that while little consensus had been reached regarding the positive value of heterosexuality, DSM-III should include recognition that at least some homosexual men and women viewed their sexual orientation as a problem and presumably were distressed by their inability to experience heterosexual arousal; these men and women might seek psychiatric intervention in order to develop a "normative sexual arousal pattern" (Spitzer 1981, 213). Spitzer's comment seems somewhat misplaced and suggests that he failed to take seriously the anguish experienced by gay men and women who regarded their sexuality as a source of personal fulfillment which was but a part of an otherwise rewarding and creative life, who nonetheless experienced stereotyping and stigma.

There is extensive documentation of the effort, first, to remove homosexuality as a form of sexual deviation in the DSM-II and, later, to modify the concept of ego-dystonic homosexuality by placing response to stigma under the category of adjustment reaction, quite apart from sexual orientation as such. However, there is much less discussion regarding the subsequent decision to remove all mention of homosexuality as a diagnostic category from the 1987 revision of the DSM (DSM-IIIR). Kutchins and Kirk (1997) suggest that gay activists used the continuing feminist debate regarding women and psychiatric disorder as a means for realizing removal of ego-dystonic homosexuality from the DSM. The term "sexual disorder not otherwise specified" (NOS) could then be used as a replacement for the category of ego-dystonic homosexuality.

One possible compromise was to drop any reference to homosexuality and instead adopt the more general term ego-dystonic sexuality. Although Spitzer had initially insisted on retaining the term ego-dystonic homosexuality in the DSM-IIIR, and although no additional evidence had been brought forward on either side, there was little passion for continuing the debate and the category of ego-dystonic homosexuality quietly disappeared from debates within the higher reaches of APA committees reviewing the nomenclature. It is still not clear exactly how and why the category of ego-dystonic homosexuality finally disappeared (Bayer 1987, 217). Bayer has noted that pressure from vocal segments of the American Psychological Association was important in the decision to remove any explicit mention of homosexuality from the 1987 revision of the nomenclature. The term "gender identity disorder" was retained to refer to effeminate boys as portrayed by Green (1987); Isay (1997) has urged that even this category be deleted from the DSM since so many gay men had reported having been effeminate during childhood that the DSM might label effeminate boys as mentally disordered because of the perception that they were likely later to become gay. However, as Coates's (1992) review has suggested, it is important to differentiate between such effeminate or "sissy boys" (R. Green 1987) and those boys with gender-atypical interests, some of whom may later report same-gender sexual orientation.

Several political considerations are important in understanding the quiet disappearance of the category of ego-dystonic homosexuality from the diagnostic nomenclature. The combined activism of gay and lesbian psychologists and psychiatrists, together with the discomfort expressed by feminist groups regarding such diagnostic categories as masochistic personality disorder, posed image problems for the APA at a time when it was acutely aware of declining public sympathy toward psychiatry and its focus on disorder rather than means for realizing optimal functioning. Bayer (1987) also suggests that those within psychoanalysis who were anxious to retain a diagnostic category for homosexuality were reluctant to become embroiled in further conflict with the APA. At a time when medical psychoanalysis was confronting legal pressure for inclusion of nonmedical practitioners, maintaining APA support for psychoanalysis as a medical specialty had become a priority. This larger issue of retaining the good will of APA may well have overshadowed the concerns of a minority of analysts who continued to view homosexuality as a reflection of psychiatric illness.

Sexual Orientation and Mental Health: Findings from Systematic Study

Much of what has been written about the presumably impaired mental health of gay men and women is a reflection primarily of the effect of antigay prejudice and resulting feelings of stigma over a lifetime, not of attributes intrinsic to same-gender sexual orientation. Indeed, virtually all systematic study has shown sexual orientation to be independent of psychopathology. For example, to the extent that Brian's "cruising" in Lynch's important presentation (1999), discussed in chapter 7, is regarded as evidence of suboptimal adjustment (Bollas 1992), the meaning of this experience is founded in the analysand's internalization of shame and effort to prove himself deserving of heterosexist criticism, rather than some failure of personality development early in the course of life.

Evelyn Hooker and Comparative Study of
Sexual Orientation and Mental Health

The first systematic comparison of adjustment and sexual orientation was undertaken by the psychologist Evelyn Hooker (1956, 1957, 1968) at the prompting of several of her gay doctoral students. These students, who had never sought psychiatric assistance, were self-reflective and well regarded by other students and faculty in the UCLA clinical psychology program. Hooker decided to explore this issue in greater depth, studying a group of gay men living in the community who had never sought psychiatric assistance. Working with a local homophile society (in the mid-1950s it was potentially compromising to one's career to disclose a same-gender sexual orientation), Hooker obtained a group of thirty gay and thirty straight men ranging in age from twenty-five to fifty, with the modal age in the mid-thirties, individually matched on age, verbal intelligence, and years of formal education. No participant was informed of the goals of the study and each was administered a battery of semistructured (projective) tests, including the Rorschach ("ink-blot"); these were scored by Hooker and the results made available to psychologists not informed of the goals of the study.

Two senior clinicians, well versed in the interpretation of psychological tests, were asked to evaluate the adjustment of each of the sixty participants on a five-point scale and to sort the protocols into groups of gay and straight participants on the basis of the projective test materials, particularly the Rorschach. Judges knew at the outset that half of the protocols were those of gay men. Differences in the adjustment scores of the men in the gay and straight groups were found not to differ more than what might be expected by chance, and neither judge could sort the Rorschach protocols according to sexual orientation at a level exceeding chance. Indeed, the judges commented that all the Rorschach protocols seem to be of persons far better adjusted than those which they had encountered in their practice.

Hooker's report was a landmark in the study of homosexuality and mental health, showing conclusively that gay and straight men not seeking psychiatric intervention could not be distinguished on the basis of psychological tests. Ratings of the life-history information provided by these gay and straight men supported this conclusion. Most remarkable about the life-history interviews was the extent of comfort with themselves expressed by participants, together with absence of evidence of psychological distress. However, it is important to recognize that Hooker's study, as with nearly all subsequent study of this issue, relied upon convenience samples of gay men and women involved in homophile groups.

Systematic Study of Sexual Orientation and Mental Health

Research focusing on sexual orientation and mental health in the decades since the 1969 Stonewall riots and the birth of gay liberation must be understood in terms of cohorts: first, men and women self-defining as gay even prior to Stonewall, and the subject of the first studies of the relation between sexual orientation and adjustment; second, young adults who participated in the social activism of the 1970s; third, gay men and lesbians coming to terms with their sexual orientation in the 1980s during the first awareness of the AIDS epidemic; and, most recently, gay men and lesbians living in urban areas with dense social networks, protection from discrimination in the workplace, support for extending benefits to same-gender partners, and even discussion of recognition of same-gender marriage. Social and historical circumstances are important as the context in which gay and bisexual men and women understand their own developmental course and present adjustment.

Hooker's initial study was conducted more than a decade before Stonewall and the emergence, in subsequent cohorts, of enhanced self-consciousness regarding sexual orientation. Bell and Weinberg (1978) and Weinberg and Williams (1974), among others, later reported on the adjustment of gay men in the decade preceding the Stonewall riots and across the period of significant social change that followed. Much of the research concerning the relation of sexual orientation and psychological adjustment in the 1970s has been summarized by Hart et al. (1978), while findings from the 1980s have been reviewed by Ross, Paulsen, and Stålström (1988), Gonsiorek (1991), Herek (1991), and Meyer (1993). Discussion of the impact of sexual orientation on adjustment must be considered in terms of the measures used to assess adjustment and personality, the time at which the research was carried out, and the community context of the research (access to affirmative social networks, such as exist in cities, is a significant factor), as well as method for obtaining participants. Recruitment from newspaper advertisements, homophile groups, and venues such as bars may provide groups for study quite different in lifestyle and adjustment.

PSYCHOLOGICAL TESTS, ADJUSTMENT, AND SEXUAL ORIENTATION. Virtually all research to date has relied on convenience samples of urban-dwelling gay men and women active in community organizations or frequenting such public spaces as bars. Few of these studies meet criteria established for psychiatric epidemiology (Robins and Regier, 1991). Two studies contrasting the mental health of HIV-positive and HIV-negative gay men and straight counterparts, although reporting conflicting findings, begin to meet such criteria (Atkinson et al. 1988; J. Williams et al. 1991). However, most studies do at least employ a design including both gay and straight groups with raters blind to group membership.

Reviewing extant studies of mental health indices of gay and straight men and women, Meyer (1993) has organized findings in terms of those relying upon psychometric trait scales, symptom scales, and epidemiological findings of prevalence and incidence of psychiatric disorder with and without comparison groups of heterosexual men and women. Many of the personality trait studies were reported in the early 1970s, often based on groups of gay men from homophile organizations who volunteered for study in the epoch prior to Stonewall and gay liberation. These volunteers were likely to be nonconformist and unconventional (Cohler, Woolsey, et al. 1968) and perhaps more psychologically distressed as well (Burdick and Stewart, 1974).

In the aftermath of early study of gay men using semistructured psychological measures, particularly the work of Evelyn Hooker (1956, 1957), there was a spate of research reporting on comparisons of gay and straight groups using paper-and-pencil measures. Summarizing the first decade of comparative study of gay and straight men, Reiss (1980) and Meredith and Reister (1980) concur that few differences had been discerned. (1980) reviews a total of fifty-eight comparative studies (twenty-three founded on semistructured or projective tests, and thirty-five founded on paper-and-pencil measures), concluding that

> there are no psychological test techniques which successfully separate homosexual men and women from heterosexual comparisons. . . . The commonly used psychological assessment tools do not show any evidence of greater pathology among homosexual women or men than among heterosexuals. That large numbers of mental health professionals still, a priori, identify homosexuality as pathology leads one to conclude that professional practice may blind one to the reality of experimentally established fact. (1980, 308)

In an earlier review, Reiss, Safer, and Yotive (1974), reported on findings from six studies using projective test measures (including two case studies of lesbians in psychotherapy) and six reports using paper-and-pencil measures (three used both projective and self-report measures) and conclude both that findings from studies of male homosexuality are not relevant in studying lesbian groups and that it is difficult to differentiate projective test protocols of lesbian women from those of heterosexual counterparts. As in studies of gay men, much of the early comparative study of lesbians and straight women contrasted groups of lesbians in psychotherapy with straight women living in the community. While some studies reviewed by Reiss, Safer, and Yotive (1974) suggested that lesbian women had more disturbed perceptions of their mothers and greater anxiety about the maternal role than heterosexual counterparts, other studies found that lesbian women volunteering from a community homophile group were better adjusted than their heterosexual counterparts who did not participate in a tightly knit community support group.

Other studies found essentially no significant group differences in comparisons of large numbers of both patient and nonpatient lesbian and straight women living in the community. On the basis of their review, Reiss, Safer, and Yotive conclude that "lesbians are not necessarily more neurotic than heterosexual women but are, rather, more dominant, autonomous, assertive and detached—in fact more like the stereotypic man" (1974, 82), but also note that this conclusion is founded largely on case reports and comparison of lesbian women in treatment or in homophile organizations with psychologically well counterparts living in the community. As Reiss, Safer, and Yotive had earlier lamented, such methodological shortcomings as comparison of patient groups with community living counterparts make it difficult to draw any conclusions regarding the comparative adjustment of gay and straight men and women.

Meredith and Reister (1980) report in detail on eighteen comparative studies of homosexual and heterosexual men and women and note that three studies report differences on paper-and-pencil measures favoring the adjustment of heterosexual groups; however, the homosexual group consisted of persons seeking psychological intervention, most often as a consequence of discharge from military service following discovery of their sexual orientation, while the heterosexual comparison group consisted of heterosexual men in a nonpatient group. Dysfunction appeared more common among those men recently discharged by the military, and those men seeking treatment for their distress. Meredith and Reister (1980) caution that there is a group of homosexual men at risk for adjustment difficulties, particularly alcoholism and suicidal potential, but that this group does not represent gay men living in the community and not seeking psychological intervention. Clinicians tend to assume that gay men are necessarily less well adjusted than straight men because the gay men in their practice are those seeking help. However, similar claims are not made about the straight men who seek psychological help—no claim is made that because some straight men seek treatment, all straight men show psychological distress.

Many of these early comparative studies of the adjustment and gender identity of gay and straight men and women use the Masculinity-Femininity scale from the Minnesota Multiphasic Personality Inventory (MMPI) developed by Hathaway (1956). This "criterion-based" scale was initially constructed in the years following the Second World War by contrasting the responses of male and female outpatient visitors to the University of Minnesota hospitals, then cross-validating those items differentiating between men and women. Several problems are posed by these studies. First, gender and education are highly confounded. Nearly every study of college-educated men and women shows that they score in the direction of the other gender. Second, these studies often confuse same-gender sexual orientation with gender identity disorder, too often assuming that men or women who express desire primarily for others of the same gender necessarily wish to be of the other gender. And third, this scale is heavily biased in the direction of stereotyped views of gender and has relatively little relevance to the study of sexual orientation. For example, present cohorts of college-educated men score above the mean (in the direction of "femininity") because their cultural interests are different from those of the initial validation cohort. While the recently introduced MMPI-2 attempts to bring the norms for the test up to date, the studies reported in the literature regarding the M–F scale were based on the original version of the test.

Meyer (1993) has most recently reviewed personality trait studies; in fifteen studies of group differences on personality trait measures, gay men scored in the direction of less adequate adjustment in six studies, heterosexual in one, with eight studies reporting no significant group differences. None of the four studies reporting group-based scores showed significant differences between groups of gay and straight men. Finally, two of the three studies comparing psychiatric "caseness" across gay and straight men showed greater caseness among the group of gay than straight men. Meyer notes that the report by Williams and her colleagues (1991) is particularly interesting in showing higher lifetime rates but lower current prevalence rates for depression among gay men, which suggests that this cohort may have had particular problems dealing with issues of stigma earlier in life which were overcome in adulthood by moving to a more acceptant urban community.

In general, Meredith and Reister (1980), Reiss (1980), and Reiss, Safer, and Yotive (1974), as well as Hart et al. (1978), have found that of the dozens of psychometric test comparisons of gay and straight men and women reported in the psychological literature, few show systematic differences between these two groups. Of the differences reported some favor one group, some the other; where scales refer to mental health outcomes, differences are generally within the "normal" range (in the case of the MMPI, having T-scores less than 60).

COMMUNITY SURVEY STUDIES OF MENTAL HEALTH AND SEXUAL ORIENTATION. Following Hooker's (1956, 1957) pioneering study, Saghir and Robins (1973) obtained information regarding life history and mental health from homophile organizations in three cities, ultimately recruiting about one hundred gay men and sixty lesbians who reported that they had never been hospitalized for psychiatric illness. Since this was a group of relatively affluent volunteers, a comparison group of presumably heterosexual unmarried young adults living in an upper middle-class housing development was selected as a comparison group. No effort was made to eliminate from either group men and women who had sought psychotherapy. Indeed, about a fourth of the gay men and 6 percent of the straight men reported having been in psychotherapy at present or in the past, while more than a third of gay women and a quarter of straight women had sought mental health services. Among the gay men and women, failure of a relationship or difficulties in realizing a homosexual adjustment were the predominant reasons for seeking psychotherapy; lesbians were primarily referred by family members or self because of depression. A similar pattern emerged among straight women seeking psychotherapy.

While mental health services were used by a number of gay men and both gay and straight women, this is not necessarily an adequate marker of personal distress. Both lifetime and point (present) prevalence of psychopathology were measured by a structured clinical interview, an early version of a measure that later became the Research Diagnostic Criteria (RDC) of the Washington University assessment project (Goodwin and Guze 1996; Mezzich and Jorge 1993). Using this early version of the RDC measure, about three-quarters of both gay and straight men were free of manifest psychopathology, using either lifetime or point prevalence measures of psychiatric disorder. A number of the men in each group (15–17 percent) reported lifetime problems with alcoholism.

While the groups of gay and straight men could not be differentiated on any measure of psychiatric disorder, more than three-quarters of lesbians and more than one-half of the comparison group of heterosexual women (a difference not statistically significant) showed lifetime prevalence of psychiatric disorder, principally what were then termed psychoneurotic disorders (depression and psychophysiological reactions). Point-prevalence figures showed that, at the time of the interview, there were continuing significant differences between the groups of gay and straight women, with lesbians reporting a greater frequency of problems with alcoholism (about a fifth of the lesbian women but none of the straight women); a significantly greater proportion of heterosexual women (14 percent) than lesbians (5 percent) reported problems with anxiety neurosis or phobias. Much of the psychiatric distress indicated by the lifetime figures was no longer evident at the time of the interview for either group of women. Overall, at the time of the interview, there was little evidence of psychopathology among either gay or straight men or women. The elevated figures for women seeking psychotherapeutic services and reported psychoneurosis are consistent with other findings from epidemiologic study, which show elevated rates of both distress and help-seeking among women (Gove and Tudor 1972; Robins and Regier 1991).

Other studies contrasting the adjustment of gay and straight men and women have reported findings essentially similar to those reported by Saghir and Robins (1973) in the first large-scale, multisite exploration of sexual orientation and mental health among nonclinical groups following the Stonewall riots. These studies have continued in the tradition of using convenience groups obtained either through political and social organizations or on the basis of recommendations from other study participants (the so-called "snowball" technique); it is likely that less well adjusted or more troubled participants would have avoided participation in these studies, which are founded on groups of urban-dwelling, well-educated, politically active gay men and women who may be more socially comfortable with their homo-sexuality.

Many early studies of adjustment and sexual orientation relied upon paper-and-pencil measures in comparing groups of gay and straight men and women. For example, Thompson, McCandless, and Strickland (1971) used self-report measures and contrasted trait measures for self-acknowledged gay men and women individually matched for age and education with men and women self-defining as heterosexual. As in much of the psychological study of adjustment among gay men and women, respondents were well educated, urban, and well connected within the emerging gay community. Findings from this study showed that heterosexual men were both more self-confident and less defensive than gay counterparts. However, gay women were more self-confident that their heterosexual counterparts. No other differences were found among either men or women in the contrasting groups of gay and straight participants.

Siegelman (1972a, 1972b) reported findings from a community study us-ing a similar approach. Gay and lesbian groups were recruited from homo-phile organizations and gay gathering places such as bookstores in New York. The comparative group of heterosexual respondents was made up of college students. Respondents in each group were administered paper-and-pencil measures of adjustment. Group differences on scale scores occurring by chance alone less than five times in a hundred showed that gay men were more sensitive, less depressed, and showed greater self-acceptance, nurtur-ance, goal-directedness, and interpersonal autonomy than their heterosexual counterparts. Similar findings were reported contrasting gay and straight women on these trait measures of adjustment (Siegelman 1972a). The lesbian group was notable for being self-reliant, self-acceptant, and goal-directed, with less overall neuroticism than was reported among the heterosexual women. Siegelman notes that these findings were consistent with previous unpublished data by others, also showing few differences in adjustment among groups of gay and straight men and women.

CROSS-NATIONAL RESEARCH AND ADJUSTMENT OF GAY AND LESBIAN MEN AND WOMEN. The most ambitious community survey studies reported in the 1970s were ethnographic and survey studies reported by Weinberg and Williams (1974) and Bell and Weinberg (1978). The former study reported on the lives of gay men participating in homophile organizations and the "bar scene" in a number of European and U.S. cities characterized by large concentrations of gay men. This study, which ultimately enrolled more than a thousand well-educated, middle-class men in the United States and another thousand in Denmark and the Netherlands, was begun even prior to the Stonewall riots, which occurred in the midst of the fieldwork. The study documented significant changes taking place in the lives of gay men at a critical point in the emergence of recognition of same-gender sexual orientation as a developmental course rather than as psychopathology.

Weinberg and Williams (1974) reported little psychopathology on the basis of self-report measures. In the first place, age was found unrelated to indices of depression. Older gay men were somewhat better adjusted on this measure than younger counterparts and showed little of either the concern with accelerated aging or the consequences of aging assumed for older gay men. This study did not provide comparison with heterosexual counterparts, although it took advantage of findings from a comparison group of presumably straight men recruited for a study of occupation and socialization (Kohn 1969), nor did it use what have come to be accepted as psychometrically reliable measures for anxiety, depression, and other dysphoric states. Gay men living in the United States were, on the whole, less psychologically troubled than their counterparts in the Netherlands and Denmark.

There was little evidence that the more tolerant European societies led to a social climate in which homosexual men had markedly greater morale and self-acceptance than in the United States (where groups in New York and San Francisco were studied). However, comparing responses to questions concerning morale and interpersonal trust with those from a social class and conformity study reported by Kohn (1969), gay men in the United States reported significantly lowered morale and lowered levels of interpersonal trust than the group of presumably straight men whose answers Kohn had reported. However, on measures of self-acceptance and psychosomatic symptoms there was little difference between the homosexual respondents in any of the three nations and Kohn's normative sample.

Men who had little social involvement within the community reported more depression and anxiety. Based on the psychometrically reliable scales constructed for the study, about a quarter of the group of gay respondents across the three nations reported being unhappy, while 42 percent reported having believed at some time that they might be on the verge of a "nervous breakdown," In the United States group, as contrasted with gay men in the Netherlands and Denmark, more than two-fifths of men had sought psychiatric intervention at some point in their adult life, although only 8 percent were presently in treatment.

SEXUAL ORIENTATION AND MENTAL HEALTH IN A SUPPORTIVE URBAN CONTEXT. The more detailed survey study reported by Bell and Weinberg (1978) recruited respondents in San Francisco and the Bay area through contacts in homophile organizations, bars, and other venues frequented by the gay community. Recognizing the many possible sources of sampling bias, great care was taken to contact organizations in different parts of the community in order to obtain a group of study participants that was diverse in terms of ethnicity and age. Particular effort was expended to recruit African Americans, who had been underrepresented in much prior study.

Bell and Weinberg also included older respondents, since much prior study had focused on younger respondents, typically those in their thirties. The final group of homosexual respondents included 575 European-American men, 229 European-American women, 111 African-American men, and 64 African-American women. The contrasting group of hetero-sexual respondents, obtained through a national survey organization and intended to represent the population characteristics of the Bay area, included 284 European-American men, 101 European-American women, 39 African-American women, and 53 African-American men. More than a quarter of the European-American gay men and a fifth of the European-American gay women were over age forty-five. With federal grant support, a lengthy and detailed interview instrument was developed and administered by a cadre of trained interviewers to the group of nearly a thousand gay men and women and the contrasting group of nearly five hundred men and women.

A notable aspect of this lengthy and detailed report was the effort to differentiate between groups of gay respondents in terms of lifestyle. Among gay men, five patterns of social adjustment and sexuality were found on the basis of correlational study: those men who were close-coupled or living in a "quasi-marriage" (about 14 percent), those men identifying a partner but also engaged in sexual experiences outside of the relationship (about a fourth of the group), those men who reported frequent and generally satisfying sexual activity with a large number of partners (about a fifth of the total group), those men reporting difficulty in finding partnership, feelings of failure as a sexual partner, or regret regarding their sexual orientation (less than a fifth of the group), and a group of asexual men, nearly a fourth of the total group of gay men, who reported that they were gay but experienced little explicit same-gender sexual interest or activity. In sum, only about a fifth of these gay men expressed personal distress or regrets regarding their sexual orientation.

Among lesbians, close-coupled respondents (about two-fifths of the group) and open-coupled respondents (about a fourth of the group) were identified. Women enjoying multiple sexual partners represented 14 percent of the total group, while women dissatisfied with their sexual orientation represented less than 10 percent of the group. A fifth group of women, who acknowledged same-gender sexual orientation but little interest in sexuality,

comprised about 16 percent of the group of homosexual women. Expectably, nearly two-thirds of the women reported continuing stable relationships, as contrasted with about two-fifths of the men. The groups of asexual
men and women were somewhat older than the other groups. Further, there
were many more men than women in the group characterized by high levels
of sexual activity but little satisfaction with sexual activity and many regrets
regarding sexual orientation.

The report on this large and systematic interview study interweaves findings from the detailed and lengthy survey with those based on ethnographic
observation. Overall, findings from this extensive study indicated that

> homosexuality is not necessarily related to pathology. Thus, decisions about
> homosexual men and women . . . should never be made on the basis of sexual
> orientation alone. Moreover, it should be recognized that what has survival
> value in a heterosexual context may be destructive in a homosexual con-
> text. . . . Life-enhancing mechanisms used by heterosexual men or women
> should not necessarily be used as the standard by which to judge the degree of
> homosexuals' adjustment. (Bell and Weinberg 1978, 233)

While the asexual men reported less favorable general health than other
homosexual or heterosexual men (they were also older), there were few
other notable differences based on the typologies discussed above for gay
men and women. Those men who had enjoyed partnership of some duration
and those men who were sexually active and satisfied with their sexuality
reported the greatest happiness. The finding that the gay men as a group
were less self-acceptant than the straight men is largely a function of the
lower self-acceptance reported by men who were distressed about their sexual orientation and by those characterized as asexual who reported being
particularly lonely (approximately 16 percent of the total number of gay men
in the study). African-American gay men were overrepresented among the
so-called dysfunctional and asexual gay men and appeared to be particularly
at risk in terms of psychological adjustment.

The groups of lesbians and their heterosexual counterparts were very
much alike in terms of personal adjustment. With the exception of a very
small number of women expressing problems in adjusting to the lesbian role,
there were few differences in morale or psychological symptoms. Once
again, African-American lesbians, subjected to triple discrimination as a consequence of ethnicity, gender, and sexual orientation, appeared most at risk
in terms of psychological adjustment; these women reported greater loneliness, tension, and suspiciousness than other lesbian respondents. Among the
remaining lesbian respondents, their general health and happiness, sense of
self-acceptance, and experience of anxiety did not differ from that of their
heterosexual counterparts.

ADULT SUICIDE AND SEXUAL ORIENTATION. A significant issue posed by Bell and Weinberg's large-scale study concerns the greater preoccupation with suicide reported within the groups of both gay men and lesbians as contrasted with heterosexual counterparts. More than half of gay men and women (particularly the European-American group) reported considering suicide at one time or another, compared to less than 5 percent of heterosexual men (comparable figures for heterosexual women were not provided). This is a figure much greater than that earlier reported by Saghir and Robins (1973) and may be explained, at least in part, by the greater preoccupation with suicide reported more generally in San Francisco (Bell and Weinberg 1978, 211–12).

It was clear that gay adolescents continue to be at somewhat greater risk for suicide than heterosexual counterparts. At the same time, there may be significant cohort effects in suicidal ideation. As gay men and women find a more comfortable place in society, suicidal ideation and attempts may diminish from adolescence to later life. Studying a small group of completed suicides in southern California, all involving men between the ages of twenty-one and thirty, Rich et al. (1986) report findings regarding the "psychological autopsy" or follow-back study of thirteen cases in which the man had been identified though detailed interviews with family and friends as clearly homosexual. Using the other 106 suicides by men under thirty as a comparison group, the investigators found no difference across the two groups in the number of prior suicide attempts. The thirteen homosexual suicide completers were all rated in their psychological autopsies as having manifested substance abuse as defined in the DSM-III, and eleven of the thirteen had a comorbid diagnosis, most often atypical depression. Stressors contributing to the suicide were most often a loss, such as the breakup of a relationship or a parental death. These findings regarding diagnosis and stressors were similar to those among the other 106 men suicide completers. Nearly all suicide completers, both men and women, had an assignable DSM-III diagnosis.

The authors conclude that "there may be few if any differences between young gay and straight males who commit suicide" (C. Rich et al. 1986, 452). They also note that social isolation appears to have played little role in the decision to commit suicide. Interviews with family and friends, a part of the psychological autopsy process, did not reveal that these thirteen young men had struggled over issues of sexual identity. As in much of the other study to date, however, gay men were more likely than heterosexual counterparts to have sought mental health services.

ETHNICITY, HIV STATUS, MENTAL HEALTH, AND SEXUAL ORIENTATION. The study by Rich et al. of a small group of completed suicides did not suggest, bases on either psychological autopsies or demographic and psychological characteristics, that gay men succeeding in suicide differ from their hetero-sexual counterparts. This finding mirrors much of the literature comparing the mental health of gay men and women with that of their heterosexual counterparts (Herek 1991; Gonsiorek 1991; Ross, Paulsen, and Stålström 1988). This literature has been well summarized by Meyer (1993), who notes that only two studies, those reported by Atkinson et al. (1988) and by Pillard (1988), have reported increased rates of personal distress among community-living, middle-class, European-American gay men in their mid-thirties as contrasted with a heterosexual comparison group.

Atkinson and his colleagues reported on a study examining lifetime and point prevalence rates for psychiatric disorders meeting DSM-III criteria, using the Diagnostic Interview Schedule (DIS), among groups of homosex-ual men with and without HIV/AIDS. Eleven seronegative men were re-cruited as a comparison group and evaluated on measures of psychopa-thology against both the HIV/AIDS groups and a group of twenty-two heterosexual men recruited through a local service organization in the south-ern California community in which the study was conducted. Reviewing lifetime prevalence, anxiety disorders and depressive disorders were more common within the group of homosexual men than within the group of heterosexual men. For present purposes, the important group comparison is between the eleven HIV-negative (HIV−) gay men, who show elevated lifetime prevalence for anxiety and depressive disorders, and the twenty-two heterosexual men in the comparison group. On the one hand, this was the first study to use a structured interview measure in the study of mental health among men or women differing in sexual orientation. On the other hand, the very small size of the samples and the borderline significance levels makes it difficult to evaluate the implications of this comparison showing impaired mental health among groups of gay as contrasted with straight men.

While the enhanced stress reflected in the DIS may be characteristic of gay men more generally, these studies used very small samples of HIV-negative gay men; particular caution should be used in generalizing from such small numbers. It should also be noted that Williams et al. (1991), using a later version of the structured psychiatric interview schedule (the Struc-tured Clinical Interview for the DSM-IIIR, or SCID) and groups of sero-positive and seronegative gay men of similar social background to the groups included in the study reported by Atkinson et al. (1988), report rates of anxi-ety and depressive disorders which were "broadly equivalent to ECA one month prevalence rates for men aged 25 to 44 years" (Williams et al. 1991, 126). That is, the point prevalence rates of psychopathology for the gay men in this study, compared with those of the Epidemiologic Catchment Area study described in greater detail in Robins and Regier (1991), are not in excess of what might be expected among heterosexual counterparts in the community.

Commenting on the differences between their own findings and those of Atkinson et al. (1988), Williams et al. (1991) note that the SCID is a different measure from the DIS, and also that their findings are based on six-month rather than lifetime prevalence. Williams and her colleagues note further the very small size of the sample studied by Atkinson et al. (1988), in which three of the eleven HIV-negative men contributed to the finding of supposed group differences in depressive disorders. The differences in reported anxiety disorders across the two studies may be due to changes in how depressive disorders are classified within the psychiatric nomenclature; earlier definitions of depressive disorder tended to be overinclusive when compared with that used by Williams and her colleagues.

The only other study to report a more adverse mental health outcome among gay than among straight adults (Pillard 1988) suggests that as contrasted with counterpart straight men, gay men between the ages of eighteen and thirty-five report a greater prevalence of depression and substance abuse. More gay than straight men also reported seeking psychotherapy, most often in relation to issues of coming out or in seeking to understand issues of sexual identity. However, the study includes only a small number (fifty-one) of urban-living gay men and a similar number of volunteering counterpart straight men; only a few of the men within the homosexual group reported problems of excess drinking or substance abuse or symptoms of affective disorder, and it is difficult to generalize on the basis of such a small number of persons to differences between the two groups. Further, as Friedman and Downey (1994) comment, findings from studies showing greater frequency of substance abuse or alcoholism among either gay men or lesbians, as contrasted with straight counterpart groups, are difficult to interpret both because data are sparse and because bars are frequently used as a means of recruitment of gay volunteers. Friedman and Downey (1994) question whether any conclusions may be drawn from studies on the relationship of substance abuse and sexual orientation that use convenience samples of bar patrons.

In Review: Method and Problem in the Study
of Sexual Orientation and Mental Health

Discussing findings from more than two decades of systematic comparative study of the adjustment of gay and straight men and women, Gonsiorek (1991) has observed that efforts to prove that homosexuality is an illness or disturbance have, in the main, failed. There is very little evidence to suggest that homosexuality represents the illness portrayed by a small group of psychiatrists and by segments of the Christian right. At the same time, much additional study is required in order to finally resolve the question of the relation of sexual orientation and mental health. Gonsiorek deplores the failure of those still regarding same-gender sexual orientation as evidence of impaired adjustment to consider findings from systematic studies such as those reviewed in the present work. Gonsiorek notes that the proportion of troubled gay and straight adults is similar—that is, sexual orientation in itself makes little difference in rates of psychiatric distress across groups over time. However, consistent with the perspective emphasized by Ross (1978), Ross, Paulsen, and Stålström (1988), Meyer (1995), and Young-Bruehl (1996), as well as the present work, stigma and antigay prejudice may impose a psychological burden which interferes with maintenance of positive morale and self-esteem.

Problems of method of study pose significant obstacles to understanding the role of sexual orientation in mental health outcome. It is important not only to contrast gay with straight comparison groups, but also to estimate the variance attributable to mode of recruiting groups, gender, partnership or marriage, geographic residence, cohort, and health status. For example, there is little to be learned from contrasting gay men who are HIV-positive with groups of HIV-negative heterosexual men on mental health measures; such differences as might be observed could hardly then be taken as a consequence of their sexual orientation. Nearly all research to date contrasting the mental health of gay and straight men and women has relied upon convenience samples gathered through urban networks such as gay community centers, voluntary associations, and newspapers, which tend to reach those gay adults better acquainted with community resources. A study by Paul, Catania, and their associates using telephone interviews to survey neighborhoods in four cities (San Francisco, Los Angeles, New York, and Chicago) known to have large populations of gay men represents an important step away from reliance on such convenience samples (Catania 1999). The advantages of this survey approach have been discussed by Harry (1990) and Meyer and Colten (1999).

Findings reported by Weinberg and Williams (1974), Meyer (1993, 1995), Shidlo (1994), and Ostrow et al. (1989) have suggested that gay men who are more involved in community organizations report higher levels of life satisfaction and more favorable adjustment because they receive support in combating antigay prejudice and associated feelings of stigma. Indeed, as Harry (1990) has suggested in reviewing findings from a probability study of gay and lesbian adults, convenience samples favor those urban-dwelling men who receive support from community organizations and maintain a social network supportive of their sexual orientation. Men and women living in small towns and rural areas have a much more difficult time locating such support and may experience more negative self-esteem as a consequence of prejudice.

Consistent with Harry's observation, Levitt and Klassen (1974) have reported that antigay prejudice is most common in small towns and rural areas. Nungesser (1983) has observed that outside of urban areas, where people are relatively likely to know someone who is gay, the lives of gay men and women may be perceived as particularly different from the expectable course of life and social stereotyping is most likely to be more intense. This social psychological perspective on the origins of prejudice suggests that the lack of a social network among rural gay men and women is compounded by greater hostility towards their developmental course than might be found in urban areas. Finally, cohort issues are intertwined with sampling issues: groups of men and women recruited from homophile organizations, necessarily secretive in the pre-Stonewall era, are inevitably different from men and women recruited across the past two decades.

One of the major problems with groups gathered from within community organizations is that more troubled gay men or lesbians might not be willing to volunteer for research. Inclusion of married heterosexual men in comparison groups makes comparison additionally difficult. Hart et al. (1978) suggest that two groups of heterosexual men or women should be used in studies comparing gay and straight groups, those who are married and those presently not married. Recent study showing the extent of partnership within the gay community similarly suggests that gay men and women should be divided into those who do and those who do not presently report having a partner.

The significance of singlehood to mental health across the course of life is particularly complex, among both gay and straight men and women (Hostetler and Cohler 1997). Findings reviewed by Cohler and Boxer (1984) on variation in morale across the "stable adult years," from the time one enters the world of work until midlife, roughly the decade of the fifties, suggest that married men are the happiest, followed by single women, married women, and single men. Married men enjoyed the support provided by their wives even though, as Siassi, Crocetti, and Spiro (1974) have reported, role strain and overload is passed on from husbands to wives, which explains the lowered morale reported among wives. Clearly this is an issue which requires additional study.

Continuing comparative ethnographic study of an inner-city neighborhood, in which African-American men and women who define themselves simply as sometimes preferring others of the same gender for sexual intimacies, and a more affluent and organized gay community (Cohler 1997) suggests that there is little awareness within the inner-city community of the larger gay community and little awareness of community health organizations seeking to prevent spread of sexually transmitted diseases. While the geographic distance between the two is not large, the social distance is very large and the resulting social isolation significant. Harry's (1990) caution about assuming that all gay men are affluent, well-educated urban residents is particularly important in considering issues of group composition. Cody and Welch's (1997) report on gay men in rural New England communities focuses on men living in less affluent circumstances than their counterparts in urban neighborhoods with many self-identified gay men. However, even within these urban neighborhoods, respondents who volunteer for studies of gay adjustment are generally better educated and less conventional and more likely to come from affluent non–ethnic minority groups than respondents in the same neighborhoods contacted through random digit dialing (Meyer and Colten 1999). Gonsiorek (1991) cautions further that gay men volunteering for psychological studies may be less well adjusted than counterparts not volunteering, particularly within communities where particularly strong stigma and antigay prejudice further compromises the mental health of gay men and lesbians.

Conclusion

This review of studies regarding mental health and sexual orientation has suggested there are few group differences attributable to sexual orientation alone, although as Herek (1991) and Meyer (1993) all caution, antigay prejudice and stigma, particularly in the absence of an effective support network, such as among men and women living in rural areas, may compromise personal adjustment (Harry 1990). Where there is little social support and substantial antigay prejudice, higher rates of depression, anxiety, attempted suicide, and substance abuse have been reported among gay men and women than among heterosexual counterparts. Clearly, gay adolescent boys and girls are particularly at risk for negative mental health outcomes when living in communities with few social supports and attending high schools where antigay prejudice among both students and teachers is rampant, and where parents are unable to understand and provide support for adolescents struggling with issues of sexual identity.

Gonsiorek writes, "The general conclusion is clear: These studies overwhelmingly suggest that homosexuality per se is not related to psychopathology or psychological adjustment" (1991, 131). Indeed, he notes that much of the literature comparing homosexual and heterosexual groups was published more than a decade earlier; findings from more recent comparative study had suggested few differences in personality attributes or mental health which could be traced to sexual orientation alone. This apparently counterintuitive finding had led to intensive study of the relation between sexual orientation and mental health. And since such study has reported few group differences attributable to sexual orientation, the question of psychopathology being inherent in same-gender sexual orientation has been clearly answered in the negative and little additional study of this issue is required. In sum, there is little evidence of any intrinsic relation between sexual orientation and adverse mental health outcomes as determined either by personality trait measures or psychiatric evaluation. As Marmor observed:

> Homosexuals, both male and female, function responsibly and honorably in positions of the highest trust and live emotionally stable, mature, and well-adjusted lives that are indistinguishable from those of well-adjusted heterosexuals except for their different sexual orientation. The issue of homosexual object choice should be regarded as essentially irrelevant, therefore, to the issue of mental illness. (1980, 400)

Almost three decades after the American Psychiatric Association removed homosexuality from the psychiatric nomenclature of its Diagnostic and Statistical Manual, the lives of gay men and lesbian are regarded as virtually normal (A. Sullivan 1995) among the mental health professions. At the same time, issues of stigma remain salient within the community, particularly in rural areas, where gay men and women may lack the social support available to urban counterparts while also facing greater antigay prejudice, among urban members of ethnic groups in which same-gender sexual identity is particularly subject to stigmatization (C. Chan 1995; Espin 1993; Loiacano 1989), and among gay and lesbian adolescents and young adults (G. Remafedi 1994b). There is an urgent need for the development of additional services for these groups of gay women and men.

Nine

Psychodynamics of Sexual Orientation

Clinical psychoanalysis involves an attempt to develop a nuanced understanding of the wishes or intentions that give meaning to the analysand's
relations with others and attributes of self across a lifetime. Within the experiential setting of the psychoanalytic situation, analyst and analysand together
study these wishes and their significance for the analysand's life. Near-daily
sessions at regular times across some duration, in which the analyst is endowed with salient meanings, provide a context in which the analysand is
able to explore these wishes within an empathic climate. As a result of this
sustained self-inquiry, the analysand is able to realize an enhanced awareness
of his or her own wishes and their reflection in action and an enhanced
sense of vitality and integrity. As Schafer (1980, 1981, 1992) has suggested,
analysand and analyst together construct a narrative of lived experience that
fosters an enhanced sense of integration of lived experience, and one
founded less on wishes out of awareness than on that which the analysand
brings to the analysis at the outset.

The analyst contributes uniquely to this ambiance; as a consequence of a
personal analysis and continuing self-inquiry (Gardner 1983), the analyst
is able to maintain a listening stance, "tasting" the analysand's experiences
through concordant identifications which include the capacity to bear the
analysand's anxiety and dysphoric feelings without projective identification
or complementary identifications (Fliess 1944, 1953; Schafer 1959; Kohut
[1959] 1978; Greenson 1960; Racker 1968). As Kohut (1984) has noted, this
ability of the analyst to listen empathically is a critical factor in the "curative"
effect of psychoanalysis.

This brief review of the manner in which psychoanalysis fosters reintegration of personality and enhanced vitality and coherence of lived experience
makes few assumptions about the course of development. Across the course
of the analysis itself, the past is continually reworked in order to maintain a
coherent narrative of lived experience (Schafer 1992). Analyst and analysand
together explore this narrative, with the goal of rewriting the life story with
which the analysand begins analysis in a manner intended to resolve past
disappointments and loss and thus to foster greater vitality.

If psychoanalysis is viewed from this perspective, as a collaboration between an analyst, aware through personal analysis and continuing self-analytic work of complex and conflicting desires, and an analysand struggling to come to terms with conflicting desires, it is puzzling that there should still be discussion of sexual orientation as other than a developmental pathway. Study of the many meanings for an analysand of sexuality and sexual orientation is little different from study of other issues within the psychoanalytic situation. Analyst and analysand together explore intention, including its expression in fantasy and action, in an effort to understand the significance of sexuality for the course of lived experience (Schafer 1995). The complex and multifaceted nature of sexuality is among the most salient issues posed for psychoanalytic study precisely because of the significance of the erotic for lives from infancy through oldest age. The many ways in which sexual wishes are experienced and enacted inevitably becomes a focus of psychoanalytic exploration. Desire and its expression may be among the most intense and pleasurable aspects of our experience but also, over time, among the most personally distressing and disappointing.

There is little in the definition of one's own sexual orientation, or determination of the gender of the partner toward whom desires are expressed, which inherently reflects distress or disappointment. No form of sexual wish and associated enactment is privileged as a sign of enhanced vitality or integration. While there may be a bias in favor of so-called heterosexual intimacy because of normative proscription, there is little reason to presume one expression of desire is optimal or inherently more mature than another. Rather, as Chodorow (1992, 1999) has emphasized, we are interested in the meanings persons provide regarding all aspects of desire enacted within lives over time.

Just as heterosexuality is not privileged, or exempt from study within the psychoanalytic situation, the many wishes and meanings reflected in expression of same-gender desire and adoption of sexual identity as a gay or bisexual man or woman do not privilege same-gender sexual orientation as beyond understanding within the psychoanalytic situation. As in all aspects of psychoanalytic work, there must not be any a priori assumption of a privileged position, for either heterosexuality or homosexuality. The sole focus is on the meaning for the analysand of any aspect of sexuality and on fostering an enhanced sense of vitality and responsiveness to such aspects of lived experience as an intimate relationship with partner or spouse. As this report has repeatedly emphasized, there is little evidence to suggest that the clinical theory in psychoanalysis should privilege any one expression of sexual desire as necessarily more mature or adaptive than another. It is ironic that psychoanalytic study of desire and meaning, requiring less presumptive study of development than any other approach to the study of lives, should have become entangled within a hierarchical theory of motivation so far removed from the evidence of the clinical situation.

The method of clinical psychoanalysis is unique within the human sciences in making use of the analyst's empathic understanding as a principal method of study. However, as both Merton Gill (1976) and George Klein (1976) had shown, this clinical method of study has too often been confused with a theory of mental functions and with mechanisms inherent in Freud's philosophy of science, which, as he notes in his discussion of regression in his essay on Leonardo ([1910c] 1957), provides only an analogy useful only in clinical psychoanalytic study.

From Epigenesis to Developmental Study Within Psychoanalysis

Freud's lifelong fascination with the archaeological study of ancient civilizations, important in mid-nineteenth-century German scholarship at the time of his childhood, together with his later interest in Darwin and developmental neurobiology, led to his interest in an epigenetic psychology in which the past was presumed to coexist in the present as a determinant of present wish and intent, in a form recognizable as a representation of both childhood and culture. This epigenetic psychology Freud ([1913] 1958) regarded as the cornerstone of psychoanalysis. The portrayal of species and personal development resulting from Freud's reading of history and biology was instrumental in the construction of what Freud portrayed in his letters to Fliess, following Kipling's short stories, as a "just-so" story of a realm lying behind psychology. By analogy to Aristotle's *Metaphysics,* which he had read together with the psychologist-philosopher Brentano during his student days, Freud termed this realm "metapsychology" (Freud 1897–1904).

The epigenetic perspective, based on an analogy to Freud's prepsychoanalytic study and founded on assumptions regarding the course of development similar to those of both ethology and social learning theory,[1] has become the

1. The genetic approach, systematized in psychoanalysis by Abraham ([1921] 1927, [1924a] 1927, [1924b] 1927), and Erikson ([1951] 1963), received apparent support from animal studies of "critical periods," or moving windows in development when the occurrence or absence of events permanently effects functions of the evolving organism. Critical periods were clearly demonstrated for certain animal behaviors, e.g., imprinting in ducks (Lorenz [1937] 1965; Tinbergen 1951). The concept was generalized to human development without empirical evidence. In the same manner, both social learning approaches and Piaget's genetic epistemology emphasize the developmental primacy of early over later experiences. Further, although the Piagetian model shares the functionalism implicit in Freud's own mechanistic metapsychology (Wolff 1960; Basch 1977; Cohler 1988), it is at least partially consistent with contemporary views of development in emphasizing at least partial discontinuity of thought between earlier and later points in development.

The epigenetic model of psychological development presumes a necessary, causal connection between earlier and later states. However, this rigid connection has been called into question by both clinical and systematic empirical studies of lives over time. For example, ethological models are

foundation for a general understanding of Freud's contribution to the study of development. This point of view assumes that it is possible to show

> how the past is contained in the present. Genetic propositions describe why, in past situations of conflict, a specific solution was adopted; why the one was retained and the other dropped, and what causal relation exists between these solutions and later development. Genetic propositions refer to the fact that in an adult's behavior, anxiety may be induced by outdated conditions, and they explain why these conditions may still exercise influence. (Hartmann and Kris 1945, 14)

This perspective on the origin of intention has been widely disseminated in texts and the popular press, where it was shown to be insufficient to account for the subtlety of the human condition (Cohler 1987; Cohler and deBoer 1996; G. Klein 1976; Sulloway 1979). However, this exposition of the genetic perspective fails to recognize Freud's signal contribution to developmental study: emphasizing the extent to which intention is founded on the totality of lived experience as continually transformed in the present although often kept out of awareness (G. Klein 1976). Further, this portrayal of Freud's views of the past fails to account for his own caution (Freud [1920] 1955), that it is easier to reconstruct the past than to predict from earlier to later developmental stages.

Nowhere is this misplaced concreteness more evident than in the psychoanalytic study of lives over time, in which enactment of the totality of lived experience within the context of the relationship of analysand and analyst becomes the particular focus of study. Psychoanalytic study of same-gender sexual orientation provides a particularly salient means for understanding this distinction between the epigenetic perspective, reflecting Freud's particular late-nineteenth-century scientific worldview, and a prospective developmental perspective founded on shared exploration of intention and meaning by analyst and analysand (Abrams 1977; Cohler 1987).

George Klein (1976) has posited two theories of psychoanalysis: a worldview based on the philosophy of science relevant in the late nineteenth century, and a clinical theory founded on Freud's detailed observations within the consulting room. The former theory deals with such concepts as fixation and regression in developmental study, while the latter deals with such questions as the significance of silence within the psychoanalytic hour, momen-

---

largely irrelevant to the study of human infant development: imprinting plays a minimal role in human learning and development (Kagan, Kearsley, and Zelazo 1978; Emde 1981; Colombo 1982; Berenthal and Campos 1987; Cohler 1987). Longitudinal studies of personality from childhood through middle and late life demonstrate that lives are less continuous and predictably ordered than is assumed in epigenetic models (Neugarten 1969, 1979; Gergen 1977; Clarke and Clarke 1976; Kagan 1980; Emde 1981; Skolnick 1986; Cohler and Freeman 1983).

tary forgetting and remembering, and the experience of analyst and analysand working together within what Gill (1994) has termed a "two-person" psychology. As Cohler and Galatzer-Levy (1995) have suggested, following Klein's pioneering reformulation of Freud's contribution, Freud's scientific worldview has too often been confused with the clinical theory founded on the study of lives.

Sulloway (1979) and Gay (1988) both have observed that much of Freud's discussion of human development was argued by analogy to his laboratory study and was not founded on clinical study. Freud introduced the study of wish and intent into psychoanalysis while striving to remain within the new laboratory psychology and neuroscience of the school of Helmholtz, emphasis on demonstration and experiment in science had, since the mid-nineteenth century, epitomized positivist Enlightenment thinking within the biological sciences and medicine. Freud was deeply affected by the views of Helmholtz and his followers while he worked in the University of Vienna laboratory of Brücke (1819–1892), whom Helmholtz called "our ambassador to the East" (Bernfeld 1941, 1949; E. Jones 1953; Sulloway 1979).

As Sulloway (1979) has observed, even while a student Freud had been attracted to Haeckel's ([1868] 1968) concept of the biogenetic principle, which proposed that "philogeny recapitulates ontogeny." Haeckel had argued that the human fetus passes, in the course of its development, through all the evolutionary phases, from that of a simple one-cell organism to full human complexity. While little credence has been given to Haeckel's speculation regarding the course of evolution, his position was particularly attractive to Freud who, working under Brücke's supervision, initiated exploration in the laboratory of Haeckel's proposition, working with the brook lamprey. Indeed, much of what came to be known as the epigenetic perspective (Erikson [1951] 1963), or the genetic point of view in psychoanalysis (Rapaport and Gill 1959), is founded on Freud's prepsychoanalytic study (Gay 1988). Freud himself ([1910c] 1957, [1914a] 1957) noted the importance for his later discussion of fixation and regression of this early scientific study (Freud 1905–24; Abraham 1924a). Freud used the findings from his early laboratory study as a metaphor for his speculations on the course of human development, but he did not use this metaphor in clinical study, other than the speculative literary effort to reconstruct the experiences of Leonardo (Stengel 1963; S. Jackson 1969).[2]

2. Problems arise to the extent that clinical observation from the psychoanalytic setting is used as a means of confirming assumptions regarding the relationship of past and present, which may have been derived from biological analogy. Viewed from a life-course perspective, the formulation of metapsychology may have permitted Freud to realize an increased sense of meaning and direction

In the essay on Leonardo, Freud comments that "impressive analogies from biology have prepared us to find that the individual's mental development repeats the course of human development in abbreviated form" ([1910c] 1957, 97). Freud ([1913] 1958) relied upon this analogy rather than only clinical observation as the foundation for his genetic psychology, which he maintained was the most fundamental tenet in a scientific psychoanalytic worldview. Indeed, Freud was not able to move beyond the scientific worldview first formulated in Brücke's laboratory and reinforced by his reading of Darwin (Ritvo 1990) and other nineteenth-century natural philosophers. This experience-distant perspective seeks to discover possible connections between present psychological states and modes of experiencing earlier maturational processes, which at certain "critical periods," particularly in the first years of life, are believed to have been formative of such later outcomes as the capacity for intimate relations with others or the ability to resolve troubling tension states.

The genetic point of view both poses problems and offers promise for study of the manner in which the past is used in understanding present wishes and intents. Freud was clearly aware of the problems posed by epigenetic as contrasted with prospective developmental study. As he observed:

> So long as we trace the development from its final outcome backwards, the chain of events appears continuous, and we feel we have gained an insight which is completely satisfactory or even exhaustive. But if we proceed the reverse way, if we start from premises inferred from the analysis and try to follow these up to the final result, we no longer get the impression of an inevitable sequence of events which could not have been otherwise determined. . . . The synthesis is thus not so satisfactory as the analysis; in other words, from a knowledge of the premises we could not have foretold the nature of the results. ([1920] 1955, 167)

The study of sexual orientation and psychopathology is founded on the assumptions that experiences early in the course of life cumulatively determine later life outcomes, and that development follows a course in which the sequential negotiation of expectable tasks at particular points over time fosters continued adjustment (Bibring 1959). The assumption regarding the cumulative nature of psychological development, portrayed by Rapaport and Gill (1959) as the genetic point of view, was founded largely on a particular reading of psychoanalysis, principally Freud's *Three Essays* on the Theory of

---

in his own life, integrating his prepsychoanalytic laboratory study and his later clinical work, maintaining a coherent narrative of his career that was consistent with biological knowledge available to him at the end of the nineteenth century (Bernfeld 1941, 1949; Pribram and Gill 1976; Sulloway 1979).

Sexuality ([1905–24] 1953), Karl Abraham's influential essays ([1916] 1927, [1924a] 1927, [1924b] 1927) and Erikson's ([1951] 1963) reformulation of this epigenetic model. However, findings from the study of lives among persons followed over periods of several decades have challenged these assumptions about the linear nature of lives.

Even when, as in Zetzel and Meissner's (1973) reformulation the present is included as "co-active" with the past, it is assumed that past memories and associated feelings are recalled in the present, in circumstances experienced as historically similar. Erikson ([1951] 1963) may be credited with the extension of this epigenetic perspective to the study of the adult years; both Erikson and others relying upon this cumulative perspective assume that earlier experiences largely determine the outcome of such adult issues as work attainment and management of the capacity for intimacy (R. Gould 1993; Vaillant and Koury 1993; Vaillant and Milofsky 1980). Controversy continues as to the nature of contributions which clinical psychoanalysis might make to an understanding of the course of life, particularly the years of middle and later adulthood.

Much of traditional psychoanalytic study, particularly that of Abraham and his protege Melanie Klein, was founded on the belief that the most significant aspects of psychological development are completed across the first years of life, and that the rest of life represents simply the amplification of psychological issues connected with the "family romance" that took place across the nursery years. This genetic point of view, the dominant intellectual position of psychoanalysis on development, poses problems with regard to the significance of psychoanalysis as a means for understanding adult lives. As Freud ([1920] 1955) emphasized, historical explanation is not simply prediction "turned upside down" (Scriven 1959); rather, it is predicated upon an autonomous mode of understanding, fundamentally different from modes of understanding linked to prospective inquiry. For this reason, although problematic for the realization of psychoanalysis as a human science, Freud's concern with the genetic approach provides the conceptual foundation for the study of life history as a narrative of experience.

Although findings from experimental psychology have led to a substantial revision in dynamic and economic metapsychological approaches (Rosenblatt and Thickstun 1977; Horowitz 1977), findings from normative developmental study have had much less impact in fostering revision of the genetic approach (Escoll 1977; Abrams 1978). Findings emerging from experimental study have too often been viewed as scientific verification of assumptions derived from genetic propositions on the origins of behavior in earliest infancy (Basch 1977, 1982, 1985; Lichtenberg 1983; Silver 1985) and in the adult outcome of particular early experiences (Sternschein 1973; Tolpin and Kohut 1980).

Remaining preoccupied with Freud's scientific worldview rather than his clinical theory emphasizing wish and intent, psychoanalysis has largely ignored the findings from study of lives over time which suggest that the course of development may not be as predictable as previously maintained (Gergen 1977, 1983; Grunes 1980; Kagan 1980; Kohlberg, Ricks, and Snarey 1984). These reports suggest that changes taking place across the course of life, often in response to unexpected, generally adverse circumstances, provide challenges to adjustment, responses to which may be difficult to predict based on a cumulative theory of development. Such cumulative models fail to acknowledge the possibly transformative impact of later experiences upon earlier experiences, and the significance of a presently maintained portrayal of the course of life as critical in understanding the experience of self and others (Emde 1981, 1983). Galatzer-Levy's (1978, 1995) discussion of catastrophe theory and the course of human development was consistent with Gergen's (1977) suggestion that much of the course of adult lives may be understood in terms of response to chance events. In a report following up on the study of adult lives over a period of more than a decade, Marjorie Fiske and David Chiriboga (1990) provided findings confirming the significance of chance events as determinants of the subsequent course of life. While the men and women in their ten-year longitudinal study (across four interview points) were generally able to maintain a sense of coherence and to take advantage of a continuing conception of self and personal style in responding to adversity, disruptive adjustment followed from such chance events as life-threatening illness early in adulthood or illness and other problems affecting adult offspring or other close relatives. Particularly among middle-aged and older adults, physical illness, even if expectable, ushers in a series of secondary consequences, such as an increased sense of personal vulnerability and an accelerated sense of aging.

Fiske and Chiriboga (1990) observe that the very diversity of opportunities in contemporary society leaves many persons bewildered regarding life choices. Their observations tally with observations of Kaufman (1986) and Gergen (1994), which suggest that this flexibility takes a toll on adult adjustment: there are just too many options for persons to comprehend. Sudden adversity appears to impose further limits on coping ability. At the same time, it is always tempting to assume that the present is the worst of times; historical study tends to raise questions regarding the privileged status of any particular time as presenting unusual challenges for personal adjustment.

The question of the impact of earlier upon later experience was systematically studied in several studies, eventually merged into one, at Berkeley's Institute of Human Development (M. Jones et al. 1971; Elder [1974] 1998; Eichorn, Clausen, et al. 1981) and in the report by Kagan and Moss (1962), based on data from the Fels longitudinal study in Ohio. Significantly, findings from these two longitudinal studies have suggested that little of the variance of later outcomes can be explained on the basis of childhood factors, including childrearing attitudes and practices. Disappointing findings from longitudinal studies of child development have increasingly led investigators to wonder if we have not overstated the case for the continuity of childhood and adult experience in human development (Neugarten 1969; Brim 1976). Indeed, as findings from both longitudinal reports across the adult years and clinical reports have suggested (H. Moss and Sussman 1980; Kohlberg, Ricks, and Snarey 1984; Colarusso and Nemiroff 1981; Nemiroff and Colarusso 1985b), the question of factors accounting for continuity or change in personality and adjustment from early adulthood through oldest age is more significant than discussion of the primacy of childhood versus adult experiences (Neugarten 1969, 1979).

Contrasting Epigenetic and Developmental Perspectives Regarding Sexual Orientation

Many of the issues confounding the genetic point of view in psychoanalysis are highlighted in psychoanalytic discussions of homosexuality as a distortion of expectable development. Freud ([1905–24] 1953), following his reading of Havelock Ellis (1897), portrayed homosexuality as an inversion of sexuality. An admirer of Darwin (Ritvo 1990), Freud assumed that the goal of sexual intercourse was to perpetuate the species; therefore, any aspect of sexual activity not specifically directed toward procreation, such as foreplay or selection of an object of desire other than a opposite-sex partner, was presumed as evidence of immaturity in psychological development. Early psychoanalytic perspectives assumed that same-gender sexual orientation was an example of such immaturity in personality development. Over time, it came to regarded as evidence of psychopathology; Choosing sexual partners of the same gender was presumed to reflect either a compromise formation founded on failure to completely resolve the nuclear neurosis of the preschool era, or pre-oedipal psychopathology founded on regression from the issues posed by the nuclear neurosis. Clinical psychoanalytic study of gay, lesbian, and bisexual men and women, focusing on how persons make and enact meanings of such aspects of lived experience as sexual desire, suggests that additional understandings of personal change across the course of life, beyond those provided within an epigenetic perspective, are required.

Waddington (1956) has suggested that development might be compared with water running downhill to a stream. The water inevitably encounters resistance from obstacles in its path, but it moves around these obstacles, changing direction yet always tracing a downward course. We may attempt to trace this downhill journey, to chart the manner in which the water responds to each obstacle. It is not that one path to the stream is better than another, but rather that there are a number of pathways which might be taken.

Applied to the course of human development, including sexual orientation, the analogy suggests that within lives studied over time a particular forward development of the capacity for tension resolution, for experience of self as integrated and coherent, and for realizing satisfaction within intimate relations will emerge as the outcome of response to obstacles—particular, often unpredictable life changes: the birth of a younger brother or sister in the second year of life, at a time when maternal presence is particularly significant; the loss of a parents' parent during the early childhood years, leading to parental preoccupation and emotional withdrawal; the loss through death of a parent; or even a collective tragedy, such as flood or warfare. All such changes have an impact on the course of development. The outcome of these experiences cannot be predicted but depends upon both individual variation in temperament and the point in the course of life at which the change occurs. Perspectives on life course provided by Waddington (1956) and Galatzer-Levy and Cohler (1993) highlight the problems inherent in epigenetic or hierarchical conceptions of human development which presume a necessary course of human development (Freud [1905–24] 1953; Abraham [1924a] 1927, [1924b] 1927; Erikson [1951] 1963; Gedo 1993; Gedo and Goldberg 1973).

Understanding meanings presently attributed to the life story, including the expression of sexual desire across a lifetime, inevitably leads to reflection on psychoanalysis as a method of inquiry, with particular relevance as a means for understanding continuity and change across the adult years. For example, as already noted, men and women who seek heterosexual relationships at one point in the course of their adult years may subsequently search for same-gender partnership. Psychoanalytic approaches to developmental study must be able to account for such changes, and must be able to understand the impact of fluidity of desire in terms of the course of adult lives studied over personal and social time within the psychoanalytic situation.

Development as Metaphor: Sexual Orientation and
the Issue of Immaturity or Inversion

As noted in chapter 2, Freud's initial interest in same-gender sexual orientation was founded on his reading of late-nineteenth-century sexology, particularly the work of Havelock Ellis. Ellis, in turn, had been influenced by the tragic life story of the elite British writer John Symonds, who had struggled to make sense of his own homosexuality and had contacted Ellis for advice. Within the intellectual climate of late-nineteenth-century Central European letters, Schliemann's excavations at Troy, together with the natural science study of Haeckel and Darwin, had sparked much interest in the role of the past for the present. As Jacobsen and Steele (1979) and Sulloway (1979) have shown, Freud's own interest in the archaeology of mental development was very much influenced by these reports and by that of the British neurologist James Hughlings Jackson (1884), which had captured the public imagination.

From Freud's early neurodevelopmental study to his later ([1905–24] 1953) extension of this study to human development, his inquiry was undertaken in the spirit of this tradition (D. Jackson 1969). Freud himself acknowledges these intellectual antecedents to what later became known as the genetic point of view in his biography of Leonardo da Vinci ([1910c] 1957), where he acknowledges that concepts of fixation and regression represent an "analogy" to study in the natural sciences. This (epi)genetic point of view primarily reflects Freud's scientistic worldview and has little relevance for the psychoanalytic study of lives, which is founded on dynamic and topographic points of view stressing the power of wish or intent, which seek satisfaction through a series of compromise formations (Kohut and Seitz [1963] 1978; G. Klein 1976). Were it not for the influence of Freud's early collaborators, particularly Ferenczi ([1913] 1950), Abraham (1924a, 1924b), and Stekel, who urged the fateful 1910, 1915, and 1920 revisions to the 1905 essays on sexuality, this mechanistic, deterministic epigenetic perspective, derived largely from theory rather than from study of lives, might never have assumed the dominant role it played particularly in the psychoanalytic study of desire in the period following the Second World War.

FIXATION, REGRESSION, AND THE ORIGINS OF DESIRE IN FREUD'S *THREE ESSAYS*. Considering the later focus on same-gender sexual desire as reflecting either fixation at the point of effort to resolve the nuclear conflict, between the third and fifth years of life, or even earlier pre-oedipal efforts at reunion with the maternal care of early childhood, Freud's initial perspective on the study of homosexuality was much less complex. Freud was concerned both with the origins of sexuality, considered in terms of metapsychology, and with the specific determinants in family and development which led to same-gender sexual preference. The latter of these issues has been addressed in the discussion of personal development and the emergence of same-gender sexual desire. In the present section, the focus is on the implications of this epigenetic perspective for mental health and for understanding of the developmental psychopathology presumed to stem either from disturbance in the early mother–child relationship or later failure to resolve the nuclear conflict, perhaps as a result of this earlier disturbance.

These outcomes were for Freud a reflection of developmental immaturity associated with the pre oedipal epoch, or else evidence of the failure to completely resolve the nuclear neurosis. Living in culture, failure to completely resolve the neurosis is inevitable, leading to compromise formations which include the totality of lived experience. This failure is symbolically expressed through dreams, so-called unintended actions, psychoneuroses, sublimations, the transference neurosis, and like manifestations such as the defense transference, which is evoked anew within the psychoanalytic situation (Freud 1900, [1914c] 1958, [1927] 1961; Schlessinger and Robbins 1983). These compromise formations inevitably reflect developmental immaturity, in which present modes of relating to others are presumed to be determined by events originally taking place in earliest childhood.

However, as Mitchell (1978) has noted, Freud did not equate such developmental immaturity with psychopathology. Rather, as Freud emphasized, even prior to the 1915 revision of the *Three Essays* and the formulation of the developmental stages of the libido later popularized by Fliess (1948) and Erikson ([1951] 1963), all sexuality remains a problem to be understood, without privileging one or another form of sexual expression. If all sexual expression is to be regarded as representing a compromise formation reflecting wishes first associated with the infantile era, then evidence of such developmental immaturity, attempting to resolve unresolved wishes stemming originally from the preschool years, is as characteristic of heterosexual as of homosexual ties (Chodorow 1992). It may thus be questioned whether labeling any phenomena as evidence of "developmental immaturity" adds to our understanding of the meanings persons make of their particular experiences.

Several aspects of Freud's discussion of the implications of his metapsychological portrayal of same-gender desire for psychopathology should be noted. First, Freud explicitly distinguished between inversion, or expressed desire for others of the same gender, and perversion, or the substitution of a part of a person or an object as the focus of desire. Second, Freud attributed the preference for desire of others of the same gender to an immaturity or inhibition stemming from early childhood. As he suggested in a footnote added to the *Three Essays on the Theory of Sexuality* in 1910 ([1905–24] 1953, 144–45), the impact of the unresolved tie to the mother may lead the future homosexual man to proceed from a narcissistic basis, finding another man to love even as his mother loved him. (As in so much of the discussion of same-gender desire, Freud was concerned primarily with the genesis of homosexuality among men, although his effort to construct a genetic psychology would be equally relevant to homosexuality among women.)

The purpose of the present discussion is not to highlight this fixation on the mother and its consequences as a possible "explanation" for homosexuality, but only to indicate the manner in which Freud approached this developmental pathway. Freud regarded homosexuality and heterosexuality alike as reflections of a compromise formation. A careful reading of the *Three Essays* shows that while genital union for the purpose of procreation was viewed as species-adaptive, aspects of lovemaking prior to genital union were seen as reflecting developmental immaturity, as was same-gender sexual expression. However, since same-gender sexual union does not foster perpetuation of the species, Freud viewed it as entirely a reflection of developmental immaturity and a reflection of a developmental inhibition preventing the achievement of "normal" genital union.

Significantly, while Freud here followed closely a Darwinian argument, he remained uncertain regarding the implications of same-gender desire for adjustment. Freud notes, with some perplexity, that persons characterized as inverts "exhibit no other serious deviations from the normal" and that their "efficiency is unimpaired and [they] are indeed distinguished by specially high intellectual development and ethical culture," adding in a footnote that inversion characterized "some of the most prominent men in all recorded history" ([1905–24] 1953, 138–39). Finally, in a footnote added in 1915, Freud attributes all selection of object choice to events taking place in the childhood of both persons and societies.

Viewing personal childhood development as an expression of a larger historical developmental process—in which persons repeat first, in prenatal life, the history of all species starting with the first one-celled organism and then, in development across the childhood years, the history of humankind from the beginning of culture—Freud maintained that sexual inversion demonstrated personal immaturity in much the same way that continuing fascination with fire, as a cultural expression, reflected collective immaturity. However, even granted Freud's genetic focus, there is little evidence in his discussion of a link between developmental immaturity and psychopathology. Freud ([1905–24] 1953, [1921b] 1977, [1935] 1951) does acknowledge that in respects other than preferring same-gender sexual intimacy, men expressing desire for other men do not appear to be compromised in their adjustment. As contrasted with the perversions, where attachment to things becomes more important than attachment to people, men expressing same-gender desire seem able to form intimate relations; capacity for loving is not impaired but rather redirected.

SAME-GENDER DESIRE AND ASSUMED DEVELOPMENTAL IMMATURITY. Subsequent contributions in the early psychoanalytic literature by Ferenczi ([1911] 1950), who sought to distinguish between men seeking another to love as their mother loved them (subject homosexuality) and men seeking another to love them (object homosexuality), were followed by a series of papers focusing on the presumed link between homosexuality and paranoia (Rosenfeld 1949; Frosch 1983). This study was initiated by Freud's detailed discussion ([1911] 1958, [1915a] 1957) of the memoirs of Judge Schreber. Freud had suggested an equation between paranoia and homosexuality in which homosexual wishes represented a projection of unacceptable impulses. Ferenczi ([1911] 1950, [1914] 1950) enlarged on Freud's original formulation, suggesting an inevitable connection between what he termed latent homosexuality and paranoia; Ferenczi also suggested that same-gender desire represented a regression and fixation of the libido at the stage of narcissism.

Citing Melanie Klein's ([1932] 1969) account of the paranoid position and persecutory anxiety in her collection *The Psychoanalysis of Children*, Rosenfeld (1949) reviewed three psychoanalytic case accounts of homosexual men in which issues of persecution for their sexual desire represented displacement of unacceptable wishes and fear of retaliation on the part of the now persecuting other. Within the transference, and relying upon the mechanism of projective identification, the analyst was endowed with these wishes and then made into the person of the persecutor. Rosenfeld's comprehensive review of the psychoanalytic literature shows that most accounts following Freud's formulation and Ferenczi's extension of Freud's views stress the close association between homosexuality and paranoia as representing regression to the fixation of the oral-aggressive stage.

Frosch (1983) views homosexuality as the factor underlying the construction of a paranoid process. He assumes that the prospectively paranoid (homosexual) man is inevitably humiliated in early childhood by the parent of the same gender, which leads to an experience of helplessness and powerlessness; later, in the adult years, particular sensitivity to even the possibility of a slight evokes regression to the anal-sadistic stage of early childhood, at which the trauma of the humiliating parent and the consequent helplessness was first experienced. This regression leads both to a fear of once again having to submit to anal aggression and to the reprojection of the rage of the anal period onto others seen as humiliating and attacking.

Reviewing Frosch's formulation, Friedman (1988) noted both the contradiction between the emphasis in much of the theoretical work on paranoia on an oral rather than anal origin of the mechanism of projection and its subsequent expression in psychological symptoms, and Frosch's vague use of the term "homosexual," including a positing of so-called latent homosexuality that is never clearly defined in terms of either fantasy or action. Carefully considering the extensive psychoanalytic literature on the mechanism of projection and expression of paranoia in relation to the lives of gay men, Friedman concluded, "The body of material discussed . . . discourages simplistic, mechanistic interpretations of the relationship between unconscious homosexuality and paranoid phenomena. Freud's theory of a universal homosexual dynamic in paranoid considerations does not rest on a firm empirical base" (1988, 177). Friedman also observed "The contemporary clinician no longer need consider why homosexual men are paranoid, since there is no evidence that they generally are" (1988, 178).

In fact, as Friedman wryly observes, considering the continuing experience of antigay prejudice in society, it might be expected that most gay men would be justified in being paranoid. It may be that homosexual imagery appears within the disordered thinking of paranoid persons less because of early childhood fixations than as a reflection of the stigma widely recognized as attached to same-gender sexual orientation. Persons with paranoid thinking make use of such stigma in their disordered cognition. If this premise is correct, then, as homosexuality becomes more widely accepted as another developmental course, there should be an accompanying decline in the role of homosexual ideation among persons with paranoid personalities.

Following the Second World War, developmental study began to focus on the significance of the child's tie to caregivers in infancy as central to determining later development. Freud's initial contributions, so well formulated at the 1936 Marienbad conference on the theory of psychoanalytic technique, had stressed the importance of recognizing instincts or drives both in development and in intervention (Friedman 1988). However, psychoanalysis was quick to embrace this new focus on caregivers (primarily the mother), which resonated with analysands' accounts within the psychoanalytic process. This perspective informed both understanding of personality development and the theory of psychoanalytic change (Gitelson 1962; Friedman 1988). Consistent with the concept of developmental arrest, same-gender sexual orientation, and much other experience, was now conceived as the outcome of deficits in the mother–child relationship.

Mahler's portrayal of the so-called mother–child symbiosis (Mahler, Pine, and Bergman 1975) informed much of this early study, just as the presumed vicissitudes of the nature of the child's attachment to the mother has informed more recent psychoanalytic discussion (Sroufe 1981). When used in a manner similar to epigenetic ordering of development (Erikson [1951] 1963; Fliess 1948), such reliance upon a necessarily linear, cumulative portrayal of development may interfere with focus on the particular meanings of wish and action endowed by an analysand and presume a predictability in development which may not be warranted on the basis of actual prospective developmental study (Cohler 1987; Galatzer-Levy and Cohler 1993). Indeed, relying upon such constructs as separation-individuation or attachment leads to studying much of the developmental process outside of the observational field of vicarious introspection or empathic understanding which is distinctive of the psychoanalytic method, focusing on social psychology rather than on the analysand's particular understanding of experiences over a lifetime (Fliess 1944, 1953; Schafer 1959; Kohut [1959] 1978, 1971). Most significantly, both the more traditional epigenetic formulation and the more recent focus on early family antecedents understand homosexuality not only as evidence of developmental immaturity but also as evidence of developmental arrest or deficit. Such as is reflected in the concept of narcissism as the basis for same gender partnership choice (Leavy 1983/85).

Wiedeman (1962, 1974), Lewes ([1988] 1995), Friedman (1988), and Meyer (1995) all have reviewed psychoanalytic formulations of same-gender sexual orientation as the outcome of an arrest in psychological development founded either in disturbance of the mother-child tie or in failure to resolve the nuclear conflict during the preschool era. Again, much of this literature is written by men and focuses on same-gender desire among men. As Nungesser (1983) has suggested, same-gender sexual expression among men evokes far greater anxiety among men than does same-gender sexual expression among women in either men or women, reflecting a social problem stemming from socialization of men across the course of life rather than simply a particular gender bias in the study of same-gender sexuality.

Early psychoanalytic study emphasized the pre-oedipal nature of same-gender sexual orientation. Nunberg (1938) and Bergler (1956) stressed oral-sadistic efforts to incorporate a strong man, as well as revenge against the mother for weaning, while Jones (1932) viewed male homosexuality in terms of the oedipus complex, proposing that men seeking same-gender sexual pleasure fear castration in retaliation for their wishes. However, Nunberg (1947) observed that the distinction between what is masculine and what is feminine had not been clearly discussed in the psychoanalytic literature. Summarizing this early literature, Wiedeman observes:

> If we examine the literature with the aim of finding a typical picture of pregenital libidinal fixation in homosexuality, we will find that any disturbance or combination of disturbances of the libidinal development, be it oral, anal, or phallic, may become manifest in overt homosexuality. However, there is no agreement that a specific libidinal fixation accounts for inversion in the male. (1962, 394)

Other early formulations emphasized structural considerations in the origin of homosexuality among men, focusing on feelings of narcissistic vulnerability (DéMonchy 1965) or guilt regarding oedipal issues and even an effort to punish oneself masochistically for such incestuous wishes (Bergler 1949, 1956; Bychowski 1954). Wiedeman noted the obvious paradox that the early psychoanalytic literature could not stress such structural considerations prior to the introduction of the structural point of view in Freud's ([1923] 1961) reformulation of the metapsychology. Bergler's account is even more complex, emphasizing the importance of the mother of early childhood as a feared person but also the focus of intense rage, against which adult homosexuality is a regressive defense. According to Bergler's formulation, homosexual ties represent reenactment of the maternal cruelty experienced in infancy, with a simultaneous effort to make reparation and to gratify this childhood tie to the cruel mother. However, assumptions of homosexuality as a reflection of either a positive or negative oedipal solution may not be sufficient to explain male homosexuality. Finally, Freeman (1955), Gillespie (1956), and Socarides (1959) all view same-gender sexual orientation among men as a reflection of a splitting of the ego, in the service of structures defending the continuation in adult life of developmental deficits first incurred in early childhood.

A significant contradiction which emerged in this psychoanalytic discussion of male homosexuality was the replacement of Freud's concept of inversion by a concept of perversion. Freud had insisted that wishes and actions related to same-gender sexual orientation had little bearing on a person's capacity for realizing satisfying relationships and an otherwise characteristically adult perspective regarding self and others. This view is reflected in the careful distinction Freud made between inversion and perversion. However, as Schafer (1995) has observed, psychoanalytic discussion of homosexuality in the ensuing decades returned to the prepsychoanalytic moral and psychopathological conception of same-gender sexual orientation as a reflection of a fundamental disturbance in the capacity for sexual intimacy, repeating an error which Freud had cautioned against in the *Three Essays*.

Much of the confusion regarding homosexuality as perversion, hence as psychopathology, and even as a gender identity disorder, is reflected in two panels on homosexuality among men, at the 1959 meetings of the American Psychoanalytic Association (Socarides 1960) and at the meetings of the International Psycho-Analytic Congress in 1963 (Gillespie 1964; Pasche 1964; Wiedeman 1964), together with Wiedeman's (1974) review of eight books published over the postwar period focusing on male homosexuality. Reporting on the 1959 panel, which included presentations by Wiedeman, Bychowski, Weiss, Fleischmann, Socarides, and Clyne and Bacon, Socarides summarized the discussion as reflecting the importance of primitive defense mechanisms in the male homosexual, the fear of maternal separation as intrinsic to the origin of homosexuality, and the inevitability of homosexual object choice as necessarily narcissistic. Although Wiedeman noted that Freud had rejected the notion of homosexuality as necessarily reflecting psychopathology, other panelists emphasized the necessary connection between homosexuality and psychopathology. Bychowski asserted that there are no well-adjusted homosexual men and that male homosexuality represents an impulsive instinctual discharge and projection of early rage against the mother, which wards off depressive affect but unwittingly leads to paranoia (Socarides 1960, 557–58). Even Weiss, who suspected that homosexuality might reflect psychopathology, doubted Bychowski's claim that it would be impossible to imagine a well-adjusted homosexual man.

Panelists were in agreement with the claims of Fleischmann, Bacon, and Wiedeman that male homosexuality necessarily reflects a profound disturbance in the early relationship to the mother which leads the prospectively homosexual man to flee from all sexual intimacy with women. The panel also made specific recommendations regarding the active intervention of the analyst in order to foster a shift to a heterosexual orientation. (This position was reviewed in some detail in chapter 2. Here, however, we are concerned with reviewing traditional psychoanalytic perspectives on the presumed relation between homosexuality and psychopathology before the period of social and intellectual ferment in the United States and Western Europe between the late 1960s and the mid-1970s.)

A similar theme was echoed in the 1963 panel of the International Psycho-Analytic Congress in presentations by Gillespie, Pasche, and Wiedeman. Gillespie (1964), while acknowledging Freud's important distinction between inversion and perversion, nevertheless retreated into portraying homosexuality as a perversion similar to bestiality. Citing then-accessible evidence, Gillespie maintained that there may be innate bisexuality, varying in quantity, which leads to such perverse activity as homosexuality, but he maintained that otherwise homosexual activity is a consequence of a disturbed tie between the prospectively homosexual child and his caregivers rather than a regressive flight from oedipal issues. Pasche (1964), however, viewed homosexuality largely in terms of this latter model, as a regressive flight from oedipal confrontation with the father and adoption of a feminine attitude characteristic of the negative oedipal conflict. In this sense, homosexuality is for Pasche simply another expression of a neurosis. Pasche also acknowledged the possibility of another type of homosexuality reflecting pre-oedipal origins in the boy's disturbed relationship with his mother, although he observed that the very capacity to symbolize wishes as homoerotic suggests that early developmental factors may be less salient as an explanation than has sometimes been maintained.

Wiedeman (1964) urged a more complex conception of the psychopathology underlying homosexuality than was suggested by any one theoretical perspective. In remarks consonant with his earlier and later reviews (Wiedeman 1962, 1974), and directed as much at understanding gender identity disorders as same-gender sexual orientation, Wiedeman supported a dual genetic and family interaction focus. It should be noted that such a focus leaves little room for consideration of the meaning of homosexuality for the analysand. In Wiedeman's view, factors impinging upon the prospective homosexual man from the outside largely determine sexual orientation. Wiedeman's (1974) review of books on homosexuality published across the preceding decade continues this focus on issues apart from those of meaning, intention, and the understanding of same-gender sexual orientation as a developmental pathway. At the same time, Wiedeman (1974) cautioned that few generalizations can be made about all men seeking same-gender intimacy. He noted efforts by the Kinsey group and others to represent sexual orientation in terms of exclusivity of fantasy and action and reviewed formulations such as those of Socarides (1968) and Ovesey (1969). Consistent with the adaptational perspective of Rado ([1945–55] 1995, 1949), Wiedeman urged psychoanalysis not to forsake Freud's effort to provide an understanding of sexual orientation in other than pejorative terms. However, he then largely disregarded Freud's ([1905–24] 1953) effort to distinguish between inversion and perversion and reviewed eight books which implicitly or explicitly led to the reinclusion of male homosexuality as necessarily perverse and inevitably interfering in realizing intimate ties.

Reviewing same-gender sexual orientation as a reflection of the complex primitive defense mechanisms of disavowal, Lachmann (1975) essentially endorses a view of homosexuality as a perversion, presenting five case vignettes designed to demonstrate that, while complex, homosexuality among both men and women represents a malignant process reflecting ego deficit. Lachmann does, however, qualify his review by acknowledging that knowledge of sexual orientation has little predictive value for other aspects of an analysand's life.

Isay (1989, 1996a) posits yet another explanation of the origins of adult same-gender sexual orientation in at least some men. He begins his discussion with the observation that many gay men report difficult relationships with their fathers across the years of adolescence and adulthood. Consistent with the findings reported by Bieber et al. (1962), although with a quite different explanation, Isay suggests that the prospectively gay man develops an intense erotic attachment to his father during the preschool years, then as an adult maintains psychological distance in order to avoid acknowledgment of this childhood erotic tie. Significantly, Isay's portrayal of the gay man's experience of the parents of early childhood is founded on study of the fantasies of gay men whom he has analyzed, including expression of these wishes within the transference, rather than on experience-distant clinician ratings, the basis of the Bieber group's study.

Isay (1989, 1996a, 1996b), Goldsmith (1995), and Lewes ([1988] 1995) all suggest a twist on the course of the resolution of the infantile neurosis: instead of the expectable "negative" oedipal constellation (Freud [1909a] 1955, Nagera 1966; A. Freud 1971) in which the son seeks to offer himself to his father in order to forestall the father's retaliation for the son's erotic wishes for the mother, some prospectively homosexual boys develop an erotic tie to the father. Instead of experiencing sexual desire for their mothers and regarding their fathers as rivals, these boys take their fathers as the object of their early childhood sexual wishes; Isay (1989, 1996a, 1996b) does not explicitly indicate whether the mother is then regarded as a rival for the little boy's desire. Later, in adolescence and adulthood, the homosexual son's perception of his father as distant may follow from the son's need to protect himself from awareness of his childhood romance with the father. At the same time, the father may withdraw from his young son because he senses the son's intense wishes, which makes him feel uncomfortable. Ultimately, the prospectively gay boy experiences rage at the father, which may be displaced onto a sibling with whom the father feels more comfortable.

Early familial circumstances are highlighted as factors contributing to same-gender sexual orientation among men in both the more traditional formulations summarized by Wiedeman (1962, 1974) and, more critically, by Friedman (1988), as well as in Isay's (1989, 1996a, 1996b) restatement of the outcome of the nuclear conflict among prospectively homosexual men. While Wiedeman's reviews supported findings reported by the Biebers and their colleagues, reviewed in greater detail in chapter 4, Isay (1989) suggests that the Bieber group relied on extra-analytic data in proposing a developmental schema which failed to consider the nature of the wishes of the prospectively homosexual man as observed within the transference, which is a distinctively psychoanalytic method of study. As a result, their influential study led to a view of homosexuality as perversion or psychopathology determined largely by factors outside the analysand's control, including biological predisposition and family-wide psychopathology. Lachmann (1975) makes this point in even greater detail.

Critically reviewing conceptions of homosexuality among men as the outcome of either a pre-oedipal or oedipal struggle leading to masochistic or paranoid personality traits, Friedman (1988) observed that there had been little support other than anecdotal case examples for much of this speculation regarding the childhood origins of homosexuality among men. As he observed, "There is no evidence to date indicating that consolidated masochistic motivation is aggregated among men at any point on the Kinsey scale, nor is there empirical support for the view that most masochists are predominately or exclusively homosexual or that most homosexuals (however defined) are masochistic" (1988, 161). At the same time, Friedman did observe that gay men may indeed act masochistically, as when they publicly acknowledge their homosexuality at a time or place where there are likely to be serious social consequences. Friedman noted that it is important to remain anchored in the reality of a particular life story unfolding across the course of psychoanalysis rather than imposing some a priori formulation.

While less extensive discussion had been devoted to homosexuality as evidence of psychopathology among women, a companion panel to the earlier panel on male homosexuality was organized for the 1960 meetings (Socarides 1962), with presentations by Socarides, Edoardo Weiss, Irving Clyne, and Judith Kestenberg. Socarides reiterated Freud's assumption of the complementarity of the nuclear conflict among men and women; however, he followed Freud's later discussion regarding the presumed consequences of anatomical distinctions between men and women, including the woman's sense of inferiority and need for rebellion and protest resulting in a masculinity complex and the choice of another woman as the desired sexual object. Faced with the choice between renouncing her femininity or her erotic attachment to her father, the prospectively homosexual woman renounces her femininity and converts her bond with her father to an identification.

In considering the possibility a more complex relationship between mothers and daughters than between mothers and sons—including the daughter's reproach toward her mother for her apparent castration and the temptation of turning toward her father, but also the greater danger of violation of the incest taboo which that represents—Socarides located an additional motive for female homosexuality. Following Jones's (1927) report on five cases of analyzed female homosexuality, Socarides suggested that identification with the father was common to all forms of female homosexuality. In a lengthy and comprehensive review of formulations of female sexuality following Freud, Socarides summarized a number of studies pointing to same-gender female sexuality as a perversion defending against recognition of femininity and resulting from disappointment rather than, as originally assumed by Freud, psychological conflict resulting from the young girl's effort to resolve the nuclear neurosis.

Other contributions to this panel echoed Socarides's assertion that, as with male homosexuality, female homosexuality represented a perversion. Weiss stressed the impact for the woman of constitutional bisexuality; the little girl identifies with little boys and feels mutilated because of presumed castration.

Expectably, a woman then realizes that an intimate relationship with a man is able to provide both expression of her own femininity and also a new solution to the loss of the penis. Weiss suggests that women turning to homosexuality are unable to master their own repressed incestuous wishes or else continue to suffer from early disturbances in the daughter-father relationship. In any event, female homosexuality reflects failure to resolve the nuclear conflict together with flight from the threatened breakthrough of incestuous wishes. According to Weiss, women who turn to homosexuality, which in terms of Freud's original formulation is a perversion rather than a neurosis, seek to relieve sexual tension through identification with another (sexually aroused) woman, with the early childhood pregenital pleasure now enriched by adult genital sexuality. Further, Weiss maintained that these homosexual women may become preoccupied by the search for a passive position in relation to some more assertive woman in order to re-create the mother-child tie of early infancy, making them unable to maintain the more characteristic feminine desire to have and care for children.

Kestenberg, the sole woman on the panel, suggested that homosexual women have renounced wishes regarding their father and instead play out a mother-child relationship with a female partner. Among homosexual women, she maintained, the shift from vaginal to clitoral libido has been incomplete or has been interfered with, leading to the glorification of virginity, the renunciation of motherhood, and the equation of baby and vagina. Further, Kestenberg asserted that both homosexual men and women are unable to experience a range of pleasure, relying instead upon narrow modes of excitation and discharge, which prevents then from adjusting to opposite-sex partners. Finally, Kestenberg joined with the other panelists in agreeing that homosexual women are at high risk for suicide attempts due to perceived loneliness when their intense needs are not met. According to Kestenberg's formulation, the high rates of alcoholism sometimes reported among homosexual women are due to the desire to realize a state of stupor or somnolence when confronted by overwhelming stimulation.

This panel reflected the problem also found in the earlier panel on same-gender sexual orientation among men: while, Herman Serota, the chair of the panel, emphasized the variety of factors and kinds of homosexuality among women, panelists opted for single, overriding explanations founded on Freud's pronouncements regarding female sexuality, ignoring, however, the fact that Freud had carefully defined homosexuality as inversion rather than perversion. Presenters continually emphasized both the importance and the difficulty of effecting change in sexual orientation. Panelists shared the view that suicidal efforts and substance abuse were common among homosexual women, although there is limited support for such a position reported in systematic studies, such as those reviewed in chapter 8; there is little evidence of increased suicidal ideation among homosexual women or men following the adolescent years when, as already discussed in chapter 5, some enhanced risk for suicide has been reported, most often the consequence of stigma. Clearly, as in the earlier panel on same-gender sexual orientation among gay men, this panel left little room for study of lesbian lives as alternative developmental pathways or as other than evidence of psychopathology.

QUESTIONING THE DEFICIT VIEW: PSYCHOLOGICAL DEVELOPMENT AND THE ISSUE OF MEANING. Mitchell (1978) was among the first within psychoanalysis to explicitly question the assumption that adult homosexuality necessarily represents a pathological position. Noting that psychodynamic formulations need not imply psychopathology and that difference need not equal psychopathology, a view shared by psychoanalytic and nonpsychoanalytic authors alike, Mitchell decries much of the contemporary literature as a kind of "strategic obscurantism" (1978, 255) which, in its preoccupation with behavioral genetics and family process, overlooks the fundamental contribution of psychoanalysis as a means of fostering understanding of sexuality in terms of all aspects of the analysand's life. Most significantly, preoccupation with homosexuality as pre-oedipal in origin and therefore necessarily pathological, poses problems for understanding the place of sexuality within the life of the analysand. As Mitchell has observed:

> The simple schema of the libidinal fixation theory of neurosis, in which sexual functioning is the center-piece of personality, determining the level of integration and development, has generally been superseded by a more complex vision of personality functioning in which ego development and richness of object relations may or may not be correlated with sexual functioning. (1978, 256)

Mitchell urges a view of sexuality as but one aspect of present adjustment and a view of homosexuality as multifaceted in its meanings and implications for adjustment. Indeed, he suggests that it may be useful to consider adult homosexuality in terms of its present meanings for the analysand apart from presumed origins in early childhood. Phrased in terms of secondary autonomy of the ego (Hartmann 1952; Beres 1972), adult sexuality, even while founded within the instinctual vicissitudes of early childhood, represents a kind of secondary autonomy apart from its instinctual origins. As Mitchell observes, "As later relationships . . . develop, the original conflicts and anxieties may no longer be the salient motives for the behavior" (1978, 278).

While this view is not inconsistent with that proposed by Stoller (1985) and by Chodorow (1992), Mitchell suggests that the presumed origin of variation in sexual orientation among adult men and women may be more complex than is acknowledged by a focus solely on failures in managing the nuclear conflict marking the transition from early to middle childhood. Schafer (1995) has expressed a similar perspective, urging that we recognize the complexities involved within lives over time, including the complex transformations taking place in adulthood regarding earlier childhood experiences.

Much of this perspective, so different from the formulations of homosexuality in the era prior to the late 1960s, is reflected in another panel at the fall meetings of the American Psychoanalytic Association in 1983 (Isay and Friedman 1986), with panelists Stanley Leavy, Richard Isay, Robert Stoller, and Richard Friedman. Panelists expressed the view that same-gender desire is not tantamount to psychopathology but that such social circumstances as antigay prejudice impose interference in the course of development. Panelists expressed concern with the use of such terms as "narcissism" in a pejorative context as a means of explaining the dynamics of same-gender sexual orientation; there is little evidence that homosexual adults are either more or less narcissistic than their heterosexual counterparts. Indeed, the term "homosexuality" is itself difficult to define. Too often the concept is used within psychoanalysis without clarification to include wish or impulse, as well as action. Panelists urged more detailed study of homosexuality in terms of typologies and the meanings for persons of their sexuality.

This reconsideration of the presumed relationship between same-gender sexual orientation and psychopathology has also been extended to the study of lesbian lives. A panel at the 1984 spring meetings of the American Psychoanalytic Association (Wolfson 1987), with presentations by Robert Stoller, Martha Kirkpatrick, and Joyce McDougall, reflected a major shift from the 1962 panel on homosexuality among women. The composition of the panel, mostly women, one of whom was lesbian, is itself a reflection of this shift. However, there were several departures from the views of the earlier panel significant in this more recent consideration of same-gender sexual orientation among women. Foremost among these departures from traditional perspectives was the panelists' willingness to challenge Freud's assumptions regarding penis envy and the penis-baby equation. In a challenge from the floor Socarides maintained that homosexuality serves to alleviate guilt and reflects various anxieties, depression, and ego despair (Wolfsen 1987, 173). The psychiatrist Carol Nadelson spoke from the floor and countered that the discussion regarding homosexuality and mental health has too long been clouded by unsupported claims, which she addressed through reference to studies such as those reviewed in the present chapter showing that the entire issue of a presumed association between homosexuality and impaired mental health is based more on social values and antigay prejudice than on fact.

Nadelson urged more detailed systematic study of psychodynamic factors entering into all forms of sexuality.

Anticipating more recent critiques such as those of Chodorow (1989), Dorsey (1996), Deutsch (1995), Mayer (1996), Richards (1996), and Suchet (1995), panelists challenged many of the assumptions stemming from Freud's work and endorsed without question the conclusions of the panel of some two decades earlier regarding the nature of castration anxiety among women, together with questions regarding the assumption that the superego of women is necessarily inferior to that of men since women don't have to struggle with wishes stimulated by the childhood family romance and subsequent fear of castration. While women may desire a penis, this is most often a means for dealing with issues of the mother-daughter tie, including the effort to show loyalty to the mother through renunciation of being a girl and attracting her father's attention.

Stoller presented a case in which a woman analysand had adopted a lesbian identity in order to realize psychological differentiation from her mother, who tried to bind her to her as a desperate bid to maintain her own identity and not be abandoned. The analysand's father was complicit in this binding relationship, so well reflected in Stierlin's (1974) discussion of separating parents and their adolescents. McDougall suggested that this maternal demand for dependence, from which the daughter was able to free herself through the emergence of a lesbian identity, inevitably led to selection of women partners able to function as reparative mother substitutes, providing tenderness the daughter had sought but not found in her own childhood. Adoption of a lesbian position represented a triumph both over the dangerous mother and over the father, since it proved that a man was not necessary in order to feel loved or to experience sexual completion. However, McDougall cautioned that dependence upon the lover could also lead to feelings of resentment and envy and resurgence of a sense of the partner as the narcissistic and demanding mother. Psychoanalytic intervention in work with this analysand sought to highlight this problem in order that she might enjoy a successful relationship with her partners. For McDougall, this represented a significant departure from her earlier position regarding the inherently destructive nature of lesbian relationships (J. McDougall [1965] 1970).

Kirkpatrick and McDougall both rejected the notion of a lack of interest in motherhood among lesbian women, reporting maternal desires within the women whom they have studied, a wish they believe follows a different developmental line than the presumed wish for a penis. Finally, panelists agreed that both boys and girls worry about the integrity of their genitals, although the worries of girls may be more diffuse and vague than those of boys. Fear regarding possible damage to internal or external genitalia is different from presumptions of a castration complex or fear of or belief in castration.

Kirkpatrick's findings have been reviewed in greater detail in chapter 6; findings presented at the panel focused on mental health implications of her study for lesbian women. Kirkpatrick reported much less hostility toward men among the twenty lesbian women she had interviewed than she had expected. These women, who had been married before seeking a lesbian lifestyle had marriages lasting at least as long as that in the comparison group of heterosexual mothers and maintained more cordial ties and enhanced capacity for parental alliance with their former husbands than did women in the heterosexual group. Reasons for ending their marriages were founded less on lack of sexual satisfaction than on feelings of lack of communication with their spouses. Kirkpatrick concluded that genital release may be less of a factor organizing and motivating psychological development among women than the quest for intimacy. This observation is consistent with that of Gilligan (1982, 1990) and subsequent study of girls and women by Gilligan and her colleagues, Burch (1993), Herbert (1996), and others.

As Chodorow (1992) has emphasized, and as Stoller observed in the 1983 panel on male homosexuality (R. C. Friedman 1986), neither heterosexuality nor homosexuality, understood either as fantasy or intention or as action, is, as such, necessarily either pathological or nonpathological. Indeed, the concept of different developmental pathways need not imply psychopathology. For example, assuming that Isay (1989, 1996a) has defined a group of men who, as boys, developed an erotic attachment to their father rather than, as classically presumed, to their mother, there is still little evidence that such difference is equivalent to pathology. Understood as a compromise formation of a particular sort, in terms of the dynamic point of view, this erotic tie to the father may lead to a different construction of sexuality in adulthood than that among boys who first experience an erotic tie to the mother. As a consequence, sexual wishes may be expressed differently than among boys experiencing the nuclear conflict and resulting compromise formations in more traditional ways.

Conclusion

As this chapter has shown, following psychoanalytic understanding of personality development, differences in the experience of the nuclear conflict within the family of early childhood lead both to particular variation in developmental pathways and to particular modes of understanding self, others, and sexuality. These different outcomes need not necessarily imply psychopathology. Further, inversion as first portrayed by Freud ([1905–24] 1953) is not tantamount to psychopathology (A. Blum, Danson, and Schneider 1997). Consistent with this perspective, the 1983 American Psychoanalytic Association panel on male homosexuality concluded that "homosexuality in any form, as far as we know, is not associated with any syndrome of psycho-pathology more than any other" (R. C. Friedman 1986, 201).

As Schafer has commented, "In psychoanalysis, the words pregenital, pre-oedipal, perverse, and inverse are disorienting as well as judgmental, and so they tend to limit further . . . curiosities about the individual case" (1995, 198). The question for psychoanalysis must always the meaning for the anal-ysand of any aspect of the life history, particularly as evident within the psy-choanalytic situation. Focus either on psychodynamics as psychopathology or on biological or social theory apart from understanding the social context of lived experience, may detract from the clinical encounter.

Further, as both Mitchell (1978) and Blum, Danson, and Schneider (1997) have commented, and consistent with the present discussion, there is little reason to assume that the vicissitudes of early life experience must inevitably lead to one or another means for the expression of desire in adulthood. Rather, it is as a consequence of lack of support from family, school, and community, and implicit sense of being ashamed for wishes perceived as be-ing socially unacceptable, that leads to purported narcissistic psychopathol-ogy and disavowed desire among gay men and women. As Blum, Danson, and Schneider observe:

> What is almost universal . . . is the fact that somewhere in a gay man's develop-ment, he will experience rejection, hatred, and even physical abuse for his sex-ual and affectional expression. The adaptation to this—the self-hatred, the contorting of oneself to maintain object ties, or even any semblance of accept-ability—are responsible for many of the aberrations of normal homosexual ex-pression in gay men who enter treatment. (1997, 10)

As this chapter has suggested, focus in psychoanalytic intervention with gay men must focus at least in part upon the lifelong effects of this self-criticism resulting from the antigay prejudices so characteristic within both family and community.

Ten

"Ego-Dystonic" Homosexuality and the
Issue of Reparative Therapy

The present work has focused primarily on the life course of people who find themselves at some point experiencing same-gender sexual desire and who realize that desire through involvement in the gay community. Despite often having mixed feelings, these women and men express an enduring positive commitment to a gay lifestyle and seek psychoanalysis and psychotherapy for issues other than sexual orientation. Gay people commonly seek therapy because of struggles with issues of intimacy and partnership, losses such as a partner's death, problems at work, or feelings of malaise. But they do not seek to change their sexual orientation and do not view their experience of homoerotic fantasies and dreams as an unwanted intrusion.

Defensive Homosexuality

There is a group of people, often men at midlife, who feel uncertain about their sexuality and who experience same-gender sexual fantasy and activity but not as in any way integral to their life stories. Meyer (1985) suggested "ego-dystonic homosexuality" as a term for this condition, which, observed, may emerge from unresolved problems arising from deficits in the emotional availability of caregivers in early life. Men affected by this condition are often preoccupied with homoerotic fantasies and may act on them in transitory sexual encounters, but these fantasies and activities feel like disruptive intrusions similar to a perversion (Goldberg 1995).

Such sexual encounters most often reflect a search for excitement intended to forestall a sensed lack of vitality. For example, a successful professional who was seen in consultation, married and with two adolescent boys, was tempted to engage in reciprocal oral sex in the back room of a bar which he had heard from a gay colleague was a refuge for gay men who commuted to work but maintained straight suburban lives. Twice he had gone to the bar but stopped, disgusted with the thought that he had allowed himself to go even that far. Exploration of factors that led this man to seek sexual activity in a gay venue suggested that he felt depressed and futile in his present life, hated his work, and resented his wife, who had found a creative vocation, and offspring, who seemed engaged and happy with their high school lives.

The client described a life that was perfectly ordered in terms of timing of expectable life changes. He was reasonably successful, consistent with the expectations of his parents, who were very religious small-town shopkeepers. They were already near middle-age when he was born and maintained distant and empty relationships with the client, their only child. His childhood had been marked by overt success as an athlete and a scholar, but also by a pervasive sense of loneliness. In midlife he grew restless and sought a sense of being alive. He was jealous of his gay coworker, who seemed lively and engaged with the gay community, and of his relationship with his partner of five years. Referred for psychotherapy, the client was able to work through his disappointments at the care and empathy he felt had been missing in his life. Ultimately, this man decided to change professions, becoming a minister after talking with his wife, who agreed to provide financial support while he returned to school. As he developed an interest in his new profession and took advantage of intensive psychotherapy with a warm woman psychiatrist, the emergence and resolution of a mirroring transference fostered enhanced psychological structure. Although his psychotherapy focused little on the intrusion into his awareness of ego-dystonic homosexual wishes and fears, his homosexual wishes and fears ceased to be troubling and he lost interest in transitory same-gender sexual activities. The emergence of same-gender sexual preoccupations had been an attempt to realize enhanced connections to others and did not arise from a specific longing for a gay sexual lifeway.

While Meyer (1985) views ego-dystonic sexual expression in adult life as rooted in deficits in provision of care experienced in earlier life, Isay (1989) focuses primarily on men who have failed to resolve issues associated with the nuclear conflict. These men remain in a negative oedipal configuration, protecting themselves against fears of castration, the father's retaliation for their wish for the mother, by fantasizing about offering themselves to the father as homosexual lovers. These men, described by Ovesey (1969) as "pseudo-homosexual," often present for psychoanalysis or dynamic psychotherapy with fears of impotence and sexual inadequacy. Isay suggests that as they gain awareness, through interpretation of transference, of their unresolved competitiveness with their fathers and rage with their mothers, these men are once more able to enjoy their work and to find sexual pleasure with women.

These straight men, who use homoerotic fantasies defensively as one aspect of their effort to resolve the nuclear conflict, may express feminine strivings out of the unconscious belief that as men they are vulnerable to the father's retaliation. Success at school or work is associated with anxiety, because it is unconsciously viewed as part of the striving for masculine, competitive success. Over the course of the analysis, focusing on issues of competition and aggression expressed through the transference, initial reports of troubling homoerotic fantasies and dreams tend to disappear from the analysand's life.

Isay (1989) reviews the case of a young man who began analysis with problems completing postbaccalaureate education and using his considerable talent in his chosen field. He felt equally inadequate in his sexual life. His father was a highly successful competitive businessman, who radiated no personal warmth. In contrast, his mother was warm and even seductive. In the transference, issues of competition emerged, and as he worked through his feelings of rage toward his mother and disappointment with his father's inability to recognize human feelings, he reported the desire to seduce his male analyst. This desire was understood as reflecting a sense that his analyst would not retaliate for his newly found vocational and sexual success. With interpretation and working-through of these issues, the analysand became more comfortable with his angry wishes, more accepting of his parents, and less preoccupied with issues of competitiveness. These changes were accompanied by a diminution of homoerotic fantasies.

Isay stresses that analyses with men who experience homoerotic fantasies as unwanted intrusions must be conducted within a context that is neither manipulative nor directed toward forcing them to accept a straight sexual lifeway. It is important to ensure that homoerotic wishes toward the analyst which repeat the oedipal child's solution to the anxiety that father will harm him are, like any transference, appropriately interpreted. These issues should no more be approached through education or manipulation than any other aspect of an oedipal situation that emerges in analysis.

Though homoerotic fantasies may be the focus of self-criticism by some gay men and women, they are generally not experienced as an intrusion to the extent reported among straight men and women. The analytic process, if not biased by the analyst's belief that one or another lifeway is preferable, will reveal the extent to which the analysand's concern with issues of same-gender sexuality is a reparative effort provoked by early deficits in caregiving, a defense against unresolved aspects of nuclear conflict, or an alternative lifeway. The oedipal configurations of gay men also involve erotic ideas about the father, but these ideas are not primarily defensive against sexual wishes toward the mother. These configurations may be problematic because they may stimulate anxiety in the father, who withdraws from the boy (Isay 1986a), a situation which may be repeated in analysis if the analyst withdraws in the face of the analysand's erotic interests.

As is generally the case in considering the dynamics of homosexuality, one should not presume that same-gender sexual desire necessarily serves either defensive or self-reparative functions or that it constitutes an attempt to maintain a sense of being alive through engagement in novel and brief erotic encounters. Nonetheless, alternative developmental pathways into sexuality are still sufficiently the subject of taboo and stigma that among some persons experiencing psychological insufficiency, same-gender sexual activity is one means of sexualizing and thus animating a life otherwise lacking in vitality and coherence. As Khan (1979) and Goldberg (1995) acknowledge, from somewhat different theoretical perspectives within psychoanalysis, this potential use of such nonnormative sexual practices. It is important, however, to differentiate such use from the experience of gay men and women for whom same-gender sexual orientation is ego-syntonic and a part of a coherent developmental lifeway. These people come to psychotherapy or psychoanalysis in order to resolve problems not related to sexual orientation as such.

Throughout the mid-twentieth century most analysts believed that same-gender sexual orientation reflected psychopathology. In addition to being consistent with the dominant culture's position, their beliefs were based on general psychoanalytic theories. Such theories are far from personal experience and have been of questionable value in understanding people. In contrast, the psychoanalytic focus on reports of wish or intent as recounted in a life story and enacted in the psychoanalytic situation has vastly enriched our understanding. These enactments include not only new editions of the oedipal situation, but also enactment of lived experience from earliest childhood onward (P. King 1980). The analyst comes to understand these enactments partly through intellectual knowledge of psychology but primarily through empathy and other personal responses (Kohut [1959] 1978, 1977; Racker 1968). This understanding is enhanced by knowledge of the expectable course of development and an appreciation of the limitations of this knowledge, especially as it is affected by social and historical change. While the phenomenon of transference is timeless, the enactments that are played out in the transference reflect the interplay of particular life circumstances and the larger context in which persons lead their lives. Psychoanalysis provides an ideal opportunity to study how context and personal meanings become interrelated (P. King 1980).

Distinguishing between inversion, as reflected in choice of an object, and perversion, as reflected in alteration of the aim of a drive, and following Darwin's focus on natural selection, Freud maintained that because sexual intercourse (without contraception) among biologically mature men and women insured species survival, it alone could be considered as genital maturity. Any aspect of sexuality intended solely to enhance pleasure reflected an element of psychobiological immaturity. Examples of this immaturity ranged from kissing and foreplay to solitary or same-sex gratification. All remnants of pregenital life were considered immature—but not necessarily undesirable.

There has been much confusion about the clinical significance of same-sex desire. For some analysts, Freud's classification of same-sex desire as immature became a call to cure it. Consistent with the medicalization of human conduct, variation in sexual preference became a form of psychopathology to be eradicated through psychiatric intervention. But Freud did not view same-gender sexual expression as necessary evidence of personal distress or psychopathology (Freud [1935] 1951). It was only in the postwar period that psychoanalysis began to view same-gender sexual orientation as more than a problem in theory formation and adopted a prejudicial attitude in which same-gender sexual orientation was viewed as necessarily pathological (Lewes [1988] 1995).

From Gay to Straight: Reparative or Conversion Therapy

Social and historical changes of the past three decades have profoundly changed how we understand sexual expression in our culture. It is now generally understood that recognition that sexuality might be organized in terms of wishes originating in the family does not, in itself, imply that this organization is immature or represents deficiencies in adult personality structure. Unfortunately, a group of psychoanalysts and analytically oriented therapists who were educated in a tradition which regarded same-gender sexual orientation solely as evidence of unresolved conflict continue to equate it with illness. These analysts may explicitly try to "convert" gay men from same- to opposite-gender sexual interests. It is understandable, although unfortunate, that psychiatry once regarded same-gender sexual orientation as itself evidence of psychological impairment. There is little justification for maintaining this perspective now, in the light of the accumulated evidence from clinical and systematic study that sexual orientation is independent of mental health outcomes except as mediated by antigay prejudice and resulting stigma. The history of this ideologically conservative movement within psychoanalysis has been reviewed by Lewes ([1988] 1995), who reports in detail on the emergence of a view of homosexuality as a developmental personality deficit during the interwar period.

Because therapists who view homosexuality as a disturbance remain a vocal and politically active group, it is important to review their claims and to understand the factors that lead them to maintain this belief. It is also useful to describe their viewpoint so as to clearly differentiate it from other psychoanalytic positions.

The goal of reparative therapy is usually to convert men seeking psychoanalytic intervention who are gay but whose manifest distress is not associated with sexual orientation to a preference for opposite-gendered sexual intimacy. Though these analysts claim to try to change only individuals who seek to change their sexual orientation, analysts identified with this tradition assume all gay people would seek to change their sexual orientation but for the psychopathology which masks their true wish.

The Logic of Reparative Therapy

From the time of Breuer and Freud's first contribution it has been a central tenet of psychoanalysis that understanding the meanings we attribute to lived experience leads to an enhanced sense of personal integrity and vitality. However, the significance of wishes may change over time and across cultures. This is no less the case in the study of sexual orientation than in that of any other aspect of lived experience. The psychoanalytic method is properly concerned with the meanings for the analysand of all aspects of any particular sexual orientation or lifeway (Chodorow 1992), including associated wishes, fears, and disappointments. Homoerotic wishes and their realization in sexuality are among the many aspects of intention over a lifetime which are properly a focus of psychoanalytic study.

While much earlier psychoanalytic study focused on the importance of the nuclear neurosis, postwar psychoanalysis, as Friedman (1988) has shown, has more fully explored the origin of current experience in the young child's experience with caregivers, and particularly the mother (Ainsworth 1973; Main 1995a, 1995b; Sroufe 1981, 1989; Stern 1985, 1989a, 1989b, 1995). Variation in the experience caregiving is presently presumed as the most important of the templates which provide the configuration for later sense of self and others. This is the dominant or master narrative on which much of contemporary psychoanalysis is based, from that of the contemporary Kleinians of London (Schafer 1994) to relational psychology (S. A. Mitchell 1988). It is important, however, in this effort to understand the template for subsequent experience (Sandler and Sandler 1994), that the focus of psychoanalytic inquiry remain with understanding meanings reflected in thought and action with the goal of facilitating enhanced personal vitality and integrity. It is critical that we differentiate between the use of the psychoanalytic method as a means of fostering self-knowledge and efforts at directing lifestyle and personal choice.

In work spanning more than four decades, Charles Socarides has sought to understand and change the sexual lifeways of analysands. His focus on tracing meanings reflected in aspects of the analysand's lived experience, including fantasies associated with enactment of sexual desire, is impressive.

The problem is that Socarides also seeks to change sexual lifeways in accordance with his own values. In this use of the power implicit in the transference (Foucault 1975), he and his colleagues go beyond the analytic task and seek to force analysands into a particular moral position. Recently, Socarides's moral position has led him to join forces with those on the Christian right who regard same-gender sexual orientation as sinful, including the Christian psychotherapist Joseph Nicolosi ([1991] 1997, [1993] 1997). Socarides serves as president and Nicolosi as executive director of the National Association for Research and Therapy of Homosexuality (NARTH), which has an avowed goal of "converting" gay men and women to a heterosexual lifeway.

Though it may reflect some limitations in the analyst, it is appropriate for analysts to decline to work with people whose lifestyle, religious beliefs, or values they reject. However, it is not appropriate to begin an analysis with the implicit or avowed goal of using the psychoanalytic situation as a means to coerce the analysand to adopt the analyst's values. This present position of Socarides and NARTH poses therapeutic and ethical challenges to psychoanalysis.

Socarides and the Study of the Psychodynamics of Homosexuality

Understanding Socarides's contributions to study of same-gender sexual orientation, primarily among men, requires a careful evaluation of his work. Socarides ([1978] 1989, 1988) has posed a typology of the origins of same-gender desire and has given detailed case study accounts, including a follow-up report on one analysand. His work is within the tradition of clinical psychoanalytic accounts. Socarides should be viewed as a representative of a generation of New York psychoanalysts that includes Irving Bieber and his colleagues (whose contributions we reviewed in chapter 4), Lionel Ovesey and his colleagues, and other distinguished analysts whose own early education at the Columbia University Psychoanalytic Institute was influenced by the adaptational perspective of one of its founders and major intellectual figures, Sander Rado. Socarides's theoretical perspective largely reflects his teacher's outlook, founded in the psychology of drives. He seems reluctant to accept theoretical and clinical innovations in a discipline which has shown significant change over the past five decades. Socarides's exposition of theory borrows heavily from such earlier contributions as those of Hans Sachs ([1923] 1978), early postwar drive psychology, and, more recently, the separation-individuation paradigm (Mahler, Pine, and Bergman 1975).

Drescher (1998a, 1998b, 1998c) has reviewed the intellectual impact of Rado's "adaptational" perspective on the formative psychoanalytic education of this generation of analysts. Rado ([1945–55] 1995) maintained that anatomy is destiny, that sexual pleasure properly serves the reproduction of the species, and thus that adult heterosexual adjustment is the expectable outcome of childhood development. Any deviation from this expectable pattern reflects fears attributed to the oedipal situation: the patient's fear of castration leads to perversion. While recognizing the possibility of female homosexuality due to fear of the penis as a destructive organ, or parental preference for a son rather than a daughter, homosexual deviation is mainly conceptualized as a symbolic but disguised representation of the conventional male-female sexual situation. In Rado's words, "Homosexuality is a deficient adaptation evolved by the organism in response to its own emergency overreaction and dyscontrol" (213). In his response to Rado's presentation of the role of fear in the foundation of same-gender sexual desire, Hoch (1949) raised questions about the connection between fear and perversion and about Rado's somewhat naïve biological assumptions.

In Rado's perspective, same-gender sexual orientation reflects severe and pervasive psychopathology and must be the result of personality development gone awry, most often as a consequence of parental conflict or failure to foster the child's psychological autonomy. The concept of the overinvolved mother and distant father was subsequently developed by Bieber and his colleagues (Bieber 1965; Bieber and Bieber 1979; Bieber et al. 1962) and Socarides ([1978] 1989, 1988). The adaptational perspective presumes further that early developmental trauma may be resolved through psychoanalytic intervention and that an appropriately cooperative and motivated analysand who is predominately homosexual may be returned to "normal" heterosexual functioning.

Socarides's (1968, [1978] 1989, 1988, 1995) contributions, based on Rado's adaptational perspective, emphasize homosexuality as a reflection of developmental arrest. He builds on the concept of "repressive compromise" founded in the work of Hans Sachs ([1923] 1978), adding a focus on the child's experience of a destructive mother unable to support psychological autonomy for separation and individuation (Mahler, Pine, and Bergman 1975). Sachs held that perversions result when repressed fantasy breaks through into consciousness. Pregenital wishes, which would ordinarily produce ego-alien neurotic symptoms, are then experienced as ego-syntonic. Socarides also draws on Bergler's (1956) application of the concept of masochism to homosexual activity. In sum, Socarides observes homosexuality as a living relic of the past, the remnant of a conflict involving an especially strong component instinct in which complete victory was impossible for the ego and repression was only partially successful. The ego had to be content with repressing the greater part of infantile libidinal strivings (primary identification with the mother, intense unneutralized aggression toward her, dread of separation, and fear of fusion) at the expense of sanctioning and taking into itself the smaller part—instead of the mother's body being penetrated, sucked, injured, or incorporated, it is the male partner's body which undergoes this fate; instead of the mother's breast, it is the penis with which the patient interacts. Homosexuality thus becomes the choice of the lesser evil, "serving the repression of a pivotal fixation in which there is a desire for, and dread of, merging with mother in order to reinstate the primitive mother-child unity" (Socarides [1978] 1989, 70). Elaborating this view, Socarides summarizes his assessment of the psychodynamics of homosexuality as:

> fixat[ion] on the wish for mother-child unity. This connotes, however, a threat of total destruction of the self, which is to be avoided at any cost. All further activities of his life are designed to ward off the realization of this unity. Homosexual behavior appears to be the solution for forestalling a powerful affective state which threatens to destroy the individual both by anxiety and by the loss of personal identity with a return to the less differentiated stages of the ego. The homosexual chooses a partner of the same sex to aid repression of he basic conflict: the wish for the mother-child unity accompanied by the dire fear of loss of self. ([1978] 1989, 224)

Socarides views male homosexuality as a true perversion resulting from a regression provoked by oedipal conflicts. This theory predicts subtypes of male homosexuality ranging from oedipal homosexuality to more severe pre-oedipal disorders involving developmental arrest or ego deformity. In Socarides's view, obligatory (or reparative) homosexuality begins in early fears; depending on the level of fixation, the pre-oedipal homosexual object reflects anxiety related to engulfment, loss of self and ego boundaries, or lack of psychological autonomy. While this "true" homosexuality is based in an attempt to ensure ego survival, oedipal forms of homosexuality are more directly related to anxiety of the father's retaliation for oedipal wishes. Socarides ([1978] 1989, 1988) maintains that oedipal homosexuality is more ego-alien and less driven and stereotypic than pre-oedipal forms.

Socarides views homosexual women as terrified of men due to an admixture of hatred and guilt felt toward her mother with feelings of disappointment and rejection from her father. Heterosexual relations would repeat the castration performed by the mother, stimulating wishes to retaliate against her mother for the castration and consequent feelings of guilt, which lead her to turn the rage against herself. Socarides maintains that all homosexual women identify with their fathers, since they need to renounce femininity, and describes the retreat into homosexuality following marriage as a response to the fear-guilt connection awoken by heterosexual relations. Socarides doubts that homosexual women are motivated to change their sexual orien-

348   CHAPTER TEN

tation. They most often come for treatment following rejection or the breakup of a lesbian relationship.

Dorpat (1990) and Jacobs (1990) discuss the origins of female homosexuality in a developmental deficit of the pre-oedipal epoch. Dorpat suggests that lesbians suffer from defective body images linked with early life failure to develop positive identifications with their mothers, particularly the mother as a mature sexual person. Dorpat maintains that so-called obligatory homosexual men and women show deficits in capacity for (satisfying) object relations. Dorpat also traces the problems of homosexual women to failure to consolidate superego development. These women (and, presumably, obligatory homosexual men as well) have formed representations with their parents' moral injunctions but have not been able to establish their own superego moral regulations. They continue to look to others rather than maintaining stable and autonomous values and see object relations as still between self and others rather than as stable parts of oneself. This early failure may be partially corrected through the transference, in which the analysand is able to realize missing superego functions through selective identifications with the analyst. One implication of this view is that attribution of antigay prejudice to the community is merely an externalization of an object-relations conflict reflected in incomplete superego development. Like other contributors to a volume edited by Socarides and Volkan (1990), Dorpat sees the origin of obligatory homosexuality as dyadic and views the role of psychoanalytic intervention as being to foster enhanced superego functioning, which in turn fosters resolution of aggressive wishes toward the same-gender parent and establishment of a positive, gender-appropriate identification (L. Jacobs 1990; Apprey and Bagley 1990).

Translating his theoretical perspectives into clinical psychoanalytic intervention, Socarides (1968, [1978] 1989, 1988) established three types of male homosexuality: pre-oedipal type I, pre-oedipal type II, and oedipal. Socarides also recognizes a schizo-homosexuality whose dynamics are those Freud (1911) described in the Schreber case. These individuals are less relevant to the discussion of psychoanalytic intervention with gay men and women whose community adaptation ranges from adequate to superior. The oedipal type of homosexuality follows closely from Socarides's understanding of the emergence and resolution of the nuclear conflict. The two pre-oedipal forms differ in terms of severity of psychopathology, predominance of pre-oedipal over oedipal factors, capacity for object relations, and predominant narcissistic balance. The pre-oedipal type II homosexual man shows a borderline adaptation and has a less favorable prognosis than the pre-oedipal type I homosexual man.

Socarides provides case examples of each type of homosexuality in two books. Socarides ([1978] 1989) provides reports of the analyses of one oedipal homosexual man, one "latent" oedipal man, one pre-oedipal type I male homosexual, and three pre-oedipal type II homosexual men; a detailed psychoanalytic seven-year follow-up interview with a pre-oedipal type I man reported as appendix A; one case each of oedipal, preoedipal type I, and pre-oedipal type II homosexual women; and one account of the analysis of a schizo-homosexual man. Two additional cases of pre-oedipal type II homosexual men are reported in Socarides's (1988) later book. Socarides states that all of these patients came to analysis deliberately seeking to change sexual orientation.

Accounts of the transference are missing from several of these case reports. None of them describes the countertransference or the analyst's experience of the analytic process. They focus instead on the interpretation of the analysand's psychodynamics in terms of Socarides's theoretical position which implicitly assumes underlying heterosexual interests.

The case of Paul (pre-oedipal type II), who started analysis at age twenty-seven, is perhaps most interesting because of the inclusion of follow-up material from two interviews conducted seven years following conclusion of the analysis. At the start of his analysis, Paul could have heterosexual intercourse only when he felt more powerful than the woman, a reenactment of his childhood fear of maternal possession and overstimulation; heterosexual relations were risky because he feared the loss of his mother's love for betraying her. Homosexual relations were characterized by a desire to dominate and sadistically attack men, reenacting the wish for his father of childhood to give him the love of which he felt deprived. Socarides reports that late in his analysis, Paul described homosexual relations as a "wild-type groping thing." In heterosexual intercourse he now experienced feelings of warmth and a newfound confidence. The five-year analysis ended when the analysand was capable of initiating and enjoying intimate sexual relations with a woman, and the seven-year follow-up showed that he had maintained a successful heterosexual adjustment. He had married, fathered three children, and acquired considerable capacity and expertise in heterosexual intercourse. Indeed, good heterosexual technique becomes an important criterion for therapeutic success. The analysand attests that his years of homosexual exploration had been of assistance in learning to enjoy the bodies of women and that he is able to enjoy all aspects of foreplay as well as highly satisfying genital penetration with his wife. At times he feels a twinge of homosexual desire, but he has learned that such recurrences come at times when he has a setback in his life. Paul concludes that "gay" is the wrong term for describing homosexuality, which is hardly carefree and a mere façade for life, not even satisfying at the moment.

Other case reports are less detailed. Claude, a thirty-five-year-old engineer (oedipal type), had a five-year analysis and was followed up five years later. Unconscious guilt was reflected in incomplete projects and not seeking opportunities for career advancement. Inhibitions were removed through interpretation of underlying psychodynamics. He married and advanced in his career.

Sumner (pre-oedipal type II) was a troubled thirty-nine-year-old engineer who had suffered in childhood with a violent mother, whose explosive temper terrified him. After initial success as a student and athlete, a transient homosexual affair in college led Sumner to seek counseling. Ultimately he dropped out of college, returning some years later as an aesthete and loner (although highly qualified to work). He found it difficult to sustain work on complex independent projects. A transient bisexual episode involving his wife and a coworker, followed by his wife's rejection of him, led him to treatment. The analytic work helped Sumner regulate self-esteem, work through his early fear and rage toward his mother (which was expressed in adulthood as masochistic and narcissistic rage), and overcome his desire to remain a child. Analysis of transference fantasies and dreams led, by the third year of analysis, to renewed self-confidence, an increased capacity to recognize the destructive import of his narcissistic rage, overcoming archaic superego enactments, formation and resolution of a transference neurosis, and recognition that the pseudo-object relations of homosexual relationships reflect pathological narcissism. The analysis was characterized by externalization of the analysand's pathologically grandiose self onto the person of the analyst, whom he loved, feared, blamed, and hated. It was only with the interpretation of these components of the narcissistic disorder that emergence of a transference neurosis was possible. Socarides provides no information on the outcome of this case.

The three presentations of analyses of pre-oedipal type I, pre-oedipal type II, and oedipal women all stress fears of maternal abandonment documented with wishes to merge with the feared and rejecting mother. Anna, the most troubled of these women (pre-oedipal type I), could not believe that she would be desirable as a woman. Following analysis of her disappointing homosexual activities and her choice of weak men, the analysand met an appropriate man, whose subsequent rejection led her into a year-long homosexual relationship and interruption of the analysis. She returned because her partner became jealous when the analysand sought sexual ties with men. During this interruption she consolidated her career goals. The analysis was interrupted after four and a half years when her work took her to a distant city. The feelings of self-depredation, depression, anxiety, body distortions, and depersonalization which had initially led her to seek treatment had been resolved. Long-standing ties to a mother whom she experienced as malevolent yet the object of desire for merger had been resolved, and she could now seek tender and appropriate men as sexual partners.

The two other women whose cases are reported had similar difficult relationships, described as more or less subtly destructive, and conflicted parental ties. Sarah (pre-oedipal type II), a thirty-five-year-old who had her first homosexual experience in college, had continued homosexual ties until entering analysis, though she feared their oral destructiveness and jealousy, and retaliatory unfaithfulness. Her oral-destructive urges were ultimately directed at her mother, with whom she also feared merger and loss of identity. Her fear of her partner's potential destructiveness replayed her concerns with her mother's retaliation for aggressive oral wishes. No conclusion or follow-up data are presented.

Joanna (oedipal type), a nineteen-year-old college student, had made a suicide gesture following abandonment by a homosexual lover. She had enormous intellectual abilities and came from a wealthy family. At first she denied her fear of women and played the role of a man in homosexual intimacies, imagining that she had a penis that brought her female partner to orgasm. She attempted heterosexual intercourse to please her analyst but denied deriving any satisfaction from it. Sexualized feelings as part of the transference were so intense that she fled treatment. After two years, she returned for another eight months. She fell in love with a man and ultimately married. Hostility toward men had disappeared. Socarides saw her disturbance as regression from the oedipal conflict to wishes for closeness to her mother. Female partners substituted for her mother. Her early attraction to men and wish for intimacies with her father so terrified her that she sought to be rid of all wishes toward men. This analysand's wishes reflected negative oedipal struggles and submission to women to forestall their attack. She experienced her homosexual wishes as ego-alien, was able to establish a significant transference, and showed little deficit in ego functions.

Socarides concluded that homosexuality was more than a phobic response. Projective identifications must be highlighted and interpreted. Fears of castration must be interpreted as well as fears of oral dependence on the opposite sex and of same-sex identifications. The fear of male homosexuals that, at climax, they will turn into women, needs to be interpreted, as does the fear of women that they will become like their mothers. According to Socarides, these interpretations lead to "cure" of homosexuality and conversion to heterosexuality.

One of the most controversial aspects of Socarides's presentations are his claims about the number of analysands he has successfully treated through conversion therapy. Noting that he had seen more homosexual analysands than any other analyst besides Bergler, who claimed to have seen more than a thousand such patients, and Bieber (1976), who claimed to have seen more than 850, all of whom had troubled lives and deeply wished to change, marry, and have children, Socarides ([1978] 1989) reported that over a decade he saw fifty-five overt homosexuals in treatment, together with more than eighteen latent homosexuals, for a total of sixty-three analysands (Socarides [1978] 1989). Not only do these numbers not add up, Socarides then reported that of forty-four homosexual analytic patients, twenty, or nearly half, became fully functioning heterosexual men or women. Two thirds of these patients were pre-oedipal type I or type II, and all, he claimed, were strongly motivated to change their sexual orientation. Ralph Roughton (personal communication) observes:

> This error eluded both Dr. Socarides and his editor, and is repeated in his [1993] affidavit when, arguing in support of Amendment 2 [which would have repealed civil rights protections for homosexuals], the same figures are presented. Is it 55 or 44 or 34 overt homosexuals who were treated? No combination with the 18 latent homosexuals adds up to the 63 he gives as the total. . . . His carelessness with figures does not inspire confidence in those that he does give.

Roughton notes the one follow-up case report, concerning Paul, and the two follow-up interviews but notes that this is the full extent of any detailed follow-up information. Roughton also reviews an interview with the *New York Times* (24 December 1995) in which Socarides claims to have helped two-thirds of a group of more than a thousand patients to control their sexual impulses. Moreover, he estimates that he has assisted more than 35 percent of his homosexual analysands in converting their sexual orientation. This is a drop in success rate of about 10 percent, based on Socarides's own reports. However, Macintosh's (1994) survey reports that fewer than 5 percent of analysts believe that such changes as Socarides reports take place with any frequency. He also notes that less than 1 percent of analysts surveyed believed that analysts should seek to change sexual orientation as part of the analytic process. Finally, Roughton questions the practical plausibility of these figures, noting that if a quarter of Socarides's patients are homosexual, as he claims, and he has had a thousand homosexual patients, one would infer that the total number of persons he has seen in analysis or consultation exceeds four thousand—or the equivalent of new patients every year for forty years!

Actions like arguing to deny gay men and women civil rights protections transform Socarides from a conservative analyst following a particular understanding of personality development and psychopathology into a controversial and troubling figure in psychoanalysis. In Colorado and Tennessee, Socarides testified in support of repealing recently enacted laws extending civil rights protection to lesbians and gay men. The judge in the Tennessee case rebuffed Socarides's testimony, noting that "Dr. Socarides' view that homosexuality is a psychiatric psychopathological condition is rejected by the psychiatric profession. It escapes the Court why this view, which he expounds throughout the affidavit, is relevant to the case" (*Campbell* v. *Sundquist,* 1995).

From Psychoanalytic to Moral Perspectives in Reparative Therapy

While Socarides's theoretical and clinical perspective derives from the tradition of psychoanalytic theory and therapy in the interwar and postwar period (R. C. Friedman 1988), the efforts of the psychologist Joseph Nicolosi have in large part been stimulated by the belief that only the union of man and woman is "natural" (Nicolosi [1991] 1997), a view commensurate with that of conservative Catholic theologians and of some Protestant and Jewish clergy (*NARTH Bulletin,* December 1995, December 1996). Nicolosi describes this position in two books. The term "reparative" stems from Socarides's observation "Reparative homosexuality initiated by early unconscious fears and characterized by inflexibility and stereotypy is the only type that can be considered true (obligatory) homosexuality" ([1978] 1989, 90).

Nicolosi views male homosexuality as a developmental deficit and a symptom of gender identity psychopathology, largely the result of intrafamily conflict and parental unavailability. He maintains (Nicolosi, [1993] 1997) that "sex is never a part of healthy male friendships." Consistent with the view of the Bieber group and Socarides, Nicolosi ([1991] 1997) particularly faults fathers of homosexual men, whose emotional distance prevents young boys from developing an appropriate masculine identification; the boy destined to become homosexual experience his mother as intrusive and overinvolved and his father as underinvolved and uninterested.

Nicolosi states that all his patients complain of the emotional and often physical absence of their fathers from their childhood. Feeling angry about this rejection, these men reject the father and, along with him, the masculine role. Nicolosi maintains that their fathers often have personality deficits and transfer to their sons their feelings of unresolved hostility and jealousy toward their own fathers and brothers. Disappointed with his father, the son protects himself from further hurt by defensive detachment from all he represents. In middle childhood, these sons become "kitchen window boys," watching with fascination as their peers engage in gender-affirmative rough-and-tumble play, but not participating. As the boy become ever more detached from other boys and his masculinity, women become familiar while men grow mysterious. Consistent with the view of the social psychologist Daryl

Bem (1996, 1997) that the exotic becomes erotic, across the adolescent years these mysterious boys become the object of erotic interest. Women, who are familiar, are not the object of sexual interest, since people are drawn to the "other-than-me" (Nicolosi [1991] 1997). In ways which are not fully explicated, affectional hunger for the attention of other men is transformed into sexual strivings. Homosexual desire is viewed by Nicolosi as the way these men enter the special male world, finding acceptance not through personal strength but, vicariously, through sexual power. The male sexual partner becomes the twin who supplies the missing sense of power, but this is accompanied by hostility, distrust, and ambivalence. According to Nicolosi, homosexual relationships are inherently unstable because they bring together two men, each of whom has the same gender identity deficit. This inevitably results in brief and unsatisfying relationships as each partner tries to fulfill missing gender identifications in the other partner. Disillusionment and disruption inevitably result. As a result, Nicolosi states, "I do not believe that any man can ever be truly at peace in living out a homosexual orientation" ([1991] 1997, 149). The clients he accepts into psychoanalytically informed psychotherapy are those he terms "nongay" homosexual men, men distressed by their same-gender sexual desire and seeking to change their sexual orientation.

Reparative therapy seeks to reconnect men with their masculinity in ways consistent with the "men's movement." Nicolosi believes that when men can be emotionally close to other men, homoerotic wishes will subside. As he states:

> The basic premise of reparative therapy is that the majority of homosexual clients suffer from a syndrome of male gender-identity deficit. It is this internal sense of incompleteness of one's own masculinity that is the essential foundation for homoerotic attraction. The causal role of reparative therapy is: "gender identity determines sexual orientation." We eroticize what we are not identified with. The focus of treatment therefore is the full development of the client's masculine gender identity. ([1993] 1997, 211–12)

This goal is realized through active, directive mentoring activities by a man who, as therapist and role model, is able to reconnect men with their masculine identity. Individual and group therapy are used to foster a sense of male power and competitiveness (qualities Nicolosi views as intrinsic to being a man). This requires that the therapist be both supportive and confrontational, enacting the role of the good father to make up for the missing father of childhood. As the client becomes more self-assertive, same-gender desire diminishes, returning only fleetingly at times of self-doubt. As he comes to realize the real needs which lie behind his unwanted behavior, the formerly homosexual man begins to recognize his unwanted homosexual attractions as rooted in a deficit, as disguised legitimate love needs for the triad of attention, affection, and approval from other men. When these needs are met, the male-to-male relationship is robbed of any sexual element. The client thus reaches out, becomes assertive and competitive in his relationships with other men, and bonds with them. The developmental clock restarts (Nicolosi [1991] 1997) and the man's natural desire for sexual relations with women is released.

Nicolosi documents his position with several interviews and eight case studies. Each report describes how men came to experience relationships with other men that are healthy, characterized by masculine roughhousing and competition. In each case, men were helped to realize their disappointment with the father of early childhood and encouraged to bond with other men in a way that will meet their needs for attention, affection, and approval. Group therapy is a particularly important element in this process since it provides men whose feelings of anger and disappointment have long been suppressed an opportunity to be assertive in a safe and protective environment as the prelude to increased effectiveness in society.

Nicolosi emphasizes the hurt and rejection homosexual men are presumed to have encountered in early childhood because of ignoring and disinterested fathers. Indeed, this hurt is central to the dominant or master narrative of reparative therapy: by providing a corrective for the lasting effects of this presently recounted rejection by the father, in the form of stereotypically masculine activities, the therapy allows homosexual men to change their sexual orientation. Nicolosi's concept of masculinity as already noted, favors participation in (and watching) competitive team sports, roughhouse play, and enjoyment of competition and the exercise of power, a sort of "Iron John" view (Bly 1990).

Nicolosi's reports are replete with assumptions, ranging from the notion that men cannot have lasting partnerships founded in both sexuality and love to the presumption of a universal dynamic in which the kitchen-window boy longs for connection with his competitive peers. He confuses biological and social roles and presumes an essentialist, biological foundation for the concept of gender-appropriate relationships in men. As we have seen, not only can gay men and women have lasting partnerships founded on love and esteem, but no single dynamic adequately explains what Socarides ([1978] 1989) terms obligatory homosexuality. Voicing a position similar to Nicolosi's, Dickes (1991) maintains, "In each case of homosexuality I have treated, aberrant gender identity was present, aberrant because by far the great majority of individuals develop identity consistent with their anatomy.

Those who have not developed gender and anatomical congruence have indeed deviated from the usual pattern." For Dickes, the goal of treatment is to bring gender identity in line with anatomy.

Some gay men and women report non–gender-stereotyped interests as children but, as discussed in chapter 4, an important distinction must be made between non–gender-stereotyped interests and the gender identity syndromes. Certainly, there are men who find their same-gender sexual orientation to be dysphoric, and is important that they be able to resolve the issues that led them into a sexual lifeway which they find discordant. However, it is important to understand the meaning of this dysphoric homosexuality in the context of a therapeutic relationship marked by respect and focused on the effort to foster in the analysand enhanced self-knowledge.

The master narrative associated with reparative therapy is used as the framework for eliciting a life story. Not surprisingly, patients often produce stories consistent with its model of binding, seductive mothers and distant, uninvolved fathers. Nicolosi's assumptions reflect a stereotyped view in which a particular family configuration is seen as the source of the boys's turn to homosexuality and reparative therapy is seen as the appropriate corrective.

Drescher (1998a) provides a careful critique of the assumptions underlying this clinical perspective. He comments on the lack of respect shown gay men and women in reparative psychotherapy. Not only is such disrespect contrary to the spirit of analysis, it is particularly problematic for the many gay men and women who have had to hide their desire over a lifetime and who desperately need a climate of safety in the psychoanalytic situation. Drescher maintains that it is not in the analysand's interest for the therapist to have an investment in how the analysand's sexual orientation unfolds, particularly if that interest is based on a theory which conflates conventional values with supposedly scientifically validated theories about the nature of masculinity.

As Drescher (1997b) emphasizes, neither therapeutic ambitions nor moral persuasions should interfere with the analysand's efforts at enhanced self-understanding. It is impossible at the outset of an analysis to know its outcome in terms of the solutions the analysand will find. It is precisely this suspension of judgment that Freud ([1914c] 1958) advocated when describing psychoanalytic technique. The analyst, through awareness of his own values, works to insure that they not unduly influence the analysand's life or important lifestyle decisions. In contrast to the suspended judgment deemed so important in the psychoanalytic situation, reparative therapy states from the outset that a goal of the therapeutic process is to change the analysand's sexual orientation. This goal is set in advance of shared understanding of the meaning of sexuality and sexual lifeway for the analysand, a practice antithetical to psychoanalysis as a means of study and intervention founded on attention to personal meaning.

Drescher faults the essentialist, religious stance of reparative therapy, which equates mental health with conformity to traditional values and norms. Reparative therapy views human nature in a heterosexist manner and coerces responses from clients that conform with these stereotypes. Drescher observes:

> Reparative therapists . . . project a heterosexist image of human nature onto patients and then define their own projections as the patients' True Selves. In doing so, they countertransferentially enact anew the role of Winnicott's impinging mother who coerces responses from her child to satisfy her own needs. The impinging mother treats the child as an extension of herself and cannot see him for who he may actually be. To maintain the relationship, the child is compelled to create a compliant, False Self that will satisfy her. (1998b, 26)

Socarides, Nicolosi, and others working within the reparative framework demand that their homosexual patients change their sexual orientation as a requisite for maintaining their therapist's support and concern. Nicolosi explicitly says that unless the client wishes to change his sexual orientation he can do little to be of assistance. Ironically, Nicolosi in particular cites Winnicott and others, maintaining that the "True Self" is a heterosexist self.

As Drescher observes, reparative therapy shares the client's view of the self as flawed and supports the client's justifications for self-hatred. Most tragically, reparative therapy adopts a disrespectful attitude toward the client and makes it difficult for the client to find safety and empathic understanding, for the therapist fosters is necessarily combative, goading the homosexual client to become a "real man." As portrayed by Nicolosi, the therapist engages in combat designed to provoke the client's nascent masculinity. Anything less than the client's adoption of a traditional masculine position is regarded as therapeutic failure.

Since one of the goals of the psychoanalyst's personal analysis, as a part of psychoanalytic education, is to increase awareness of one's wishes and desires, psychoanalytic education should enhance, not reduce, tolerance of others' views and wishes. Recalling Nungesser's (1983) observations about the concern nominally heterosexual men, including male therapists, feel regarding gay men, the fervor with which Socarides and Nicolosi condemn nonheterosexual lifeways suggests that such nonnormative sexual expression must have particular significance for them. Efforts to deprive gay men and women of civil rights by explicitly supporting elements in the community that seek to repeal laws protecting those rights, expression of antigay prejudice, and reparative or conversion therapy contradict the values central to psychoanalysis (Ferguson 1994).

The Ethics of Reparative Therapy

Reparative therapy shows a fundamental disregard and disrespect for modes of sexual expression not consistent with conservative social values. This position is not in the client's best interests. Reflecting values widespread in the American medical and mental health professions, the American Medical Association issued a statement in 1994 calling for "nonjudgmental recognition of sexual orientation by physicians with respect and concern for their lives and values" (Hausman 1995). This position statement elicited an angry retort from Socarides and Nicolosi's National Association for Research and Therapy of Homosexuality: "One wonders how reasonable it is for the AMA to mandate respect (rather than simply tolerance) for every person's life and values." The NARTH position is that some lives may be tolerated but not respected.

The National Association of Social Work has declared conversion or reparative therapy to be unethical. The American Psychological Association adopted the position that, while not necessarily unethical, conversion or reparative therapy has not been shown to be effective in changing sexual orientation and that it is not a recommended treatment. NARTH regards as ill informed the statements of dismay by several committees of the American Psychological Association regarding the necessarily coercive nature of the conversion therapy. The NARTH position (*NARTH Bulletin,* December 1995) holds that, in any event, the American Psychological Association can go no further, because any stronger statement would be regarded by NARTH as restraint of trade and would lead to a lawsuit.

Haldeman (1991, 1994), reviewing findings on reparative therapy in the model presently advocated by NARTH, maintained that the American Psychological Association code of ethics takes an affirmative position regarding homosexuality. On this ground alone, reparative therapy should be faulted as not ethical. Additional ethical issues concern the therapist's responsibility to clients and concern for consumer welfare. Haldeman notes that outcome data must be questioned since it is largely anecdotal. Careful reading of these anecdotal reports suggests that some increased heterosexual competence is about the most that reparative therapy effects. Homosexual men continue at the end of therapy to have homosexual desire. Haldeman observes:

> Evidence for the efficacy of sexual conversion programs is less than compelling. All research in this area has evolved from unproven hypothetical formulations about the pathological nature of homosexuality. The illness model has never

been empirically validated; to the contrary, a broad literature validates the non-pathological view of homosexuality, leading to its declassification as a mental disorder. . . . In short, no consistency emerges from the extant database which suggests that sexual orientation is amenable to redirection or significant influence from psychological intervention. (1994, 224)

These findings lead both Haldeman (1994) and T. O. Murphy (1997) to suggest that the lack of empirical support for conversion therapy calls in question the judgment of clinicians who practice or endorse it. Conversion therapy poses a particular ethical problem because it is "predicated on a devaluation of homosexual identity and behavior" (Haldeman 1994, 226). Even Nicolosi ([1993] 1997) is concerned with this issue. He reports that shortly before Irving Bieber's death he inquired of Bieber whether there really had been psychological changes among the men he had worked with, since so many of his clients continued at the end of therapy to harbor homosexual desire. Bieber acknowledged this problem. The best answer seemed to be that the propensity for same-gender desire could be evoked once again when clients faced stressful situations. Haldeman (1991), quoting Buie's (1990) report in the monthly newspaper, the *Monitor,* published by the American Psychological Association, says:

> California psychologist Joseph Nicolosi, a specialist in "reparative therapy" with what he refers to as "nongay" homosexuals, is reported to have acknowledged that he has never had a client who left his office "cured" of homosexuality and that one of his most "successful" clients, married and the father of three, still reported "homosexual fantasies that lingered like a gnat buzzing around your ear." (1991, 156)

This is consistent with the observation of Birk (1980), who integrated behavioral perspectives with those of Bieber's research group:

> In speaking of heterosexual shifts, I want to make it clear that it is my belief that these represent shifts in a person's salient sexual adaptation to life, not total metamorphosis. Most if not all people who have been homosexual continue to have some homosexual feelings, fantasies, and interests. More often than not they also have occasional, or more than occasional, homosexual outlets, even while being "happily" married. (1980, 387)

Other psychologists and psychiatrists, not associated in any way with the debate between NARTH and its opponents, have taken stronger position than professional groups regarding the ethics of reparative or conversion therapy. Davison (1976) had initially observed that programs seeking to change sexual orientation serve to strengthen prejudices against homosexuality, leading to shame and excessive self-criticism, and induce some gay men and women to become heterosexual. Davison (1991) notes that while there is a large literature on efforts to change sexual orientation among gay men, there is a paucity of literature on helping those harboring antigay prejudice to change their attitudes.

Davison notes further that therapists are seldom truly neutral on issues such as sexual orientation. Recognition of the effects of social stigma, together with the assumption that same-gender sexual orientation is highly correlated with impairment in adjustment, leads many therapists to the a priori assumption that gay men and women would be helped to have a more successful life if they could change their sexual orientation. When these gay men and women then show up at a therapist's office, the therapist presumes that the root cause of their distress must be their sexual orientation.

Davison suggests that much ego-dystonic homosexuality (of the sort portrayed by Nicolosi) may be viewed as internalized reactions to a hostile society (1991). Murphy (1997) is similarly concerned that conversion therapy stresses the patient's pathology at the expense of recognizing social conditions that lead gay men to feel self-hatred and criticism. Halleck (1976) notes that clients' requests for change in sexual orientation should be greeted with suspicion since there are such enduring social pressures urging change that it is difficult to know if the patient really experiences his or her homosexuality as dysphoric. Haldeman (1991) also notes that, since there is little evidence that reparative therapy can change sexual orientation, homosexual clients are likely to feel both disappointed with the failure of treatment and worse about being gay after being subjected to it. Following Martin (1984), Davison (1991) and Murphy (1997) worry that the inevitable failure of reparative therapy reinforces homosexual men's self-hatred and their belief that antigay prejudice is justified. Reviewing a number of published accounts by men who felt rejected by analysts who seemed to collude with and support their own feelings of self-hatred, Mitchell (1981) expresses similar concern.

Halleck (1976) is equally concerned that therapists seeking to change sexual orientation are imposing their values on their patients. Halleck and Murphy both maintain that it is unethical to attempt to change sexual orientation because we have very limited understanding of what patients seeking such change really want; they question whether homosexual men can really give informed consent when feeling social duress to change their sexual orientation. To the extent that these men do not have all the facts about the course and outcome of reparative therapy, it is unethical to undertake such intervention programs.

Conclusion

Findings reported in this chapter regarding the claims of so-called reparative or conversion therapy suggest that these programs appear unable to deliver on their promise to change sexual orientation. Recognizing the extent of antigay prejudice and social intolerance, homosexual patients seeking such therapy may not be attending to their best interest but instead responding to social and family demands.

Addressing the problems of reparative or conversion therapy, Mitchell observes that, while many therapists engaging in this practice claim allegiance to psychoanalysis, they fail to facilitate a therapeutic situation in which meaningful self-inquiry can occur. Rather than fostering the transference and its resolution, they ignore the transferential implications of the client's submissive, compliant efforts to win affirmation and admiration and fail to consider their own countertransference. In such a treatment the patient is deprived of the opportunity to resolve issues that could properly be addressed through analysis. When called analysis, reparative therapy denies the analysand that method of personality change for which the analysand sought treatment. Mitchell comments:

> Psychoanalysis itself is looked to for behavioral standards and moral direction. In this context, the dangers of influence have become enormous. If psychoanalysis is to remain the most radical form of human transformation, it must rest on value-free inquiry. Departing from this process by transmitting values overtly or covertly through the influence of the analyst may, perhaps, be a more effective instrument for altering behavior. Yet, the price of this possible increase in efficacy is clear indeed, both for those who are "cured" as well as for those who are not. For the former, behavioral alterations occur, but the repetitive, maladaptive, internal structures remain and, in fact, may have been reinforced, while for the later, the experience in analysis leaves behind a residue of shame and self-blame. (1981, 77)

The goal of reparative therapy appears to be that of eradicating rather than understanding wishes and meanings associated with same-gender sexual orientation. It thus creates an emotional climate that makes it impossible to use the analysis of the transference to help patients make peace with their presently experienced past and realize a more coherent and integrated life story than at the outset of their analysis. Sadly, reparative therapy, which seeks to free men from their distress about same-gender sexual orientation, may only reaffirm that they are indeed unworthy and that their self-hatred is justified, as evident in the values expressed by the analyst who appears to mirror the larger society.

Eleven

Psychoanalytic Intervention among Gay Men and Women

For much of its history psychoanalysis has studied the expression of same-gender sexual desire in the context of psychological conflict. Following the Second World War, a focus on the first years of life led some analysts to view same-gender sexual desire as a reflection of an enduring deficit in psychological development arising from early disturbances in attachment or caretaker response. More recently, analysts have concluded that, while gay men and women may differ in sexual orientation from their straight counterparts, this difference is not tantamount to psychopathology (Isay and Friedman 1986). In fact, the distinction between homosexuality and heterosexuality may be less sharp and reflect more about society's view of sexuality than is implicitly assumed in much psychoanalytic writing (Chauncey 1994).

The following vignette reflects the need for a new perspective on sexual orientation in the life course.

> A thirty-seven-year-old woman with two school-aged children sought psychoanalysis following the end of a difficult marriage. A few years previously, her husband advanced in his company and was transferred to a distant city. He used the transfer as an opportunity to ask for a divorce. The couple had met at work, courted briefly, and decided to marry. She had found him very attractive despite his reputation as a playboy, a reputation that continued after the marriage. The couple settled into a comfortable life in a fashionable neighborhood where the children were able to walk to an elite, progressive private school. Partly because of the husband's heavy travel schedule and increased responsibilities, the marriage grew ever more distant. Still, the family remained together and appeared close-knit.
>
> Sometime after her husband announced his desire for a divorce, this woman met the mother of one of her children's classmates while working on a committee. The two women became increasingly close. Their families often shared activities and the children got along well. One day, visiting at her friend's house while the children were in school, this woman was overcome by sexual desire for her friend. An exchange of looks suggested that the friend was similarly inclined and the two women soon were enjoying a sexual relationship, which they found far more satisfying than what either had had with her husband. Eventually, several years before the present search for analysis, mothers and children in the two families moved in together. The children accepted and even

benefited from their mothers' closeness, which contrasted to the tension in each woman's marriage. As her children grew up, this woman struggled with issues of career and intimacy. Feeling guilty about an otherwise satisfying relationship with her partner, and unsure what to do with her life as her children left for college, she sought analysis to foster a sense of well-being and to help her make career decisions and confront worries about her own aging.

This woman was unaware of same-gender desire before her marriage broke up. Now, except for the minor tensions of any long partnership, her relationship with her partner was psychologically and physically satisfying. Her story represents one developmental pathway which led to same-gender partnership at a particular time of life. She does not consider herself lesbian, though she guesses that is how the community regards her. She sees herself simply as loving another woman, who responds with affection.

This woman's life story challenges clinical psychoanalytic thought. There is little evidence that her choice of another woman as a life partner reflects psychopathology. Yet the analyst wishes to understand the meaning of her choice. Our discussion of this matters rests on a view of psychoanalysis as a distinctive mode of understanding leading to change, founded in a "two-person psychology" (J. Sandler 1976; Gill 1994). What is distinctive about psychoanalysis as a method of study is its reliance upon the analyst's vicarious introspection (Kohut [1959] 1978), using the analysand's presently narrated account to understand lived experience. This perspective places a burden on analysts to continue self-inquiry (Gardner 1983; T. Jacobs 1991). It recognizes both the analysand's enactments and the analyst's counterenactments or countertransference (Jacobs 1999b) as means to explore a totality of the presently remembered past, experienced present, and anticipated future (Schafer 1982, 1992). It attends not only to the origins of the analysand's and analyst's experience in early childhood and the oedipal period but to experiences across the entire life course as central to psychoanalytic understanding (Nemiroff and Colarusso 1985a, 1990; Colarusso and Nemiroff 1981; P. King 1980).

This focus on the totality of lived experience as the foundation for the present expression of wish and intent is common to both classical views of the dynamics of psychoanalysis and more recent relational and self psychology. Thus, this chapter seeks to integrate clinical psychoanalytic study of personal distress and psychological change, not only from the traditional perspectives of drive and ego psychology but also from interpersonal, intersubjective, and self perspectives, as these contributions aid clinical psychoanalytic study and intervention with gay and bisexual men and women seeking treatment.

Sexual Orientation and Contemporary Clinical Psychoanalysis

As we have seen, little evidence supports the assumption that same-gender sexual orientation is evidence of psychopathology. Except as a result of living in communities where antigay prejudice leads to a sense of stigma, gay and bisexual men and women show the same range of satisfactions and discomforts with their lives as their straight counterparts. In addition, rather being an essential characteristic, sexual orientation is fluid across the life course.

Psychoanalytic inquiry tries to understand the psychological significance of all aspects of the analysand's life experiences and their foundations. As Chodorow emphasizes in her discussion of the varieties of sexuality, all choices reflect an effort to resolve conflicts enduring since early childhood:

> Clinically, there is no normal heterosexuality; any heterosexuality is a developmental *outcome* reflected in transference, whatever the admixture of biology or culture (and whether we define "culture" as gender identity, sexual rules, dominant cultural fantasies, or mother's and father's gender identifications) that may contribute to it. This developmental and transferential outcome results from fantasy, conflict, defenses, regressions, making and breaking relationships internally and externally, and trying to constitute a stable self and maintain self-esteem. . . . Sexual development and orientation, fantasy and erotism need explaining and describing in the individual clinical case. (1992, 285)

Chodorow observes that it has been difficult for psychoanalysis to adopt a view of either homosexual or heterosexual orientation that does not privilege heterosexuality. Yet heterosexuality is but one of many outcomes of the effort to resolve the nuclear conflict of early childhood, and its significance is fluid across the course of life. We must move beyond viewing the sexual partner's gender as the core of the significance of sexual ties and the relationships of which they are a part, and focus instead on the meanings of relationships and sexuality for psychological well-being in terms of the analysand's experiences of a lifetime.

At the same time, the quandary for psychoanalysis regarding the significance of sexual orientation for personal adjustment must be acknowledged and discussed. It has been less than two decades since the first discussion appeared in the psychoanalytic literature repudiating the received wisdom that homosexuality represented psychological illness requiring remediation. Macintosh's (1994) informal survey showed that many analysts had changed their views about the place of same-gender sexual orientation. While analysts who volunteered to report the outcome of analysis of gay analysands were still concerned with efforts to alter sexual orientation (albeit with little success), they were also able to recognize alternative views.

It is important to recognize that cohort differences have led to a generation gap in understanding the place of same-gender sexual orientation across the course of life. Most senior analysts completed their psychoanalytic education when homosexuality was considered psychopathology. These analysts had almost no openly lesbian or gay colleagues or friends, so personal experience could not foster attitude change. Many younger analysts have gay and lesbian friends and have gone through training programs with openly gay and lesbian colleagues. Those who have completed their psychoanalytic education within the past decade are less likely than older colleagues to equate same-gender sexual orientation with impaired mental health.

Macintosh (1994) reported that a majority of analysts, reflecting these gradual changes in psychoanalytic conceptions of homosexuality, believed that directed efforts at changing sexual orientation are misguided, that few analysts continue to insist on such change as a criterion of a successful analysis, and that efforts at changing sexual orientation are unlikely to succeed. Though Friedman and Lilling's (1996) survey findings are consistent with Macintosh's report they also observe that many analysts still believe that male homosexuality serves as a defense against heterosexual wishes.

Mitchell's (1996b) discussion also reflects this quandary regarding the many meanings of same-gender sexual orientation within the clinical psychoanalytic situation. He notes that once sexuality and reproduction are viewed as separate, there is no obvious reason to take homosexuality as evidence of psychopathology. Commenting on Chodorow's observation that if we "need a story to account for the development of any person's particular heterosexuality . . . it is very hard to know where to draw the line on what needs accounting for in anyone's sexual development" (1992, 273), Mitchell wonders how we will be able to find a position from which to help a person struggling with issues of sexual orientation and sexual identity. His own solution to the quandary of understanding sexual orientation when heterosexuality has lost its privileged position in psychoanalysis and society is to maintain an open and honest reflection of this dilemma in analytic work, recognizing that we do not know (and may never know) the "true" origins of a particular sexual orientation while acknowledging personal bias and uncertainty. Mitchell suggests that the analyst and analysand jointly explore the factors that foster and interfere with the analysand's sense of well-being, sort out the choices the analysand has made and might make, and collaborate on a new life story that is more flexible in responding to life circumstances. While Schwartz (1996) properly rejects the essentialist assumptions underlying Mitchell's discussion, Mitchell honestly reflects the uncertainty which besets psychoanalysts trying to remake understandings of the development of sexual orientation and the place of psychoanalytic intervention for gay and bisexual men and women.

In his discussion of a formerly straight man who found his way into being gay but expressed awareness of the implications of the choice of being either straight or gay, Mitchell admits to his own perplexity but also to his own lack of understanding of the significance of either choice. Remaining open to all options, Mitchell provides a situation in which his analysand can explore the meaning of his options, recognize the problems of choosing to remain gay in terms of antigay prejudice, and decide for himself. It is important to note that Mitchell remained aware of his own prior assumptions of an association of homosexuality and pathology, an almost inevitable consequence of membership in the cohort of analysts educated before much of the reconsideration of this issue. Mitchell was genuinely uncertain what point of view to adopt, so he listened to and was guided by his analysand's continuing exploration of the meaning of sexual orientation in his life.

Precisely because clinical psychoanalytic inquiry is founded on the assumption that everything it addresses can be studied within the analytic process, discussion of sexual orientation and psychoanalytic inquiry is difficult. Many analysts have tried to avoid this problem by bringing what they believe to be truth established outside the psychoanalytic situation to bear on the problem. Whether one assumes, as Socarides ([1978] 1989) does, that heterosexuality is the norm and that there should be a directed analytic goal of changing the homosexual analysand's sexual orientation, or adopts Isay's (1989, 1996b) position that whatever their nature the origins of sexual orientation are beyond psychoanalytic inquiry and influence or Friedman and Downey's (1993b) implied position that homosexuality is a fixed, constitutional attribute, the basic tenet of clinical psychoanalysis that all is open to scrutiny has been abandoned.

Same-gender sexual orientation involves meaningful fantasies and, usually, actions designed to satisfy desire. These meanings are expressed through the transference. From a psychoanalytic perspective, little is gained by claiming that because still-to-be-identified biological factors may play a role in shaping sexual orientation, it should be regarded as either immutable or pathological and thus beyond discussion.

It is difficult to know, at the outset of an analysis, how things will turn out years later, when analyst and analysand agree that the analysand is able to continue self-inquiry on his or her own (Gardner 1983). With respect to sexual orientation, many outcomes are possible, including the decision by a presumably straight man to seek same-gender ties as an aspect of what Winnicott called the true self or the converse decision by a man or woman presently self-defining as gay to adopt a new identity as straight. The only danger in the latter case is that the analysand might arrive at this decision because of an unresolved wish for acceptance and approval from an analyst who is biased in the direction of believing that heterosexuality is desirable. Society's anti-gay prejudice suggests that this outcome is more likely than that an analysand would seek to become lesbian or gay to please the analyst.

Work with gay and lesbian patients brings certain issues of the analytic compact into sharp focus (Gould 1995). Gill (1982), commenting on Lipton's (1977, 1988) discussion of Freud's ([1909c] 1955) technique in the analysis of the Rat Man, observed that the analyst can do much to create the ambiance that is a precondition for the analysand's struggle to recognize and resolve conflicting wishes and fears. The analyst's overconcern to avoid ordinary human responsiveness may stalemate the analysis; as Kohut (1984) and Gill (1994) noted from quite different perspectives, the analyst's responsiveness and the creation of conditions for empathic listening facilitate the emergence of the analytic relationship and "cure." Creation of a working relationship (Greenson 1965) is essential to the process which ultimately permits understanding and resolution of conflicts, especially the gay analysand's sense of shame and self-criticism (Drescher 1996a, 1998b, 1998c).

As we discuss distinctive issues arising in psychoanalytic intervention with lesbians, gay men, and bisexual men and women, it is important to reemphasize that personal distress is not more characteristic of gay than of straight people and that psychopathology is no more common in one group than the other (Herron et al. 1982; T. Stein 1988). The bias that same-gender orientation represents psychopathology, in particular that it may be a marker of severe narcissistic pathology, leads some analysts to believe that gay or bisexual men or women are too psychologically impaired to tolerate the therapeutic regression of the psychoanalytic process, or even to assume that such men and women could not profit from insight-oriented therapy.

Though sexual orientation and personal distress are generally independent, partly because of antigay prejudice and consequent stigma in the larger society, including the individual's supporting social networks, and partly because of troubled personal histories, gay and bisexual men and women may seek psychoanalytic or psychotherapeutic assistance to deal with issues related to sexuality, morale, and adjustment. It is important to keep this chapter's discussion of clinical issues in the context of the larger work. That some gay men and women seek treatment and that in treatment they often want to address their sexuality, an important part of life, is not evidence of an intrinsic link between alternative sexual orientation and impaired mental health. These patients may be damaged if the analyst assumes such a link.

The issue of the analyst's personal response within the psychoanalytic situation has been a focus of concern since Freud's initial interest in Breuer's response to Anna O.'s confession of love for him (Breuer and Freud [1893–95] 1955); Gay, 1988). In the final essay of the volume, Freud acknowledges the impact upon the person of the physician of the analysand's wishes as enacted within the psychoanalytic process. The issue of the analyst's response to the analysand, founded on the "patient's influence on his unconscious feelings" (Freud [1910b] 1957, 144) and the resistances which this raises for the analyst require continuing self-inquiry (Gardner 1983). Blum and Goodman (1995) have provided a succinct discussion of the analyst's many responses to the analysand's expression of the transference. Reviewing the literature on countertransference, Blum and Goodman (1995) caution that such self-inquiry must proceed outside the field of the analytic situation in order that the analysand not be burdened with the analyst's own unresolved conflicts. Fliess (1944, 1953), Jaffe (1986), A. Reich (1951), and Racker (1968) are among the theorists of the psychoanalytic situation who note that the analyst has a wide range of responses to the analysand. These issues are particularly salient with regard to matters such as sexual orientation, where shared societal prejudice may obscure the analyst's countertransferences or even rationalize them through analytic theory. The question confronting analyst and analysand is whether the analyst's heterosexism, an almost inevitable part of the personality of individuals raised in our society, is sufficiently resolved that problems of the gay person's shame in analysis can be meaningfully worked through or whether the analytic situation will simply involve another, if more subtle, powerful, and therefore more damaging, experience of being stigmatized.

Transference and Enactment

Freud (1900, [1905–24] 1953, [1913] 1958, [1914–18] 1955, [1916–17] 1963) understood much of human behavior as derived from the "nuclear neurosis," the young child's fundamental wish for erotic intimacy with family members combined with the taboo against incest present in all cultures (Parsons 1952). Freud (1900) maintained that this wish presses for satisfaction while social reality demands repression. A compromise formation, however, may provide partial satisfaction, in disguised form, while yet meeting the demands of social reality. Included among these compromise formations are dreams, slips of the tongue and other unintended actions, psychoneurotic symptoms (hysteria and the obsessional neurosis), and creative activity or sublimation.

ENACTMENT OF INTENT IN THE PSYCHOANALYTIC SITUATION. Freud saw in the experience of all relationships a disguised effort to satisfy the nuclear wish. This occurred in a particularly clear way in analysis, where he saw feelings and thoughts toward the analyst as representing elements of the nuclear situation. The person of the analyst provides a point of attachment for partial and disguised satisfaction of the nuclear wishes. In analysis this process of transference is interpreted; the underlying conflicts are brought into awareness. As a result they are partially resolved and become less potent as unconscious influences on daily living.

Clinical and developmental studies over the last half century suggest that the nuclear wish was not the only issue enacted as transference. Early forms of attachment and the conflicts regarding them have also been recognized as shaping transference (Winnicott [1951] 1953, 1960b; L. Friedman 1988; Gitelson 1962; Mahler, Pine, and Bergman 1975). In addition, theoretical considerations about the nature of mental activity have led to a different view of transference than Freud originally proposed (A. Cooper 1987).

Ironically, as we will discuss later, analysts at both extremes of psychoanalytic attitudes on same-gender orientation (Isay 1989; Socarides [1978] 1989) maintain highly traditional views about the inevitable repetition of the nuclear conflict in the psychoanalytic situation.

Recently, analysts have focused on enactments, situations in which the analysand puts important aspects of the transference into action, as opposed to speaking of a wish or fantasy (T. Jacobs 1986, 1991; McLaughlin 1991; Chused 1991; Johan 1992; Roughton 1983). An important aspect of these unconscious dramatizations is the extent to which they evoke responses in the analyst, which are sometimes initially expressed in the analyst's actions. Underlying the concept of enactment is the recognition that we emplot all relationships with meanings based on the totality of lived experienced and express these meanings in fantasy, word, and deed. These meanings include the many ways people experience others, not only in the realm of competition and erotic longing but also as sources of sustenance, comfort, and solace (Blos 1980; Gill 1994; P. King 1980; Neubauer 1980; Sandler and Sandler 1994, 1997a). When they appear as attitudes, wishes, and actions directed at the analyst they may be observed and interpreted. Early analysts conceptualized these happenings as bringing the patient's illness into the analysis and called the central transference the transference neurosis (which was presumed to repeat the earlier form of the patient's neurosis, the infantile neurosis) (Reed 1994). While the nuclear conflict or family romance, which ordinarily emerges during transition from early to middle childhood, may be regarded as a typical model of the phenomena, today most analysts recognize that transferences may be associated with many other eras. In addition, rather than being isomorphic with early experience, as Freud believed, transferences are founded on unconscious and transformed memories of these experiences (A. Cooper 1987). Thus transference is a ubiquitous aspect of experience. However, it is uniquely accessible to observation and understanding in

the psychoanalytic situation, where analyst and analysand share a commitment to study how the analysand makes meanings (Stone 1961).

Kohut ([1959] 1978, 1977, 1984) added to thinking about transference by
examining how analysands use the analyst to support the experience of the
self. He characterized "transferencelike" phenomena, in which the analysand's intense engagement with the analyst compensates for perceived missed
experience, as opposed to transferences, in which the analysand directs feelings such as love and hate toward the analyst, who is important to the analysand as another person. These transferencelike phenomena include idealization, mirroring, and experience of merger or twinship with the analyst, who
is then said to function as a self-object. Ordinary living provides numerous
supports for the self through relationships to other people and groups
(Galatzer-Levy and Cohler 1993). Expectable life changes, such as retirement, and unexpected adversity, such as personal illness or the illness or loss
of family members, may bring the issues of the self's integrity and self-object
function into sharp focus.

ROLE RESPONSIVENESS AND THE PSYCHOANALYTIC SITUATION. When analysts abandon assumptions about the nature of possible transferences an enormous range of transference phenomena are observed (S. Roth 1988; Feinsilver 1999; Renik 1990; Rapaport 1958; P. King 1980; J. Sandler 1976).
For example Roth (1988) reports the analysis of a woman who experienced
the analyst as a lesbian lover; as she came to appreciate her competitive strivings and aggression toward her mother, sexual wishes toward the analyst re-
ceded.

Renik (1990) describes a similar situation, observing that focus on the
transference to (male) analyst in traditional gender-based terms would have
missed significant longings for the analyst as a loving woman. Male analysts,
struggling with anxieties about their feminine wishes, may collude with the
resistance of women analysands in avoiding acknowledging wishes toward
the analyst as a female lover. The patient, a married mother in her late thirties
sought analysis to resolve career inhibition. Late in the second year of analysis, she focused on the meaning of having children and of deprecation of
her husband in favor of sexual wishes toward her analyst. Analysis of her
fantasy during intercourse of watching her husband being penetrated from
behind by another man led first to fantasies of her penetrating her husband
as he penetrated her, then to wondering if the analyst was aroused by her
sexual fantasies and imagining him masturbating in the session by rubbing
his legs together like a masturbating woman, and then to fantasies of penetrating her analyst in the manner of the intercourse fantasy and of being penetrated by another woman with whom she would have a baby. Finally, she

embarrassedly admitted that during intercourse she enjoyed having her husband insert objects into her vagina and rectum. After exploring other possibilities, Renik and his analysand came to understand her experience of him as a homosexual lover in terms of her early wish to impact her often distant mother and to care for women bearing children. Her wish to sexually excite women having children, and her analyst in the maternal transference, was associated with her wish for her mother's response.

Working with gay male analysands, Isay (1986a, 1989) reports a similar reversal of the heterosexual family romance. He understands these transferences as emerging from wishes founded in a childhood search for emotional connection with a distant father. Isay (1989) suggests that some young boys are predominantly sexually attracted to their father, whereas most young boys are predominantly attracted to their mothers. (Presumably a parallel "reverse" expression of the nuclear conflict would be observed in gay women, who were attracted in early childhood to their mother rather than to their father.) He further suggests that the boy's father implicitly understands the nature of his son's wishes and, disturbed by their import, distances himself from the boy. This leads to the son's experience of his father as emotionally unavailable. The wish for a sexual tie to the father is enacted anew in the analysis, where the analysand sees the analyst as like the distant father and anticipates shock and distancing in response to his erotic longings.

Alternatively, the analysand may try to regain this childhood experience by searching for sexual satisfaction from the analyst, either by appearing supermasculine so that the analyst-father will finally take an interest in him or by trying to become "daddy's little girl," acting feminine and helpless to win the analyst-father's love and affection. Isay (1996a) reports how one gay man, angry that his womanizing father paid him little attention, was convinced that his analyst also preferred other analysands. The analysand arrived for an hour with his fly unzipped and seemed unaware of this until his analyst called his attention to this "unintended action." The idea that his open fly was like a dress unzipped at the side came to the analysand's mind. He fantasized that were he a girl he could win the attention of the men he sought. This wish, in turn, was related to his belief, founded in his childhood experiences, that if he was like the women who got his father's attentions, then his father and the analyst would attend to him too.

UNDERSTANDING THE EROTICIZED TRANSFERENCE WITH GAY AND BISEXUAL MEN AND WOMEN. Descriptions of transference in the analysis of gay and bisexual patients are surprisingly rare (Bergmann 1994; Gabbard 1994; Kwawer 1980). Erotic transferences between men and their male analysts are often difficult to express because of men's charged experience of same-gender erotic ties (Nungesser 1983; Person 1985, McWilliams 1996). In contrast, women often directly express erotic fantasies about their female analysts (McWilliams 1996).

Some authors have noted that compliance appears to be a particular issue in the transference among gay men and women (S. A. Mitchell 1981). For example, a case reported by Thomson (1968) involved a young professional man lonely and depressed in the context of being unable to realize same-gender desire. His passive longings and his wish to be cared for, admired, and esteemed by the analyst were expressed early in the transference. At the same time he was demanding in a way that suggested strong destructive wishes. This transference was understood as a replication of his experience of a binding but exploiting mother. Interpretations of this wish and fear fostered emergence of a paternal transference, expressed in wishes to mutilate the competitive analyst and fears of retaliation for this aggression, accompanied by new interests in heterosexuality and again fears of retaliation from the analyst-father. Integration of oral sadism and mourning the loss of the symbiotic destructive mother led to an enhanced sense of psychological autonomy and a "normal" heterosexual adjustment. Thus compliance with the analyst-mother and fear of the analyst's magical powers, together with the fear and need to submit to the analyst-father in order to avoid castration, were important factors contributing to the patient's compliance. Whether his ultimate "good" social and personal adjustment reflected the resolution or the continuation of this compliance is unclear.

Anna Freud (1949, 1951) attributed the particular transference compliance of homosexual analysands to passivity which resulted from feminine identification formed as a result of the nuclear conflict. This idea is difficult to sustain, as contemporary analytic understanding no longer equates femininity with passivity (see chapter 3). Isay (1989) notes that compliance with the analyst's often covert wish for change in the analysand's sexual orientation may also reflect an unresolved erotic or loving relationship to the analyst.

Though compliance itself may not relate to gender orientation, the analyst's attitude toward compliance may. Generally, analysts regard compliance as a resistance to insight and analyze it as such. However, several analysts who regard same-gender sexual intimacy as a psychological symptom recommend using transference-induced compliance in curtailing homosexual activity (Bieber 1965; Kolb and Johnson 1955; Ovesey 1969; Ovesey, Gaylin, and Hendin 1963; Ovesey and Woods 1980; Socarides 1968, [1978] 1989; Socarides and Volkan 1991). They maintain that manipulation of the transference is needed to realize their goal of converting the gay analysand to heterosexuality. It may be that the compliance described in gay men and lesbians in analysis has less to do with the dynamics of sexual orientation than with the particular segment of that population who view their sexual orientation and desires so negatively that they voluntarily seek treatment with analysts who regard this orientation as profoundly disturbed.

Other descriptions of transference in the analysis of same-gender–oriented individuals include Thompson's (1947) hypothesis that homosexual men and women unconsciously wish to put themselves into danger from the criminal justice system, an idea that gained support from the harsh external realities of the time, and Gabbard's (1994) emphasis on the negative oedipal configuration.

Overall, though, there has been little discussion of erotic transferences in gay analysands or their significance for the analytic process (Wrye and Welles 1994; Gould and Rosenberger 1994). The concept of an eroticized transference is complex (Bergman 1994; D. Hill 1994). Erotic transferences are often regarded as an aspect of the defense transference, the characterological way analysands avoid recognition and exploration of other transferences (Schlessinger and Robbins 1983), or the analysand's means of protection against feelings of loss and emptiness (H. Blum 1973; Coen 1981). Schafer (1977) suggests that erotized transferences are not different from other transferences in which the analysand shapes current experience out of current needs, wishes, and the experienced past. This eroticized transference can be seen in the following clinical situation, observed by one of the present authors:

> A gay therapist working in a psychodynamically oriented community counseling center for gay and bisexual men and women noted that the client was unusually silent. The client had come to the center hoping to overcome inhibitions about approaching other men in settings where he might meet a prospective boyfriend. Based on Luborsky's (1967) research finding that lengthy silences often reflect (often unconscious) sexual wishes toward the therapist, the therapist gently inquired what his client was thinking. With pain and embarrassment, the client reported that he had been fantasizing about meeting the therapist at a well-known, local gay bar, imagining that the therapist might make an overture and encourage conversation and that they would go home together and begin an intimate relationship. In tears, he confessed that he loved his therapist and often masturbated imagining sex with him. The therapist acknowledged that such wishes, while painful to talk about, might help them to figure out why it was so difficult for the client to initiate conversations with men he found attractive.
>
> This therapist viewed his client's sexual fantasies about him as an acknowledgment that the therapist could help the client in overcoming his inhibition. The client said that what made it easier to imagine intimacy with the therapist was the therapist's open and honest manner and support for the client's efforts to understand his own wishes. Thus this erotic transference was understood

not primarily as a resistance to insight but as an opportunity to explore a possibility in a context where previous interferences in erotic longings could be temporarily put aside by virtue of the patient's underlying idealizing transference (Wolf 1994). Historically, the client's father always expected the client to initiate any conversation between them. The client felt angry and unable to take so much of the relationship on himself. This situation was unconsciously reawakened when, at a bar, he felt required to assume all responsibility for initiating interactions.

The client felt that the therapist was willing to assume some responsibility for reciprocity. He experienced therapy as a role rehearsal for finding men who could respond rather than avoid the client's bid for intimacy. The client's sexual wishes toward the therapist were understood as a resolution, in the here and now in the treatment (Schafer 1982), of a longstanding discomfort with paternal demand that the client take the initiative in their relationship. The erotic transference was an adaptive effort to resolve this struggle. The therapist's understanding of the client's expression of sexual wishes, acknowledging the significance of the client's idealization expressed as sexual wishes, facilitated the resolution of the client's struggles.

Gabbard (1994) reports similar expression of an eroticized transference in the analysis of a man whose father was a career military office and away for much of the analysand's early childhood. In the transference the analysand longed for a reliable and supportive father. He masturbated with fantasies about the analyst and wished for a homosexual encounter with him. Gabbard understood this material differently from the counselor in the case vignette. He focused on the analysand's effort to satisfy passive longings for anal penetration through the analyst's active interpretations of his homoerotic wishes, rather than on the analysand's experience of the analyst as the idealized father. He describes the patient as enacting a sadomasochistic script.

A client's awareness that the therapist is gay may affect the form of erotic transferences. This may be particularly the case when therapist and patients cross paths outside of treatment in situations that might be sexually suggestive, such as health clubs or in "gay neighborhoods" where they both reside (Shelby 1997). For example, a psychoanalytically informed gay therapist met a client in the shower after a workout. The client had never mentioned his membership in the same health club, so the therapist was not aware that they worked out in the same place. At their next appointment, the client reported on an experience of meeting a man he was attracted to and feeling rebuffed by him. The therapist asked whether there might be a connection between this experience and meeting him at the health club. Reluctantly and with embarrassment, the client admitted that he had felt stimulated and rebuffed by the therapist when they met in the shower. Naked together in a circumstance where a sexual liaison could be imagined, stimulated by knowing his therapist was gay and so might be receptive to a sexual overture, the client felt disappointed that his therapist had not approached him sexually. The therapist acknowledged this disappointment but noted that in reality such contact between therapist and client would not be in the client's best interest and was prohibited. The client then related several instances in his childhood when he felt rebuffed by his father when they were naked together in the swimming pool or around the house. He recalled being attracted to his father's genitals and longing to fondle his father's penis but knew that his father sensed his wish and felt uncomfortable. The client guessed that his therapist had experienced the same discomfort that his father had felt, just as he had had the same sense of disappointment at not being able to fondle his therapist's genitals, which he believed to be larger and more powerful than his own, and so a source of potency and masculinity. The therapist acknowledged his own discomfort about meeting his client in the shower because of his concern with the possible stimulation and sense of disappointment which his client might experience. While clearly awkward for client and therapist alike, it was possible this chance meeting was therapeutically useful through focus on the erotic transference.

Patients may actively seek the therapist's sexual interest. One client arrived for his midsummer therapeutic hour wearing a ragged tank top and cutoff shorts. As he sprawled in his chair with his legs wide apart, the therapist, whom the client knew to be gay, experienced the client's dress and demeanor as seductive. When the therapist described this situation, the client acknowledged that the only way he had ever received attention was by acting seductive. The client wished and feared that he could elicit his therapist's interest. Moreover, he feared such interest would lead his therapist to abandon him, justifying a pervasive belief that he would be abandoned by those with whom he tried to be close, just as he felt he had been by his father, a corporate officer who was often out of town on business. The client wished to scare off the therapist, just as he believed he had scared off his father in childhood through his seductive overtures. Further discussion revealed that this wish and fear had been repeatedly played out in the client's erotic relationships. When he sensed a man might be interested in him he emphasized his sexual allure. Then, as the possibility of a relationship developed, he pulled back, proving again that other men could not be trusted and that being abandoned was inevitable.

While this situation raises important issues regarding the erotic transference likely to occur regardless of the sexual orientation of the therapist, the client's awareness of his therapist's sexual orientation as similar to his own contributes to fantasies that it is possible. It may also lead to an inaccurate assumption that the therapist and patient share a vision of being gay, which is all the more problematic if it remains implicit. It is important that the analyst not permit the silent assumption of similarity by failing to examine these meanings (Drescher 1998; S. Phillips 1996).

Consistent with Sandler's (1976) discussion of "role-responsiveness" and Casement's (1991) enlargement of this concept, the client in this example was able to use the transference as a means to reenact a long-standing experience of his father, and simultaneously to use the therapist's approachable but not seductive style to help overcome this expectation of abandonment and to consider alternative approaches leading to more vital relationships. While they may also serve as enactments of the unresolved transference to the desired father of early childhood (Isay 1989, 1996a), in the here and now of the therapeutic relationship, fantasized erotic experiences represent acknowledgment of the possibility of "conditions for loving" made possible anew by psychoanalytic intervention (Schafer 1977). Though McWilliams (1996) reports on the experience of working as a straight woman analyst with gay women, while Drescher (1996a, 1996b) and Phillips (1996) have reported on the experience of working as a gay analyst with straight men and women, there is still little discussion of the nature and resolution of specifically erotic transferences as a function of the analysand's sexual lifeway.

The Psychoanalytic Situation and the Gay or Bisexual Analysand

The social and historical changes of the past two decades, which have led to our understanding alternative sexual lifeways as reflecting different but not necessarily deviant developmental processes, have made it possible for self- and publicly acknowledged gay and bisexual men and women not only to seek analysis, but also to pursue psychoanalytic education. As openly gay and lesbian psychoanalysts have begun to report on their work, it has been possible for the first time to understand the interplay of psychoanalytic process and sexual orientation of analyst and analysand and to provide a gay or lesbian analyst for analysands seeking such a referral (Domenici and Lesser 1995; Rochlin 1982). In particular, it is important to understand the impact of the analyst's sexual orientation upon the psychoanalytic situation. While many gay and bisexual analysts may not be known as such within the larger community, issues about the analyst's sexual orientation are inevitably posed during the analysis.

Sexual Orientation of Analyst and Analysand
and the Presumption of Compatibility

The issue of the analyst's sexual orientation and the analysand's knowledge of it needs to be considered in the larger context of how the analyst impacts the patient. An analytic tradition grew up in the United States following the

Second World War that emphasized neutrality, abstinence, and anonymity as the foundations of psychoanalytic technique. Analysis was seen as operating through interpretations, primarily interpretation of transference. An attempt was made to ensure that the transference was determined, as much as possible, by the analysand. It was believed that by avoiding introducing aspects of the analyst personality into the situation, transferences would stand out with great clarity. In an attempt to do this analysts scrupulously avoided providing patients with information about themselves (anonymity), acceding to patients' wishes (abstinence), or taking positions about any matter (neutrality). It should be mentioned that neutrality in this sense has a substantially different meaning than it does in other analytic contexts. A major problem with these technical recommendations was that absence of activity communicates as much as activity. Thus refusal to tell an analysand whether one is married is at least as powerful a communication as a direct reply. The recommendation leads to an interpersonal situation between analyst and patient which is at best odd.

Reconsideration of "curative" factors in the psychoanalytic situation has highlighted the contributions of Freud's work style (Lipton 1977, 1988), characterized by a friendly, personable, and engaging approach to the analytic collaboration. Cooper (1987), Viederman (1991), and Wolf (1983), working in different psychoanalytic traditions, arrive at a similar position. While Freud was not particularly abstinent in his own practice (Lipton 1977, 1988; Lynn and Vaillant 1998), he feared that other analysts in the emotionally charged, often erotic, atmosphere of the psychoanalytic situation might be led to reciprocate their patient's sexual interest (Gay 1988) so recommended a strictly abstinent analytic technique.

Too often, concern with the analyst's possible erotic or other unwarranted counterenactments has led to the belief that analysts should withhold even ordinary courtesy. Such extreme positions have been rationalized by long discarded energic views that the motive for analysands to do the analytic work comes from frustration, so that gratified analysands will lack motivation. Attempts to make analysis more scientific have also led some analysts to avoid any action that might "contaminate" the analytic situation (Lipton 1977). For a time avoiding "parameters" (Eissler 1953), or possible deviations from presumed standard technique, was regarded as a major problem for analytic work. Cooper (1987) suggests that exclusive focus on transference interpretation as the significant factor in analytic work has obscured other aspects of the analytic collaboration that contribute to change.

Starting in the 1930s analysts recognized that the analysand's adoption of certain of the analyst's values and standards plays an important role in analytic change (L. Friedman 1988). Transference interpretations themselves are only possible through focus on the here and now of the analytic collaboration (Schafer 1982; Gill 1994). This, in turn, depends on the analysand's underlying experience of the analyst's benign and passionate concern for the analysand's welfare and the rapport of their collaboration.

The inclusion of all aspects of what is experienced within this unique collaboration of analyst and analysand does not vitiate the importance of fostering shared understanding of the meaning of all aspects of this collaboration. What it does mean is that the analysand begins analysis with knowledge of who the analyst is and that this knowledge grows. Acknowledgment of this knowledge and its significance for the analysis contributes to therapeutic change.

The analysand's awareness of the analyst's sexual orientation. These considerations apply to the analyst's sexual orientation. For example, in Phillips's (1996) account of an analysis of a straight man by a gay analyst it is retrospectively clear that the patient knew Phillips was gay nearly from the outset of their work together. The psychoanalytic community is so small that most analysands know much more about their analysts than is generally recognized. Furthermore, the patient is highly motivated to learn about the analyst and few human beings can hide much from a truly curious observer. The choice is often not between the analysand's knowing and not knowing—it is between acknowledging and not acknowledging the information. Shared acknowledgement of aspects of the analyst's life serves the best interests of the analysand (Cooper 1987).

> As a candidate Heinz Kohut had a reputation as a meticulously careful student deeply committed to classical psychoanalysis. Thus he was surprised when two days following his marriage (for which he had not taken time off from work) a patient reported a dream that clearly referred to Kohut's marriage. As he presented the case to his classmates he characteristically drummed the fingers of his left hand against his forehead, only becoming aware as a result of his classmates' laughter that no elaborate theory was needed to explain the analysand's knowledge of the marriage, only the observation that Kohut was now wearing a wedding band.

In contrast with more visible characteristics like gender and ethnicity, sexual orientation is seldom publicly visible and requires the analyst's self-disclosure. Yet many psychoanalytic communities are so cross-connected and intimate that it is hard for a gay analyst to ensure that his or her sexual orientation will remain unknown to analysands (Phillips 1996). The choice is usually how, rather than whether, the gay analysand will learn of the analyst's gay sexual orientation. Our discussion presumes that, at least at a conscious level, gay analysts can be comfortable and open about their sexual orientation and recognize the impact of this sexual lifeway upon colleagues, analysands, and the larger community, even while recognizing the many and complex issues discussed throughout this work, including continuing internalized homophobia. The issue of disclosure can itself be a fruitful topic for analytic work:

> A bright, intuitive young professional who valued interpersonal honesty sought a referral to a mental health center primarily serving the gay community. At the first meeting with his therapist he repeated his interest in working with a gay therapist and wished to confirm that reality. His therapist assented that he was indeed gay but noted that it was important for them to explore what this meant to the client. The client's lifelong struggle with his own self-hatred was repetitively enacted through tearoom encounters followed by self-denigration and shame. He feared being "out," though he worked at a newspaper with an accepting atmosphere where other people were out.
>
> After a year of work devoted to the client's problems realizing a sustained intimate relationship, his therapist canceled an appointment scheduled during the following month. The client asked where the therapist was going. The therapist honestly replied that he was going to a professional meeting, without providing additional information. The client then asked if the therapist was going with anyone, which led to another somewhat impulsively posed question—whether the therapist had a partner. Following the perspective provided by Cooper (1987), with tact and consideration for the client's sensitivity about feeling rebuffed as he felt had been within his family when he was a child, the therapist noted that that either a yes or no answer might pose a burden for the client. After a few minutes' pause, the client grinned and said that his therapist was right in not disclosing this information; a yes answer would lead the client to feel envious and angry, while a no answer would mean that his therapist was as unable as he of finding a relationship. In so doing he began to explore the meanings of both these ideas for himself.

Thus, disclosure of sexual orientation and related matters may be viewed as like other disclosures by the analyst, not a matter to be prejudged or resolved by reference to authoritative prescriptions but an issue to be evaluated in each instance based on what is likely to move the analytic work forward.

Viewing psychotherapy as a relationship between two people designed both to foster enhanced self-knowledge and capacity for understanding others, Jourard (1971) argued in a now classic paper that the therapist's self-revelations make the therapist seem more human and so enhance therapeutic progress. Jourard's findings suggest that the therapist's self-disclosure fosters enhanced self-disclosure by patients. However, Lane and Hull (1990), reviewing both traditional and contemporary perspectives on the role of the therapist in psychodynamic therapeutic processes, note that the issue of the analyst's responsiveness to the analysand's needs should be paramount. The question is always what is in the analysand's best interests. Gitelson (1952) and Greenson (1967), anticipating such contemporary psychoanalytic approaches as relational psychology and Gill's (1994) "two-person" psychology, stress that problems may arise if the analysand cannot see the analyst as a real person.

Menaker (1990) suggests that a view of psychoanalysis as a process of mutual affective sharing assumes that the analyst will convey empathic understanding, including self-disclosure which conveys an understanding of the analysand's struggles. He maintains that the goal of the psychoanalytic process is to find a way to arrive at a mutually acceptable understanding of the analysand's own reality or, put differently, to coconstruct an account of the analysand's life story (Schafer 1980, 1992).

The issue of disclosure was first raised by Freud, who cautioned "young and eager psycho-analysts [who might be] tempted to bring their own individuality freely into the discussion, in order to . . . lift him over the barriers of his own narrow personality" not to attempt to overcome the analysand's resistance by giving glimpses into the analyst's own "mental defects and conflicts . . . and information about his own life" ([1912c] 1958, 117). Freud believed that such disclosure makes it even more difficult for the analysand to overcome resistance. Rather, "the doctor should be opaque to his patients and, like a mirror, should show them nothing but what is shown to him" (118). It should be noted that Freud was not famous for following his own advice (Lipton 1977, 1988; Lynn and Vaillant 1998). Freud regularly dispatched advice, gave his analysands books to read, and discussed his own views on politics and the arts. Indeed, actual practice often deviates in marked ways from the model of the analyst as mirror. While it is a two-person relationship, the analytic relationship is beyond doubt asymmetric; the analyst knows far more about the analysand's life and personality than the analysand knows about the analyst.

The question is whether and in what circumstances the analyst's self-disclosure is in the best interest of the analysand and of facilitating the analytic alliance (Josephs 1990, 1995). The assumption is that, as a result of the analyst's own personal analysis and continuing self-inquiry (Gardner 1983), the decision to disclose some aspect of his or her own life will be well considered apart from issues of so-called countertransference responses or complementary identifications (T. Jacobs 1999a; Racker 1968; Feinsilver 1999). Renik (1993, 1995) has discussed this issue in particular detail and notes the paradox in contemporary psychoanalytic practice, in which the analyst is presumed to withhold personal revelations even as the model for practice has become one of recognition of the personal relationship of analyst and analysand. Renik disputes presumptions about self-analysis as a guide to self-disclosing, nothing that such self-inquiry follows rather than precedes self-disclosure.

He suggests that our model is still one of objective neutrality, presumably always a fiction, while our practice is in reality intersubjective (Hoffman 1998; Stolorow, Atwood, and Brandchaft 1994).

While Wasserman (1999) laments that this perspective is not in accord with a classical psychoanalytic model, it may be questioned whether there ever was such a classical model. As we have stressed throughout this book, over time social and historical change leads to changes in our understanding of the manner in which lives are understood and portrayed. The intellectual revolution beginning in the 1960s affected both clinical theory and practice, within psychoanalysis as elsewhere in the human sciences. Renewed emphasis upon the dynamics of the therapeutic relationship, including increased focus on the analyst's contribution to this relationship, is reflected in clinical reports such as those of the object relations tradition, self psychology, interpersonal theory, and intersubjective perspectives.

The reality, as Renik (1993) sagely observes, is that it is the younger, beginning analyst who tends to error on the side of stiffness, while experienced analysts are more likely to foster a real and more personal relationship within the analytic setting. Further, Renik observes: "Every effective clinician learns that appropriate gratifications for analyst and analysand are an essential feature of the successful analytic process. . . . In practice we struggle to determine which gratifications are effective appropriate and which are counterproductive and exploitative" (1993, 565). There can be no arbiter of this struggle outside of the relationship of analyst and analysand (Hoffman 1983, 1998; Orange and Stolorow 1998). That is to say, it is important for analyst and analysand to understand the meanings of all aspects of their relationship, including the analyst's personal disclosures, as these meanings bear on the analysand's search after greater self-understanding. Further, there are times in any analysis when analyst and analysand alike feel uncomfortable as a result of some issues in their relationship. Psychoanalysis departs from other modes of psychotherapy in making explicit that which is implicit, because a source of discomfort, in conventional social reality. It is the ability to talk about the analysand's response to this gratification and to understand what the analysand's response means to the analysand and within their relationship that is central to psychoanalysis as a psychotherapeutic process (S. Rosenbaum 1998; Viederman 1991), rather than the objectivity sometimes regarded as central (Wasserman 1999).

The issue of self-disclosure becomes particularly complex in the case of the gay analyst and either gay or straight analysands. While the analyst's partnership status is always an issue within the transference, the stigma and prejudice still attached to same-gender sexual orientation makes it likely that gay analysts will be confronted with particular issues. There is no real way of avoiding this, given that the analytic community is small and that analysands often know far more about their analysts than analysts realize. Further, analysands look for even the most subtle cues regarding their analyst's marital status. In contemporary bourgeois society almost all married women and most married men wear wedding rings. The analysand often silently digests such information starting in the first diagnostic interview before beginning analysis. The lack of a wedding ring poses unique transference fantasies including the analyst's sexual availability. Some lesbian and gay analysts have commitment rings, often worn on the right hand, which convey yet other information. The analyst listens for evidence regarding the manner in which the analysand interprets the presence or absence of a ring, as well as other cues, including the analyst's dress and demeanor, office furniture, books and pictures, and even the analytic couch itself.

At the outset, the gay analyst is presented with the issue of whether to include information about his or her own sexual orientation in what is told to the analysand at the beginning of the analysis. Many gay men and women specifically request a gay analyst and arrive for the first appointment assured that they are being referred to a gay analyst. However, there may be dynamic reasons for such disclosure even in the unlikely circumstance that the analysand is not aware of the analyst's sexual orientation as gay. For example, Isay (1996a, 1996b) argues that many gay men, having experienced the emotional withdrawal of their own fathers in response to awareness of their boyhood erotic attraction, need an affirmative and caring man who can provide a good role model and who can see that sexuality and intimacy can be found together. Further, the reality of antigay prejudice within the community requires that the psychoanalytic situation provide a sense of safety from such prejudice, uniquely possible when gay analysands know that their analyst shares their sexual lifeway. Finally, Isay believes that the analyst's acknowledgment of shared sexual orientation acknowledges to the patient that details of his lifestyle are implicitly understood.

While generally sympathetic with the work of Isay (1989, 1996a, 1996b), among the first gay psychoanalysts to publicly acknowledge his gay sexual lifeway, Drescher is more cautious in recommending self-disclosure, and for precisely the reasons that Isay (1996b) urges it. Drescher observes that precisely because the gay analysand is aware of a shared lifeway with his analyst, the analysand may seek to avoid talking about such issues as the meaning of being gay, which otherwise would come into the analytic process. Raphling and Chused (1988) have raised the issue of gender similarity in the analytic relationship. They note that whether the analyst's gender is the same or different from that of the analysand that fact raises distinctive issues for the course of the analysis. Shared gender may be a source either of increased safety and comfort, as the analysand presumes a set of shared life experiences (Jones and Gabriel 1999) or as Drescher (1998) suggests, of resistance to analysis, promoting a failure to consider the meanings of such status characteristics as gender, marital status, sexual orientation, or even ethnicity and race for the analysand's lived experience (Holmes 1992).

The question of the role of similarity of analyst and analysand in terms of shared gay sexual orientation also raises the larger question of analyst-analysand "match" (J. Kantrowitz 1995). Following Cooper (1987) and Viederman (1991), Kantrowitz suggests that compatibility in terms of character structure may be more significant in fostering a productive collaboration than such apparent sources of similarity as gender, ethnicity, or sexual orientation. While the analysand may believe that an analyst who is also gay may be the most likely to understand what it means to be gay or lesbian, and most able to provide a source of mirroring, other, less obvious aspects of the analyst may contribute more to fostering a working alliance and a positive facilitating transference. A straight analyst able and willing to learn about gay lifeways from gay and lesbian analysands might more readily foster such an alliance than an ideological gay analyst with specific views regarding the impact of sexual orientation upon personality and lifestyle. Kantrowitz's (1995) discussion highlights particularly subtle aspects of the analyst's personality likely to be important in determining a good match between analyst and analysand.

The expectation of automatic understanding by virtue of shared sexual orientation may obscure both the content of particular fantasies and implicit ideas of "perfect" relationships.

> A talented aspiring actor developed characters in his work by merging with the character, attempting to think as his character would in similar circumstances. He had sought referral to a gay therapist. This technique of merger with the character was enacted anew in the transference. He assumed his therapist shared his experiences and could be one with him as he described both his search for intimacy and his almost compulsive cruising. When his therapist asked him to describe in greater detail his experience while cruising, the client regarded this query as a failure to acknowledge what the client had assumed were shared experiences.

Presumption of a shared set of experiences and implicit understandings by either or both analyst and analysand can easily permit the analysand to avoid personally painful topics by appealing to the analyst's shared understanding of, for example, "what it means to be gay." Sometimes knowledge of the analyst's sexual lifeway does not foster a sense of safety in the therapeutic situation. A young adult seen in intensive psychoanalytic psychotherapy at a mental health center serving the gay and lesbian community feared that his therapist might seduce him; assuming that his therapist must be gay because of the nature of the clinic, he was afraid that a lifelong pattern would be enacted once again: an older man, in the first instance a distant relative, would befriend him only to try to sexually exploit him. Another gay man explicitly stated that he did not want a gay therapist; he was sure that a gay therapist would be the object of social disparagement and, like himself, hate himself and be self-disparaging, while a straight therapist would be able to feel good about himself.

Analysands often seek analysts who seem like themselves, especially in terms of obvious qualities like gender and ethnicity. Often this reflects a conviction that such analysts will more readily understand the analysand's struggle or mistrust of individuals who are thought likely to misunderstand the analysand. Women, for example, often seek female analysts, who they believe will understand them better and be less likely to be sexist than male analysts. Lesbians and gay men often make similar considerations in choosing analysts and are supported in doing so by the writings of some gay therapists (Isay 1996a).

For example, Rochlin believes that gay and lesbian therapists can enhance a gay or lesbian client's sense of safety in therapy:

> The issue of client–therapist similarity has special significance for gay male and lesbian clients. Along with the feeling of being alone, the reality of difference and alienation even in the family of origin constitutes the distinctive pain of early gay experience, unparalleled in the family experiences of members of other oppressed groups. In the author's clinical experience, the perpetuation of that pain in therapy with a non-gay therapist is one of the commonly reported reasons for gay male and lesbian clients' dissatisfaction or failure in traditional psychotherapy. (1982, 23)

Rochlin's claim has several important elements. First is the assertion that the therapy should provide a corrective for the isolation that is assumed to have been a specific result of the client's already present sexual orientation during childhood. Second, Rochlin implies that the therapist, having dealt with issues of self-criticism and public acknowledgment of sexual orientation, can be a role model and, thus, facilitate resolution of the client's own struggles with these issues. The gay therapist is assumed to be more readily able to follow the gay client's references to gay settings and issues that would be outside the experience of straight therapists. Finally, the gay therapist is assumed to be familiar with the gay world and able to guide the client in avoiding the pitfalls of being gay and in using the resources of the community. Isay (1989, 1996a, 1996b) maintains a similar position, asserting that as a result of the antigay prejudice in our society gay women and men are likely to feel safer and more accepted working with a gay rather than a straight analyst.

Issues of safety and shared understanding of the problems and possibilities of being gay may be more complex than Rochlin and Isay acknowledge. A group of problems arise when analyst and analysand are motivated to presume they share a vision, because that vision is then unlikely to become the focus of analytic scrutiny. For example, the experience of being gay has changed in dramatic and surprising ways between cohorts of gay men, as we have shown in previous chapters. The middle-aged gay analyst who relies on his own experience is almost as likely to misunderstand the gay adolescent's experience as a straight analyst but may be at greater risk of not acknowledging this misunderstanding, especially if easy understanding between analyst and patient is seen as highly desirable. Furthermore, as Malyon (1982) maintains, heterosexism is so ubiquitous in our society that the gay analyst is as likely as straight counterparts to maintain some residual sense of antigay prejudice. Further, as Blechner (1995) and Drescher (1995) note, gay people who completed a psychoanalytic education before the opening of the institutes to gay individuals are likely to have particularly complex and unsatisfactory experiences of integrating homosexuality into their larger lives and their personal analyses.

Unlike ethnicity and gender, sexual orientation is neither obvious nor customarily acknowledged in a professional setting. Thus the process of gay patients going to gay therapists requires some sort of public announcement of an aspect of life ordinarily held private in our society.

Isay's concern that the analysand find a positive role model in a gay man well adapted to his sexual lifeway ignores the reality of a lifetime of exposure to antigay prejudice experienced by analyst and analysand alike (Herek 1991, 1996), which itself must become a part of the therapeutic situation. A part of the work with gay and lesbian analysands consists precisely in working through these often personally painful experiences; it is neither desirable or even possible to avoid this therapeutic work. Isay (1996b) tries to emphasize that gay men can have satisfactory lives and fulfilling intimate relationships. He believes that through adopting a gay-affirmative position and fostering an idealizing transference, it is possible to provide a sort of "corrective emotional experience." Given the life experiences of his cohort of middle-aged gay men, it is understandable that he should express such ideas. However, for many younger adults this is not an issue; these gay and bisexual men and women implicitly understand that there is little necessary connection between sexual lifeway and well-being.

At some point during the resolution of the analytic relationship, it is necessary for analyst and analysand to understand together the significance for the analysand of idealizing and mirroring transferences. The very search for a role model, so often presumed necessary among analysands from erotic and other minority groups, must itself be understood. The request for referral to a gay or gay-friendly therapist, while undoubtedly reflecting a wish for safety and understanding in the therapeutic relationship, often involves a host of other factors.

A problem shared by all therapists, meeting clients in social situations, may be particularly troublesome for gay therapists. In many cities, the gay and lesbian community is geographically and socially tightly knit. Clients and therapists often live in the same neighborhood. While straight analysands may meet their analyst and his or her spouse or partner in a restaurant or at the theater, the gay or lesbian analysand may well encounter his or her therapist in more awkward social settings. Knowledge of the analyst's sexual orientation and factors such as whether the analyst has a partner or wears a ring indicating partnership can lead to interesting and challenging issues within analysis. Phillips's (1996) description of the impact of such knowledge on the analysis of a "straight" patient illustrates not only the richness of meaning the analysand may attribute to the analyst's orientation but also the complex defenses that can be mounted by an anxious patient confronted with such information. While Phillips was able to work through the multiple layers of this process masterfully, one can easily imagine how in less skilled hands the analysis could have become irreparably bogged down.

THE ANALYST'S DISCLOSURE OF SEXUAL ORIENTATION. One way to deal with the problem so well illustrated in Phillip's account of his analysand's growing awareness of his gay sexual lifeway is for the analyst to acknowledge his or her gay sexual orientation at the outset of the analysis (Gabriel and Monaco 1995; Isay 1986b, 1991; Kooden 1991; Rochlin 1982; T. Stein 1988). This may facilitate the psychoanalytic process with both gay and straight analysands. The analysand will likely learn of the therapist's sexual orientation in any case, and may feel guilty and embarrassed about possessing knowledge which the analyst, by choosing to withhold, has indicated a reluctance to disclose (Cornett 1995). Acknowledging sexual orientation at the outset allows the many meanings of this disclosure to be examined as part of the analytic process.

Writing about gay men who seek psychodynamic psychotherapy and their gay male therapists, gay senior clinicians (Isay 1991; Cornett 1991; Gabriel and Monaco 1995; T. Stein 1988) justify this self-disclosure in terms of the therapeutic alliance (Josephs 1990, 1995). They argue that disclosure of sexual orientation supports the client's struggle with self-criticism and helps counteract the low self-esteem generated by growing up in antigay society. In addition, they claim, it enhances the client's sense of personal safety and fosters the sense that his therapist will accept his sexuality. As Isay observes:

> The gay analyst or therapist who hides or disguises his sexual orientation by refusing to acknowledge it implies that he is heterosexual and may further damage the self-esteem of his patients by conveying his shame, self-depreciation, or fear of disclosure. Equally important, he fails to provide a corrective for his patients' injured self-esteem that derives from internalized attitudes and parental and peer rejection. Self-revelation through confrontation or confirmation at some appropriate point is . . . necessary and important to an effective therapeutic effort for a gay man in treatment with a gay therapist. (1991, 203)

Gabriel and Monaco (1995) affirm Isay's position on self-disclosure when working with lesbian analysands. They note that most analysands assume that their analyst is straight, which may create unnecessary problems for the therapeutic alliance and the gay or lesbian analyst's complementary identifications. They further note that self-disclosure need not compromise the fundamental principle of the "neutrality" of the psychoanalytic situation if the information is provided in a planned, matter-of-fact way and, consistent with discussions in Stricker and Fisher's (1990) collection, and Palombo's (1987) perspective on self-disclosure in general, is not an enactment of complementary identification. Such self-disclosure reflects the reality that the psychoanalytic situation is a two-person relationship. (In contrast, if the information is urgently blurted out, the self-revelation is probably based on inadequately analyzed unconscious responses to the analysand.) It also provides a context in which to explore the analysand's response and so to foster the analysand's self-knowledge, regardless of the analysand's sexual orientation.

Isay believes that affirmative self-disclosure benefits gay and straight analysands alike by demonstrating the analyst's positive self-regard. Conversely, Stein (1988) suggests that the gay therapist's reluctance to reveal sexual orientation signals to the client that the therapist has difficulties accepting being gay. Isay (1991, 1986b) and Kooden (1991) stress that the therapist's self-disclosure lets the therapist serve as a role model and foster the client's self-acceptance through identification with his gay therapist. Isay cautions, however, that it is essential for the gay male therapist to have achieved some level of understanding of the meaning for himself of being gay before beginning psychotherapy with gay men. There has been less discussion of this issue of self-disclosure in psychodynamic psychotherapy with lesbian clients.

An additional advantage of explicit acknowledgment of the analyst's sexual orientation at the outset is that the meanings for the analysand, whether gay or straight, may enter more directly and explicitly into the analytic process. While the analysand may still find it difficult to talk about the meaning of the analyst's sexual orientation, the burden of bearing presumably secret knowledge regarding the analyst's life, learned more or less inadvertently, is short-circuited (Isay 1991). This controversial recommendation presumes that the analyst is at ease publicly acknowledging sexual orientation.

The gay therapist who feels reluctant to disclose his or her sexual orientation, as opposed to the therapist who decides that such disclosure does not reflect optimal analytic technique, should carefully consider the situation. In the contemporary urban mental health culture, there are few legal or social sanctions related to sexual orientation. Covertly gay therapists who are uncomfortable with their sexual orientation or its acknowledgment in the community should therefore ask themselves whether further personal analytic work is in order. Having grown up in a society with widespread antigay prejudice, the gay analyst may remain sensitive to issues of stigma beyond what is reasonable within the community. Clearly the analyst's concern with the meanings of sexual orientation for the analysand may stem from complementary identifications (Kooden 1991). The analyst's self-revelation may then reflect erotic wishes toward the analysand, perhaps out of awareness, which are enacted by informing the analysand of sexual orientation or presuming that this is a paramount aspect of the emerging transference. Similarly, in opposite-gender analyses revelations of same-gender orientation may be unconsciously used to reassure the analysand that there is no risk of sexual activity in the analysis.

The issue of the analyst as positive role model is complex; idealization of the analyst inevitably arises with the emergence of a positive alliance (Greenson 1965; Kohut 1977, 1984; Zetzel 1958) and must itself become the focus of collaborative study at some point in the course of the analytic work.

Knowledge of the analyst's sexual orientation might also, however, be the source of a negative therapeutic reaction. Among gay men who disparage their own sexuality, in response to the attitudes of family and society, acknowledgment that the analyst shares this devalued attribute may be viewed as evidence of the analyst's failings. Clearly, the analyst's decision to disclose sexual orientation, perhaps as a consequence of material emerging in the course of the analysis suggesting that the analysand is aware of the analyst's sexual lifeway—through extraanalytic information or through often implicit cues within the emerging two-person relationship—suggests that such disclosure is necessary. Only continuing self-inquiry will provide a guide as to whether and when the analyst should make such a disclosure.

Beyond the analyst's explicit acknowledgment of sexual orientation, it is assumed that other questions posed by the analysand will be regarded as questions more generally are regarded within the psychoanalytic situation, always keeping in mind the best interests of the analysand. As in other aspects of the psychoanalytic situation, great care must be given to understanding those aspects of the analyst's own life which must be communicated to the analysand. Questions about partnership or lifestyle must be considered in terms of both implications for the transference and the analyst's possible complementary identifications with the analysand's life struggles. Self-revelation poses somewhat different issues in work with straight and gay analysands. The small size and limited connections of the gay community in even large cities increases the likelihood that the analysand may meet the analyst in a social situation or learn about the analyst's life from mutual friends.

> A gay analysand recounted at his Monday hour meeting a gay, non–analytically oriented psychiatrist at a dinner party attended by a number of gay couples the prior weekend. Inevitably, conversation got around to his analysis and analyst. The psychiatrist, who had met the analyst and his partner at a social event and had known the analyst's partner as a former lover of his own partner's best friend, made less than flattering comments about analysis in general and his analyst's partner in particular. The many meanings of this conversation were explored across the course of the analysis, including feelings of envy of the partner for being special in the analyst's life, of resentment that he was not able to achieve a relationship such as he imagined his analyst to have, and of abandonment over weekends and holidays, when he imagined the close and sexually satisfying relationship between his analyst and his analyst's partner. These issues, closely tied to his own efforts at resolving issues from his childhood, were accompanied by idealization of his analyst as a gay man who was able to maintain a long-term partnership, in contrast with the stereotypical gay man unable to realize such ties.

Matching Gender and Sexual Orientation of Analysand and Analyst

Clearly, in the analysis of gay and bisexual men and women by analysts sharing the same sexual orientation—as in other situations in which similarity is presumed, on the basis of gender, ethnicity, race, or other status—it is important to pay close attention to the analyst's enactments of complementary identifications. As already noted, issues of shame and embarrassment shared by analyst and analysand may lead the analyst to such an identification: unable to bear the analysand's feelings of shame and embarrassment, which resonate with similar issues in his or her life, the analyst may be reluctant to acknowledge these issues.

Several recent clinical reports focus on the countertransference issues arising among straight analysts working with gay men and women and, reciprocally, gay analysts working with straight analysands. Still, Mann (1997) and R. Tyson (1986) note the paucity of either analytic discussion or literature dealing with the analyst's personal experience working with gay or lesbian patients. In particular, there is little discussion of the gay analyst's experience of his or her own same-gender desire evoked reciprocally in the transference of gay or lesbian analysands. Assuming that we are all familiar with the variety of sexual wishes common to the human condition, maintaining a focus on assisting each patient to find the best solutions to the particular dilemmas for which he or she sought psychotherapy resolves many of the potential problems of therapists working with patients of the opposite gender or a different sexual orientation. An affirmative position recognizing that same-gender desire is as "natural" for a gay person as opposite-gender desire is for a straight person, acknowledging the compelling nature of such desire, makes it possible to maintain an empathic stance regardless of sexual orientation.

McWilliams (1996) suggests that lesbian and bisexual women have particularly erotic transferences to their woman therapists and that the therapist must pay particular attention to the analysand's experience of the woman therapist as seductive. She suggests that, regardless of the gender and gender orientation of the patient, interventions focusing on the meaning for the analysand of her possible sexual attraction most often lead the analysand to recognize the nature of his or her own wishes. McWilliams also notes that what gay men and women had found missing in their youth was a sense that they could feel safe with their desire and that their desire would be understood and accepted by others.

Drescher (1996a) suggests that McWilliams's is overly optimistic in her view of the analyst as acceptant of the gay man or woman seen in analysis. However, he suggests that a major motivation for the wish of many gay men for a gay analyst is, ironically, in order to avoid having to reflect on their own experience and self-criticism; with a straight therapist it is all too easy to displace these feelings of self-hatred onto the person of the therapist, while, with a gay therapist, these men believe they can finesse issues related to their sexuality and seek their therapist's complicity. The gay analyst able to recognize his or her own residual antigay prejudice is able to help these gay men to deal with their own feelings of self-hatred. Isay (1991) also acknowledges the problems potentially posed by the analyst's self-disclosure of sexual orientation. Particularly with straight analysands, such information may crystallize antigay prejudice, which interferes in the therapeutic alliance, particularly when the analysand's response stimulates complementary responses based on rage and projective identification on the part of the analyst.

Antihomosexual countertransferences among gay analysts result from the analysts' experience of criticism by others, including members of the larger community and the psychoanalytically oriented mental health community (Blechner 1995). It is all too easy for the gay analyst to join with the analysand's own self-critical antigay attitudes, thus avoiding examination of important but personally painful issues (Drescher 1996a). Gay analysts must attend to complementary identifications different from those confronted by straight analysts. However, as Isay (1989, 1996a) testily observes, gay men and women have decades of experience working with analysts unable to understand or accept their sexual lifeway.

Conversely unresolved same-gender desire makes straight therapists, particularly men, uncomfortable working with gay analysands (Mann 1997; Nungesser 1983). For example, the analyst may experience an analysand's comments as a bid for a sexual encounter and unconsciously defensively respond by having intense heterosexual fantasies. Similarly the analyst may avoid any response to the analysand's experience. Mann wonders, for instance, whether it is possible that Bollas (1992) could in fact have had no personal response to his analysand's casual sexual encounters. Mann (1997) details his own response to a young male artist who reported pursuing a gay sexual lifeway since childhood. Raised by strict and aloof parents who were reportedly sadistic in their punishments, the analysand escaped his cold environment through fantasies of living on another planet. His loneliness resonated with Mann's experience of his own childhood as one of emotional emptiness, allowing him to recognize his analysand's loneliness. His sharing this recognition with the analysand then led the analysand to acknowledge his own feeling for the analyst as a longed-for paternal figure. Over the course of a summer holiday, the analysand met a man with whom he had a close but nonsexual relationship, which Mann interpreted as an effort to deal with his analyst's absence. Mann became aware of his own erotic admiration for his handsome and well-proportioned analysand during the same summer break, when he came across some T-shirts similar to those worn by his analysand. Trying one on, he was pleased to see that he could still wear such a shirt, and recognized this pleasure at still having a trim enough figure to permit such a youthful shirt as an expression of his own erotic attraction to his analysand.

Conclusion

The past three decades have witnessed significant changes both in the theory of psychoanalytic technique and in psychoanalytic practice. Lipton (1977, 1988) and Gill (1994) have sympathetically noted that contemporary practice has shifted back toward the tradition in which the Freuds practiced (Couch 1995), away from Sigmund Freud's often misunderstood, perhaps politically motivated, writing (particularly in volume 12 of the Standard Edition) on clinical psychoanalytic technique. The reality is that clinical psychoanalysis is founded on a real relationship between two participants (Gill 1994; Hoffman 1998). While asymmetrical, the psychoanalytic process is founded on the analyst's effort to understand the meanings which the analysand has made of the experiences of a lifetime.

At the same time, consistent with Mannheim's ([1928] 1993) understanding of the interplay of generations in the formation of idea systems and Toulmin's (1990) perspective on the philosophy of science, the terms in which the analyst seeks to make sense of the analysand's experiences are themselves a consequence of the analyst's own, time-bound experience as an analysand, together with the analysand's course work and supervised clinical work as a candidate. The most senior generation of analysts, completing their psychoanalytic studies in the aftermath of the Second World War, saw in psychoanalysis a means of understanding the nonrationality of international aggression. Grounded in a natural science perspective, so much a part of ego psychology, these analysts continue to view psychoanalytic theory and practice in the terms of their own postwar psychoanalytic education.

The intellectual ferment of the past three decades has had a profound impact upon our understanding of psychoanalysis as a human science. In the first place, changes in our understanding of the foundation of knowledge have had an impact upon our understanding of the theory underlying clinical technique (Toulmin 1986). In the second place, reconsideration of presumptions regarding, for example, the inevitable sequence of psychological development and the foundation of personal vulnerability, have also had an impact upon our understanding of change in clinical psychoanalysis (Cohler, Stott, and Musick 1995; Galatzer-Levy and Cohler 1990; Kagan 1998; Lewis 1997; Masten and Coatsworth 1995).

Of particular relevance for the present book, larger social changes regarding our understanding of sexuality and sexual identity (Clendinen and Nagourney 1999; D'Emilio [1983] 1998) have forced a reconsideration of the understanding of sexual identity within psychoanalysis. Following earlier work of Thompson (1947) and Mitchell (1978, 1981), clinical theory and technique is being rapidly reshaped within the context of contemporary reports concerning gay men and lesbians seeking psychoanalytic intervention (C. Friedman 1998; Frommer 1994a; Glazer 1998; Herron et al. 1982; Phillips 1998; P. Lynch 1999; Drescher 1998b; Schafer 1995). On the one hand, work with gay and lesbian analysands by both gay and straight analysts is changing our understanding of the psychoanalytic process, as we focus on such issues as the analyst's experience of countertransference, the analyst's disclosure of salient personal information to the analysand, and the many meanings of sexual desire and enaction for the analysand's experience of personal integrity or self (Cohler and Galatzer-Levy 1995; Shelby 1998; Tolpin 1997a).

This chapter has pointed to a number of issues which, while not unique to work with gay and lesbian analysands, often becomes central in such work. While it is not necessary for the analyst of the gay or lesbian analysand to be gay, it is necessary for the analyst, whether gay or straight, to have become aware of his or her own lifelong prejudice, the inevitable result of growing up in a heterosexist society, and to be prepared to explore these issues with the analysand. At the same time, it is important to explore the many meanings for the gay or lesbian analysand of such issues as the process leading to the expression of their particular sexual identity, choice of partner and preferred sexual expression, fantasies related to partner and sexuality, and the impact of being gay or lesbian on relations with friends and family. Psychoanalysis is about making meanings of life experiences within the context of a unique relationship in which meanings ordinarily implicit in social life become explicit and central (Sandler and Sandler 1987, 1994). As this work proceeds, analyst and analysand alike must remain aware of the discomfort and even anxiety that may be evoked by this focus on sexuality and identity (Mann 1997; Wrye and Welles 1994). It is important that both remain focused on the possibility that their own prejudices may interfere in this exploration of the analysand's sexual identity. It is also essential that such exploration be undertaken in an atmosphere of mutual respect and appreciation of the significance for the analysand of this sexual lifeway (Herdt 1997; Hostetler and Herdt 1998). The important difference between contemporary and earlier perspectives on psychoanalytic work with gay and lesbian analysands is that sexual orientation as such is not regarded as a "problem" to be resolved or corrected. Sexuality is approached in the same manner as other aspects of lived experience. Further, recognizing that all aspects of sexuality inevitably become a part of the psychoanalytic situation, and that heterosexuality is as much an experience to be understood as homosexuality, no one aspect of sexuality is privileged as beyond analysis (Stoller 1985; Chodorow 1994).

Perhaps the most distinctive aspect of psychoanalytic intervention among lesbians and gay men is the enduring sense of shame which so often pervades their sense of self and their relationships with family, friends, and lovers. Particularly where the analyst is also a gay man or woman, this sense of shame may be shared, requiring the analyst's continuing self-inquiry into the manner in which residual antigay prejudice learned over a lifetime enters into the therapeutic relationship (Malyon 1982; Herek 1996). While able to inform concordant identifications, the analysand's struggles with issues of shame and discomfort with sexual identity as gay may also evoke complementary identifications, which interfere with the analyst's ability to maintain the empathic attitude so important in fostering change within the therapeutic situation.

The issue of shared sexual identity among analysand and analyst continues as a major issue in the discussion of psychotherapy for gay women and men. Responding to the activist stance of many members of the gay community, many lesbians and gay men seek an analyst sharing their sexual identity (Isay 1996b). This preference may be understood as an aspect of the larger issue of the analysand-analyst match (J. Kantrowitz 1995). Overall, compatibility of personality and the analyst's capacity for empathic listening—consequent upon enhanced awareness of his or her own wishes and fears, particularly in the realm of sexuality—is much more important than the analyst's sexual orientation. Assuming that the analyst is comfortable with his or her own sexual identity and able to integrate the feelings inevitably revoked reciprocal to the struggles of a gay or lesbian analysand seeking to understand his or her sexuality within the context of the analytic relationship (Mann 1997), there is little evidence that the analyst's own avowed sexual identity is an important factor in the psychoanalytic situation. Indeed, as Drescher (1998) has cautioned, there is a danger that gay men and women working with gay analysts may avoid dealing with personally painful issues in analysis by appealing to shared understanding of gay and lesbian lived experience.

Overall, as we discussed in chapter 7, realization of ambiance in the psychoanalytic situation is particularly important in psychoanalytic work with lesbians and gay men, particularly those whose life story is one of early awareness of being different from others, often accompanied by a sense of this difference as wrong or bad. Entering the psychoanalytic situation, much of this sense of shame may be disavowed or censored in the manner portrayed by Kris (1990) and Sandler and Sandler (1987, 1994). The analyst's own personal comfort in dealing with issues of sexuality, along with an enhanced awareness of his or her own residual antigay prejudice, makes possible the analyst's empathic listening.

Unrecognized complementary identifications (Racker 1968), experienced by the analyst as anxiety evoked by the analysand's account, may lead to an empathic break or withdrawal from the empathic listening stance. This stance is critical in facilitating the analysand's increased understanding and resolution of shame, as well as his or her recognition of the deleterious effect of this sense of shame on personal vitality over a lifetime. The struggle with shame and its continuing adverse impact upon the life of gay and lesbian analysands continues throughout the analysis and may become a silent aspect of the transference. Attention to this issue is critical in the analysis of men and women within sexual minorities, as more generally among men and women identified with stigmatized minority groups.

Twelve

Self, Sexual Identity, and the Psychoanalytic Situation

Mann's (1997) review of his work with a gay analysand (discussed at the end of chapter 11) reflects the use of concordant identifications, which let him recognize how his analysand's account of his childhood resonated with his own childhood experiences. The resulting understanding led to interpretations that empathically expressed his appreciation of the analysand's struggles. Continuing self-inquiry later revealed his erotic attraction to his analysand, which let him be more comfortable with the analysand's sexuality and fostered an accepting attitude in the analytic setting, making it possible for the analysand to reveal and resolve his wish for his analyst to be his lover.

The analyst's enhanced awareness of the analysand's lived experience may lead to counterenactments. At the same time, enhanced awareness of one's own lived experience may lead to more empathic responses. Enactments are inevitable in human relationships—the question is not whether they will occur in the analysis but how they will be handled. The extent to which enactments reciprocally evoked in the analyst on hearing the analysand's life story lead to impasse or interfere in analytic listening relates to the analyst's capacity for continuing self-inquiry.

Empathy and Self-Object Experiences

There is no "other" apart from one's own present experience of that other. Vicarious introspection, commonly called empathy (Kohut [1959] 1978), provides a means to transform meanings evoked by "essential others" (Galatzer-Levy and Cohler 1993) into enhanced understanding of oneself and others. Anxiety generated in this process, especially if not available to awareness, may lead to enactments that interfere with such understanding. Continuing self-inquiry is essential to maintaining awareness of counterenactments and taking advantage of the experience of another as a means of enhancing understanding.

The concept of empathy is not well understood in psychoanalysis and the human sciences (Beres and Arlow 1974). In psychoanalysis the term has a meaning much more specific than the common experience of fellow-feeling

(D. Buie 1981; Pigman 1995; T. Shapiro 1981; Schwaber 1981). It refers to a particular mode of knowing another's experiences through vicarious introspection (D. Buie 1981; Greenson 1960; Kohut [1959] 1978; Racker 1968; Schafer 1959). The analyst in a sense "tastes" the analysand's experience and intervenes based on the resulting emotional and cognitive understanding (Jaffe 1986). This process, sometimes called counteridentification (Fliess 1944, 1953) or concordant identification (Racker 1968), represents a mediated encounter with another's world of lived experience. Kohut notes that empathy as a method of study can be used to many ends, including negative ones involving inappropriate influence or terror. It represents a method of study distinctive to the human sciences. Empathy is not intuition but a mode of listening founded on the analyst's continuing self-exploration and appreciation of others (Kohut [1959] 1978; T. Shapiro 1981).

Kohut (1984) and Jackson (1992) have suggested that the experience of being listened to and of the effort by another to understand one's experience itself contributes to personality change in psychoanalysis. Since Alexander (1956) first formulated the concept, the idea of the "corrective emotional experience," by means of which the analyst could provide needed developmental experiences within the analysis, has been controversial in psychoanalysis. The view that aspects of the psychoanalytic setting might themselves foster change (Stone 1961) has been viewed as antithetical to the view of psychoanalysis as a process of bringing irrational aspects of thought and action under conscious control (Pigman 1995). This critique ignores the automatic role of the analyst as "essential other" (Galatzer-Levy and Cohler 1993) and the significance of the therapist's ability to maintain an empathic mode of listening when confronted with analysand's experiences and enactments. The analyst's capacity to "taste" or experience and interpret experiences and enactments facilitates personality change by bringing previously unacceptable sentiments and intents into awareness and making them available for reconsideration. Freud's (1900, [1912b] 1957, [1915b] 1958) original concept of "evenly suspended attention" assumed an experience-near collaborative process similar to those more thoroughly explored by Schafer (1959), Kohut ([1959] 1978, 1971), and Schwaber (1983) rather than the more experience-distant and scientist role often assumed as the ideal for psychoanalysis. Optimally, the analyst is attuned to the analysand's wishes, thoughts, and feelings through listening to the analysand's narrative, experiencing the pain and joy of the analysand's life world, and fostering the analysand's enhanced self-awareness through interpretive integration, organization, and focus of this narrative, which further extends the analysand's range of self-observation and capacity for self-inquiry. Abend (1986) suggests at least three kinds of empathic experiences: awareness of the analysand's unconscious efforts at evoking the analyst's interest or opprobrium; awareness of the analysand's enaction of wishes founded on the totality of the analyst's own life experiences; and awareness of the analysand's present feeling states.

It is important to emphasize that psychoanalytic empathy is different from sympathetic understanding (Greenson 1960). Wolf (1983) and Pigman (1995) note that the term sympathy is a mistranslation of *Einfühlung*, which refers to a focus on putting oneself in the analysand's place, leading to tact and understanding of the analysand's experiential world. Wolf maintains that Freud so clearly and implicitly viewed empathy as a central aspect of the psychoanalytic process that there was little need to elaborate on the term, which in German has a quite straightforward significance.

Empathy and Construction of a Psychoanalytic Story

Vygotsky and Bakhtin showed the way to understanding the inherently so-cial nature of all thought, which is dialogically or jointly constructed within shared discourse (Hoffman 1991; A. Wilson and Weinstein 1992, 1996). In analysis the analysand's life story is enacted, examined, and refashioned through collaborative work by means of a dialogic process. Any life story thus (re)constructed is a shared construction of the two participants (Hoff-man 1991). The new, jointly crafted narrative optimally permits the analy-sand a greater sense of personal congruity and vitality than the narrative im-plicit at the beginning of the analysis (Schafer 1980, 1981). Note that analyst and analysand, as any teller and listener, live within the constraints of the larger social order. The nature of the life stories that emerge as satisfactory from analyses changes with social conditions. (Commonly, analysts treat these various life stories as though they reflected truths independent of the wider social situation and claim that the currently useful story is truer than older ones.)

The psychoanalytic life story, as any life story, is a performance in which telling is a mode of acting. Gesture and speech, recognition of audience, and other aspects of performance are intrinsic elements of the story. The teller and listener each bring a lifetime history of meanings and varying capacities for self-inquiry and listening. The analyst's own analysis fosters listening which is less burdened by personal pain, aided by a capacity for self-inquiry and awareness of his or her own wishes and feelings which, at the start of the analysis, is presumably greater than that of the analysand. By the completion of the analysis, as a result of collaborative inquiry, the analysand has acquired many of these same attributes and becomes both a different and more reflec-tive listener and teller.

Thus, the interplay of empathy and other experiences of the analyst leads to the construction of a new life story founded on the sharing of affective states (Beres and Arlow 1974). T. Shapiro (1981) asks, however, whether at least some of what is thought to be empathy really results from the analyst's contertransferences. Reliance upon vicarious introspection as the foundation for knowing another requires the analyst's own analysis, which makes continuing self-analysis possibly the single most important aspect of psychoanalytic education. Abend observes:

> The identical psychological abilities and functions that provide an analyst with his essential empathic capability also constitute his potential for countertransference. Empathy and countertransference are distinguished by their *result,* that is to say, by the degree of accuracy of responsivity, and not by the nature of the forces in operation in the analyst's unconscious. In the analytic situation, to put it bluntly, countertransference is empathy when the analyst is wrong. (1986, 569)

Enactment and Empathy in the Analysis of Gay Men and Women

Gay and bisexual analysands bring to the psychoanalytic situation feelings of embarrassment and shame founded on a lifetime of living in a society in which their sexual orientation is at best a controversial issue and often the source of stigma and prejudice. Such prejudice has often become a part of the selves of the analysands, who have learned that their desire is deemed reprehensible in the larger society. This is particularly evident in the cohort of now middle-aged men growing up in the post-Stonewall epoch. Many of these men seek to publicly acknowledge their sexual lifeway to achieve an enhanced sense of personal integrity, but still often experience criticism from family and friends and a sense of embarrassment and shame. The discourse about AIDS has exacerbated this feeling of embarrassment. Clinical psychoanalytic work with gay men and lesbians must first provide an environment of safety and then focus on the present unconscious and on the analysand's lifelong experience of shame.

As discussed in chapter 7, any analyst reared in our society, regardless of sexual orientation, shares its antigay prejudice (De Monteflores 1986; Herek 1995, 1996; Malyon 1982; I. Meyer 1993; T. Stein 1988). The struggle with this prejudice is well reflected in S. A. Mitchell's (1996b) discussion of the place of gender and sexual orientation in the postmodern age, which focuses on meanings rather than presumed categories. The analyst's personal analysis and continued self-inquiry should lead to an increased awareness of the conflicting sexual wishes that are ubiquitous in our society (Freud 1905b). The analyst working with gay people is particularly aware of residual feelings of shame and embarrassment in even talking about issues of same-gender physical intimacy (R. Stein 1997). This shame and embarrassment may lead to identifications complementary to the analysand's sense of shame, manifest as slips, such as forgetting the name of the analysand's same-gender partner; reluctance to explore the meaning for the analysand of sexual experiences; or even concern about the possible problems for the analysand of acknowledging his or her sexual lifeway to others (Morrison 1999).

This perspective is well illustrated in a recent exchange between Trop and Stolorow (1992) and their critics (Blechner 1993; Lesser 1993; S. A. Mitchell 1992; D. Schwartz 1993a; Stolorow and Trop 1992, 1993). Trop and Stolorow reported a case in order to show the difference between the ways self psychologists and other analysts understand the means people use to protect themselves from the perceived danger of wishes. The case in part concerned a homosexual conflict expressed as repudiated conscious homosexual wishes. The analysand's narrative was similar to those reported by many gay men. It included having felt different since childhood, nontraditional gender interests, explicit homosexual wishes in adolescence and adulthood, and feelings of self-loathing. The homosexual wishes were interpreted as an effort to avoid feelings of worthlessness and to restore some sense of being alive. At termination of the analysis, the analysand reported an enhanced sense of himself as heterosexual.

The analyst, by endorsing a heterosexual perspective, supported the analysand's shame and self-criticism about homosexual wishes. The analyst clearly viewed heterosexuality as a superior outcome and found it difficult to be empathic with the analysand's homosexual desire. Frommer (1995) maintains that this shared sense of shame is reflected in the analyst's theory of the origins and "meaning" of sexual orientation for the analysand, which, like any preexisting theory, interferes with empathy and suggests complementary identifications (Racker 1968). While Stolorow and Trop (1992) maintain that the analyst merely saw the homosexual material as having meanings that needed to be understood, Blechner (1993), Lesser (1993), and D. Schwartz (1993a) disagree. Blechner (1993) calls attention to the analyst's clear antigay prejudice, which is reciprocal to the analysand's shame. The problem of the analyst's complementary identifications are compounded by the analysand's fragile adjustment and his idealization of the analyst.

Blechner argues that analyst and analysand were both responding to society's norms and joined in disavowing a significant aspect of the analysand's self. Lesser (1993) observes that the analyst was preoccupied with the analysand's interest in women and frankly encouraged his pursuit of them. She wonders why the analysand's homosexual desire was analyzed with the goal of diminishing interest in same-gender sexuality, while heterosexual desire was not subject to analytic scrutiny. D. Schwartz (1993a) notes further that psychoanalysts often overvalue intimate heterosexual relationships. They start with the presumption that same-gender intimacy has a defensive-reparative function while opposite-gender intimacy does not. The analysand's difficulties might best be understood as a struggle with never-affirmed same-gender desire.

In response to these critiques, Stolorow and Trop (1993) maintain that had the analysand been able to establish satisfying intimate relationships with partners of either gender, they would have formulated the case differently. The problem with this response is that the analyst identified so completely with the analysand's shame that he could not recognize and support this struggle for same-gender intimacy. Given the analyst's repeated indications that heterosexuality is desirable in response to the analysand's statement that with women he felt alive as never before, it might be maintained that the analysand was manifesting elements of a compliant here-and-now transference (Schafer 1982) reflecting a wish to please the analyst (S. A. Mitchell 1981). This rich exchange reflects the complexity of understanding in a context where assumptions about the origin of same-gender desire have been, at least partly, abandoned but shame about such desire remains significant for both analyst and analysand.

Self Psychological Perspectives on Psychoanalytic Intervention among Gay Men and Women

Self psychologists, starting with Heinz Kohut (1971), bring a new perspective to the study of the dynamics of same-gender sexual orientation (Cornett 1993, 1995; Gonsiorek and Rudolph 1991; Shelby 1994a, 1998). Noting that Freud's ([1921a] 1955, [1923] 1961) description of self-criticism in the structural theory did not explain aspects of the phenomena of shame and low self-esteem encountered in some analyses, Kohut posited that these states arise because early failures in the provision of care make maintaining a sense of personal integrity and vitality difficult throughout life. Subsequently this perspective was extended to include the recognition that across the entire life course others ordinarily function to support the self. The self psychological perspective is particularly useful in studying the self-criticism and disavowal often observed in analyses of gay people. In the first place, self psychological perspectives on personal distress focus less on the object of desire (Bollas 1992; Coen 1981; Khan 1979; H. Rich 1991) than on the role of the object in maintaining psychological vitality and warding off feelings of psychological vulnerability (Goldberg 1995). In addition, self psychologists view understanding self-criticism and shame as critical to restoring psychological vitality and integrity.

Its focus on the origins and consequence of self-criticism suggests that self psychological perspectives have particular relevance for psychoanalytic intervention with distressed gay and bisexual people. For example, homosexual cruising has often been portrayed as a classic instance of sexualization (Bollas 1992). However, cruising can also be a search for another to provide affirmation and companionship. Multiple trial encounters may be needed to define the characteristics of this good partner. The important factor in understanding the significance of sexuality for personal adjustment is less a concern with decoding the symbolic meanings of the events during an evening at a dance bar than the analysand's experience of this evening and the significance that emerges as analyst and analysand come increasingly to understand cruising encounters (Shelby 1994a). The psychological function of a manifest behavior may change over time so that what begins with sexualization is transformed into a search for an affirming person. Self psychology attempts to restore personal vitality and a sense of well-being by understanding how the analysand uses the analyst to enhance self-regard, through identification with the experience of the analyst's affirming support and assurance. Over time this leads to greater self-understanding, capacity to bear transitory increases in tension, increased capacity for solace, maintenance of sense of well-being, and an enhanced sense of personal integration and vitality.

> A young professional man had struggled since puberty to suppress homoerotic desires that he found particularly repugnant because they involved fantasies of controlling and being controlled by a sexual partner. His analyst's conviction that these longings made sense, even though he did not as yet understand their significance, led the patient to feel less ashamed and, for the first time, to go to a leather bar. His initial encounters there involved several people whose sexual desires did not mesh with his own. However, identifying with his analyst's openness and curiosity he was able to see the humanity of the people who wanted to engage in activities that held little appeal for him. He was even able to experience compassionate humor about a situation in which a man he had met wanted him to glowingly describe the man's genitalia and the patient wanted mostly to feel the man's "bearlike" embrace. In time, the patient began to experience the bar as a companionable place where, more important than meeting sexual partners, he could sit quietly and regulate the encounters he had with other people. The right to be uninterested in men who cruised him let him regulate interactions more successfully than he ever had before. He gradually became friendly with another regular at the bar, also a well-educated man with high ideals. Their erotic engagement was an aspect of their friendship, an entirely new experience for the analysand, and developed into his first experience of adult love.

Kohut and his associates (Elson 1986; Goldberg 1988, 1995; Kohut 1971, 1977, 1979, 1984; Kohut and Wolf 1978; Wolf 1988) have explored how people protect themselves from shame and embarrassment. A sense of per-

sonal coherence or integrity is commonly maintained through disavowal of
disturbing experiences and associated affects. Though the information that
an event occurred remains accessible to awareness, its significance and emotional impact are put aside. Disavowal, or vertical splitting, is a very common
means of protection against troubling thoughts or feelings that permits
people to go on with their lives despite knowing about grave realities, such
as ongoing war, poverty, personal limitation, and the inevitability of their
own deaths (Basch 1983; Goldberg 1999). For most people the issues involved are neither worked through nor repressed but exist in a split-off
awareness, which can be put aside almost all of the time. This same mechanism can be used to protect against less universal but equally disturbing experiences, such as having engaged in action the individual thinks of as immoral
or disgusting. Thus, when people engage in sexual acts of which they are
ashamed and which they cannot integrate into their self experiences, they
commonly disavow the experience. If they asked themselves whether it happened they know it did, but the question of how it fits with the rest of their
lives or how they feel about it remains carefully unaddressed.

In the safety of the analytic situation, created in part by the analyst's tact,
respect, and empathy, analysands can admit and speak of such experiences.
The dialogue with the analyst and, equally important, the admission to
themselves serve to reduce their sense of fragmentation as these disavowed
experiences are integrated as part of a more coherent life story.

Looking again at the issue of cruising, we note it is often associated with
feelings of self-criticism and shame (Shelby 1998; P. Lynch 1999). Many of
those engaged in this activity implicitly share the views of some analysts (Bollas 1992; Calef and Weinshel 1984; Khan 1979; H. Rich 1991) that it is
intrinsically demeaning and unsatisfactory because it substitutes fleeting sexual encounters for real intimacy. That very similar heterosexual behavior,
currently referred to as "hooking up" by late adolescents and young adults,
carries little of the self-condemnation, suggests that shame about cruising is
neither evidence of simple dissatisfaction with a substitute activity nor intrinsically masochistic. Rather this shame is in large measure a rationalized aspect
of the internalized hatred of same-gender attraction. The use of public places
such as men's rooms and parks for some of this activity should first be addressed in terms of the social realities of the participants before being explained by elaborate unconscious masochistic fantasies (Humphreys 1970).

Self psychological perspectives focus on cruising less as a route to sexual
satisfaction than as an effort to manage feelings of being overwhelmed,
empty, or fragmented. This focus naturally leads to consider why means
more congruent with the analysand's conception of self are not available.
One could also ask whether by cruising the analysand is making his internal

sense of shame about his erotic desires more concrete and angrily punishing himself for being unworthy and shameful (Lynch 1999). Analytic attention to cruising, particularly as a means to deal with feelings of depletion or threatened fragmentation while away from the analyst's soothing and protective presence, helps the analysand appreciate some of the meanings of the analyst and the analytic situation in his life. As Shelby (1998) notes, the analysand's accounts of cruising and associated affects reflect a deepening of the analytic process. The analysand's ability to speak in detail of this behavior suggests he has begun to feel safe enough to admit previously warded-off material into awareness and dialogue. The analysis of cruising allows access to disavowed affects and meanings and indications of important deficits in tension regulation.

The Psychological Use of Others

The need for solace and comfort, and for assistance in maintaining a sense of coherence and vitality, may be met in various ways over the course of life, but it is never absent. Disorders of the self may result from disturbances of self-object function not only in infancy but at any time in the life course (Wolf 1988; Cohler and Galatzer-Levy 1990; Galatzer-Levy and Cohler 1993; Gilbert 1994). Some find it difficult to let themselves make psychological use of others during times of distress. Some cannot obtain solace from the memory of the past experience of others. Adverse life changes may lead to transformations in the sense of self and others so intense as to interfere with existing abilities to find solace. However, most adults can rely on others for these functions and implicitly recognize that interdependence is expectable across the course of life, though its expression may be shaped by circumstances. One "curative" factor in psychoanalysis is the restoration of the capacity to appropriately use others to maintain a sense of personal integrity and vitality and to enlarge this capacity through interpretation of reactions to disappointments and frustrations in the analysis.

Self psychology has reconsidered the origins and course of personal distress in terms of the self and its supports. For example, Wolf (1988) understands most neurosis as resulting not from conflicted wishes of the oedipal period but from failures of the experienced caretaker of the preschool years to modulate this conflict. This view is consistent with Kohut's (1977, 1984) observation that the transition from early to middle childhood, marked by the appearance and resolution of the nuclear conflict, need not be a source of disturbance and becomes problematic only as a result of the failure to support the expectable assertiveness and sexuality of the preschool and early school-aged child. Kohut argues that the primary source of personal distress lies in the inability to provide adequate means for supporting the self. These issues can become the focus of the analytic process. This view contrasts with ego and drive psychological formulations, which posit an inevitable conflict between wish, sense of reality, and internalized social values as the root of psychopathology (Brenner 1982).

The psychological conflict perspective assumes that the primary goal of pathology is the disguise of wish and intent while providing gratification (A. Freud [1936] 1946). From this perspective, the goal of analysis is to bring these conflicts into awareness in their full emotional intensity so that they may be reworked in light of the present reality. The analysand is assumed to resist recognition of wish and intent in order to insure continued partial satisfaction of repressed wishes and avoid the anxiety that conscious aware-ness of them would bring. Thus, analysis is a continuing struggle between the analyst and the analysand's mature ego, on one hand, and the forces of repression and disguised infantile gratification, on the other. The ambiance in the analytic setting may be best characterized as respectful warfare.

Self psychology views analysands as doing their best to maintain a sense of integrity and vitality. Psychological symptoms may best be characterized as failures to maintain this sense or efforts to maintain it that substantially inter-fere with other aspects of living. Since the sense of self is maintained through relations with others, much symptomatology manifest in this area involves the vicissitudes of maintaining relationships. (Note that "relationships" here refers to an intrapsychic happening, of which interpersonal relations may be one manifestation.) This understanding leads to a different attitude in lis-tening, but it does not, as some analysts mistakenly believe, imply that self psychologists hold that kindness cures. From the point of view of conflict psychology, the assumption that patients mean something close to what they say is an error. While recognizing that attempts to protect against psycholog-ical pain may lead some people to disguise feelings and intents from them-selves and others, self psychology does not hold that people inevitably are trying to hide their real intents. These different understandings of the patient naturally engender different attitudes and responses in the analyst.

Self psychology's most important contribution to psychoanalysis is this emphasis on the continuing use of others in a psychological function across the course of life. Most obvious in the first year of life, self-object or essential other relationships continue more subtly across the life course, providing a sense of coherence and vigor of the self (Winnicott [1960a] 1965, 1960b; Stechler and Kaplan 1980; Galatzer-Levy and Cohler, 1993). To the extent that young children receive "good enough" care, the caregiving fosters a sense that the world is "good enough," and the child develops optimism and a sense of effectiveness. In the process of "transmuting internalization," manageable fluctuation in caregiver's provision for needs allow the individual to take in capacities to perform for themselves what was previously done by others. If, however, because caregivers lack attunement or empathy with the young child's needs, caretaking is not "good enough," the child is likely to grow pessimistic, feel ineffective, and find tension states difficult to deal with.

Whether caretakers are good enough depends on both caretaker and child. Babies clearly differ in their temperament and in their ability to be quieted, just as caregivers vary in their capacity for providing this care. Also, caregivers' abilities to remain attuned to a child's needs vary over time, depending, for example, on what other issues demand their attention. The caregiver's emotional state clearly interplays with the child's temperament in determining the child's experience of the availability of the caretaker and so the child's experience of vitality and integrity.

The problem is not in the need for essential others but in the extent to which others fail to provide a sense of organizing vitality or in problematic feelings toward essential others. Self-object functions continue across the course of life, although their form varies with maturity (Galatzer-Levy and Cohler 1993). However, much of the study of self-object functioning has focused on the immature and disturbed modes of experiencing others associated with personal distress.

Varieties of Self-Object Transferences

Children who receive caregiving that is not "good enough" (Winnicott 1960b) experience the deficits as their failures and not those of the caregiver. For example, an external observer might describe a mother as preoccupied with a loss in her own life or with career issues and so not remaining attuned to her baby. This is likely to be experienced by the baby as a deficit in its capacity for tension regulation. This deficit is subsequently experienced as a sense of depletion or inner deadness, lack of creativity, and experience of feeling overwhelmed. Psychotherapy has a restorative function first through the therapist's very concern and effort to empathically understand the patient's distress (Kohut 1984), and then through the emergence of enactments such as idealization of the therapist, identification with the therapist, mirroring-merger enactments designed to obtain the therapist's appreciation and recognition, and twinship or alter-ego enactments that use the therapist to supply a missing function (Elson 1986; Wolf 1988).

De Monteflores (1986) suggest that being the object of stigma may exacerbate the experience of deficit in disorders of the self. As a result particular effort is required to foster a sense of trust in people who are members of sexual (or ethnic) minorities, so increased congruence of ethnicity, gender, and sexual orientation of therapist and client are desirable.

The self-object transferences are manifestations of continuing needs for archaic self-objects which result from failures to internalize early self-object functions. The therapist is experienced not as an independent individual but as an aspect of the self. His self-object function seems essential to the patient's continued psychological existence. These needs are defended against, both because of the danger of repeated self-object failures and because of their potential interference with whatever means the patient has found for stabilizing his self. Usually denial, disavowal, and splitting are the principle defenses employed.

Kohut (1971) divided the self-object transferences into two major groups: "mirror transferences" involved the stabilization of the grandiose self, while "idealizing transferences" involved the self-object functioning as part of the ideal self. Generally self-object transferences are silent when they are functioning effectively. In this silent phase they provide the patient with missing functions necessary to sustain the self. This "silence" is in marked contrast with the fully engaged transference neurosis in which ever more explicit and explicitly frustrated transference longings lead to intense distress. For the patient whose psychopathology is primarily related to a disorder of the self, distress is felt only when the self-object fails. Two typical such failures are disruptions in continuity (e.g., weekend or vacation interruption) or breaks in empathy (e.g., the therapist's inevitable failure to appreciate the significance of a particular external event). Kohut's initial distinction between the various self-object transferences is conceptually useful but inconsistent with clinical observations. The transferences tend to merge, with one or another aspect dominating at a given moment. To be an adequate mirror of grandiosity, the mirroring person must be admirable. Similarly, merger with an idealized object results in feelings of grandeur.

THE IDEALIZING TRANSFERENCES.   In the idealizing transferences the therapist is viewed as the incarnation of strength, goodness, and power. Through his relation to the idealized therapist, the patient feels vigorous, good, and whole. Initially idealization tends to be coarse. Aspects of the therapist such as appearance, manner of speech, and office décor may be included in the idealization. As a result of working through, the idealization becomes increasingly specific and related to the patient's needs. Appreciation of the nondefensive idealizing transference is an instance of the expanded possibilities associated with self psychology theory. Therapists who believe that all transferences are aspects of the nuclear neurosis are bound to interpret manifest idealization as a disguise for underlying competition. Self psychological perspectives point to the possibility of other motives than defense against competition.

THE MIRROR TRANSFERENCES. Kohut (1971) described three overlapping forms of mirror transference—merger transference, alter-ego transference, and mirror transference proper. In the merger transference the patient's grandiose self is supported by the idea of a single entity, the analyst-patient ("We are great!"). The alter-ego transference is characterized by the fantasy that patient and analyst share a worldview as twins who are well and good because they are the same. In the mirror transference proper, the patient feels well because of the therapist's appreciative response to his grandiosity. He can experience his own glory confidently, as it is reflected back to him by the therapist.

COMPLEMENTARY COUNTERTRANSFERENCES. Among Kohut's most important contributions to the study of the psychoanalytic process was his focus on the quality of the analytic relationship and on understanding the place of empathic processes. Freud addressed this issue, but more recent contributions had portrayed the therapeutic alliance as the silent carrier of the psychoanalytic process (Greenson 1965; Zetzel 1958). Kohut brought rapport into focus as a central aspect of the psychoanalytic process. The analyst's anxieties may interfere with this rapport. Transferences involving nuclear conflicts may stimulate complementary countertransferences in the analyst (e.g., the analyst may become competitive with the patient). Idealizing transferences may be less than optimally managed when the analyst, overstimulated by the idealization, fails to recognize them. Some analysts confront analysands with "reality" or question the need to idealize, or idealizations may be mistakenly and prematurely interpreted, usually as a resistance against recognizing the analysand's hostility. These efforts impede emergence and resolution of the transference, and may lead to interruption of treatment as the analysand is forced to search elsewhere for idealized objects.

Another major error is the use of such idealizations to make oneself a model for the analysand. This is particularly a temptation among gay and lesbian analysts who have succeeded in establishing affirmative identities and believe that their analysands should work out their own destiny in a similar way. Offering oneself as a source of idealization may forestall analysands' working through their own feelings toward sexual orientation and personal goals. This leaves the analysand with the analyst's aspirations and thus may lead to a greater sense of personal incoherence. When idealized transferences become the explicit focus of shared study of analyst and analysand, analysands can develop ideas beyond those of their analysts without necessarily rejecting their analyst's important contributions. When the analyst believes an idealization is deserved, the analysand may come to believe that the analyst actually possesses some marvelous quality that the analysand can find nowhere else, for example, some wisdom about leading the good life. This interferes with recognition and resolution of idealizing transferences.

Mirror transferences may be expressed as a desire on the part of the analysand for a sexual relationship with the analyst. The experience of being as one through the analyst's anal penetration or through masturbating together may enter into the analysand's fantasies and is often expressed with much shame. S. Shapiro (1985) describes this mirroring response on the part of an analysand who sought closeness through such sexual encounters.

Commonly, analysts respond to mirroring transferences with discomfort at being treated as part of another's self, as without independent will. Boredom, fatigue, and emotional withdrawal, perhaps alternating with feelings of discouragement with the progress of the analysis, are common when chronically (and, often, coercively) treated as though one's purpose for being is satisfaction of the analysand's self-object needs. The gay or lesbian analysand's heightened sensitivity to the emotional responses of others, the consequence of long-term experiences of shame and stigma, may lead to a reciprocal disengagement in which analyst and analysand both feel apart from their relationship (Morrison and Stolorow 1997).

Analysts often deal with the distress of being treated as an extension of the analysand through increased therapeutic activism, for example, elaborate interpretation, confrontations, or suggestions that demonstrate to the analyst that the analyst is still alive. It is common for the analyst, with the conscious motive of improving the analysand's interpersonal relations, to sermonize about the importance of treating others as people in their own right. Pejorative diagnostic labels, such as "borderline" or "primitive object relations," may be attached to analysands who are particularly strident in their demand that the analyst function as a mirroring self-object.

Another group of countertransference responses involves manifest fears that the analysand's grandiosity will become unmanageable or intolerable. Interpretations are replaced with "emergency" educational measures or prohibitions designed to prevent the analysand from damaging himself and others. Particularly with gay analysands, whose sexual activity may entail health risks, there is often the desire to caution or to give advice regarding risky actions. Being acquainted with the current medical literature, the analyst may believe it necessary to caution the analysand or to give advice. The analyst's own incompletely analyzed grandiosity may be stimulated to such an extent that he tries to convince the analysand that he appreciates external reality better than the analysand. Generally, such measures only lead the analysand to feel out of control and evoke increased disorganization. There is, on the other hand, a group of patients whose psychological state might be likened to a chronic tantrum, who indeed need to be firmly and calmly held psychologically because they continue to create escalating difficulties for themselves. It sometimes brings these patients considerable relief to be forbidden self-destructive enactments. The therapist's position in such cases differs from the countertransference-determined response described here in that the patient usually has a long history of genuinely dangerous behavior and the therapist does not experience a pressing urgency when making these interventions.

The most effective therapeutic strategy at such times may be recognition and acceptance of the analysand's need for mirroring. This understanding leads analysands to a stabilized sense of self and, as a consequence, both increases their capacity to understand how others may be psychologically used to provide stability of self and decreases the urgency of action. This acknowledgment of the need for mirroring may be the most effective means of assisting the analysand to engage in safer sex. Since risky actions may be in response to issues not yet acknowledged and discussed within the therapeutic relationship, focus on the analysand's experience of the therapeutic relationship may provide the most effective means of fostering the analysand's sense of personal integrity and, as a consequence, increased desire to provide good self-care (Cohler 1999a, 1996).

A third group of responses involves efforts to directly satisfy the analysand's transference needs. Most analysts would regard this as a distortion of the psychoanalytic process, but leading clinical theorists like Ferenczi and Winnicott ([1960a] 1965) have regarded them as essential in work with certain types of patients. Activities such as literally holding (Little 1981) or feeding (Sechehaye 1951) patients, inviting them to community or social functions, or proffering books and articles, even if without explicit intimate elements, are intended to provide supplies which the analysand had missed earlier in life. The belief that the analyst can provide "reparenting" reflects the analyst's wish to undo past deprivations. This often results from a fantasy that the analyst's own defective development can be remedied in similar fashion. Strachey (1934) observed that interpretations were the best feed. Rephrased in the language of self psychology, maintenance of an empathic situation in which the analysand feels understood and appreciated, with assistance in recognizing the variety of ways in which the analyst may be used to support an enfeebled self, is the best means of helping the analysand to overcome feelings of vulnerability and helplessness. From this perspective, therapists who become sexually involved with patients are often attempting to magically and concretely provide for the narcissistic needs of the patient. At the same time they reflect the therapist's rage at the patient, which leads to the enactment taking a destructive form and a sexualized attempt to reassert the vigor of the therapist's self in a context where (the often seriously narcissistically depleted therapist) feels particularly unresponded to.

Self-object transferences may challenge the analyst by evoking overstimulation or feelings associated with lack of mirroring responses. As in the analysis of drives and conflicts, where countertransference responses arise based on the analyst's unresolved nuclear neurosis, it is essential that the analyst have adequately worked through issues involving the self for countertransference responses not to interfere with an empathic stance towards the analysand.

The curative elements of psychoanalysis are understood differently in self psychology than in more traditional psychoanalytic approaches. Analysts have long maintained that new psychological structure is laid down through internalization of psychological functions in response to object loss (Freud [1923] 1961; Schafer 1960, 1968). Kohut (1971, 1977, 1984) maintained that the process of cure in disorders of the self occurred as new psychological structure was realized through nontraumatic interruption of the analysand's disrupted capacity for using others for self-object functions.

Using the analyst's empathic understanding to foster awareness of the impact of even minor frustrations on his or her morale, the analysand grows increasingly able to provide self-regulation. In treatment, after working through the resistance to awareness of the analyst's significance, the analysand begins to use the analyst more effectively and with lessened disavowal, as a "self-object." When, as is inevitable, the analyst fails in his self-object function for the analysand, the analysand, supported by the analyst's empathic comprehension of this failure (Goldberg 1988), develops increasing capacity for managing such disappointments without the loss of spontaneity and vigor of the self, a process Kohut called "transmuting internalization." Functions that were performed by the external self-object are now taken on by the analysand.

Self Perspectives Regarding Intervention among Gay Men and Women

Several factors have led to a focus in contemporary psychoanalysis on the experience of self and others: changes in the social context of psychoanalysis since the Second World War, the advent of interest in early childhood and antecedents then of the experience of self, and the metaphorical use of childhood as a means of understanding the origins of personal distress. Regardless of whether this focus is portrayed as object relations theory (Winnicott [1951] 1953, 1958, [1960a] 1965, 1960b; Guntrip 1971; Summers 1994), relational psychology (Greenberg and Mitchell 1983; S. A. Mitchell 1988, 1993a), or self psychology (Kohut 1971, 1977, 1984), the concern is with factors that interfere with maintenance of a sense of integrity or congruence, and with the collaborative construction by analyst and analysand of a life story or "working model" which more effectively and comfortably integrates wish and experience across a lifetime than the story told by the patient at the outset of treatment (Freud [1909c] 1955).

Accompanying the elaboration of this concern with self, others, and experience, there has been a shift in the therapist's perspective on therapy. While issues of competition initiated in early childhood conflict with the parent retained analysts' attention—both the "positive" constellation, described by Freud as the nuclear neurosis, and the "negative" or "inverted" form emphasized by Isay (1989) as an explanation for psychic conflict among gay men—maintenance of personal integrity and coherence also became an major focus in psychoanalysis. This focus has specific relevance for study and intervention among men and women whose sexual orientation is different from the majority.

Recognition of the importance of the experience of integrity and congruence for continued mental health across the course of life is central to self psychological perspectives (Fairbairn 1952; Winnicott [1951] 1953, 1958, 1960a; Kohut [1959] 1978, 1971, 1977, 1984). This focus need not contradict more traditional psychoanalytic perspectives focusing on the family romance and consequent concerns with issues of competition, envy, and rivalry. However, recent perspectives do question the assumption of a primary aggressive drive or instinct and tend to see aggression as reactive to failures of affirmation (Guntrip 1971). They also question the assumption, prevalent in Western European and American psychology and social thought, that individuality and autonomy is the goal of psychological development. Rather, concern is with the role of an experienced other as the foundation for a continued sense of coherence. Kohut has observed:

> Each person has his own favorite ways of dealing with the world. Certainly it is fully compatible with mental health to be, under stress, capable of turning toward another person and confiding in him and, as it were, merging in and with him, allowing his comparative strength temporarily to infuse oneself. It is an irrational or pre-rational kind of mechanism, but a very important one. . . . An arm over the shoulder, physical closeness, or quietly sitting next to one another has its place in certain trying moments in life . . . one has to choose somebody with whom one has ties of friendship. One must be capable of tolerating the delay until one reaches somebody with whom this kind of appeal for pre-rational support is an appropriate one. (Kohut 1987, 84–85)

While Freud ([1909a] 1955, [1913] 1958), Schafer (1968a), Meissner (1981), and others have discussed the foundations of the capacity to use the memory of others as an aspect of adjustment, much of this inquiry has been focused on the use of this capacity as an outcome of mourning following a loss, including that expectable as a child moves off into the larger world of school and community. This perspective assumes that the problem in psychological development is one of becoming differentiated from others and maintaining a sense of personal autonomy (E. Jacobson 1964; Mahler, Pine, and Bergman 1975). Kohut's (1971) important reformulation of this concept, however, regards continuing close relationships with others, not as a narcissistic failure to attain psychological autonomy, but as a lifelong source of sustenance and support. This support fosters enhanced congruence and integrity, referred to as self-object functions, or as termed by Galatzer-Levy and Cohler (1993), the "essential (experienced) other." Problems arise only when persons are unable to take advantage of this support, or when support is not sustaining or fulfilling. Self psychological perspectives suggest that, initially, the child experiences the care provided by others as care provided for oneself (Cohler 1980).

Kohut (1977, 1979) has questioned whether in psychoanalysis we have a bias toward outcomes which emphasize increased capacity for intimate relationships. It may well be that the analysand's own goals as they emerge in the course of collaborative work focus primarily on realizing an enhanced capacity for creativity rather than on intimacy. Overall, the goal should be to create conditions which foster an enhanced sense of personal vitality and well-being without specific regard for the therapist's own values. Increasing attention should be paid to the therapist's awareness, gained through continuing self-inquiry, of factors which interfere in maintaining an empathic attitude toward the analysand and which interfere in the analysand's experience of the analyst as an aid to restoration of personal integrity (Gardner 1983).

Kohut has explicitly related this changed conception of narcissism as a new mode of understanding intimate relationships. Writing about sexuality and this function of the other used as a means of providing enhanced personal integration, Kohut observes:

> There are some types of heterosexual relationships which are highly narcissistic, and there are some very developed homosexual relationships in which the partner is very much recognized as an individual in his own right. There are stable long-term relationships among homosexuals in which the partner is recognized and loved very much as an independent human being who is permitted a certain degree of being different from oneself. And there is no love relationship in which the partner is totally permitted to be different. (1987, 29–30)

The capacity to use the experienced other as a means for reducing tension and enhancing personal integration is critical for maintenance of adjustment. One the foremost concerns of psychoanalytic psychotherapy should be to foster the further development of this capacity for providing supports of the self through relationships with others, memory of past experience, and activities which provide a sense of personal vitality and involvement.

For example, Greenson (1971) portrays a British RAF flier downed in the English Channel during the Second World War. While awaiting his rescuers, this flier recalled strains of a nursery rhyme which his Flemish mother sang to comfort him in early childhood. This comforted him. The capacity to use his experience of early parental care as a source of soothing and comfort was important in maintaining psychological equilibrium until help could arrive. Similarly, we all use the experience of remembered past care and concern as sustenance during times of distress.

There have been at least five reports on the significance of self psychological perspectives in psychotherapy with homosexual men and women, in addition to Kohut's initial report of Mr. Z. (Kohut 1979), in which the patient's brief homosexual relationship with a camp counselor was understood as part of a desire for acceptance within the context of a mirroring relationship. S. Shapiro (1985) reported on the emergence of a mirroring transference in the lengthy analysis of a middle-aged bisexual man who resolved his homosexual wishes and improved his marriage; here homosexuality was regarded as a sexualization and a reflection of fragmentation resolved through analysis of the mirroring transference. De Monteflores (1986) reported on psychotherapy with a Hispanic lesbian woman in which an idealizing transference was understood in terms of the therapist's similarity in terms of ethnicity and sexual orientation as acknowledged to the patient. Magid (1993) reviewed Freud's ([1920] 1955) case of a homosexual woman whose infatuation with an older woman was understood as a "sexualized breakdown product" of expectable adolescent needs for mirroring and idealization. Cornett (1993) reported in detail on the use of self psychological perspectives in the treatment of gay men, in which issues of personal integration and self-affirmation appeared as paramount.

In what is perhaps the most detailed report on the use of self psychological perspectives in psychotherapeutic intervention with gay men, Shelby (1997) reported on his work as a publicly acknowledged gay therapist with a man who shared many of the characteristics of those now middle-aged men who came of age in the epoch after the Stonewall riots of 1969 and the resulting emergence of gay liberation. Sexually active but, like the rest of this cohort before the mid-1980s, unaware of the transmission of HIV, Mr. G. became HIV-positive. Shelby described his work helping his client first to mourn the loss of his partner to AIDS and then to use the experience of this loss as a source of strength. This period of mourning was marked by times when the client began to fall apart psychologically; personal fragmentation was expressed in terms of functioning in a world which "no longer made sense." As the client recovered from his acute grief following his partner's death, he became increasingly anxious about his growing dependence on his therapist.

Focusing on the client's mirroring transference and his bid for merger with the therapist, an eroticized transference which also reflected the client's place within a highly psychologically enmeshed immigrant family, Shelby helped Mr. G. foster an enhanced sense of personal stability and vitality. Gradually, the client could begin to talk about past disappointments, particularly those involving the failure of family members to recognize or admire his artistic efforts. Feeling his therapist's appreciation for his struggles led the client to characterize the therapist as the gay uncle he wished had been available as a source of strength in his childhood. The client began to express increased curiosity about his therapist, his lifestyle and partnership status, and, all reflecting a mirroring transference, trying to use his therapist's life as the foundation for a more stable self-structure. Ultimately, he met another man, also HIV-positive, and began to rebuild his fragile sense of self as a coherent self. He expressed an interest in learning new skills, began to reconsider childhood and adolescent memories which suggested that he had been both more competent and more highly regarded than he had previously acknowledged to himself, and renewed contact with old high school friends, including several who were gay. Most significantly, he established a close tie with a nephew who idolized him and connected anew with other family members, who he discovered were indeed appreciative of his achievements.

Interpretation of this mirroring-idealizing "gay uncle" transference, an expression of the client's wish for someone to mediate between father and son and to assure the parents that it was alright to be gay, enabled the client to reintegrate split-off aspects of self, bolstered by the therapist's appreciation of his client's strengths and support of a view of sexual pleasure as an important and positive aspect of life (Shelby 1994a, 74). Solomon (1997) comments on the parallel between the "gay uncle" transference and Mr. G's creation of a relationship with an admiring nephew. Solomon notes that lack of affirming parental responsiveness (perhaps because the father is frightened off by his preschool son's positive erotic tie) leads to expression of a deficit within the therapeutic situation in terms of an idealizing transference. Sexualization of the transference may be a first self-protective effort as the analysand begins to experience the pull of this idealization and the emerging importance of the analyst as a stabilizing figure in his life. Clearly, the analysand's experience of the analyst must remain a focus of collaborative effort, and interpretation of the analysand's wish for an idealizing-mirroring transference fosters the analysand's enhanced self-understanding and ability to make sense of disturbing feelings arising in response to the discovery of the importance of the analyst as a stabilizing function in his life.

The Sexual Partner as Self-Object

Self psychology has struggled to make sense of same-gender sexual orientation. Kohut tried to understand the selection of a sexual partner of the same gender in terms of what was then termed a narcissistic resolution, noting that this term should not carry with it a pathological connotation (Elson 1987; Tolpin and Tolpin 1996). What Kohut had in mind was that selecting a partner of the same gender involved an attempt to complete the sense of self. Generally, across the course of life all people form relationships with evoked or essential others as a means of fostering personal integrity or congruence (Galatzer-Levy and Cohler 1993; Shelby 1994). Thus, choice of a same-gender partner serves fundamentally the same purpose as any object choice. More mature self-object ties are those which endure in the absence of the loved one and lead to enhanced self-valuation beyond the immediate physical and social encounter. They also involve the integration of more forms of satisfaction into the relationship.

Self psychology provides an important means for understanding mirroring, idealizing, and twinship phenomena in relationships. Paradoxically, little has been written about mature self-object relations, and when there has been consideration of these issues, it has generally involved exploring same-gender sexual preference in the context of perversion (S. Shapiro 1985; Goldberg 1995). These presentations describe men who use homosexual activity to protect against fragmentation of the self. Because sex provides stimulation that relieves the unremitting pressure of a sense of personal depletion, sexuality assumes particular importance among psychologically fragile persons who fear personal collapse.

Shapiro's (1985) reported an archaic transference in a middle-aged man. This man searched for an idealization of another man, first experienced with a favorite uncle in childhood. The patient had slept with this uncle, who deserted him during the transition from early to middle childhood. He attempted to recapture this experience in transient, illicit affairs with other men. This needed relationship was repeated in the transference, in which he viewed the analyst as his "lifeline." When he felt his analyst was insufficiently responsive, he would find a partner for a homosexual affair who would provide him with the acknowledgment and response he felt missing within the analytic relationship. Goldberg's discussion of perversions also refers to same-gender sexuality in terms of cases such as that of "Jan" who nightly, desper-

ately, cruised local parks in search of other men for anonymous sex. At points
when he felt disappointed in the idealizing transference with his analyst, his
cruising intensified.

As Isay (1989) has observed, desperately driven or disorganized sexual activity may signify serious psychological disturbance. However, the question
must always be the meaning for an analysand of all aspects of wish and intention, including sexuality. It is important not to presume that one form
of sexual expression is "normal" and another a perversion (Schafer 1995).
Rather, it is important to understand all forms of sexual expression in terms
of their meaning within the life story constructed collaboratively within the
analysis. This alternative perspective is well reflected in Shelby's (1994) account of enactments among gay men seen in psychoanalytic psychotherapy.
One patient sought big, burly partners as a means of providing the masculinity he had been criticized by his family for lacking in childhood. Work with
this person's feelings of lowered self-esteem led him to find a more appropriate and attentive partner who did not have to display stereotypic prowess.

"Cruising" and the Search for Personal Vitality

Few aspects of same-gender sexual orientation elicit such intense controversy as the search for anonymous or "recreational" sex. Though such activity is associated with all sexual preferences, it has been particularly noted
among gay men. Anonymous sex in the back rooms of bars, pornographic
bookstores, parks, or public rest rooms ("tearooms") is commonly described
as a search for erotic pleasure. The extent of opprobrium expressed by the
mental health professions and the larger community alike is puzzling. First,
both gay and straight young adults in contemporary society are likely to regard sexuality in a more casual manner than those previous cohorts (Bollas
1992). The singles bars of the straight community are little different in function from those within the gay community. Gay and straight men and
women alike take advantage of these social arenas in their developmentally
appropriate exploration of partnership and intimacy. Second, the use of sexuality in the search for a sense of excitement and vitality as a means to escape
feelings of depletion is little different among straight and gay men and
women.

Finally, for some this activity may represent an enactment of the sense of
self-hatred engendered by internalization of society's disapproval of same-
gender desire. Anonymous sex in public places is potentially dangerous because of surveillance for illegal or illicit activity, failure to use good judgment
regarding safer sex, and involvement in activities pleasurable only because
debasing. Psychoanalytically informed discussion of cruising most often de-

scribes this activity in terms either of the dynamics associated with failure to resolve the nuclear conflict or as an effort to overcome a sense of depletion depression associated with particular psychological fragility and effort of an enfeebled self to regain coherence.

Khan (1979) proposed that cruising is, for a homosexual man, an archaic response to regressive yearnings accompanied by primitive, sadistic desires to retaliate against another man's sexuality, which unconsciously represent a wish to attack the alternatively seductive and emotionally unavailable mother who impinged on his emerging sense of self. Continuing this idea Coen (1981) and H. Rich (1991) both view cruising as an overvaluing of sexuality used as a (regressive) defense against acknowledgment of painful affects or psychological conflict, or even as the enactment of maternal seduction during early childhood. Coen described the situation of a man in his late twenties, completing analysis but feeling that his analyst was pushing him out. This feeling was dealt with by increased homosexual fantasies and vague efforts at telephone sex and finding a gay escort.

This sexualization reflected a recycling (Schlessinger and Robbins 1983) of affects and associated enactments from earlier in the analysis when this analysand had fantasized that his analyst was on the other end of the telephone and that he was attempting to elicit his analyst's interest through sexual arousal. This effort was associated with the experience of a mother who was depressed and emotionally unavailable but who used bodily stimulation to counter her depletion depression. Fear of his incestuous wishes, together with anger at his alternatively seductive and withdrawn mother was played out anew in the transference in which the analyst became the unavailable sexualized mother of early childhood.

Thus, sexual behavior and fantasy may be used as a defense against incestuous wishes arising from early experiences of having been used by a depressed mother who acted seductively in an effort to feel alive. The child identifies with and internalizes this mode of defense in order to maintain a tie with his mother (Khan 1979; Schafer 1968a). As Coen observes, "Sexual seductiveness then becomes the child's predominant mode for relating to others and for expressing his intense object hunger" (1981, 509). Bollas (1992) also viewed cruising as an enactment of earlier experienced impingement by the powerfully and personally absorbing mother, which leaves the child with no sense of private self. Search for an anonymous sexual encounter, sometimes disavowed even as it is taking place, reflects a dreamlike effort to recreate "the homosexual's experience of cumulative moment when he feels erased by the mother's usage of him as her 'it' within her own fantasy world. . . . [The homosexual intimate stranger] represents this mother in the arena when he seeks a stranger for it-to-it erotics" (1992, 153).

This focus on the meaning of cruising as an enactment of deficits experienced in the infantile maternal tie contrasts with formulations that view cruising as an enactment of wishes stemming from unresolved aspects of the nuclear conflict. In that formulation men and women wish to rob and murder the same-gender parent and feel guilt and a need for reparation through offering themselves as sexual objects (Calef and Weinshel 1984).

Shelby (1998) questions the tradition of understanding cruising enactments in terms of the meaning of the partner rather than the significance for oneself. Reporting on his therapeutic work with men and women seeking such encounters, and following Goldberg's (1995) discussion of nonnormative sexual behavior enacted in response to aspects of the therapeutic situation, Shelby urged consideration less of the significance of the object of the cruising than of the self state of the person who is cruising and of the adaptive significance of such enactments either in providing a sense of excitement and aliveness in a world otherwise experienced as depleted or in satisfying wishes for admiration by an anonymous partner. Shelby notes that cruising may be associated with enactments related to the inevitable disappointments and frustrations of breaks in the analytic situation over weekends and holidays. Further, consistent with Lynch's (1999) observation, cruising provides further justification for self-criticism in response to being gay.

Self Psychology and Complementary Identifications in the Analysis of Gay Men and Women

Discussion of the analyst's contribution to the analytic relationship is among the most complex and emotion-laden issues in the psychoanalytic literature. While Freud was humane and honest in his discussion of his relationship with his analysands (Lipton 1977, 1988), discussion of the analyst's response to the analysand has been beclouded both by a more traditional view that the analysand brings material to the analytic process which is then interpreted and by a view which has emphasized the extent to which the analyst's own experience of the analysand might interfere with the course of the analysis. More recently, influenced by developments in criticism (Bakhtin 1986), Schafer (1992), Cohler and Freeman (1993), and others have portrayed analysis as a dialogic process to which the analysand brings a particular life story which is then revised through a collaboration in which both analysand and analyst are active.

To date, and particularly since Anne Reich's (1951) contribution, much of this discussion of the analyst's experience of the relationship has been subsumed under the term countertransference. Racker (1968) has differentiated between complementary and concordant identifications, with the complementary identifications with the analysand evoked as a consequence of the failure of concordant identifications or empathy. As Kohut ([1959] 1978) and Schafer (1959) note, the capacity to remain attuned to the analysand's experience and to use vicarious introspection as a means of tasting this experience (Fliess 1944, 1953) fosters a lively encounter in which the analyst's attitude is reflected in the effort to understand, which may be a central curative dynamic in the psychoanalytic process.

The question then remains of the nature of the therapist's experience and response in the analysis of gay, lesbian, and bisexual analysands. As Shelby (1994a) observes, sexual orientation cannot be separated from other aspects of self-organization. The experience of sexual orientation is part of the totality of the analysand's experience of self. Issues of stigma and of internalized heterosexism complicate both the analysand's enactments and the analyst's experience of these enactments. Cornett (1995), Isay (1989, 1996a), and Shelby (1994a) note that as a consequence of experiences of stigma or heterosexism, the gay or lesbian analysand may be particularly sensitive to the analyst's own experience of sexuality and may be particularly likely to experience fragmentation, evoked even by the expectable momentary fluctuations of the therapist's attentive listening. Further, the analysand's long-term experience of marginality may make particular demands on the analyst's own sense of authenticity and honest response when confronted by the analysand's personal struggles and often intense sense of shame (Morrison 1989, 1999). The analyst must be able to maintain continuing self-inquiry to remain fully responsive and attuned when confronted by the demands of the analysand for such authenticity, and willing to acknowledge lapses in empathy which would be less of a problem for an analysand with a more robust, less stigmatized sense of self.

Conclusion

Focus on issues of self and realization of a sense of personal integrity both complements and extends other perspectives within psychoanalysis concerned with fostering enhanced experience of personal vitality through increased self-understanding. Lifelong issues of stigma and experience of anti-gay prejudice may become part of the sense of self experienced by gay women and men. Issues of shame, often supported by analysand, family, and community, adversely impact self-esteem over a lifetime. Disappointment that others have not been able to respond affirmatively to the analysand's bid for support in realizing an enhanced sense of self, as true to feelings and wishes; the experience of loss, particularly within the cohort of middle-aged men and women struggling with the death of partners and friends from the

AIDS pandemic; and the struggle to understand a life course that is not clearly charted and expectable within the larger community, all become issues properly addressed in psychoanalysis and psychodynamic psychotherapy.

The perspective of self psychology reflects enduring issues not always as fully recognized in approaches seeking to assist personally distressed gay men and women: attention by analyst and analysand alike to the manner in which the analysand experiences the therapist, concern with realizing affirmation from another experienced as idealized, and the search for an enhanced sense of personal integrity and vitality. This perspective focuses on the combination of family and community stigma that lead to compromised capacity for positive self-regard and appreciation, which is essential in realizing a continuing sense of well-being and positive morale. Psychoanalytic work with these stigmatized gay men and women, when it fosters both grieving the past and reconciliation with disappointments and losses of a lifetime, can facilitate realization of enhanced ability to maintain self-regard. As a consequence of attention to these issues of disappointment and failure of others as the support of personal regard, the analysand is helped to make more effective use of others and to realize more complete development of personal integrity.

Conclusion

Toward a Developmental Perspective on Gay and Lesbian Lives

The Context of the Present Book

This book integrates findings from the study of biological hypotheses about the origins of same-gender sexual orientation, the course of development from early childhood to oldest age, relations of gay and lesbian parents and their offspring, adjustment of offspring of gay and lesbian parents, mental health of gay and lesbian adults, including factors relevant to the emergence of personal distress, and implications of a developmental perspective on homosexuality for psychoanalytic intervention.

We found that nonnormative expression of sexual desire and same-gender sexual orientation has little relationship to adjustment or experience of personal distress. Social theory and study of the lives of gay and straight men and women converge to show that the experience of sexual desire is not fixed but varies across the course of life. Sexual orientation should not be viewed from an essentialist perspective that regards sexual desire as predetermined by either innate or developmental factors; sexual desire is fluid and changing in its significance for society and persons over historical time and in lived experience within lifetimes. Little is known about factors leading to either heterosexuality or homosexuality. The meaning of same-gender desire is founded in social and historical circumstances which change over time and across generations or cohorts. Social contexts and personal life circumstances alike influence the presently told life story narrated and collaboratively reconstructed in psychoanalysis.

Biology and Sexual Orientation

Our summary of published findings on social biology, behavioral genetics, prenatal development, and brain anatomy suggests that, while future study may show a relation between biology and sexual orientation, there is scant evidence at present of such an association. Much of the research in this area is methodologically flawed and has not been replicated. To date little evidence suggests difference between brain structures in gay and straight men and women. Much of the study of hormonal factors is flawed by unsupported assumptions about the relation of gender to the sexual practices of gay women and men.

Biological study of the determinants of sexual orientation has been confounded by the assumption that homosexual and heterosexual are essential and fixed categories. Much of it assumes that same-gender sexual orientation, expressed either in fantasy or in action, is not only nonnormative but also aberrant. It incorrectly presumes that gay men must be like women since, like women, they seek men as sexual partners, while lesbians must be like men since they seek women as sexual partners.

Philosophy of science perspectives suggest that the principal factor underlying the continuing search for a "cause" of same-gender sexual orientation is preoccupation with a late Victorian theory of "normal love" which takes heterosexuality is the ideal expression of romantic love. Much biological study of sexual orientation fails to recognize that the origins of *both* heterosexuality and homosexuality need to be explained (Chodorow 1994). To date, there is little evidence of biological factors as relevant in understanding sexual orientation. However, as Freud ([1920] 1955, 230) has reminded us, any "recognition of the organic factor in homosexuality does not relieve us of the obligation of studying psychical process connected with its origin."

Life Course and Expression of Same-Gender Sexual Orientation

Much of this book reviews what is known about the course of same-gender sexual orientation from early childhood through later adulthood. We emphasize the changes that have taken place in how successive cohorts of men and women understand sexuality and sexual orientation. Recognizing that conceptions of what it means to be gay or straight are changing in contemporary culture and that society and history preclude some options while making others available, there is little evidence that factors founded in the course of lifetime development are particularly significant in determining sexual orientation. Development across the course of life is always a complex negotiation between life circumstances, which lead to a particular experience of desire, and constraints imposed by culture and history. For example, there is little evidence, as was earlier claimed, that the particular family constellation of overinvolved mother and cold and distant father will lead to their offspring adopting a homosexual orientation.

The literature on preadult development and sexual orientation focuses largely on boys—our culture seems preoccupied by same-gender desire among men. Much of the literature on same-gender sexual orientation among women is concerned less with its development than with the often destructive role of family and community in subjugating women and diminishing their self-esteem. Much of the psychoanalytic literature regarding the presumed development of male homosexuality focuses on aspects of the early mother-child relationship or on failure to resolve the nuclear conflict or "oedipal complex." This literature presumes both lasting impact of often subtle aspects of family life upon later personality development and a linear course of development; neither assumption is supported by study of personality development across the course of life.

Historically, the psychoanalytic literature after Freud presumed that homosexuality inevitably reflects psychopathology and sought the psychological "cause" of male homosexuality in personality deficit or developmental aberration. The resulting personality flaws were seen as expressed in homosexual "acting out." This psychoanalytic literature was largely silent on the psychopathology of homosexuality among women. While appreciating that this earlier literature carefully studied adult lives using clinical psychoanalytic methods, more recent clinical and developmental study raises important questions about its assumptions.

The literature on the emergence of homosexuality in the adolescent decade reflects a somewhat more balanced concern with gay girls and boys. It is characterized by prospective developmental study rather than presumptions about the earlier course of development. Clearly, there are several developmental paths to same-gender sexual orientation. Some adolescents and young adults, as also adults, report having always known that they were "gay;" other youth and adults first become aware of same-gender desire in high school or college. First-person accounts of gay youth suggest that, in the absence of experienced antigay prejudice and stigma, they are similar in their adjustment and interests to counterpart straight adolescents and young adults. If they are fortunate enough to grow up in families and communities that support variation in sexual orientation, these young people do not experience their own sexual identity either as a problem or as interfering in their pursuits of intellectual and professional goals.

Continuing study of the course of gay and lesbian lives across the adult years shows that the interplay of lifetimes and social change significantly affects the story of sexual orientation successively recounted across the course of life. Presently middle-aged and, particularly, young adult cohorts of gay men and women have a dominant or master narrative of being gay which is characterized by the theme of *always* having been gay. The cohort of older men and women focus less on such constancy of sexual desire and more on their adult experiences in finding partnership and the nature of their often tentative participation in the emerging socially visible gay community. It appears that cohort is more significant than age or place in the course of life as a factor influencing the presently told narrative of sexuality and life history.

A striking feature of the life stories told by both younger and older gay men and women is the extent to which the generally well educated gay men and women most commonly studied are conversant with the available biological and psychological literature on the gay experience. However, it is important to recognize that virtually all life-course developmental study of gay and lesbian lives to date is founded on convenience groups of urban-living gay men and women with access to extensive social networks and resources relevant to the gay experience. Indeed, it is largely through gay media and political groups that these men and women are recruited for study. Much less is known about the development and present lifestyle of men and women living outside major metropolitan areas or about those urban-living gay men and women not identified with visible geographic and social gay communities.

We reviewed issues of intimacy and parenthood among gay and lesbian adults. A stereotype regarding gay men and women is that they cannot maintain intimate ties and enduring relationships. Comparative study of heterosexual marriage and gay and lesbian partnership reveals few differences in duration of relationship or factors leading to dissolution. Younger adult gay men and women question whether the model of heterosexual marriage is even appropriate in understanding their partnerships. Interdependence, mutual influence, and loyalty are important as defining features of gay and lesbian partnership. Among gay men, a model stressing the concept of "best friend" may be the most appropriate in understanding long-term partnership.

A majority of both gay women and men at midlife have been in a heterosexual marriage at some point across the course of life. Reasons for the dissolution of such heterosexual marriages have less to do with the discovery by one or the other partner of same-gender desire, although that is often mentioned, than with problems of intimacy in the marital relationship, which appears to precede realization of same-gender sexual orientation. Often pre-adult offspring are cared for by one or both parents, who may or may not be remarried or living with a same-gender partner.

Our review of systematic developmental study has shown that there are few differences in the personal adjustment or sexual orientation of children living either part- or full-time with parents and their same-gender partners or of children born to a lesbian couple through donor insemination. Systematic study of offspring living in gay and lesbian unions suggests that they may, however, be more experimental in their lifestyles and less conservative in their social attitudes and their sexual orientation than counterpart young people growing up in more traditional families. Finally, there is little evidence that children whose parents are living in same-gender partnerships encounter any greater problems at school or with peers than children growing up in more traditional households. In fact, these children seem to have greater self-esteem and perspective on self and society than children growing up in more traditional straight households.

The parenting alliance appears more easily maintained among women formerly in a heterosexual marriage and now living with same-gendered partners than among straight women divorced from their husband, whether living alone or in another relationship. Lesbian mothers also report lower levels of role strain and overload and higher morale than straight counterpart mothers. Partners of lesbian mothers are more involved in household chores and childcare than has been noted among husbands in heterosexual marriages. Lesbian couples report being better able than straight couples to divide household labor.

Gay men with children either from a previous marriage or adopted report somewhat greater difficulty than gay women with young children. In many states, the courts are reluctant to grant custody to openly gay fathers; gay partners of fathers provide less support and assistance than lesbian partners. Fathers more comfortable and acceptant of their own sexuality are better able to maintain a positive relationship with their sons and to arrange for appropriate custody arrangements. Gay fathers appear to be somewhat more nurturing and child-centered than self-identified straight counterpart fathers, and also somewhat more explicitly concerned with setting limits for the boys. Finally, gay fathers report making an explicit effort to be sure that their boys receive traditional gender role socialization.

Much of the study of gay women and men at midlife has presumed that, particularly among gay men, attainment of midlife would be marked by a sense of accelerated aging relative to straight counterparts. This assumption was founded both on the often noted emphasis on youth within the gay community and on the losses over the past two decades of partners and friends to AIDS. Systematic study has not confirmed a sense of accelerated aging among gay men at midlife. Many men and women first become aware of their own same-gender sexual desire only in midlife. Others come to midlife following identification as gay or lesbian at some earlier point, childhood or their young adult years. The social network becomes "family" among both gay men and women, although the one large-scale study to date of gay women at midlife has reported that these women often prefer living alone, while maintaining close ties with friends for support and assistance.

Systematic study suggests that lesbians at midlife appear to be particularly successful, resilient, and self-aware as contrasted with counterpart straight women. These women are also particularly determined to keep personal and professional life separate and to prevent work from interfering in personal satisfaction. Gay men and women both report a greater sense of life satisfaction at midlife than earlier in adulthood. Further, gay men and women are more introspective and self-reflective at midlife than at younger ages.

Study of gay men and women across later life reflects particularly the impact of social change over the past three decades. Already in midlife at the time of the June 1969 riots that followed gay patrons' resistance to a police raid at New York's Stonewall Inn, the older men and women in this cohort have lived their lives "beneath the social radar." They were not aware of their sexual orientation as a particular source of stigma in their professional lives, established partnerships during early to midadulthood, and have led quiet lives in the intervening years. Many of those in the present cohort of older gay men were already living in monogamous relationships during the decade following the Stonewall riots, when sexual experimentation among gay men became more pronounced. Consequently they had little contact with friends living and dying with AIDS. Some of these gay elders have more recently begun participation in political activities related to the gay community. Studies suggest that gay men and women do not view their own aging in ways different from straight counterparts and that these men and women are comfortable with both their sexuality and their aging. When partners are still alive, gay men and women maintain extensive social ties. While they acknowledge that the social changes of the past three decades have made things much easier for the gay community as a whole, these men and women do not report the same involvement with these changes as has been reported among middle-aged gay and lesbian counterparts. Study has generally concluded that sexual orientation, as such, has little association with adjustment to aging or morale.

Sexual Orientation and Mental Health

The relationship of the mental health professions to sexual orientation has been problematic. Psychoanalysis in particular long assumed that nonnormative sexualities indicate psychopathology. More than a half century of comparative study of gay and straight adults, however, provides little confirmation of this hypothesis. From studies of convenience samples to more systematic community surveys, findings contrasting personality tests, interviewer ratings, and self-reports have found few differences between counterpart groups of straight and gay men and women.

Study of sexual orientation and mental health suggests that antigay prejudice and stigma does take a toll on mental health. Antigay prejudice often becomes part of self-definition, leading gay men and women to feel shame about their sexual orientation. Antigay prejudice remains a major problem reported in one study of a large number of young people seeking psychological intervention associated with feelings of lowered morale and self-esteem.

Antigay prejudice experienced in junior high and high schools, college, and community has been particularly pronounced within prior cohorts of adults. The self-criticism and shame learned as a result of experiencing such prejudice becomes a particular focus of psychotherapeutic and psychoanalytic intervention. Indeed, self-criticism is a central dynamic in development over a lifetime of both men and women characterized by nonnormative sexuality, and is often a major factor in their decisions to seek psychoanalytic intervention. Issues of shame and stigma, experienced over a lifetime, are inevitably evoked once again within the transference. This model recognizes the significance of censorship of these feelings of shame and embarrassment within the "here and now" of the transference.

Those gay men and women who participate in political and social activities within the gay and lesbian community report less impact of antigay prejudice than those who are less involved. Continuing support from other gay men and women appears important in reducing the otherwise adverse impact of antigay prejudice. Since issues of shame and self-criticism have been the focus of considerable prior psychoanalytic study, means for restoring sense of personal vitality and integrity have also been documented. Psychoanalysis and psychodynamic psychotherapy are effective intervention for those gay men and women experiencing enhanced awareness of self-criticism and its impact on their present morale.

Psychoanalytic Intervention

The same heightened self-criticism which endures among many gay men and women who seek psychoanalytic intervention is reciprocally a problem for the gay or straight therapists they consult. Recognition of this shared sense of stigma highlights the importance of studying the therapeutic relationship. Focus on self-criticism and a lifetime of living with antigay prejudice is an important feature of clinical psychoanalytic intervention. Other issues include the analyst's own efforts at dealing with feelings evoked by the accounts of self and lived experience presented by gay and lesbian analysands.

Problems of self-disclosure on the part of the analyst are particularly significant among more politically active gay and lesbian prospective analysands who seek either a gay analyst or an analyst sympathetic to gay issues. However, search for a gay analyst may often serve as cover for the analysand's effort to evade painful experiences and wishes. The analyst must be alert for the enactment of feelings of shame and self-criticism in the psychoanalytic situation. We have outlined a model of therapeutic intervention relevant for dealing with these issues of self-criticism. It is important to remember that some men and women who express same-gender sexual desire may try and protect themselves against other issues in their life.

The mental health community must confront the ethics of directed efforts at changing sexual orientation. Generally these efforts are not successful. But more importantly, there is no place in psychoanalytic understanding of the human condition for a perspective that promises a certain outcome prior to analysis, even if its claims were plausible. Directed approaches used in psychoanalytic intervention with gay and lesbian analysands only serve to exacerbate self-criticism by presuming that the ideal outcome among gay men and women who seek psychoanalysis as a means of resolving personal distress is a change in sexual orientation. Indeed, such directed approaches are ethically inconsistent with the goals of clinical psychoanalysis, which seeks enhanced personality integration, not maintenance of a false self.

Freud stated explicitly that sexual orientation was not a factor relevant either in considering personal well-being or in the selection of candidates for psychoanalytic education. Responding to a letter from Ernst Jones and Otto Rank informing him that the British society had rejected the application of an "overt homosexual," Freud replied that "we cannot exclude such persons without other sufficient reasons, as we cannot agree with their legal prosecution. We feel that a decision in such cases should depend upon a thorough examination of the other qualities of the candidate" (Freud [1921b] 1977, quoted in Lewes [1988] 1995, 33). However, many in psychoanalysis demurred from Freud's views, assuming that selection of a sexual partner of the same gender represented psychopathology, which, possibly, could be modified through psychoanalytic intervention. As this book is being completed, claims of a "cure" for homosexuality have arisen once more, despite evidence that such purportedly therapeutic efforts do not work and may cause harm.

With the growing influence of the most socially conservative voices in national political life, a nonnormative but not psychologically disruptive developmental pathway has been branded as a moral evil and character flaw. Elected national leaders deplore the many ways in which homosexuality is allegedly destructive to society. Scientists who claim to be studying homosexuality from an objective position maintain that should genetic research identify a "gay" gene, prospective parents would be justified in seeking abortion. Scholars who have studied the expression of antigay prejudice (Herek 1991, 1996; Nungesser 1983) have shown that disparagement of alternative sexualities can readily evoke profound personal responses that resonate with the enduring self-criticism of gay men and women subjected to such criticism from earliest childhood. Discussion regarding the meaning of all aspects of sexuality cannot be carried out in a climate of hostility and rancor. Psychoanalysis provides a means for understanding the meanings both of sexuality and of prejudice, and so may serve to foster a more balanced debate regarding the place of sexuality within lives over time and within the larger society.

Over the past two decades, there has been a shift within the larger society regarding understanding of sexual orientation. Stemming from the social and intellectual revolution of the mid-1960s to the mid-1970s, views regarding sexuality changed as did much of our understanding of self and society. Psychoanalysis is never isolated from larger social and historical changes. Indeed, much of our understanding of changes within lives over time is founded on presently shared understandings. Each generation shapes knowledge as a consequence of present social and historical changes, and knowledge can only be understood in terms of these cohort-related changes.

The theory of psychoanalytic technique has changed dramatically in the past two decades, largely in response to larger social and historical changes. The psychological development of women has been the subject of intense scrutiny; the dynamics of change within psychoanalysis have been reconsidered, including a renewed focus on the analytic relationship itself. Similar scrutiny has been given to the questions of sexual orientation, psychological development, and adjustment. The removal of homosexuality from the Diagnostic and Statistical Manual of the American Psychiatric Association reflects this change, as does the decision by the American Psychoanalytic Association to remove sexual orientation as a consideration of suitability for psychoanalytic education.

While the meaning of sexual orientation is always significant as a part of the psychoanalytic process, sexual orientation in itself is independent of psychopathology or present adjustment and should not be relevant as a factor in evaluating change in psychoanalysis. This position follows from contemporary perspectives on sexuality and sexual orientation in the larger society, which do not regard variation in sexual orientation as evidence of maladjustment. There is little evidence at the present time to suggest that the experience of same-gender sexual desire is biologically determined through genetic transmission of sexual orientation, prenatal hormonal influences, or structural changes in the central nervous system at some point over the course of life. However, there is overwhelming evidence that the experience of same-gender sexual desire is not fixed in childhood and that it may best be characterized as a particular sexual lifeway whose expression in fantasy, and generally in action as well, through the search for same-gender intimacy, is fluid across the course of life.

Same-gender sexual desire may be nonnormative, but it is not necessarily evidence of personal immaturity or psychopathology. It is important that psychoanalytic study and intervention in gay and lesbian lives take advantage of the empathic method of clinical psychoanalysis in an effort to understand the variety of meanings which are made of sexual orientation and sexual identity over a lifetime. This focus on the analyst's empathic appreciation of the analysand's experience, over a lifetime of self-criticism founded on the antigay prejudices of the larger society, may be useful in resolving the impact of such self-criticism as a determinant of lowered morale and in fostering enhanced experience of personal understanding, congruence, vitality, and personal coherence.

References

Abend, S. 1974. Problems of identity. *Psychoanalytic Quarterly* 43:606–37.

———. 1986. Countertransference, empathy, and the analytic ideal: The impact of life stresses on analytic capability. *Psychoanalytic Quarterly* 55:563–74.

———. 1995. Identity. In *Psychoanalysis: The major concepts,* ed. B. E. Moore and B. O. Fine. New Haven, Conn.: Yale University Press, 471–74.

Abraham, K. [1916] 1927. The first pregenital stage of the libido. In *Selected papers of Karl Abraham, M.D.* London: Hogarth Press, 248–79.

———. [1921] 1927. Contributions to the theory of the anal character. In *Selected papers of Karl Abraham, M.D.* London: Hogarth Press, 370–92.

———. [1924a] 1927. The influence of oral erotism on character formation. In *Selected papers of Karl Abraham, M.D.* London: Hogarth Press, 393–406.

———. [1924b] 1927. A short study of the development of the libido, viewed in the light of mental disorders. In *Selected papers of Karl Abraham, M.D.* London: Hogarth Press, 418–501.

———. [1925] 1927. Character-formation on the genital level of the libido. In *Selected papers of Karl Abraham, M.D.* London: Hogarth Press, 407–17.

Abrams, S. 1977. The genetic point of view: Antecedents and transformations. *Journal of the American Psychoanalytic Association* 25:417–25.

———. 1978. The teaching and learning of psychoanalytic developmental psychology. *Journal of the American Psychoanalytic Association* 26:387–406.

Adams, C. L., and D.C. Kimmel. 1997. Exploring the lives of older African-American gay men. In *Ethnic and cultural diversity among lesbians and gay men,* ed. B. Greene. Thousand Oaks, Calif.: Sage Publications, 132–51.

Adams, H. [1907] 1961. *The education of Henry Adams.* Boston: Houghton-Mifflin.

Adelman, M. 1987. *Long time passing: Lives of older lesbians.* Boston, Mass.: Alyson.

———. 1990. Stigma, gay lifestyles, and adjustment to aging: A study of later-life gay men and lesbians. In *Gay midlife and maturity,* ed. J. A. Lee. New York: Harrington Park Press, 7–32.

Adorno, T., E. Frenkel-Brunswik, D. Levinson, and R. Sanford. 1950. *The authoritarian personality.* New York: Harper.

Agero, J., L. Bloch, and D. Byrne. 1984. The relationships among sexual beliefs, attitudes, experience, and homophobia. *Journal of Homosexuality* 14:95–107.

Aguilera, D. 1994. *Crisis intervention: Theory and methodology.* 7th ed. Saint Louis, Mo.: Mosby.

Ainsworth, M. D. S. 1973. The development of infant-mother attachment. In *Review of child development research,* ed. B. Caldwell and H. Ricciuti. Vol. 3. Chicago: University of Chicago Press, 1–94.

Aldous, J. 1996. *Family careers: Rethinking the developmental perspective.* Thousand Oaks, Calif.: Sage Publications.

Alexander, F. 1956. *Psychoanalysis and psychotherapy.* New York: Norton.

Alexander, J., and K. Sufka. 1993. Cerebral lateralization in homosexual males: A preliminary EEG investigation, *International Journal of Psychophysiology* 15:269–74.

Alexander, R. D. 1975. The search for a general theory of behavior. *Behavioral Science* 2:77–100.

Allen, D. J., and T. Oleson. 1999. Shame and internalized homophobia in gay men. *Journal of Homosexuality* 37:33–43.

Allen, G. 1997. The double-edged sword of genetic determinism: Social and political agendas in genetic studies of homosexuality, 1940–1994. In *Science and homosexualities,* ed. V. Rosario. New York: Routledge, 242–70.

———. 1999. Modern biological determinism: The violence initiative, the Human Genome Project and the new eugenics. In *The practices of human genetics,* ed. M. Fortun and E. Mendelsohn. Amsterdam: Kluwer Academic Publishers, 1–24.

Allen, L., and R. Gorski. 1992. Sexual orientation and size of the anterior commissure in the human brain. *Proceedings of the National Academy of Sciences* 89:7199–7202.

Allen, L., M. Hines, J. Shryne, and R. Gorski. 1989. Two sexually dimorphic cell groups in the human brain. *Journal of Neuroscience* 9:497–506.

Allen, L. S., M. F. Richey, Y. M. Chai, and R. A. Gorski. 1991. Sex differences in the corpus callosum of the living human being. *Journal of Neuroscience* 11:933–42.

Allen, M., and N. Burrell. 1996. Comparing the impact of homosexual and heterosexual parents on children: Meta-analysis of existing research. *Journal of Homosexuality* 32: 19–35.

Allport, G. W. 1954. *The nature of prejudice.* Cambridge, Mass.: Addison-Wesley.

Almvig, C. 1982. *The invisible minority: Aging and lesbianism.* Syracuse, N.Y.: Utica College of Syracuse.

Alquijay, M. A. 1997. The relationship among self-esteem, acculturation, and lesbian identity formation in Latina lesbians. In *Ethnic and cultural diversity among lesbians and gay men,* ed. B. Greene. Thousand Oaks, Calif.: Sage Publications, 249–65.

Alwin, W. 1995. Taking time seriously: Studying social change, social structure and human lives. In *Examining lives in context: Perspectives on the ecology of human development,* ed. P. Moen, G. H. Elder Jr., and Kurt Lüscher. Washington, D.C.: American Psychological Association, 211–62.

Andrews, F., and S. Withey. 1976. *Social indicators of well being: Americans' perception of life quality.* New York: Plenum Press.

Antonucci, T. 1990. Social supports and social relationships. In *Handbook of aging and the social sciences,* ed. R. Binstock and L. K. George. New York: Academic Press, 205–27.

Apperson, L., and G. McAdoo. 1968. Parental factors in the childhood of homosexuals, *Journal of Abnormal Psychology* 73:201–6.

Apprey, M., and H. Bagley. 1990. On the usefulness of the diagnostic profile (Anna Freud) in evaluating adult male homosexuality. In *The homosexualities: Reality, fantasy, and the arts,* ed. C. W. Socarides and V. D. Volkan. Madison, Conn.: International Universities Press, 161–75.

Aries, P. 1962. *Centuries of childhood: A social history of family life.* Trans. R. Baldwick. New York: Random House.

Atkinson, J. H., I. Grant, C. J. Kennedy, D. D. Richman, S. A. Spector, and J. A. McCutchan. 1988. Prevalence of psychiatric disorders among men infected with human immunodeficiency virus. *Archives of General Psychiatry* 45:859–64.

Atwood, G., and R. Stolorow. 1984. *Structures of subjectivity: Explorations in psychoanalytic phenomenology.* Hillsdale, N.J.: Analytic Press.

Back, K. 1974. Transition to aging and the self-image. In *Normal aging: II,* ed. E. Palmore. Durham, N.C.: Duke University Press, 207–216.

Bailey, J. M., and A. P. Bell. 1993. Familiality of female and male homosexuality. *Behavior Genetics* 23:313–20.

Bailey, J. M., and D. Benishay. 1993. Familial aggregation of female sexual orientation. *American Journal of Psychiatry* 150:272–77.

Bailey, J. M., D. Bobrow, M. Wolfe, and S. Mikach. 1995. Sexual orientation of adult sons of gay fathers. *Developmental Psychology* 31:115–23.

Bailey, J. M., J. Miller, and L. Willerman. 1993. Maternally rated childhood gender non-conformity in homosexuals and heterosexuals. *Archives of Sexual Behavior* 22:461–69.

Bailey, J. M., and R. Pillard. 1991. A genetic study of male sexual orientation. *Archives of General Psychiatry* 48:1089–96.

———. 1993. Reply to Dr. Lidz. *Archives of General Psychiatry* 50:240–41.

Bailey, J. M., R. Pillard, M. Neale, and Y. Agyei. 1993. Heritable factors influence sexual orientation in women. *Archives of General Psychiatry* 50:217–23.

Bailey, J. M., L. Willerman, and C. Parks. 1991. A test of the maternal stress theory of human male homosexuality. *Archives of Sexual Behavior* 20:277–93.

Bailey, M. 1995. Biological perspectives on sexual orientation. In *Lesbian, gay, and bisexual identities over the life span,* ed. A. R. D'Augelli and C. Patterson. New York: Oxford University Press, 102–35.

Bailey, M. J., and K. Dawood. 1998. Behavioral genetics, sexual orientation, and the family. In *Lesbian, gay, and bisexual identities in families: Psychological perspectives,* ed. C. J. Patterson and A. R. D'Augelli. New York: Oxford University Press, 3–18.

Bailey, M., and K. Zucker. 1995. Childhood sex-typed behavior and sexual orientation: A conceptual analysis and quantitative review. *Developmental Psychology* 31:43–55.

Bakhtin, M. M. 1981. *The dialogic imagination.* Trans. C. Emerson and M. Holquist. Austin: University of Texas Press, 1981.

———. 1986. The problem of speech genres. In *Speech genres and other late essays.* Austin: University of Texas Press, 60–102.

Bakwin, H. 1968. Deviant gender-role behavior in children: Relation to homosexuality. *Pediatrics* 43:620–29.

Baltes, P. H. 1979. Life-span developmental psychology: Some converging observations on history and theory. In *Life-span development and behavior,* ed. P. Baltes and O. G. Brim Jr. New York: Academic Press, 2:256–81.

Baltes, P., S. Cornelius, and J. Nesselroade. 1979. Cohort effects in developmental psychology. In *Longitudinal research in the study of behavior and development,* ed. J. R. Nesselroade and P. B. Baltes. New York: Academic Press, 61–87.

Baltes, P. B., and K. W. Schaie. 1968. Longitudinal and cross-sectional sequences in the study of age and generation effects. *Human Development* 11:145–71.

Bancroft, J. 1975. Deviant sexual behavior. Oxford: Clarendon Press.

Bane, M. J. 1976. *Here to stay: American families in the twentieth century.* New York: Basic Books.

Banks, A., and N. Gartrell. 1995. Hormones and sexual orientation: A questionable link. *Journal of Homosexuality* 28:247–68.

Barker, R. G. 1968. *Ecological psychology: Concepts and methods for studying the environment of human behavior.* Stanford, Calif.: Stanford University Press.

Baruch, G. K., and J. Brooks-Gunn, eds. 1984. *Women in midlife.* New York: Plenum Press.

Basch, M. 1977. Developmental psychology and explanatory theory in psychoanalysis. *Annual of Psychoanalysis* 5:229–63.

———. 1982. The significance of infant development studies for psychoanaloytic theory. In *Infant Research: The Dawn of Awareness,* ed. M. Mayman. Psychoanalytic Inquiry, vol. 1, no. 4. New York: International Universities Press, 731–38.

———. 1983. The perception of reality and the disavowal of meaning. *Annual for Psychoanalysis* 11:125–53.

———. 1985. Some clinical and theoretical implications of infant research. In *Commentaries on Joseph Lichtenberg's psychoanalysis and infant research,* ed. D. Silver. Psychoanalytic Inquiry, vol. 5, no. 3. Hillsdale, N.J.: Analytic Press, 509–16.

Baum, M. J., R. S. Carroll, M. S. Erskine, and S. A. Tobet. 1985. Neuroendocrine response to estrogen and sexual orientation [letter]. *Science* 23 (4728): 960–61.

Bauman, Z. 1991. *Modernity and ambivalence.* Ithaca, N.Y.: Cornell University Press.

———. 1992. *Intimations of postmodernity.* New York: Routledge.

Baumrind, D. 1995. Commentary on sexual orientation: Research and social policy implications. *Developmental Psychology* 31:130–36.

Bayer, R. 1987. *Homosexuality and American psychiatry: The politics of diagnosis.* Princeton, N.J.: Princeton University Press.

Bayer, R., and R. Spitzer. 1982. Edited correspondence on the status of homosexuality in DSM-III. *Journal of the History of the Behavioral Sciences* 18:32–52.

Becker, H. 1963. *Outsiders: Studies in the sociology of deviance.* New York: Free Press.

Beeler, J. 1997. Coming out in young adulthood: Relations among parents and offspring. Unpublished manuscript. Committee on Human Development, University of Chicago.

Beeler, J., and V. Di Prova. 1999. Family adjustment following disclosure of homosexuality by a member: Themes discerned in narrative accounts. *Journal of Marriage and Family Counseling* 25:443–59.

Behrens, M. 1954. Childbearing and the character structure of the mother. *Child Development* 25:225–38.

Bell, A. P., M. Weinberg, and S. Hammersmith. 1981. *Sexual preference: Its development in men and women.* 2 vols. Bloomington: Indiana University Press.

Bell, R. Q. 1971. Stimulus control of parent or caretaker behavior by offspring. *Developmental Psychology* 4:63–72.

———. 1977. Socialization findings reexamined. In *Child effects on adults,* ed. R. Q. Bell and L. Harper. Hillsdale, N.J.: Erlbaum, 53–84.

Bell, R. Q., and L. Harper. 1977. *Child effects on adults.* Hillsdale, N. J.: Erlbaum.

Belsky, J., and R. Isabella. 1985. Marital and parent-child relationships in family of origin and marital change following the birth of a baby: A retrospective analysis. *Child Development* 56:342–49.

Belsky, J., M. Lang, and M. Rovine. 1985. Stability and change in marriage across the transition to parenthood: A second study. *Journal of Marriage and the Family* 47:855–865.

Belsky, J., and J. Rovine. 1988. Nonmaternal care in the first year of life and the security of infant-parent attachment. *Child Development* 59:157–67.

Belsky, J., G. Spanier, and M. Rovine. 1983. Stability and change in marriage across the transition to parenthood. *Journal of Marriage and the Family* 45:567–77.

Bem, D. 1996. Exotic becomes erotic: A developmental theory of sexual orientation. *Psychological Review* 103:320–35.

————. 1997. The exotic-becomes-erotic theory of sexual orientation. In *Same sex: Debating the ethics, science, and culture of homosexuality,* ed. J. Corvino. Lanham, N.J.: Rowman and Littlefield, 121–34.

Bene, E. 1965. On the genesis of male homosexuality: An attempt at clarifying the role of the parents. *British Journal of Psychiatry* 111:803–13.

Benedek, T. [1958] 1973. Parenthood as a developmental phase. In *Psychoanalytic investigations: Selected papers.* New York: Quadrangle, 378–401.

————. 1973. Discussion: Parenthood as a developmental phase. In *Psychoanalytic investigations: Selected papers.* New York: Quadrangle, 401–7.

Bengtson, V., M. Furlong, and R. Laufer. 1974. Time, aging, and the continuity of social structure: Themes and issues in generational analysis. *Journal of Social Issues* 30:1–30.

Benjamin, J. 1995a. *Like subjects, love objects: Essays on recognition and sexual difference.* New Haven, Conn.: Yale University Press.

————. 1995b. Sameness and difference: Toward an "overinclusive" model of gender development. *Psychological Inquiry* 15:125–42.

————. 1998. *In the shadow of the other: Intersubjectivity and gender in psychoanalysis.* New York: Routledge.

Bennett, K., and N. Thompson. 1990. Accelerated aging and male homosexuality: Australian evidence in a continuing debate. In *Gay midlife and maturity,* ed. J. A. Lee. New York: Harrington Park Press, 65–77.

Berenbaum, S., and E. Snyder. 1995. Early hormonal influences on childhood sex-typed activity and playmate preferences: Implications for the development of sexual orientation. *Developmental Psychology* 31:31–42.

Berenthal, B., and J. Campos. 1987. New directions in the study of early experience. *Child Development* 58:560–67.

Beres, D. 1972. Ego autonomy and ego pathology. *Psychoanalytic Study of the Child* 26: 3–23.

Beres, D., and J. Arlow. 1974. Fantasy and identification in empathy. *Psychoanalytic Quarterly* 42:26–50.

Berger, P., and T. Luckmann. 1967. *The social construction of reality: A treatise in the sociology of knowledge.* Garden City, N.Y.: Doubleday-Anchor Books.

Berger, R. M. 1980. Psychological adaptation of the older homosexual male. *Journal of Homosexuality* 5:161–75.

————. [1982] 1996. *Gay and gray: The older homosexual man.* 2d ed. New York: Harrington Park Press.

————. 1982. Research on older gay men: What we known, what we need to know. In *Lesbian and gay lifestyles: A guide for counseling and education,* ed. N.J. Woodman. New York: Irvington, 217–34.

————. 1984. Realities of gay and lesbian aging. *Social Work* 29:57–62.

————. 1990. Men together: Understanding the gay couple. *Journal of Homosexuality* 19:31–49.

Berger, R., and J. Kelly. 1996. Gay men and lesbians grown older. In *Textbook of homosexuality and mental health,* ed. R. Cabaj and T. S. Stein. Washington, D.C.: American Psychiatric Press, 305–18.

Bergler, E. 1949. *The basic neurosis.* New York: Harper and Brothers.

————. 1956. *Homosexuality: Disease or way of life.* New York: Hill and Wang.

————. 1961. *Curable and incurable neurotics: Problems of "neurotic" versus "malignant" psychic masochism.* Madison, Conn.: International Universities Press.

Bergmann, M. 1994. The challenge of erotized transference to psychoanalytic technique. *Psychoanalytic Inquiry* 14:499–518.

Bernfeld, S. 1941. Freud's earliest theories on the school of Helmholtz. *Psychoanalytic Quarterly* 13:341–62.

———. 1949. Freud's scientific beginnings. *Imago* 6:163–96.

Bernstein, P. (panel reporter). 1993. Gender identity disorder in boys. *Journal of the American Psychoanalytic Association* 41:729–42.

Berrill, K. 1990. Anti-gay violence in the United States: An overview. *Journal of Interpersonal Violence* 5:274–94.

Bertaux, D. 1981a. From the life-history approach to the transformation of sociological practice. In *Biography and society: The life history approach in the social sciences,* ed. D. Bertaux. Newbury Park, Calif.: Sage Publications, 28–46.

———. 1981b. Introduction. In *Biography and society: The life history approach in the social sciences,* ed. D. Bertaux. Newbury Park, Calif.: Sage Publications.

Bertaux, D., and M. Kohli. 1984. The life-story approach: A continental view. *Annual Review of Sociology* 10:215–37.

Bettelheim, B. 1951. *Love is not enough.* New York: Free Press/Macmillan.

———. 1954. *Symbolic wounds: Puberty rites and the envious male.* New York: Free Press/Macmillan.

———. 1955. *Truants from life.* New York: Free Press/Macmillan.

Bettelheim, B., and M. Janowitz. 1950. *The dynamics of prejudice: A psychological and sociological study of veterans.* Glencoe, Ill.: Free Press.

Bettinger, M. 1997. Gay male couples and families. In *On the road to same-sex marriage,* ed. R. Cabaj and D. Purcell. San Francisco: Jossey-Bass, 59–88.

Bibring, E. 1959. Some considerations of the psychological process in pregnancy. *Psychoanalytic Study of the Child* 14:113–21.

Bibring, E., T. Dwyer, D. Huntington, and A. Valenstein. 1961. A study of the psychological processes of pregnancy and the earliest mother-child relationship. *Psychoanalytic Study of the Child* 9:9–72.

Bieber, I. 1965. Clinical aspects of male homosexuality. In *Sexual inversion: The multiple roots of homosexuality,* ed. J. Marmor. New York: Basic Books, 248–67.

———. 1976a. A discussion of "Homosexuality: The ethical challenge." *Journal of Consulting and Clinical Psychology* 44:163–66.

———. 1976b. Psychodynamics and sexual object choice, I: A reply to Dr. Richard C. Friedman's paper. *Contemporary Psychoanalysis* 12:366–69.

Bieber, I., and T. Bieber. 1979. Male homosexuality. *Canadian Journal of Psychiatry* 24: 409–21.

Bieber, I., H. Dain, P. Dince, M. Drellich, H. Grand, R. Gundlach, M. Kremer, A. Rifkin, C. Wilbur, and T. Bieber. 1962. *Homosexuality: A psychodynamic study of male homosexuals.* New York: Basic Books.

Bigner, J., and F. Bozett. 1990. Parenting by gay fathers. In *Homosexuality and family relations,* ed. F. W. Bozett and M. B. Sussman. New York: Haworth/Harrington Park Press, 155–76.

Bigner, J., and R. Jacobsen. 1989a. The value of children to gay and heterosexual fathers. In *Homosexuality and the family,* ed. F. W. Bozett. New York: Harrington Park Press, 163–72.

———. 1989b. Parenting behaviors of homosexual and heterosexual fathers. In *Homosexuality and the family,* ed. F. W. Bozett. New York: Harrington Park Press, 173–86.

Bird, B. 1957. A consideration of etiology of prejudice. *Journal of the American Psychoanalytic Association* 5:490–513.

Birk, L. 1980. The myth of classical homosexuality: Views of a behavioral psychotherapist. In *Homosexual behavior: A modern reappraisal,* ed. J. Marmor. New York: Basic Books, 376–90.

Birke, L. 1982. Is homosexuality hormonally determined? *Journal of Homosexuality* 6: 35–49.

Blanchard, R., and A. Bogaert. 1996. Homosexuality of men and number of older brothers. *American Journal of Psychiatry* 153:27–31.

Blanchard, R., K. Zucker, S. Bradley, and C. Hume. 1995. Birth order and sibling sex ratio in homosexual male adolescents and probably prehomosexual feminine boys. *Developmental Psychology* 31:22–30.

Blasband, D., and L. Peplau. 1985. Sexual exclusivity versus openness in gay male couples. *Archives of Sexual Relations* 14:395–412.

Blechner, M. J. 1992. Commentary on J. L. Trop and R. D. Stolorow's "Defense analysis in self-psychology." *Psychoanalytic Dialogues* 2:627–37.

———. 1993. Homophobia in psychoanalytic writing and practice. *Psychoanalytic Dialogues* 3:627–38.

———. 1995. The shaping of psychoanalytic theory and practice by cultural and personal biases about sexuality. In *Disorienting sexuality: Psychoanalytic reappraisals of sexual identities,* ed. T. Domenici and R. C. Lesser. New York Routledge, 265–88.

———, ed. 1997a. *Hope and mortality: Psychodynamic approaches to AIDS and HIV.* Hillsdale, N.J.: Analytic Press.

———. 1997b. Psychodynamic approaches to AIDS and HIV. In *Hope and mortality: Psychodynamic approaches to AIDS and HIV,* ed. M. J. Blechner. Hillsdale, N.J.: Analytic Press, 3–62.

Bleier, R., W. Byne, and I. Siggelkow. 1982. Cytoarchitectonic sexual dimorphisms of the medial preoptic and anterior hypothalamic areas in guinea pig, rat, hamster, and mouse. *Journal of Comparative Neurology* 212:118–30.

Blood, R., and D. Wolfe. 1960. *Husbands and wives.* New York: Free Press.

Blos, P. 1967. The second individuation process of adolescence. *Psychoanalytic Study of the Child* 22:162–87.

———. 1979. *The adolescent passage: Developmental issues.* Madison, Conn.: International Universities Press.

———. 1980. The life cycle as indicated by the nature of the transference in the psychoanalysis of adolescents. *International Journal of Psychoanalysis* 61 (2): 145–51.

Blum, A., M. Danson, and S. Schneider. 1997. Problems of sexual expression in adult gay men: A psychoanalytic reconsideration. *Psychoanalytic Psychology* 14:1–12.

Blum, A., and V. Pfetzing. 1997. Assaults to the self: The trauma of growing up gay. *Gender and Psychoanalysis* 2:427–42.

Blum, H. 1973. The concept of eroticized transference. *Journal of the American Psychoanalytic Association* 29:61–76.

Blum, H., and W. Goodman. 1995. Countertransference. In *Psychoanalysis: The major concepts,* ed. B. E. Moore and B. O. Fine. New Haven, Conn.: Yale University Press, 121–29.

Blumstein, P., and P. Schwartz. 1983. *American couples: Work, money, sex.* New York: Morrow.

———. 1989. Intimate relationships and the creation of sexuality. In *Gender in intimate relationships,* ed. B. Rismamn and P. Schwartz. Belmont, Calif.: Wadsworth Publishing Company, 120–29.

———. 1990. Intimate relationships and the creation of sexuality. In *Homosexuality/ heterosexuality: Concepts of sexual orientation,* ed. D. P. McWhirter, S. A. Sanders, and J. M. Reinisch. New York: Oxford University Press, 307–20.

Bly, R. 1990. *Iron John: A book about men.* Reading, Mass.: Addison-Wesley.

Bollas, C. 1992. Cruising in the homosexual arena. In *Being a character: Psychoanalysis and self-experience.* New York: Hill and Wang, 144–64.

———. 1997. Wording and telling sexuality. *International Journal of Psychoanalysis* 78: 363–367.

Bone, J. 1995. Gay gene claim thrown into doubt. *Australian,* 11 July, 14.

Booth, W. [1961] 1983. *The Rhetoric of Fiction.* 2d ed. Chicago: University of Chicago Press.

Borden, W. 1989. Life review as a therapeutic frame in the treatment of young adults with AIDS. *Health and Social Work* 14:253–59.

Borden, W. 1992. Narrative perspectives in psychosocial intervention following adverse life events. *Social Work* 37:135–41.

Boxer, A. 1990. Life-course transitions of gay and lesbian youth: Sexual identity, development, and parent-child relationships. Unpublished doctoral dissertation, University of Chicago.

———. 1997. Gay, lesbian, and bisexual aging into the twenty-first century: An overview and introduction. *Journal of Gay, Lesbian, and Bisexual Identity* 2:1997, 187–97. (Special issue: Coming of age: Gays, lesbians, and bisexuals in the second half of life, ed. G. Herdt, A. Hostetler, and B. Cohler.)

Boxer, A., and B. Cohler. 1989. The life course of gay and lesbian youth: An immodest proposal for the study of lives. In *Gay and lesbian youth,* ed. G. Herdt. New York: Harrington Park Press, 315–55.

Boxer, A., B. Cohler, G. Herdt, and F. Irvin. 1993. The study of gay and lesbian teenagers: Life-course, "coming out" and well being. In *Handbook of clinical research and practice with adolescents,* ed. P. Tolan and B. Cohler. New York: Wiley-Interscience, 249–80.

Boxer, A. M., J. A. Cook, and B. J. Cohler. 1986. Grandfathers, fathers, and sons: Intergenerational relations among men. In *Elder abuse: Conflict in the family,* ed. K. Pillemer and R. Wolf. Dover, Mass: Auburn House, 93–121.

Boxer, A., J. Cook, and G. Herdt. 1990. Double jeopardy: Identity transformations and parent-child relations among gay and lesbian youth. In *Parent-child relations across the life-span,* ed. K. Pillemer and K. McCartney. Hillsdale, N.J.: Lawrence Erlbaum.

Boxer, A., H. Gershenson, and D. Offer. 1984. Historical time and social change in adolescent experience. In *Patterns of adolescent self-image,* ed. D. Offer, E. Ostrow, and K. Howard. New Directions for Mental Health Services, no. 22. San Francisco: Jossey-Bass, 83–95.

Boxer, A., R. Levinson, and A. Petersen. 1989. Adolescent sexuality. In *The adolescent as decision maker,* ed. J. Worrell and F. Danner. New York: Academic Press, 209–43.

Boxer, A. M., and A. C. Petersen. 1986. Pubertal change in a family context. In *Adolescence in families,* ed. G. K. Leigh and G. W. Petersen. Cincinnati, Ohio: South-Western Publishing, 73–103.

Boyer, D. 1989. Male prostitution and homosexual identity. In *Gay and lesbian youth,* ed. G. Herdt. New York: Harrington Park Press, 151–84.

Bozett, F. 1980a. Gay fathers: Evolution of the gay father identity. *American Journal of Orthopsychiatry* 51:552–59.

———. 1980b. Gay fathers: How and why they disclose their homosexuality to their children. *Family Relations* 29:173–79.

———. 1987. Gay fathers. In *Gay and lesbian parents,* ed. F. W. Bozett. New York: Praeger, 3–22.

———. 1988. Gay fatherhood. In *Fatherhood today: Men's changing roles in the family,* ed. P. Bornstein and C. P. Cowan. New York: Wiley, 214–35.

———. 1993. Gay fathers: A review of the literature. In *Psychological perspectives on lesbian and gay male experiences,* ed. L. Garnets and D.C. Kimmel. New York: Columbia University Press, 437–58.

Bradford, J., and C. Ryan. 1991. Who we are: Health concerns of middle-aged lesbians. In *Lesbians at midlife: The creative transition,* ed. B. Sang, J. Warshow, and A. Smith. San Francisco: Spinsters Ink, 147–63.

Bradford, J., C. Ryan, and E. Rothblum. 1994. National lesbian health care survey: Implications for mental health care. *Journal of Clinical and Consulting Psychology* 62: 228–42.

Bradley, S. J., and K. J. Zucker. 1997. Gender identity disorder: A review of the past 10 years. *Journal of the American Academy of Child and Adolescent Psychiatry* 36:872–80.

Breakwell, S. 1986. *Threatened identities.* London: Methuen.

Breedlove, S. 1994. Sexual differentiation of the human nervous system. *Annual Review of Psychology* 45:389–418.

Brenner, C. 1982. *The mind in conflict.* New York: International Universities Press.

Breuer, J., and S. Freud. [1893–95] 1955. Studies in hysteria. In *The standard edition of the complete psychological works of Sigmund Freud.* Ed. and trans. J. Strachey. Vol. 2. London: Hogarth Press.

Brim, O. G., Jr. 1976. Life-span development of the theory of oneself: Implications for child development. In *Advances in child development and behavior,* ed. H. Reese and L. Lipsitt. New York: Academic Press, 2:241–51.

Bronfenbrenner, U. 1977. Toward an experimental ecology of human development. *American Psychologist* 32:513–31.

Brooks-Gunn, J., and A. C. Petersen. 1983. *Girls at puberty: Biological and psychosocial perspectives.* New York: Plenum Press.

Brooks-Gunn, J., A. C. Petersen, and D. Eichorn, eds. 1985a, 1985b. Timing of maturation and psychosocial functioning in adolescence. Parts 1 and 2 (two issues). *Journal of Youth and Adolescence* 14, nos. 3 and 4.

Brown, L. M., and C. Gilligan. 1992. *Meeting at the crossroads: Women's psychology and girls' development.* Cambridge, Mass.: Harvard University Press.

Browning, C. 1992. *Ordinary men: Reserve police battalion 101 and the final solution in Poland.* New York: Basic Books.

Bruner, J. 1990. *Acts of meaning.* Cambridge, Mass.: Harvard University Press.

———. 1987. Life as narrative. *Social Research* 54:11–32.

———. 1986. *Actual minds, possible worlds.* Cambridge, Mass.: Harvard University Press.

Buchanan, C., E. Maccoby, and S. Dornbusch. 1996. *Adolescents after divorce.* Cambridge, Mass.: Harvard University Press.

Buchholz, E. S. 1997. *The call of solitude: Alonetime in a world of attachment.* New York: Simon and Schuster.

Buhrich, N., J. M. Bailey, and N. G. Martin. 1991. Sexual orientation, sexual identity, and sex-dimorphic behaviors in male twins. *Behavior Genetics* 21:75–96.

Buie, D. 1981. Empathy: Its nature and limitations. *Journal of the American Psychoanalytic Association* 29:281–306.

Buie, J. 1990. "Heterosexuality ethic" mentality is decried. *American Psychological Association Monitor,* March, 20.

Buloff, B., and M. Osterman. 1995. Queer reflections: Mirroring and the lesbian experience of self. In *Lesbians and psychoanalysis: Revolutions in theory and practice,* ed. J. Glassgold and S. Iasenza. New York: Free Press, 93–106.

Burch, B. 1993. *On intimate terms: The psychology of difference in lesbian relationships.* Urbana: University of Illinois Press.

———. 1995. Gender identities, lesbianism, and potential space. In *Lesbians and psychoanalysis: Revolutions in theory and practice,* ed. J. Glassgold and S. Iasenza. New York: Free Press, 287–308.

Burdick, J., and D. Stewart. 1974. Differences between "show" and "no-show' volunteers in a homosexual population. *Journal of Social Psychology* 92:159–60.

Burke, K. [1945] 1969. *A Grammar of Motives.* Berkeley: University of California Press.

———. [1950] 1969. *A Rhetoric of Motives.* Berkeley: University of California Press.

Burke, N., and B. Cohler. 1992. Countertransference and psychotherapy with the anorectic adolescent. In *Countertransference in Child and Adolescent Psychotherapy,* ed. J. Brandell. New York: Aronson, 163–89.

Burke, R., T. Weir, and R. Duwors. 1980. Work demands on administrators and spouse well-being. *Human Relations* 33:253–78.

Butler, J. P. 1997. *The psychic life of power.* Stanford, Calif.: Stanford University Press.

Butler, R. 1963. The life-review: An interpretation of reminiscence in the aged. *Psychiatry* 26:65–76.

Bychowski, G. 1954. The structure of homosexual acting out. *Psychoanalytic Quarterly* 23:48–61.

Byne, W. 1994. The biological evidence challenged. *Scientific American* 270 (May): 50–55.

———. 1995. Science and belief: Psychobiological research on sexual orientation. *Journal of Homosexuality* 28:303–44.

———. 1996. Biology and homosexuality: Implications of neuroendocrinological and neuroanatomical studies. In *Textbook of homosexuality and mental health,* ed. R. Cabaj and T. S. Stein. Washington, D.C.: American Psychiatric Press, 129–46.

———. 1997a. LeVay's thesis reconsidered. In *A queer world: The Center for Lesbian and Gay Studies reader,* ed. M. Duberman. New York: New York University Press, 318–27.

———. 1997b. Why we cannot conclude that sexual orientation is primarily a biological phenomenon. *Journal of Homosexuality* 34:73–80.

Byne, W., and M. Lasco. 1997. The origins of sexual orientation: Possible biological contributions. In *Same sex: Debating the ethics, science, and culture of homosexuality,* ed. J. Corvino. Lanham, N.J.: Rowman and Littlefield, 107–20.

Byne, W., and B. Parsons. 1993. Human sexual orientation: The biological theories reappraised. *Archives of General Psychiatry* 50:228–39.

Byne, W., and E. Stein. 1997. Varieties of biological explanation. *Harvard Gay and Lesbian Review* 4 (1): 13–15.

Cadwell, S., R. Burnham, and M. Forstein. 1994. *Therapists on the front line: Psychotherapy with gay men in the age of AIDS.* Washington, D.C.: American Psychiatric Association Press.

Cain, L. 1964. Life-course and social structure. In *Handbook of Modern Sociology*, ed. R. Faris. Chicago: Rand-McNally, 272–309.

Calef, V., and E. Weinshel. 1984. Anxiety and the restitutional function of homosexual cruising. *International Journal of Psychoanalysis* 64:45–53.

Campbell, A., P. Converse, and W. Rodgers. 1976. *The quality of American life: Perceptions, evaluations and satisfactions*. New York: Russell Sage.

Carleton, F. 1999. Contested identity: The law's construction of gay and lesbian subjects. In *The construction of attitudes toward lesbians and gay men*, ed. L. Pardie, L. Luchetta, and T. Luchetta. Binghamton, N.Y.: Haworth Press.

Carney, J., and B. Cohler. 1993. Developmental continuities and adjustment in adulthood: Social relations, morale, and the transformation from middle to late life. In *The course of life*, vol. 6: *Late Adulthood*, ed. G. Pollock and S. Greenspan. Madison, CT: International Universities Press, 199–226.

Carr, D. 1986. *Time, Narrative, and History*. Bloomington: Indiana University Press.

Carrier, J. 1989. Gay liberation and coming out in Mexico. In *Gay and lesbian youth*, ed. G. Herdt. New York: Harrington Park Press, 225–52.

———. 1995. *De los otros: Intimacy and homosexuality among Mexican men*. New York: Columbia University Press.

Casement, P. 1991. *Learning from the patient*. New York: Guilford Press.

Cass, V. C. 1979. Homosexual identity formation: A theoretical model. *Journal of Homosexuality* 4:219–35.

———. 1983/84. Homosexual identity: A concept in need for definition. *Journal of Homosexuality* 10:105–26.

———. 1984. Homosexual identity formation: Testing a theoretical model. *Journal of Sex Research* 20:143–67.

———. 1990. The implications of homosexual identity formation for the Kinsey model and scale of sexual preference. In *Homosexuality/heterosexuality: Concepts of sexual orientation*, ed. D. P. McWhirter, S. A. Sanders, and J. M. Reinisch. New York: Oxford University Press, 239–66.

———. 1996. Sexual orientation and identity formation. In *Textbook of homosexuality and mental health*, ed. R. Cabaj and T. S. Stein. Washington, D.C.: American Psychiatric Press, 227–51.

Catania, J. A. 1999. Sexual development and mental health among men who have sex with men. Paper presented at New Approaches to Research on Sexual Orientation, Mental Health, and Substance Abuse. Bethesda, Md.: National Institute of Mental Health, September.

Cerbone, A. 1997. Symbol of privilege, object of derision: Dissonance and contradictions. In *Ethnic and cultural diversity among lesbians and gay men*, ed. B. Greene. Thousand Oaks, Calif.: Sage Publications, 117–32.

Chan, C. 1995. Issues of sexual identity in an ethnic minority: The case of Chinese American lesbians, gay people and bisexual people. In *Lesbian, gay, and bisexual identities over the life span*, ed. A. R. D'Augelli and C. Patterson. New York: Oxford University Press, 87–101.

———. 1997. Don't ask, don't tell, don't know: The formation of a homosexual identity and sexual expression among Asian American lesbians. In *Ethnic and cultural diversity among lesbians and gay men*, ed. B. Greene. Thousand Oaks, Calif.: Sage Publications, 240–48.

Chan, R. W., B. Raboy, and C. J. Patterson. 1998. Psychosocial adjustment among children conceived via donor insemination by lesbian and heterosexual mothers. *Child Development* 69:443–57.

Chang, J., and J. Block. 1960. A study of identification in male homosexuals. *Journal of Consulting and Clinical Psychology* 24:307–10.

Charbonneau, C., and P. Lander. 1991. Redefining sexuality: Women becoming lesbian at midlife. In *Lesbians at midlife: The creative transition,* ed. B. Sang, J. Warshow, and A. Smith. San Francisco: Spinsters Ink, 35–43.

Chauncey, G. 1994. *Gay New York: Gender, urban culture and the making of the gay male world, 1890–1940.* New York: Basic Books.

Cherlin, A. 1981. *Marriage, divorce, remarriage.* Cambridge, Mass.: Harvard University Press.

Chodorow, N. 1978. *The reproduction of mothering.* Berkeley: University of California Press.

———. 1989. *Feminism and psychoanalytic theory.* New Haven: Yale University Press.

———. 1992. Heterosexuality as a compromise formation: Reflections on the psychoanalytic theory of sexual development. *Psychoanalysis and Contemporary Thought* 15: 267–304.

———. 1994. *Femininities, masculinities, sexualities: Freud and beyond.* Lexington: University Press of Kentucky.

———. 1999. *The power of feelings: Personal meaning in psychoanalysis, gender and culture.* New Haven, CT: Yale University Press.

Christensen, L., and R. Gorski. 1978. Independent masculinization of neuroendocrine systems by intracerebral implants of testosterone or estradiol in the neonatal female rat. *Brain Research* 146:325–40.

Chused, J. 1991. The evocative power of enactments. *Journal of the American Psychoanalytic Association* 39:615–39.

Clark, K. 1965. *Dark ghetto.* New York: Harper and Row.

Clarke, A. M., and A. B. D. Clarke, eds. 1976. *Early experience: Myth and evidence.* New York: Free Press.

Clarke, A. B. D., and A. M. Clarke. 1981. "Sleeper effects" in development: Fact or artifact? *Developmental Review* 1:344–60.

Clarke-Stewart, A. 1978. Popular primers for parents. *American Psychologist* 33:359–69.

Clausen, J. A. 1975. The social meaning of differential physical and sexual maturation. In *Adolescence in the life cycle,* ed. S. Dragastin and G. H. Elder Jr. Washington, D.C.: Hemisphere, 25–47.

———. 1993. *American lives: Looking back at the children of the Great Depression.* New York: Free Press.

Clendinen, D., and A. Nagourney. 1999. *Out for good: The struggle to build a gay rights movement in America.* New York: Simon and Schuster.

Coates, S. 1985. Extreme boy femininity: Overview and new research findings. In *Sexuality: New perspectives,* ed. Z. De Fries, R. Friedman, and R. Corn. Westport, Conn.: Greenwood Press, 101–24.

———. 1992. The etiology of boyhood gender identity disorder: An integrative model. In *Interface of psychoanalysis and psychology,* ed. J. Barron, M. Eagle, and D. Wolitzky. Washington, D.C.: American Psychological Association, 245–65.

Coates, S., and S. Wolfe. 1995. Gender identity disorder in boys: The interface of constitution and early experience. *Psychological Inquiry* 15:6–38.

Coates, T. J., A. C. Petersen, and C. Perry. 1982. *Promoting adolescent health: A dialog on research and practice.* New York: Academic Press.

Coates, S., and S. Wolfe. 1995. Gender identity disorder in boys: The interface of constitution and early experience. *Psychoanalytic Inquiry* 15:6–38. (Special issue, Feminine and masculine gender identity, ed. F. D. Barth.)

Cody, P., and P. Welch. 1997. Rural gay men in northern New England: Life experiences and coping styles. *Journal of Homosexuality* 33:51–67.

Coen, S. J. 1978. Sexual interviewing, evaluation, and therapy: Psychoanalytic emphasis on the use of sexual fantasy. *Archives of Sexual Behavior* 7:229–41.

———. 1981. Sexualization as a predominant mode of defense. *Journal of the American Psychoanalytic Association* 29.893–920.

Cohen, C., and T. Stein. 1986. Reconceptualizing individual psychotherapy with gay men and lesbians. In *Contemporary perspectives on psychotherapy with lesbians and gay men,* ed. T. Stein and C. Cohen. New York: Plenum Medical Book Company, 27–56.

Cohen, J., and J. Abramowitz. 1990. AIDS attacks the self: A self-psychological exploration of the psychodynamic consequences of AIDS. In *The realities of the transference: Progress in self psychology,* ed. A. Goldberg. Hillsdale, N.J.: Analytic Press, 6:157–71.

Cohen, K., and R. Savin-Williams. 1996. Developmental perspectives on coming out to self and others. In *The lives of lesbians, gays, and bisexuals,* ed. R. C. Savin-Williams and K. M. Cohen. Fort Worth, Tex.: Harcourt Brace, 113–51.

Cohen, R., and S. Weissman. 1984. The parenting alliance. In *Parenthood: A psychodynamic perspective,* ed. R. Cohen, B. Cohler, and S. Weissman. New York: Guilford Press, 119–47.

Cohler, B. 1980. Developmental perspectives on the psychology of self in early childhood. In *Advances in self psychology,* ed A. Goldberg. New York: International Universities Press, 69–115.

———. 1982. Personal narrative and life course. In *Life-span development and behavior,* ed. P. Baltes and O. G. Brim Jr. New York: Academic Press, 4:205–41.

———. 1984. Parenthood, psychopathology, and child-care. In *Parenthood: A psychodynamic perspective,* ed. R. S. Cohen, B. J. Cohler, and S. Weissman. New York: Guilford Press, 119–48.

———. 1987. Approaches to the study of development in psychiatric education. In *The role of psychoanalysis in psychiatric education: Past, present, and future,* ed. S. Weissman and R. Thurnblad. Madison, Conn.: International Universities Press, 225–70.

———. 1988. The human studies and the life-history: The Social Service Review lecture. *Social Service Review* 62 (4): 552–75.

———. 1996. Self, sexual orientation, and lived experience: Implications for the analytic relationship. Annual meetings, Society for Self Psychology, Washington, D.C., November 1996.

———. 1997. Psychoanalytic psychotherapy with a man practicing unsafe sex. Unpublished manuscript, Committee on Human Development and the Evelyn Hooker Center on Gay and Lesbian Mental Health, University of Chicago.

———. 1998. Clinical psychoanalysis and the study of older adult lives. Unpublished manuscript, Committee on Human Development, University of Chicago.

———. 1999a. Sexual orientation, psychoanalysis and intervention among lesbians and gay men. *Journal of Gay and Lesbian Psychotherapy,* in press.

———. 1999b. The gay therapist's response to a gay client practicing unsafe sex (barebacking). *Journal of Analytic Social Work,* in press.

Cohler, B., and K. Altergott. 1995. The family of the second half of life: Connecting theories and findings. In *Handbook of Aging and the Family,* ed. R. Blieszner and V. Hilkevitch Bedford. Westport, Conn.: Greenwood Press, 59–94.

Cohler, B., and J. Beeler. 1996. The construction of sexuality at mid-life: Reports from a focus group of gay men. Unpublished paper.

Cohler, B., and A. Boxer. 1984. Middle adulthood: Settling into the world-person, time, and context. In *Normality and the life-cycle,* ed. D. Offer and M. Sabshin. New York: Basic Books, 145–204.

Cohler, B., and D. deBoer. 1996. Psychoanalysis and the study of adult lives. In *Psychoanalytic perspectives on developmental psychology,* ed. J. M. Masling and R. E. Bornstein. Washington, D.C.: American Psychological Association, 151–220.

Cohler, B., and M. Freeman. 1993. Psychoanalysis and the developmental narrative. In *The course of life,* ed. G. Pollock and S. Greenspan. Rev. ed. Vol. 5, *Early adulthood.* Madison, Conn.: International Universities Press, 99–177.

Cohler, B., and R. Galatzer-Levy. 1988. Self-psychology and psychoanalytic psychotherapy. In *New Concepts in Psychoanalytic Psychotherapy,* ed. J. Ross and W. A. Myers. New York: American Psychiatric Association Press, 204–25.

———. 1990. Self, meaning, and morale across the second-half of life. In *New dimensions in adult development,* ed. R. Nemiroff and C. Colarusso. New York: Basic Books, 214–59.

———. 1995. What kind of a science is psychoanalysis? Unpublished manuscript. Library of the Institute for Psychoanalysis, Chicago.

———. 1996. Self-psychology perspectives on homosexuality. In *Textbook of homosexuality and mental health,* ed. R. Cabaj and T. S. Stein. Washington, D.C.: American Psychiatric Press, 207–26.

Cohler, B., and H. Grunebaum. 1981. *Mothers, grandmothers and daughters: Personality and child care in three generation families.* New York: John Wiley-Interscience.

Cohler, B., and A. Hostetler. In press. Aging, intimate relations, and the life-story among gay men. In *A meaningful age,* ed. R. S. Weiss and S. A. Bass. New York: Cambridge University Press.

Cohler, B., A. Hostetler, and A. Boxer. 1998. Generativity, social context and lived experience: Narratives of gay men in middle adulthood. In *Generativity and adult experience: Psychosocial perspectives on caring and contributing to the next generation,* ed. D. McAdams and E. de St. Aubin. Washington, D.C.: American Psychological Association Press, 265–309.

Cohler, B., and M. Lieberman. 1979. Personality change across the second half of life: Findings from a study of Irish, Italian and Polish-American men and women. In *Ethnicity and aging,* ed. D. Gelfand and A. Kutznik. New York: Springer Publishing, 227–45.

———. 1980. Social relations and mental health: Middle-aged and older men and women from three European ethnic groups. *Research on Aging* 2:454–69.

Cohler, B., and J. Nakamura. 1996. Self and experience across the second half of life. In *Comprehensive review of geriatric psychiatry,* ed. J. Sadavoy, L. Lazarus, L. Jarvik, and G. Grossberg. 2d ed. Washington, D.C.: American Psychiatric Association Press, 153–96.

Cohler, B., F. Stott, and J. Musick. 1995. Adversity, vulnerability, and resilience: Cultural and developmental perspectives. In *Manual of developmental psychopathology,* vol. 2, ed. D. Cicchetti and D. Cohen. New York: Wiley, 753–800.

Cohler, B., S. Woolsey, J. Weiss, and H. Grunebaum. 1968. Child-rearing attitudes among young mothers volunteering and revolunteering for a psychological study. *Psychological Reports* 23:603–12.

Colarusso, C., and R. Nemiroff. 1979. Some observations and hypotheses about the psychoanalytic theory of adult development. *International Journal of Psychoanalysis* 60: 59–71.

———. 1981. *Adult development: A new dimension of psychodynamic theory and practice.* New York: Plenum.

Coleman, E. 1982. Developmental stages of the coming-out process. *American Behavioral Scientist* 25:469–82.

———. 1987. Assessment of sexual orientation. *Journal of Homosexuality* 13:9–24.

———. 1990. Toward a synthetic understanding of sexual orientation. In *Homosexuality/ heterosexuality: Concepts of sexual orientation,* ed. D. P. McWhirter, S. A. Sanders, and J. M. Reinisch. New York: Oxford University Press, 267–76.

Coleman, J. C. 1980. *The nature of adolescence.* New York and London: Methuen.

Coleman, P. 1986. *Ageing and reminiscence: Social and clinical implications.* New York: Wiley.

Coles, R. 1967. *Children of crisis: A study of courage and fear.* Boston: Little-Brown.

Colgan, P. 1987. Treatment of identity and intimacy issues in gay males. *Journal of Homosexuality* 13:101–23.

Colombo, J. 1982. The critical period concept: Research, methodology, and theoretical issues. *Psychological Bulletin* 91:260–75.

Connell, R. 1992. A very straight gay: Masculinity, homosexual experience, and the dynamics of gender. *American Sociological Review* 57:735–51.

Connerton, P. 1989. *How societies remember.* Cambridge: Cambridge University Press.

Conway, M. 1990. *Autobiographical memory: An introduction.* Philadelphia: Open University Press/Milton Keynes.

Coons, N. 1987. Modern prom: A night to remember. *Chicago Magazine,* June, 162–73.

Coontz, S. 1992. *The way we never were: American families and the nostalgia trap.* New York: Basic Books.

———. 1997. *The way we really are: Coming to terms with America's changing families.* New York: Basic Books.

Cooper, A. J. 1974. Aetiology of homosexuality. In *Understanding homosexuality: Its biological and psychological bases,* ed. J. A. Loraine. New York: American Elsevier Publishing Company, 1–24.

———. 1987. The transference neurosis: A concept ready for retirement. *Psychoanalytic Inquiry* 7:569–85.

Cooper, B. 1987. *Ageism in the lesbian community.* Freedom, Calif.: Crossing Press.

Corbett, K. 1993. The mystery of homosexuality. *Psychoanalytic Psychology* 10:345–57.

———. [1997] 1999. Homosexual boyhood: Notes on girlyboys. In *Sissies and tomboys: Gender nonconformity and homosexual childhood,* ed. M. Rottnek. New York: New York University Press, 107–39.

———. 1997. Speaking queer: A response to Richard C. Freedman. *Gender and Psychoanalysis* 2:495–514.

———. 1998. Gross-gendered identifications and homosexual boyhood: Toward a more complex theory of gender. *American Journal of Orthopsychiatry* 68:352–60.

Cornett, C. 1991. The "risky" intervention: Twinship self-object impasses and therapist self-disclosure in psychodynamic psychotherapy. *Clinical Social Work Journal* 19:49–61.

———. 1993. Dynamic psychotherapy of gay men: A view from self psychology. In *Affirmative dynamic psychotherapy with gay men,* ed. C. Cornett. Northvale, N.J.: Jason Aronson, 45–76.

———. 1995. *Reclaiming the authentic self: Dynamic psychotherapy with gay men.* Northvale, N.J.: Jason Aronson.

Cornett, C., and R. Hudson. 1987. Middle adulthood and the theories of Erikson, Gould, and Vaillant: Where does the gay man fit? *Journal of Gerontological Social Work* 10:61–73.

Cottle, T., and S. Klineberg. 1974. *The present of things future*. New York: Free Press.

Couch, A. S. 1995. Anna Freud's adult psychoanalytic technique: A defence of classical analysis. *International Journal of Psychoanalysis* 76:153–71.

Cowan, C., and P. Cowan. 1992. *When partners become parents: The big life change for couples*. New York: Basic Books.

———. 1987. Men's involvement in parenthood: Identifying the antecedents and understanding the barriers. In *Men's transition to parenthood,* ed. P. Berman and F. Pedersen. Hillsdale, N.J.: Erlbaum, 145–74.

Cowan, C., P. Cowan, G. Heming, E. Garrett, W. Coysh, H. Curtiss-Boles, and I. A. Boles. 1985. Transitions to parenthood: His, hers, theirs. *Journal of Family Issues* 6:451–81.

Cox, M. 1985. Progress and continued challenges in understanding the transition to parenthood. *Journal of Family Issues* 6:395–408.

Cramer, D., and A. Roach. 1988. Coming out to Mom and Dad: A study of gay males and their relationships with their parents. *Journal of Homosexuality* 15:79–91.

Crane, R. D. 1953. *The language of criticism and the structure of poetry*. Toronto: University of Toronto Press.

Crapanzano, V. 1980. *Tuhami: Portrait of a Moroccan*. Chicago: University of Chicago Press.

———. 1989. On self characterization. In *Cultural Psychology,* ed. J. Stigler, R. Shweder, and G. Herdt. Cambridge: Cambridge University Press.

Crosbie-Burnett, M., and L. Helmbrecht. 1993. A descriptive empirical study of gay male stepfamilies. *Family Relations* 42:256–62.

Cruikshank, M. 1990. Lavender and gray: A brief survey of lesbian and gay aging studies. In *Gay midlife and maturity,* ed. J. A. Lee. New York: Harrington Park Press, 77–88.

Csikszentmihalyi, M., and R. Larson. 1984. *Being adolescent: Conflict and growth in the teenage years*. New York: Basic Books.

Cumming, E., and W. Henry. 1961. *Growing old*. New York: Basic Books.

Cuneot, R., and S. Fugita. 1982. Perceived homosexuality: Measuring heterosexual attitudinal and nonverbal reactions. *Personality and Social Psychology Bulletin* 8:100–106.

Daniels, P., and K. Weingarten. 1982. *Sooner or later: The timing of parenthood in adult lives*. New York: Norton.

Dank, B. 1971. Coming out in the gay world. *Psychiatry* 34:180–97.

Dannecker, M. 1984. Towards a theory of homosexuality: Socio-historical perspectives. *Journal of Homosexuality* 10:1–8.

Dannefer, D. 1984. Adult development and social theory: A paradigmatic reappraisal. *American Sociological Review* 49:100–116.

Dannefer, D., and P. Uhlenberg. 1999. Paths of the life course: A typology. In *Handbook of theories of aging,* ed. V. L. Bengtson and K. W. Schaie. New York: Springer Publishing Company, 306–26.

Datan, N., A. Antonovsky, and B. Maoz. 1981. *A time to reap: The middle age of women in five Israeli subcultures*. Baltimore, Md.: Johns Hopkins University Press.

D'Augelli, A. R. 1991. Gay men in college: Identity processes and adaptations. *Journal of College Student Development* 32:140–46.

———. 1992. Lesbian and gay male undergraduates' experiences of harassment and fear on campus. *Journal of Interpersonal Violence* 7:383–95.

———. 1994. Lesbian and gay male development: Steps toward an analysis of lesbians' and gay men's lives. In *Lesbian and gay psychology: Theory, research and clinical applications,* ed. B. Greene and G. M. Herek. Psychological Perspectives on Lesbian and Gay Issues, vol. 1. Thousand Oaks, Calif.: Sage Publications, 118–32.

———. 1996. Lesbian, gay, and bisexual development during adolescence and young adulthood. In *Textbook of homosexuality and mental health,* ed. R. Cabaj and T. S. Stein. Washington, D.C.: American Psychiatric Press, 267–88.

———. 1998. Developmental implications of victimization of lesbian, gay, and bisexual youths. In *Stigma and sexual orientation: Understanding prejudice against lesbians, gay men and bisexuals,* ed. G. Herek. Thousand Oaks, Calif.: Sage Publications, 187–210.

D'Augelli, A. R., and S. L. Hershberger. 1993. Lesbian, gay and bisexual youth in community settings: Personal challenges and mental health problems. *American Journal of Community Psychology* 21:421–48.

D'Augelli, A. R., S. L. Hershberger, and N. W. Plinkington. 1998. Lesbian, gay, and bisexual youth and their families: Disclosure of sexual orientation and its consequences. *American Journal of Orthopsychiatry* 68:361–71.

D'Augelli, A. R., and C. Patterson, eds. 1995. *Lesbian, gay, and bisexual identities over the life span.* New York: Oxford University Press.

D'Augelli, A. R., and M. Rose. 1990. Homophobia in a university community: Attitudes and experience of white heterosexual freshman. *Journal of College Student Development* 31:484–91.

D'Augelli, J.-F., and A. R. D'Augelli. 1979. Sexual development and relationship involvement: A cognitive developmental view. In *Social exchange in developing relationships,* ed. R. Burgess and T. Huston. New York: Academic Press, 307–49.

Davics, P. 1992. The role of disclosure in coming out among gay men. In *Modern homosexualities: Fragments of lesbian and gay experience,* ed. K. Plummer. New York: Routledge, 75–83.

Davis, C. 1994. Genes, hormones and nuclei: The limits of biological understandings of homosexuality. Unpublished manuscript, Committee on Biopsychology, University of Chicago.

Davison, G. C. 1976. Homosexuality: The ethical challenge. *Journal of Consulting and Clinical Psychology* 44:157–62.

———. 1991. Constructionism and morality in therapy for homosexuality. In *Homosexuality: Research implications for public policy,* ed. J. C. Gonsiorek and J. D. Weinrich. Thousand Oaks, Calif.: Sage Publications, 137–48.

De Cecco, J. 1982. Definition and meaning of sexual orientation. *Journal of Homosexuality* 6:51–67.

———. 1987. Homosexuality's brief recovery: From sickness to health and back again. *Journal of Sex Research* 23:106–29.

De Cecco, J., and J. Elia. 1993. A critique and synthesis of biological essential and social constructionist views of sexuality and gender. *Journal of Homosexuality* 24:1–26.

De Cecco, J., and D. Parker. 1995. The biology of homosexuality: Sexual orientation or sexual preference? *Journal of Homosexuality* 28:1–27.

De Cecco, J., and M. Shively. 1984. From sexual identity to sexual relationships: A contextual shift. *Journal of Homosexuality* 10:1–26.

Deenen, A. A., L. Gijs, and A. X. van Naerssen. 1994. Intimacy and sexuality in gay male couples. *Archives of Sexual Behavior* 23:421–31.

D'Emilio, J. [1983] 1998. *Sexual politics, sexual communities: The making of a homosexual minority in the United States, 1940–1970.* 2d ed. Chicago: University of Chicago Press.

Dé Monchy, R. 1965. A clinical type of male homosexuality. *International Journal of Psychoanalysis* 46:218–25.

De Monteflores, C. 1986. Notes on the management of difference. In *Contemporary perspectives on psychotherapy with lesbians and gay men,* ed. T. Stein and C. Cohen. New York: Plenum Medical Book Company, 73–138.

Demos, J. 1986. *Past, present and personal: The family and the life course in American history.* New York: Oxford University Press.

Deutsch, L. 1995. Out of the closet and on to the couch: A psychoanalytic exploration of lesbian development. In *Lesbians and psychoanalysis: Revolutions in theory and practice,* ed. J. Glassgold and S. Iasenza. New York: Free Press, 19–38.

Devereux, G. 1967. *From anxiety to method in the behavioral sciences.* The Hague: Mouton.

DeVine, J. L. 1984. A systemic inspection of affectional preference orientation and the family of origin. *Journal of Social Work and Human Sexuality* 2:9–17.

Dickemann, M. 1993. Reproductive strategies and gender construction: An evolutionary view of homosexualities. *Journal of Homosexuality* 24:55–71.

———. 1995. Wilson's Panchreston: The inclusive fitness hypothesis of sociobiology re-examined. *Journal of Homosexuality* 28:147–83.

Dickes, R. 1991. Observations on the treatment of homosexual patients. In *The homosexualities: Reality, fantasy, and the arts,* ed. C. W. Socarides and V. D. Volkan. Madison, Conn.: International Universities Press, 9–28.

DiPlacido, J. 1998. Minority stress among lesbians, gay men, and bisexuals: A consequence of heterosexism, homophobia, and stigmatization. In *Stigma and sexual orientation: Understanding prejudice against lesbians, gay men and bisexuals,* ed. G. Herek. Thousand Oaks, Calif.: Sage Publications, 138–15.

Doell, R. 1995. Sexuality in the brain. *Journal of Homosexuality* 28:345–54.

Domenici, T. 1995. Exploding the myth of sexual psychopathology. In *Disorienting sexuality: Psychoanalytic reappraisals of sexual identities,* ed. T. Domenici and R. C. Lesser. New York: Routledge, 33–63.

———. 1997. Antihomosexuality, bad faith, and psychoanalysis: Response to commentaries. *Gender and Psychoanalysis* 2:225–40.

Domenici, T., and R. Lesser. 1995. *Disorienting sexuality: Psychoanalytic reappraisals of sexual identities.* New York: Routledge.

Dorell, B. 1991. Being there: A support network of lesbian women. *Journal of Homosexuality* 20:89–98.

Dörner, G. 1976. *Hormones and brain sexual differentiation.* Amsterdam: Elsevier Scientific.

———. 1980. Sexual differentiation of the brain. *Vitamins and Hormones* 38:325–81.

———. 1988. Neuroendocrine response to estrogen and brain differentiation in heterosexuals, homosexuals and transsexuals. *Archives of Sexual Behavior* 17:57–75.

———. 1989. Hormone-dependent brain development and neuroendocrine prophylaxis. *Experimental and Clinical Endocrinology* 94:4–22.

Dörner, G., F. Döcke, F. Götz, W. Rohnde, F. Stahl, and R. Tuonjes. 1987. Sexual differentiation of gonadotropin secretion, sexual orientation and gender role behavior. *Journal of Steroid Biochemistry* 27:1081–87.

Dörner, G., T. Geiser, L. Ahrens, L. Krell, H. Sieler, E. Kittner, and J. Muller. 1980. Prenatal stress and possible aetiogenetic factor homosexuality in human males. *Endokrinologie* 75:365–68.

Dörner, G., F. Götz, T. Ohkawa, W. Rohde, F. Stahl, and R. Tönjex. 1987. Prenatal stress and sexual brain differentiation in animal and human beings. International Academy of Sex Research, 13th annual meeting, Tutzing, Germany.

Dörner, G., and G. Hinz. 1968. Induction and prevention of male homosexuality by androgens. *Journal of Endocrinology* 40:387–88.

Dörner, G., I. Popper, F. Stahl, J. Kolzsch, and R. Uebelhack. 1991. Gene-and-environment-dependent neuroendocrine etiogenesis of homosexuality and transsexualism. *Experimental and Clinical Endocrinology* 98:141–50.

Dörner, G., W. Rohde, F. Stahl, L. Krell, and W. Masius. 1975. A neuroendocrine predisposition for homosexuality in men. *Archives of Sexual Behavior* 4:1–8.

Dörner, G., B. Schenk, B. Schmiedel, and L. Ahrens. 1983. Stressful events in prenatal life of bi- and homosexual men. *Experimental and Clinical Endocrinology* 81:88–90.

Dorpat, T. 1990. Female homosexuality: An overview. In *The homosexualities: Reality, fantasy, and the arts,* ed. C. W. Socarides and V. D. Volkan. Madison, Conn.: International Universities Press, 111–38.

Dorsey, D. 1996. Castration anxiety or feminine genital anxiety? In "Psychology of women: Psychoanalytic perspectives," ed. A. Richards and P. Tyson. *Journal of the American Psychoanalytic Association* 44 (supplement): 283–302.

Douvan, E., and J. Adelson. 1966. *The adolescent experience.* New York: Wiley.

Downey, J., and R. C. Friedman. 1995. Internalized homophobia in lesbian relationships. *Journal of the American Academy of Psychoanalysis* 23:435–48.

———. 1996a. The negative therapeutic reaction and self-hatred in gay and lesbian patients. In *Textbook of homosexuality and mental health,* ed. R. Cabaj and T. S. Stein. Washington, D.C.: American Psychiatric Press, 471–84.

———. 1996b. The psychoanalytic theory of female homosexuality: A contemporary view. American Psychoanalytic Meetings, Fall, New York.

Downs, A., and M. Fuller. 1991. Recollections of spermarche: An exploratory investigation. *Current Psychology: Research and Reviews* 10:93–102.

Drescher, J. 1994. Contemporary psychoanalytic psychotherapy with gay men. American Psychiatric Association, annual meetings.

———. 1995. Anti-homosexual bias in training. In *Disorienting sexuality: Psychoanalytic reappraisals of sexual identities,* ed. T. Domenici and R. C. Lesser. New York: Routledge, 227–42.

———. 1996a. A discussion across sexual orientation and gender boundaries: Reflections of a gay male analyst to a heterosexual female analyst. *Gender and Psychoanalysis* 1: 223–37.

———. 1996b. Psychoanalytic subjectivity and male homosexuality. In *Textbook of homosexuality and mental health,* ed. R. Cabaj and T. S. Stein. Washington, D.C.: American Psychiatric Press, 173–90.

———. 1997a. The analyst's authority and the patient's sexuality. Unpublished manuscript, William Alanson White Foundation.

———. 1997b. A brief history of the psychoanalytic theory of homosexuality. *Academy Forum* 41:4–6.

———. 1997c. From preoedipal to postmodern: Changing psychoanalytic attitudes toward homosexuality. *Gender and Psychoanalysis* 2:203–16.

———. 1998a. Contemporary psychoanalytic psychotherapy with gay men: With a commentary on reparative therapy of homosexuality. *Journal of Gay and Lesbian Psychotherapy* 2:51–74.

————. 1998b. I'm your handyman: A history of reparative therapies. *Journal of Homosexuality,* 36:19–42.

————. 1998c. *Psychoanalytic therapy and the gay man.* Hillsdale, N.J.: Analytic Press.

Duberman, M. 1993. *Stonewall.* New York: St. Martin's Press.

Durkheim, E. [1912] 1995. *The Elementary Forms of the Religious Life.* Trans. Karen Fields. New York: Basic Books.

Duvall, E. [1951] 1971. *Family Development.* Philadelphia: Lippincott.

Dyer, E. 1963. Parenthood as crisis: A restudy. *Journal of Marriage and Family Living* 25: 196–201.

Easterlin, R. 1987. *Birth and fortune: The impact of numbers on personal welfare.* 2d ed. Chicago: University of Chicago Press.

————. 1996. Economic and social implications of demographic patterns. In *Handbook of aging and the social sciences,* ed. R. Binstock and L. George. 4th ed. New York: Academic Press, 73–93.

Echols, A. 1989. *Daring to be bad: Radical feminism in America, 1967–1975.* Minneapolis: University of Minnesota Press.

Ehrenberg, M. 1996. Aging and mental health: Issues in the gay and lesbian community. In *Gay and lesbian mental health: A sourcebook for practitioners,* ed. C. Alexander. New York: Harrington Park Press, 189–209.

Ehrhardt, A. A. 1978. Behavioral sequelae of perinatal hormonal exposure in animals and man. In *Pharmacology: A generation of progress,* ed. M. Lipton, A DiMascio, and K. Killam. New York: Raven Press.

Eichorn, D., J. Clausen, N. Haan, M. Honzik, and P. Mussen. 1981. *Present and past in middle life.* New York: Academic Press.

Eichorn, D., P. Mussen, J. Clausen, N. Haan, and M. Honzik. 1981. Overview. In *Present and past in middle life,* ed. D. Eichorn, J. Clausen, N. Haan, M. Honzik, and P. Mussen. New York: Acadmeic Press, 411–34.

Eisold, B. 1998. Recreating mother: The consolidation of "heterosexual" gender identification in the young sons of homosexual men. *American Journal of Orthopsychiatry* 68:433–42.

Eissler, K. R. 1953. The effect of the structure of the ego on psychoanalytic technique. *Journal of the American Psychoanalytic Association* 1:104–43.

Elder, G. H., Jr. [1974] 1998. *Children of the Great Depression: Social change in life experience.* Boulder, Colo.: Westview Press/Harper Collins.

————. 1975. Age differentiation and the life course. *Annual Review of Sociology.* Palo Alto, Calif.: Annual Reviews.

————. 1979. Historical change in life patterns and personality. In *Life-span development and behavior,* ed. P. Baltes and O. G. Brim Jr. New York: Academic Press, 1:117–59.

————. 1980. Adolescence in historical perspective. In *Handbook of adolescent psychology,* ed. J. Adelson. New York: Wiley, 3–46.

————. 1986. Military times and turning points in mens' lives. *Developmental Psychology* 22:233–45.

————. 1987. War mobilization and the life course: A cohort of World War II veterans. *Sociological Focus* 2:449–72.

————. 1995. The life-course paradigm: Social change and individual development. In *Examining lives in context: Perspectives on the ecology of human development,* ed. P. Moen, G. H. Elder Jr., and Kurt Lüscher. Washington, D.C.: American Psychological Association, 101–39.

————. 1996. Human lives in changing societies: Life course and developmental insights. In *Developmental science: Multiple perspectives,* ed. R. Cairns, G. H. Elder Jr., and E. Costello. New York: Cambridge University Press, 31–62.

————. 1997. The life-course and human development. In *Handbook of child psychology,* vol. 1, *Theory,* ed. R. M. Lerner (general editor W. Damon). New York: Wiley, 939–91.

Elder, G. H., Jr., and A. Caspi. 1988. Human development and social change: An emerging perspective on the life course. In *Persons in context: Developmental processes,* ed. N. Bolger, A. Caspi, G. Downey, and M. Moorehouse. New York: Cambridge University Press, 77–113.

————. 1990. Studying lives in a changing society: Sociological and personological explorations. In *Studying persona and lives,* ed. A. I. Rabin, R. A. Zucker, R. A. Emmons, and S. Frank. New York: Springer Publishing, 201–47.

Elder, G. H., Jr., and T. Hareven. 1993. Rising above life's disadvantage: From the Great Depression to war. In *Children in time and place: Developmental and historical insights,* ed. G. H. Elder Jr., J. Modell, and R. Parke. New York: Cambridge University Press, 47–72.

Elder, G. H., M. Shanahan, and E. Clipp. 1994. When war comes to men's lives: Life course patterns in family, work, and health. *Psychology of Aging* 9:5–16.

Ellis, H. 1936. *Studies in the psychology of sex.* New York: Random House.

Ellis, H., and J. A. Symonds. [1897] 1975. *Sexual inversion.* New York: Arno Press.

Ellis, L. 1996a. Theories of homosexuality. In *The lives of lesbians, gays, and bisexuals: Children to adults,* ed. R. C. Savin-Williams and K. M. Cohen. Fort Worth, Tex.: Harcourt Brace, 11–34.

————. 1996b. The role of perinatal factors in determining sexual orientation. In *The lives of lesbians, gays, and bisexuals: Children to adults,* ed. R. C. Savin-Williams and K. M. Cohen. Fort Worth, Tex.: Harcourt Brace, 35–70.

————. 1997. Perinatal influences on behavior and health, with special emphasis on sexual orientation and other sex-linked behavior. In *Sexual orientation,* ed. L. Ellis and I. Ebertz. Westport, Conn.: Praeger, 71–90.

Ellis, L., and M. Ames. 1987. Neurohormonal functioning and sexual orientation: A theory of homosexuality-heterosexuality. *Psychological Bulletin* 101:233–58.

Ellis, L., M. A. Ames, W. Peckham, and D. Burke. 1988. Sexual orientation of human offspring may be altered by severe maternal stress during pregnancy. *Journal of Sex Research* 25:152–57.

Elson, M. 1986. *Self-psychology in clinical social work.* New York: Norton.

————. 1987. *The Kohut seminars on self-psychology and psychotherapy with adolescents and young adults.* New York: Norton.

Emde, R. 1981. Changing the models of infancy and the nature of early development: Remodeling the foundation. *Journal of the American Psychoanalytic Association* 29: 179–219.

————. 1983. From adolescence to midlife: Remodeling the structure of adult development. *Journal of the American Psychoanalytic Association* 33 (supplement): 59–61.

Entwisle, D., and S. Doering. 1981. *The first birth: A family turning point.* Baltimore: Johns Hopkins University Press.

Epstein, J. 1992. AIDS, stigma, and narratives of containment. *American Imago* 49: 293–310.

Epstein, S. 1987. Gay politics, ethnic identity: The limits of social constructionism. *Socialist Review* 93/94:9–54.

Erikson, E. H. [1951] 1963. *Childhood and society.* New York: Norton.

――――. 1958. *Young man Luther: A study in psychoanalysis and history.* New York: Norton.

――――. 1959. *Identity and the life cycle.* New York: Norton.

――――. 1964. Psychological reality and historical actuality. In *Insight and responsibility.* New York: Norton, 159–256.

――――. 1968. *Identity, youth and crisis.* New York: Norton.

――――. 1982. *The life-cycle completed.* New York: Norton.

Erikson, E. H., E. Erikson, and H. Kivnick. 1986. *Vital involvement in old age: The experience of old age in our time.* New York: Norton.

Escoll, P. 1977. The contribution of psychoanalytic developmental concepts to adult analysis. *Journal of the American Psychoanalytic Association* 25:219–34.

Espin, O. M. 1993. Issues of identity in the psychology of Latina lesbians. In *Psychological perspectives on lesbian and gay male experiences,* ed. L. Garnets and D. Kimmel. New York: Columbia University Press, 348–63.

――――. 1997. Crossing borders and boundaries: The life narratives of immigrant lesbians. In *Ethnic and cultural diversity among lesbians and gay men,* ed. B. Greene. Thousand Oaks, Calif.: Sage Publications, 191–215.

Evans, N., and A. D'Augelli. 1996. Lesbians, gay men, and bisexual people in college. In *The lives of lesbians, gays, and bisexuals: Children to adults,* ed. R. C. Savin-Williams and K. M. Cohen. Fort Worth, Tex.: Harcourt Brace, 201–26.

Evans, R. 1969. Childhood parental relationships of homosexual men. *Journal of Consulting and Clinical Psychology* 33:129–35.

Everall, I. P., P. J. Luthert, and P. L. Lantos. 1991. Neuronal loss in the frontal cortex in HIV infection. *Lancet* 337:1119–21.

Fairbarin, W. R. D. 1952. *On object-relations theory of the personality.* New York: Basic Books.

Falbo, T., and L. Peplau. 1980. Power strategies in intimate relationships. *Journal of Personality and Social Psychology* 38:618–28.

Falk, P. 1989. Lesbian mothers: Psychosocial assumptions in family law. *American Psychologist* 44:941–47.

Farber, S. L. 1981. *Identical twins reared apart: A reanalysis.* New York: Basic Books.

Farnham-Diggory, S. 1966. Self, future, and time: A developmental study of the concepts of psychotic, brain injured and normal children. Monographs of the Society for Research in Child Development, no. 33.

Fausto-Sterling, A. [1985] 1992. *Myths of gender: Biological theories about women and men.* Rev. ed. New York: Basic books.

――――. 1995. Animal models for the development of human sexuality: A critical evaluation. *Journal of Homosexuality* 28:217–36.

――――. 1997a. Beyond difference: A biologist's perspective. *Journal of Social Issues* 53:233–58.

――――. 1997b. How to build a man. In *Science and homosexualities,* ed. V. Rosario. New York, Routledge, 219–25.

Fein, R. 1976. Men's entrance into parenthood. *Family Coordinator* 25:341–48.

Feinsilver, D. 1999. Countridentification, comprehensive countertransference, and therapeutic action: Toward resolving the intrapsychic-interactional dichotomy. *Psychoanalytic Quarterly* 8:248–63.

Feldman, D. A. 1988. Gay youth and AIDS. *Journal of Homosexuality* 17:185–93.

Feldman, L. 1971. Deprssion and marital interaction. *Family Process* 20:389–95.

Feldman, S., and S. Nash. 1984. The transition from expectancy to parenthood: Impact of the firstborn child on men and women. *Sex Roles* 11:61–78.

Fellows, W. 1996. *Farm boys: Lives of gay men from the rural midwest.* Madison: University of Wisconsin Press.

Ferenczi, S. [1911] 1950. On the part played by homosexuality in the pathogenesis of paranoia. In *Sex in psychoanalysis,* ed. E. Jones. New York, Basic Books, 154–86.

———. [1913] 1950. Stages in the development of the sense of reality. In *Sex in psychoanalysis,* ed. E. Jones. New York, Basic Books, 213–39.

———. [1914] 1950. On the nosology of male homosexuality. In *Sex in psychoanalysis,* ed. E. Jones. New York, Basic Books, 296–318.

Ferguson, M. 1994. Fixation and regression in the psychoanalytic theory of homosexuality: A critical evaluation. *Journal of Homosexuality* 27:309–27.

Firth, R., J. Hubert, and A. Forge. 1970. *Families and their relatives: Kinship in a middle-class sector of London.* London: Humanities Press.

Fischer, J., and A. Fischer. 1963. The New Englanders of Orchard Town. In *Six cultures: Studies of childrearing,* ed. B. Whiting. New York: Wiley, 869–1010.

Fishman, J. M. 1994. Countertransference, the therapeutic frame and AIDS: One psychotherapist's response. In *Therapists on the front line: Psychotherapy with gay men in the age of AIDS,* ed. S. Cadwell, R. Burnham Jr., and M. Forstein. Washington, D.C.: American Psychiatric Association Press, 497–516.

Fiske, M. 1980. Tasks and crises of the second half of life: The interrelationship of commitment, coping, and adaptation. In *Handbook of Mental Health and Aging,* ed. J. Birren and R. B. Sloane. Englewood Cliffs, N.J.: Prentice-Hall, 337–73.

Fiske, M., and D. Chiriboga. 1990. *Change and continuity in adult life.* San Francisco: Jossey-Bass.

Fitzgerald, J. M. 1996. Intersecting meanings of reminiscence in adult development and aging. In *Remembering our past: Studies in autobiographical memory,* ed. D.C. Rubin. New York: Cambridge University Press.

Fivush, R., C. Haden, and E. Reese. 1996. Remembering, recounting, reminiscing: The development of autobiographical memory in social context. In *Remembering our past: Studies in autobiographical memory,* ed. D.C. Rubin. New York: Cambridge University Press, 341–59.

Flaks, D., I. Fischer, F. Masterpasqua, and G. Joseph. 1995. Lesbians choosing motherhood: A comparative study of lesbian and heterosexual parents and their children. *Developmental Psychology* 31:105–14.

Fliess, R. 1944. The metapsychology of the analyst. *Psychoanalytic Quarterly* 11:211–27.

———. 1953. Countertransference and counteridentification. *Journal of the American Psychoanalytic Association* 1:268–84.

Fliess, R., ed. 1948. *The psychoanalytic reader.* New York: International Universities Press.

Forger, N., and S. Breedlove. 1987. Motoneuronal death during early human fetal development. *Journal of Comparative Neurology* 264:118–22.

Foucault, M. [1961] 1988. *Madness and civilization: A history of insanity in the age of reason.* Trans. R. Howard. New York: Random House/Vintage Books.

———. [1966] 1970. *The order of things: An archaeology of the human sciences.* New York: Random House/Vintage House Books.

———. 1975. *Discipline and punish.* New York: Pantheon.

———. [1976] 1990. *The history of sexuality,* vol. 1, *An introduction.* Trans. R. Hurley. New York: Random House.

————. [1984a] 1990. *The history of sexuality,* vol. 2, *The use of pleasure.* Trans. R. Hurley. New York: Random House.

————. [1984b] 1990. *The history of sexuality,* vol. 3, *The care of the self.* Trans. R. Hurley. New York: Random House.

Foulkes, M. 1994. Single worlds and homosexual lifestyles: Patterns of sexuality and intimacy. In *Sexuality across the life course,* ed. A. Rossi. Chicago: University of Chicago Press, 151–84.

Fowles, M. 1994. Single worlds and homosexual lifestyles: Patterns of sexuality and intimacy. In *Sexuality across the life course,* ed. A. Rossi. Chicago: University of Chicago Press, 151–86.

Freedman, N. 1975. Homosexuals may be healthier than straights. *Psychology Today* 8: 28–32.

Freeman, M. 1985. Psychoanalytic narration and the problem of historical knowledge. *Psychoanalysis and Contemporary Thought* 8:133–82.

————. 1993. *Rewriting the self: History, memory, narrative.* New York: Routledge.

Freeman, T. 1955. Clinical and theoretical observations on male homosexuality. *International Journal of Psychoanalysis* 36:335–47.

Frencher, J., and J. Henkin. 1973. The menopausal queen: Adjustment to aging and the male homosexual. *American Journal of Orthopsychiatry* 43:670–74.

Freud, A. [1936] 1946. *The ego and the mechanisms of defense.* New York: International Universities Press.

————. [1941–45] 1973. Monthly reports to the Foster Parents' Plan for War Children, Inc., New York. In A. Freud, *The Writings of Anna Freud,* vol. 3, *1939–1945.* New York: International Universities Press, 3–540.

————. 1949. Some clinical remarks concerning the treatment of cases of male homosexuality. *International Journal of Psychoanalysis* 30:196.

————. 1951. Clinical observations on the treatment of male homosexuality. *Psychoanalytic Quarterly* 20:337–38.

————. 1958. Adolescence. *Psychoanalytic Study of the Child* 16:225–78.

————. 1965. *Normality and psychopathology in childhood: Assessments of development.* New York: International Universities Press.

————. 1971. The infantile neurosis: Genetic and dynamic considerations. *Psychoanalytic Study of the Child* 26:79–90.

Freud, A., and D. Burlingham. [1944] 1973. Infants without families: The case for and against residential nurseries. In A. Freud, *The Writings of Anna Freud,* vol. 3, *1939–1945.* New York: International Universities Press, 543–664.

Freud, S. 1897–1904. *The complete letters of Sigmund Freud to Wilhelm Fliess, 1887–1904.* Ed. J. Masson. Cambridge, Mass.: Harvard University Press.

————. [1891] 1953. *On aphasia.* New York: International Universities Press.

————. [1895] 1966. Project for a scientific psychology. In *The standard edition of the complete psychological works of Sigmund Freud.* Ed. and trans. J. Strachey. London: Hogarth Press, 1:295–398.

————. 1900. The interpretation of dreams. In *The standard edition of the complete psychological works of Sigmund Freud.* Ed. and trans. J. Strachey. London: Hogarth Press, vols. 4–5.

————. [1901] 1960. The psychopathology of everyday life. In *The standard edition of the complete psychological works of Sigmund Freud.* Ed. and trans. J. Strachey. London: Hogarth Press, vol. 6.

———. [1905a] 1953. Fragment of an analysis of a case of hysteria. In *The standard edition of the complete psychological works of Sigmund Freud*. Ed. and trans. J. Strachey. London: Hogarth Press, 7:7–124.

———. [1905b] 1953. On psychotherapy. In *The standard edition of the complete psychological works of Sigmund Freud*. Ed. and trans. J. Strachey. London: Hogarth Press, 7:257–70.

———. [1905–24] 1953. Three essays on the theory of sexuality. In *The standard edition of the complete psychological works of Sigmund Freud*. Ed. and trans. J. Strachey. London: Hogarth Press, 7:130–243.

———. [1909a] 1955. Analysis of a phobia in a five-year old boy. In *The standard edition of the complete psychological works of Sigmund Freud*. Ed. and trans. J. Strachey. London: Hogarth Press, 10:5–147.

———. [1909b] 1959. Family Romances. In *The standard edition of the complete psychological works of Sigmund Freud*. Ed. and trans. J. Strachey. London: Hogarth Press, 9:235–44.

———. [1909c] 1955. Notes upon a case of obsessional neurosis. In *The standard edition of the complete psychological works of Sigmund Freud*. Ed. and trans. J. Strachey. London: Hogarth Press, 10:153–320.

———. [1910a] 1957. Five lectures on psychoanalysis (The Clark Lectures). In *The standard edition of the complete psychological works of Sigmund Freud*. Ed. and trans. J. Strachey. London: Hogarth Press, 11:9–58.

———. [1910b] 1957. The future prospects of psycho-analytic therapy. In *The standard edition of the complete psychological works of Sigmund Freud*. Ed. and trans. J. Strachey. London: Hogarth Press, 11:141–61.

———. [1910c] 1957. Leonardo Da Vinci and a memory of his childhood. In *The standard edition of the complete psychological works of Sigmund Freud*. Ed. and trans. J. Strachey. London: Hogarth Press, 11:63–138.

———. [1910d] 1957. A special type of object choice made by men (Contributions to the psychology of love—I). In *The standard edition of the complete psychological works of Sigmund Freud*. Ed. and trans. J. Strachey. London: Hogarth Press, 11:163–75.

———. [1911] 1958. Psycho-analytic notes on an autobiographical account of a case of paranoia (dementia paranoides). In *The standard edition of the complete psychological works of Sigmund Freud*. Ed. and trans. J. Strachey. London: Hogarth Press, 12:3–82.

———. [1912a] 1958. The dynamics of the transference. In *The standard edition of the complete psychological works of Sigmund Freud*. Ed. and trans. J. Strachey. London: Hogarth Press, 12:97–108.

———. [1912b] 1957. On the universal tendency to debasement in the sphere of love (Contributions to the psychology of love—II). In *The standard edition of the complete psychological works of Sigmund Freud*. Ed. and trans. J. Strachey. London: Hogarth Press, 11:177–90.

———. [1912c] 1958. Recommendations to physicians practicing psychoanalysis. In *The standard edition of the complete psychological works of Sigmund Freud*. Ed. and trans. J. Strachey. London: Hogarth Press, 12:109–20.

———. [1913] 1958. The claims of psychoanalysis to scientific interest. In *The standard edition of the complete psychological works of Sigmund Freud*. Ed. and trans. J. Strachey. London: Hogarth Press, 13:165–92.

———. [1914a] 1957. On the history of the psychoanalytic movement. In *The standard edition of the complete psychological works of Sigmund Freud*. Ed. and trans. J. Strachey. London: Hogarth Press, 14:7–66.

————. [1914b] 1957. On narcissism: An introduction. In *The standard edition of the complete psychological works of Sigmund Freud*. Ed. and trans. J. Strachey. London: Hogarth Press, 14:67–104.

————. [1914c] 1958. Remembering, repeating and working through: Further recommendations on the technique of psychoanalysis. In *The standard edition of the complete psychological works of Sigmund Freud*. Ed. and trans. J. Strachey. London: Hogarth Press, 12:146–56.

————. [1914–18] 1955. From the history of an infantile neurosis. In *The standard edition of the complete psychological works of Sigmund Freud*. Ed. and trans. J. Strachey. London: Hogarth Press, 17:7–122.

————. [1915a] 1957. A case of paranoia running counter to the psychoanalytic theory of the disease. In *The standard edition of the complete psychological works of Sigmund Freud*. Ed. and trans. J. Strachey. London: Hogarth Press, 14:261–72.

————. [1915b] 1958. Observations on transference love (further recommendations on the technique of psycho-analysis, III). In *The standard edition of the complete psychological works of Sigmund Freud*. Ed. and trans. J. Strachey. London: Hogarth Press, 12:157–71.

————. [1915c] 1957. The unconscious. In *The standard edition of the complete psychological works of Sigmund Freud*. Ed. and trans. J. Strachey. London: Hogarth Press, 14:159–216.

————. [1916–17] 1963. Introductory lectures on psychoanalysis. In *The standard edition of the complete psychological works of Sigmund Freud*. Ed. and trans. J. Strachey. London: Hogarth Press, vols. 15–16.

————. [1920] 1955. The psychogenesis of a case of homosexuality in a woman. In *The standard edition of the complete psychological works of Sigmund Freud*. Ed. and trans. J. Strachey. London: Hogarth Press, 18:147–72.

————. [1921a] 1955. Group psychology and the analysis of the ego. In *The standard edition of the complete psychological works of Sigmund Freud*. Ed. and trans. J. Strachey. London: Hogarth Press, 18:67–144.

————. [1921b] 1977. Letter (to E. Jones). *Body Politic* 9:7.

————. [1922] 1955. Some neurotic mechanisms in jealousy, paranoia, and homosexuality. In *The standard edition of the complete psychological works of Sigmund Freud*. Ed. and trans. J. Strachey. London: Hogarth Press, 18:221–32.

————. [1923] 1961. The ego and the id. In *The standard edition of the complete psychological works of Sigmund Freud*. Ed. and trans. J. Strachey. London: Hogarth Press, 19:12–59.

————. [1924] 1961. The economic problem of masochism. In *The standard edition of the complete psychological works of Sigmund Freud*. Ed. and trans. J. Strachey. London: Hogarth Press, 19:157–70.

————. [1925] 1959. An autobiographical study. In *The standard edition of the complete psychological works of Sigmund Freud*. Ed. and trans. J. Strachey. London: Hogarth Press, 20:7–76.

————. [1927] 1961. Civilization and its discontents. In *The standard edition of the complete psychological works of Sigmund Freud*. Ed. and trans. J. Strachey. London: Hogarth Press, 21:64–148.

————. [1930] 1977. Open letter to *Wiener Arbeitzeitung* (16 May 1930). Trans. and reprinted in *Body Politic* (Toronto, May 1977), 8.

————. [1933] 1964. New introductory lectures on psycho-analysis. In *The standard edition of the complete psychological works of Sigmund Freud*. Ed. and trans. J. Strachey. London: Hogarth Press, 22:7–184.

————. [1935] 1951. A letter from Freud. *American Journal of Psychiatry* 107:786.

————. [1937] 1964. An outline of psychoanalysis. In *The standard edition of the complete psychological works of Sigmund Freud*. Ed. and trans. J. Strachey. London: Hogarth Press, 23:144–254.

————. [1940] 1964. Constructions in analysis. In *The standard edition of the complete psychological works of Sigmund Freud*. Ed. and trans. J. Strachey. London: Hogarth Press, 23:255–70.

Freund, K., and R. Blanchard. 1983. Is the distant relationship of fathers and homosexual sons related to the sons' erotic preference for male partners, or to the sons' atypical gender identity or both? *Journal of Homosexuality* 9:7–25.

Fricke, A. 1981. *Reflections of a rock lobster*. Boston, Mass.: Alyson Publications.

Fricke, A., and W. Fricke. 1991. *Sudden strangers: The story of a gay son and his father*. New York: St. Martin's Press.

Friedman, C. 1998. Eros in a gay dyad: A case presentation. *Gender and Psychoanalysis* 3:335–46.

Friedman, L. 1988. *The anatomy of psychotherapy*. Hillsdale, N.J.: Analytic Press.

Friedman, R. C. 1976a. Psychodynamics and sexual object choice. *Contemporary Psychoanalysis* 12:94–108.

————. 1976b. Psychodynamics and sexual object choice. III. A rereply to Drs. I. Bieber and C. W. Socarides. *Contemporary Psychoanalysis* 12:379–85.

————. 1988. *Male homosexuality: A contemporary psychoanalytic perspective*. New Haven, Conn.: Yale University Press.

————. 1997. Response to Ken Corbett's "Homosexual boyhood." *Gender and Psychoanalysis* 2:487–94.

Friedman, R. C., and J. Downey. 1998a. Psychoanalysis and the model of homosexuality as psychopathology: A historical overview. *American Journal of Psychoanalysis* 58: 249–70.

————. 1993a. Neurobiology and sexual orientation: Current relationships. *Journal of Neuropsychiatry and Clinical Neuroscience* 5:131–53.

————. 1993b. Psychoanalysis, psychobiology, and homosexuality. *Journal of the American Psychoanalytic Association* 41:1159–98.

————. 1994. Homosexuality. *New England Journal of Medicine* 331 (14): 923–30.

————. 1995. MacIntosh study faulted. *Journal of the American Psychoanalytic Association* 43:304–5.

Friedman, R. C., and A. Lilling. 1996. An empirical study of the beliefs of psychoanalysts about scientific and clinical dimensions of male homosexuality. *Journal of Homosexuality* 32:79–89.

Friedman, R. C., and L. Stern. 1980. Fathers, sons, and sexual orientation: Replication of a Bieber hypothesis. *Psychiatric Quarterly* 52:175–89.

Friend, R. 1980. Gayaging: Adjustment and the older gay male. *Alternative Lifestyles* 3:231–48.

————. 1987. The individual and social psychology of aging: Clinical implications for lesbians and gay men. *Journal of Homosexuality* 4:307–31 .

————. 1990a. Older lesbian and gay people: A theory of successful aging. In *Gay midlife and maturity*, ed. J. A. Lee. New York: Harrington Park Press, 99–118.

————. 1990b. Older lesbian and gay people: Responding to homophobia. In *Homosexuality and family relations*, ed. F. W. Bozett and M. B. Sussman. New York: Haworth/ Harrington Park Press, 241–63.

Frommer, S. 1994a. Homosexuality and psychoanalysis: Technical considerations revisited. *Psychoanalytic Dialogues* 4:215–34.

———. 1994b. Reply to Renik and Spezzano. *Psychoanalytic Dialogues* 4:247–52.

———. 1995. Countertransference obscurity in the psychoanalytic treatment of homosexual patients. In *Disorienting sexuality: Psychoanalytic reappraisals of sexual identities,* ed. T. Domenici and R. C. Lesser. New York: Routledge, 65–82.

Frosch, J. 1983. *The psychotic process.* New York: International Universities Press.

Furstenberg, F., J. Brooks-Gunn, and S. Morgan. 1987. *Adolescent mothers in later life.* New York: Cambridge University Press.

Fusco, J. 1993. How gay men at midlife achieved generativity through selfobject relationships. Unpublished doctoral dissertation, Chicago School of Professional Psychology.

Futuyma, D., and S. Risch. 1984. Sexual orientation, sociobiology, and evolution. *Journal of Homosexuality* 10:157–67.

Gabbard, G. 1994. On love and lust in erotic transference. *Journal of the American Psychoanalytic Association* 42:385–403.

Gabriel, M., and G. Monaco. 1995. Revisiting the question of self disclosure: The lesbian therapist's dilemma. In *Lesbians and psychoanalysis: Revolutions in theory and practice,* ed. J. Glassgold and S. Iasenza. New York: Free Press, 161–72.

Gaddis, A., and J. Brooks-Gunn. 1985. The male experience of pubertal change. *Journal of Youth and Adolescence* 14:61–69.

Gagnon, J., and W. Simon. 1973. *Sexual conduct.* Chicago: Aldine.

Gair, S. 1995. The false self, shame, and the challenge of self-cohesion. In *Lesbians and psychoanalysis: Revolutions in theory and practice,* ed. J. Glassgold and S. Iasenza. New York: Free Press, 107–24.

Galatzer-Levy, R. 1978. Qualitative change from quantitative change: Mathematical catastrophe theory in relation to psychoanalysis. *Journal of the American Psychoanalytic Association* 26:921–36.

———. 1995. Psychoanalysis and dynamical systems theory: Prediction and self. *Journal of the American Psychoanalytic Association* 43:1085–1113.

Galatzer-Levy, R., and B. Cohler. 1990. The developmental psychology of the self and the changing world-view of psychoanalysis. *Annual for Psychoanalysis* 17:1–44.

———. 1993. *The essential other.* New York: Basic Books.

———. 1998. *Contemporary psychoanalysis.* New York: Basic Books.

Gardner, R. 1983. *Self-Inquiry.* Boston: Little-Brown and Atlantic Monthly Press.

Garfinkel, H. [1967] 1984. Passing and the managed achievement of sex status in an "intersexed" person, pt. 1 and appendix. In *Studies in ethnomethodology.* Cambridge, Mass.: Polity Press, 116–85.

Garnets, L. D., G. M. Herek, and B. Levy. 1990. Violence and victimization of lesbians and gay men: Mental health consequences. *Journal of Interpersonal Violence* 51:366–83.

Garnets, L., and D. Kimmel. 1993. Adolescence, mid-life, and aging. In *Psychological perspectives on lesbian and gay male experiences,* ed. L. Garnets and D. Kimmel. New York: Columbia University Press, 460–67.

Gartrell, N., A. Banks, J. Hamilton, N. Reed, H. Bishop, and C. Rodas. 1999. The national lesbian family study: 2. Interviews with mothers of toddlers. *American Journal of Orthopsychiatry* 69:362–69.

Gay, P. 1988. *Freud: A life for our times.* New York: Norton.

———. 1998. *Pleasure wars: The bourgeois experience,* vol. 5, *Victoria to Freud.* New York: Norton.

Gebhard, P. H. 1965. Situational factors affecting human sexual behavior. In *Sex and behavior*, ed. F. A. Beach. New York: John Wiley and Sons.

Gebhard, P. H., J. H. Gagnon, W. B. Pomeroy, and C. V. Christenson. 1965. *Sex offenders: An analysis of types.* New York: Harper and Row.

Gedo, J. 1993. The hierarchical model of mental functioning: Sources and applications. In *Hierarchical concepts in psychoanalysis: Theory, research and clinical practice,* ed. A. Wilson and J. E. Gedo. New York: Guilford Press, 129–52.

Gedo, J., and A. Goldberg. 1973. *Models of the mind.* Chicago. University of Chicago Press.

Geertz, C. 1973. Thick description: Toward an interpretive theory of culture. In *The interpretation of cultures.* New York: Basic Books, 3–30.

———. [1974] 1983. "From the native's point of view": On the nature of anthropological understanding. In *Local knowledge: Further essays in interpretive anthropology.* New York: Basic Books, 55–72.

George, L. 1993. Sociological perspectives on life transitions. *Annual Review of Sociology* 19:353–73.

———. 1996. Missing links: The case for a social psychology of the life-course. *Gerontologist* 36:248–55.

Gergen, K. 1977. Stability, change and chance in understanding human development. In *Life-span developmental psychology: Dialectical perspectives on experimental research,* ed. N. Datan and H. Reese. New York: Academic Press, 32–65.

———. 1994. *Realities and relationships: Soundings in social construction.* Cambridge, Mass.: Harvard University Press.

Gerstel, C. J., A. J. Feraios, and G. Herdt. 1989. Widening circles: Am ethnographic profile of a youth group. In *Gay and lesbian youth,* ed. G. Herdt. New York: Harrington Park Press, 75–92.

Gibson, P. 1989. Gay male and lesbian youth suicide. In *Report of the secretary's task force on youth suicide,* vol. 3, *Preventions and interventions in youth suicide,* ed. R. Feinlieb. Rockville, Md.: Department of Health and Human Services, 110 42.

———. 1994. Gay male and lesbian youth suicide. In *Death by denial: Studies of suicide in gay and lesbian teenagers,* ed. G. Remafedi. Boston: Alyson Publications, 15–68.

Gilbert, H. 1994. Selfobjects throughout the life span: Research with nonclinical subjects. In *Progress in self psychology,* ed. A. Goldberg. Hillsdale, N.J.: Analytic Press, 10:31–51.

Gill, M. 1976. Metapsychology is not psychology. In *Psychology versus metapsychology,* ed. M. Gill and P. Holzman. New York: International Universities Press, 71–105. Psychological Issues Monograph, no. 71.

———. 1982. *Analysis of transference,* vol. 1, *Theory and technique.* Madison, Conn.: International Universities Press.

———. 1994. *Psychoanalysis in transition: A personal view.* Hillsdale, N.J.: Analytic Press.

Gillespie, W. 1956. The general theory of sexual perversion. *International Journal of Psychoanalysis* 37:396–403.

———. [1956] 1995. The structure and aetiology of sexual perversions. In *Life, sex, and death: Selected writings.* Ed. M. D. A. Sinason. New York: Routledge.

———. 1964. Symposium on homosexuality. *International Journal of Psychoanalysis* 45: 203–9.

Gilligan, C. 1982. *In a different voice: Psychological theory and women's development.* Cambridge, Mass.: Harvard University Press.

———. 1990. Remapping the moral domain: New images of the self in relationship. In

Essential papers on the psychology of women, ed. C. Zanardi. New York: New York University Press, 480–96.

Gilligan, C., N. Lyons, and T. Hanmer. 1990. *Making connections: The relational worlds of adolescent girls at Emma Willard School.* Cambridge, Mass.: Harvard University Press.

Gillis, J. 1994. *Commemorations: The politics of nation identity.* Princeton, N.J.: Princeton University Press.

———. 1996. *A world of their own making: Myth, ritual and the quest for family values.* New York: Basic Books.

Gitelson, M. 1952. The emotional position of the analyst in the psychoanalytic situation. *International Journal of Psychoanalysis* 33:1–10.

———. 1962. The first phase of psycho-analysis: Symposium on the curative factors in psycho-analysis. *International Journal of Psychoanalysis* 43:194–205.

Gitlin, T. 1987. *The sixties: Years of hope, days of rage.* New York: Bantam Books.

Gladue, B. 1988. Hormones in relationship to homosexual/bisexual/heterosexual gender orientation. In *Handbook of sexology: The pharmacology and endrincology of sexual function,* ed. M. J. A. Sitzen. Amsterdam: Elsevier, 6:388–409.

Gladue, B., R. Green, and R. Hellman. 1984. Neuroendocrine response to estrogen and sexual orientation. *Science* 225:1469–99.

Glassgold, J. 1995. Psychoanalysis with lesbians: Self-reflection and agency. In *Lesbians and psychoanalysis: Revolutions in theory and practice,* ed. J. Glassgold and S. Iasenza. New York: Free Press, 203–28.

Glassgold, J., and S. Iasenza, eds. *Lesbians and psychoanalysis: Revolutions in theory and practice.* New York: Free Press.

Glazer, D. 1998. Homosexuality and the analytic stance: Implications for treatment and supervision. *Gender and Psychoanalysis* 3:397–412.

Glick, P. 1989. The family life-cycle and social change. *Family Relations* 38:123–29.

Goffman, E. 1959. *The presentation of self in everyday life.* Garden City, N.Y.: Doubleday-Anchor Books.

———. 1963. *Stigma: Notes on the management of spoiled identity.* Englewood-Cliffs, N.Y.: Prentice-Hall.

Goldberg, A. 1988. *A fresh look at psychoanalysis.* Hillsdale: Analytic Press.

———. 1993. Sexualization and desexualization. *Psychoanalytic Quarterly* 62:383–99.

———. 1995. *The problem of perversion: The view from self-psychology.* New Haven, Conn.: Yale University Press.

———. 1999. *Being of two minds: The vertical split in psychoanalysis and psychotherapy.* Hillsdale, N.J.: Analytic Press.

Golden, C. 1996. What's in a name? Sexual self-identification among women. In *The lives of lesbians, gays, and bisexuals: Children to adults,* ed. R. C. Savin-Williams and K. M. Cohen. Fort Worth, Tex.: Harcourt Brace, 227–49.

———. 1997. Diversity and variability in women's sexual identities. In *Same sex: Debating the ethics, science, and culture of homosexuality,* ed. J. Corvino. Lanham, N.J.: Rowman and Littlefield, 149–66.

Goldsmith, S. 1995. Oedipus or Orestes? Aspects of gender identity development in homosexual men. *Psychoanalytic Inquiry* 15:112–24. (Special issue, Feminine and masculine gender identity, ed. F. D. Barth.)

Goldstein, E. 1994. Self-disclosure in treatment: What therapists do and don't talk about. *Clinical Social Work Journal* 22:417–33.

Goldstein, M. J. 1983. Family interaction: Patterns predictive of the onset and course of schizophrenia. In *Psychosocial Intervention in Schizophrenia: An International View*, ed. H. Stierlin, L. C. Wynne, and M. Wirsching. New York: Springer-Verlag, 5–20.

———. 1987. Psychosocial issues. *Schizophrenia Bulletin* 13:157–71.

Goldstein, M. J., I. Hand, and K. Hahlweg, eds. 1986. *Treatment of Schizophrenia: Family assessment and Intervention*. New York: Springer-Verlag.

Golombok, S., A. Spencer, and M. Rutter. 1983. Children in lesbian and single-parent households: Psychosexual and psychiatric appraisals. *Journal of Child Psychology and Psychiatry* 24:551–72.

Gonsiorek, J. 1982a. Results of psychological testing on homosexual populations. In *Homosexuality: Social, psychological, and biological issues,* ed. W. Paul, J. Weinrich, J. C. Weinrich, J. C. Gonsiorek, and M. E. Hotvedt. Beverly Hills, Calif.: Sage Publications, 71–80.

———. 1982b. Social psychological concepts in the understanding of homosexuality. *American Behavioral Scientist* 25:483–92.

———. 1988. Mental health issues of gay and lesbian adolescents. *Journal of Adolescent Health Care* 9:114–22.

———. 1991. The empirical basis for the demise of the illness model of homosexuality. In *Homosexuality: Research implications for public policy,* ed. J. C. Gonsiorek and J. D. Weinrich. Thousand Oaks, Calif.: Sage Publications, 115–36.

———. 1995. Gay male identities: Concepts and issues. In *Lesbian, gay, and bisexual identities over the life span,* ed. A. R. D'Augelli and C. Patterson. New York: Oxford University Press, 24–47.

———. 1996. Mental health and sexual orientation. In *The lives of lesbians, gays, and bisexuals: Children to adults,* ed. R. C. Savin-Williams and K. M. Cohen. Fort Worth, Tex.: Harcourt Brace, 462–78.

Gonsiorek, J. C., and J. Rudolph. 1991. Homosexual identity: Coming out and other developmental events. In *Homosexuality: Research implications for public policy,* ed. J. C. Gonsiorek and J. D. Weinrich. Thousand Oaks, Calif.: Sage Publications, 161–76.

Gonsiorek, J. C., and J. D. Weinrich. 1991. The definition and scope of sexual orientation. In *Homosexuality: Research implications for public policy,* ed. J. C. Gonsiorek and J. D. Weinrich. Thousand Oaks, Calif.: Sage Publications, 1–12.

Good, B. 1994. *Medicine, rationality, and experience: An anthropological perspective*. New York: Cambridge University Press.

Goodwin, D., and S. Guze. 1996. *Psychiatric diagnosis*. 4th ed. New York: Oxford University Press.

Gooren, L. 1984. Sexual dimorphism and transsexuality: Clinical observations. *Progress in Brain Research* 61:399–406.

———. 1986a. The neuroendocrine response of luteinizing hormone to estrogen administration in heterosexual, homosexual, and transsexual subjects. *Journal of Clinical Endocrinology* 15:3–14.

———. 1986b. The neuroendocrine response of luteinizing hormone to estrogen administration in the human is not sex-specific but dependent on the hormonal environment. *Journal of Clinical Endocrinology and Metabolism* 63:588–93.

———. 1990. Biomedical theories of sexual orientation: A critical examination. In *Homosexuality/heterosexuality: Concepts of sexual orientation,* ed. D. P. McWhirter, S. A. Sanders, and J. M. Reinisch. New York: Oxford University Press, 71–87.

———. 1995. Biomedical concepts of homosexuality: Folk belief in a white coat. *Journal of Homosexuality* 28:237–46.

Gooren, L., E. Fliers, and K. Courtney. 1990. Biological determinants of sexual orientation. *Annual Review of Sex Research* 1:175–96.

Gordon, K., E. Eli, and K. Gordon. 1965. Factors in post-partum emotional adjustment.
Obstetrics and Gynecology 25:158–66.

Gorski, R., J. Gordon, J. Shrune, and A. Southern. 1978. Evidence for a morphological
sex difference within the medial preoptic area of the rat brain. *Brain Research*
148:333–46.

Gottman, J. 1990. Children of gay and lesbian parents. In *Homosexuality and family relations,* ed. F. W. Bozett and M. B. Sussman. New York: Haworth/Harrington Park
Press, 177–96.

Gould, D. 1995. A critical examination of the notion of pathology in psychoanalysis. In
Lesbians and psychoanalysis: Revolutions in theory and practice, ed. J. Glassgold and S. Iasenza. New York: Free Press, 3–18.

Gould, E., and J. Rosenberger. 1994. Erotic transference: Contemporary perspectives.
Psychoanalytic Inquiry 14, no. 4. Hillsdale, N.J.: Analytic Press.

Gould, R. 1993. Transformational tasks in adulthood. In *The course of life,* vol. 6, *Late
adulthood,* ed. G. H. Pollock and S. Greenspan. Madison, Conn.: International Universities Press, 23–68.

Gove, W., and M. Geerken. 1977. The effect of children and employment on the mental
health of married men and women. *Social Forces* 56:66–76.

Gove, W., and C. Peterson. 1980. An update on the literature on personal and marital
satsifaction: The effect on children and the employment of wives. *Marriage and Family
Review* 3:63–96.

Gove, W, C. Style, and M. Hughes. 1990. The effect of marriage on the well-being of
adults: A theoretical analysis. *Journal of Family Issues* 11:4–35.

Gove, W., and J. Tudor. 1972. Adult sex roles and mental illness. *American Journal of Sociology* 78:812–35.

Gray, H., and P. Dressel. 1985. Alternative interpretations of aging among gay males.
Gerontologist 25:83–87.

Green, G. D., and F. W. Bozett. 1991. Lesbian mothers and gay fathers. In *Homosexuality:
Research implications for public policy,* ed. J. C. Gonsiorek and J. D. Weinrich. Thousand
Oaks, Calif.: Sage Publications, 197–214.

Green, R. 1987. *The "sissy boy syndrome" and the development of homosexuality.* New Haven,
Conn.: Yale University Press.

Green, R. J., J. Mandel, M. Hotvedt, J. Gray, and L. Smith. 1986. Lesbian mothers and
their children: A comparison with solo parent heterosexual mothers and their children.
Archives of Sexual Behavior 15:167–84.

Greenberg, D. 1988. *The construction of homosexuality.* Chicago: University of Chicago
Press.

Greenberg, J., and S. Mitchell. 1983. *Object relations in psychoanalytic theory.* Cambridge,
Mass.: Harvard University Press.

Greenblatt, D. 1966. Semantic differential analysis of the "triangular system" hypothesis
in "adjusted" male homosexuals. Unpublished doctoral dissertation, University of California at Los Angeles.

Greene, A. L. 1986. Future time perspective in adolescence: The present of things future
revisited. *Journal of Youth and Adolescence* 15:99–113.

———. 1990. Great expectations: Constructions of the life-course during adolescence.
Journal of Youth and Adolescence 19:289–306.

Greene, A. L., and A. M. Boxer. 1986. Daughters and sons as young adults: Restructuring the ties that bind. In *Life-span developmental psychology: Intergenerational relations,* ed. N. Datan, A. L. Greene, and H. W. Reese. Hillsdale, N. J.: L. Erlbaum, 125–49.

Greene, A. L., and S. Wheatley. 1992. "I've got a lot to do and I don't think I'll have the time": Gender differences in late adolescents' narratives of the future. *Journal of Youth and Adolescence* 21:667–86.

Greene, B. 1994. Ethnic-minority lesbians and gay men: Mental health and treatment issues. *Journal of Consulting and Clinical Psychology* 62:243–51.

———. 1995. Addressing racism, sexism, and heterosexism in psychoanalytic psychotherapy. In *Lesbians and psychoanalysis: Revolutions in theory and practice,* ed. J. Glassgold and S. Iasenza. New York: Free Press, 145–60.

———. 1997. Ethnic minority lesbians and gay men: Mental health and treatment issues. In *Ethnic and cultural diversity among lesbians and gay men,* ed. B. Greene. Thousand Oaks, Calif.: Sage Publications, 216–39.

———. 1998. Family, ethnic identity, and sexual orientation: African-American lesbians and gay men. In *Lesbian, gay, and bisexual identities in families: Psychological perspectives,* ed. C. J. Patterson and A. R. D'Augelli. New York: Oxford University Press, 40–52.

Greenson, R. 1960. Empathy and its vicissitudes. *International Journal of Psychoanalysis* 41:418–24.

———. 1964. On homosexuality and gender identity. *International Journal of Psychoanalysis* 45:217–19.

———. 1965. The working alliance and the transference neurosis. *Psychoanalytic Quarterly* 34:155–81.

———. 1967. *The technique and practice of psychoanalysis.* Madison, Conn.: International Universities Press.

———. 1971. A dream while drowning. In *Separation-individuation: Essays in honor of Margaret S. Mahler,* ed. J. McDevitt and C. Settlage. Madison, Conn.: International Universities Press, 377–84.

Grellert, E., M. Newcomb, and P. Bentler. 1982. Childhood play activities of male and female homosexuals and heterosexuals. *Archives of Sexual Behavior* 11:451–78.

Grossman, F., L. Eichler, and S. Winickoff. 1980. *Pregnancy, birth and parenthood.* San Francisco: Jossey-Bass.

Grube, J. 1996. Natives and settlers: An ethnographic note on early interaction of older homosexual men with younger gay liberationists. In R. Berger, *Gay and gray: the older homosexual man.* 2d ed. New York: Harrington Park Press, 245–48.

Grunes, J. 1980. Reminscence, regression, and empathy: A psychotherapeutic approach to the impaired elderly. In *The course of life,* vol. 3, *Adulthood and the aging process,* ed. S. Greenspan and G. Pollock. Washington, D.C.: U.S. Government Printing Office, 545–48.

Gundlach, R. 1969. Childhood parental relationships and the establishment of gender roles of homosexuals. *Journal of Consulting and Clinical Psychology* 33:136–39.

Guntrip, H. 1971. *Psychoanalytic theory, therapy, and the self.* New York: Basic Books.

Gutmann, D. 1975. Parenthood: Key to the comparative study of the life-cycle. In *Life-span develpmental psychology: Normative life-crises,* ed. N. Datan and L. Ginsberg. New York: Academic Press, 167–84.

———. 1987. *Reclaimed powers: Toward a psychology of men and women in later life.* New York: Basic Books.

Gutmann, D., B. Griffin, and J. Grunes. 1982. Developmental contributions to the late onset affective disorders. In *Life-span development and behavior,* ed. P. Baltes and O. G. Brim Jr. New York: Academic Press, 4:244–63.

Haeckel, E. [1868] 1968. *Natural history of creation* (Naturaliche Schopfungsgeschichte). Berlin: Georg Reimmer.

———. 1874. *The evolution of man: A popular exposition of the principal points of human ontogeny and phylogeny.* 2 vols. New York: A. L. Fowle: International Science Library.

Hägestad, G. 1974. Middle aged women and their children: Exploring changes in a role relationship. Unpublished doctoral dissertation, University of Minnesota.

———. 1990. Social perspectives on the life course. In *Handbook of aging and the social sciences,* ed. R. Binstock and L. K. George. 3d ed. New York: Academic Press, 151–68.

———. 1996. On-time, off-time, out of time? Reflections on continuity and discontinuity from an illness process. In. *Aging and adulthood: Research on continuities and discontinuities,* ed. V. Bengtson. New York: Springer Publishing, 204–22.

Hägestad, G., and B. Neugarten. 1985. Age and the life-course. In *Handbook of aging and society,* ed. R. Binstock and E. Shanas. 2d ed. New York: Van Nostrand-Reinhold, 35–61.

Halbwachs, M. [1952] 1992. *On collective memory.* Trans. and ed. L. Coser. Chicago: University of Chicago Press.

Haldeman, D. 1991. Sexual orientation conversion therapy for gay men and lesbians: A scientific examination. In *Homosexuality: Research implications for public policy,* ed. J. C. Gonsiorek and J. D. Weinrich. Thousand Oaks, Calif.: Sage Publications, 149–60.

———. 1994. The practice and ethics of sexual orientation conversion therapy. *Journal of Clinical and Consulting Psychology* 62:211–27.

Hall, G. S. 1904. *Adolescence: Its psychology and its relation to physiology, anthropology, sociology, sex, crime, religion and education.* New York: Appleton.

Hall Carpenter Archives. 1989. *Walking after midnight: Gay men's life stories.* New York: Routledge.

Halleck, S. L. 1976. Another response to "Homosexuality: The ethical challenge." *Journal of Consulting and Clinical Psychology* 44:167–70.

Halpern, D. F., and M. Crothers. 1997. Sex, sexual orientation, and cognition. In *Sexual orientation,* ed. L. Ellis and L. Ebertz. Westport, Conn.: Praeger, 181–98.

Hamer, D. H, and P. Copeland. 1994. *The science of desire: The search for the gay gene and the biology of behavior.* New York: Simon and Schuster.

———. 1998. *Living with our genes: Why they matter more than you think.* New York: Doubleday.

Hamer, D. H., S. Hu, V. Magnusson, N. Hu, and A. Pattatucci. 1993. A linkage between DNA markers on the X chromosome and male sexual orientation. *Science* 261:321–27.

———. 1994. Response. *Science* 262:2065.

Hamill, J. A. 1995. Dexterity and sexuality: Is there a relationship. *Journal of Homosexuality* 28:375–96.

Hamilton, W. 1964. The genetical evolution of social behavior. 2 pts. *Journal of Theoretical Biology* 7:1–52.

Hammersmith, S., and M. Weinberg. 1973. Homosexual identity: Commitment, adjustment, and significant others. *Sociometry* 36:56–79.

Hanson, G., and L. Hartmann. 1996. Latency development in prehomosexual boys. In *Textbook of homosexuality and mental health,* ed. R. Cabaj and T. S. Stein. Washington, D.C.: American Psychiatric Press, 253–66.

Hare-Mustin, R., and P. Broderick. 1979. The myth of motherhood. *Psychology of Women Quarterly* 4:114–28.

Hareven, T. 1980. The life-course and aging in historical perspective. In *Life-course: Integrative theories and exemplary populations,* ed. K. W. Back. Boulder, Colo.: Westview Press, 9–26.

———. 1986. Historical changes in the construction of the life-course. *Human Development* 29:171–80.

Harris, M., and P. Turner. 1985/86. Gay and lesbian parents. *Journal of Homosexuality* 12:101–13.

Harrison, P. J., I. Everall, and J. Catalan. 1994. Editorial: Is homosexual behavior hardwired? *Psychological Medicine* 24:811–16.

Harry, J. 1982a. Decision making and age differences among gay male couples. *Journal of Homosexuality* 8:9–21.

———. 1982b. *Gay children grown up: Gender, culture and gender deviance.* New York: Praeger.

———. 1983. Gay male and lesbian relationships. In *Contemporary families and alternative lifestyles: Handbook on research and theory,* ed. E. Macklin and R. H. Rubin. Beverly Hills, Calif.: Sage Publications, 217–34.

———. 1984a. *Gay couples.* New York: Praeger.

———. 1984b. Sexual orientation as destiny. *Journal of Homosexuality* 10:111–24.

———. 1990. A probability sample of gay males. *Journal of Homosexuality* 19:89–103.

Harry, J., and W. DeVall. 1978. *The social organization of gay males.* New York: Praeger.

Hart, M., H. Roback, B. Tittler, L. Weitz, B. Walston, and E. McKee. 1978. Psychological adjustment of non-patient homosexuals: Critical review of the research literature. *Journal of Clinical Psychiatry* 39:604–8.

Hartmann, H. [1939] 1958. *Ego-psychology and the problem of adaptation.* Trans. D. Rapaport. New York: International Universities Press.

———. 1952. The mutual influences in the development of ego and id. *Psychoanalytic Study of the Child Psychoanalysis* 7:9–30.

Hartmann, H., and E. Kris. 1945. The genetic approach in psychoanalysis. *Psychoanalytic Study of the Child* 1:1–29.

Hartstein, N. 1996. Suicide risk in lesbian, gay, and bisexual youth. In *Textbook of homosexuality and mental health,* ed. R. Cabaj and T. S. Stein. Washington, D.C.: American Psychiatric Press, 819–38.

Harwood, G. 1997. *The oldest gay couple in America: A 70 year journey through same-sex America.* Secaucus, N.J.: Carol Publishing.

Hathaway, S. 1956. Scales 5 (masculinity-femininity), 6 (paranoia), and 8 (schizophrenia). In *Basic readings on the MMPI in psychology and medicine,* ed. G. S. Welsh and W. G. Dahlstrom. Minneapolis: University of Minnesota Press, 104–11.

Haumann, G. 1995. Homosexuality, biology, ideology. *Journal of Homosexuality* 28:57–77.

Hausman, K. 1995. AMA reverses stand on homosexual issues. *Psychiatric News* 30 (2): 1.

Havighurst, R. J. 1948. *Developmental Tasks and Education.* New York: David McKay.

Havighurst, R., and B. Neugarten. 1957. *Society and education.* Boston: Allyn and Bacon.

Havighurst, R., B. Neugarten, and S. Tobin. 1961. The measurement of life-satisfaction. *Journal of Gerontology* 16:134–43.

Haynes, J. 1995. A critique of the possibility of genetic inheritance of homosexual orientation. *Journal of Homosexuality* 28:91–113.

Hazan, H. 1980. *The limbo people: A study of the constitution of the time universe among the aged.* London: Routledge and Kegan Paul.

Hendricks, S. E., B. Graber, and J. F. Rodriguez-Sierra. 1989. Neuroendocrine responses in exogenous estrogen: No differences between heterosexual and homosexual men. *Psychoneuroendocrinology* 14:177–85.

Herbert, S. 1996. Lesbian sexuality. In *Textbook of homosexuality and mental health,* ed. R. Cabaj and T. S. Stein. Washington, D.C.: American Psychiatric Press, 723–42.

Herdt, G. 1981. *Guardians of the flutes: Idioms of masculinity.* New York: McGraw-Hill.

———. 1987. *The Sambia: Ritual and gender in New Guinea.* New York: Holt, Rinehart and Winston.

———. 1989. Introduction: Gay and lesbian youth, emergent identities, and cultural scenes at home and abroad. In *Gay and lesbian youth,* ed. G. Herdt. New York: Harrington Park Press, 1–42.

———. 1991a. Representations of homosexuality: An essay on cultural ontology and historical comparison, pt. 1. *Journal of the History of Sexuality* 1:481–504.

———. 1991b. Representations of homosexuality: An essay on cultural ontology and historical comparison, pt. 2, *Journal of the History of Sexuality,* 2:603–32.

———. 1997. *Same sex different cultures.* Boulder, Colo.: Westview Press.

Herdt, G., and J. Beeler. 1998. Older gay men and lesbians in families. In *Lesbian, gay, and bisexual identities in families: Psychological perspectives,* ed. C. J. Patterson and A. R. D'Augelli. New York: Oxford University Press, 177–96.

Herdt, G., J. Beeler, and T. Rawls. 1997. Life course diversity among older lesbians and gay men. *Journal of Lesbian, Gay and Bisexual Identity* 2:231–47. (Special issue: Coming of age: Gays, lesbians, and bisexuals in the second half of life, ed. G. Herdt, A. Hostetler, and B. Cohler.)

Herdt, G., and A. Boxer. 1996. *Children of horizons.* 2d ed. Boston: Beacon Press.

Herdt, G., and J. Davidson. 1988. The Sambia "Turnim-Man": Sociocultural and clinical aspects of gender formation in male pseudohermaphrodites with 5-alpha-reductase deficiency in Papua New Guinea. *Archives of Sexual Behavior* 17:33–55.

Herdt, G., and R. Stoller. 1990. *Intimate communications: Erotics and the study of culture.* new York: Columbia University Press.

Herek, G. M. 1984a. Attitudes towards lesbians and gay men: A factor analytic study. *Journal of Homosexuality* 10:39–51.

———. 1984b. Beyond "homophobia": A social psychological perspective on attitudes toward lesbians and gay men. *Journal of Homosexuality* 10:1–21.

———. 1985. On doing, being, and not being: Prejudice and the social construction of sexuality. *Journal of Homosexuality* 12:135–51.

———. 1991. Myths about sexual orientation: A lawyer's guide to social science research. *Law and Sexuality: A Review of Lesbian and Gay Legal Issues* 1:133–72.

———. 1995. Psychological heterosexism in the United States. In *Lesbian, gay, and bisexual identities over the life span,* ed. A. R. D'Augelli and C. Patterson. New York: Oxford University Press, 321–46.

———. 1996. Heterosexism and homophobia. In *Textbook of homosexuality and mental health,* ed. R. Cabaj and T. S. Stein. Washington, D.C.: American Psychiatric Press, 101–13.

———. 1999. AIDS and stigma. *American Behavioral Scientist* 42:1105–16.

Herek, G., and J. P. Capitanio. 1999. AIDS, stigma, and sexual prejudice. *American Behavioral Scientist* 42:1130–47.

Herek, G., and E. Glunt. 1988. An epidemic of stigma: Public reactions to AIDS. *American Psychologist* 43:886–91.

Herrn, R. 1995. On the history of biological theories of homosexuality. *Journal of Homosexuality* 28:31–56.

Herron, W., T. Kinter, I. Sollinger, and J. Trubowith. 1982. Psychoanalytic psychotherapy for homosexual clients: New concepts. In *A guide to psychotherapy with gay and lesbian clients,* ed. J. C. Gonsiorek. New York: Harrington Park Press, 177–92.

Hershberger, S., and A. D'Augelli. 1995. the impact of victimization on the mental health and suicidality of lesbian, gay, and bisexual youths. *Developmental Psychology* 31:65–74.

Heston, L. L., and J. Shields. 1968. Homosexuality in twins: A family study and a registry study. *Archives of General Psychiatry* 18:149–50.

Hetherington, E. M., and W. G. Clingempeel. 1988. Coping with marital transitions: A family systems perspective. Monographs of the Society for Research in Child Development, no. 57. (Serial 227. Chicago: University of Chicago Press.)

Hetrick, E., and A. Martin. 1987. Developmental issues and their resolution for gay and lesbian adolescents. *Journal of Homosexuality* 14:25–43.

Hildebrand, P. 1992. A patient dying with AIDS. *International Review of Psychoanalysis* 19:457–69.

Hill, D. 1994. The special place of the erotic transference in psychoanalysis. *Psychoanalytic Inquiry* 14:483–99.

Hill, R. 1986. Life cycle stages for types of single parent families: Of family development theory. *Family Relations* 35:19–29.

Hill, R., and P. Mattessich. 1979. Family development theory and life-span development. In *Life-span development and behavior,* ed. P. Baltes and O. G. Brim Jr. New York: Academic Press, 2:161–204.

Hill, R., and R. Rodgers. 1964. The developmental approach. In *Handbook of marriage and the family,* ed. H. Christensen. Chicago: Rand-McNally, 171–211.

Hirsch, E. D. 1976. *The aims of interpretation.* Chicago: University of Chicago Press.

Hirsch, I. 1987. Varying modes of analytic participation. *Journal of the American Academy of Psychoanalysis* 15:205–22.

———. 1996. Observing-participation, mutual enactment, and the new classical models. *Contemporary Psychoanalysis* 20:358–83.

Hirschfeld, M. 1932. *Sexual pathology,* trans. J. Gibbs. Newark, N.J.: Julian. (Abridged version of *Sexualpathologie.* 3 vols. Bonn: A. Marcus and E. Weber, 1917–20.)

Hobbs, D. 1965. Parenthood as crisis: A third study. *Marriage and Family Living* 27:367–72.

———. 1968. Transition to parenthood: A replication and extension. *Journal of Marriage and the Family* 30:413–17.

Hobbs, D., and S. P. Cole. 1976. Transition to parenthood: A decade of replication. *Journal of Marriage and the Family* 38:723–31.

Hoch, P. 1949. Clinical and psychoanalytic approach: Discussion II. In *Psychosexual development in health and disease,* ed. P. H. Hoch and J. Zubin. New York: Grune and Stratton, 206–12.

Hochschild, A. 1975. Disengagement theory: A critique and a proposal. *American Sociological Review* 40:553–69.

Hoffman, I. 1983. The patient as interpreter of the analyst's experience. *Contemporary Psychoanalysis* 19:287–304.

———. 1991. Discussion: Toward a social-constructionist view of the psychoanalytic situation. *Psychoanalytic Dialogues* 1:74–105.

———. 1998. *Ritual and spontaneity in the psychoanalytic process.* Hillsdale, N.J.: Analytic Press.

Hogan, D. 1981. *Transitions and social change: The early lives of American men.* New York: Academic Press.

———. 1984. The demography of life-course transitions: Temporal and gender considerations. In *Gender and the life-course,* ed. A. Rossi. New York: Aldine/Atherton, 65–78.

———. 1987. Demographic trends in human fertility, and parenting across the life span. In *Parenting across the life-span: Biosocial dimensions,* ed. J. Lancaster, J. Altmann, A. Rossi, and L. Sherrod. New York: Aldine de Gruyter, 315–49.

Hogan, D., and N. Astone. 1986. The transition to adulthood. *Annual Review of Sociology* 12:101–30.

Holeman, R. E., and G. Winokur. 1965. Effeminate homosexuality: A disease of childhood. *American Journal of Orthopsychiatry* 35:48–56.

Holmes, D. E. 1992. Race and transference in psychoanalysis and psychotherapy. *International Journal of Psychoanalysis* 73:1–11.

Holtzen, D. W. 1997. Sexual orientation and handedness: A reanalysis of recent data and research considerations for future inquiry. In *Sexual orientation,* ed. L. Ellis and L. Ebertz. Westport, Conn.: Praeger, 151–62.

Hooker, E. 1956. A preliminary analysis of group behavior of homosexuals. *Journal of Psychology* 42:217–25.

———. 1957. The adjustment of the male overt homosexual. *Journal of Projective Techniques* 21:18–31.

———. 1965. Male homosexuals and their "worlds." In *Sexual inversion: The multiple roots of homosexuality,* ed. J. Marmor. New York: Basic Books, 83–107.

———. 1967. The homosexual community. In *Sexual deviance,* ed. J. H. Gagnon and W. Simon. New York: Harper and Row, 167–84.

———. 1968/69. Homosexuality. In *National Institute of Mental Health Task Force on homosexuality: Final report and background papers,* ed. J. Livingood. Rockville, Md.: National Institute of Mental Health, 11–21.

———. 1969. Parental relations and male homosexuality in patient and nonpatient samples. *Journal of Consulting and Clinical Psychology* 33:140–42.

Hopcke, R. 1992. Midlife, gay men and the AIDS epidemic. *Quadrant* 25:101–9.

Horowitz, M. 1977. The quantitative line of approach in psychoanalysis: A clinical assessment of its current status. *Journal of the American Psychoanalytic Association* 25:559–80.

Hostetler, A., and B. Cohler. 1997. Partnership, singlehood and the lesbian and gay life course: A research agenda. *Journal of Lesbian, Gay and Bisexual Identities* 2:199–230. (Special issue: Coming of age: Gays, lesbians, and bisexuals in the second half of life, ed. G. Herdt, A. Hostetler, and B. Cohler.)

Hostetler, A., and G. Herdt. 1998. Culture, sexual lifeways, and developmental subjectivities: Rethinking sexual taxonomies. *Social Research* 65:249–90.

Hotvedt, M., and G. Mandel. 1982. Children of lesbian mothers. In *Homosexuality: Social, psychological, and biological issues,* ed. W. Paul, J. Weinrich, J. C. Weinrich, J. C. Gonsiorek and M. E. Hotvedt. Beverly Hills, Calif.: Sage Publications, 275–85.

Hoult, T. 1984. Human sexuality in biological perspective: Theoretical and methodological considerations. *Journal of Homosexuality* 10:137–55.

Howard, J., P. Blumstein, and P. Schwartz. 1986. Sex, power, and influence tactics in intimate relationships. *Journal of Personality and Social Psychology* 51:102–9.

Hu, S., A. Pattatucci, C. Patterson, L. Li, D. Fulker, S. Cherny, L. Kuglyak, and D. Hamer. 1995. Linkage between sexual orientation and chromosome Xq28 in male but not females. *Nature Genetics* 11:248–56.

Huggins, S. 1989. A comparative study of self-esteem of adolescent children of divorced lesbian mothers and divorced heterosexual mothers. In *Homosexuality and the family,* ed. F. W. Bozett. New York: Harrington Park Press, 123–35.

Humphreys, L. 1970. *Tearoom trade: Impersonal sex in public places.* Chicago: Aldine.

Humphreys, L., and B. Miller. 1980. Identities in the emerging gay culture. In *Homosexual behavior: A modern reappraisal,* ed. J. Marmor. New York: Basic Books, 142–56.

Husserl, E. 1960. Cartesian meditations: An introduction to phenomenology. Trans. D. Cairns. The Hague: Martinus Nijoff.

Hutchinson, G. 1959. A speculative consideration of certain possible forms of sexual selection in man. *American Naturalist* 93:81–91.

Imperato-McGinley, J., L. Guerrero, T. Gautier, and R. E. Peterson. 1974. Steroid 5a-reductase deficiency in man: An inherited form of male pseudohermaphroditism. *Science* 286:1213–15.

Imperato-McGinley, J., R. Peterson, T. Gautier, and E. Sturla. 1979. Androgens and the evolution of male gender identity among male pseudohermaphrodites with 5a-reductase deficiency. *New England Journal of Medicine* 300:1233.

———. [1981] 1985. The impact of androgens on the evolution of male gender identity. In *Sexuality: New perspectives,* ed. Z. De Fries, R. Friedman, and R. Corn. Westport, Conn.: Greenwood Press, 125–40.

Irvine, J. 1994. Cultural differences in adolescent sexualities. In *Sexual cultures and the construction of adolescent identities,* ed. J. M. Irvine. Philadelphia: Temple University Press, 3–28.

Isay, R. 1986a. The development of sexual identity in homosexual men. *Psychoanalytic Study of the Child* 41:467–89.

———. 1986b. On the analytic therapy of gay men. In *Contemporary perspectives on psychotherapy with lesbians and gay men,* ed. T. Stein and C. Cohen. New York: Plenum Medical Book Company, 139–56.

———. 1989. *Being homosexual: Gay men and their development.* New York: Farrar, Strauss and Giroux.

———. 1991. The homosexual analyst: Clinical considerations. *Psychoanalytic Study of the Child* 46:199–216.

———. 1993. On the analytic therapy of homosexual men. In *Affirmative dynamic psychotherapy with gay men,* ed. C. Cornett. New York: Aronson, 23–44.

———. 1996a. *Becoming gay: The journey to self-acceptance.* New York: Pantheon.

———. 1996b. Psychoanalytic therapy with gay men: Developmental considerations. In *Textbook of homosexuality and mental health,* ed. R. Cabaj and T. S. Stein. Washington, D.C.: American Psychiatric Association Press, 451–69.

———. 1997. Remove gender identity disorder from DSM. *Psychiatric News,* 28 November.

Isay, R., and R. C. Friedman. 1986. Toward a further understanding of homosexual men. *Journal of the American Psychoanalytic Association* 34:193–208.

Jackson, D. 1969. The history of Freud's concept of regression. *Journal of the American Psychoanalytic Association* 17:743–84.

Jackson, J. H. 1884. Evolution and dissolution of the nervous system. In *Selected papers,* vol. 2. New York: Basic Books.

Jackson, S. 1992. The listening healer in the history of psychological healing. *American Journal of Psychiatry* 149:1623–32.

Jacobs, L. 1990. Preoedipal determinants of female homosexuality. In *The homosexualities: Reality, fantasy, and the arts,* ed. C. W. Socarides and V. D. Volkan. Madison, Conn.: International Universities Press, 139–60.

Jacobs, T. 1986. On countertransference enactments. *Journal of the American Psychoanalytic Association* 34:289–307.

———. 1991. *The use of the self: Countertransference and communication in the analytic situation.* Madison, Conn.: International Universities Press.

———. 1999a. On the question of self disclosure by the analyst: Error or advancement in technique. *Psychoanalytic Quarterly* 68:159–83.

———. 1999b. Countertransference past and present: A review of the concept. *Psychoanalytic Quarterly* 80:575–94.

Jacobsen, P. B., and R. S. Steele. 1978. From present to past: The development of Freudian theory. *International Review of Psychoanalysis* 5:393–412.

———. 1979. From present to past: Freudian archaeology. *International Review of Psychoanalysis* 6:349–62.

Jacobson, E. 1964. *The Self and the Object World.* Madison, Conn.: International Universities Press.

Jacobson, S., and A. Grossman. 1996. Older lesbians and gay men: Old myths, new images and future directions. In *The lives of lesbians, gays, and bisexuals: Children to adults,* ed. R. C. Savin-Williams and K. M. Cohen. Fort Worth, Tex.: Harcourt Brace, 345–74.

Jacoby, A. 1969. Transition to parenthood: A reassessment. *Journal of Marriage and the Family* 31:720–27.

Jaffe, D. 1986. Empathy, counteridentification, countertransference: A review with some personal perspectives on the "analytic instrument." *Psychoanalytic Quarterly* 55:215–43.

Jagose, A. 1996. *Queer theory: An introduction.* New York: University Press.

James, S. E. 1998. Fulfilling the promise: Community response to the needs of sexual minority youth and their families. *American Journal of Orthopsychiatry* 68:447–54.

James, S. E., and B. C. Murphy. 1998. Gay and lesbian relationships in a changing social context. In *Lesbian, gay, and bisexual identities in families: Psychological perspectives,* ed. C. J. Patterson and A. R. D'Augelli. New York: Oxford University Press, 99–121.

Jaques, E. 1965. Death and the mid-life crisis. *International Journal of Psychoanalysis* 46 (4): 502–14.

———. [1980] 1993. The midlife crisis. In *The course of life,* vol. 5, *Early Adulthood,* ed. G. Pollock and S. Greenspan. Madison, Conn.: International Universities Press, 201–31.

Jaspers, K. 1963. *General psychopathology.* Trans. J. Hoenig and M. W. Hamilton. Chicago: University of Chicago Press.

Jay, K., and A. Young. 1977. *The gay report: Lesbians and gay men speak out about sexual experiences and lifestyles.* New York: Summit Books.

Johan, M. (panel reporter). 1992. Enactments in psychoanalysis. *Journal of the American Psychoanalytic Association* 40:827–41.

Jones, E. 1927. The early development of female sexuality. *International Journal of Psychoanalysis* 8:459–72.

———. 1932. The phallic phase. In *Papers on psychoanalysis.* Baltimore: Williams and Wilkins, 452–84.

———. 1953. *The life and work of Sigmund Freud,* vol. 1. New York: Basic Books.

Jones, M., N. Bayley, and J. MacFarlane. 1971. *The course of human development.* Waltham, Mass.: Xerox College Publishing.

Jones, M. A., and M. A. Gabriel. 1999. Utilization of psychotherapy by lesbians, gay men, and bisexuals: Findings from a nationwide survey. *American Journal of Orthopsychiatry* 69:209–19.

Jones, R., and J. DeCecco. 1982. The femininity and masculinity of partners in heterosexual and homosexual relationships. *Journal of Homosexuality* 8:37–44.

Josephs, L. 1990. Self-disclosure and the psychology of the self. In *Self-disclosure in psychotherapy,* ed. G. Stricker and M. Fisher. New York: Plenum.

———. 1995. Countertransference as an expression of the analyst's narrative strategies. *Contemporary Psychoanalysis* 31:345–79.

Jourard, S. 1971. *Self-disclosure: An experimental analysis of the transparent self.* New York: John Wiley and Sons.

Jung, C. G. 1933. *Modern man in search of a soul.* New York: Harcourt, Brace and World.

Kagan, J. 1980. Perspectives on continuity. In *Constance and change in human development,* ed. O. G. Brim Jr. and J. Kagan. Cambridge, Mass.: Harvard University Press, 26–74.

———. 1998. *Three seductive ideas.* Cambridge, Mass.: Harvard University Press.

Kagan, J., R. Kearsley, and P. Zelazo. 1978. *Infancy.* Cambridge, Mass.: Harvard University Press.

Kagan, J., and H. Moss. 1962. *From birth to maturity.* New York: John Wiley.

Kahn, R., and T. Antonucci. 1981. Convoys of social support: A life-course approach. In *Aging: Social change,* ed. S. Kiesler, J. Morgan, and V. Oppenheimer. New York: Academic Press, 383–405.

Kalish, R., ed. 1971. *Death, dying, transcending.* Farmingdale, N.Y.: Baywood Publishing Company.

———. 1989. *Midlife loss: Coping strategies.* Newbury Park, Calif.: Sage Publications.

Kallman, F. 1952. Comparative twin study on the genetic aspects of male homosexuality. *Journal of Nervous and Mental Diseases* 115:283–93.

Kaminsky, M. 1984. The uses of reminiscence: A discussion of the formative literature. In *The uses of reminiscence: New ways of working with older adults,* ed. M. Kaminsky. New York, Haworth Press, 137–56 (*Journal of Gerontological Social Work* 7, nos. 1/2.)

Kandel, D., and G. S. Lesser. 1972. *Youth in two worlds.* San Francisco: Jossey Bass.

Kandel, E. 1998. A new intellectual framework for psychiatry. *American Journal of Psychiatry* 155:457–69.

Kantrowitz, A. [1977] 1996. *Under the rainbow: Growing up gay.* New York: St. Martin's Press.

Kantrowitz, J. 1995. The beneficial aspects of the patient-analyst match. *International Journal of Psychoanalysis* 76:299–314.

Kaplan, G., V. Barell, and A. Lusky. 1988. Subjective state of health and survival in elderly adults. *Journal of Gerontology* 43:114–20.

Katz, J. N. 1990. The invention of heterosexuality. *Socialist Review* 20:7–33.

———. 1995. *The invention of heterosexuality.* New York: Dutton/Plume Books.

Kaufman, S. 1986. *The ageless self: Sources of meaning in late life.* Madison: University of Wisconsin Press.

Kehoe, M. 1986. Lesbians over 65: A triple invisible minority. *Journal of Homosexuality* 12:139–52.

———. 1989. *Lesbians over 60 speak for themselves.* New York: Harrington Park Press.

Keith, J. 1982. *Old people as people: Social and cultural influences on aging and old age.* Boston: Little-Brown.

Kelly, J. 1977. The aging male homosexual: Myth and reality. *Gerontologist* 17:328–32.

———. 1980. Homosexuality and aging. In *Homosexual behavior: A modern reappraisal,* ed. J. Marmor. New York: Basic Books, 176–93.

Kendell, K. 1997. Lesbian couples creating families. In *On the road to same-sex marriage,* ed. R. Cabaj and D. Purcell. San Francisco: Jossey-Bass, 41–58.

———. 1998. "When a woman loves a woman" in Lesotho: Love, sex, and the (Western) construction of homophobia. In *Boy-wives and female husbands: Studies of African homosexualities,* ed. S. O. Murray and W. Roscoe. New York: St. Martin's Press, 223–41.

Kenen, S. 1997. Who counts when you're counting homosexuals? Hormones and homosexuality in mid-twentieth century America. In *Science and homosexualities,* ed. V. Rosario. New York, Routledge, 197–218.

Keniston, K. [1960] 1965. *The uncommitted: Alienated youth in American society.* New York: Harcourt, Brace, and World.

Kernberg, O. 1980. Normal narcissism in middle age. In *Internal world and external reality: Object relations theory applied.* New York: Aronson, 121–53.

Kertzer, D. I. 1983. Generation as a social problem. *Annual Review of Sociology* 9:125–49.

Kertzner, R. M. 1997. Entering midlife: Gay men, HIV and the future. *Journal of the Gay and Lesbian Medical Association* 1:87–95.

———. In press. Self-appraisal of life experience and psychological adjustment in midlife gay men. *Journal of Psychology and Human Sexuality.*

Kertzner, R. M., and M. Sved. 1996. Midlife gay men and lesbians: Adult development and mental health. In *Textbook of homosexuality and mental health,* ed. R. Cabaj and T. S. Stein. Washington, D.C.: American Psychiatric Press, 289–304.

Khan, M. 1974. *The privacy of the self.* Madison, Conn.: International Universities Press.

———. 1979. *Alienation in perversions.* Madison, Conn.: International Universities Press.

Kimmel, D. 1978. Adult development and aging: A gay perspective. *Journal of Social Issues* 34:113–30.

———. 1979–80. Life-history interviews of gay men. *International Journal of Aging and Human Development* 10:239–48.

———. 1993. Adult development and aging: A gay perspective. In *Psychological perspectives on lesbian and gay male experiences,* ed. L. Garnets and D. Kimmel. New York: Columbia University Press, 517–34.

Kimmel, D., and B. Sang. 1995. Lesbians and gay men in midlife. In *Lesbian, gay, and bisexual identities over the life span,* ed. A. R. D'Augelli and C. Patterson. New York: Oxford University Press, 190–214.

Kindlon, D., and M. Thompson. 1999. *Raising Cain: Protecting the emotional life of boys.* New York: Ballantine Books.

King, M., and E. McDonald. 1992. Homosexuals who are twins: A study of 46 probands. *British Journal of Psychiatry* 160:407–9.

King, P. 1980. The life cycle as indicated by the nature of the transference in the psychoanalysis of the middle-aged and elderly. *International Journal of Psychoanalysis* 61:153–60.

Kinsey, A., W. Pomeroy, C. Martin, and P. Gebhard. 1953. *Sexual behavior in the human female.* Philadelphia: W. B. Saunders.

Kinsey, A., W. Pomeroy, and C. Martin. 1948. *Sexual behavior in the human male.* Philadelphia: W. B. Saunders.

Kinsley, C. H., K. G. Lambert, and H. E. Jones. 1997. Experimental alterations of prenatal determinants of sexual orientation and sex-typed behavior in nonhuman mammals. In *Sexual orientation,* ed. L. Ellis and L. Ebertz. Westport, Conn.: Praeger, 21–40.

Kirkpatrick, M. 1987. Clinical implications of lesbian mother studies. *Journal of Homosexuality* 13:201–11.

———. 1996. Lesbians as parents. In *Textbook of homosexuality and mental health,* ed. R. Cabaj and T. S. Stein. Washington, D.C.: American Psychiatric Press, 353–70.

Kirkpatrick, M., and C. Morgan. 1980. Psychodynamic psychotherapy of female homosexuality. In *Homosexual behavior: A modern reappraisal,* ed. J. Marmor. New York: Basic Books, 357–75.

Kirkpatrick, M., C. Smith, and R. Roy. 1981. Lesbian mothers and their children. *American Journal of Orthopsychiatry* 51:545–51.

Kirsch, J., and J. Weinrich. 1991. Homosexuality, nature and biology: Is homosexuality natural? Does it matter? In *Homosexuality: Research implications for public policy,* ed. J. C. Gonsiorek and J. D. Weinrich. Thousand Oaks, Calif.: Sage Publications, 13–31.

Kite, M. 1984. Sex differences in attitudes toward homosexuals: A meta-analytic review. *Journal of Homosexuality* 10:69–81.

Kitzinger, C. 1987. *The social construction of lesbianism.* Thousand Oaks, Calif.: Sage Publications.

———. 1995. Social constructionism: Implications for lesbian and gay psychology. In *Lesbian, gay, and bisexual identities over the life span,* ed. A. R. D'Augelli and C. Patterson. New York: Oxford University Press, 136–64.

Kitzinger, C., and S. Wilkinson. 1995. Transitions from heterosexuality to lesbianism: The discursive production of lesbian identities. *Developmental Psychology* 31:95–104.

Klein, F., B. Sepekoff, and T. Wolff. 1985. Sexual orientation: A multi-variate dynamic process. *Journal of Homosexuality* 11:35–49.

Klein, G. 1976. *Psychoanalytic theory: An exploration of essentials.* Ed. M. Gill. Madison, Conn.: International Universities Press.

Klein, M. [1932] 1969. *The psychoanalysis of chidlren.* London: Hogarth Press.

Klinger, R. 1996. Lesbian couples. In *Textbook of homosexuality and mental health,* ed. R. Cabaj and T. S. Stein. Washington, D.C.: American Psychiatric Press, 339–52.

Kohlberg, L., D. Ricks, and J. Snarey. 1984. Childhood development as a predictor of adaptation in adulthood. *Genetic Psychology Monographs,* no. 110, 91–172.

Kohli, M., and J. Meyer. 1986. Social structure and social construction of life stages. *Human Development* 29:145–80.

Kohn, M. 1969. *Class and conformity: A study in values.* Homewood, Ill.: Dorsey Press.

Kohut, H. [1959] 1978. Introspection, empathy and psychoanalysis: An examination of the relationship between mode of observation and theory. In *The search for the self: Selected writings of Heinz Kohut, 1950–1978.* Ed. P. Ornstein. New York: International Universities Press, 1:205–32.

———. 1971. *The analysis of the self.* Madison, Conn.: International Universities Press.

———. 1976. Creativeness, charisma, group psychology: Reflections on the self-analysis of Freud. In *Freud: The fusion of science and humanism,* ed. J. Gedo and G. H. Pollock. New York: International Universities press, 379–425. (*Psychological Issues* Monograph 34/35.)

———. 1977. *The restoration of the self.* Madison, Conn.: International Universities Press.

———. 1979. The two analyses of Mr. Z. *International Journal of Psychoanalysis* 60:3–27.

———. 1982. Introspection, empathy, and the semi-circle of mental health. *International Journal of Psychoanalysis* 63:395–407.

————. 1984. *How does analysis cure?* Chicago: University of Chicago Press.

————. 1985. *Self-psychology and the humanities: Reflections on a new psychoanalytic approach.* New York: Norton.

————. 1987. *The Kohut seminars: On self-psychology and psychotherapy with adolescents and young adults.* Ed. M. Elson. New York: Norton.

Kohut, H., and P. Seitz. [1963] 1978. Concepts and theories of psychoanalysis. In *The search for the self: Selected writings of Heinz Kohut, 1950–1978.* Ed. P. Ornstein. New York: International Universities Press, 337–74.

Kohut, H., and E. Wolf. 1978. The disorders of the self and their treatment: An outline. *International Journal of Psychoanalysis* 59:413–25.

Kolb, L. C., and A. M. Johnson. 1955. Etiology and therapy of overt homosexuality. *Psychoanalytic Quarterly* 24:506–15.

Kooden, H. 1991. Self-disclosure: The gay male therapist as an agent of social change. In *Gays, lesbians, and their therapists,* ed. C. Silverstein. New York: Norton, 143–54.

Kotre, J. 1984. *Outliving the self: Generativity and the interpretation of lives.* Baltimore, Md.: Johns Hopkins University Press.

Kourany, R. F. C. 1987. Suicide among homosexual adolescents. *Journal of Homosexuality* 13:111–17.

Kovel, J. 1989. *The radical spirit: Essays on psychoanalysis and society.* New York: Columbia University Press.

Kozulin, A. 1990. *Vygotsky's psychology: A biography of ideas.* Cambridge, Mass.: Harvard University Press.

Krafft-Ebing, R. 1889–90. Angeborne konträre sexualemfindung: Erfolgreiche hypnotische absuggerierung homosexualer empfindungen. *Internationales centralblatt für die physiologie und pathologie der harn-und sexual-organe* 1:7–11.

Kretzner, R., and M. Sved. 1996. Midlife gay men and lesbians: Adult development and mental health. In *Textbook of homosexuality and mental health,* ed. R. Cabaj and T. S. Stein. Washington, D.C.: American Psychiatric Press, 289–304.

Kris, A. O. 1982. *Free associations.* New Haven, Conn.: Yale University Press.

————. 1990. Helping patients by analyzing self-criticism. *Journal of the American Psychoanalytic Association* 38:605–36.

Kris, E. 1956. The personal myth: A problem in psychoanalytic technique. *Journal of the American Psychoanalytic Association* 4:653–81.

Krajeski, J. 1996. Homosexuality and the mental health professions: A contemporary history. In *Textbook of homosexuality and mental health,* ed. R. Cabaj and T. S. Stein. Washington, D.C.: American Psychiatric Press, 17–39.

Kurdek, L. 1988. Relationship quality of gay and lesbian cohabiting couples. *Journal of Homosexuality* 15:93–118.

————. 1994. The nature and correlates of relationship quality in gay, lesbian, and heterosexual cohabiting couples: A test of the contextual, investment, and discrepancy models. In *Lesbian and gay psychology: Theory, research and clinical applications,* ed. B. Greene and G. M. Herek. Psychological Perspectives on Lesbian and Gay Issues, vol. 1. Thousand Oaks, Calif.: Sage Publications, 135–55.

————. 1995a. Developmental changes in relationship quality in gay and lesbian cohabitating couples. *Developmental Psychology* 31:86–92.

————. 1995b. Lesbian and gay couples. In *Lesbian, gay, and bisexual identities over the life span,* ed. A. R. D'Augelli and C. Patterson. New York: Oxford University Press, 243–61.

————. 1998. Relationship outcomes and their predictors: Longitudinal evidence from heterosexual married, gay cohabiting and lesbian cohabiting couples. *Journal of Marriage and the Family* 60:553–68.

Kurdek, L., and J. P. Schmitt. 1986. Relationship quality of gay men in closed or open relationships. *Journal of Homosexuality* 12:85–99.

———. 1987a. Partner homogamy in married, heterosexual cohabiting, gay, and lesbian couples. *Journal of Sex Research* 23:212–32.

———. 1987b. Perceived emotional support from family and friends in members of homosexual, married, and heterosexual cohabiting couples. *Journal of Homosexuality* 14:57–68.

Kus, R. 1988. Alcoholism and non-acceptance of gay self: The critical link. *Journal of Homosexuality* 15:25–41.

Kutchins, H., and S. A. Kirk. 1997. *Making us crazy: DSM: The psychiatric bible and the creation of mental disorders.* New York: Free Press.

Kwawer, J. 1980. Transference and countertransference in homosexuality: Changing psychoanalytic views. *American Journal of Psychotherapy* 34:72–80.

Labov, W., and D. Fanshel. 1977. *Therapeutic Discourse: Psychotherapy as Discourse.* New York: Academic Press.

Labov, W., and J. Waletzky. 1967. Narrative analysis: Oral versions of personal experience. In *Essays on the Verbal and Visual Arts,* ed. J. Helm. Seattle: University of Washington Press and The American Ethnological Society, 12–44.

Lachmann, F. 1975. Homosexuality: Some diagnostic perspectives and dynamic considerations. *American Journal of Psychotherapy* 29:254–60.

Laird, J. 1998. Invisible ties: Lesbians and their families of origin. In *Lesbian, gay, and bisexual identities in families: Psychological perspectives,* ed. C. J. Patterson and A. R. D'Augelli. New York: Oxford University Press, 197–230.

Lane, R. C., and J. W. Hull. 1990. Self-disclosure and classical psychoanalysis. In *Self-disclosure in the therapeutic relationship,* ed. G. Stricker and M. Fisher. New York: Plenum Press, 31–59.

Laner, M. R. 1977. Permanent partner priorities: Gay and straight. *Journal of Homosexuality* 3:21–39.

———. 1978. Growing older male: Heterosexual and homosexual. *Gerontologist* 18: 496–501.

Lansky, M. 1999. Shame and the idea of a central affect. In *Is shame the central affect of disorders of the self?* ed. E. M. Carr. Hillsdale, N.J.: Analytic Press (*Psychological Inquiry* 19:347–72).

Lansky, M. R., and A. P. Morrison. 1997. *The widening scope of shame.* Hillsdale, N.J.: Analytic Press.

Larson, R., M. Csikszentmihalyi, and R. Graef. 1980. Mood variability and the psychosocial adjustment of adolescents. *Journal of Youth and Adolescence* 9:469–90.

Laufer, R., and V. Bengtson. 1974. Generation, aging and social stratification: On the development of generational units. *Journal of Social Issues* 30:181–206. (Special issue: Youth, generations and social change, ed. V. Bengtson and R. Laufer.)

Lazarus, R., and S. Folkman. 1984. *Stress, appraisal and coping.* New York: Springer Publishing Company.

Leavy, S. 1983/85. Male homosexuality reconsidered. In *Sexuality: New perspectives,* ed. Z. De Fries, R. Friedman, and R. Corn. Westport, Conn.: Greenwood Press, 141–58.

Lebovitz, P. 1972. Feminine behavior in boys: Aspects of its outcome. *American Journal of Psychiatry* 128:1283–89.

Lee, G. 1979. Children and the elderly: Interaction and morale. *Research on Aging* 1:335–39.

Lee, J. A. 1977. Going public: A study into the sociology of homosexual liberation. *Journal of Homosexuality* 3:49–78.

———. 1987. What can homosexual aging studies contribute to theories of aging? *Journal of Homosexuality* 13:43–71.

———. 1988. Invisible lives of Canada's gray gays. In *Aging in Canada,* ed. V. Marshall. Toronto: Fitzhenry and Whiteside, 138–55.

———. 1991a. Can we talk? Can we *really* talk? Communication as a key factor in the maturing homosexual couple. *Journal of Homosexuality* 20:143–68.

———. 1991b. Through the looking glass: Life after Isherwood—A conversation with Don Bachardy. *Journal of Homosexuality* 20:33–63.

Leff, J., and C. Vaughn. 1985. *Expressed emotion in families.* New York: Guilford Press.

Lejeune, P. 1989. *On autobiography.* Trans. K. Leary. Minneapolis: University of Minnesota Press. (Theory and History of Literature, vol. 52.)

LeMasters, E. E. 1957. Parenthood as crisis. *Marriage and Family Living* 19:352–55.

———. 1970. *Parents in modern America.* Homewood, Ill.: Dorsey Press.

Lerner, R., and N. Busch-Rossnagel. 1981. Individuals as producers of their development: Conceptual and empirical bases. In *Individuals as producers of their development: A life-span perspective,* ed. R. Lerner and N. Busch-Rossnagel. New York: Academic Press, 1–36.

Lesser, R. 1993. Commentary on J. L. Trop and R. D. Stolorow's "Defense analysis in self-psychology." *Psychoanalytic Dialogues* 3:639–41.

LeVay, S. 1991. A difference in hypothalamic structure between heterosexual and homosexual men. *Science* 253:1034–37.

———. 1993. *The sexual brain.* Cambridge, Mass.: MIT Press.

LeVay, S., and D. Hamer. 1994. Evidence for a biological influence in male homosexuality. *Scientific American* 270:44–49.

Levine, M, P. Nardi, and J. Gagnon, eds. 1997. *In changing times: Gay men and lesbians encounter with HIV/AIDS.* Chicago: University Chicago Press.

LeVine, R. A. 1973. *Culture, behavior, and personality.* Chicago: Aldine.

Levinson, D. 1978. *The seasons of a man's life.* New York: Alfred Knopf.

———. 1996. *The seasons of a woman's life.* New York: Alfred Knopf.

Levitt, E., and A. Klassen, A. 1974. Public attitudes toward homosexuality: Part of the 1970 national survey by the Institute for Sex Research. *Journal of Homosexuality* 1:29–43.

Lewes, K. [1988] 1995. *The psychoanalytic theory of male homosexuality.* 2d ed. New York: Jason Aronson.

———. 1992. Homophobia and the heterosexual fear of AIDS. *American Imago* 49: 343–56.

———. 1995. Introduction: 1995: Nature and culture. In *The psychoanalytic theory of male homosexuality.* 2d ed. New York: Jason Aronson.

———. 1998. A special oedipal mechanism in the development of male homosexuality. *Psychoanalytic Psychology* 15:341–59.

Lewin, E. 1993. *Lesbian mothers: Accounts of gender in American culture.* Ithaca, N.Y.: Cornell University Press.

Lewin, K. [1946] 1964. Behavior and development as a function of the total situation. In *Field theory in social science,* ed. K. Lewin. New York: Harper Torchbooks, 238–304.

Lewinsohn, P., P. Rohde, and P. Seeley. 1994. Psychosocial risk factors for future adolescent suicide attempts. *Journal of Consulting and Clinical Psychology* 62:297–305.

Lewis, M. 1997. *Altering fate: Why the past does not predict the future*. New York: Guilford Press.

Lewontin, R. 1974. *The genetic basis of evolutionary change*. New York: Columbia University Press.

Lewontin, R., S. Rose, and L. Kamin. 1984. *Not in our genes*. New York: Pantheon Books.

Lichtenberg, J. 1983. *Psychoanalysis and infant research*. Hillsdale, N.J.: Analytic Press

Lidz, T. 1973. *The origin and treatment of schizophrenic disorders*. New York: Basic Books.

———. 1993. Reply to "A genetic study of male sexual orientation." *Archives of General Psychiatry* 50:240.

Lidz, T., S. Fleck, A. Cornelison, and associates. 1965. *Schizophrenia and the family*. New York: International Universities Press.

Lieberman, M., and J. Falk. 1971. The remembered past as a source of data for research on the life cycle. *Human Development* 14:132–41.

Lieberman, M., and S. Tobin. 1983. *The experience of old age: Stress, coping, and survival*. New York: Basic Books.

Linsk, N. 1997. Experience of older gay and bisexual men living with HIV/AIDS. *Journal of Lesbian, Gay and Bisexual Identities* 2:285–308. (Special issue: Coming of age: Gays, lesbians, and bisexuals in the second half of life, ed. G. Herdt, A. Hostetler, and B. Cohler.)

Lippmann, W. 1922. *Pubic Opinion*. New York: Harcourt, Brace.

Lipton, S. 1977. The advantages of Freud's technique as shown in his analysis of the Rat Man. *International Journal of Psychoanalysis* 58:255–74.

———. 1988. Further observations on the advantages of Freud's technique. *Annual for Psychoanalysis* 16:19–32.

Little, M. 1981. *Transference neurosis and transference psychosis: Toward basic unity*. New York: Aronson.

Litwak, E. 1965. Extended kin relations in an industrial democratic society. In *Social structure and the family: Generational relations*, ed. E. Shanas and G. Streib. Englewood-Cliffs, N.J.: Prentice-Hall, 290–325.

Livson, N., and H. Peskin. 1980. Perspectives on adolescence from longitudinal research. In *Handbook of adolescent psychology*, ed. J. Adelson. New York: Wiley, 47–96.

Lock, J. 1998. Treatment of homophobia in a gay male adolescent. *American Journal of Psychotherapy* 52:202–14.

Locke, J., and H. Steiner. 1999. Gay, lesbian, and bisexual youth risks for emotional, physical, and social problems: Results from a community based survey. *Journal of the American Academy of Child and Adolescent Psychiatry* 38:297–304.

Loiacano, D. 1989. Gay identity issues among Black Americans: Racism, homophobia, and the need for validation. *Journal of Counseling and Development* 68:21–25.

Long, D. 1997. Scientific authority and the search for sex hormones. In *A queer world: The Center for Lesbian and Gay Studies reader*, ed. M. Duberman. New York: New York University Press, 298–308.

Lorenz, K. [1937] 1965. *Evolution and modification of behavior*. Chicago: University of Chicago Press.

Loughery, J. 1998. *The other side of silence: Men's lives and gay identities: A twentieth century history*. New York: Henry Holt/Owl Books.

Lowenthal, M. F. 1964. Social isolation and mental illness in old age. *American Sociological Review* 29:54–70.

Lowenthal, M. F., and B. Robinson. 1976. Social networks and isolation. In *Handbook of aging and the social sciences,* ed. R. Binstock and E. Shanas. New York: Van Nostrand, 432–56.

Lowenthal, M. F., M. Thurnher, D. Chiriboga, and associates. 1975. *Four states of life.* San Francisco: Jossey-Bass.

Luborsky, L. 1967. Momentary forgetting during psychotherapy and psychoanalysis: A theory and research method. In *Motives and thought: Psychoanalytic essays in honor of David Rapaport,* ed. R. Holt. Madison, Conn.: International Universities Press, 175–217.

Lynch, F. R. 1987. Non-ghetto gays: A sociological study of suburban homosexuals. *Journal of Homosexuality* 13:13–42.

Lynch, P. 1999. Debasement in the sphere of homosexual love as understood through Freud's formulation of the universal tendency to debasement. *Journal of the American Psychoanalytic Association,* in press.

Lynn, D. J., and G. E. Vaillant. 1998. Anonymity, neutrality, and confidentiality in the actual methods of Sigmund Freud: A review of 43 cases, 1907–1939. *American Journal of Psychiatry* 155:163–71.

Maas, H., and J. Kuypers. 1974. *From thirty to seventy: A forty year longitudinal study of adult life.* San Francisco: Jossey-Bass.

Maccoby, E. 1990. Gender and relationships: A developmental account. *American Psychologist* 45:523–20.

———. 1998. *The two sexes: Growing up apart, coming together.* Cambridge, Mass.: Harvard University Press.

Maccoby, E. E., and R. Mnookin. 1992. *Dividing the child: Social and legal dilemmas of custody.* Cambridge, Mass.: Harvard University Press.

MacIntosh, H. 1994. Attitudes and experiences of psychoanalysts in analyzing homosexual patients. *Journal of the American Psychoanalytic Association* 42:1183–1207.

———. 1995. Reply to Friedman and Downey. *Journal of the American Psychoanalytic Association* 43:305–8.

MacIntyre, A. 1984. *After virtue: A study in moral theory.* Notre Dame, Ind.: University of Notre Dame Press.

MacLean, C. R. K., K. G. Walton, S. R. Wenneberg, D. K. Levitsky, et al. 1997. Effects of the transcendental meditation program on adaptive mechanisms: Changes in hormone levels and responses to stress after 4 months of practice. *Psychoneuroendocrinology* 221:277–95.

Magee, M., and D. Miller. 1996a. Psychoanalytic views of female homosexuality. In *Textbook of homosexuality and mental health,* ed. R. Cabaj and T. S. Stein. Washington, D.C.: American Psychiatric Press, 191–206.

———. 1996b. What sex is an amaryllis? What gender is lesbian? Looking for something to hold it all. *Gender and Psychoanalysis* 139–69.

———. 1997. *Lesbian lives: Psychoanalytic narratives old and new.* Hillsdale, N.J.: Analytic Press.

Magid, B. 1993. The homosexual identity of a nameless woman. In *Freud's case studies: Self-psychological perspectives,* ed. B. Magid. Hillsdale, N.J.: Analytic Press, 189–200.

Mahler, M., F. Pine, and A. Bergman. 1975. *The psychological birth of the human infant.* New York: Basic Books.

Main, M. 1995a. Discourse, prediction, and recent studies in attachment: Implications for psychoanalysis. In *Research in psychoanalysis: Process, development, and outcome,* ed. T. Shapiro and R. N. Emde. Madison, Conn.: International Universities Press, 209–44.

———. 1995b. Recent studies in attachment: Overview with selected implications for clinical work. In *Attachment theory: Social, developmental, and clinical perspectives,* ed. S. Goldberg, R. Muir, and J. Kerr. Hillsdale, N.J.: Analytic Press, 407–74.

Makari, G. J. (panel reporter). 1997. Current conceptions of neutrality and abstinence. *Journal of the American Psychanalytic Association* 45:1231–39.

Malyon, A. 1982. Psychotherapeutic implications of internalized homophobia in gay men. *Journal of Homosexuality* 72:59–69.

Manasse, G., and J. Swallow. 1995. *Making love visible: In celebration of gay and lesbian families.* Freedom, Calif.: Crossing Press.

Mandler, J. 1984. *Stories, scripts, and scenes: Aspects of schema theory.* Hillsdale, N.J.: Erlbaum.

Mandler, J., and N. Johnson. 1977. Remembrance of things parsed: Story structure and recall. *Cognitive Psychology* 9:111–51.

Mann, D. 1997. *Psychotherapy: An erotic relationship.* London: Routledge.

Mannheim, K. [1928] 1993. The problem of generations. In *From Karl Mannheim,* 2d exp. ed., ed. K. H. Wolff. New Brunswick, N.J.: Transactions Books, 351–98.

Marecek, J., S. Finn, and M. Cardell. 1982. Gender roles in the relationships of lesbians and gay men. *Journal of Homosexuality* 8:45–49.

Marini, M. 1984. Age and sequencing norms in the transition to adulthood. *Social Forces* 63:229–44.

Marmor, J. 1980. Epilogue: Homosexuality and the issue of mental illness. In *Homosexual behavior: A modern reappraisal,* ed. J. Marmor. New York: Basic Books, 391–402.

Marshall, E. 1995. NIH'S "gay gene" study questioned. *Science* 268:1841.

Marshall, V. 1975. Age and awareness of finitude in developmental gerontology. *Omega* 6:113–29.

———. 1981. *Last chapters: A sociology of death and dying.* Belmont, Calif.: Wordsworth Publishing Company.

———. 1986. A sociological perspective on aging and dying. In *Later life: The social psychology of aging,* ed. V. Marshall. Beverly Hills, Calif.: Sage Publications, 125–46.

Martin, A. D. 1982. Learning to hide: The socialization of the gay adolescent. *Adolescent Psychiatry* 10:52–65.

———. 1984. The emperor's new clothes: Modern attempts to change sexual orientation. In *Innovations in psychotherapy with homosexuals,* ed. E. S. Hetrick and T. S. Stein. Washington, D.C.: American Psychiatric Association, 23–58.

———. 1998. Clinical issues in psychotherapy with lesbian-, gay-, and bisexual-partnered families. In *Lesbian, gay, and bisexual identities in families: Psychological perspectives,* ed. C. J. Patterson and A. R. D'Augelli. New York: Oxford University Press, 270–92.

Martin, A. D., and E. Hetrick. 1988. The stigmatization of the gay and lesbian adolescent. *Journal of Homosexuality* 15:163–83.

Marx, K. [1845] 1978. The German ideology, part 1. In *The Marx-Engels Reader.* 2d ed. Ed. and trans. R. Tucker. New York: Norton, 146–200.

Masten, A., and D. Coatsworth. 1995. Competence, vulnerability, and psychopathology. In *Manual of developmental psychopathology,* vol. 2, ed. D. Cicchetti and D. Cohen. New York: Wiley, 715–52.

Matthews, S. 1986. Friendships in old age: Biography and circumstance. In *Later Life: The Social Psychology of Aging,* ed. V. Marshall. Beverly Hills, CA: Sage Publications, 233–270.

Mattison, A., and D. McWhirter. 1987. Stage discrepancy in male couples. *Journal of Homosexuality* 13:89–99.

Mayer, E. L. 1996. Psychoanalytic stories about gender: Moving toward an integration of mind and body. *Gender and Psychoanalysis* 1:239–47.

Mayson, S. (panel reporter). 1989b. Personal reflections on the role of sexuality in the etiology and treatment of the neuroses. *Journal of the American Psychoanalytic Association* 37:803–12.

McAdams, D. 1985. *Power, intimacy, and the life-story.* Homewood, Ill.: Dorsey Press, 252–79.

———. 1989. The development of a narrative identity. In *Personality psychology: Recent trends and emerging directions,* ed. D. Buss and N. Cantor. New York: Sprigner-Verlag, 160–274.

———. 1991. Self and story. In *Perspectives in personality: A research annual,* vol. 3, pt. B, ed. A. Stewart, J. Healy Jr., and D. Ozer. London: Jessica Kingsley Publishers, 133–60.

———. 1993. *Stories we live by: Personal myths and the making of the self.* New York: William Morrow and Company.

———. 1996. Narrating the self in adulthood. In *Aging and biography: Explorations in adult development,* ed. J. Birren, G. Kenyon, J-E Ruth, J. J. F. Schroots, and T. Svensson. New York: Springer, 131–48.

McAdams, D., and E. de St. Aubin. 1992. A theory of generativity and its assessment through self-report, behavioral acts and narrative themes in autobiography. *Journal of Personality and Social Psychology* 62:1003–15.

McAdams, D., E. de St. Aubin, and R. Logan. 1993. Generativity among young, midlife and older adults. *Psychology and Aging* 8:221–30.

McAdams, D., H. Hart, and S. Maruna. 1998. The anatomy of generativity. In *Generativity and adult experience: Psychosocial perspectives on caring and contributing to the next generation,* ed. D. McAdams and E. de St. Aubin. Washington, D.C.: American Psychological Association Press, 7–43.

McAdams, D., B. Hoffman, E. Mansfield, and R. Day. 1996. Themes of agency and communion in significant autobiographical scenes. *Journal of Personality* 64:339–77.

McAdams, D., K. Ruetzel, and J. Foley. 1986. Complexity and generativity at mid-life: Relation among social motives, ego development, and adults' plans for the future. *Journal of Personality and Social Psychology* 50:800–807.

McCabe, A., E. Capron, and C. Peterson. 1991a. The voice of experience: The recall of early childhood and adolescent memories by young adults. In *Developing narrative structure,* ed. A. McCabe and C. Peterson. Hillsdale, N.J.: Lawrence Erlbaum and Associates, 137–74.

McCall, G., and J. Simmons. 1978. *Identities and interactions: An examination of human associations in everyday life.* Rev. ed. New York: Free Press.

McCandlish, B. 1987. Against all odds: Lesbian mother family dynamics. In *Gay and lesbian parents,* ed. F. W. Bozett. New York: Praeger, 23–38.

McClintock, M., and G. Herdt. 1997. Rethinking puberty: The development of sexual attraction. *New Directions in Psychological Science* 5:178–83.

McDougall, G. 1993. Therapeutic issues with gay and lesbian elders. In *The forgotten aged: Ethnic, psychiatric and social minorities,* ed. T. L. Brink. New York: Haworth Press, 45–58.

McDougall, J. [1965] 1970. Homosexuality in women. In *Female sexuality,* ed. J. Chasseguet-Smirgel, C. Luquet-Parat, B. Grunberger, J. McDougall, M. Torok, and C. David. Ann Arbor: University of Michigan Press, 171–212.

McFadden, D., and E. G. Pasanen. 1998. Comparison of the auditory systems of heterosexuals and homosexuals: Click-evoked otoacoustic emissions. *Proceedings of the National Academy of Science* 95:2709–13.

McGee, M., and D. Miller. 1997. *Lesbian lives: Psychoanalytic narratives old and new.* Mahweh, N.J.: Analytic Press/Erlbaum.

McGuire, T. 1995. Is homosexuality genetic? A critical review and some suggestions. *Journal of Homosexuality* 28:115–45.

McKnight, J. 1997. *Straight science? Homosexuality, evolution and adaptation.* London: Routledge.

McKusick, L., J. A. Wiley, T. J. Coates, R. Stall, G. Saika, S. Morin, K. Charles, and W. R. Horstman. 1985. Reported changes in the behavior of men at risk for AIDS: 1982–1984: The AIDS Behavioral Research Project. San Francisco: AIDS Behavioral Research Project, Public Health Reports 100:622–29.

McLanahan, S., and J. Adams. 1987. Parenthood and psychological well-being. *Annual Review of Sociology* 5:237–57.

McLaughlin, J. 1991. Clinical and theoretical aspects of enactment. *Journal of the American Psychoanalytic Association* 39:595–614.

McMahon, A., and P. Rhudick. 1964. Reminiscing: Adaptational significance in the aged. *Archives of General Psychiatry* 10:292–98.

———. 1967. Reminiscing in the aged: An adaptational response. In *Psychodynamic studies on aging: Creativity, reminiscing, and dying,* ed. S. Levin and R. Kahana. New York: International Universities Press, 64–78.

McWhirter, D. P., and A. M. Mattison. 1984. *The male couple: How relationships develop.* Englewood Cliffs, N. J.: Prentice-Hall.

———. 1996. Male couples. In *Textbook of homosexuality and mental health,* ed. R. Cabaj and T. S. Stein. Washington, D.C.: American Psychiatric Press, 319–37.

McWilliams, N. 1996. Therapy across the sexual orientation boundary: Reflections of a heterosexual female analyst on working with lesbian, gay, and bisexual patients. *Gender and Psychoanalysis* 1:203–21.

Mead, M. [1928] 1961. Coming of age in Samoa. New York: Morrrow Quill Paperbacks.

Meissner, W. 1981. *Internalization in psychoanalysis.* New York: International Universities Press. (Psychology Issues monograph, no. 50.)

Mendola, M. 1980. *The Mendola report: A new look at gay couples.* New York: Crown Publishers.

Menaker, E. 1990. Transference, countertransference, and therapeutic efficacy in relation to self-disclosure by the analyst. In *Self-disclosure in the therapeutic relationship,* ed. G. Stricker and M. Fisher. New York: Plenum Press, 103–16.

Meredith, R., and R. Reister. 1980. Psychotherapy responsibility and homosexuality: Clinical examination of socially deviant behavior. *Professional Psychology* 11:174–93.

Meyer, I. 1993. Prejudice and pride: Minority stress and mental health in gay men. Doctoral dissertation, Columbia University. Ann Arbor, Mich.: UMI Dissertation Services.

———. 1995. Minority stress and mental health in gay men. *Journal of Health and Social Behavior* 36:38–56.

Meyer, I. H., and M. E. Colten. 1999. Sampling gay men: Random digit dialing versus sources in the gay community. *Journal of Homosexuality* 37:99–110.

Meyer, I. H., and L. Dean. 1998. In *Stigma and sexual orientation: Understanding prejudice against lesbians, gay men and bisexuals,* ed. G. Herek. Thousand Oaks, Calif.: Sage Publications, 160–86.

Meyer, J. K. 1982. The theory of gender identity disorders. *Journal of the American Psychoanalytic Association* 30 (2): 381–418.

———. 1985. Ego-dystonic homosexuality. In *Comprehensive textbook of psychiatry/IV,* vol. 1, ed. H. I. Kaplan and B. J. Sadock. 4th ed. Baltimore, Md.: Williams and Wilkins, 1056–65.

———. 1995. Homosexuality. In *Psychoanalysis: The major concepts,* ed. B. E. Moore and B. O. Fine. New Haven, Conn.: Yale University Press, 346–63.

Meyer-Bahlburg, H. 1984. Psychoendocrine research on sexual orientation: Current status and future options. *Progress in Brain Research* 61:367–90.

———. 1997a. Psychobiologic research on homosexuality. In *A queer world: The Center for Lesbian and Gay Studies reader,* ed. M. Duberman. New York: New York University Press, 285–97.

———. 1997b. The role of prenatal estrogens in sexual orientation. In *Sexual orientation,* ed. L. Ellis and L. Ebertz. Westport, Conn.: Praeger, 41–52.

Meyer-Bahlburg, H., A. Ehrhardt, L. Rosen, R. Gruen, N. Veridiano, F. Vann, and H. Neuwalder. 1995. Prenatal estrogens and the development of homosexual orientation. *Developmental Psychology* 31:12–21.

Meyerowitz, J., and H. Feldman. 1966. Transition to parenthood. *Psychiatric Research Reports* 20:78–84.

Mezzich, J., and M. Jorge. 1993. *Psychiatric epidemiology: Assessment, concepts and methods.* Baltimore, Md.: Johns Hopkins University Press.

Michaels, S. 1996. The prevalence of homosexuality in the United States. In *Textbook of homosexuality and mental health,* ed. R. Cabaj and T. S. Stein. Washington, D.C.: American Psychiatric Press, 43–64.

Millan, G., and M. W. Ross. 1987. AIDS and gay youth: Attitudes and lifestyle modifications in young male homosexuals. *Community Health Studies* 11:50–53.

Miller, B. 1979a. Gay fathers and their children. *Family Coordinator* 28:544–52.

———. 1979b. Unpromised paternity: The life-styles of gay fathers. In *Gay men,* ed. M. Levine. New York: Harper and Row, 240–52.

Miller, B., and D. Sollie. 1980. Normal stresses during the transition to parenthood. *Family Relations* 29:459–65.

Miller, E. 1987. The Oedipus complex and rejuvenation fantasies in the analysis of a seventy-year-old-woman. *Journal of Geriatric Psychiatry* 20:29–51.

Miller, J., R. Jacobsen, and J. Bigner. 1981. The child's home environment for lesbian v. heterosexual mothers: A neglected area of research. *Journal of Homosexuality* 7:49–56.

Miller, N. 1995. Out of the past: Gay and lesbian history from 1869 to the present. New York: Random House/Vintage Books.

Miller, P., and L. Sperry. 1988. Early talk about the past: The origins of conversational stories of personal experience. *Journal of Child Language* 15:293–315.

Miller, T. 1997. *Shirts and skins.* Los Angeles: Alyson Books.

Mink, L. O. 1965. The anatomy of historical understanding. *History and Theory* 5: 24–47.

———. 1981. Everyman his or her own annalist. *Critical Inquiry* 7:777–92.

Minnigerode, F. 1976. Age-status labeling in homosexual men. *Journal of Homosexuality* 1:263–76. Reprinted in R. Berger, *Gay and gray: The older homosexual man* (2d ed.; New York: Harrington Park Press, 1996), 245–48.

Minnigerode, F., and M. Adelman. 1978. Elderly homosexual women and men: Report on a pilot study. *Family Coordinator* 27:451–56.

Minton, H., and G. McDonald. 1984. Homosexual identity formation as a developmental process. *Journal of Homosexuality* 10:91–104.

Minturn, L., and W. Lambert. 1964. *Mothers of six cultures: Antecendents of childrearing.* New York: Wiley.

Mishler, E. 1986a. The analysis of interview-narratives. In *Narrative Psychology: The Storied Nature of Human Conduct*, ed. T. Sarbin. New York: Praeger, 233–55.

———. 1986b. *Research interviewing: Context and narrative*. Cambridge, Mass.: Harvard University Press.

———. 1990. Validation: The social construction of knowledge—A brief for inquiry-guided research. *Harvard Educational Review* 60:415–42.

Mishler, E., and N. Waxler. [1965] 1968. Family interaction process and schizophrenia: A review of current theories In *Family processes and schizophrenia*, ed. E. Mishler and N. Waxler. New York: Science House, 3–62.

———. 1968. *Schizophrenia in families: An experimental study of family process and schizophrenia*. New York: Wiley, 1968.

Mitchell, J. 1997. Sexuality, psychoanalysis, and social change. *International Psychoanalysis: The Newsletter of the International Psychoanalytical Society* 6 (1): 28–29.

Mitchell, S. A. 1978. Psychodynamics, homosexuality, and the question of pathology. *Psychiatry* 41:254–63.

———. 1981. The psychoanalytic treatment of homosexuality: Some technical considerations. *International Review of Psychoanalysis* 8:63–80.

———. 1988. *Relational concepts in psychoanalysis: An integration*. Cambridge, Mass.: Harvard University Press.

———. 1992. Commentary on J. L. Trop and R. D. Stolorow's "Defense analysis in self-psychology." *Psychoanalytic Dialogues* 2:443–53.

———. 1993a. Commentaries on J. L. Trop and R. D. Stolorow's "Defense analysis in self-psychology" (Introduction). *Psychoanalytic Dialogues* 3:623–25.

———. 1993b. *Hope and dread in psychoanalysis*. New York: Basic Books.

———. 1996a. Constructions of gender and sexuality, sandcastles on the shore: A response to Mayer and Schwartz. *Gender and Psychoanalysis* 1:261–69.

———. 1996b. Gender and sexual orientation in the age of postmodernism: The plight of the perplexed clinician. *Gender and Psychoanalysis* 1:45–73.

Mitchell, V. 1998. The birds and the bees . . . and the sperm banks: How lesbian mothers talk with their children about sex and reproduction. *American Journal of Orthopsychiatry* 68:400–409.

Mohr, R. 1992. *Gay ideas: Outing and other controversies*. Boston: Beacon Press.

Moll, A. 1897a. Probleme in der homosexualität. *Zeitschrift für criminal-anthropologie, Gefängnis-wissenschaft und prostitution* 1:157–89.

———. 1897b. *Untrsuchungen über die libido sexualis*. Berlin: Fischer's medicinische buch-handlung, H. Kornfeld.

Mondimore, F. M. 1996. *A natural history of homosexuality*. Baltimore, Md.: Johns Hopkins University Press.

Money, J. 1988. *Gay, straight, and in-between: The sexology of erotic orientation*. New York: Oxford University Press.

———. 1997. Sex as science and as philosophy. *Harvard Gay and Lesbian Review* 4 (1): 16–17.

Money, J., and A. Ehrhardt. 1972. *Boy and girl: The differentiation and dimorphism of gender identity from conception to maturity*. Baltimore, Md.: Johns Hopkins University Press.

Moore, B. E., and D. Fine. 1990. *Psychoanalytic terms and concepts*. New Haven, Conn.: Yale University Press.

Moore, C., H. Dou, and J. Juraska. 1992. Maternal stimulation affects the number of motor neurons in a sexually dimorphic nucleus of the lumbar spinal cord. *Brain Research* 572:52–56.

Moraitis, G. 1985. The psychoanalyst's role in the biographer's quest for self-awareness. In *Introspection in biography: The biographer's quest for self-awareness,* ed. S. Baron and C. Pletsch. Hillsdale, N.J.: Analytic Press, 319–54.

Morrison, A. 1989. *Shame: The underside of narcissism.* Hillsdale, N.J.: Analytic Press.

———. 1999. Walking taller, though still wounded: A discussion of "Wounded but still walking: One man's effort to move out of shame." In *Is shame the central affect of disorders of the self?* ed. E. M. Carr. Hillsdale, N.J.: Analytic Press (*Psychological Inquiry* 19:320–46.)

Morrison, A. P., and R. Stolorow. 1997. Shame, narcissism, and intersubjectivity. In *The widening scope of shame,* ed. M. R. Lansky and A. P. Morrison. Hillsdale, N.J.: Analytic Press, 63–88.

Moses, A., and R. Hawkins. 1982. *Counseling lesbian women and gay men: A lie-issues approach.* St. Louis: C. V. Mosby.

Moss, D. 1992. Hating in the first person plural: The example of homophobia. *American Imago* 49:277–91.

———. 1997a. "Disorienting sexuality"—a commentary. *Gender and Psychoanalysis* 2: 185–90.

———. 1997b. On situating homophobia. *Journal of the American Psychoanalytic Association* 45:201–15.

Moss, H., and E. Sussman. 1980. Longitudinal study of personality development. In *Constancy and change in human development,* ed. O. G. Brim Jr. and J. Kagan. Cambridge, Mass.: Harvard University Press, 530–95.

Mossey, J. M., and E. Shapiro. 1982. Self-rated health: A predictor of mortality among the elderly. *American Journal of Public Health* 72:800–08.

Muller, A. 1987. *Parents matter.* New York: Naiad Press.

Munnichs, J. 1966. *Old age and finitude: A contribution to psychogerontology.* New York: Karger.

Murphy, B. 1989. Lesbian couples and their parents: The effects of perceived parental attitudes on the couple. *Journal of Counseling and Development* 68:46–51.

Murphy, T. F. 1984. Freud reconsidered: Bisexuality, homosexuality, and moral judgment. *Journal of Homosexuality* 10:65–77.

———. 1997. *Gay science: The ethics of sexual orientation research.* New York: Columbia University Press.

Murray, S. O. 1984. *Social theory, homosexual realities.* New York: Gay Academic Union.

———. 1995a. Homosexual categorization in cross-cultural perspective. In *Latin-American male homosexualities,* ed. S. O. Murray. Albuquerque: University of New Mexico Press, 3–32.

———. 1995b. Machismo, male homosexuality, and Latino culture. In *Latin-American male homosexualities,* ed. S. O. Murray. Albuquerque: University of New Mexico Press, 49–69.

———. 1995c. Modern male homosexuality in Mexico and Peru. In *Latin-American male homosexualities,* ed. S. O. Murray. Albuquerque: University of New Mexico Press, 145–49.

———, ed. 1995d. *Latin-American male homosexualities.* Albuquerque: University of New Mexico Press.

———. 1996. *American gay.* Chicago: University of Chicago Press.

———. 1998. "A feeling within me": Kamau, a twenty-five year old Kikuyu. In *Boy-wives and female husbands: Studies of African homosexualities,* ed. S. O. Murray and W. Roscoe. New York: St. Martin's Press, 41–62.

Murray, S. O, and W. Roscoe, eds. 1998. *Boy-wives and female husbands: Studies of African homosexualities.* New York: St. Martin's Press, 41–62.

Murphy, T. O. 1992a. Freud and sexual reorientation therapy. *Journal of Homosexuality* 23:21–38.

———. 1992b. Redirecting sexual orientation: Techniques and justifications. *Journal of Sex research* 29:501–23.

———. 1997. *Gay science: The ethics of sexual orientation research.* New York: Columbia University Press.

Mussen, P., and M. Jones. 1957. Self-conceptions, motivations, and interpersonal attitudes of early maturing and late maturing boys. *Child Development* 28:243–56.

Myerhoff, B. 1978. A symbol perfected in death. In *Life's career-aging: Cultural variations in growing old,* ed. B. Myerhoff and A. Simic. Beverly Hills, Calif.: Sage Publications, 163–205.

———. 1979. *Number our days.* New York: Dutton.

———. 1992. *Remembered lives: The work of ritual, storytelling, and growing older,* ed. M. Kaminsky. Ann Arbor: University of Michigan Press.

Myers, G. 1990. Demography of aging. In *Handbook of aging and the social sciences,* ed. R. H. Binstock and L. K. George. 3d ed. San Diego, Calif.: Academic Press, 19–44.

Nagera, H. 1966. *Early childhood disturbances, the infantile neurosis and the adult disturbances.* New York: International Universities Press.

Nardi, P. 1999. *Gay men's friendships: Invincible communities.* Chicago: University of Chicago Press.

Nash, J. 1993. The heterosexual analyst and the gay man. In *Affirmative Dynamic Psychotherapy with Gay Men,* ed. C. Cornett. Northvale, N.J.: Jason Aronson, 199–228.

Nash, J., and F. Hayes. 1965. The parental relationships of male homosexuals: Some theoretical issues and a pilot study. *Australian Journal of Psychology* 17:35–43.

Neff, L. 1997. The kids are all right. *Windy City Times,* 28 August, 12 (51): 1.

Nemiroff, R., and C. Colarusso. 1985a. Adult development and transference. In *The race against time: Psychotherapy and psychoanalysis in the second half of life,* ed. R. A. Nemiroff and C. Colarusso. New York: Plenum Press, 59–72.

———. 1985b. *The race against time: Psychotherapy and psychoanalysis in the second half of life.* New York: Plenum.

———. 1990. Frontiers of adult development in theory and practice. In *New dimensions in adult development,* ed. R. Nemiroff and C. Colarusso. New York: Basic Books, 97–124.

Neubauer, P. B. 1980. The life cycle as indicated by the nature of the transference in the psychoanalysis of children. *International Journal of Psychoanalysis* 61:137–44.

Neugarten, B. 1967. The awareness of middle age. In *Middle Age,* ed. R. Owen. London: British Broadcasting Company, 1967. (Reprinted in *Middle Age and Aging,* ed. B. L. Neugarten. Chicago: University of Chicago Press, 1968, 93–98.)

———. 1969. Continuities and discontinuities of psychological issues into adult life. *Human Development* 12:121–30.

———. 1970. Dynamics of transition of middle age to old age. *Journal of Geriatric Psychiatry* 4:71–87.

———. 1973. Personality change in late life: A developmental perspective. In *The psychology of adult development,* ed. C. Eisorfer and M. Lawton. Washington, D.C.: American Psychological Association, 311–38.

———. 1979. Time, age, and the life-cycle. *American Journal of Psychiatry* 136:887–94.

———. 1996. *The meanings of age.* Ed. D. A. Neugarten. Chicago: University of Chicago Press.

Neugarten, B., and associates. 1964. *Personality in middle and later life.* New York: Atherton-Aldine.

Neugarten, B., and N. Datan. 1974a. The middle years. In *American handbook of psychiatry,* ed. S. Arieti. New York: Basic Books, 1:592–606.

———. 1974b. Sociological perspectives on the life cycle. In *Life-span developmental psychology: Personality and socialization,* ed. P. Baltes and K. Schaie. New York: Academic Press, 53–69.

Neugarten, B., and G. Hagestad. 1976. Age and the life course. In *Handbook of aging and the social sciences,* ed. R. Binstock and E. Shanas. New York: Van Nostrand-Reinhold, 35–55.

Neugarten, B., and J. Moore. 1968. The changing age-status system. In *Middle-age and aging: A reader in social psychology,* ed. B. Neugarten. Chicago: University of Chicago Press, 5–20.

Neugarten, B., J. Moore, and J. Lowe. [1965] 1996. Age norms, age constraints, and adult socialization. In *The meanings of age: Selected papers of Bernice Neugarten.* Ed. D. Neugarten. Chicago: University of Chicago Press, 24–33.

Nichols, M. 1990. Lesbian relationships: Implications for the study of sexuality and gender. In *Homosexuality/heterosexuality: Concepts of sexual orientation,* ed. D. P. McWhirter, S. A. Sanders, and J. M. Reinisch. New York: Oxford University Press, 350–64.

Nicolosi, J. [1991] 1997. *Reparative therapy of male homosexuality: A new clinical approach.* Northvale, N.J.: Jason Aronson.

———. [1993] 1997. *Healing homosexuality: Case studies of reparative therapy.* Northvale, N.J.: Jason Aronson.

Novey, S. 1968. *The second look.* Baltimore, Md.: Johns Hopkins University Press.

Nunberg, H. 1938. Homosexuality, magic and aggression. *International Journal of Psychoanalysis* 19:1–16.

———. 1947. Circumcision and problems of bisexuality. *International Journal of Psychoanalysis* 28:145–79.

Nungesser, L. 1980. Theoretical bases for research on the acquisition of social sex-roles by children of lesbian mothers. *Journal of Homosexuality* 5:189–204.

———. 1983. *Homosexual acts, actors, and identities.* New York: Praeger.

Nussbaum, M. 1998. Of paederasty and proposition two. *Harvard Gay and Lesbian Review* 5:12–15.

Nydegger, C. 1980. Role and age transitions: A potpourri of issues. In *New methods of old age research: Anthropological alternatives,* ed. C. Fry and J. Keith. Chicago: Loyola University of Chicago Center for Urban Studies, 127–45.

———. 1981. On being caught up in time. *Human Development* 24:1–12.

O'Brien, K. 1992. Primary relationships affect the psychological health of homosexual men at risk for AIDS. *Psychological Reports* 71:147–53.

O'Connor, N., and J. Ryan. 1993. *Wild desires and mistaken identities: Lesbianism and psychoanalysis.* New York: Columbia University Press.

Odets, W. 1995. *In the shadow of the epidemic: Being HIV-negative in the age of AIDS.* Durham, N.C.: Duke University Press.

Offer, D. 1969. *The psychological world of the teenager: A study of normal adolescent boys.* New York: Basic Books.

———. 1987. In defense of adolescents. *Journal of the American Medical Association* 257 (24): 3407–8.

Offer, D., and D. Offer. 1975. *From teenage to young manhood: A psychological study.* New York: Basic Books.

Offer, D., E. Ostrov, and K. Howard. 1981. The mental health professional's concept of the normal adolescent. *Archives of General Psychiatry* 38:149–52.

Offer, D., and M. Sabshin, eds. 1984. *Normality and the life cycle.* New York: Basic Books.

Offer, D., and C. Strozier, eds. 1985. *The leader: Psychohistorical essays.* New York: Plenum Press.

Orange, D., and R. Stolorow. 1998. Self-disclosure from the perspective of intersubjectivity theory. *Psychoanalytic Inquiry* 18:530–37.

Orbuch, T. 1997. People's accounts count: The sociology of accounts. *Annual Review of Sociology* 23:455–78.

Osofsky, J., and H. Osofsky. 1984. Psychological and developmental perspectives on expectant and new parenthood. *Review of Child Development Research,* vol. 7. Chicago: University of Chicago Press.

Ostrow, D., A. Monjan, J. Joseph, M. VanRaden, R. Fox, L. Kingsley, J. Dudley, and J. Phair. 1989. HIV-related symptoms and psychological functioning in a cohort of homosexual men. *American Journal of Psychiatry* 146:737–42.

Oudshoorn, N. 1995. Female or male: The classification of homosexuality and gender. *Journal of Homosexuality* 28:79–68.

Ovesey, L. 1969. *Homosexuality and pseudohomosexuality.* New York: Science House.

Ovesey, L., W. Gaylin, and H. Hendin. 1963. Psychotherapy of male homosexuality: Psychodynamic formulation. *Archives of General Psychiatry* 9:19–31.

Ovesey, L., and S. Woods. 1980. Pseudohomosexuality and homosexuality in men: Psychodynamics as a guide to treatment. In *Homosexual behavior: A modern reappraisal,* ed. J. Marmor. New York: Basic Books, 325–41.

Palombo, J. 1987. Spontaneous disclosures in psychotherapy. *Clinical Social Work Journal* 15:107–20.

Parke, R. 1986. Fathers: An intrafamilial perspective. In *In support of families,* ed. M. Yogman and T. Brazelton. Cambridge, Mass.: Harvard University Press, 59–68.

Parker, D., and J. De Cecco. 1995. Sexual expression: A global perspective. *Journal of Homosexuality* 28:427–30.

Parks, C. 1999. Lesbian identity development: An examination of differences across generations. *American Journal of Orthopsychiatry* 69:347–61.

Parsons, T. 1949. The social structure of the family. In *The family: Its function and destiny,* ed. R. Anshen. New York: Harper and Row 173–201.

———. 1952. The superego and the theory of social systems. *Psychiatry* 15:15–24.

———. 1955. Family structure and the socialization of the child. In T. Parsons and R. Bales, *Family, socialization and interaction process.* New York: Free Press, 35–131.

Parsons, T., and K. Clark, eds. 1966. *The Negro American.* Boston: Houghton-Mifflin.

Pasche, F. 1964. Symposium on homosexuality. *International Journal of Psychoanalysis* 45:210–13.

Pattatucci, A. M. L. 1998. Biopsychological interactions and the development of sexual orientation. In *Lesbian, gay, and bisexual identities in families: Psychological perspectives,* ed. C. J. Patterson and A. R. D'Augelli. New York: Oxford University Press, 19–39.

Pattatucci, A., and D. Hamer. 1995. Development and familiality of sexual orientation in females. *Behavior Genetics* 25:407–20.

Patterson, C. 1992. Children of lesbian and gay parents. *Chid Development* 63:1025–42.

———. 1994. Children of the lesbian baby boom: Behavioral adjustment, self-concepts, and sex role identity. In *Lesbian and gay psychology: Theory, research and clinical applications,* ed. B. Greene and G. M. Herek. Psychological Perspectives on Lesbian and Gay Issues, vol. 1. Thousand Oaks, Calif.: Sage Publications, 156–75.

———. 1995a. Families of the lesbian baby boom: Parents' division of labor and childrens' adjustment. Developmental Psychology 31:115–23.

———. 1995b. Lesbian mothers, gay fathers, and their children. In Lesbian, gay, and bisexual identities over the life span, ed. A. R. D'Augelli and C. Patterson. New York: Oxford University Press, 262–92.

———. 1995c. Sexual orientation and human development: An overview. Developmental Psychology 31:3–11.

———. 1996. Lesbian and gay parents and their children. In The lives of lesbians, gays, and bisexuals: Children to adults, ed. R. C. Savin-Williams and K. M. Cohen. Fort Worth, Tex.: Harcourt Brace, 274–304.

———. 1998. The family lives of children born to lesbian mothers. In Lesbian, gay, and bisexual identities in families: Psychological perspectives, ed. C. J. Patterson and A. R. D'Augelli. New York: Oxford University Press, 154–76.

Patterson, C., and R. Chan. 1996. Gay fathers and their children. In Textbook of homosexuality and mental health, ed. R. Cabaj and T. S. Stein. Washington, D.C.: American Psychiatric Press, 371–96.

Patterson, C., S. Hurt, and C. D. Mason. 1998. Families of the lesbian baby boom: Childrens' contact with grandparents and other adults. American Journal of Orthopsychiatry 68:390–99.

Paul, J. 1993. Childhood cross-gender behavior and adult homosexuality: The resurgence of biological models of sexuality. In If your seduce a straight person, can you make them gay? Issues in biological versus social constructionism in gay and lesbian identities, ed. J De Cecco and J. P. Elia. New York: Harrington Park Press, 41–54.

———. 1996. Bisexuality: Exploring/exploding the boundaries. In The lives of lesbians, gays, and bisexuals: Children to adults, ed. R. C. Savin-Williams and K. M. Cohen. Fort Worth, Tex.: Harcourt Brace, 436–61.

Paul, J. P., R. B. Hays, and T. J. Coates. 1995. The impact of the HIV epidemic on U.S. gay male communities. In Lesbian, gay, and bisexual identities over the lifespan, ed. A. R. D'Augelli and C. J. Patterson. New York: Oxford University Press, 347–97.

Paykel, E., B. Prusoff, and E. Uhlenhuth. 1971. Scaling of life events. Archives of General Psychiatry 25:340–47.

Payne, E. (panel reporter). 1977. Psychoanalytic treatment of male homosexuality. Journal of the American Psychoanalytic Association 25:183–99.

Pearlin, L. 1980. Life strains and psychological distress among adults. In Themes of work and love in adulthood, ed. E. Erikson and N. Smelser. Cambridge, Mass.: Harvard University Press, 174–92.

Pearlin, L., and M. Lieberman. 1979. Social sources of emotional distress. In Research in community and mental health, ed. R. Simmons. Greenwich, Conn.: JAI Press, 1:217–48.

Pearlin, L., B. Menaghan, M. Lieberman, and J. Mullan. 1981. The stress process. Journal of Health and Social Behavior 22:337–56.

Pellegrini, A. D., and P. K. Smith. 1998. The development of play during childhood: Forms and possible functions. Child Psychology and Psychiatry Review 3:51–57.

Penelope, J., and S. Wolfe. 1989. The original coming out stories. Expanded ed. Freedom, Calif.: Crossing Press.

———. 1993. Lesbian culture, an anthology: The lives, work, ideas, art and visions of lesbians, past and present. Freedom, Calif.: Crossing Press.

Pennebaker, J. W., and B. L. Banasik. 1997. On the creation and maintenance of collective memories: History as social psychology. In *Collective memory of political events: Social psychological perspectives,* ed. J. W. Pennebaker, D. Paez, and B. Rimé. Mahwah, N.J.: Lawrence Erlbaum Associates, 3–20.

Peplau, L. 1982. Research on homosexual couples: An overview. *Journal of Homosexuality* 8:3–8.

———. 1991. Lesbian and gay relationships. In *Homosexuality: Research implications for public policy,* ed. J. C. Gonsiorek and J. D. Weinrich. Thousand Oaks, Calif.: Sage Publications, 177–96.

———. 1993. Lesbian and gay relationships. In *Psychological perspectives on lesbian and gay male experiences,* ed. C. Garnets and D.C. Kimmel. New York: Columbia University Press, 395–419.

Peplau, L., and S. Cochran. 1990. A relationship perspective on homosexuality. In *Homosexuality/heterosexuality: Concepts of sexual orientation,* ed. D. P. McWhirter, S. A. Sanders, and J. M. Reinisch. New York: Oxford University Press, 321–49.

Peplau, L., C. Padesky, and M. Hamilton. 1982. Satisfaction in lesbian relationships. *Journal of Homosexuality* 8:23–36 .

Peplau, L. A., R. Veniegas, and S. M. Campbell. 1996. Gay and lesbian relationships. In *The lives of lesbians, gays, and bisexuals: Children to adults,* ed. R. C. Savin-Williams and K. M. Cohen. Fort Worth, Tex.: Harcourt Brace, 250–73.

Person, E. 1985. The erotic transference in women and men: Differences and consequences. *Journal of the American Academy of Psychoanalysis* 13:159–80.

———. 1988a. *Dreams of love and fateful encounters: The power of romantic passion.* New York: Norton.

———. 1988b. A psychoanalytic approach. In *Theories of human sexuality,* ed. J. H. Geer and W. T. O'Donohue. New York: Plenum Press, 385–410.

Peskin, N., and N. Livson. 1981. Use of the past in adult psychological health. In *Present and past in middle-life,* ed. D. Eichorn, J. Clausen, N. Haan, M. Honzik, and P. Mussen. New York: Academic Press, 154–83.

Petersen, A. 1981. The development of the self-concept in adolescence. In *The self-concept,* ed. D. M. Lynch, A. Norem-Heibeisen, and K. Gergen. New York: Balinger, 191–202.

———. 1985. Pubertal development as a cause of disturbance: Myths, realities, and unanswered questions. *Genetic, Social and Psychological Monographs* 111:205–22.

Petersen, A. C., and A. Boxer. 1982. Adolescent sexuality. In *Promoting adolescent health: A dialog on research and practice,* ed. A. J. Coates, A. C. Petersen, and C. Perry. New York: Academic Press, 237–53.

Petersen, A. C., and L. Crockett. 1985. Pubertal timing and grade effects. *Journal of Youth and Adolescence* 14:191–206.

Petersen, A. C., and B. Taylor. 1980. The biological approach to adolescence: Biological change and psychological adaptation. In *Handbook of adolescent psychology,* ed. J. Adelson. New York: Wiley, 117–55.

Petersen, A. C., M. Tobin-Richards, and A. M. Boxer. 1983. Puberty: Its measurement and its meaning. *Journal of Early Adolescence* 3:47–62.

Peterson, B., and E. Klohnen. 1995. Realization of generativity in two samples of women at midlife. *Psychology and Aging* 10:20–29.

Peterson, B., and A. Stewart. 1993. Generativity and social motives in young adults. *Journal of Personality and Social Psychology* 65:186–98.

———. 1996. Antecedents and contexts of generativity motivation at midlife. *Psychology and Aging* 11:21–33.

Peterson, C., and A. McCabe. 1983. *Developmental psycholinguistics: Three ways of looking at a child's narrative.* New York: Plenum Press.

Petrucelli, J. 1997. "Playing with fire": Transference-countertransference configurations in the treatment of a sexually compulsive HIV-Positive gay man. In *Hope and mortality: Psychodynamic approaches to AIDS and HIV,* ed. M. Blechner. Hillsdale, N.J.: Analytic Press, 143–62.

Phillips, M., and S. Murrell. 1994. Impact of psychological and physical health, stressful events, and social support on subsequent mental health help seeking among older adults. *Journal of Consulting and Clinical Psychology* 62:270–75.

Phillips, S. 1996. A new analytic dyad: Homosexual analyst and heterosexual patient. Paper presented at Fall meetings, American Psychoanalytic Association, New York, December.

———. 1998. A new analytic dyad: Homosexual analyst, heterosexual patient. *Journal of the American Psychoanalytic Association* 46:1195–1219.

Phoenix, C., R. Goy, A. Grall, and W. Young. 1959. Organizing action of prenatally administered testosterone propionate on the tissues mediating mating behavior in the female guinea pig. *Endocrinology* 65:369.

Piaget, J. [1975] 1985. *The equilibration of cognitive structures: The central problem of cognitive development.* Trans. T. Brown and K. J. Thampy. Chicago: University of Chicago Press.

Pies, C. 1990. Lesbians and the choice to parent. In *Homosexuality and family relations,* ed. F. W. Bozett and M. B. Sussman. New York: Haworth/Harrington Park Press, 137–54.

Pigman, G. 1995. Freud and the history of empathy. *International Journal of Psychoanalysis* 76:237–56.

Pillard, R. 1982. Psychotherapeutic treatment for the invisible minority. *American Behavioral Scientist* 25:407–22.

———. 1988. Sexual orientation and mental disorders. *Psychiatric Annals* 18:52–56.

———. 1991. Masculinity and femininity in homosexuality: "Inversion" revisited. In *Homosexuality: Research implications for public policy,* ed. J. C. Gonsiorek and J. D. Weinrich. Thousand Oaks, Calif.: Sage Publications, 32–43.

———. 1996. Homosexuality from a familial and genetic perspective. In *Textbook of homosexuality and mental health,* ed. R. Cabaj and T. S. Stein. Washington, D.C.: American Psychiatric Press, 115–28.

———. 1997. The search for a genetic influence on sexual performance. In *Science and homosexualities,* ed. V. Rosario. New York, Routledge, 216–41.

Pillard, R., J. Poumadere, and R. Carretta. 1981. Is homosexuality familial? A review, some data, and a suggestion. *Archives of Sexual Behavior* 10:465–75.

Pillard, R., and J. Weinrich. 1986. Evidence of familial nature of male homosexuality. *Archives of General Psychiatry* 43:808–12.

Plath, D. 1980. Contours of consociation: Lessons from a Japanese narrative. In *Lifespan development and behavior,* ed. P. Baltes and O. G. Brim Jr. New York: Academic Press, 3:287–305.

Plummer, K. 1975. *Sexual stigma: An interactionist account.* London: Routledge, Kegan Paul.

———. 1981. Going gay: Identities life cycles and life styles in the male gay world. In *The theory and practice of homosexuality,* ed. J. Hart and D. Richardson. London: Routledge and Kegan Paul, 93–110.

———. 1989. Lesbian and gay youth in England. In *Gay and lesbian youth,* ed. G. Herdt. New York: Harrington Park Press, 195–224.

———. 1995. *Telling sexual stories: Power, change, and social worlds*. New York: Routledge.

———. 1996. Symbolic interactionism and the forms of homosexuality. In *Queer theory/sociology*, ed. S. Seidman. London: Blackwell, 64–82.

Polanyi, L. 1989. *Telling the American story: A structural and cultural analysis of conversational storytelling*. Cambridge, Mass.: MIT Press.

Polkinghorne, D. 1983. *Methodology for the human sciences: Systems of inquiry*. Albany: State University of New York Press.

———. 1988. *Narrative knowing and the human sciences*. Albany: State University of New York Press.

Pollock, G. 1989. *The mourning-liberation process*, 2 vols. Madison, Conn.: International Universities Press.

Ponse, B. 1978. *Identities in the lesbian world: The social construction of self*. Westport, Conn.: Greenwood Press.

———. 1980a. Finding self in the lesbian community. In *Women's sexual development*, ed. M. Kirkpatrick. New York: Plenum, 181–200.

———. 1980b. Lesbians and their world. In *Homosexual behavior: A modern reappraisal*, ed. J. Marmor. New York: Basic Books, 157–75.

Pope, M., and R. Schulz. 1990. Sexual attitudes and behavior in midlife and aging homosexual males. In *Gay midlife and maturity*, ed. J. A. Lee. New York: Harrington Park Press, 169–78.

Porter, K., and J. Weeks. 1991. *Between the acts: Lives of homosexual men, 1885–1967*. London: Routledge.

Pribram, K. H., and M. M. Gill. 1977. *Freud's "Project" re-assessed: Preface to contemporary cognitive theory and neuropsychology*. New York: Basic Books.

Purifoy, F. E., and L. H. Koopmans. 1980. Androstenedione, testosterone, and free testosterone concentrations in women of various occupations. *Social Biology* 26:179–88.

Quam, J., and G. Whitford. 1992. Adaptation and age-related expectations of older gay and lesbian adults. *Gerontologist* 32:367–74.

Racker, H. 1968. *Transference and counter-transference*. New York: Universities Press.

Rado, S. [1945–55] 1995. *Adaptational psychodynamics*. Ed. J. Jameson and H. Klein. New York: Jason Aronson.

———. 1949. An adaptational view of sexual behavior. In *Psychosexual development in health and disease*, ed. P. H. Hoch and J. Zubin. New York: Grune and Stratton, 159–89.

Rand, C., D. Graham, and E. Rawlings. 1982. Psychological health and factors the court seeks to control in lesbian mother custody trials. *Journal of Homosexuality* 8:27–39.

Rapaport, D. 1960a. On the psychoanalytic theory of motivation. In *The collected papers of David Rapaport*. Ed. M. Gill. New York: Basic Books, 8853–8915.

———. 1960b. Psychoanalysis as a developmental psychology. In *The collected papers of David Rapaport*. Ed. M. Gill. New York: Basic Books, 820–52.

Rapaport, D., and M. Gill. 1959. The points-of-view and assumptions of metapyschology. *International Journal of Psychoanalysis* 40:153–62.

Raphael, S., and K. Robinson. 1980. The older lesbian. *Alternative Life-Styles* 3:207–29.

Raphling, D., and J. F. Chused. 1988. Transference across gender lines. *Journal of the American Psychoanalytic Association* 36:77–104.

Rappaport, E. 1958. The grandparent syndome. *Psychoanalytic Quarterly* 27:518–38.

Raymond, D. 1994. Homophobia, identity, and the meanings of desire: Reflections on the cultural construction of gay and lesbian adolescent sexuality. In *Sexual cultures and the construction of adolescent identities*, ed. J. M. Irvine. Philadelphia: Temple University Press, 115–50.

Rebelsky, F., and C. Hanks. 1971. Fathers: Verbal interaction with infants in the first three months of life. *Child Development* 42:63–68.

Reed, G. 1994. *Transference neurosis and psychoanalytic experience*. New Haven, Conn.: Yale University Press.

Reich, A. 1951. On countertransference. *International Journal of Psychoanalysis* 32:25–31.

Reich, W. [1933] 1949. *Character analysis*. Trans. T. P. Wolfe. New York: Straus and Cudahy.

———. 1970. *The mass psychology of fascism*. Trans. V. Carfagno. New York: Farrar, Straus and Giroux.

Reid, J. [1973] 1993. *The best little boy in the world*. Rev. ed. New York: Ballantine Books.

———. 1995. Development in late life: Older lesbian and gay lives. In *Lesbian, gay, and bisexual identities over the life span,* ed. A. R. D'Augelli and C. Patterson. New York: Oxford University Press, 215–42.

Reilly, M. E., and J. Lynch. 1990. Power-sharing in lesbian partnerships. *Journal of Homosexuality* 19:1–30.

Reinisch, J. M., and S. Sanders. 1984. Prenatal gonodal sterioidal influences on gender related behavior. *Progress in Brain Research* 61:407–16.

Reiss, B. 1980. Psychological tests in homosexuality. In *Homosexual behavior: A modern reappraisal,* ed. J. Marmor. New York: Basic Books, 296–311.

Reiss, B., J. Safer, and W. Yotive. 1974. Psychological test data on female homosexuality. *Journal of Homosexuality* 1:71–85.

Reite, M., J. Sheeder, D. Richardson, and P. Teale. 1995. Cerebral laterality in homosexual males: Preliminary communication using magnetoencephalography. *Archives of Sexual Behavior* 24:585–95.

Remafedi, G. 1987a. Adolescent homosexuality: Psychosocial and medical implications. *Pediatrics* 79:331–37.

———. 1987b. Homosexual youth: A challenge to contemporary society. *Journal of the American Medical Association* 258:222–25.

———. 1987c. Male homosexuality: The adolescent's perspective. *Pediatrics* 79:326–30.

———. 1991. Risk factors for attempted suicide in gay and bisexual youth. *Pediatrics* 87:869–75.

———. 1994a. The state of knowledge on gay, lesbian, and bisexual youth suicide. In *Death by denial: Studies of suicide in gay and lesbian teenagers,* ed. G. Remafedi. Boston: Alyson Publications, 7–14.

Remafedi, G., ed. 1994b. *Death by denial: Studies of suicide in gay and lesbian teenagers*. Boston: Alyson Publishrs.

Remafedi, G., J. Farrow, and R. Deisher. 1993. Risk factors for attempted suicide in gay and bisexual youth. In *Psychological perspectives on lesbian and gay male experiences,* ed. L. Garnets and D. Kimmel. New York: Columbia University Press, 469–85.

Remafedi, G., M. Resnick, R. Blum, and L. Harris. 1992. Demography of sexual orientation in adolescents. *Pediatrics* 89:869–75.

Renik, O. 1990. Analysis of a woman's homosexual strivings by a male analyst. *Psychoanalytic Quarterly* 59:41–53.

———. 1993. Analytic interaction: Conceptualizing technique in light of the analyst's irreducible subjectivity. *Psychoanalytic Quarterly* 621:553–71.

———. 1994. Commentary on Martin Stephen Frommer's "Homosexuality and psychoanalysis." *Psychoanalytic Dialogues* 4:235–39.

———. 1995. The idea of the anonymous analyst and the problem of self-disclosure. *Psychoanalytic Quarterly* 64:466–95.

Rice, G., C. Anderson, N. Risch, and G. Ebers. 1999. Male homosexuality: Absence of linkage to microsatellite markers at Xq28. *Science* 284 (23 April): 665–67.

Rich, C., R. Fowler, D. Young, and M. Blenkush. 1986. San Diego suicide study: Comparison of gay to straight males. *Suicide and Life-Threatening Behavior* 16:448–57.

Rich, H. L. 1991. Homosexual cruising compulsion. In *The homosexualities and the therapeutic process,* ed. C. W. Socarides and V. D. Volkan. Madison, Conn.: International Universities Press, 227–40.

Richards, A. 1996. Primary femininity and female genital anxiety. In Psychology of women: Psychoanalytic perspectives, ed. A. Richards and P. Tyson. *Journal of the American Psychoanalytic Association* 44 (supplement): 261–82.

Richardson, D. 1981. Lesbian identities. In *The theory and practice of homosexuality,* ed. J. Hart and D. Richardson. London: Routledge and Kegan Paul, 111–24.

———. 1992. Constructing lesbian identities. In *Modern homosexualities,* ed. K. Plummer. New York: Routledge, 187–99.

Ricketts, W. 1984. Biological research on homosexuality: Ansell's cow or Occam's razor. *Journal of Homosexuality* 10:65–93.

Ricketts, W., and R. Achtenberg. 1990. Adoption and foster parenting for lesbians and gay men: Creating new traditions in family. In *Homosexuality and family relations,* ed. F. W. Bozett and M. B. Sussman. New York: Haworth/Harrington Park Press, 83–118.

Ricks, S. 1985. Father-infant interactions: A review of empirical research. *Family Relations* 34:505–11.

Ricoeur, P. 1971. The model of the text: Meaningful action considered as text. *Social Research* 38:529–62 .

———. 1977. The question of proof in Freud's psychoanalytic writings. *Journal of the American Psychoanalytic Association* 25:835–72.

Riley, M. 1973. Aging and cohort succession: Interpretations and misinterpretations. *Public Opinion Quarterly* 37:35–49.

———. 1976. Age strata in social systems. In *Handbook of aging and the social sciences,* ed. R. Binstock and E. Shanas. New York: Van Nostrand-Reinhold, 189–217.

Ring, M., and E. McDonald. 1992. Homosexuals who are twins: A study of 46 probands. *British Journal of Psychiatry* 160:407–9.

Ritchey, P. N., and C. S. Stokes. 1974. Correlates of childlessness and expectations to remain childless: U.S. 1967. *Social Forces* 52:349–56.

Ritvo, L. 1990. *Darwin's influence on Freud: A tale of two sciences.* New Haven, Conn.: Yale University Press.

Rivera, R. R. 1991. Sexual orientation and the law. In *Homosexuality: Research implications for public policy,* ed. J. C. Gonsiorek and J. D. Weinrich. Thousand Oaks, Calif.: Sage Publications, 81–100.

Robins, L., and D. Regier. 1991. *Psychiatric disorders in America: The epidemiologic catchment area study.* New York: Free Press.

Robinson, B. E., L. H. Walters, and P. Skeen. 1989. Response of parents to learning that their child is homosexual and concern over AIDS: A national study. *Journal of Homosexuality* 18:59–80 .

Robinson, M. K. 1979. The older lesbian. Unpublished master's thesis, California State University at Dominguez Hills.

Robinson, P. 1999. *Gay lives.* Chicago: University of Chicago Press.

Rochlin, M. 1982. Sexual orientation of the therapist and therapeutic effectiveness with gay clients. *Journal of Homosexuality* 7:21–29.

Roesler, T., and R. W. Deisher. 1972. Youthful male homosexuality. *Journal of the American Medical Association* 219:1018–23.

Rollins, B., and R. Galligan. 1978. The developing child and marital satisfaction of parents. In *Child influences on marital and family interaction: A life-span perspective,* ed. R. Lerner and G. Spanier. New York: Academic Press, 71–102.

Rook, K. 1989. Strains in older adults' friendships. In *Old adult friendship: Structure and process,* ed. R. Adams and R. Blieszner. Newbury Park, Calif.: Sage Publications, 166–92.

Roopnarine, J., and B. Miller. 1985. Transitions to fatherhood. In *Dimensions of fatherhood,* ed. S. Hanson and F. Bozett. Beverly Hills, Calif.: Sage Publications, 49–63.

Rorty, R. 1979. *Philosophy and the mirror of nature.* Princeton, N.J.: Princeton University Press.

Rosenbaum, S. 1998. Abstinence, anonymity, and the avoidance of self-disclosure. *Psychoanalytic Inquiry* 18:530–37.

Rosenblatt, A., and J. Thickstun. 1977. Energy, information and motivation: A revision of psychoanalytic theory. *Journal of the American Psychoanalytic Association* 25:537–58.

Rosenfeld, H. 1949. Remarks on the relation of male homosexuality to paranoia, paranoid anxiety and narcissism. *International Journal of Psychoanalysis* 30:36–47.

Rosenwald, G. 1993. Conclusion: Reflections on narrative self-understanding. In *Storied lives: The cultural politics of self-understanding,* ed. G. Rosenwald and R. Ochberg. New Haven, Conn.: Yale University Press, 265–90.

Rosow, I. 1974. *Socialization to old age.* San Francisco: University of California Press.

———. 1978. What is a cohort and why? *Human Development* 21:65–75.

Ross, B. 1991. *Remembering the personal past: Descriptions of autobiographical memory.* New York: Oxford University Press.

Ross, J. 1975. The development of paternal identity: A critical review of the literature on nurturance and generativity in boys and men. *Journal of the American Psychoanalytic Association* 23 (4): 783–817.

———. 1979. Fathering: A review of some psychoanalytic contributions on paternity. *Journal of the American Psychoanalytic Association* 60:317–27.

———. 1982a. In search of fathering: A review. In *Father and child: Developmental and clinical perspectives,* ed. S. Cath, A. Gurwit, and J. Ross. Boston: Little, Brown, 21–32.

———. 1982b. Oedipus revisited: Laius and the "Laius complex." *Psychoanalytic Study of the Child* 37:169–200.

Ross, M. 1978. The relationship between perceived societal hostility, conformity, and psychological adjustment in homosexual males. *Journal of Homosexuality* 4:157–68.

———. 1980. Retrospective distortion in homosexual research. *Archives of Sexual Behavior* 9:523–31.

———. 1988. Ego-dystonic heterosexuality: A case study. *Journal of Homosexuality* 14: 7–23.

———. 1989. Gay youth in four cultures: A comparative study. In *Gay and lesbian youth,* ed. G. Herdt. New York: Harrington Park Press, 299–314.

———. 1990. Married homosexual men: Prevalence and background. In *Homosexuality and family relations,* ed. F. W. Bozett and M. B. Sussman. New York: Haworth/Harrington Park Press, 35–57.

Ross, M., J. Paulsen, and O. Stålström. 1988. Homosexuality and mental health: A cross-cultural review. *Journal of Homosexuality* 14:131–51.

Rossi, A. 1968. Transition to parenthood. *Journal of Marriage and the Family* 30:26–39.

———. 1972. Family development in a changing world. *American Journal of Psychiatry* 128:1057–66.

———. 1980a. Aging and parenthood in the middle years. In *Life-span development and behavior,* ed. P. Baltes and O. G. Brim Jr. New York: Academic Press, 3:138–207.

———. 1980b. Life-span theories and womens' lives. *Signs* 6:4–32.

———. 1985. Gender and parenthood. In *Gender and the life-course,* ed. A. Rossi. New York: Aldine, 161–91.

———. 1987. Parenthood in transition: From lineage to child to self-orientation. In *Parenting across the life-span: Biosocial dimensions,* ed. J. Lancaster, J. Altmann, A. Rossi, and L. Sherrod. New York: Aldine de Gruyter, 31–84.

Rossi, A., and P. Rossi. 1990. *Of human bonding: Parent-child relations across the life course.* New York: Aldine de Gruyter.

Roth, J. 1963. *Timetables: Structuring the passage of time in hospital treatment and other careers.* Indianapolis: Bobbs-Merrill.

Roth, S. 1988. A woman's homosexual transference with a male analyst. *Psychoanalytic Quarterly* 57:28–55.

Rothblum, E. 1994a. Introduction to the special section: Mental health of lesbians and gay men. *Journal of Clinical and Consulting Psychology* 62:211–12.

———. 1994b. "I only read abut myself on bathroom walls": The need for research on the mental health of lesbians and gay men. *Journal of Clinical and Consulting Psychology* 62:213–20.

Rotheram-Borus, M., J. Hunter, and M. Rosario. 1994. Suicidal behavior and gay-related stress among bisexual male adolescents. *Journal of Adolescent Research* 9:498–508.

Rotheram-Borus, M. J., M. Rosario, R. Van Rossem, H. Reid, and R. Gillis. 1995. Prevalence, course, and predictors of multiple problem behaviors among gay and bisexual male adolescents. *Developmental Psychology* 31:75–85.

Rottnek, M., ed. 1999. *Sissies and tomboys: Gender nonconformity and homosexual childhood.* New York: New York University Press.

Roughton, R. 1983. Useful aspects of acting out: Repetition, enactment and actualization. *Journal of the American Psychoanalytic Association* 41:443–72.

———. 1996. Personal communication.

Rousseau, J. J. [1762] 1979. *Emile, or On Education.* Trans. A. Bloom. New York: Basic Books.

Rowe, J, and R. Kahn. 1987. Human aging: Usual and successful. *Science* 237:143–49.

Rubin, D., ed. 1996. *Remembering our past: Studies in autobiographical memory.* New York: Cambridge University Press.

Ruse, M. 1982. Are there gay genes? Sociobiology and homosexuality. *Journal of Homosexuality* 8:5–34.

Russell, C. 1974. Transition to parenthood: Problems and gratifications. *Journal of Marriage and the Family* 36:294–302.

———. 1980. Unscheduled parenthood: Transition to "parent" for the teenager. *Journal of Social Issues* 36:45–63.

Russell, G., and E. M. Greenhouse. 1995. Homophobia in the supervisory relationship: An invisible intruder. In *Lesbians and psychoanalysis: Revolutions in theory and practice,* ed. J. Glassgold and S. Iasenza. New York: Free Press, 145–60.

Rust, P. 1993. Coming out in the age of social constructionism: Sexual identity formation among lesbians and bisexual women. *Gender and Society* 7:50–77.

Ryan, J. 1997. Reflections on "Disorienting sexuality." *Gender and Psychoanalysis* 2:177–84.

Ryder, N. 1965. The cohort as a concept in the study of social change. *American Sociological Review* 30:843–61.

Sachs, H. [1923] 1978. On the genesis of perversions. Trans. H. F. Bernays. In C. W. Socarides, *Homosexuality: psychoanalytic therapy.* Northvale, N.J.: Jason Aronson, 531–46.

Saghir, M., and E. Robins. 1973. *Male and female sexuality: A comprehensive investigation.* Baltimore, Md.: Williams and Wilkins.

Sagrin, E., and R. Kelly. 1980. Sexual deviance and labelling perspectives. In *The labelling of deviance: Evaluating a perspective,* ed. W. Gove. 2d ed. Thousand Oaks, Calif.: Sage Publications, 347–79.

Salais, D., and R. Fischer. 1995. Sexual preference and altruism. *Journal of Homosexuality* 28:185–96.

Sameroff, A., and M. Haith, eds. 1996. *The five to seven year shift: The age of reason and responsibility.* Chicago: University of Chicago Press.

Sampson, R., and J. Laub. 1996. The military as a turning point in the lives of disadvantaged men. *American Sociological Review* 61:347–67.

Sandler, J. 1960a. The background of safety. *International Journal of Psychoanalysis* 41: 352–56.

———. 1960b. On the concept of the superego. *Psychoanalytic Study of the Child* 15: 128–62.

———. 1976. Countertransference and role-responsiveness. *International Review of Psychoanalysis* 3:43.

———. 1996. Comments on the psychodynamics of interaction. *Psychoanalytic Inquiry* 16:88–95.

Sandler, J., ed. 1989. *Projection, identification, projective identification.* London: Karnac Books.

Sandler, J., and A. M. Sandler. 1987. The past unconscious, the present unconscious and the vicissitudes of guilt. *International Journal of Psychoanalysis* 68:331–41.

———. 1994. The past unconscious and the present unconscious: A contribution to a technical frame of reference. *Psychoanalytic Study of the Child* 49:278–92.

———. 1997a. On remembering, repeating and working through. In *Reason and passion: A celebration of the work of Hanna Segal,* ed. D. Bell. London: Duckworth, 128–38.

———. 1997b. A psychoanalytic theory of repression and the unconscious. In *Recovered memories of abuse: True or false,* ed. J. Sandler and P. Fonagy. Madison, Conn.: International Universities Press, 163–81.

Sang, B. 1991. Moving towards balance and integration. In *Lesbians at midlife: The creative transition,* ed. B. Sang, J. Warshow, and A. Smith. San Francisco: Spinsters Ink, 206–14.

———. 1993. Existential issues of midlife lesbians. In *Psychological perspectives on lesbian and gay male experiences,* ed. L. Garnets and D. Kimmel. New York: Columbia University Press, 500–516.

Savin-Williams, R. 1989. Parental influences on the self-esteem of gay and lesbian youths: A reflected appraisals model. In *Gay and lesbian youth,* ed. G. Herdt. New York: Harrington Park Press, 93–110.

———. 1990. *Gay and lesbian youth: Expression of identity.* Washington, D.C.: Hemisphere Publications.

———. 1994. Verbal and physical abuse as stressors in the lives of lesbian, gay male and bisexual youths: Associations with school problems, running away, substance abuse, prostitution, and suicide. *Journal of Clinical and Consulting Psychology* 62:261–69.

———. 1995a. An exploratory study of pubertal maturational timing and self-esteem among gay and bisexual male youths. *Developmental Psychology* 31:56–64.

———. 1995b. Lesbian, gay male, and bisexual adolescents. In *Lesbian, gay, and bisexual identities over the life span,* ed. A. R. D'Augelli and C. Patterson. New York: Oxford University Press, 165–89.

———. 1996a. Dating and romantic relationships among gay, lesbian, and bisexual youth. In *The lives of lesbians, gays, and bisexuals: Children to adults,* ed. R. C. Savin-Williams and K. M. Cohen. Fort Worth, Tex.: Harcourt Brace, 166–80.

———. 1996b. Ethnic- and sexual-minority youth. In *The lives of lesbians, gays, and bisexuals: Children to adults,* ed. R. C. Savin-Williams and K. M. Cohen. Fort Worth, Tex.: Harcourt Brace, 152–65.

———. 1996c. Memories of childhood and early adolescent sexual feelings among gay and bisexual boys: A narrative approach. In *The lives of lesbians, gays, and bisexuals: Children to adults,* ed. R. C. Savin-Williams and K. M. Cohen. Fort Worth, Tex.: Harcourt Brace, 94–109.

———. 1997. *. . . And then I became gay: Young men's stories.* New York: Routledge.

———. 1998. Lesbian, gay, and bisexual youths' relationships with their parents. In *Lesbian, gay, and bisexual identities in families: Psychological perspectives,* ed. C. J. Patterson and A. R. D'Augelli. New York: Oxford University Press, 75–98.

Savin-Williams, R., and K. Cohen. 1996. Psychosocial outcomes of verbal and physical abuse among lesbian, gay, and bisexual youths. In *The lives of lesbians, gays, and bisexuals: Children to adults,* ed. R. C. Savin-Williams and K. M. Cohen. Fort Worth, Tex.: Harcourt Brace, 181–200.

Savin-Williams, R., and R. Dubé. 1998. Parental reactions to their child's disclosure of a gay/lesbian identity. *Family Relations* 47:7–13.

Savin-Williams, R., and R. Rodriguez. 1993. A developmental, clinical perspective on lesbian, gay male, and bisexual youths. In *Adolescent sexuality: Advances in adolescent development,* ed. T. P. Gullotta, G. R. Adams, and R. Montemayor. 5:77–101.

Schafer, R. 1959. Generative empathy in the treatment situation. *Psychoanalytic Quarterly* 28:342–73.

———. 1960. The loving and beloved superego in Freud's structural theory. *Psychoanalytic Study of the Child* 15:163–88.

———. 1968a. *Aspects of internalization.* New York: International Universities Press.

———. 1968b. The mechanisms of defence. *International Journal of Psychoanalysis* 49 (1): 49–62.

———. 1972. Internalization: Process or fantasy? *Psychoanalytic Study of the Child* 27: 411–36.

———. 1977. The interpretation of transference and the conditions of loving. *Journal of the American Psychoanalytic Association* 25:335–62.

———. 1980. Narration in the psychoanalytic dialogue. *Critical Inquiry* 7:29–53.

———. 1981. *Narrative actions in psychoanalysis.* Heinz Werner Lecture Series, vol. 14. Worcester, Mass: Clark University Press.

———. 1982. The relevance of the "here-and-now" transference interpretation to the reconstruction of early development. *International Journal of Psychoanalysis* 63:77–82.

———. 1992. *Retelling a life: Narration and dialogue in psychoanalysis.* New York: Basic Books.

———. 1994. The contemporary Kleinians of London. *Psychoanalytic Quarterly* 63: 409–32.

———. 1995. The evolution of my views on nonnormative sexual practices. In *Disorienting sexuality: Psychoanalytic reappraisals of sexual identities,* ed. T. Domenici and R. C. Lesser. New York: Routledge, 187–202.

Schaffer, D., P. Fisher, R. Hicks, M. Parides, and M. Gould. 1995. Sexual orientation in adolescents who commit suicide. *Suicide and Life-Threatening Behavior* 25:64–71.

Schaffner, B. H. 1997. Modifying psychotherapeutic methods when treating the HIV-positive patient. In *Hope and mortality: Psychodynamic approaches to AIDS and HIV,* ed. M. J. Blechner. Hillsdale, N.J.: Analytic Press, 63–80.

Schaie, K. W. 1984. The Seattle Longitudinal Study: A 2-year exploration of the psychometric intelligence of adulthood. In *Longitudinal studies of personality,* ed. K. W. Schaie. New York: Guilford Press, 64–135.

———. 1995. *Intellectual development in adulthood: The Seattle Longitudinal Study.* New York: Cambridge University Press.

Schlessinger, N., and F. Robbins. 1983. *A developmental view of the psychoanalytic process: Follow-up studies and consequences.* New York: International Universities Press.

Schmidt, G., and U. Clement. 1995. Does peace prevent homosexuality. *Journal of Homosexuality* 28:269–75.

Schneider, M. 1989. Sappho was a right-on adolescent: Growing up lesbian. In *Gay and lesbian youth,* ed. G. Herdt. New York: Harrington Park Press, 111–30.

Schneider, S., N. Farberow, and G. Kruks. 1989. Suicidal behavior in adolescent and young adult gay men. *Suicide and Life-Threatening Behavior* 19:381–94.

Schofeld, M. 1965. *Sociological aspects of homosexuality.* Boston: Little-Brown.

Schucker, E. 1996. Toward further analytic understanding of lesbian patients. *Journal of the American Psychoanalytic Association* 44 (supplement): 485–510.

Schüklenk, U., and M. Ristow. 1996. The ethics of research into the cause(s) of homosexuality. *Journal of Homosexuality* 31:1996.

Schuman, H., R. Belli, and K. Bischoping. 1997. The generational basis of historical knowledge. In *Collective memory of political events: Social psychological perspectives,* ed. J. W. Pennebaker, D. Paez, and B. Rimé. Mahwah, N.J.: Lawrence Erlbaum Associates, 47–78.

Schuman, H., and J. Scott. 1989. Generations and collective memory. *American Sociological Review* 54:359–81.

Schutz, A. 1970. *On phenomenology and social relations.* Ed. H. R. Wagner. Chicago: University of Chicago Press.

Schutz, A., and T. Luckmann. 1973. *The structures of the life-world.* Vol. 1. Trans. T. Luckmann. Evanston, ILL.: Northwestern University Press.

———. [1983] 1989. *The structures of the life-world.* Vol. 2. Trans. R. M. Zaner and D. J. Parent. Evanston, IlL.: Northwestern University Press.

Schwaber, E. 1981. Empathy: A mode of analytic listening. *Psychoanalytic Inquiry* 1:357–92.

———. 1983. A particular perspective on analytic listening. *Psychoanalytic Study of the Child* 38:519–46.

Schwartz, A. 1998. *Sexual subjects: Lesbians, gender and psychoanalysis.* New York: Routledge.

Schwartz, D. 1993a. Commentary on J. L. Trop and R. D. Stolorow's "Defense analysis in self-psychology." *Psychoanalytic Dialogues* 3:643–52.

———. 1993b. Heterophilia: The love that dare not speak its name. *Psychoanalytic Dialogues* 3:643–52.

———. 1996. Questioning the social construction of gender and sexual orientation. *Gender and Psychoanalysis* 1:249–60.

———. 1999. Is a gay Oedipus a Trojan horse? Commentary on Lewes's "A special oedipal mechanism in the development of male homosexuality." *Psychoanalytic Psychology* 16:88–93.

Schwartzberg, S. 1996. *A crisis of meaning: How gay men make sense of AIDS*. New York: Oxford University Press.

Scriven, M. 1959. Truisms as the grounds for historical explanations. In *Theories of history*, ed. P. Gardiner. New York: Free Press, 443–75.

Sealey, J. D. 1997. *Per scientism ad justitiam:* Mangus Hirschfeld and the sexual politics of innate homosexuality. In *Science and homosexualities*, ed. V. A. Rosario. New York: Routledge, 133–54.

Sears, J. 1991. *Growing up gay in the South: Race, gender, and journeys of the spirit*. New York: Harrington Park Press.

———. 1997. *Lonely hunters: An oral history of lesbian and gay Southern life, 1948–1968*. Boulder, Colo.: Westview Press/Harper-Collins.

Sears, R. R., L. Rau, and R. Alpert. 1965. *Identification and child rearing*. Stanford, Calif.: Stanford University Press.

Sechehaye, M. 1951. *Symbolic realization*. New York: International Universities Press.

Sedgwick, E. 1992. *Epistemology of the closet*. Berkeley: University of California Press.

Seidman, S., C. Meeks, and F. Traschen. 1999. Beyond the closet? The changing social meaning of homosexuality in the United States. *Sexualities* 2:9–34.

Seltzer, M. M. 1976. Suggestions for examination of time-disordered relationships. In *Time, roles and self in old age*, ed. J. Gubrium. New York: Human Sciences Press, 111–25.

Seltzer, M. M., and C. Ryff. 1996. The parental experience in midlife: Past, present, and future. In *The parental experience of midlife*, ed. C. D. Ryff and M. M. Seltzer. Chicago: University of Chicago Press, 641–64.

Sengers, W. 1969. *Homosexualiteit als Klacht Ein psychiatrische studie* (Homosexuality as a complaint: A psychiatric study). Hilversum, Netherlands: Brand.

Settersten, R. A., Jr. 1999. *Lives in time and place: The problems and promises of developmental science*. Amityville, N.Y.: Baywood Publishing Company.

Settersten, R. A., Jr., and G. Hägestad. 1996. What's the latest? Cultural age deadlines for family transitions. *Gerontologist* 36:178–88.

Settersten, R. A., Jr., and K. O. Mayer. 1997. The measurement of age, age structuring, and the life course. *Annual Review of Sociology* 23:233–61.

Shanas, E. 1979. Social myth as hypothesis: The case of family relations of old people. *Gerontologist* 19:3–9.

Shanas, E., P. Townsend, D. Wedderburn, and associates. 1968. *Old people in three industrial societies*. London: Routledge and Kegan Paul.

Shapiro, S. 1985. Archaic selfobject transferences in the analysis of a case of male homosexuality. *Progress in Self Psychology* 1:164–77.

———. 1997. There but for the grace of . . . : Countertransference during the psychotherapy of a young HIV-Positive woman. In *Hope and mortality: Psychodynamic approaches to AIDS and HIV*, ed. M. Blechner. Hillsdale, N.J.: Analytic Press, 115–32.

Shapiro, T. 1981. Empathy: A critical evaluation. *Psychoanalytic Inquiry* 1:423–48.

Sharp, C. n. d. Lesbianism and later life: How does the development of one affect anticipation of the other? Unpublished manuscript, Psychology Department, University of Western Sydney, Macarthur, Australia.

———. 1997. Lesbianism and later life in an Australian sample: How does the development of one affect anticipation of the other? *Journal of Gay, Lesbian, and Bisexual Identity* 2:247–63.

Shelby, R. D. 1994a. Homosexuality and the struggle for coherence. In *Progress in self psychology,* ed. A. Goldberg, 10:55–78. Hillsdale, N.J.: Analytic Press.

———. 1994b. Mourning within a culture of mourning. In *Therapists on the front line: Psychotherapy with gay men in the age of AIDS,* ed. S. Cadwell, R. Burnham Jr., and M. Forstein. Washington, D.C.: American Psychiatric Association Press, 53–79.

———. 1995. *People with HIV and those who help them.* New York: Harrington Park Press/ Haworth Press.

———. 1997. The self and orientation: The case of Mr. G. In *Progress in self psychology,* ed. A. Goldberg. Hillsdale, N.J.: Analytic Press, 181–202.

———. 1998. About cruising and being cruised. Unpublished paper, Library of the Institute for Psychoanalysis (Chicago).

Shereshefsky, P., and L. Yarrow, eds. 1973. *Psychological aspects of a first pregnancy and early postnatal adaptation.* New York: Raven Press.

Sherman, S. 1992. *Lesbian and gay marriage: Private commitments, public ceremonies.* Philadelphia: Temple University Press.

Shidlo, A. 1994. Internalized homophobia: Conceptual and empirical issues in measurement. In *Lesbian and gay psychology: Theory, research and clinical applications,* ed. B. Greene and G. M. Herek. Psychological Perspectives on Lesbian and Gay Issues, vol. 1. Thousand Oaks, Calif.: Sage Publications, 176–205.

Shields, S., and R. Harriman. 1984. Fear of male homosexuality: Cardiac responses of low and high homonegative males. *Journal of Homosexuality* 10:53–67.

Shively, M., and J. De Cecco. 1977. Components of sexual identity. *Journal of Homosexuality* 3:41–48.

Shively, M., C. Jones, and J. De Cecco. 1984. Research on sexual orientation: Definitions and methods. *Journal of Homosexuality* 10:127–36.

Shyer, M., and C. Shyer. 1996. *Not like other boys.* Los Angeles: Alyson Books.

Siassi, G., G. Crocetti, and H. Spiro. 1974. Loneliness and dissatisfaction in a blue collar population. *Archives of General Psychiatry* 30:261–65.

Siegelman, M. 1972a. Adjustment of homosexual and heterosexual women. *British Journal of Psychiatry* 120:477–81.

———. 1972b. Adjustment of male homosexuals and heterosexuals. *Archives of Sexual Behavior* 2:9–26.

———. 1974. Parental background of male homosexuals and heterosexuals. *Archives of Sexual Behavior* 3:3–18.

———. 1981. Parental backgrounds of homosexual and heterosexual men: A cross-national replication. *Archives of Sexual Behavior* 10:505–13.

Signorile, M. 1997. *Life outside: The Signorile report on gay men: Sex, drugs, muscles, and the passages of life.* New York: HarperCollins.

Silver, D., ed. 1985. *Commentaries on Joseph Lichtenberg's psychoanalysis and infant research.* Hillsdale, N.J.: Analytic Press.

Simmel, G. [1908] 1950. The stranger. In *The sociology of Georg Simmel.* Ed. K. H. Wolff. New York: Free Press, 402–8.

Simmons, R. G., D. A. Blyth, E. F. Van Cleave, and D. M. Bush. 1979. Entry into early adolescence: The impact of school structure, puberty, and early dating on self-esteem. *American Sociological Review* 44:948–67.

Simmons, R., M. F. Rosenberg, and M. C. Rosenberg. 1973. Disturbance in the self-image at adolescence. *American Sociological Review* 38:553–68.

Simon, W., and J. Gagnon. 1984. Sexual scripts. *Transaction* 22:53–60.

————. 1988. A sexual scripts approach. In *Theories of human sexuality*, ed. J. H. Geer and W. T. O'Donoghue. New York: Plenum, 363–83.

Singer, J., and P. Salovey. 1993. *The remembered self: Emotion and memory in personality.* New York: Free Press.

Sinnott, J. 1982. Correlates of sex roles of older adults. *Journal of Gerontology* 37:587–94.

Skolnick, A. 1986. Early attachment and personal relationships across the life course. In *Life-span development and behavior*, ed. P. B. Baltes, D. Featherman, and R. Lerner. Hillsdale, N.J.: Lawrence Erlbaum Associates, 7:173–206.

Slater, S. 1999. *The lesbian family life cycle.* Urbana: University of Illinois Press.

Slavney, P., and P. McHugh. 1984. Life stories and meaningful connections: reflections on a clinical method in psychiatry and medicine. *Perspectives in Biology and Medicine* 27:279–88.

Slijper, F. 1984. Androgens and gender role behavior in girls with congenital adrenal hyperplasia (CAH). *Progress in Brain Research* 61:417–22.

Smith, A. 1997. Cultural diversity and the coming-out process: Implications for clinical practice. In *Ethnic and cultural diversity among lesbians and gay men*, ed. B. Greene. Thousand Oaks, Calif.: Sage Publications, 279–300.

Smith, J. 1988. Psychopathology, homosexuality, and homophobia. *Journal of Homosexuality* 15:59–73.

Smith, M. B., J. Bruner, and R. W. White. 1956. *Opinions and Personality.* New York: Wiley.

Snarey, J. 1993. *How fathers care for the next generation: A four-decade study.* Cambridge, Mass.: Harvard University Press.

Snortum, J. R. 1969. Family dynamics and homosexuality. *Psychological Reports* 24:763–70.

Socarides, C. W. 1959. Meaning and content of a pedophiliac perversion. *Journal of the American Psychoanalytic Association* 7:84–94.

———— (panel reporter). 1960. Theoretical and clinical aspects of overt male homosexuality. *Journal of the American Psychoanalytic Association* 8:552–66.

———— (panel reporter). 1962. Theoretical and clinical aspects of overt female homosexuality. *Journal of the American Psychoanalytic Association* 10:579–92.

————. 1968. *The overt homosexual.* New York: Grune and Stratton.

————. 1976. Psychodynamics and sexual object choice. II: A reply to Dr. Richard C. Friedman's paper. *Contemporary Psychoanalysis* 12:371–77.

————. [1978] 1989. *Homosexuality: Psychoanalytic therapy.* New York: Jason Aronson.

————. 1988. *The preoedipal origin and psychoanalytic therapy of sexual perversions.* Madison, Conn.: International Universities Press.

————. 1990. The homosexualities: A psychoanalytic classification. In *The homosexualities: Reality, fantasy, and the arts*, ed. C. W. Socarides and V. D. Volkan. Madison, Conn.: International Universities Press, 9–46.

————. 1991. The specific tasks in the psychoanalytic treatment of well-structured sexual deviations. In *The homosexualities and the therapeutic process*, ed. C. W. Socarides and V. D. Volkan. Madison, Conn.: International Universities Press, 277–92.

————. 1992. Sexual politics and scientific logic: The issue of homosexuality. *Journal of Psychohistory* 19:307–29.

————. 1995. William H. Gillespie's psychoanalysis of sexual perversions: An appreciation and integration. In W. H. Gillespie, *Life, sex, and death*, ed. M. D. A. Sinason. New York: Routledge, 35–53.

Socarides, C., and V. D. Volkan. 1990. Introduction. In *The homosexualities: Reality, fantasy, and the arts,* ed. C. Socarides and V. D. Volkan. Madison, Conn.: International Universities Press, 1–8.

Socarides, C., and V. Volkan, eds. 1991. *The homosexualities and the therapeutic process.* Madison, Conn.: International Universities Press.

Solomon, B. 1997. Discussion of Shelby's "The self and orientation: The case of Mr. G." In *Progress in self psychology,* ed. A. Goldberg. Hillsdale, N.J.: Analytic Press, 203–12.

Sontag, S. 1989. *AIDS and its metaphors.* New York: Farrar, Strauss Giroux.

Sorokin, P., and R. Merton. 1937. Social time: A methodological and functional analysis. *American Journal of Sociology* 42:615–29.

Spacks, P. M. 1981. *The adolescent idea: Myths of youth and the adult imagination.* New York: Basic Books.

Spanier, G. 1976. Use of recall data in survey research on human sexual behavior. *Social Biology* 23:244–53.

Spease, A. 1999. A road to nowhere: Complications of life course for men due to the HIV epidemic. Unpublished manuscript, College of the University of Chicago.

Spence, J. T., and R. Helmreich. 1978. *Masculinity and femininity: Their psychological dimensions.* Austin: University of Texas Press.

Spezzano, C. 1994. Commentary on Martin Stephen Frommer's "Homosexuality and psychoanalysis." *Psychoanalytic Dialogues* 4:241–45.

Spitzer, R. 1973. A proposal about homosexuality and the APA nomenclature: Homosexuality as an irregular form of sexual behavior and sexual orientation disturbance as a psychiatric disorder. *American Journal of Psychiatry* 130:1214–16.

———. 1981. The diagnostic status of homosexuality in DSM-III: A reformulation of the issues. *American Journal of Psychiatry* 138:210–15.

Sroufe, A. 1981. The organization of emotional development. *Psychoanalytic Inquiry* 1:575–600.

———. 1989. Relationships, self, and individual adaptation. In *Relationship disturbance in early childhood: A developmental approach,* ed. A. Sameroff and R. N. Emde. New York: Basic Books, 70–94.

Stearns, D.C., and J. Sabini. 1997. Dyadic adjustment and community involvement in same-sex couples. 1998. Life course diversity among older lesbians and gay men. *Journal of Lesbian, Gay and Bisexual Identities* 2:265–84.

Stechler, G., and S. Kaplan. 1980. The development of the self. *Psychoanalytic Study of the Self* 35:85–105.

Steckel, A. 1987. Psychosocial development of children of lesbian mothers. In *Gay and lesbian parents,* ed. F. W. Bozett. New York: Praeger, 75–85.

Stein, A. 1997. *Sex and sensibility: Stories of a lesbian generation.* Berkeley: University of California Press.

Stein, E. 1994. The relevance of scientific research about sexual orientation to lesbian and gay rights. *Journal of Homosexuality* 27:269–308.

———. 1997. The ethical relevance of scientific research on sexual orientation. In *Same sex: Debating the ethics, science, and culture of homosexuality,* ed. J. Corvino. Lanham, N.J.: Rowman and Littlefield, 135–48.

———. 1999. *The mismeasure of desire: The science, theory, and ethics of sexual orientation.* New York: Oxford University Press.

Stein, N., and S. Folkman, T. Trabasso, and T. A. Richards. 1997. Appraisal and goal processes as predictors of psychological well-being in bereaved caregivers. *Journal of Personality and Social Psychology* 72:872–84.

Stein, N., and M. Policastro. 1984. The concept of a story: A comparison between children's and teacher's viewpoints. In *Language and comprehension of text,* ed. H. Mandl, N. Stein, and T. Trabasso. Hillsdale, N.J.: Erlbaum, 113–58.

Stein, R. 1997. The shame experiences of the analyst. In *Progress in self psychology,* ed. A. Goldberg. Hillsdale, N.J.: Analytic Press, 109–23.

Stein, T. 1988. Theoretical considerations in psychotherapy with gay men and lesbians. *Journal of Homosexuality* 15:75–96.

———. 1996. The essentialist/social constructionist debate about homosexuality and its relevance for psychotherapy. In *Textbook of homosexuality and mental health,* ed. R. Cabaj and T. S. Stein. Washington, D.C.: American Psychiatric Press, 83–100.

———. 1997. Deconstructing sexual orientation: Understanding the phenomena of sexual orientation. *Journal of Homosexuality* 34:81–86.

Steinberg, L. 1981. Transformations in family relations at puberty. *Developmental Psychology* 17:833–40.

———. 1985. *Adolescence.* New York: Alfred A. Knopf.

Stengel, E. 1963. Highlings Jackson's influence on psychiatry. *British Journal of Psychiatry* 109:348–55.

Stern, D. N. 1985. *The interpersonal world of the infant.* New York: Basic Books.

———. 1989a. Developmental prerequisites for the sense of a narrated self. In *Psychoanalysis: Towards the second century,* ed. A. Cooper, O. Kernberg, and E. Person. New Haven, Conn.: Yale University Press, 168–80.

———. 1989b. The representation of relational patterns: Some developmental considerations. In *Relationship disorders,* ed. A. Sameroff and R. N. Emde. New York: Basic Books, 52–69.

———. 1995. *The motherhood constellation: A unified view of parent-infant psychotherapy.* New York: Basic Books.

Sternschein, I. 1973. The experience of separation-individuation in infancy and its reverberations through the course of life. III: Maturity, senescence, and sociological implications. *Journal of the American Psychoanalytic Association* 21:633–45.

Stewart, A., and J. Healy Jr. 1989. Linking individual development and social change. *American Psychologist* 44:30–42.

Stewart, A., and E. Vandewater. 1998. The course of generativity. In *Generativity and adult experience: Psychosocial perspectives on caring and contributing to the next generation,* ed. D. McAdams and E. de St. Aubin. Washington, D.C.: American Psychological Association Press, 75–100.

Stierlin, H. 1974. *Separating parents and their adolescents.* New York: Quadrangle Books.

Stoller, R. 1964. A contribution to the study of gender identity. *International Journal of Psychoanalysis* 45:220–26.

———. 1968. *Sex and gender: On the development of masculinity and femininity.* New York: Science House/Aronson.

———. 1985. *Presentations of gender.* New Haven, Conn.: Yale University Press.

Stoller, R., and G. Herdt. 1982. The development of masculinity: A cross-cultural contribution. *Journal of the American Psychoanalytic Association* 30:29–59.

———. 1985. Theories of origins of male homosexuality. *Archives of General Psychiatry* 42:399–404.

Stoller, R., J. Marmor, I. Bieber, R. Gold, C. Socarides, R. Green, and R. Spitzer. 1973.

A symposium: Should homosexuality be in the APA nomenclature. *American Journal of Psychiatry* 130:1207–16.

Stolorow, R., and G. Atwood. 1992. *Contexts of being: The intersubjective foundations of psychological life*. Hillsdale, N.J.: Analytic Press.

Stolorow, R., G. Atwood, and B. Brandchaft, eds. 1994. *The intersubjective perspective*. New York: Jason Aronson.

Stolorow, R. D., and J. L. Trop. 1991. Homosexual enactments. In *The homosexualities and the therapeutic process,* ed. C. W. Socarides and V. D. Volkan. Madison, Conn.: International Universities Press, 207–26.

———. 1992a. Reply to A. D. Richards and S. A. Mitchell. *Psychoanalytic Dialogues* 3:653–56.

———. 1993. Reply to M. J. Blechner, R. C. Lesser, and D. Schwartz. *Psychoanalytic Dialogues* 3:653–56.

Stone, L. 1961. *The psychoanalytic situation: An examination of its development and essential nature*. New York: International Universities Press.

———. 1995. Transference. In *Psychoanalysis: The major concepts,* ed. B. E. Moore and B. O. Fine. New Haven, Conn.: Yale University Press, 110–20.

Storr, A. 1988. *Solitude: A return to the self*. New York: Free Press.

Strachey, J. 1934. The nature of the therapeutic action of psychoanalysis. *International Journal of Psychoanalysis* 15:127–59.

Stricker, G., and M. Fisher. 1990. *Self-disclosure in the therapeutic relationship*. New York: Plenum Press.

Strickland, B. 1995. Research on sexual orientation and human development: A commentary. *Developmental Psychology* 31:137–40.

Strommen, E. [1989] 1993. "You're a what?": Family member reactions to the disclosure of homosexuality. In *Psychological perspectives on lesbian and gay male experiences,* ed. L. Garnets and D. Kimmel. New York: Columbia University Press, 248–66.

Sturken, M. 1997. *Tangled memories: The Vietnam war, the AIDS epidemic, and the politics of remembering*. Berkeley: University of California Press.

Suchet, M. 1995. "Having it both ways": Rethinking female sexuality. In *Lesbians and psychoanalysis: Revolutions in theory and practice,* ed. J. Glassgold and S. Iasenza. New York: Free Press, 63–92.

Sullivan, A. 1995. *Virtually normal: An argument about homosexuality*. New York: Knopf.

———. 1998. *Love undetectable: Notes on friendship, sex, and survival*. New York: Knopf.

Sullivan, G. 1990. Discrimination and self-concept of homosexuals before the gay liberation movement: A biographical analysis examining social context and identity. *Biography* 13:203–21.

Sullivan, H. 1953. *The interpersonal theory of psychiatry*. New York: Norton.

Sulloway, S. 1979. *Freud, biologist of the mind: Beyond the psychoanalytic legend*. New York: Basic Books.

Summers, F. 1994. *Object relations and clinical practice*. Hillsdale, N.J.: Analytic Press.

Suppe, F. 1994. Explaining homosexuality: Philosophical issues and who cares anyhow? *Journal of Homosexuality* 27:223–68.

———. 1997. Explaining homosexuality: Who cares anyhow. In *Same sex: Debating the ethics, science, and culture of homosexuality,* ed. J. Corvino. Lanham, N.J.: Rowman and Littlefield, 167–75.

Sussman, M. B. 1959. The isolated nuclear family: Fact or fiction. *Social Problems* 6: 333–40.

————. 1965. Relationships of adult children with their parents in the United States. In *Social structure and the family: Generational relations,* ed. E. Shanas and G. Streib. Englewood-Cliffs, N.J.: Prenctice-Hall, 62–92.

Swaab, D. F., and E. Fliers. 1985. A sexually dimorphic nucleus in the human brain. *Science* 228:1112–15.

Swaab, D., L. Gooren, and M. Hofman. 1992. The human hypothalamus in relation to gender and sexual orientation. *Progress in Brain Research* 93:205–19.

————. 1995. Brain research, gender, and sexual orientation. *Journal of Homosexuality* 28:283–301.

Swaab, D., and M. Hofman. 1984. Sexual differentiation of the human brain: A historical perspective. *Progress in Brain Research* 61:361–74.

Swaab, D. F., J.-N. Zhou, M. Fodor, and M. A. Hofman. 1997. Sexual differentiation of the human hypothalamus: Differences according to sex, sexual orientation, and transexuality. In *Sexual orientation,* ed. L. Ellis and L. Ebertz. Westport, Conn.: Praeger, 129–50.

Sweet, J. 1977. Demography and the family. *Annual Review of Sociology* 3:363–405.

Symonds, J. A. 1984. *The memoirs of John Addington Symonds.* Ed. P. Grosskurth. New York: Random House.

Tanner, J. M. 1971. Sequence, tempo, and individual variation in the growth and development of boys and girls aged twelve to sixteen. *Daedalus* 100:907–30.

Tasker, F. L., and S. Golombok. 1997. *Growing up in a lesbian family: Effects on child development.* New York: Guilford Press .

Thompson, C. 1947. Changing concepts of homosexuality in psychoanalysis. *Psychiatry* 10:183–88.

Thompson, C. P., J. J. Skowronski, S. F. Larson, and A. L. Betz, eds. 1996. *Autobiographical memory: Remembering what and remembering when.* Mahweh, N.J.: Lawrence Erlbaum Associates.

Thompson, E. P. 1963. *The making of the English working class.* New York: Random House/Vintage.

Thompson, N. L., Jr., B. McCandless, and B. Strickland. 1971. Personal adjustment of male and female homosexuals and heterosexuals. *Journal of Abnormal Psychology* 78: 237–40.

Thompson, N. L., Jr., D. M. Schwartz, B. R. McCandless, and D. A. Edwards. 1973. parent–child relationships and sexual identity in male and female homosexuals and heterosexuals. *Journal of Consulting and Clinical Psychology* 41:120–27.

Thompson, P. [1978] 1988. *The voice of the past.* 2d ed. New York: Oxford University Press.

————. 1992. "I don't feel old": Subjective aging and the search for meaning in later life. *Ageing and Society* 12:23–47.

Thomson, P. 1968. Vicissitudes of the transference in a male homosexual. *International Journal of Psychoanalysis* 49:629–39.

Tinbergen, N. 1951. *The study of instinct.* Oxford: Clarendon Press.

Tipton, S. 1982. *Getting saved from the sixties: Moral meaning in conversion and social change.* Berkeley: University of California Press.

Tobias, A. 1998a. *The best little boy in the world grows up.* New York: Random House.

————. 1998b. Gay like me: In and out of the closet at Harvard, 1653–1998. *Harvard Magazine* 100 (3): 50–59, 100–103.

Tobin, S. 1991. *Personhood in advanced old age.* New York: Springer Publications.

Tobin, S., and M. Lieberman. 1976. *Last home for the aged: Critical implications of institutionalization.* San Francisco: Jossey Bass.

Tolpin, M. 1997a. Compensatory structure: Paths to the restoration of the self. In *Conversations in self psychology (Progress in self psychology),* ed. A. Goldberg. Hillsdale, N.J.: Analytic Press, 13:3–20.

———. 1997b. Response to Fossage. In *Conversations in self psychology (Progress in self psychology),* ed. A. Goldberg. Hillsdale, N.J.: Analytic Press, 13:29–31.

Tolpin, M., and H. Kohut. 1980. The disorders of the self: The psychopathology of the first years of life. In *The course of life,* vol. 1, *Infancy and early childhood,* ed. S. Greenspan and G. Pollock. Washington, D.C.: U.S. Government Printing Office, 425–42.

Tolpin, P., and M. Tolpin, eds. 1996. *Heinz Kohut: The Chicago Institute lectures.* Mahwah, N.J.: Analytic Press.

Tonkin, E. 1992. *Narrating our pasts: The social construction of oral history.* New York: Cambridge University Press.

Toulmin, S. 1986. Self psychology as post-modern science. In *Commentaries on Heinz Kohut's "How does analysis cure,"* ed. M. F. Bornstein, E. Wolf, and associates. Hillsdale, N.J.: Analytic Press, 459–78.

———. 1990. *Cosmopolis: The hidden agenda of modernity.* New York: Free Press.

Townsend, M. 1997. Mental health issues and same-sex marriage. In *On the road to same-sex marriage,* ed. R. Cabaj and D. Purcell. San Francisco: Jossey-Bass, 89–108.

Treas, J. 1995. Older Americans in the 1990s and beyond. *Population Bulletin* 50 (2). Washington, D.C.: Population Reference Bureau.

Treichler, P. 1988. AIDS, homophobia and biomedical discourse: An epidemic of signification. In *AIDS: Cultural analysis, cultural criticism,* ed. D. Crimp. Cambridge, Mass.: MIT Press, 31–70.

Tripp, C. A. 1975. *The homosexual matrix.* New York: McGraw-Hill.

Trivers, R. 1974. Parent-offspring conflict. *American Zoologist* 14:249–64.

Troiden, R. 1979. Becoming homosexual: A model of gay identity acquisition. *Psychiatry* 42:362–73.

———. 1984. Self, self-concept, identity, and homosexual identity: Constructs in need for definition and differentiation. *Journal of Homosexuality* 10:97–109.

———. 1988. *Gay and lesbian identity: A sociological analysis.* New York: General-Hall.

———. 1989. The formation of homosexual identities. In *Gay and lesbian youth,* ed. G. Herdt. New York: Harrington Park Press, 43–74.

———. 1993. The formation of homosexual identities. In *Psychological perspectives on lesbian and gay male experiences,* ed. L. Garnets and D. Kimmel. New York: Columbia University Press, 191–217.

Troll, L. 1970. Issues in the study of generations. *International Journal of Aging and Human Development* 9:199–218.

Trop, J., and R. Stolorow. 1992. Defense analysis in self psychology: A developmental view. *Psychoanalytic Dialogues* 2:427–42.

Trujillo, C. M. 1997. Sexual identity and the discontents of difference. In *Ethnic and cultural diversity among lesbians and gay men,* ed. B. Greene. Thousand Oaks, Calif.: Sage Publications, 266–78.

Turner, V. 1967. *The forest of symbols: Aspects of Ndembu ritual.* Ithaca, N.Y.: Cornell University Press.

Turner, W. J. 1995. Homosexuality, type 1: An Xq28 phenomenon. *Archives of Sexual Behavior* 24:109–34.

Tuttle, W., Jr. 1993. America's home front children in World War II. In *Children in time and place: Developmental and historical insights,* ed. G. Elder, J. Modell, and R. D. Parke. New York: Cambridge University Press, 27–46.

Tyson, P. 1982. A developmental line of gender identity, gender role, and choice of love object. *Journal of the American Psychoanalytic Association* 30:61–86.

Tyson, R. 1986. Countertransference evolution in theory and practice. *Journal of the American Psychoanalytic Association* 34:251–74.

Ulrichs, K. H. [1864–79] 1994. *The riddle of "man-manly love": The pioneering works on male homosexuality* (Forschungen über das rätsel der mannmännlichen lieben). Trans. M. A. Lombardi-Nash. 2 vols. Buffalo: Prometheus Books.

U.S. Bureau of the Census. 1984. *Current Population Reports.* Series P-23, no. 138. Washington, D.C.: Government Printing Office.

———. 1993. *Current Population Reports.* Series P-25, no. 1104. Washington, D.C.: Government Printing Office.

Vacha, K. 1985. *A quiet fire: Memoirs of older gay men.* Truansburg, N.Y.: Crossing Press.

Vaillant, G. 1977. *Adaptation to life.* Boston: Little-Brown.

———. 1993. *The wisdom of the ego.* Cambridge, Mass.: Harvard University Press.

Vaillant, G., and S. Koury. 1993. Late midlife development. In *The course of life,* vol. 6, *Late adulthood,* ed. G. Pollock and S. Greenspan. Madison, Conn.: International Universities Press, 1–22.

Vaillant, G., and E. Milofsky. 1980. Natural history of the male psychological life-cycle: IX. Empirical evidence for Erikson's model of the life cycle. *American Journal of Psychiatry* 137:1348–58.

Vance, C. S. 1989. Social construction theory: Problems in the history of sexuality. In *Homosexuality, which homosexuality?* ed. D. Altman, C. Vance, M. Vicenus, and J. Weeks.. Amsterdam: An Dekker/Schorer; London: GMP Publishers, 13–34.

Van Gennep, A. [1912] 1960. *Rites of passage.* Chicago: University of Chicago Press.

Van Wyk, P., and C. Geist. 1995. Biology of bisexuality: Critique and observations. *Journal of Homosexuality* 28:357–73.

Varnes, R., U. Holger, D. Austin, and R. Lambe. 1982. Endocrine response patterns and psychological correlates. *Journal of Psychosomatic Research* 26:123–31.

Vaughan, S. 1997a. The developmental and social experience of homosexuality. Paper presented at the fall meetings, American Psychoanalytic Association, New York.

———. 1997b. *The talking cure: The science behind psychotherapy.* New York: Grosset/ Putnam.

———. 1998. Clinical intervention in lesbian lives: Implications for the study of development and sexuality. Paper presented at the winter meetings, American Academy of Psychoanalysis, New York.

Ventura, J. 1987. The stresses of parenthood reexamined. *Family Relations* 36:26–29.

VerMeulen, M. 1982. The gay plague. *New York Magazine,* 31 May.

Veroff, J., E. Douvan, and R. Kulka. 1981. *The inner American: A self-portrait from 1957–1981.* New York: Basic Books.

Veroff, J., and S. Feld. 1970. *Marriage and work in America.* New York: Van Nostrand and Reinhold.

Vetere, V. 1983. The role of friendship in the development and maintenance of lesbian love relationships. *Journal of Homosexuality* 8:51–65.

Veevers, J. 1979. Voluntary childlessness: A review of issues and evidence. *Marriage and Family Review* 2:1–26.

Viederman, M. 1991. The real person of the analyst and his role in the process of psychoanalytic cure. *Journal of the American Psychoanalytic Association* 39:451–90.

Vygotsky, L. [1924–34] 1987. *The collected works of L. S. Vygotsky.* 2 vols. Ed. R. W. Rieber and A. S. Carton. Trans. N. Minick. New York: Plenum Press.

Waddington, C. 1956. *Principles of embryology.* London: Allen and Unwin.

Wallace, J. B. 1992. Reconsidering the life review: The social construction of talk about the past. *Gerontologist* 32:120–25.

Ward, I. 1977. Exogenous androgen activates female behavior in copulating, prenatally stressed rats. *Journal of Comparative and Physiological Psychology* 91:465–71.

Warren, C. 1980. Homosexuality and stigma. In *Homosexual behavior: A modern reappraisal,* ed. J. Marmor. New York: Basic Books, 123–41.

Warrner, M. 1993. *Fear of a queer planet: Queer politics and social theory.* Minneapolis: University of Minnesota Press.

Warshaw, C. 1990. Youth at risk for abuse. Chicago: Library of the Michael Reese Hospital and Medical Center.

Warshow, J. 1991. Eldercare as a feminist issue. In *Lesbians at midlife: The creative transition,* ed. B. Sang, J. Warshow, and A. Smith. San Francisco: Spinsters Ink, 65–72.

Wasserman, M. D. 1999. The impact of psychoanalytic theory and a two-person psychology on the empathizing analyst. *International Journal of Psychoanalysis* 80:449–64.

Waxler, N. 1974. Parent and child effects on cognitive performance: An experimental approach to the etiological and responsive theories of schizophrenia. *Family Process* 13:1–23.

Wayment, H., and L. Peplau. 1995. Social support and well being among lesbian and heterosexual women: A structural modeling approach. *Personality and Social Psychology Bulletin* 21:1189–99.

Weber, M. [1904–5] 1955. *The Protestant ethic and the spirit of capitalism.* Trans. T. Parsons. New York: Scribners.

Weeks, J. 1983. The problem of older homosexuals. In *The theory and practice of homosexuality,* ed. J. Hart and D. Richardson. London: Routledge and Kegan Paul, 177–85.

———. 1985. *Sexuality and its discontents: Meanings, myths, and modern sexualities.* London: Routledge and Kegan Paul.

———. 1991. *Against nature: Essays on history, sexuality, and identity.* London: Rivers Oram Press.

———. 1996. The construction of homosexuality. In *Queer theory/sociology,* ed. S. Seidman. London: Blackwell, 41–63.

Weinberg, G. 1972. *Society and the healthy homosexual.* Boston: Alyson.

Weinberg, M., and C. Williams. 1974. *Male homosexuals: Their problems and adaptations.* New York: Oxford University Press.

Weinberg, M. S., C. J. Williams, and C. W. Pryor. 1994. *Dual attraction: Understanding bisexuality.* Oxford: Oxford University Press.

Weinberg, T. 1984. Biology, ideology, and the reification of developmental stages in the study of homosexual identities. *Journal of Homosexuality* 10:77–84.

Weinrich, J. 1976. Human reproductive strategy: I. Environmental predictability and reproductive strategy: Effects of social class and race. II. Homosexuality and non-reproduction: Some evolutionary models. Unpublished doctoral dissertation, Harvard University.

———. 1995. Biological research on sexual orientation: A critique of the critics. *Journal of Homosexuality* 28:197–213.

Weissman, M. 1978. Rates and risks of depressive symptoms in a United States community. *Acta Psychiatrica Scandinavica* 57:219–31.

Weissman, M., and G. Klerman. 1978. Epidemiology of mental disorders: Emerging trends in the United States. *Archives of General Psychiatry* 35:705–11.

Weissman, M., J. K. Myers, and P. Hardin. 1978. Psychiatric disorders in a U.S. urban community. *American Journal of Psychiatry* 135:459–62.

Weissman, M., J. K. Myers, and D. Thompson. 1981. Depression and its treatment in a U.S. urban community, 1975–1976. *Archives of General Psychiatry* 38:417–21.

Wertsch, J. 1985. *Vygotsky and the social formation of mind.* Cambridge, Mass.: Harvard University Press.

———. 1991. *Voices of the mind: A sociocultural approach to mediated action.* Cambridge., Mass.: Harvard University Press.

West, D. 1959. Parental figures in the genesis of male homosexuality. *International Journal of Social Psychiatry* 5:85–97.

Weston, K. 1997. *Families we choose: Lesbians, gays, kinship.* New York: Columbia University Press.

Whitam, F. 1977. Childhood indicators of male homosexuality. *Archives of Sexual Behavior* 6:89–96.

Whitam, F., M. Diamond, and J. Martin. 1993. Homosexual orientation in twins: A report on 61 pairs and three triplet sets. *Archives of Sexual Behavior* 22:187–206.

White, B. 1965. Evidence for a hierarchical arrangement of learning processes. In *Advances in child development and behavior,* ed. L. Lipsitt and C. Spiker. New York: Academic Press, 187–220.

White, H. 1972–73. Interpretation in history. In *Tropics of discourse: Essays in cultural criticism,* ed. H. White. Baltimore, Md.: Johns Hopkins University Press, 51–80.

———. 1980. The value of narrativity in the representation of reality. *Critical Inquiry* 7:5–29.

———. 1981. Critical response, III: The narrativization of real events. *Critical Inquiry* 7:789–93.

———. 1987. The question of narrative in contemporary historical theory. In *The content of the form: Narrative discourse and historical representation.* Baltimore, Md.: Johns Hopkins University Press, 26–58.

Whiting, B., and J. Whiting. 1975. *Children of six cultures.* Cambridge, Mass.: Harvard University Press.

Whitman, F. I., M. Diamond, and J. Martin. 1993. Homosexual orientation in twins: A report on 61 pairs and three triplet sets. *Archives of Sexual Behavior* 22:187–206.

Wickelgren, I. 1999. Discovery of "gay gene" questioned. *Science* 284:571.

Wiedeman, G. 1962. Survey of psychoanalytic literature on overt male homosexuality. *Journal of the American Psychoanalytic Association* 10:386–409.

———. 1964. Symposium on homosexuality. *International Journal of Psychoanalysis* 45:214–16.

———. 1974. Homosexuality: A survey. *Journal of the American Psychoanalytic Association* 22:651–96.

Williams, J., J. Rabkin, R. Remien, J. Gorman, and A. Ehrhardt. 1991. Multidisciplinary baseline assessment of homosexual men with and without human immunodeficiency virus infection: II. Standardized clinical assessment of current and lifetime psychopathology. *Archives of General Psychiatry* 48:124–30.

Williams, M. K. L. 1999. *Sexual pathways: Adapting to dual sexual attraction.* Westport, Conn.: Praeger.

Williams, W. L. 1998. Social acceptance of same-sex relationships in families: Models from other cultures. In *Lesbian, gay, and bisexual identities in families: Psychological perspectives,* ed. C. J. Patterson and A. R. D'Augelli. New York: Oxford University Press, 53–74.

Wilson, A., and L. Weinstein. 1992. An investigation into some implications of a Vygotskian perspective on the origins of the mind: Psychoanalysis and Vygotskian psychology, Part 1. *Journal of the American Psychoanalytic Association* 40:349–79.

———. 1996. Transference and the zone of proximal development. *Journal of the American Psychoanalytic Association* 44:167–200.

Wilson, E. O. 1975. *Sociobiology: The new synthesis.* Cambridge, Mass.: Belknap/Harvard University Press.

———. 1978. *On human nature.* Cambridge, Mass.: Harvard University Press.

Winnicott, D. W. 1951/53. Transitional objects and transitional phenomena. In *Collected papers: Through pediatrics to psychoanalysis.* New York: Basic Books, 229–42.

———. 1958. The capacity to be alone. In *The maturational process and the facilitating environment.* New York: International Universities Press, 29–36.

———. 1960a/65. Ego distortion in terms of the true and false self. In *The maturational process and the facilitating environment.* New York: International Universities Press, 140–52.

———. 1960b. The theory of the parent–infant relationship. *International Journal of Psychoanalysis* 41:585–95.

Wittig, M., and A. Petersen, eds. 1979. *Sex related differences in cognitive functioning: Developmental issues.* New York: Academic Press.

Wittman, C. [1972] 1992. A gay manifesto. In *Out of the closet: Voices of gay liberation,* ed. K. Jay and A. Young. 2d ed. New York: New York University Press, 330–42.

Wolf, E. 1988. *Treating the self: Elements of clinical self-psychology.* New York: Guilford Press.

———. 1983. Empathy and countertransference. In *The future of psychoanalysis: Essays in honor of Heinz Kohut,* ed. A. Goldberg. Madison, Conn.: International Universities Press, 309–26.

———. 1994. Narcissistic lust and other vicissitudes of sexuality. *Psychoanalytic Inquiry* 14:519–34.

Wolf, E., and S. Nebel. 1978. Psychoanalytic excavations: The structure of Freud's cosmography. *American Imago* 35:178–202.

Wolff, P. 1960. The developmental psychologies of Jean Piaget and psychoanalysis. *Psychological Issues,* monograph 17. New York: International Universities Press.

———. 1986. Discussion: Alternative theories of development and their implications for studying the ontogeny of behavior and social adaptation. *American Journal of Psychoanalysis* 46:153–66.

———. 1996. The irrelevance of infant observations for psychoanalysis. *Journal of the American Psychoanalytic Association* 44:369–92.

Wolfson, A. (panel reporter). 1987. Towards the further understanding of homosexual women. *Journal of the American Psychoanalytic Association* 35:165–812.

Woodward, K. 1984. Reminiscence and the life review: Prospects and retrospects. In *What does it mean to grow old: Reflections from the humanities,* ed. T. Cole and S. Gadow. Durham, N.C.: Duke University Press, 135–62.

Woolf, V. [1929] 1957. *A room of one's own.* San Diego, Calif.: Harcourt Brace Jovanovich.

Worthington, E., and B. Buston. 1987. The marriage relationship during the transition to parenthood: A review and a model. *Journal of Family Issues* 7:443–73.

Wrye, H. K., and J. K. Welles. 1994. *The narration of desire: Erotic transferences and counter-transferences.* Hillsdale, N.J.: Analytic Press.

Wyatt, F. 1967. Clinical notes on the motives of reproduction. *Journal of Social Issues* 23:29–56.

———. 1971. A clinical view of parenthood. *Bulletin of the Menninger Clinic* 35:167–80.

Wylie, H., and M. Wylie. 1987. The older analysand: Countertransference issues in psychoanalysis. *International Journal of Psychoanalysis* 68:343–52.

Wynne, L. 1981. Current concepts about schizophrenics and family relationships. *Journal of Nervous and Mental Disease* 169:82–89.

Wynne, L., M. Singer, K. Bartko, and M. Toohey. 1977. Schizophrenics and their families: Recent research on parental communication. In *Developments in psychiatric research,* ed. J. M. Tanner. London: Hodder and Stoughton, 254–86.

Yalom, I., R. Green, and N. Fisk. 1973. Prenatal exposure to female hormones. *Archives of General Psychiatry* 28:554–59.

Yarrow, M. R., J. D. Campbell, and R. V. Burton. 1970. Recollections of childhood: A study of the retrospective method. Monographs of the Society for Research in Child Development 35. (Serial no. 138.)

Young, I. 1995. *The Stonewall experiment: A gay psychohistory.* London: Cassell.

Young-Bruehl, E. 1988. *Anna Freud: A biography.* New York: Summit Books.

———. 1996. *The anatomy of prejudices.* Cambridge, Mass.: Harvard University Press.

———. 1998. *Subject to biography: Psychoanalysis, feminism, and writing women's lives.* Cambridge, Mass.: Harvard University Press.

Zetzel, E. 1958. The analytic situation and the analytic process. In *The capacity for emotional growth.* New York: International Universities Press, 197–215.

Zetzel, E., and W. Meissner. 1973. *Basic concepts of psychoanalytic psychiatry.* New York: Basic Books.

Zucker, K. J. 1990. Gender identity disorders in children: Clinical descriptions and natural history. In *Clinical management of gender identity disorders in children and adults,* ed. R. Blanchard and B. Steiner. Washington, D.C.: American Psychiatric Press, 1–24.

Zuger, B. 1966. Effeminate behavior present in boys from early childhood: I. The clinical syndrome and follow-up studies. *Journal of Pediatrics* 69:1098–1107.

———. 1974. Effeminate behavior in boys: Parental age and other factors. *Archives of General Psychiatry* 30:173–77.

———. 1978. Effeminate behavior present in boys from childhood: Ten additional years of follow-up. *Comprehensive Psychiatry* 19:363–69.

———. 1980. Homosexuality and parental guilt. *British Journal of Psychiatry* 137:55–57.

———. 1984. Early effeminate behavior in boys: Outcome and significance for homosexuality. *Journal of Nervous and Mental Disease* 172:90–97.

Zuger, B., and P. Taylor. 1969. Effeminate behavior present in boys from early childhood: II. Comparison with similar symptoms in non-effeminate boys. *Pediatrics* 44:375–80.

Author Index

Subject Index